Access regular text updates, online study materials, interactive assessments, and other Internet resources at

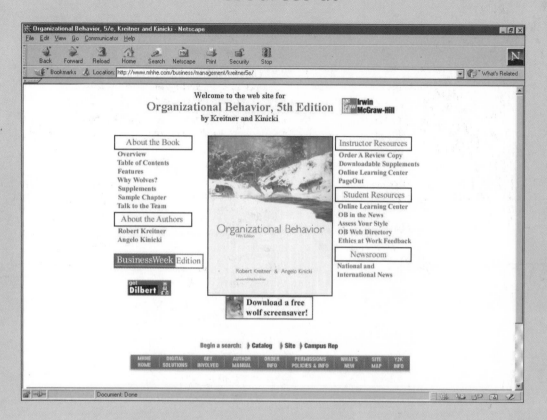

www.mhhe.com/kreitner

- **OB in the News**—Check out news briefs that relate the latest organizational behavior news stories to chapter concepts (updated regularly by the text authors).

- **Self-Assessment Activities**—Curious about your decision-making style, your listening skills, or your political aptitude? Log on and find out!

- **Directory of OB Web Links**—Jump to other websites of interest in studying organizational behavior.

- **Online Learning Center**—Review and apply text concepts with interactive practice quizzes, PowerPoint slides, Internet exercises, and other materials.

A password-protected portion of the site is also available to instructors, offering downloadable supplements and other teaching resources including PageOut!—an exclusive McGraw-Hill product that helps you create and customize a course website free of charge.

Organizational Behavior

Fifth Edition

Robert Kreitner

Angelo Kinicki

Both of Arizona State University

Boston   Burr Ridge, IL   Dubuque, IA   Madison, WI   New York   San Francisco
St. Louis   Bangkok   Bogotá   Caracas   Lisbon   London   Madrid
Mexico City   Milan   New Delhi   Seoul   Singapore   Sydney   Taipei   Toronto

McGraw-Hill Higher Education

A Division of The McGraw-Hill Companies

ORGANIZATIONAL BEHAVIOR

This book is printed on acid-free paper.

domestic   2 3 4 5 6 7 8 9 0 VNH/VNH 0 9 8 7 6 5 4 3 2 1
international   2 3 4 5 6 7 8 9 0 VNH/VNH 0 9 8 7 6 5 4 3 2 1

ISBN 0-07-231500-8

Vice president/Editor-in-chief: *Michael W. Junior*
Executive editor: *John E. Biernat*
Senior developmental editor: *Laura Hurst Spell*
Marketing manager: *Brad Schultz*
Project manager: *Kimberly D. Hooker*
Production supervisor: *Rose Hepburn*
Senior designer: *Kiera Cunningham*
Cover photo: *©Daniel J. Cox/Natural Exposures*
Inside back cover: *©Corbis*
Interior wolf images: *©Photodisc*
Photo research coordinator: *Sharon Miller*
Supplement coordinator: *Betty Hadala*
New media: *Barb Block*
Compositor: *Carlisle Communications, Ltd.*
Typeface: *10.5/12 Times Roman*
Printer: *Von Hoffmann Press, Inc.*

Library of Congress Cataloging-in-Publication Data
Kreitner, Robert.
    Organizational behavior / Robert Kreitner, Angelo Kinicki.—5th ed.
       p. cm.
    Includes index.
    ISBN 0-07-231500-8
    1. Organizational behavior. I. Kinicki, Angelo. II. Title.
HD58.7 .K766 2000
658.3—dc21   99-086384

www.mhhe.com

To the joys of life: Margaret's love and laughter, Mom's strength and courage, good friends, learning and teaching, purring cats, mountain hikes, desert rain, trees and birds, home-grown tomatoes, woodcarving, fishing, and almond M&Ms.

—B.K.

To Henry Kinicki, my dad, and to my wife and best friend Joyce Kinicki. Dad, your strength and faith have shown me what it really means to have courage in the face of adversity. Joyce, I am blessed and thankful to have you in my life. Your love, support, encouragement, and friendship helped me to grow and develop beyond my wildest dreams. You are the best!

—A.K.

About the Authors

ROBERT (BOB) KREITNER, PHD is a part-time Senior Lecturer in Management at Arizona State University. Prior to joining ASU in 1975, where he attained the rank of tenured Full Professor of Management, Bob taught at Western Illinois University. He also has taught organizational behavior at the American Graduate School of International Management (Thunderbird). Bob is a popular speaker who has addressed a diverse array of audiences worldwide on management topics. Bob has authored articles for respected journals such as *Organizational Dynamics, Business Horizons,* and *Journal of Business Ethics.* He also is the co-author (with Fred Luthans) of the award-winning book *Organizational Behavior Modification and Beyond: An Operant and Social Learning Approach,* and the author of *Management,* 8th edition, a best-selling introductory management text.

Among his consulting and executive development clients have been American Express, SABRE Computer Services, Honeywell, Motorola, Amdahl, the Hopi Indian Tribe, State Farm Insurance, Goodyear Aerospace, Doubletree Hotels, Bank One–Arizona, Nazarene School of Large Church Management, US Steel, and Allied-Signal. In 1981–82 he served as Chairman of the Academy of Management's Management Education and Development Division.

On the personal side, Bob is a native of Buffalo, New York. After a four-year tour of duty in the US Coast Guard, including service on the icebreaker EASTWIND in Antarctica, Bob attended the University of Nebraska–Omaha on a football scholarship. Bob also holds an MBA from the University of Nebraska–Omaha and a PhD from the University of Nebraska–Lincoln. While working on his PhD in Business at Nebraska, he spent six months teaching management courses for the University in Micronesia. In 1996, Bob taught two courses in Albania's first-ever MBA program (funded by the US Agency for International Development and administered by the University of Nebraska–Lincoln). He taught a summer leadership program in Switzerland from 1995 to 1998. Bob and his wife, Margaret, live in Phoenix with three cats and an orphaned wild bird, and they enjoy travel, hiking, woodcarving, and fishing.

ANGELO KINICKI is a Professor and Dean's Council of 100 Distinguished Scholar at Arizona State University. He joined the faculty in 1982, the year he received his doctorate in business administration from Kent State University. His specialty is Organizational Behavior.

Angelo is recognized for both his research and teaching. He has published over 60 articles in a variety of leading academic and professional journals devoted to organizational behavior. Angelo's success as a researcher also resulted in his selection to serve on the editorial review boards for the *Academy of Management Journal, Journal of*

Vocational Behavior, and the *Journal of Management.* He also received the All Time Best Reviewer Award from the *Academy of Management Journal* for the period of 1996–1999. Angelo's outstanding teaching performance resulted in his selection as the Graduate Teacher of the Year and the Undergraduate Teacher of the Year in the College of Business at Arizona State University. He also was acknowledged as the Instructor of the Year for Executive Education from the Center for Executive Development at Arizona State University.

One of Angelo's strengths is his ability to teach students at all levels within a university. He uses an interactive environment to enhance undergraduates' understanding about organizational behavior and management. He focuses MBAs on applying organizational behavior theories to solve complex problems. The PhD students learn the art and science of conducting scholarly research.

Angelo also is a busy consultant and speaker with companies around the world. His clients are many of the *Fortune* 500 companies as well as a variety of entrepreneurial firms. Much of his consulting work focuses on creating organizational change aimed at increasing organizational effectiveness and profitability. One of Angelo's most important and enjoyable pursuits is the practical application of his knowledge about organizational behavior.

Angelo and his wife Joyce have enjoyed living in the beautiful Arizona desert for 18 years, but are natives of Cleveland, Ohio. They enjoy traveling, hiking, and golfing.

Preface

Things move very fast in today's Internet-linked global economy. Competition is intense. Speed, cost, and quality are no longer the trade-offs they once were (meaning improvement in one came at the expense of one or both of the others). Today's customers want immediate access to high-quality products and services at a reasonable price. Thus, managers are challenged to simultaneously speed up the product creation and delivery cycle, cut costs, and improve quality. (And to do so in an ethical manner.) Regardless of the size and purpose of the organization and the technology involved, *people* are the common denominator when facing this immense challenge. Success or failure hinges on the ability to attract, develop, retain, and motivate a diverse array of appropriately-skilled people. The *human factor* drives everything. To know more about workplace behavior is to gain a valuable competitive edge. The purpose of this textbook is to help present and future managers better understand and manage people at work.

Although this Fifth Edition of *Organizational Behavior* is aimed at undergraduate business students in similarly named courses, previous editions have proven highly versatile. *Organizational Behavior* has been used effectively in MBA programs, executive education and management development programs, and industrial and organizational psychology programs around the world. (Note: A special European edition is available.) This textbook is the culmination of our combined 48 years of teaching experience and research into organizational behavior and management in the United States, Pacific Rim, and Europe. Thanks to detailed feedback from students, professors, and practicing managers, this Fifth Edition is more refined and better organized. Many new changes have been made in this edition, reflecting new research evidence, new management techniques, and the fruits of our own learning process.

Organizational Behavior, Fifth Edition, is a product of the *total quality management* (TQM) process described in Chapter 1. Specifically, it is *user driven* (as a result of carefully listening to our readers), developed through close *teamwork* between the authors and the publisher, and the product of *continuous improvement.* Our TQM approach has helped us achieve a difficult combination of balances. Among them are balances between theory and practice, solid content and interesting coverage, and instructive detail and readability. Students and instructors say they want an up-to-date, relevant, and interesting textbook that actively involves the reader in the learning process. Our efforts toward this end are evidenced by many new topics and real-life examples, a stimulating art program, timely new cases and boxed inserts, end-of-chapter experiential exercises for both individuals and teams, and more than two dozen exercises integrated into the text. We realize that reading a comprehensive textbook is hard work, but we also firmly believe the process should be interesting (and sometimes fun).

Structural Changes in the Fifth Edition

Part One in this Fifth Edition provides a foundation of understanding as well as a cultural context for the study of organizational behavior. In Parts Two through Five, the material flows from micro (individuals) to macro (groups and organizations) topics. Once again, we have tried to achieve a workable balance between micro and macro topics. As a guide for users of the previous edition, the following structural changes need to be noted:

- The single chapter on power, politics, conflict, and negotiation has been divided into two chapters: Chapter 14, Managing Conflict and Negotiation, and Chapter 16, Influence Tactics, Empowerment, and Politics. This improved topical alignment includes extensive new coverage of conflict.

- Two macro chapters in the Fourth Edition (Chapters 18 and 19) have been combined into a single chapter. Chapter 19, now titled Organizational Effectiveness and Design, provides more efficient coverage of essential macro topics.

- As a result of user feedback, the Behavior Modification and Self-Management chapter (now

Chapter 10) has been moved forward to Part Two: This creates a smoother topical flow from motivation to feedback and rewards to behavior modification.

- Individual and Group Decision Making (Chapter 11) is now the lead-in chapter for Part Three on Group and Social Processes. This creates the good bridge between micro and macro topics our users prefer.

- As requested by users, the chapters on group dynamics and teams and teamwork are now paired as Chapters 12 and 13 in Part Three.

- Performance appraisal is now covered in an optional module following Chapter 9 on feedback and rewards.

- Chapter numbers for Chapters 10 through 12 and 14 through 19 have been changed from the prior edition to reflect these topical realignments.

AACSB/IAME Coverage

In keeping with curriculum recommendations from the AACSB/International Association for Management Education for greater attention to managing in a global economy, managing cultural diversity, improving product/service quality, and making ethical decisions, we feature these chapters:

- A full chapter on international organizational behavior and cross-cultural management (Chapter 4). To ensure integrated coverage of international topics, 29 boxed features titled "International Organizational Behavior" can be found throughout the text.

- Chapter 2 offers comprehensive and up-to-date coverage of managing diversity.

- Principles of total quality management (TQM) and the legacy of W Edwards Deming are discussed in Chapter 1 to establish a quality-improvement context for the entire textbook. Also, many quality-related examples have been integrated into the textual presentation.

- Ethics is covered early in the text (Chapter 3) to set a proper moral tone for managing people at work. Ethical issues are raised throughout the text. New to this Fifth Edition are 20 interactive "Ethics at Work" pop-out boxes integrated into the textual flow (one per chapter). They raise hard-hitting ethical issues, ask tough

questions, and have corresponding interpretations on our Web site. They are a constant reminder of the importance of ethical management.

New and Expanded Coverage

Our readers kindly tell us how much they appreciate our efforts to keep this textbook up-to-date and relevant. Toward that end, you will find new or significantly improved coverage of the following topics in this Fifth Edition: knowledge management, layers of diversity, glass ceiling, espoused versus enacted values, types of organizational culture, individualist versus collectivist cultures, North American women on foreign assignments, organizational identification, attitude stability, emotional intelligence, disability stereotypes, the set-up-to-fail syndrome, a new job performance model of motivation, distributive/procedural/interactional justice, race and feedback, role of trust in 360-degree feedback, pay inequality, performance appraisal concepts and techniques, managing antecedents at UPS, judgmental/availability/representativeness heuristics, decision-making styles, extension of Tuckman group development model (group decay), group effectiveness and value diversity, virtual teams, cooperative versus competitive team goals, conflict-producing trends, desired conflict outcomes, types of conflict, personality conflict, workplace incivility, value conflict, intergroup conflict, cross-cultural conflict, conflict triangles, alternative dispute resolution (ADR), ethics in negotiation, messages sent by different communication media, Extranets, drawbacks of E-mail, videoconferencing, updated list of influence tactics, empowerment and information sharing, barriers to delegation, personal initiative in delegation, trust and delegation, new empowerment research, cross-cultural impression management, culture and charismatic leadership, effects of leadership across different organizational levels, eustress, perceived stress, new treatment of organizational decline, virtual organizations, information technology as a force of change, and organizational causes of resistance to change.

Pedagogical and Cooperative Learning Features

The Fifth Edition of *Organizational Behavior* is designed to be a complete teaching/learning tool that captures the reader's interest and imparts useful knowledge. Some of the most significant pedagogical features of this text are:

- Classic and modern topics are given balanced treatment in terms of the latest and best available theoretical models, research evidence, and practical applications.

- Several concise learning objectives open each chapter to focus the reader's attention and serve as a comprehension check.

- Every chapter opens with a real-name, real-world case study to provide an interesting and relevant context for the material at hand. Nineteen of these brief cases are new to this Fifth Edition. They highlight male and female role models as well as US and foreign companies.

- A colorful and lively art program includes captioned photographs and figures.

- Hundreds of real-world examples involving large and small, public and private organizations have been incorporated into the textual material to make this edition up-to-date, interesting, and relevant.

- Women play a prominent role throughout this text, as is befitting their large and growing presence in the workplace. Lots of female role models are included. Special effort has been devoted to uncovering research insights about relevant and important gender-related differences.

- New to this Fifth Edition are 20 interactive "Ethics at Work" pop-out boxes integrated into the textual flow (one per chapter), which raise hard-hitting ethical issues and ask tough questions. Feedback is provided on the book Web site at **www.mhhe.com/kreitner.**

- Key terms are emphasized in bold print where they are first defined and featured in the adjacent margins for review purposes.

- Twenty-seven OB Exercise boxes are distributed throughout the text to foster personal involvement and greater self-awareness. Readers will gain experiential insights about their cultural orientation toward time, self-esteem, perception, motives, sense of fairness, roles, power, impression management tactics, conflict handling style, work group autonomy, decision-making style, upward communication, stress, and readiness for change.

- A "Summary of Key Concepts" feature at the end of each chapter restates the chapter learning objectives and concisely answers them.

- Ten discussion questions at the end of every chapter challenge the reader to explore the personal and practical implications of what has just been covered. These questions also are useful for classroom discussion and cooperative learning.

- The Internet Exercises found at the end of each chapter have been completely updated for the Fifth Edition, offering more interactivity, variety, and link durability. These exercises encourage and aid students in navigating the Internet to learn more about topics and organizations covered in the text. The Internet Exercises also can serve as a valuable tool for cooperative learning when students team up to track down relevant new information.

- Forty end-of-chapter exercises foster hands-on experiential and cooperative learning. Every chapter is concluded with a Personal Awareness and Growth Exercise and a Group Exercise. Each exercise has learning objectives, an introduction, clear instructions, and discussion questions to facilitate interaction and learning.

Also available with this Fifth Edition is a complete set of supplement materials for students and instructors:

For the Student

- *Student CD-ROM.* Packaged free with every new copy of the text the CD contains the integrative case video featuring the Specialized Bicycle Ponients Company with discussion questions, chapter quizzes, selected PowerPoint slides, and Web links. The CD helps students prepare for exams and conduct Internet searches related to text examples. Instructors can assign the video and discussion questions in preparation for classroom discussion.

- *Web site www.mhhe.com/kreitner.* The student portion of the Web site features Internet exercises (from book), OB in the News (weekly text updates from the authors), Self-Assessment activities, a directory of Web links, and an online learning center, including online quizzing and text review materials. Several just-for-fun links have been added to the site as well, such as Why Wolves? (where you can access a series of links to wolf Internet sites) and the Dilbert Zone.

For the Instructor

- *Instructor's Resource Manual,* prepared by Kim J Wade, Washington State University. Lecture outlines, case solutions, exercise notes, supplemental lecture material, additional exercises, and more can be found in this substantive and convenient resource volume. Also provided in the manual is a continuing case involving an in-depth study of a first-time manager tackling a department with a variety of organizational behavior–related problems. This case (a.k.a. the Roberta case) illustrates in detail how topics from the text can actually affect an individual manager's job. A set of discussion questions for each International OB issue is provided, allowing the instructor to more easily incorporate this important material into a lesson plan. Teaching notes for the video series and transparency masters are also included.

- *Test Bank,* prepared by Kim J Wade, Washington State University. The test bank has been expanded in the Fifth Edition to offer more than 1,500 true/false, multiple-choice, and essay questions. Essay questions now include suggested answers. All questions have been reevaluated and revised as needed to ensure an emphasis on testing concepts rather than definitional memorization. Every question is conveniently tagged with a difficulty rating and a page reference to the text.

- *Computest.* A computerized version of the test bank allows the instructor to generate random tests and to add his or her own questions.

- *Videos.* An integrative video case has been added to the package for the Fifth Edition, featuring Specialized—an innovative bike manufacturer with global operations and headquarters in Morgan Hill, California, where "building bikes isn't a job . . . it's a full-bore, hardcore religion." This four-part video (complementing the major sections in the text) explores Specialized unique organizational culture, commitment to employee development and teamwork, and organizational design and strategy. The video shows how the various levels of an organization fit together and what makes a successful organization tick. A corresponding written case appears in the text, and a digital version of the video is available on the Student CD-Rom.

In addition to the new integrative case video on Specialized, a comprehensive set of **chapter videos** is available, consisting of NBC News broadcast footage and original business documentaries. Most of the chapter videos are new to the Fifth Edition and are related

to specific examples and cases in the text. Highlights include "Bill Gates Discusses His Book 'Business at the Speed of Thought,' " "*Fortune* Magazine's Best Companies for Minorities," "EuroDisney," "How Safe Is Our Work Environment?," "Challenger Space Shuttle Disaster," and "Computer Culture: Stress for Workers in Cyberspace." An icon in the text indicates when there is a video that corresponds to a textbook example or case.

- *PowerPoint Presentation Software,* prepared by Janet Drez of Kinicki and Associates. More than 200 colorful PowerPoint slides are provided, complementing the 20 chapters in the text. These slides consist of both original lecture materials and key textual material. In response to suggestions from our adopters, the Fifth Edition presentation has been expanded to include representations of *all* figures and tables in the text.

- *Color Acetates* or *Transparency Masters.* All of the PowerPoint slides are also available as either color acetates or transparency masters.

Words of Appreciation

This textbook is the fruit of many people's labor. Our colleagues at Arizona State University have been supportive from the start. Through the years, our organizational behavior students at ASU, the American Graduate School of International Management (Thunderbird), and the University of Tirana (Albania) have been enthusiastic and candid academic "customers." We are grateful for their feedback and we hope we have done it justice in this new edition. Sincere appreciation goes to Kim Wade of Washington State University, for her skillful and dedicated work on the *Instructor's Resource Manual* and *Test Bank.* Thank you to Dale Boroviak for a very professional job of managing our permissions. Thank you to Janet Drez for creating the PowerPoint presentation.

To the manuscript reviewers spanning the five editions go our gratitude and thanks. Their feedback was thoughtful, rigorous, constructive, and above all, essential to our goal of *kaizen* (continuous improvement). Reviewers for this edition were:

Joe S. Anderson
Northern Arizona State University

Anthony F. Chelte
Western New England College

Pamela L. Cox
SUNY–Oswego

Robert Culpepper
Stephen F. Austin State University

Scott Douglas
Florida State University

Janice M. Feldbauer
Austin Community College

Jean Hanebury
St. Leo's University

Barbara L. Hassell
Indiana University–Purdue University, Indianapolis

Peter L. Henderson
Faulkner University

Eileen Hogan
Kutztown University

Gabriel Jaskolka
Tiffin University

Katryna Johnson
Concordia University–Saint Paul

Thomas J. Keefe
Indiana University Southeast

Andrew Klein
Keller Graduate School

Joseph F. Kornfeind
Muhlenberg College

Robert C. Liden
University of Illinois at Chicago

Hany H. Makhlouf
University of the District of Columbia

Barbara G. McCain
Oklahoma City University

Thomas McFarland
Mt. San Antonio College

Janice S. Miller
University of Wisconsin–Milwaukee

Clark Molstad
California State University, San Bernardino

Gordon A. Morse
George Mason University

Audrey Murrell
University of Pittsburgh

Stefanie Naumann
Louisiana State University

Linda L. Neider
University of Miami

Isaac Owolabi
Montreat College

Mark W. Phillips
University of Texas–San Antonio

Sandra Powell
Weber State University

Brooke Quigg
Pierce College

Randall G. Sleeth
Virginia Commonwealth University

Susan M. Smith
Finger Lakes Community College

B. Kay Snavely
Miami University

Kenneth C. Solano
Northeastern University

Raymond T. Sparrowe
Cleveland State University

Leigh Stelzer
Seton Hall University

Susan Stites-Doe
SUNY College at Brockport

Nell Tabor Hartley
Robert Morris College

Sandy J. Wayne
University of Illinois at Chicago

Alan R. Zeiber
Portland State University

Special thanks go to our dedicated "pack" at Irwin/McGraw-Hill: our editors, John Biernat and Laura Hurst Spell; and our design and production team, Kiera Cunningham, Sara Evertson, Kimberly Hooker, Rose Hepburn, and Sharon Miller.

Finally, we would like to thank our wives, Margaret and Joyce, for being tough and caring "first customers" of our work. This book has been greatly enhanced by their common sense, reality testing, and managerial experience. Thanks in large measure to their love and moral support, this project again was completed on time and it strengthened rather than strained a treasured possession—our friendship.

We hope you enjoy this textbook. Best wishes for success and happiness!

Bob Kreitner
Angelo Kinicki

Brief Contents

Contents

Part Two
Individual Behavior in Organizations   133

Part Three
Group and Social Processes 337

Chapter Twelve
Group Dynamics 376

Part One

The World of Organizational Behavior

Chapter One

Organizational
Behavior: Developing
People-Centered
Organizations and Skills

Learning Objectives

When you finish studying the material in this chapter, you should be able to:

1   Identify the P's in the 4-P cycle of continuous improvement and define the term *management*.

2   Identify at least 5 of the 11 managerial skills in Wilson's profile of effective managers.

3   Describe the new employment contract.

4   Characterize 21st-century managers.

5   Define the term *organizational behavior*, and explain why OB is a horizontal discipline.

6   Contrast McGregor's Theory X and Theory Y assumptions about employees.

7   Explain the managerial significance of Deming's 85–15 rule.

8   Identify the four principles of total quality management (TQM).

9   Describe the sources of organizational behavior research evidence.

I don't think people realize just how "new" the Internet is. We have yet to scratch the surface of what the Net makes possible for business. Until recently, the Net has involved an almost mindless convergence of information: You do a search using one of the popular search engines, and you still have to sift through 10,000 or 20,000 pieces of information. That kind of search is frustrating and time-consuming, and it just doesn't make sense as a business tool.

The critical next step for the Net involves increasing its relevance. That means giving people the information they need, when they need it, and eliminating the clutter that prevents people from making good decisions. That also means bringing together information from inside and outside of organizations—from partners, service providers, and merchants—to provide a console from which people can do their work. For business, that's the real promise of the Web.

The more the technology of the Web changes how we do business, the more we need to focus on people. Financial performance, growth, and wealth are all wonderful things, but it's people—your employees, your customers, your business partners—who make those things happen. When we founded PeopleSoft [a global supplier of enterprise application software], we had three core principles: Make customers happy. Have fun. Be profitable. Having fun at PeopleSoft is mandatory. People who are having fun are more

David Duffield, Chairman,
PeopleSoft, Inc.

productive, they are nicer to the other people in the organization, they become evangelists for the company, and they deliver fantastic customer service.

The most important part of my job involves working with our employees and our customers. That's another thing that's new about the new economy: The job of leadership has changed. Leadership is not about having all the answers or about issuing directives. Leadership is about getting people to do things for you without your having to ask them to. That's a real challenge, and that's where those core principles take over.[1]

FOR DISCUSSION

What must PeopleSoft's managers do to strike a workable balance between the core principles of having fun and making a profit?

True or false? *People* are the key to success in today's highly competitive global economy. Jack Welch, prior to his 2001 retirement as the successful and respected CEO of General Electric, said, "We spend all our time on people. The day we screw up the people thing, this company is over."[2] So Welch picks "true." But wait a minute. Dilbert cartoonist Scott Adams, who humorously documents managerial lapses of sanity, sees it differently. Adams ranks the often-heard statement "Employees are our most valuable asset" number one on his list of "Great Lies of Management."[3] This raises serious questions. Is Welch the exception, a manager who actually backs up the claim that people are our most valuable resource? Does the typical manager merely pay lip service to the critical importance of people? If so, what are the implications of this hypocrisy for organizational productivity and employee well-being?

Stanford University's Jeffrey Pfeffer and his colleagues recently shed instructive light on this dilemma. Generally, they concluded:

> There is a substantial and rapidly expanding body of evidence, some of it quite methodologically sophisticated, that speaks to the strong connection between how firms manage their people and the economic results achieved.[4]

Their review of research evidence from companies in both the United States and Germany showed *people-centered practices* strongly associated with much higher profits and significantly lower employee turnover. Further analysis uncovered the following seven people-centered practices in successful companies:

1. Job security (to eliminate fear of layoffs).
2. Careful hiring (emphasizing a good fit with the company culture).
3. Power to the people (via decentralization and self-managed teams).
4. Generous pay for performance.
5. Lots of training.
6. Less emphasis on status (to build a "we" feeling).
7. Trust building (through the sharing of critical information).[5]

Importantly, these factors are a *package* deal, meaning they need to be installed in a coordinated and systematic manner—not in bits and pieces.

The dark side of this study is that Scott Adams's cynical assessment is too often true. Managers tend to act counter to their declarations that people are their most important asset. Pfeffer and his colleagues blame a number of modern management trends and practices. For example, undue emphasis on short-term profit precludes long-term efforts to nurture human resources. Also, excessive layoffs, when managers view people as a cost rather than an asset, erode trust, commitment, and loyalty.[6] *Only 12 percent of today's organizations, according to Pfeffer, have the systematic*

(**DILBERT** reprinted by permission of United Feature Syndicate, Inc.)

approaches and persistence to qualify as true people-centered organizations, thus giving them a competitive advantage.[7]

To us, an 88 percent shortfall in the quest for people-centered organizations represents a tragic loss, both to society and to the global economy. There are profound ethical implications as well. We all need to accept the challenge to do better.[8] Toward that end, the mission of this book is to help increase the number of people-centered managers and organizations around the world.

Our jumping-off point is the 4-P model of strategic results in Figure 1–1 (focusing on *people, products, processes,* and *productivity*). The 4-P model emphasizes the larger

Figure 1–1   *Strategic Results: The 4-P Cycle of Continuous Improvement*

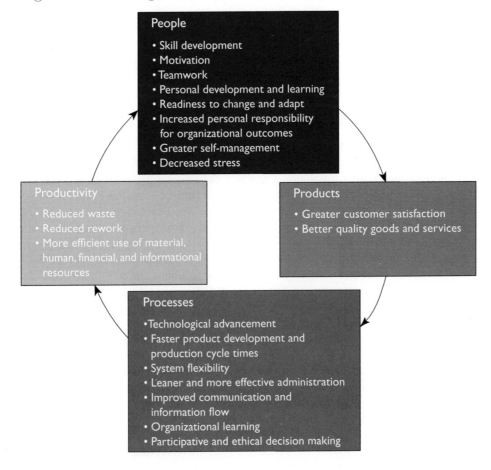

strategic context for managing people. Although people indeed are the key to organizational success today, other factors such as planning, technology, and finances also require good management. Further, the 4-P model stresses the importance of day-to-day *continuous improvement* in all aspects of organizational endeavor to cope with more demanding customers and stiffer competition.

The purpose of this first chapter is to explore the manager's job, define and examine organizational behavior and its evolution, and consider how we can learn more about organizational behavior. A topical model for the balance of the book also is introduced.

The Manager's Job: Getting Things Done through Others

Management
Process of working with and through others to achieve organizational objectives efficiently and ethically.

For better or for worse, managers touch our lives in many ways. Schools, hospitals, government agencies, and large and small businesses all require systematic management. Formally defined, **management** is the process of working with and through others to achieve organizational objectives in an efficient and ethical manner. From the standpoint of organizational behavior, the central feature of this definition is "working with and through others." Managers play a constantly evolving role. Today's successful managers are no longer the I've-got-everything-under-control order givers of yesteryear. Rather, they need to creatively envision and actively sell bold new directions in an ethical and sensitive manner. Effective managers are team players empowered by the willing and active support of others who are driven by conflicting self-interests. Each of us has a huge stake in how well managers carry out their evolving role. Henry Mintzberg, a respected management scholar, observed: "No job is more vital to our society than that of the manager. It is the manager who determines whether our social institutions serve us well or whether they squander our talents and resources."[9]

Extending our managerial thrust, let us take a closer look at the skills managers need to perform, the evolving relationship between employer and employee, and the future direction of management.

What Do Managers Do? A Skills Profile

Observational studies by Mintzberg and others have found the typical manager's day to be a fragmented collection of brief episodes.[10] Interruptions are commonplace, while large blocks of time for planning and reflective thinking are not. In one particular study, four top-level managers spent 63% of their time on activities lasting less than nine minutes each. Only 5% of the managers' time was devoted to activities lasting more than an hour.[11] But what specific skills do effective managers perform during their hectic and fragmented workdays?

Many attempts have been made over the years to paint a realistic picture of what managers do.[12] Diverse and confusing lists of managerial functions and roles have been suggested. Fortunately, a stream of research over the past 20 years by Clark Wilson and others has given us a practical and statistically validated profile of managerial *skills*[13] (see Table 1–1). Wilson's managerial skills profile focuses on 11 observable categories of managerial behavior. This is very much in tune with today's emphasis on managerial competency.[14] Wilson's unique skills-assessment technique goes beyond the usual self-report approach with its natural bias. In addition to surveying a given manager about his or her 11 skills, the Wilson approach also asks those who report directly to the manager to answer questions about their boss's skills. According to Wilson and his colleagues, the result is an assessment of skill *mastery,* not simply skill awareness.[15] The logic behind Wilson's approach is both simple and compelling. Who better to assess a manager's skills than the people who experience those behaviors on a day-to-day basis—those who report directly to the manager?

Table 1–1   *Skills Exhibited by an Effective Manager**

1. **Clarifies goals and objectives** for everyone involved.
   (See Chs. 6, 8, 15, 17, and 19)

2. **Encourages participation,** upward communication, and suggestions.
   (See Chs. 2, 12, 13, 15, 16, and 17)

3. **Plans and organizes** for an orderly work flow.
   (See Chs. 19 and 20)

4. Has **technical and administrative expertise** to answer organization-related
   questions.
   (See Chs. 1, 2, 9, 15, and 20)

5. **Facilitates work** through team building, training, coaching, and support.
   (See Chs. 3, 4, 7, 9, 13, 15, 16, 17, and 18)

6. **Provides feedback** honestly and constructively.
   (See Chs. 9, 10, 13, 15, 16, and 17)

7. **Keeps things moving** by relying on schedules, deadlines, and helpful reminders.
   (See Chs. 7, 8, 9, 10, 13, 14, 15, 16, 17, and 20)

8. **Controls details** without being overbearing.
   (See Chs. 2, 4, 5, 6, 9, 11, 15, 17, and 18)

9. Applies reasonable **pressure for goal accomplishment.**
   (See Chs. 1, 4, 5, 6, 7, 8, 9, 10, 11, 12, 14, 15, 16, 17, and 19)

10. **Empowers and delegates** key duties to others while maintaining goal clarity and
    commitment.
    (See Chs. 2, 3, 11, 13, 16, 17, and 19)

11. **Recognizes good performance** with rewards and positive reinforcement.
    (See Chs. 7, 8, 9, 10, 15, 16, and 17)

*Annotated with relevant chapters in this textbook.
SOURCE: Adapted from material in C Wilson, "Identify Needs with Costs in Mind," *Training and Development Journal,* July 1980, pp 58–62; and F Shipper, "A Study of the Psychometric Properties of the Managerial Skill Scales of the Survey of Management Practices," *Educational and Psychological Measurement,* June 1995, pp 468–79.

The Wilson managerial skills research yields three useful lessons:

1. Dealing effectively with *people* is what management is all about. The 11 skills in Table 1–1 constitute a goal creation/commitment/feedback/reward/accomplishment cycle with human interaction at every turn.

2. Managers with high skills mastery tend to have better subunit performance and employee morale than managers with low skills mastery.[16]

3. *Effective* female and male managers *do not* have significantly different skill profiles,[17] contrary to claims in the popular business press in recent years.[18]

The New Employment Contract: A Cautionary Tale

If Rip van Winkle worked for a large North American company and just woke up from a 20-year nap, he would be shocked and worried. His **employment contract,** defined as the written and implied expectations between employer and employee, would have been completely rewritten (without his input or consent).[19] When he went to sleep, his employer expected him to be loyal, hard working, and obedient. In return, Rip expected

Employment contract
Mutual written and implied expectations between employer and employee.

to get a steady stream of salary increases and promotions and the proverbial gold watch upon his retirement from the company. In short, the company was like a nurturing parent who knew what was best for Rip and his career. He loved and trusted the company.

Now Rip's head spins as he hears things about the so-called new employment contract. "Everyone is self-employed." "You own your own employability." "Build a portable career." "You're paid to add value." "Be willing to stay, but ready to leave." According to this new employment contract, Rip's employer expects him to be a creative self-starter and team player capable of doing a variety of jobs with a diverse array of people. His pay will be tied to results, not to years on the job. Moreover, Rip's company expects him to take charge of his own career and act more like a partner than an employee. Complaints and comments by co-workers tell Rip they don't love and trust the company as before. He turns to one of them and whispers, "What's a stock option? And what on earth is E-mail?" Rip certainly has a lot to learn.

The new employment contract, although couched in terms of North America in this tale, has immense implications for both individuals and organizations in advanced economies worldwide.

Implications for the Individual For employees committed to life-long learning, working smarter rather than harder, and making their own opportunities, the new employment contract is a positive situation. Organizational life will give them more opportunities to grow and be rewarded for creating value for internal and external customers. Promotions will be fewer and slower than under the old employment contract because of flatter organizations with fewer layers. But lateral moves from one project or function to another will provide lots of challenge for those who get results. The skills profile for an effective manager in Table 1–1 is a good measuring stick for personal growth and success under the new contract. Meanwhile, the new employment contract is *not* good news for employees with an entitlement mentality. They are the ones who believe the company owes them pay raises and promotions just for showing up at work. They also tend to be inflexible and resistant to change.

Implications for Organizations According to one management writer, there has been a shift from a "relational contract" to a "transactional contract."[20] Unfortunately, corporate America so far has done a better job of defining the employee's end of the bargain than it has its own. It is one thing to say everyone is self-employed, but what are the company's obligations in the new transactional environment? A survey of 3,300 employees across the United States by Towers Perrin, the New York consulting firm, outlined the expectations of today's employees (and a disturbing expectations gap):

> Most of Towers Perrin's respondents didn't consider the new deal a raw deal: They were willing to take responsibility for their careers and for producing value for the company—as long as the company delivers meaningful rewards for goals achieved, support for skill development, honest communication about mutual objectives, and reasonable flexibility in the work environment.

Ethics at Work

After nearly a decade of downsizing, restructuring and reengineering, loyalty between employee and company is being stretched thin....

Judging by all the published advice, workers now should consider themselves to be "Me Inc.," and maneuver for assignments that boost their standing. If companies are going to rightsize for every market current, then workers should suffer no guilt in accepting company-paid training even as they jump at the next best offer.

SOURCE: Excerpted from D Jones, "Workplace Loyalty: Not Dead Yet, But Strained," *USA Today*, February 4, 1998, p 4B.

You Decide . . .

Is it ethical to take full advantage of what your employer has to offer in the way of incentives and training and then pick up and leave for a better opportunity? Explain.

For an interpretation of this situation, visit our Web site **www.mhhe.com/kreitner**

But employers aren't delivering consistently: 41% of respondents disagreed when asked if policies are administered fairly and consistently; 45% did not think their company hires the most qualified people for jobs; 52% saw a gap between pay and the level of performance the company demands.[21]

Employees tend to give what they get. Thus, organizations failing to hold up their end of the new employment contract will see the erosion of key factors such as commitment, loyalty, trust, and motivation.

21st-Century Managers

Today's workplace is indeed undergoing immense and permanent changes.[22] Organizations are being "reengineered" for greater speed, efficiency, and flexibility.[23] Teams are pushing aside the individual as the primary building block of organizations.[24] Command-and-control management is giving way to participative management and empowerment.[25] Ego-centered leaders are being replaced by customer-centered leaders. Employees increasingly are being viewed as internal customers. All this creates a mandate for a new kind of manager in the 21st century. Table 1–2 contrasts the characteristics of past and future managers. As the balance of this book will demonstrate, the managerial shift in Table 1–2 is not just a good idea, it is an absolute necessity in the new workplace.

Table 1–2   *Evolution of the 21st-Century Manager*

	Past Managers	Future Managers
Primary role	Order giver, privileged elite, manipulator, controller	Facilitator, team member, teacher, advocate, sponsor, coach
Learning and knowledge	Periodic learning, narrow specialist	Continuous life-long learning, generalist with multiple specialties
Compensation criteria	Time, effort, rank	Skills, results
Cultural orientation	Monocultural, monolingual	Multicultural, multilingual
Primary source of influence	Formal authority	Knowledge (technical and interpersonal)
View of people	Potential problem	Primary resource
Primary communication pattern	Vertical	Multidirectional
Decision-making style	Limited input for individual decisions	Broad-based input for joint decisions
Ethical considerations	Afterthought	Forethought
Nature of interpersonal relationships	Competitive (win–lose)	Cooperative (win–win)
Handling of power and key information	Hoard and restrict access	Share and broaden access
Approach to change	Resist	Facilitate

The Field of Organizational Behavior: Past and Present

Organizational behavior

Interdisciplinary field dedicated to better understanding and managing people at work.

Organizational behavior, commonly referred to as OB, is an interdisciplinary field dedicated to better understanding and managing people at work. By definition, organizational behavior is both research and application oriented. Three basic levels of analysis in OB are individual, group, and organizational. OB draws upon a diverse array of disciplines, including psychology, management, sociology, organization theory, social psychology, statistics, anthropology, general systems theory, economics, information technology, political science, vocational counseling, human stress management, psychometrics, ergonomics, decision theory, and ethics. This rich heritage has spawned many competing perspectives and theories about human work behavior. By the mid-1980s, one researcher had identified 110 distinct theories about behavior within the field of OB.[26]

Organizational behavior is an academic designation. With the exception of teaching/research positions, OB is not an everyday job category such as accounting, marketing, or finance. Students of OB typically do not get jobs in organizational behavior, per se. This reality in no way demeans OB or lessens its importance in effective organizational management. OB is a *horizontal* discipline that cuts across virtually every job category, business function, and professional specialty. Anyone who plans to make a living in a large or small, public or private, organization needs to study organizational behavior.

A historical perspective of the study of people at work helps in studying organizational behavior. According to a management history expert, this is important because

Historical perspective is the study of a subject in light of its earliest phases and subsequent evolution. Historical perspective differs from history in that the object of historical perspective is to sharpen one's vision of the present, not the past.[27]

In other words, we can better understand where the field of OB is today and where it appears to be headed by appreciating where it has been. Let us examine three significant landmarks in the evolution of understanding and managing people:

1. The human relations movement.
2. The total quality management movement.
3. The contingency approach to management.

The Human Relations Movement

A unique combination of factors during the 1930s fostered the human relations movement. First, following legalization of union–management collective bargaining in the United States in 1935, management began looking for new ways of handling employees. Second, behavioral scientists conducting on-the-job research started calling for more attention to the "human" factor. Managers who had lost the battle to keep unions out of their factories heeded the call for better human relations and improved working conditions. One such study, conducted at Western Electric's Chicago-area Hawthorne plant, was a prime stimulus for the human relations movement. Ironically, many of the Hawthorne findings have turned out to be more myth than fact.

The Hawthorne Legacy   Interviews conducted decades later with three subjects of the Hawthorne studies and reanalysis of the original data with modern statistical techniques do not support initial conclusions about the positive effect of supportive supervision. Specifically, money, fear of unemployment during the Great Depression, managerial discipline, and high-quality raw materials—not supportive supervision—

Thanks to new federal legislation legalizing industrial labor unions, these Pittsburgh steel workers voted for union representation in 1937 under the watchful eye of the National Labor Relations Board. With labor in a more powerful bargaining position, management began to apply human relations concepts as a way to increase productivity.

CORBIS

turned out to be responsible for high output in the relay assembly test room experiments.[28] Nonetheless, the human relations movement gathered momentum through the 1950s, as academics and managers alike made stirring claims about the powerful effect that individual needs, supportive supervision, and group dynamics apparently had on job performance.

The Writings of Mayo and Follett   Essential to the human relations movement were the writings of Elton Mayo and Mary Parker Follett. Australian-born Mayo, who headed the Harvard researchers at Hawthorne, advised managers to attend to employees' emotional needs in his 1933 classic, *The Human Problems of an Industrial Civilization.* Follett was a true pioneer, not only as a woman management consultant in the male-dominated industrial world of the 1920s, but also as a writer who saw employees as complex combinations of attitudes, beliefs, and needs. Mary Parker Follett was way ahead of her time in telling managers to motivate job performance instead of merely demanding it, a "pull" rather than "push" strategy. She also built a logical bridge between political democracy and a cooperative spirit in the workplace.[29]

McGregor's Theory Y   In 1960, Douglas McGregor wrote a book entitled *The Human Side of Enterprise,* which has become an important philosophical base for the modern view of people at work.[30] Drawing upon his experience as a management consultant, McGregor formulated two sharply contrasting sets of assumptions about

Table 1–3   *McGregor's Theory X and Theory Y*

Outdated (Theory X) Assumptions about People at Work	Modern (Theory Y) Assumptions about People at Work
1. Most people dislike work; they avoid it when they can.	1. Work is a natural activity, like play or rest.
2. Most people must be coerced and threatened with punishment before they will work. People require close direction when they are working.	2. People are capable of self-direction and self-control if they are committed to objectives.
3. Most people actually prefer to be directed. They tend to avoid responsibility and exhibit little ambition. They are interested only in security.	3. People generally become committed to organizational objectives if they are rewarded for doing so.
	4. The typical employee can learn to accept and seek responsibility.
	5. The typical member of the general population has imagination, ingenuity, and creativity.

SOURCE: Adapted from D McGregor, *The Human Side of Enterprise* (New York: McGraw-Hill, 1960), Ch 4.

Theory Y

McGregor's modern and positive assumptions about employees being responsible and creative.

human nature (see Table 1–3). His Theory X assumptions were pessimistic and negative and, according to McGregor's interpretation, typical of how managers traditionally perceived employees. To help managers break with this negative tradition, McGregor formulated his **Theory Y,** a modern and positive set of assumptions about people. McGregor believed managers could accomplish more through others by viewing them as self-energized, committed, responsible, and creative beings.

A mid-1990s survey of 10,227 employees from many industries across the United States challenges managers to do a better job of acting on McGregor's Theory Y assumptions. From the employees' perspective, Theory X management practices are the major barrier to productivity improvement and employee well being. The researcher concluded:

> The most noteworthy finding from our survey is that an overwhelming number of American workers—some 97%—desire work conditions known to facilitate high productivity. Workers uniformly reported—regardless of the type of organization, age, gender, pay schedule, or level in the organizational hierarchy—that they needed and wanted in their own workplaces the conditions for collaboration, commitment, and creativity research has demonstrated as necessary for both productivity and health. Just as noteworthy, however, is the finding that the actual conditions of work supplied by management are those conditions that research has identified as *competence suppressors*—procedures, policies, and practices that prevent or punish expressions of competence and most characterize unproductive organizations.[3]

New Assumptions about Human Nature   Unfortunately, unsophisticated behavioral research methods caused the human relationists to embrace some naive and misleading conclusions. For example, human relationists believed in the axiom, "A satisfied employee is a hardworking employee." Subsequent research, as discussed later in this book, shows the satisfaction–performance linkage to be more complex than originally thought.

Despite its shortcomings, the human relations movement opened the door to more progressive thinking about human nature. Rather than continuing to view employees as passive economic beings, managers began to see them as active social beings and took steps to create more humane work environments.

The Total Quality Management Movement

In 1980, NBC aired a television documentary titled "If Japan Can . . . Why Can't We?" It was a wake up call for North American companies to dramatically improve product quality or continue losing market share to Japanese electronics and automobile companies. A full-fledged movement ensued during the 1980s and 1990s. Much was written, said, and done about improving the quality of both goods and services.[32] Thanks to the concept of *total quality management* (TQM), the quality of much of what we buy today is significantly better than in the past. The underlying principles of TQM are more important than ever given the growth of both E-commerce on the Internet and the overall service economy.[33] According to one business writer:

> A company stuck in the industrial-age mentality is very likely to get squashed because "zero-defect" quality has become an ante to compete, not a differentiator. Even "zero-time" operations that address customers' expectations for immediate response and gratification are becoming common in today's digital age.[34]

In a recent survey of 1,797 managers from 36 countries by the American Management Association, "customer service" and "quality" ranked as the corporate world's top two concerns.[35] TQM principles have profound practical implications for managing people today.[36]

What Is TQM?   Experts on the subject offered this definition of **total quality management:**

> TQM means that the organization's culture is defined by and supports the constant attainment of customer satisfaction through an integrated system of tools, techniques, and training. This involves the continuous improvement of organizational processes, resulting in high-quality products and services.[37]

Quality consultant Richard J Schonberger sums up TQM as "continuous, customer-centered, employee-driven improvement."[38] TQM is necessarily employee driven because product/service quality cannot be continuously improved without the active learning and participation of *every* employee. Thus, in successful quality improvement programs, TQM principles are embedded in the organization's culture.[39]

The Deming Legacy   TQM is firmly established today thanks in large part to the pioneering work of W Edwards Deming.[40] Ironically, the mathematician credited with Japan's post–World War II quality revolution rarely talked in terms of quality. He instead preferred to discuss "good management" during the hard-hitting seminars he delivered right up until his death at age 93 in 1993.[41] Although Deming's passion was the statistical measurement and reduction of variations in industrial processes, he had much to say about how employees should be treated. Regarding the human side of quality improvement, Deming called for the following:

- Formal training in statistical process control techniques and teamwork.
- Helpful leadership, rather than order giving and punishment.

Total quality management
An organizational culture dedicated to training, continuous improvement, and customer satisfaction.

- Elimination of fear so employees will feel free to ask questions.
- Emphasis on continuous process improvements rather than on numerical quotas.
- Teamwork.
- Elimination of barriers to good workmanship.[42]

One of Deming's most enduring lessons for managers is his 85–15 rule.[43] Specifically, when things go wrong, there is roughly an 85% chance the *system* (including management, machinery, and rules) is at fault. Only about 15% of the time is the individual employee at fault. Unfortunately, as Deming observed, the typical manager spends most of his or her time wrongly blaming and punishing individuals for system failures. Statistical analysis is required to uncover system failures.

Principles of TQM   Despite variations in the language and scope of TQM programs, it is possible to identify four common TQM principles:

1. Do it right the first time to eliminate costly rework.
2. Listen to and learn from customers and employees.
3. Make continuous improvement an everyday matter.
4. Build teamwork, trust, and mutual respect.[44]

Deming's influence is clearly evident in this list.[45] Once again, as with the human relations movement, we see people as the key factor in organizational success.

In summary, TQM advocates have made a valuable contribution to the field of OB by providing a *practical* context for managing people. When people are managed according to TQM principles, everyone is more likely to get the employment opportunities and high-quality goods and services they demand.[46] As you will see many times in later chapters, this book is anchored to Deming's philosophy and TQM principles.

The Contingency Approach

Scholars have wrestled for many years with the problem of how best to apply the diverse and growing collection of management tools and techniques. Their answer is the contingency approach. The **contingency approach** calls for using management techniques in a situationally appropriate manner, instead of trying to rely on "one best way." According to a pair of contingency theorists:

> [Contingency theories] developed and their acceptance grew largely because they responded to criticisms that the classical theories advocated "one best way" of organizing and managing. Contingency theories, on the other hand, proposed that the appropriate organizational structure and management style were dependent upon a set of "contingency" factors, usually the uncertainty and instability of the environment.[47]

Contingency approach
Using management tools and techniques in a situationally appropriate manner; avoiding the one-best-way mentality.

The contingency approach encourages managers to view organizational behavior within a situational context. According to this modern perspective, evolving situations, not hard-and-fast rules, determine when and where various management techniques are appropriate. For example, as discussed in Chapter 17, contingency researchers have determined that there is no single best style of leadership. Organizational behavior specialists embrace the contingency approach because it helps them realistically interrelate individuals, groups, and organizations. Moreover, the contingency approach sends a clear message to managers in today's global economy: Carefully read the situation and then be flexible enough to adapt[48] (see International OB on next page).

International OB — Three Coca-Cola Executives Address the Issue of a Globally Appropriate Management Style

Lynn Oliver, from the [United Kingdom], is responsible for Western Europe training and development. Kees van Langen, from the Netherlands, works with corporate and Asian managers. David Veale, based in the US, is manager of training and development for Coca-Cola Foods. Mr. Veale posed the questions mostly by electronic mail, occasionally commenting himself in the responses.

Do you see a homogenization of management practices down the road? Is there one best set of practices that everyone will eventually use?

Oliver: No, I don't because so much is dictated by cultural, political, and religious beliefs. Who owns the business also has an impact. The common trends I see are toward a more people-focused management style. Technology requires skilled, thoughtful people with higher education levels. Higher living standards and the increased mobility of these people give them more of a choice of where to work.

Okay, then. Who has the better or most appropriate management style: Japan, Europe, Great Britain or the US?

Oliver: I don't think any one style is best; there is value for the different approaches depending on the market. If you subscribe to the school of thought that the most successful businesses of the future will be those with the abil-

ity to learn and respond to new and uncharted environments, there may be some evidence that points to the Japanese systems of developing learning ability in people.

van Langen: The burning question is how to foster industry and commerce in a way that promotes collaboration from the strength of expressive individualism. None of the countries has found the answer as yet, so a discussion of who is best begs the question.

Veale: I have to agree with both of you. I can't see a "best" style. I don't really see much difference. Being fast, focused, and flexible in working with customers and producing and distributing great products efficiently are challenges for everyone. Lynn, you are correct in identifying learning as the key. Kees is right as well in that managing a balance between society, the individual and commerce is something that businesses face no matter what their country of origin. If anything, perhaps we in the US could learn to be more collaborative as opposed to adversarial in our approach to addressing social and individual needs. It might make the learning happen more quickly.

SOURCE: Excerpted from D Veale, L Oliver, and K van Langen, "Three Coca-Cola Perspectives on International Management Styles," *Academy of Management Executive*, August 1995, pp 74–77.

Now that we have reviewed OB's historical evolution, we need to address how we learn about OB through a combination of theory, research, and practice.

Learning about OB from Theory, Research, and Practice

As a human being, with years of interpersonal experience to draw upon, you already know a good deal about people at work. But more systematic and comprehensive understanding is possible and desirable. A working knowledge of current OB theory, research, and practice can help you develop a tightly integrated understanding of why organizational contributors think and act as they do. In order for this to happen, however, prepare yourself for some intellectual surprises from theoretical models, research results, or techniques that may run counter to your current thinking. For instance, conventional wisdom says that ulcers are caused by stress (often work related) and diet. Employees in today's fast-paced, high-pressure workplaces should be happy with this bit of research news on the stress front:

Ulcers—sores in the lining of the stomach or small intestine—affect nearly 25 million Americans, 4 million of them chronically. Each year 350,000 to 500,000 new ulcer cases are diagnosed, and about 1 million sufferers are hospitalized for complications such as bleeding or perforation.

Fully 80% to 90% of this misery is due to *Helicobacter pylori* infection. An expert panel at the National Institutes of Health [in 1994] urged patients to take antibiotic treatments to wipe out the bug and prevent ulcers from recurring, rather than downing antacids.

But ulcer patients are still pointing their finger at "the salsa that I love and the boss I don't," says the American Digestive Health Foundation. [In 1995,] the gastroenterologists' group released a survey showing 90% of ulcer sufferers cite stress and 60% of them cite diet as sources of their ulcers.

To be sure, life's excesses can churn your innards. But the undisputed champ of corrosion is H. pylori.

The discrepancy between expert advice and popular opinion has meant that adoption of the necessary antibiotic treatment hasn't been as widespread as doctors would like to see. Many sufferers, it seems, are not seeking curative treatment.[49]

Research surprises can not only make learning fun, as mentioned earlier, they also can improve the quality of our lives both on and off the job. Let us examine the dynamic relationship between OB theory, research, and practice and the value of each.

Figure 1–2 illustrates how theory, research, and practice are related. Throughout the balance of this book, we focus primarily on the central portion, where all three areas overlap. Knowledge of why people behave as they do and what managers can do to improve performance is greatest within this area of maximum overlap. For each major topic, we build a foundation for understanding with generally accepted theory. This theoretical foundation is then tested and expanded by reviewing the latest relevant research findings. After interpreting the research, we discuss the nature and effectiveness of related practical applications.

Sometimes, depending on the subject matter, it is necessary to venture into the large areas outside the central portion of Figure 1–2. For example, an insightful theory supported by convincing research evidence might suggest an untried or different way of managing. In other instances, an innovative management technique might call for an explanatory theoretical model and exploratory research. Each area—theory, research, and practice—supports and, in turn, is supported by the other two. Each area makes a valuable contribution to our understanding of, and ability to, manage organizational behavior.

Learning from Theory

Theory

A story defining key terms, providing a conceptual framework, and explaining why something occurs.

A respected behavioral scientist, Kurt Lewin, once said there is nothing as practical as a good theory. According to one management researcher, a **theory** is a story that explains "why."[50] Another calls well-constructed theories "disciplined imagination."[51] A good OB theory, then, is a story that effectively explains why individuals and groups behave as they do. Moreover, a good theoretical model

1. *Defines* key terms.

2. Constructs a *conceptual framework* that explains how important factors are interrelated. (Graphic models are often used to achieve this end.)

3. Provides a *departure point* for research and practical application.

Indeed, good theories are a fundamental contributor to improved understanding and management of organizational behavior.[52]

Figure 1–2   *Learning about OB through a Combination of Theory, Research, and Practice*

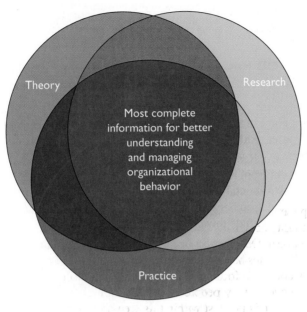

Learning from Research

Because of unfamiliar jargon and complicated statistical procedures, many current and future managers are put off by behavioral research.[53] This is unfortunate because practical lessons can be learned as OB researchers steadily push back the frontier of knowledge. Let us examine the various sources and uses of OB research evidence.

Five Sources of OB Research Insights   To enhance the instructional value of our coverage of major topics, we systematically cite "hard" evidence from five different categories. Worthwhile evidence was obtained by drawing upon the following *priority* of research methodologies:

- *Meta-analyses.* A **meta-analysis** is a statistical pooling technique that permits behavioral scientists to draw general conclusions about certain variables from many different studies.[54] It typically encompasses a vast number of subjects, often reaching the thousands. Meta-analyses are instructive because they focus on general patterns of research evidence, not fragmented bits and pieces or isolated studies.[55]

- *Field studies.* In OB, a **field study** probes individual or group processes in an organizational setting. Because field studies involve real-life situations, their results often have immediate and practical relevance for managers.

- *Laboratory studies.* In a **laboratory study,** variables are manipulated and measured in contrived situations. College students are commonly used as subjects. The highly controlled nature of laboratory studies enhances research precision. But generalizing the results to organizational management requires caution.[56]

- *Sample surveys.* In a **sample survey,** samples of people from specified populations respond to questionnaires. The researchers then draw conclusions about the

Meta-analysis
Pools the results of many studies through statistical procedure.

Field study
Examination of variables in real-life settings.

Laboratory study
Manipulation and measurement of variables in contrived situations.

Sample survey
Questionnaire responses from a sample of people.

relevant population. Generalizability of the results depends on the quality of the sampling and questioning techniques.

- *Case studies.* A **case study** is an in-depth analysis of a single individual, group, or organization. Because of their limited scope, case studies yield realistic but not very generalizable results.[57]

Three Uses of OB Research Findings   Organizational scholars point out that managers can put relevant research findings to use in three different ways:[58]

1. *Instrumental use.* This involves directly applying research findings to practical problems. For example, a manager experiencing high stress tries a relaxation technique after reading a research report about its effectiveness.

2. *Conceptual use.* Research is put to conceptual use when managers derive general enlightenment from its findings. The effect here is less specific and more indirect than with instrumental use. For example, after reading a meta-analysis showing a negative correlation between absenteeism and age,[59] a manager might develop a more positive attitude toward hiring older people.

3. *Symbolic use.* Symbolic use occurs when research results are relied on to verify or legitimize already held positions. Negative forms of symbolic use involve self-serving bias, prejudice, selective perception, and distortion. For example, tobacco industry spokespersons routinely deny any link between smoking and lung cancer because researchers are largely, but not 100%, in agreement about the negative effects of smoking. A positive example would be managers maintaining their confidence in setting performance goals after reading a research report about the favorable impact of goal setting on job performance.

By systematically reviewing and interpreting research relevant to key topics, this book provides instructive insights about OB. (The mechanics of the scientific method and OB research are discussed in detail in Learning Module A following this chapter.)

Learning from Practice

Learning to manage people is like learning to ride a bicycle. You watch others do it. Sooner or later, you get up the courage to try it yourself. You fall off and skin your knee. You climb back on the bike a bit smarter, and so on, until wobbly first attempts turn into a smooth ride. Your chances of becoming a successful manager can be enhanced by studying the theory, research, and practical examples in this textbook. Figuratively speaking, however, you eventually must climb aboard the "managerial bicycle" and learn by doing. Still, there's more.

In the world of competitive business, acquiring work-related knowledge is not enough today. According to the growing practice of *knowledge management,* key information and knowledge must be *shared* with co-workers who need it to do a better job if the organization is to gain a competitive advantage:

> Intel Corp., the Santa Clara, California-based computer chip maker, for example, has designed its knowledge management initiative to propel the company into a leadership position in the new knowledge era. The program initially facilitated the reuse of knowledge in-house and then expanded the knowledge sharing to business partners. Intel's final goal is to start revolutionary new businesses worldwide to become a leader in its field.[60]

In the spirit of knowledge management, we challenge you to not only learn from OB theory, research, and practice, but to share your insights and lessons with others who can help in our quest for more people-centered managers and organizations.

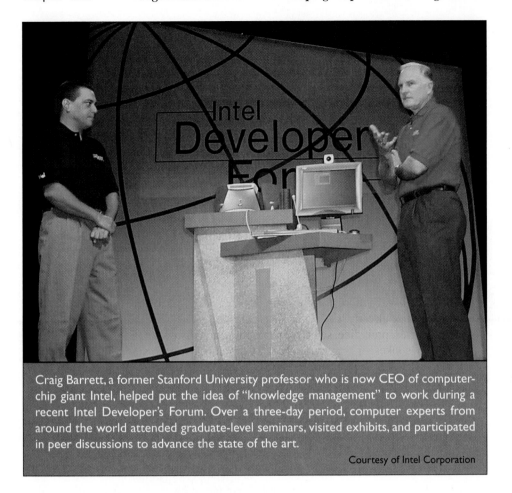

Craig Barrett, a former Stanford University professor who is now CEO of computer-chip giant Intel, helped put the idea of "knowledge management" to work during a recent Intel Developer's Forum. Over a three-day period, computer experts from around the world attended graduate-level seminars, visited exhibits, and participated in peer discussions to advance the state of the art.

Courtesy of Intel Corporation

The theory→research→practice sequence discussed in this section will help you better understand each major topic addressed later in this book. Attention now turns to a topical model that sets the stage for what lies ahead.

A Topical Model for Understanding and Managing OB

Figure 1–3 is a topical road map for our journey through this book. Our destination is organizational effectiveness through continuous improvement. Four different criteria for determining whether or not an organization is effective are discussed in Chapter 19. The study of OB can be a wandering and pointless trip if we overlook the need to translate OB lessons into effective and efficient organized endeavor.

At the far left side of our topical road map are managers, those who are responsible for accomplishing organizational results with and through others. The three circles at the center of our road map correspond to Parts Two, Three, and Four of this text. Logically, the flow of topical coverage in this book (following introductory Part One) goes from individuals, to group processes, to organizational processes and problems, to organizations. Around the core of our topical road map in Figure 1–3 is the organization. Accordingly, we end our journey with organization-related material in Part Five. Organizational structure and design are covered there in Chapter 19 to establish and develop the *organizational* context of organizational behavior. Rounding out our organizational context is a discussion of organizational change in Chapter 20. Chapters 3 and 4 provide a *cultural* context for OB.

Figure 1–3   *A Topical Model for What Lies Ahead*

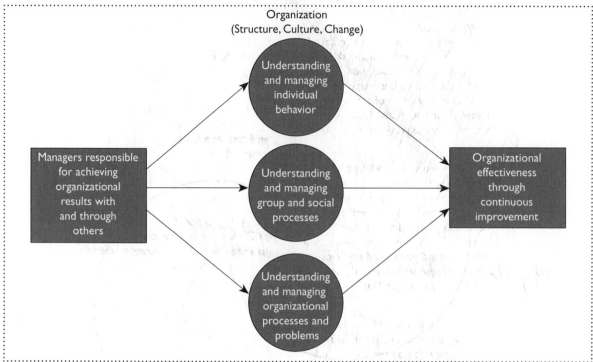

The broken line represents a permeable boundary between the organization and its environment. Energy and influence flow both ways across this permeable boundary. Truly, no organization is an island in today's highly interactive and interdependent world. Relative to the *external* environment, international cultures are explored in Chapter 4. Organization–environment contingencies are examined in Chapter 19.

Chapter 2 examines the OB implications of significant demographic and social trends, and Chapter 3 explores important ethical considerations. These discussions provide a realistic context for studying and managing people at work.

Bon voyage! Enjoy your trip through the challenging, interesting, and often surprising world of OB.

Summary of Key Concepts

1. *Identify the P's in the 4-P cycle of continuous improvement and define the term* management. The 4 P's are people, products, processes, and productivity. Management is the process of working with and through others to achieve organizational objectives in an efficient and ethical manner.

2. *Identify at least 5 of the 11 managerial skills in Wilson's profile of effective managers.* According to the Wilson skills profile, an effective manager (a) clarifies goals and objectives, (b) encourages participation, (c) plans and organizes, (d) has technical and administrative expertise, (e) facilitates

work through team building and coaching, (f) provides feedback, (g) keeps things moving, (h) controls details, (i) applies reasonable pressure for goals accomplishment, (j) empowers and delegates, and (k) recognizes and rewards good performance.

3. *Describe the new employment contract.* It is a transactional contract in which employees are expected to be flexible self-starters who are team players with multiple skills. The new contract pays employees for results, not for time spent on the job, and makes employees responsible for their own careers. The company's side of the bargain, in well-managed and ethical organizations, involves giving each employee the opportunity to grow and acquire marketable skills.

4. *Characterize 21st-century managers.* They will be team players who will get things done cooperatively by relying on joint decision making, their knowledge instead of formal authority, and their multicultural skills. They will engage in life-long learning and be compensated on the basis of their skills and results. They will facilitate rather than resist change, share rather than hoard power and key information, and be multidirectional communicators. Ethics will be a forethought instead of an afterthought. They will be generalists with multiple specialties.

5. *Define the term* organizational behavior *and explain why OB is a horizontal discipline.* Organizational behavior (OB) is an interdisciplinary field dedicated to better understanding and managing people at work. It is both research and application oriented. Except for teaching/research positions, one does not normally get a job in OB. Rather, because OB is a horizontal discipline, OB concepts and lessons are applicable to virtually every job category, business function, and professional specialty.

6. *Contrast McGregor's Theory X and Theory Y assumptions about employees.* Theory X employees, according to traditional thinking, dislike work, require close supervision, and are primarily interested in security. According to the modern Theory Y view, employees are capable of self-direction, of seeking responsibility, and of being creative.

7. *Explain the managerial significance of Deming's 85–15 rule.* Deming claimed that about 85% of organizational failures are due to system breakdowns involving factors such as management, machinery, or work rules. He believed the workers themselves are responsible for failures only about 15% of the time. Consequently, Deming criticized the standard practice of blaming and punishing individuals for what are typically *system* failures beyond their immediate control.

8. *Identify the four principles of total quality management (TQM).* (a) Do it right the first time to eliminate costly rework. (b) Listen to and learn from customers and employees. (c) Make continuous improvement an everyday matter. (d) Build teamwork, trust, and mutual respect.

9. *Describe the sources of organizational behavior research evidence.* Five sources of OB research evidence are meta-analyses (statistically pooled evidence from several studies), field studies (evidence from real-life situations), laboratory studies (evidence from contrived situations), sample surveys (questionnaire data), and case studies (observation of a single person, group, or organization).

Discussion Questions

1. Why view the typical employee as a human resource?

2. In your opinion, what are the three or four most important strategic results in Figure 1–1? Why?

3. How would you respond to a fellow student who says, "I have a hard time getting along with other people, but I think I could be a good manager"?

4. Based on either personal experience as a manager or on your observation of managers at work, are the 11 skills in Table 1–1 a realistic portrayal of what managers do?

5. How willing and able are you to work under the new employment contract?

6. What is your personal experience with Theory X and Theory Y managers (see Table 1–3)? Which did you prefer? Why?

7. How would you respond to a new manager who made this statement? "TQM is about statistical process control, not about people."

8. Do you use the contingency approach in your daily affairs? Explain the circumstances.

9. What "practical" theories have you formulated to achieve the things you want in life (e.g., graduating, keeping fit, getting a good job, meeting that special someone)?

10. From a manager's standpoint, which use of research is better: instrumental or conceptual? Explain your rationale.

Internet Exercise

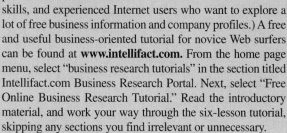

Part 1 (Note: This part is for those with little or no Internet experience, those who need to polish their Internet research skills, and experienced Internet users who want to explore a lot of free business information and company profiles.) A free and useful business-oriented tutorial for novice Web surfers can be found at **www.intellifact.com.** From the home page menu, select "business research tutorials" in the section titled Intellifact.com Business Research Portal. Next, select "Free Online Business Research Tutorial." Read the introductory material, and work your way through the six-lesson tutorial, skipping any sections you find irrelevant or unnecessary.

Questions

1. What useful online research tips did you discover?

2. What useful business-related information sources did you discover?

3. What useful information did you acquire?

Note: If you know of a better *free* online research tutorial than this one, please tell your instructor and fellow students.

   Part 2: The purpose of this exercise is to focus on one well-known company with a good general reputation (Hewlett-Packard) and look for evidence of the seven people-centered practices discussed at the beginning of this chapter (go back and review them to refresh your memory). On the Internet, go to Hewlett-Packard's home page (**www.hp.com**), and select "Company Information" from the main menu. Next, select "About HP," and then select "Corporate Objectives & the HP Way." Read the Corporate Objectives statement, focusing particularly on the sections "Our People" and "Management." At the end of this material, click on the prompt "HP Way" and read about the company's history and culture, focusing on the section "Organizational Values."

Questions

1. On a scale of 1 = low to 10 = high, how people-centered is HP?

2. What *specific* evidence of each of the seven people-centered practices did you find?

3. Which of the seven practices appears to be HP's strongest suit?

4. Do HP's culture and values give it a strategic competitive advantage? Explain.

5. Would you like to work for HP? Why or why not?

OB in Action Case Study

Steve Ballmer, CEO, Microsoft Corp.: "I'm Trying to Let Other People Dive in Before I Do"[61]

BusinessWeek Steven A Ballmer's explosive temper is legendary. Back in his bad old days, before being appointed Microsoft Corp.'s president [and then CEO], Ballmer would shout himself hoarse if a lieutenant didn't do his bidding fast enough. His motivational techniques drew heavily from Attila the Hun. When he directed the company's Windows product group, he put the fear of God into engineers by bellowing at them and pounding a baseball bat into his palm. And don't forget his outburst last May after the Justice Dept. sued Microsoft for antitrust law violations. "To heck with Janet Reno!" he blurted out.

   Today, you'll find a tamer Ballmer. Since he took over running Microsoft's day-to-day operations, the 19-year veteran has worked hard to fashion a leadership style that's diplomatic rather than bullying—more Eisenhower than Patton. He still has the booming voice, but what he does with it is more constructive. "I'm trying to temper myself. I don't think I've mellowed. But I try to redirect my energy," he says, bursting into a raucous laugh. The difference is obvious to people who know Ballmer well. "He's certainly changed. He's calmer," says Microsoft board member Jon A Shirley.

   The fact is, Ballmer, 43, is coming into his own as Microsoft's [new CEO]—and putting his mark on the company to boot. Since Ballmer got the job, he hasn't been content just to make the trains run on time. He's spearheading the effort to reshape Microsoft. He dreamed up a plan—which he calls Vision Version 2—for energizing employees, focusing them on customers, and broadening their outlook far beyond the narrow confines of the PC and Windows.

Wild Cheers

It's quite a different role for Ballmer. He has long played loyal sidekick to Chairman William H Gates III. The two met as undergraduates at Harvard in 1973. Both were math whizzes, but Ballmer was more outgoing. He managed the college football team, the *Harvard Crimson* newspaper, and the student literary magazine. Ballmer also was more firmly rooted in day-to-day tasks than the absent-minded Gates. Once, after Gates left his dorm door and window open to weather and burglars when he departed for Christmas vacation, a watchful Ballmer battened down the place for him.

Gates eventually dropped out of Harvard to form Microsoft. But he didn't forget Ballmer. In 1980, he coaxed his pal to leave Stanford business school to join the fledgling company and whip into shape its chaotic business operations. The offer: A $50,000 salary and 7% of the company—a stake now worth nearly $20 billion. Later, Gates called on Ballmer to goose delivery of Microsoft's crucial Windows operating system. Then he relied on his friend to build a sales organization to compete with IBM in large corporate accounts.

Ballmer was always the passionate heart of the company. He led wild cheers at company meetings—leaping around on stage like a burly Mick Jagger. On a dare, he once dove into a pond on the company's Redmond (Wash.) campus in November. Charismatic as he was, Ballmer always remained in Gates's shadow. Now Gates is sharing the limelight. "Of the upper management at Microsoft, Steve's the one that gets it," says a former company executive.

Not only does Ballmer get it, but he's doing something about it. As part of Vision 2, he hopes to transform a culture where he and Gates made too many decisions themselves. Now, he's pushing authority down into the ranks. And he's more inclined to listen to subordinates before he speaks. At a review of the Consumer Windows Div.'s product plans on Apr. 30, for instance, he made polite suggestions to managers, rather than quickly telling them what they ought to do. "I see him coaching more than in the past—as opposed to pushing," says Bill Veghte, the group's general manager. Ballmer admits his biggest challenge is delegating. "I'm used to diving in deeply," he says. "Now I'm trying to let other people dive in before I do."

Ballmer's getting atta-boys for his efforts. Gates praises the way he shepherded Microsoft's new E-commerce strategy. The company hopes to get 1 million businesses to use its software to create electronic stores linked to the MSN Web portal. "I think it's a brilliant idea," says Gates. Others say Ballmer has notched up the level of teamwork in the company by forming a Business Leadership Team—14 managers who meet monthly to coordinate strategies across the operating units. "Early days, but signs are good," says Paul A Maritz, executive vice-president in charge of the Developer Group.

Ballmer appears willing to do whatever it takes to make Microsoft successful. And that includes giving up his beloved baseball bat. In late March, when marketing vice-president Deborah N Willingham spotted him with the bat in a hallway and urged him to be careful, he handed it over to her. "He was saying you're the leaders—the bat swingers. It's a new world," Willingham says. Ballmer still unleashes his famous temper now and then—but at least he isn't swinging a bat anymore.

Questions for Discussion

1. Which of the seven people-centered practices discussed at the beginning of the chapter does Ballmer need to work on to be an effective top manager? Explain your choices.

2. Which people-centered practices seem to be most evident in this brief case study of Microsoft?

3. Using Table 1–1 as a guide, how would you assess Steve Ballmer's skills as an effective manager?

4. What is the connection between TQM and Ballmer's Vision Version 2?

5. Imagine yourself as a new Microsoft manager who reports directly to Steve Ballmer. How would the fact that he owns $20 billion (that's a "B") in company stock affect the way you likely would respond to him and interact with him on a daily basis?

Personal Awareness and Growth Exercise

How Strong Is Your Motivation to Manage?

Objectives

1. To introduce a psychological determinant of managerial success.

2. To assess your readiness to manage.

3. To discuss the implications of motivation to manage, from the standpoint of global competitiveness.

Introduction

By identifying personal traits positively correlated with both rapid movement up the career ladder and managerial effectiveness, John B Miner developed a psychometric test for measuring what he calls motivation to manage. The ques-

tionnaire assesses the strength of seven factors relating to the temperament (or psychological makeup) needed to manage others. One word of caution. The following instrument is a shortened and modified version of Miner's original. Our version is for instructional and discussion purposes only. Although we believe it can indicate the *general* strength of your motivation to manage, it is *not* a precise measuring tool.

Instructions

Assess the strength of each of the seven dimensions of *your own* motivation to manage by circling the appropriate numbers on the 1 to 7 scales. Then add the seven circled numbers to get your total motivation to manage score.

Factor	Description	Scale
1. Authority figures	A desire to meet managerial role requirements in terms of positive relationships with superiors.	Weak 1–2–3–4–5–6–7 Strong
2. Competitive games	A desire to engage in competition with peers involving games or sports and thus meet managerial role requirements in this regard.	Weak 1–2–3–4–5–6–7 Strong
3. Competitive situations	A desire to engage in competition with peers involving occupational or work-related activities and thus meet managerial role requirements in this regard.	Weak 1–2–3–4–5–6–7 Strong
4. Assertive role	A desire to behave in an active and assertive manner involving activities that in this society are often viewed as predominantly masculine and thus to meet managerial role requirements.	Weak 1–2–3–4–5–6–7 Strong
5. Imposing wishes	A desire to tell others what to do and to utilize sanctions in influencing others, thus indicating a capacity to fulfill managerial role requirements in relationships with subordinates.	Weak 1–2–3–4–5–6–7 Strong
6. Standing out from group	A desire to assume a distinctive position of a unique and highly visible nature in a manner that is role-congruent for managerial jobs.	Weak 1–2–3–4–5–6–7 Strong
7. Routine administrative functions	A desire to meet managerial role requirements regarding activities often associated with managerial work that are of a day-to-day administrative nature.	Weak 1–2–3–4–5–6–7 Strong
		Total = _____

Scoring and Interpretation

Arbitrary norms for comparison purposes are as follows: Total score of 7–21 = Relatively low motivation to manage; 22–34 = Moderate; 35–49 = Relatively high. How do you measure up? Remember, though, high motivation to manage is only part of the formula for managerial success. The right combination of ability and opportunity is also necessary.

Years of motivation-to-manage research by Miner and others has serious implications for America's future global competitiveness. Generally, in recent years, college students in the United States have not scored highly on motivation to manage.[62] Indeed, compared with samples of US college students, samples of students from Japan, China, Mexico, Korea, and Taiwan consistently scored higher on motivation to manage.[63] Miner believes the United States may consequently lag in developing sufficient managerial talent for a tough global marketplace.[64]

In a study by other researchers, MBA students with higher motivation-to-manage scores tended to earn more money after graduation. But students with a higher motivation to manage did not earn better grades or complete their degree program any sooner than those with a lower motivation to manage.[65]

Questions for Discussion

1. Do you believe our adaptation of Miner's motivation to manage instrument accurately assessed your potential as a manager? Explain.

2. Which of the seven dimensions do you think is probably the best predictor of managerial success? Which is the least predictive? Why?

3. Miner puts heavy emphasis on competitiveness by anchoring two of the seven dimensions of motivation to manage to the desire to compete. Some observers believe the traditional (win–lose) competitive attitude is being pushed aside in favor of a less competitive (win–win) attitude today, thus making Miner's instrument out of date. What is your position on this competitiveness debate? Explain.

4. Do you believe Miner is correct in saying that low motivation to manage hurts the United States's global competitiveness? Explain.

Group Exercise

Timeless Advice

Objectives

1. To get to know some of your fellow students.
2. To put the management of people into a lively and interesting historical context.
3. To begin to develop your teamwork skills.

Introduction

Your creative energy, willingness to see familiar things in unfamiliar ways, and ability to have fun while learning are keys to the success of this warm-up exercise. A 20-minute, small-group session will be followed by brief oral presentations and a general class discussion. Total time required is approximately 40 to 45 minutes.

Instructions

Your instructor will divide your class randomly into groups of four to six people each. Acting as a team, with everyone offering ideas and one person serving as official recorder, each group will be responsible for writing a one-page memo to your current class. Subject matter of your group's memo will be "My advice for managing people today is. . . ." The fun part of this exercise (and its creative element) involves writing the memo from the viewpoint of the person assigned to your group by your instructor.

Among the memo viewpoints your instructor may assign are the following:

- David Duffield (chapter-opening vignette).
- An ancient Egyptian slave master (building the great pyramids).
- Mary Parker Follett.
- Douglas McGregor.
- A Theory X supervisor of a construction crew (see McGregor's Theories X and Y in Table 1–3).
- W Edwards Deming.

- A TQM coordinator at 3M Company.
- A contingency management theorist.
- Steve Ballmer (end-of-chapter case study).
- A Japanese auto company executive.
- The chief executive officer of IBM in the year 2030.
- Commander of the Starship Enterprise II in the year 3001.
- Others, as assigned by your instructor.

Use your imagination, make sure everyone participates, and try to be true to any historical facts you've encountered. Attempt to be as specific and realistic as possible. Remember, the idea is to provide advice about managing people from another point in time (or from a particular point of view at the present time).

Make sure you manage your 20-minute time limit carefully. A recommended approach is to spend 2 to 3 minutes putting the exercise into proper perspective. Next, take about 10 to 12 minutes brainstorming ideas for your memo, with your recorder jotting down key ideas and phrases. Have your recorder use the remaining time to write your group's one-page memo, with constructive comments and help from the others. Pick a spokesperson to read your group's memo to the class.

Questions for Discussion

1. What valuable lessons about managing people have you heard?
2. What have you learned about how NOT to manage people?
3. From the distant past to today, what significant shifts in the management of people seem to have taken place?
4. Where does the management of people appear to be headed?
5. All things considered, what mistakes are today's managers typically making when managing people?
6. How well did your group function as a "team"?

Learning Module A
Research Methods in Organizational Behavior

As a future manager, you probably will be involved in developing and/or implementing programs for solving managerial problems. You may also be asked to assess recommendations derived from in-house research reports or judge the usefulness of management consulting proposals. These tasks might entail reading and evaluating research findings presented both in scientific and professional journal articles. Thus, it is important for managers to have a basic working knowledge of the research process. Moreover, such knowledge can help you critically evaluate research information encountered daily in newspaper, magazine, and television reports. These conclusions are all the more important when you consider them in light of results obtained from two recent studies. The first was a national survey about the extent to which Americans believe or accept poll results reported on TV or in a newspaper. Results revealed that 33% of adults generally believed in what they heard or read: 44% did not.[1] The second study, which was conducted by the National Science Foundation, indicated that most people could not tell good scientific studies from bad ones.[2] If people can not judge the difference between good and bad research, then how do they know what to believe about research results pertaining to organizational or societal problems? As a specific case in point, let us consider the issue of whether to wear rear-seat lap belts while riding in an automobile.

A study conducted by the National Transportation Safety Board (NTSB) concluded, "Instead of protecting people, rear-seat lap belts can cause serious or fatal internal injuries in the event of a head-on crash."[3] Despite previous recommendations to wear seat belts, do you now believe rear-seat lap belts are dangerous? To answer this question adequately, one needs to know more about how the NTSB's study was conducted and what has been found in related studies. Before providing you with this information, however, this advanced learning module presents a foundation for understanding the research process. Our purpose is not to make you a research scientist. The purpose is to make you a better consumer of research information, such as that provided by the NTSB.

The Research Process

Research on organizational behavior is based on the scientific method. The *scientific method* is a formal process of using systematically gathered data to test hypotheses or to explain natural phenomena. To gain a better understanding of how to evaluate this process, we discuss a model of how research is conducted, explore how researchers measure organizationally relevant variables, highlight three ways to evaluate research methods, and provide a framework for evaluating research conclusions. We also discuss how to read a research article. Finally, we return to the NTSB study and evaluate its conclusions on the basis of lessons from this advanced learning module.

A Model of the Research Process

A flowchart of the research process is presented in Figure A–1. Organizational research is conducted to solve problems. The problem may be one of current interest to an organization, such as absenteeism or low motivation, or may be derived from published

Figure A–1   *Model of the Research Process*

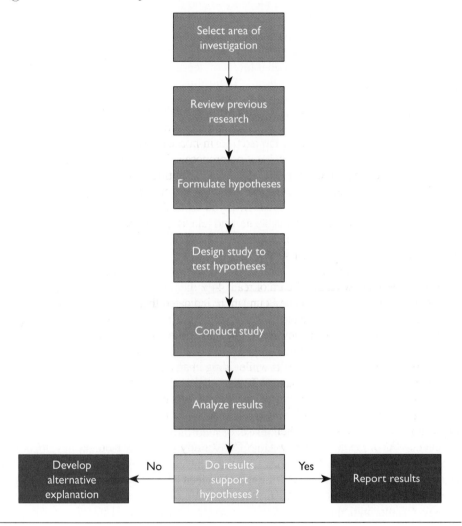

SOURCE: V R Boehm, "Research in the 'Real World': A Conceptual Model," *Personnel Psychology,* Autumn 1980, p 496. Used with permission.

research studies. In either case, properly identifying and attempting to solve the problem necessitates a familiarity with previous research on the topic. This familiarity contributes background knowledge and insights for formulating a hypothesis to solve the problem. Students who have written formal library-research papers are well-acquainted with this type of *secondary* research.

According to a respected researcher: "A *hypothesis* is a conjectural statement of the relation between two or more variables. Hypotheses are always in declarative form, and they relate, either generally or specifically, variables to variables."[4] Regarding the problem of absenteeism, for instance, a manager might want to test the following hypothesis: "Hourly employees who are dissatisfied with their pay are absent more often than those who are satisfied." Hypothesis in hand, a researcher is prepared to design a study to test it.

There are two important, interrelated components to designing a study. The first consists of deciding how to measure independent and dependent variables. An *independent variable* is a variable that is hypothesized to affect or cause a certain state of events. For example, a study demonstrated that losing one's job led to lower self-esteem and greater depression.[5] In this case, losing one's job, the independent variable, produced lower levels of self-esteem and higher levels of depression. A *dependent variable* is the variable being explained or predicted. Returning to the example, self-esteem and depression were the dependent variables (the variables being explained). In an everyday example, those who eat less (independent variable) are likely to lose weight (dependent variable). The second component of designing a study is to determine which research method to use (recall the discussion in Chapter 1). Criteria for evaluating the appropriateness of different research methods are discussed in a later section.

After a study is designed and completed, data are analyzed to determine whether the hypothesis is supported. Researchers look for alternative explanations of results when a hypothesis is not supported.[6]

Measurement and Data Collection

"In its broadest sense, measurement is the assignment of numerals to objects or events according to rules."[7] Organizational researchers measure variables. Job satisfaction, turnover, performance, and perceived stress are variables typically measured in OB research. Valid measurement is one of the most critical components of any research study because research findings are open to conflicting interpretations when variables are poorly measured.[8] Poor measurement reduces the confidence one has in applying research findings. Four techniques are frequently used to collect data: (1) direct observation, (2) questionnaires, (3) interviews, and (4) indirect methods.

Observation   This technique consists of recording the number of times a prespecified behavior is exhibited. For example, psychologist Judith Komaki developed and validated an observational categorization of supervisory behavior. She then used the instrument to identify behavior differences between effective and ineffective managers from a large medical insurance firm. Managerial effectiveness was based on superior ratings. Results indicated that effective managers spent more time monitoring their employees' performance than did ineffective managers. Komaki more recently applied the same instrument to examine the performance of sailboat captains competing in a race. Similar to the managerial study, skippers finished higher in the overall race standings when they monitored and rewarded their crews.[9] There are few "valid" observational schemes for use in OB research outside of Komaki's taxonomy.

Questionnaires   Questionnaires ask respondents for their opinions or feelings about work-related issues. They generally contain previously developed and validated instruments and are self-administered. Given their impersonal nature, poorly designed questionnaires are susceptible to rater bias. Nevertheless, a well-developed survey can be an accurate and economical way to collect large quantities of data.[10]

Interviews   Interviews rely on either face-to-face or telephone interactions to ask respondents questions of interest. In a *structured* interview, interviewees are asked the same questions in the same order. *Unstructured* interviews do not require interviewers to use the same questions or format. Unstructured interviews are more spontaneous. Structured interviews are the better of the two because they permit

Table A–1   *Assessment of Frequently Used Research Methods*

Method	Generalizability	Precision in Control and Measurement	Realistic Context
Case study	Low	Low	High
Sample survey	High	Low	Low
Field study	Moderate	Moderate	High
Laboratory experiment	Low	High	Low
Field experiment	Moderate	Moderate	Moderate

SOURCE: Adapted in part from J E McGrath, J Martin, and R A Kulka, *Judgment Calls in Research* (Beverly Hills, CA: Sage Publications, 1982).

consistent comparisons among people. Accordingly, human resource management experts strongly recommend structured interviews during the hiring process to permit candidate-to-candidate comparisons.[11]

Indirect Methods   These techniques obtain data without any direct contact with respondents. This approach may entail observing someone without his or her knowledge. Other examples include searching existing records, such as personnel files, for data on variables such as absenteeism, turnover, and output. This method reduces rater error and generally is used in combination with one of the previously discussed techniques.

Evaluating Research Methods

All research methods can be evaluated from three perspectives: (1) generalizability, (2) precision in control and measurement, and (3) realism of the context.[12] *Generalizability,* which also is referred to as external validity, reflects the extent to which results from one study are generalizable to other individuals, groups, or situations. *Precision in control and measurement* pertains to the level of accuracy in manipulating or measuring variables. A *realistic context* is one that naturally exists for the individuals participating in the research study. In other words, realism implies that the context is not an artificial situation contrived for purposes of conducting the study. Table A–1 presents an evaluation of the five most frequently used research methods in terms of these three perspectives.

   In summary, there is no one best research method. Choosing a method depends on the purpose of the specific study.[13] For example, if high control is necessary, as in testing for potential radiation leaks in pipes that will be used at a nuclear power plant, a laboratory experiment is appropriate (see Table A–1). In contrast, sample surveys would be useful if a company wanted to know the generalizable impact of a television commercial for light beer.

Evaluating Research Conclusions

There are several issues to consider when evaluating the quality of a research study.[14] The first is whether results from the specific study are consistent with those from past research. If not, it is helpful to determine why discrepancies exist. For instance, it is insightful to compare the samples, research methods, measurement of variables, statistical analyses, and general research procedures across the discrepant studies. Extreme differences suggest that future research may be needed to reconcile the inconsistent results. In the meantime, however, we need to be cautious in applying research findings from one study that are inconsistent with those from a larger number of studies.

The type of research method used is the second consideration. Does the method have generalizability (see Table A–1)? If not, check the characteristics of the sample. If the sample's characteristics are different from the characteristics of your work group, conclusions may not be relevant for your organization. Sample characteristics are very important in evaluating results from both field studies and experiments.

The level of precision in control and measurement is the third factor to consider. It is important to determine whether valid measures were used in the study. This can be done by reading the original study and examining descriptions of how variables were measured. Variables have questionable validity when they are measured with one-item scales or "ad-hoc" instruments developed by the authors. In contrast, standardized scales tend to be more valid because they are typically developed and validated in previous research studies. We have more confidence in results when they are based on analyses using standardized scales. As a general rule, validity in measurement begets confidence in applying research findings.

Finally, it is helpful to brainstorm alternative explanations for the research results. This helps to identify potential problems within research procedures.

Reading a Scientific Journal Article

Research is published in scientific journals and professional magazines. *Journal of Applied Psychology* and *Academy of Management Journal* are examples of scientific journals reporting OB research. *Management Review* and *HRMagazine* are professional magazines that sometimes report research findings in general terms. Table A–2 contains a list of 50 highly regarded management journals and magazines. You may find this list to be a useful source of information when writing term papers.

Scientific journal articles report results from empirical research studies, overall reviews of research on a specific topic, and theoretical articles. To help you obtain relevant information from scientific articles, let us consider the content and structure of these three types of articles.[15]

Empirical Research Studies

Reports of these studies contain summaries of original research. They typically comprise four distinct sections consistent with the logical steps of the research process model shown in Figure A–1. These sections are as follows:

- *Introduction.* This section identifies the problem being investigated and the purpose of the study. Previous research pertaining to the problem is reviewed and sometimes critiqued.

- *Method.* This section discusses the method used to conduct the study. Characteristics of the sample or subjects, procedures followed, materials used, measurement of variables, and analytic procedures typically are discussed.

- *Results.* A detailed description of the documented results is presented.

- *Discussion.* This section provides an interpretation, discussion, and implications of results.

Table A–2   *A List of Highly Regarded Management Journals and Magazines*

1. Administrative Science Quarterly	26. Journal of Occupational Behavior
2. Journal of Applied Psychology	27. Public Administration Quarterly
3. Organizational Behavior and Human Decision Processes	28. Journal of Organizational Behavior Management
4. Academy of Management Journal	29. Organizational Dynamics
5. Psychological Bulletin	30. Monthly Labor Review
6. Industrial and Labor Relations Review	31. Journal of World Business
7. Journal of Personality and Social Psychology	32. Journal of Business Research
8. Academy of Management Review	33. Group and Organization Management
9. Industrial Relations	34. Human Resource Planning
10. Journal of Labor Economics	35. Journal of Management Studies
11. Personnel Psychology	36. Administration and Society
12. American Psychologist	37. Negotiation Journal
13. Journal of Labor Research	38. Arbitration Journal
14. Journal of Vocational Labor	39. Compensation and Benefits Review
15. Journal of Applied Behavioral Science	40. Journal of Collective Negotiations in the Public Sector
16. Occupational Psychology	41. Public Personnel Management
17. Sloan Management Review	42. Journal of Management Education*
18. Journal of Conflict Resolution	43. Review of Business and Economic Research
19. Human Relations	44. Personnel Journal
20. Journal of Human Resources	45. Journal of Small Business Management
21. Labor Law Journal	46. SAM Advanced Management Journal
22. Harvard Business Review	47. Business Horizons
23. Social Forces	48. Business and Public Affairs
24. Journal of Management	49. HRMagazine**
25. California Management Review	50. Training and Development***

*Formerly Organizational Behavior Teaching Review

**Formerly Personnel Administrator

***Formerly Training and Development Journal

SOURCE: Adapted by permission from M M Extejt and J E Smith, "The Behavior Sciences and Management: An Evaluation of Relevant Journals," *Journal of Management,* September 1990, p 545.

Review Articles

These articles, including meta-analyses, are critical evaluations of material that has already been published. By organizing, integrating, and evaluating previously published material, the author of a review article considers the progress of current research toward clarifying a problem."[16] Although the structure of these articles is not as clear-cut as reports of empirical studies, the general format is as follows:

- A statement of the problem.
- A summary or review of previous research that attempts to provide the reader with the state of current knowledge about the problem (meta-analysis frequently is used to summarize past research).

• Identification of shortcomings, limitations, and inconsistencies in past research.

• Recommendations for future research to solve the problem.

Theoretical Articles

These articles draw on past research to propose revisions to existing theoretical models or to develop new theories and models. The structure is similar to that of review articles.

Back to the NTSB Study

This module was introduced with a National Transportation Safety Board study that suggested it is not safe to wear rear-seat lap belts while riding in an automobile. Given what we have just discussed, take a few minutes now to jot down any potential explanations for why the NTSB findings conflict with past research supporting the positive benefits of rear-seat lap belts. Now compare your thoughts with an evaluation presented in the *University of California, Berkeley Wellness Letter:*

> Critics claim that the NTSB study paints a misleadingly scary picture by focusing on 26 unrepresentative accidents, all unusually serious and all but one frontal. The National Highway Traffic Safety Administration has strongly disputed the board's findings, citing five earlier studies of thousands of crashes showing that safety belts—including lap belts—are instrumental in preventing death and injury. And a new study of 37,000 crashes in North Carolina shows that rear-seat lap belts reduce the incidence of serious injury and death by about 40% . . .
>
> In the meantime, most evidence indicates that you should continue to use rear-seat lap belts. You can minimize the risk of injury by wearing them as low across the hips as possible and keeping them tight.[17]

The NTSB findings were based on a set of unrepresentative serious frontal accidents. In other words, the NTSB's sample was not reflective of the typical automobile accident. Thus, the generalizability of the NTSB results is very limited. Buckle up!

Chapter Two

Managing Diversity: Releasing Every Employee's Potential

Learning Objectives

When you finish studying the material in this chapter, you should be able to:

1 Define diversity.

2 Discuss the four layers of diversity.

3 Explain the differences among affirmative action, valuing diversity, and managing diversity.

4 Demonstrate your familiarity with the demographic trends that are creating an increasingly diverse workforce.

5 Highlight the managerial implications of increasing diversity in the workforce.

6 Review the five reasons managing diversity is a competitive advantage.

7 Identify the barriers and challenges to managing diversity.

8 Discuss the organizational practices used to effectively manage diversity as identified by R Roosevelt Thomas, Jr, and Ann Morrison.

BusinessWeek Madoka Matsumae, 24, doesn't want to be treated like a man, just to earn as much as one. For six years, she has snapped rings onto pistons at Mazda Motor Corp.'s engine plant in Hiroshima. Yet unlike her male colleagues, Matsumae leaves work every day at 5:30 P.M. Japanese factory workers can earn up to 30% more than their regular pay by doing night shifts. But women have been banned from working after 10 P.M. or putting in more than six hours of overtime a week.

That is starting to change. On Apr. 1, [1999,] Japan revised its Equal Employment Opportunity Law to end overly protective restrictions on women's work. The law also is much tougher on sexual harassment and gender-based hiring. The most immediate impact will be felt in factories. Thanks to the greater flexibility, Japanese manufacturers are likely to hire many more women for manual jobs. An aging population means fewer young men are entering the workforce. So companies must rely more on women to keep factories humming.

Factories are even starting to refit assembly lines with lighter tools and equipment to accommodate female

Mazda Plant: With fewer men in the workforce, factories need more women.
(Tom Wagner/SABA)

workers. Toyota Motor Corp. spent $424,000 to retool two assembly lines that will be staffed by 650 women this year—up from 440 in 1998—and 1,100 later. It's also giving women more training in everything from sexual harassment policies to how to work on assembly lines. "There are more women interested in this type of work than in the past," says Tateaki Harada, a Toyota human resources manager. The attraction is a livelihood that offers more than sitting around an office. "I'd rather have a more active job," explains 18-year-old Mazda recruit Nami Kitamura. "I'm looking forward to showing that I can do as good a job as a man."

The gender gap in Japan is still wide in comparison with the West. Even with 60 new female hires this year, only 8 of every 1,000 Mazda factory workers will be women, compared with 158 per 1,000 at the North American factories of Mazda's largest shareholder, Ford Motor Co. At Toyota City, the ratio is still just 2 per 1,000. What's more, the gains will be felt more in factories than in the white-collar world. The Labor Ministry says that 1 in 10 Japanese managers is a woman. But this includes those who run their own businesses. Female executives are rare at Japan's elite corporations, and few experts expect dramatic improvement. "The good jobs are still restricted to men," contends Mizuho Fukushima, a leading women's rights activist and a House of Councillors member. "Women are so low on the totem pole that they cannot see what is happening at the top."

Women's Work. Women still suffer because most were hired and trained as clerical workers. Men are more likely to be put on a management track, while women spend most of their time filing papers and reserving bullet train tickets. "Women in these companies don't have the same training, so they don't know what to do," says human resources consultant Yuriko Miyazaki.[1]

FOR DISCUSSION
Why is the gender gap larger in Japan than it is in the United States? Explain.

M anagers are increasingly being asked to boost productivity, quality, and customer satisfaction while also reducing costs. These goals can only be met, however, through the cooperation and effort of all employees. By creating positive work environments where people feel valued and appreciated, organizations are more likely to foster the employee commitment and performance needed for organizational success. This conclusion may partly explain why Japan is trying to reduce the gender gap discussed in the opening vignette. Interestingly, however, some organizations are missing the mark when it comes to managing diversity. Consider the work environment at the Miami maintenance hangar for American Eagle, a unit of AMR Corporation.[2]

Employees regularly painted the men's bathroom to cover up the constant racial graffiti penned by mechanics. "Bulletin-board cartoons depicted black mechanics as gorillas or starving Somalians. Someone posted a jet-black, over-exposed Polaroid picture with four white dots on it and the names of two black mechanics "on the ramp at 10 PM."[3] Imagine how Tony Lee, an African-American crew chief, must have felt when he observed a noose with the name "Tony" attached by the time clock or a when another employee found a stuffed gorilla labeled "Tony Lee" with a noose around its neck. Would you be motivated to perform at your best if you were Mr. Lee? It is important to note that these terrible things occurred in spite of the fact that AMR's American Eagle unit adopted strong policies against graffiti and workplace behavior that promoted racial or sexual discrimination. As you will learn in this chapter, managing diversity entails much more than creating policies and procedures.

Managing diversity is a sensitive, potentially volatile, and sometimes uncomfortable issue. Yet managers are required to deal with it in the name of organizational survival. Accordingly, the purpose of this chapter is to help you get a better understanding of this important context for organizational behavior. We begin by defining diversity. Next, we build the business case for diversity and then discuss the barriers and challenges associated with managing diversity. The chapter concludes by describing the organizational practices used to manage diversity effectively.

Defining Diversity

Diversity represents the multitude of individual differences and similarities that exist among people. This definition underscores three important issues about managing diversity:[4] (1) There are many different dimensions or components of diversity. This implies that diversity pertains to everybody. It is not an issue of age, race, or gender. It is not an issue of being heterosexual, gay, or lesbian or of being Catholic, Jewish, Protestant, or Muslim. Diversity also does not pit white males against all other groups of people. Diversity pertains to the host of individual differences that make all of us unique and different from others. (2) Diversity is not synonymous with differences. Rather, it encompasses both differences and similarities. This means that managing diversity entails dealing with both simultaneously. (3) Diversity includes the collective mixture of differences and similarities, not just the pieces of it. Dealing with diversity requires managers to integrate the collective mixture of differences and similarities that exist within an organization.

Diversity
The host of individual differences that make people different from and similar to each other.

This section begins our journey into managing diversity by first reviewing the key dimensions of diversity. Because many people associate diversity with affirmative action, this section compares affirmative action, valuing diversity, and managing diversity. They are not the same.

Layers of Diversity

Like seashells on a beach, people come in a variety of shapes, sizes, and colors. This variety represents the essence of diversity. Lee Gardenswartz and Anita Rowe, a team of diversity experts, identified four layers of diversity to help distinguish the important ways in which people differ (see Figure 2–1). Taken together, these layers define your personal identity and influence how each of us sees the world.[5]

Figure 2–1 shows that personality is at the center of the diversity wheel. Personality is at the center because it represents a stable set of characteristics that is responsible for a person's identity. The dimensions of personality are discussed later in Chapter 5. The OB Exercise is a brief self-assessment of your personality profile. It can help you better understand how similarities and differences between your personality and that of co-workers influence your interactions with others. Take a short break from your reading to complete the

Diversity is more than just skin deep. To motivate today's diverse workforce, managers need to understand the nature of diversity and create a positive work environment where individuals feel valued and appreciated.

(David Young-Wolff/PhotoEdit)

Figure 2–1   *The Four Layers of Diversity*

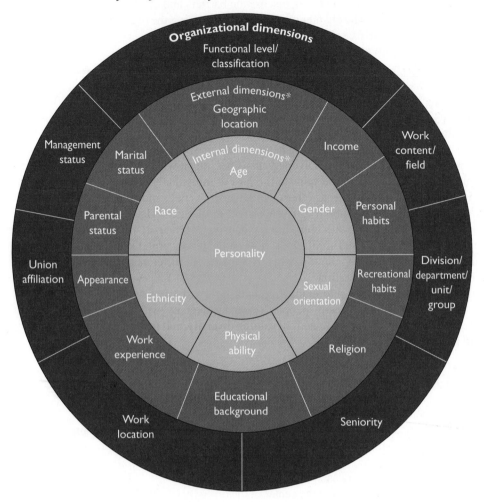

*Internal Dimensions and External Dimensions are adapted from Loden and Rosener, *Workforce America!* (Homewood, IL: Business One Irwin, 1991).

SOURCE: L Gardenswartz and A Rowe, *Diverse Teams at Work: Capitalizing on the Power of Diversity* (New York: McGraw-Hill, 1994), p. 33. © 1994. Reproduced with permission of The McGraw-Hill Companies.

exercise. What is your reaction to the exercise? Are you surprised to see how similarities and differences in personality influence your relationship with someone else? How might you improve your working relationship with this comparison person based on results from this exercise?

The next layer of diversity consists of a set of internal dimensions that are referred to as the primary dimensions of diversity.[6] These dimensions, for the most part, are not within our control, but strongly influence our attitudes and expectations and assumptions about others, which, in turn, influence our behavior. Take the encounter experienced by an African-American woman in middle management while vacationing at a resort:

> While she was sitting by the pool, "a large 50-ish white male approached me and demanded that I get him extra towels. I said, 'Excuse me?' He then said, 'Oh, you don't work here,' with no shred of embarrassment or apology in his voice."[7]

OB Exercise   Drawing Your Personality Profile

Instructions

First, evaluate the extent to which each of the following personality characteristics fits your image of yourself by marking an "X" along each continuum. There are no right or wrong evaluations. Then connect your "Xs" vertically to form your personality profile. Once completed, answer the following questions: (1) Which characteristics are likely to make you a good team player when working with others? (2) Which characteristics may cause problems when working with others? (3) Which characteristics are most important to your identity?

We now want you to take this assessment one step further by marking each continuum to form the profile of someone you have a difficult time getting along with. This can be someone that you currently or previously worked with, another student, and/or a friend or family member. Vertically connect the "Xs" for this individual's profile and consider the following questions: (1) What personality characteristics of others are hardest for you to deal with? (2) Where are the biggest gaps between the two profiles? (3) What similarities or differences seem to be at the heart of your difficulty in getting along with this individual?

Patient	_____	Impatient
Introvert	_____	Extrovert
Doer	_____	Thinker
Assertive	_____	Nonassertive
Competitive	_____	Collaborative
Leader	_____	Follower
Listener	_____	Talker
Fast-paced	_____	Slow-paced
Serious	_____	Humorous
Spontaneous	_____	Scheduled
Flexible	_____	Rigid
Relaxed	_____	Intense
Optimist	_____	Pessimist
Realist	_____	Idealist
Rational	_____	Emotional

SOURCE: This exercise was adapted from one contained in L Gardenswartz and A Rowe, *Diverse Teams at Work: Capitalizing on the Power of Diversity* (New York: McGraw-Hill, 1994), pp 34–35.

Stereotypes regarding one or more of the primary dimensions of diversity most likely influenced this man's behavior toward the woman.

Figure 2–1 reveals that the next layer of diversity is composed of external influences, which are referred to as secondary dimensions of diversity. They represent individual differences that we have a greater ability to influence or control. Examples include where you grew up and live today, your religious affiliation, whether you are married and have children, and your work experiences. These dimensions also exert a significant influence on our perceptions, behavior, and attitudes.

Consider religion as an illustration. Given that Islam is expected to surpass Judaism as the second-most commonly practiced religion in the United States (Christianity is first), organizations need to consider both Muslim employees and customers when implementing their policies, procedures, and programs. Argenbright Security Inc. in Atlanta created problems for itself when management sent home seven Muslim women for wearing Islamic headscarves at their security jobs at Dulles International Airport. Because wearing headscarves in no way affected their job performance, the company had to reimburse the women for back pay and other relief in a settlement negotiated with the Equal Employment Opportunity Commission.[8] Similarly, a lack of sensitivity regarding the Muslim faith led Nike to recall a shoe line in 1997. The shoe was imprinted with a logo that looked like the Arabic script for Allah. Nike paid refunds for returned shoes, issued a public apology, sent employees to sensitivity training, and donated money to a Muslim elementary school in the United States.[9]

As you can see from these examples, a lack of awareness about the external layer of diversity can cause bad feelings among both employees and customers. The final layer of diversity includes organizational dimensions such as seniority, job title and function, and work location.

Affirmative Action and Valuing Diversity

Valuing diversity and managing diversity require organizations to adopt a new way of thinking about differences among people. Rather than pitting one group against another, valuing diversity and managing diversity strive to recognize the unique contribution every employee can make. This philosophy is much different from that of affirmative action. This section highlights the differences among affirmative action, valuing diversity, and managing diversity. Table 2–1 compares these three approaches to managing employee differences.

Affirmative Action   As shown in Table 2–1, affirmative action focuses on achieving equality of opportunity in an organization and is legally mandated in the United States by Equal Opportunity laws. **Affirmative action** is an artificial intervention aimed at giving management a chance to correct an imbalance, an injustice, a mistake, and/or outright discrimination. Affirmative action does not legitimize quotas. Quotas are illegal. They can only be imposed by judges who conclude that a company has engaged in discriminatory practices. It also is important to note that under no circumstances does affirmative action require companies to hire unqualified people.

Affirmative action
Focuses on achieving equality of opportunity in an organization.

Although affirmative action created tremendous opportunities for women and minorities, it does not foster the type of thinking that is needed to effectively manage diversity.[10] For example, affirmative action is resisted more by white males than women and minorities because it is perceived as involving preferential hiring and treatment based on group membership. Affirmative action plans are more successful when employees view them as fair and equitable.[11]

Affirmative action programs also were found to negatively affect the women and minorities expected to benefit from them. Research demonstrated that women and minorities, supposedly hired on the basis of affirmative action, felt negatively stigmatized as unqualified or incompetent. They also experienced lower job satisfaction and more stress than employees supposedly selected on the basis of merit.[12] A recent study, however, showed that these negative consequences were reduced for women when a merit criterion was included in hiring decisions. In other words, women hired under affirmative action programs felt better about themselves and exhibited higher performance when they believed they were hired because of their competence rather than their gender.[13] Moreover, the true valuing and managing of diversity rarely occurs without affirmative action's focus on the hiring and promoting of diverse employees according

Table 2–1   *Comparison of Affirmative Action, Valuing Diversity, and Managing Diversity*

Affirmative Action	Valuing Diversity	Managing Diversity
Quantitative. Emphasizes achieving equality of opportunity in the work environment through the changing of organizational demographics. Monitored by statistical reports and analysis.	*Qualitative.* Emphasizes the appreciation of differences and creating an environment in which everyone feels valued and accepted. Monitored by organizational surveys focused on attitudes and perceptions.	*Behavioral.* Emphasizes the building of specific skills and creating policies which get the best from every employee. Monitored by progress toward achieving goals and objectives.
Legally driven. Written plans and statistical goals for specific groups are utilized. Reports are mandated by EEO laws and consent decrees.	*Ethically driven.* Moral and ethical imperatives drive this culture change.	*Strategically driven.* Behaviors and policies are seen as contributing to organizational goals and objectives such as profit and productivity and are tied to reward and results.
Remedial. Specific target groups benefit as past wrongs are remedied. Previously excluded groups have an advantage.	*Idealistic.* Everyone benefits. Everyone feels valued and accepted in an inclusive environment.	*Pragmatic.* The organization benefits; morale, profit, and productivity increase.
Assimilation model. Assumes that groups brought into system will adapt to existing organizational norms.	*Diversity model.* Assumes that groups will retain their own characteristics and shape the organization as well as be shaped by it, creating a common set of values.	*Synergy model.* Assumes that diverse groups will create new ways of working together effectively in a pluralistic environment.
Opens doors in the organization. Affects hiring and promotion decisions.	*Opens attitudes, minds, and the culture.* Affects attitudes of employees.	*Opens the system.* Affects managerial practices and policies.
Resistance due to perceived limits to autonomy in decision making and perceived fears of reverse discrimination.	*Resistance due to* fear of change, discomfort with differences, and desire for return to "good old days."	*Resistance due to* denial of demographic realities, the need for alternative approaches, and/or benefits associated with change; and the difficulty in learning new skills, altering existing systems, and/or finding time to work toward synergistic solutions.

SOURCE: L Gardenswartz and A Rowe, *Managing Diversity: A Complete Desk Reference and Planning Guide* (Homewood, IL: Business One Irwin, 1993), p 405. Reprinted with permission of The McGraw-Hill Companies.

to a study conducted by the federal Glass Ceiling Commission, a bipartisan group studying diversity in the workplace.[14]

Valuing Diversity   Table 2–1 indicates that **valuing diversity** emphasizes the awareness, recognition, understanding, and appreciation of human differences. It revolves around creating an environment in which everyone feels valued and accepted. In essence, valuing diversity entails a cultural change geared toward viewing employee differences as a valuable resource that can contribute to organizational success.[15] This generally takes place through a series of management education and training programs that attempt to improve interpersonal relationships among diverse employees and to minimize blatant expressions of sexism and racism.[16] For example, Patricia Digh, a

Valuing diversity
Emphasizes the awareness, recognition, understanding, and appreciation of human differences.

management consultant, estimated that more than 70% of *Fortune* 500 companies had implemented some type of initiative aimed at valuing diversity by 1998.[17] Simply sending employees to diversity training, however, does not guarantee changes in attitudes or behaviors. A study of 785 human resource professionals revealed that both the adoption and success of diversity training was strongly related to top management support for diversity.[18] Consider, for example, the level of top management support for the successful diversity program at Allstate Insurance Company.

> At Allstate Insurance Co., a strong commitment to the diversity of our workforce has taken on a strategic role: It helps us achieve both external and internal results and gives us a real competitive advantage. While views on affirmative action and its role in workplace diversity may differ, it has been our long-held opinion that a diverse workforce is not about political mandates or political correctness. Rather, it is about unlocking the potential for excellence among all workers by providing them with the tools, resources, and opportunities they need to succeed.... By the end of 1998, all of Allstate's nonagent employees with service of more than a year had completed diversity training, which represents an investment in excess of 640,000 hours in classroom time.[19]

In addition to top management support, the success of diversity training also was associated with mandatory attendance for all managers, long-term evaluation of training results, and managerial rewards for increasing diversity.[20]

Managing diversity
Creating organizational changes that enable all people to perform up to their maximum potential.

Managing Diversity   **Managing diversity** entails enabling people to perform up to their maximum potential. It focuses on changing an organization's culture and infrastructure such that people provide the highest productivity possible. Ann Morrison, a diversity expert, conducted a study of 16 organizations that successfully managed diversity. Her results uncovered three key strategies for success: education, enforcement, and exposure. She describes them as follows:

> The education component of the strategy has two thrusts: one is to prepare nontraditional managers for increasingly responsible posts, and the other is to help traditional managers overcome their prejudice in thinking about and interacting with people who are of a different sex or ethnicity. The second component of the strategy, enforcement, puts teeth in diversity goals and encourages behavior change. The third component, exposure to people with different backgrounds and characteristics, adds a more personal approach to diversity by helping managers get to know and respect others who are different.[21]

In summary, both consultants and academics believe that organizations should strive to manage diversity rather than only valuing it or simply using affirmative action. This conclusion was recently supported by a study of 200 African-American and white males and females employed in retail stores. Results revealed that employees viewed leaders as more accepting of diversity and more desirable to work for when they demonstrated behaviors consistent with managing diversity as opposed to valuing diversity and affirmative action.[22] More is said about managing diversity later in this chapter.

Building the Business Case for Managing Diversity

The rationale for managing diversity goes well beyond legal, social, and moral reasons. Quite simply, the primary reason for managing diversity is the ability to grow and maintain a business in an increasingly competitive marketplace. Allstate Insurance believes in this proposition. The company's diversity vision statement states that "diversity is Allstate's strategy for leveraging differences in order to create a competitive advantage."[23] Organizations cannot use diversity as a strategic advantage if employees fail to contribute their full talents, abilities, motivation, and commitment. Thus, it is essential for an organization to create an environment or culture that allows all employees to reach their full potential. Managing diversity is a critical component of creating such an organization.

This section explores the business need to manage diversity by first reviewing the demographic trends that are creating an increasingly diverse workforce. We then review the key reasons effective management of diversity creates a competitive advantage.

Increasing Diversity in the Workforce

Workforce demographics, which are statistical profiles of the characteristics and composition of the adult working population, are an invaluable human-resource planning aid. They enable managers to anticipate and adjust for surpluses or shortages of appropriately skilled individuals. For example, the US workforce is expected to grow less than 1% between 1998 and 2006.[24] However, the number of new jobs created in the United States is projected to exceed this growth. These demographics reveal that organizations need to devise strategies to manage the mismatch in labor supply and demand. Companies are using a variety of methods to deal with the shortage of labor. Consider Sears, 7-Eleven, and Omni Computer Products:

> Sears offers even part-time sales clerks tuition reimbursements of 75%, up to $5,250 a year. Others have been able to cushion the blow by attracting older workers. The average age of employees in company-owned 7-Eleven stores has risen from 32 in the 1980s to 36 in the 1990s. . . . Omni Computer Products, a Los Angeles company that sells ink-jet printers to businesses, is hiring struggling actors with the promise that they can take time off for auditions.[25]

Moreover, general population demographics give managers a preview of the values and motives of future employees. Demographic changes in the US workforce during the last two or three decades have immense implications for organizational behavior. This section explores four demographic trends that are creating an increasingly diverse workforce: (1) women continue to enter the workforce in increasing numbers, (2) people of color (non-caucasian) represent a growing share of the labor force, (3) there is a critical mismatch between workers' educational attainment and occupational requirements, and (4) the workforce is aging.

Women Entering the Workforce   Table 2–2 shows that approximately 49.6% of the new entrants into the workforce between 1996 and 2006 are expected to be women. It also shows that women will account for 44.1% of the departures from the workforce. Men account for the largest share of retirement-bound employees.

In spite of the fact that women constituted 46% of the labor force in 1996 and are expected to represent 47% by 2006, they continue to encounter the **glass ceiling.**[26] The glass ceiling represents an invisible barrier that separates women and minorities from advancing into top management positions. It can be particularly demotivating because employees can look up and see coveted top management positions through the transparent ceiling but are unable to obtain them. A variety of statistics support the existence of a glass ceiling.

Historically, female employment was concentrated in relatively lower paying and lower level occupations. As of April 1999, women were still underpaid relative to men: Women managers and professionals received 70.5% of the equivalent men's salaries.[27] Even when women are paid the same as men, they may suffer in other areas of job opportunities. For example, a recent study of 69 male and female executives from a

Workforce demographics
Statistical profiles of adult workers.

Glass ceiling
Invisible barrier blocking women and minorities from top management positions.

Table 2–2   *Projected Entrants and Departures in the US Workforce from 1996 to 2006*

	ENTRANTS*		DEPARTURES*	
	1996–2006	Percent	1996–2006	Percent
Total**	39,670	100.0%	24,768	100.0%
Men	19,978	50.4	13,839	55.9
Women	19,692	49.6	10,929	44.1
White Non-Hispanic	24,214	61.0	16,963	68.5
Men	12,132	30.6	9,728	39.3
Women	12,082	30.5	7,236	29.2
African-American	6,191	15.6	5,003	20.2
Men	2,807	7.1	2,550	10.3
Women	3,384	8.5	2,453	9.9
Hispanic	5,920	14.9	1,293	5.2
Men	3,365	8.5	776	3.1
Women	2,555	6.4	516	2.1
Asian and Other Races	3,346	8.4	1,508	6.1
Men	1,674	4.2	785	3.2
Women	1,671	4.2	724	2.9

*Labor force entrants and departures, in thousands, 1996–2006.

**All groups add to total.

Note: Numbers may not add up due to rounding.

SOURCE: Data were taken from Table 6 in H Fullerton, Jr, "Employment Projections: Entrance to the Labor Force by Sex, Race, and Hispanic Origin," *Bureau of Labor Statistics Online*, January 1998. (http://stats.bls.gov/emptab3.htm)

large multinational financial services corporation revealed no differences in base salary or bonus. However, the women in this sample received fewer stock options than the male executives, even after controlling for level of education, performance, and job function, and reported less satisfaction with future career opportunities.[28] A follow-up study of 13,503 female managers and 17,493 male managers from the same organization demonstrated that women at higher levels in the managerial hierarchy received fewer promotions than males at comparable positions.[29] Would you be motivated if you were a woman working in this organization?

Women still have not broken into the highest echelon of corporate America to any significant extent. Women held 6% of all line officer positions and represented only 3.8% of the highest officer positions—chairman, vice chairman, chief executive officer (CEO), president, chief operating officer (COO), senior executive vice president, and executive vice president—as of November 1998.[30] Women also accounted for 11% of the board of director positions for *Fortune* 500 firms in 1998.[31] As detailed in the International OB, the glass ceiling also exists around the world. The glass ceiling has been credited as one reason women are increasingly starting their own businesses. For example, the number of woman-owned businesses has more than doubled between 1987 and 1999. Women-owned businesses represented 38% of all businesses in the United States in 1999 and employed approximately one-quarter of the labor force.[32]

International OB The Glass Ceiling Exists Around the World

Businesswomen in America may complain that the glass ceiling constrains their progress up the corporate ladder— women hold only 11% of board seats of the *Fortune* 500— but in Europe and Asia, the ceiling may as well be concrete. In Britain, women hold a mere 5% of board seats in its top 200 companies. And while women hold 40% of all management positions in America, in Europe it is only 20% to 30%. The story is much the same in Asia. Despite China's two decades of formal commitment to sexual equality, there are no female business leaders of note. In Japan, the rigidity of the corporate culture keeps women out of the executive suite. The famed salaryman style can only exist with a full-time homemaker for support.

SOURCE: C Daniels, "The Global Glass Ceiling: And Ten Women Who Broke Through It," *Fortune*, October 12, 1998, p 102.

Why does the glass ceiling exist for women? A team of researchers attempted to answer this question by surveying 461 executive women who held titles of vice president or higher in *Fortune* 1000 companies and all of the *Fortune* 1000 CEOs. Respondents were asked to evaluate the extent to which they used 13 different career strategies to break through the glass ceiling. The 13 strategies are shown in the OB Exercise.[33] Before discussing the results from this study, we would like you to complete the OB Exercise.

Findings indicated that the top nine strategies were central to the advancement of these female executives. Within this set, however, four strategies were identified as critical toward breaking the glass ceiling: consistently exceeding performance expectations, developing a style with which male managers are comfortable, seeking out difficult or challenging assignments, and having influential mentors. Results further demonstrated that the CEOs and female executives differed in their assessment of the barriers preventing women from advancing to positions of corporate leadership. CEOs concluded that women do not get promoted because (1) they lack significant general management or line experience and (2) women have not been in the executive talent pool for a long enough period of time to get selected. In contrast, the female executives indicated that (1) male stereotyping and preconceptions and (2) exclusion from informal networks were the biggest inhibitors to their promotability. These findings suggest that it is important to sensitize CEOs to the corporate culture faced by female employees. Breaking the glass ceiling will only occur when senior management has a good understanding of the unique experiences associated with being in the minority.

People of Color in the US Workforce   People of color in the United States are projected to add 38.9% of the new entrants in the workforce from 1996 to 2006 (see Table 2–2). African-Americans are predicted to account for the largest share of this increase (15.6%). Because fewer Hispanics will leave the workforce between 1996 and 2005 than any other racial group (5.2%), Hispanics will account for the greatest *net* percentage increase in new workers.

Unfortunately, three additional trends suggest that people of color are experiencing their own glass ceiling. First, people of color are advancing even less in the managerial and professional ranks than women. For example, African-Americans, Hispanics, and whites held 7%, 4.5%, and 88%, respectively, of all managerial and professional jobs in 1996.[35] Further, African-Americans and Hispanics together account for less than 2% of senior executive positions in the United States in 1999.[36] Second, people of color also tend to earn less than whites. Average income in 1995 was $25,275, $27,112, and $38,770 for African-Americans, Hispanics, and whites, respectively.[37]

OB Exercise   What Are the Strategies for Breaking the Glass Ceiling?

Instructions

Read the 13 career strategies shown below that may be used to break the glass ceiling. Next, rank order each strategy in terms of its importance for contributing to the advancement of a woman to a senior management position. Rank the strategies from 1 (most important) to 13 (least important). Once this is completed, compute the gap between your rankings and those provided by the women executives who participated in this research. Their rankings are presented in Endnote 34 at the back of the book. In computing the gaps, use the absolute value of the gap. (Absolute values are always positive, so just ignore the sign of your gap.) Finally, compute your total gap score. The larger the gap, the greater the difference in opinion between you and the women executives. What does your total gap score indicate about your recommended strategies?

Strategy	My Rating	Survey Rating	Gap (Your Rating – Survey Rating)
1. Develop leadership outside office	_____	_____	_____
2. Gain line management experience	_____	_____	_____
3. Network with influential colleagues	_____	_____	_____
4. Change companies	_____	_____	_____
5. Be able to relocate	_____	_____	_____
6. Seek difficult or high visibility assignments	_____	_____	_____
7. Upgrade educational credentials	_____	_____	_____
8. Consistently exceed performance expectations	_____	_____	_____
9. Move from one functional area to another	_____	_____	_____
10. Initiate discussion regarding career aspirations	_____	_____	_____
11. Have an influential mentor	_____	_____	_____
12. Develop style that men are comfortable with	_____	_____	_____
13. Gain international experience	_____	_____	_____

SOURCE: Strategies and data were taken from B R Ragins, B Townsend, and M Mattis, "Gender Gap in the Executive Suite: CEOs and Female Executives Report on Breaking the Glass Ceiling," *The Academy of Management Executive*," February 1998, pp 28–42.

Finally, a recent study of 280 minority executives indicated that 40% believed that they had been denied well-deserved promotions because of discrimination. Fifty-two percent of these same respondents revealed that they are likely to change jobs for more challenging positions.[38] These findings are consistent with previous studies that indicated that people of color have more negative career experiences, lower upward mobility, lower career satisfaction, decreased job involvement, and greater turnover rates than their white counterparts.[39]

Mismatch between Educational Attainment and Occupational Requirements

Approximately 27% of the labor force has a college degree.[40] Unfortunately, many of these people are working in jobs for which they are overqualified. This creates underemployment. **Underemployment** exists when a job requires less than a person's full potential as determined by his or her formal education, training, or skills. In 1995, approximately 40% of those individuals with some college and 10% of college graduates were underemployed.[41] Underemployment is associated with higher arrest rates and the likelihood of becoming an unmarried parent for young adults. It also is negatively correlated with job satisfaction, work commitment, job involvement, internal work motivation, life satisfaction, and psychological well-being. Underemployment also is related to higher absenteeism and turnover.[42] On a positive note, however, underemployment is one of the reasons more new college graduates are starting businesses of their own. Moreover, research reveals that over time a college graduate's income ranges from 50% to 100% higher than that obtained by a high-school graduate.[43] It pays to graduate from college!

There is another important educational mismatch. The national high-school dropout rate is approximately 12.8%, and more than 20% of the adult US population read at or below a fifth-grade-level, a level which is below that needed to earn a living wage. More than 40 million Americans age 16 and older also are illiterate.[44] Literacy is defined as "an individual's ability to read, write, and speak in English, compute and solve problems at levels of proficiency necessary to function on the job and in society, to achieve one's goals, and develop one's knowledge and potential."[45] These statistics are worrisome because 70% of on-the-job reading materials are written for ninth-grade to college levels. Also, 41% to 44% of illiterate adults live in poverty; thus organizations are having a hard time finding qualified employees.[46] For example, a recent survey of 300 executives from manufacturing, technology, and finance firms revealed that a shortage of skilled workers limited sales by as much as 33%.[47] In contrast to underemployment, dropouts and illiterate individuals are unlikely to have the skills organizations need to remain competitive.

The Aging Workforce

America's population and workforce are getting older. Between 1995 and 2020, the number of indi-

Underemployment
The result of taking a job that requires less education, training, or skills than possessed by a worker.

A high-school student in East Rutherford, New Jersey, receives her diploma. Unfortunately, many of her peers will not. Statistics show that the national high-school dropout rate is approximately 12.8 percent, and more than 20 percent of the adult US population read at or below a fifth-grade-level, a level below that needed to earn a living wage. Workforce illiteracy poses challenges for organizations that may have difficulty finding qualified employees.

(Jeff Greenberg/PhotoEdit)

viduals in the United States over age 65 will increase by 60%, the 45- to 64-year-old population by 34%, and those between ages 18 and 44 by 4%.[48] Life expectancy is increasing as well. The number of people living into their 80s is increasing rapidly, and this group disproportionately suffers from chronic illness. The United States is not the only country with an aging population. Japan, Eastern Europe, and former Soviet republics, for example, are expected to encounter significant economic and political problems due to an aging population.

Managerial Implications of Increasing Diversity   Highly skilled women and people of color will be in high demand given future labor shortages. To attract the best workers, companies need to adopt policies and programs that meet the needs of women and people of color. Programs such as day care, elder care, flexible work schedules and benefits, paternal leaves, less rigid relocation policies, and mentoring programs are likely to become more popular.[49]

Ethics at Work

Consider the following: On Saturday morning, the boss invites his subordinates, Tom, Dick, and Harry, for a friendly game of golf. Mary, who doesn't play golf, is not invited.

SOURCE: Excerpted from L Bierman, "Regulating Reindeer Games," *Academy of Management Executive*, November 1997, p 92.

You Decide . . .

Is this Saturday morning golf game simply a friendly social occasion, or is it a subtle form of discrimination? Explain.

For an interpretation of this situation, visit our Web site **www.mhhe.com/kreitner**

Mismatches between the amount of education needed to perform current jobs and the amount of education possessed by members of the workforce are growing. Underemployment among college graduates threatens to erode job satisfaction and work motivation. As well-educated workers begin to look for jobs commensurate with their qualifications and expectations, absenteeism and turnover likely will increase. This problem underscores the need for job redesign (see the discussion in Chapter 7). In addition, organizations will need to consider interventions, such as realistic job previews and positive reinforcement programs, to reduce absenteeism and turnover. On-the-job remedial skills and literacy training will be necessary to help the growing number of dropouts and illiterates cope with job demands. For example, a recent survey conducted by the Bureau of Labor Statistics revealed that almost 93% of those companies with 50 or more employees provide or finance formal training for their employees. These companies spent $7.7 billion on in-house training and another $5.5 billion on training conducted by outside vendors.[50]

Moreover, organizations will continue to be asked to help resolve the educational problems in the United States. Supporting education is good for business and society at large. A better education system not only contributes to the United States's ability to compete internationally, but it facilitates a better quality of life for all its population.

With labor force size not expected to increase significantly during the 1990s, a shortage of qualified entry-level workers and late-career managers is predicted. This will force organizations to devise creative ways to recruit qualified employees. Consider the strategies used by Ocean Reef Club and Smithfield Packing Co.:

> The exclusive Ocean Reef Club in the Florida Keys needed groundskeepers and housekeepers, but many such workers couldn't afford to live nearby. Working with Ocean Reef, the Miami-Dade Transit Agency created an express bus route to the club from 30 miles away in southern Dade County, where many people looking for jobs lived. Ocean Reef, which used to run shuttles, now saves money; it buys 100 bus passes a month and sells them to staff at face value.
>
> Hog processor Smithfield Packing Co., a unit of Smithfield Foods Inc., Norfolk, Va., worked with transit and social-service agencies near rural Tar Heel, N.C. to transport

160 workers to its facility there. With private bus companies, the packer created routes from Fayetteville, 30 miles away, for its first- and second-shift workers and found an independent van driver to shuttle workers from other cities.[51]

However, as the baby-boom generation reaches retirement age after the turn of the century, the workforce will be top-heavy with older employees, creating the problem of career plateauing for younger workers. **Career plateauing** is defined "as that point in a career [at] which future hierarchical mobility seems unlikely."[52] Career plateauing is associated with stress and dissatisfaction.[53] Unfortunately, this problem is intensified by the fact that organizations are flattening—and reducing the number of managerial jobs— in order to save costs and increase efficiency. Managers will thus need to find alternatives other than promotions to help employees satisfy their needs and to feel successful, and employees will need to take a much more active role in managing their careers.

Career plateauing
The end result when the probability of being promoted is very small.

Six managerial initiatives may help organizations effectively adapt to an aging workforce:[54]

1. Organizations might devise more flexible and creative retirement plans because many employees are delaying retirement. Some people want to work longer, and others have inadequate savings.

2. It will become critical to match individuals' skills and desires to job requirements as people age. An appropriate match is more likely to produce positive outcomes for individuals and organizations alike.

3. Organizations can conduct succession planning for older workers who will be retiring in the future.

4. Organizations can reengineer their production processes and capital equipment so as to operate with fewer employees.

5. Organizations need to be sensitive to issues associated with elder care. The ratio of frail elderly to middle-aged people is predicted to rise 75% by 2030.[55] Many companies, including Prudential and office furniture manufacturer Herman Miller Inc., offer employees elder care as an employee benefit.[56]

6. If managers are to be more responsive to older workers, they also need to be aware of how aging affects one's values and attitudes.

Managing Diversity—A Competitive Advantage

Consultants, academics, and business leaders believe that effectively managing diversity is a competitive advantage. This advantage stems from the process in which the management of diversity affects organizational behavior and effectiveness. Effectively managing diversity can influence an organization's costs and employee attitudes, recruitment of human resources, sales and market share (see International OB), creativity and innovation, and group problem solving and productivity. This section explores the relationship between managing diversity and each of these outcomes.

Lower Costs and Improved Employee Attitudes   Effectively managing diversity can lower costs in three ways. First, if we assume that adhering to equal employment opportunity laws is a prerequisite to managing diversity, then organizations can reduce the chance of experiencing a costly discrimination lawsuit. For example, Jury Verdict Research estimates that average settlements between 1988 and 1995 were $219,000 for age discrimination, $147,799 for race discrimination, $106,728 for sex discrimination, and $100,345 for disability cases.[57] Second, diversity initiatives can reduce health care expenses and absenteeism. Consider the effect of supporting a

International OB   Cultural Insensitivity Affects Sales

Olympia reportedly tried to introduce a photocopier in Chile under the name ROTO. The copiers, however, did not sell well. Why? Two possible explanations: (1) *Roto* is the Spanish word for "broken," and (2) *roto* is the word used to delineate the lowest class in Chile.

General Motors was faced with a somewhat similar problem. It was troubled by the lack of enthusiasm among the Puerto Rican dealers for its recently introduced Chevrolet Nova. The word *nova* means "star" when translated literally. However, when spoken, it sounds like "*no va,*" which, in Spanish, means "it does not go." This obviously did little to increase consumer confidence in the new vehicle...

In the early 1980s, a German beer company launched a new brand in West Africa and named it EKU. Sales were uneven, and it took the firm two years to figure out the cause. Foreigners and some local tribe members purchased the beer, but one important tribe totally avoided it. Apparently *eku* was the local slang word in that tribe for "excrement." As word spread, members of other tribes and even the foreigners started drinking it less.

SOURCE: Excerpted from D Ricks, *Blunders in International Business* (Cambridge, MA: Blackwell Business, 1995), pp 35–36.

---

lactation or breast-feeding program. Research shows that breast-fed babies have fewer allergies, respiratory infections, ear infections, and serious diseases. Other studies show that one-day absences from work due to a baby's illness are twice as high among mothers who use formula as opposed to breast feeding. The Los Angeles Department of Water and Power offers a good illustration of the benefits associated with a lactation program. The company realized reductions of 27% in absenteeism and 35% in health care claims after implementing their program.[58] Finally, employee recruiting and training expenses can be reduced by effectively managing diversity. These savings occur through reductions in turnover by women and people of color. NationsBank and Aetna Life & Casualty were able to reduce turnover of diverse employees by implementing targeted diversity programs:

> …At NationsBank, two-thirds of employees on flexible schedules said they would have left without these policies.
>
> Aetna Life & Casualty dramatically demonstrated the effect employer policies can have on retention. Before 1988 Aetna had a 23% turnover rate among those who took family leave, especially among high-potential professional women. By modifying company policy to allow part-time return after family leave, the company cut attrition by more than 50%—resulting in an 88% to 91% retention rate of leave-takers over the past five years. Aetna calculated that reduction in turnover represents more than $1 million in annual savings.[59]

Diversity also was related to employee attitudes.

Past research revealed that people who were different from their work units in racial or ethnic background were less psychologically committed to their organizations, less satisfied with their careers, and perceived less autonomy to make decisions on their jobs. African-Americans also were found to receive lower performance ratings than whites.[60] Organizational surveys further demonstrated that between 25% and 66% of gay and lesbian employees experienced discrimination at work. Gay and lesbian employees also reported higher levels of stress than heterosexual employees, and gay and bisexual male workers earned from 11% to 27% less than heterosexual peers with similar experience and education.[61] Further, a meta-analysis of research covering 66 studies and more than 67,000 people found that men held more negative attitudes toward homosexuality and the civil rights of lesbians and gays than did women.[62] How important is the issue of sexual preference? An exit poll of voters conducted by Voter News Service on November 4, 1996, revealed that 5% of the voters indicated that they were gay or lesbian.[63] Assuming that the voting population is similar to the working population, can any organization afford to squelch the motivation and productivity of 5% of its workforce?

Employees' mental/physical abilities and characteristics are another dimension of diversity that needs to be effectively managed. The US Department of Labor estimates that one of six Americans has a disability. Although two out of three individuals with disabilities can and want to work, roughly 72% are unemployed. Individuals with disabilities tend to be employed in part-time, low-status jobs offering little chance for advancement and earn up to 35% less than their nondisabled counterparts.[64] These statistics prompted the passage of the **Americans with Disabilities Act** in 1992. This law bans discrimination against the disabled in the United States and requires organizations to reasonably accommodate an individual's disabilities. Despite the fact that most job accommodations are relatively inexpensive (e.g., nearly 20% of accommodations cost nothing, and 50% cost less than $500), disabled workers are still finding it difficult to obtain employment.[65] Do you think this segment of the population is being underutilized?

Americans with Disabilities Act
Prohibits discrimination against the disabled.

Improved Recruiting Efforts   Attracting and retaining competent employees is a competitive advantage. This is particularly true given the workforce demographics discussed in the preceding section. Organizations that effectively manage diversity are more likely to meet this challenge because women and people of color are attracted to such companies. Moreover, recruiting diverse employees helps organizations to provide better customer service. A senior vice president at Crestar Financial Corporation came to the following conclusion about recruiting diverse workers:

> We know that our customer base is very diverse. By actively recruiting from that base, our employees are representative of the communities in which we do business. This has a positive effect on our business.[66]

Increased Sales, Market Share, and Corporate Profits   Workforce diversity is the mirror image of consumer diversity. It is thus important for companies to market their products so that they appeal to diverse customers and markets. Consider how the Target discount chain is trying to obtain a larger share of the Hispanic market:

> Eager to dethrone Sears as the mass retailer most aggressively courting Hispanics, Target is remodeling stores, refashioning its merchandise mix, and developing marketing events to appeal to one of the nation's fastest-growing ethnic groups, which now accounts for 11% of the US population . . . Target also recently launched its own magazine for Hispanics, taking up a marketing tool pioneered by Sears, which publishes the nation's largest-circulation Spanish-language magazine.[67]

Sears has initiated tactics to counter Target's marketing efforts as the battle for this lucrative market continues.

Researchers are beginning to examine the effects of a top management team's (TMT's) demographic characteristics on an organization's financial performance. For example, a 1997 study of 1,000 companies conducted by the American Management Association and the Business & Professional Women's Foundation suggests that a diverse TMT can contribute to corporate profits. Results revealed that sales growth averaged 22.9%, 20.2%, and 13% for companies whose senior management team contained a majority of women, included people of color, and consisted of a majority of white men, respectively.[68] Given these impressive results, other researchers are trying to identify the exact process or manner in which a TMT's diversity positively impacts corporate success. The current thinking is that diversity promotes the sharing of unique ideas and a variety of perspectives, which, in turn, leads to more effective decision making.[69]

Increased Creativity and Innovation   Preliminary research supports the idea that workforce diversity promotes creativity and innovation. This occurs through the sharing of diverse ideas and perspectives. Rosabeth Moss-Kanter, a management expert, was one of the first to investigate this relationship. Her results indicated that innovative companies deliberately used heterogeneous teams to solve problems, and they employed more women and people of color than less innovative companies. She also noted that innovative companies did a better job of eliminating racism, sexism, and classism.[70] A recent summary of 40 years of diversity research supported Moss-Kanter's conclusion that diversity can promote creativity and improve a team's decision making.[71]

Increased Group Problem Solving and Productivity   Because diverse groups possess a broader base of experience and perspectives from which to analyze a problem, they can potentially improve problem solving and performance. Research findings based on short-term groups that varied in terms of values, attitudes, educational backgrounds, and experience supported this conclusion. Heterogeneous groups produced better-quality decisions and demonstrated higher productivity than homogeneous groups. Nevertheless, these results must be interpreted cautiously because the experimental samples, tasks, time frames, and environmental situations bear very little resemblance to actual ongoing organizational settings.[72] Additional research has attempted to control these problems.

More recent studies do not clearly support the proposed benefits of diversity. A study of culturally homogeneous and diverse groups over a period of 17 weeks showed higher performance among homogeneous groups for the first 9 weeks due to the fact that heterogeneous groups experienced less effective group processes than homogeneous groups. Over weeks 10 through 17, however, homogeneous and heterogeneous groups demonstrated similar performance. Additional studies found that work group diversity was significantly associated with increased absenteeism, turnover, and less psychological commitment and intention to stay in the organization.[73]

In summary, research shows that diversity can improve creativity and innovation, but these positive benefits may not influence productivity because diverse groups generally experience more negative group dynamics. How then do managers capitalize on the positive benefits of diversity? One lesson seems to be that organizations should not simply assemble a diverse group and then let group dynamics take care of themselves. Rather, training should be used to help group members become aware of cultural and attitudinal differences of other group members. This training should be conducted at the beginning of a group's formation because conflict is likely to be highest at this point and this conflict negatively influences subsequent group processes.[74] A second lesson revolves around the fact that the group processes and performance of diverse groups are enhanced when group members share common values and norms that promote the pursuit of common goals.[75] Managers and organizations thus are encouraged to identify ways of enhancing group members' sense of shared values and a common fate. Increasing shared values can be facilitated through an organization's culture, which is discussed in Chapter 3, and common fate can be created by making group members accountable for group or team-level performance goals. Team goals and team rewards are discussed in Chapter 13.

We introduced this chapter by noting that diversity is a sensitive, potentially volatile, and sometimes uncomfortable issue. It is therefore not surprising that organizations encounter significant barriers when trying to move forward with managing diversity. The following is a list of the most common barriers to implementing successful diversity programs;[76]

Barriers and Challenges to Managing Diversity

1. *Inaccurate stereotypes and prejudice.* This barrier manifests itself in the belief that differences are viewed as weaknesses. In turn, this promotes the view that diversity hiring will mean sacrificing competence and quality.

2. *Ethnocentrism.* The ethnocentrism barrier represents the feeling that one's cultural rules and norms are superior or more appropriate than the rules and norms of another culture.[77] This barrier is thoroughly discussed in Chapter 4.

3. *Poor career planning.* This barrier is associated with the lack of opportunities for diverse employees to get the type of work assignments that qualify them for senior management positions.

4. *An unsupportive and hostile working environment for diverse employees.* Diverse employees are frequently excluded from social events and the friendly camaraderie that takes place in most offices.

5. *Lack of political savvy on the part of diverse employees.* Diverse employees may not get promoted because they do not know how to "play the game" of getting along and getting ahead in an organization. Research reveals that women and people of color are excluded from organizational networks.[78]

6. *Difficulty in balancing career and family issues.* Women still assume the majority of the responsibilities associated with raising children. This makes it harder for women to work evenings and weekends or to frequently travel once they have children. Even without children in the picture, household chores take more of a woman's time than a man's time.

7. *Fears of reverse discrimination.* Some employees believe that managing diversity is a smoke screen for reverse discrimination. This belief leads to very strong resistance because people feel that one person's gain is another's loss.

8. *Diversity is not seen as an organizational priority.* This leads to subtle resistance that shows up in the form of complaints and negative attitudes. Employees may complain about the time, energy, and resources devoted to diversity that could have been spent doing "real work."

9. *The need to revamp the organization's performance appraisal and reward system.* Performance appraisals and reward systems must reinforce the need to effectively manage diversity. This means that success will be based on a new set of criteria. Employees are likely to resist changes that adversely affect their promotions and financial rewards.

10. *Resistance to change.* Effectively managing diversity entails significant organizational and personal change. As discussed in Chapter 20, people resist change for many different reasons.

In summary, managing diversity is a critical component of organizational success. Case studies and limited research inform us that this effort is doomed to failure unless top management is truly committed to managing diversity. The next section examines the variety of ways organizations are attempting to manage diversity.

Organizational Practices Used to Effectively Manage Diversity

Many organizations throughout the United States are unsure of what it takes to effectively manage diversity. This is partly due to the fact that top management only recently became aware of the combined need and importance of this issue.

So what are organizations doing to effectively manage diversity? Answering this question requires that we provide a framework for categorizing organizational initiatives. Researchers and practitioners have developed relevant frameworks. One was developed by R Roosevelt Thomas, Jr, a diversity expert. He identified eight generic action options that can be used to address any type of diversity issue. A second was proposed by another diversity expert, Ann Morrison. She empirically identified the specific diversity initiatives used by 16 organizations that successfully managed diversity. This section reviews these frameworks in order to provide you with both a broad and specific understanding about how organizations are effectively managing diversity.

R Roosevelt Thomas, Jr's Generic Action Options

Thomas identified eight basic responses for handling any diversity issue. After describing each action option, we discuss relationships among them.[79]

Option 1: Include/Exclude   This choice is an outgrowth of affirmative action programs. Its primary goal is to either increase or decrease the number of diverse people at all levels of the organizations. Shoney's restaurant represents a good example of a company that attempted to include diverse employees after settling a discrimination lawsuit. The company subsequently hired African-Americans into positions of dining-room supervisors and vice presidents, added more franchises owned by African-Americans, and purchased more goods and services from minority-owned companies.[80]

Option 2: Deny   People using this option deny that differences exist. Denial may manifest itself in proclamations that all decisions are color, gender, and age blind and that success is solely determined by merit and performance. Consider State Farm Insurance, for example. "Although it was traditional for male agents and their regional managers to hire male relatives, State Farm Insurance avoided change and denied any alleged effects in a nine-year gender-bias suit that the company lost."[81]

Option 3: Assimilate   The basic premise behind this alternative is that all diverse people will learn to fit in or become like the dominant group. It only takes time and reinforcement for people to see the light. Organizations initially assimilate employees through their recruitment practices and the use of company orientation programs. New hires generally are put through orientation programs that aim to provide employees with the organization's preferred values and a set of standard operating procedures. Employees then are encouraged to refer to the policies and procedure manual when they are confused about what to do in a specific situation. These practices create homogeneity among employees.

Option 4: Suppress   Differences are squelched or discouraged when using this approach. This can be done by telling or reinforcing others to quit whining and complaining about issues. The old "you've got to pay your dues" line is another frequently used way to promote the status quo.

Option 5: Isolate   This option maintains the current way of doing things by setting the diverse person off to the side. In this way the individual is unable to influence organizational change. Managers can isolate people by putting them on special projects. Entire work groups or departments are isolated by creating functionally independent entities, frequently referred to as "silos." Shoney Inc.'s employees commented to a *Wall Street Journal* reporter about isolation practices formerly used by the company:

> White managers told of how Mr. Danner [previous chairman of the company] told them to fire blacks if they became too numerous in restaurants in white neighborhoods; if they refused, they would lose their jobs, too. Some also said that when Mr. Danner was expected to visit their restaurant, they scheduled black employees off that day or, in one case, hid them in the bathroom. Others said blacks' applications were coded and discarded.[82]

Option 6: Tolerate   Toleration entails acknowledging differences but not valuing or accepting them. It represents a live-and-let-live approach that superficially allows organizations to give lip service to the issue of managing diversity. Toleration is different from isolation in that it allows for the inclusion of diverse people. However, differences are not really valued or accepted when an organization uses this option.

Option 7: Build Relationships   This approach is based on the premise that good relationships can overcome differences. It addresses diversity by fostering quality relationships—characterized by acceptance and understanding—among diverse groups. R R Donnelley is a good example of a company attempting to use this diversity option. "R R Donnelley sponsors an exchange program where counterparts in two nations swap positions for several weeks to learn about each other's countries and customs."[83]

Option 8: Foster Mutual Adaptation   In this option, people recognize and accept differences, and most importantly, agree that everyone and everything is open for change. Mutual adaptation allows the greatest accommodation of diversity because it allows for change even when diversity is being effectively managed. Some of the companies that remained on *Fortune*'s list of the 100 best companies to work for in America in 1998 appeared to use mutual adaptation. They continually offered more diversity initiatives in order to provide positive working environments for employees:

> One veteran—Alagasco, a Birmingham utility—was able not only to hang on but also to move from No. 93 to No. 72 by adding several family-friendly benefits, such as $5,000 in aid to adoptive parents. However groovy your company may be today, keeping up with the best requires constant improvement . . . Haven't heard of Synovus, the Columbus, [Georgia,] firm that displaced Southwest as the best of the best? . . . Synovus doesn't skimp on such tangibles as topnotch training, which attracts Gen Xers from all over the country, and primo benefits such as the 20 hours that employees are paid to spend in class with their kids or grandkids. What employees talk about most, though, is how Synovus promotes a sense of community both inside and outside the office.[84]

Conclusions about Action Options   Although the action options can be used alone or in combination, some are clearly better than others. Exclusion, denial, assimilation, suppression, isolation, and toleration are among the least preferred options. Inclusion, building relationships, and mutual adaptation are the preferred strategies. That said, Thomas reminds us that mutual adaptation is the only approach that unquestionably endorses the philosophy behind managing diversity. In closing this discussion, it is important to note that choosing how to best manage diversity is a dynamic process that is determined by the context at hand. For instance, some organizations are not ready for mutual adaptation. The best one might hope for in this case is the inclusion of diverse people.

Ann Morrison Identifies Specific Diversity Initiatives

As previously mentioned, Ann Morrison conducted a landmark study of the diversity practices used by 16 organizations that successfully managed diversity. Her results uncovered 52 different practices, 20 of which were used by the majority of the companies sampled. She classified the 52 practices into three main types: accountability, development, and recruitment.[85] The top 10 practices associated with each type are shown in Table 2–3. They are discussed next in order of relative importance.

Accountability Practices   **Accountability practices** relate to managers' responsibility to treat diverse employees fairly. Table 2–3 reveals that companies predominantly accomplish this objective by creating administrative procedures aimed at integrating diverse employees into the management ranks (practices number 3, 4, 5, 6, 8, 9, and 10). In contrast, work and family policies, practice 7, focuses on creating an environment that fosters employee commitment and productivity. Law firms, for example, are beginning to implement family-friendly programs:

> Goodwin, Procter & Hoar, Boston's largest law firm has started providing in-home consultants to help expectant parents plan child care. Cooley Godward, a 410-lawyer Palo Alto, [California,] firm, offers childbirth leaves of up to 29 weeks for mothers and 13

Accountability practices
Focus on treating diverse employees fairly.

Employees of Renaissance Global Logistics, owned by the O-J Group, pack vehicle kits for shipment to overseas growth markets. They are among many Ford suppliers operating thriving businesses in the metro Detroit empowerment zone through Ford's nationally recognized Minority Supplier Program. Ford views its suppliers as important partners in maintaining its competitive advantage. Their outstanding performance is one reason Ford is able to provide high-value features and cutting-edge technologies to customers quickly and efficiently.

Courtesy of Ford Corporation

Table 2–3   *Common Diversity Practices*

Accountability Practices	Development Practices	Recruitment Practices
1. Top management's personal intervention 2. Internal advocacy groups 3. Emphasis on EEO statistics, profiles 4. Inclusion of diversity in performance evaluation goals, ratings 5. Inclusion of diversity in promotion decisions, criteria 6. Inclusion of diversity in management succession planning 7. Work and family policies 8. Policies against racism, sexism 9. Internal audit or attitude survey 10. Active AA/EEO committee, office	1. Diversity training programs 2. Networks and support groups 3. Development programs for all high-potential managers 4. Informal networking activities 5. Job rotation 6. Formal mentoring program 7. Informal mentoring program 8. Entry development programs for all high-potential new hires 9. Internal training (such as personal safety or language) 10. Recognition events, awards	1. Targeted recruitment of nonmanagers 2. Key outside hires 3. Extensive public exposure on diversity (AA) 4. Corporate image as liberal, progressive, or benevolent 5. Partnerships with educational institutions 6. Recruitment incentives such as cash supplements 7. Internships (such as INROADS) 8. Publications or PR products that highlight diversity 9. Targeted recruitment of managers 10. Partnership with nontraditional groups

SOURCE: Abstracted from Tables A.10, A.11, and A.12 in A M Morrison, *The New Leaders: Guidelines on Leadership Diversity in America* (San Francisco: Jossey-Bass, 1992).

for fathers, some of the time paid, the rest unpaid . . . Perkins, Cole, Seattle's biggest firm, recently began paying for child care when a sick youngster has to stay home from school, so employees won't feel guilty about being at work.[86]

Moreover, organizations increasingly are attempting to build an accountability component into their diversity programs in order to motivate managers to effectively manage diversity. A recent survey of *Fortune* 500 companies indicated that 25% linked both compensation and performance to accomplishing diversity goals.[87] Consider the approaches used by Motorola Inc. and Sara Lee Corporation:

At Motorola Inc., tracking reports show the representation of women and minorities within each senior manager's area of responsibility. The company reviews progress twice a year and holds managers accountable for developing and retaining women and minorities. . . . The Sara Lee Corp., based in Chicago, sets diversity goals for recruiting, hiring and advancement, and operating executives are held accountable for meeting short-term and long-term goals. The company ties executives' bonuses to the objectives for the advancement of women and measures discrimination charges as part of assessing success in attaining diversity objectives.[88]

These examples illustrate that both Motorola and Sara Lee want to create a direct linkage between managing diversity and the rewards received by organizational leaders.

Development Practices   The use of development practices to manage diversity is relatively new compared with the historical use of accountability and recruitment practices. **Development practices** focus on preparing diverse employees for greater

Development practices
Focus on preparing diverse employees for greater responsibility and advancement.

responsibility and advancement. These activities are needed because most nontraditional employees have not been exposed to the type of activities and job assignments that develop effective leadership and social networks.[89] Table 2–3 indicates that diversity training programs, networks and support groups, and mentoring programs are among the most frequently used developmental practices. There is one particular developmental practice that more and more organizations are confronting: Teaching English to non-English-speaking workers. Successfully teaching English and learning to communicate in multiple languages will become increasingly important as employers continue to hire people for whom English is not their first language. Imagine the situation faced by Doubletree Hotels Corporation when it had to communicate about its revamped employee benefits to a workforce of 30,000 people who speak 20 different languages:

> Instead of being daunted by the prospect of explaining benefits in multiple languages and to many employees with limited educations, Doubletree launched an outreach program that spoke to virtually all employees in their own tongues, on their own terms. The main tools were audio cassette tapes, shipped to each work site and made available for employees to use with loaned tape players. The tapes explained changes in the benefits program, such as a greater selection of health maintenance organizations and the debut of flexible benefits.
>
> The tapes were recorded in 14 languages, including Spanish, Somali, Tongan, Creole, Mandarin, and Russian, and became very popular with employees, some of whom are illiterate and would not have understood written materials, said Lenny Sanicola, benefits manager of Phoenix-based Doubletree. The company decided to communicate in native languages with any group of at least 25 employees.[90]

Recruitment practices
Attempts to attract qualified, diverse employees at all levels.

Recruitment Practices   **Recruitment practices** focus on attracting job applicants at all levels who are willing to accept challenging work assignments. This focus is critical because people learn the leadership skills needed for advancement by successfully accomplishing increasingly challenging and responsible work assignments. As shown in Table 2–3, targeted recruitment of nonmanagers (practice 1) and managers (practice 9) are commonly used to identify and recruit women and people of color. Both Intel Corporation and Boeing Company rely on targeted recruiting:

> Intel, for example, headquartered in Santa Clara, [California,] hired a top consulting firm to compile a closely guarded list of the 10 colleges and universities with the highest minority enrollments in the field of circuitry design. At Boeing Co., in Seattle, the HR [human resources] team launched a slick, nationwide advertising campaign aimed at women and ethnic minorities who feel underutilized in their current jobs.[91]

Summary of Key Concepts

1. *Define diversity.* Diversity represents the host of individual differences that make people different from and similar to each other. Diversity pertains to everybody. It is not simply an issue of age, race, gender, or sexual orientation.

2. *Discuss the four layers of diversity.* The layers of diversity define an individual's personal identity and constitute a perceptual filter that influences how we interpret the world. Personality is at the center of the diversity wheel.

The second layer of diversity consists of a set of internal dimensions that are referred to as the primary dimensions of diversity. The third layer is composed of external influences and are called secondary dimensions of diversity. The final layer of diversity includes organizational dimensions.

3. *Explain the differences among affirmative action, valuing diversity, and managing diversity.* Affirmative action focuses on achieving equality of opportunity in an organization. It rep-

resents an artificial intervention aimed at giving management a chance to correct an imbalance, an injustice, a mistake, and/or outright discrimination. Valuing diversity emphasizes the awareness, recognition, understanding, and appreciation of human differences. Training programs are the dominant method used to accomplish this objective. Managing diversity entails creating a host of organizational changes that enable all people to perform up to their maximum potential.

4. *Demonstrate your familiarity with the demographic trends that are creating an increasingly diverse workforce.* There are four key demographic trends: (a) half of the new entrants into the workforce between 1990 and 2006 will be women, (b) people of color will account for more than a third of the new entrants into the workforce between 1990 and 2006, (c) a mismatch exists between worker's educational attainment and occupational requirements, and (d) the workforce is aging.

5. *Highlight the managerial implications of increasing diversity in the workforce.* There are six broad managerial implications: (a) To attract the best workers, companies need to adopt policies and programs that particularly meet the needs of women and people of color; (b) techniques such as job redesign, realistic job previews, and positive reinforcement are needed to reduce the problem of underemployment; (c) remedial skills training will be necessary to help the growing number of dropouts and illiterates cope with job demands; (d) organizations will need to tangibly support education if the United States is to remain globally competitive; (e) the problem of career plateauing needs to be managed; and (f) five separate managerial initiatives can help organizations effectively adapt to an aging workforce.

6. *Review the five reasons managing diversity is a competitive advantage.* (a) Managing diversity can lower costs and improve employee attitudes. (b) Managing diversity can improve an organization's recruiting efforts. (c) Managing diversity can increase sales, market share, and corporate profits. (d) Managing diversity can increase creativity and innovation. (e) Managing diversity can increase group problem solving and productivity.

7. *Identify the barriers and challenges to managing diversity.* There are 10 barriers to successfully implementing diversity initiatives: (a) inaccurate stereotypes and prejudice, (b) ethnocentrism, (c) poor career planning, (d) an unsupportive and hostile working environment for diverse employees, (e) lack of political savvy on the part of diverse employees, (f) difficulty in balancing career and family issues, (g) fears of reverse discrimination, (h) diversity is not seen as an organizational priority, (i) the need to revamp the organization's performance appraisal and reward system, and (j) resistance to change.

8. *Discuss the organizational practices used to effectively manage diversity as identified by R Roosevelt Thomas, Jr, and Ann Morrison.* There are many different practices organizations can use to manage diversity. R Roosevelt Thomas, Jr, identified eight basic responses for handling any diversity issue: include/exclude, deny, assimilate, suppress, isolate, tolerate, build relationships, and foster mutual adaptation. Exclusion, denial, assimilation, suppression, isolation, and toleration are among the least preferred options. Inclusion, building relationships, and mutual adaptation are the preferred strategies. Ann Morrison's study of diversity practices identified three main types or categories of activities. Accountability practices relate to a manager's responsibility to treat diverse employees fairly. Development practices focus on preparing diverse employees for greater responsibility and advancement. Recruitment practices emphasize attracting job applicants at all levels who are willing to accept challenging work assignments. Table 2–3 presents a list of activities that are used to accomplish each main type.

Discussion Questions

1. Whom do you think would be most resistant to accepting the value or need to manage diversity? Explain.

2. What role does communication play in effectively managing diversity?

3. Does diversity suggest that managers should follow the rule "Do unto others as you would have them do unto you"?

4. What can be done to break the glass ceiling for women and people of color?

5. What can be done to facilitate the career success of the disabled? Explain.

6. Why is underemployment a serious human resource management problem? If you have ever been underemployed, what were your feelings about it?

7. How can interpersonal conflict be caused by diversity? Explain your rationale.

8. Have you seen any examples that support the proposition that diversity is a competitive advantage?

9. Which of the barriers to managing diversity would be most difficult to reduce? Explain.

10. How can Thomas's generic action options and Morrison's specific diversity initiatives be helpful in overcoming the barriers and challenges to managing diversity?

Internet Exercise

This chapter discussed a variety of demographic statistics that underlie the changing nature of the US workforce. We discussed how a glass ceiling is affecting the promotional opportunities and pay for women and people of color. We also reviewed the mismatch between educational attainment and occupational requirements. We did not, however, discuss the employment opportunities within your chosen field of study. The purpose of this exercise is for you to conduct a more thorough examination of statistics related to the workforce as a whole and for statistics pertaining to your career goals. Visit the Web site for the Bureau of Labor Statistics at http://stats/bls.gov/blshome.html, and review information pertaining to the "Economy at a Glance" and "Other Statistics Sites." In particular, look at reports and tables pertaining to average hourly salaries, unemployment, and occupational employment statistics.

Questions

1. To what extent are income levels rising? Determine whether differences exist by race and gender.

2. Do unemployment rates vary by race? Identify which racial groups are advantaged and disadvantaged.

3. What occupational categories are projected to experience the greatest growth in employment opportunities?

4. What are the employment prospects for your chosen field of study or targeted job? Be sure to identify job opportunities and projected wages. Are you happy with your career choice?

OB in Action Case Study

Diversity and Competitive Advantage at Merck[92]

Would Merck's chemistry group necessarily discover better molecules if it were more diverse? Does a parent care whether the medicine that saves a child's life was invented by a white chemist or a black one? Would, or even should, a shareholder care?

In *The Wealth of Nations,* Adam Smith observed that "every [corporation] endeavors to employ its capital so that its produce may be of greatest value. By pursuing its own interest it frequently promotes that of society more effectually than when it really intends to promote it." It's not that we at Merck don't care about doing the right thing, but we believe, like Adam Smith, that our job is to focus on our business. Pressing for diversity, absent a business rationale, may do more harm than good.

To meet our financial goal of performing in the top-quartile of leading health care companies, we need people who can discover and develop important new medicines and market them effectively around the world. What policies and practices can help us assemble such people? Would anyone suggest seriously that pursuing workforce homogeneity would be a smart strategy? Of course not. A homogeneous workforce would inevitably exclude some superior individuals, and it would also preclude a keener understanding of the varied customer and cultural demands of the global market.

We begin, then, with the simple premise that we need to hire and develop the best people we can find. If our people achieve their full potential, Merck will succeed. We don't isolate diversity as a distinct program within the company; instead, we include it as an integral part of our business practices and training strategy. We expect all leaders at Merck to achieve key human resource goals—including diversity—and we use those goals to judge the performance not only of individual managers but also of whole divisions and the entire corporation.

How do we make sure we have access to the kind of people we need? What does it mean, in practice, to be inclusive? Consider two very different recruiting initiatives we've designed.

The first focuses on the long term. Merck has a direct stake in supporting medical and science education in a broad array of colleges and universities. In 1995, to address the shortage of talented minority students who choose biomedical research as a career, Merck made a 10-year, $20 million commitment to the United Negro College Fund to provide scholarship awards and internships. This program will expand the pool of outstanding minority researchers available to the general scientific community. More particularly, we hope that many of them will one day join the Merck Research Laboratories. In addition to our UNCF efforts, we also work with school districts near our facilities in Pennsylvania and New Jersey to improve science education.

The second recruiting initiative was tailored to handle a recent surge of new product introductions. We had to hire an unprecedented number of field reps and we had to do it quickly.

First, we asked the hiring managers to identify the traits, skills, and behaviors most critical to job performance. We then developed a process to screen for those competencies at various stages of candidate assessment: résumé screening, telephone evaluation, and final interview. Scoring each candidate on the individual criteria gave us an objective ranking of the candidates with the highest potential.

Compared with earlier recruitment efforts, this process was more efficient and gave us greater consistency throughout all regions of the country. And there was another interesting effect: The people we hired were an even more diverse group than those we had hired as reps in the past. Diversity, in other words, was a welcome outcome of an inclusive hiring process that was based entirely on business-directed criteria.

Whether it's in the lab or in the marketplace, competitive advantage in a business like ours rests on innovation.

To succeed, we must bring together talented and committed people with diverse perspectives—people who can challenge one another's thinking, people who collectively approach problems from multiple points of view. We will continue, therefore, to cast the widest net in our search for talent—because it is the smart thing to do.

Questions for Discussion

1. Which of the layers of diversity is Merck targeting in its two recruiting initiatives?

2. Why does Raymond Gilmartin, the chairman and CEO of Merck, believe that managing diversity is providing Merck a competitive advantage? Explain your rationale.

3. Which of R Roosevelt Thomas, Jr's eight generic diversity options is Merck using to manage diversity? Explain.

4. Using Table 2–3 as a point of reference, identify the various accountability, development, and recruitment practices used by Merck.

Personal Awareness and Growth Exercise

How Does Your Diversity Profile Affect Your Relationships with Other People?

Objectives

1. To identify the diversity profile of yourself and others.

2. To consider the implications of similarities and differences across diversity profiles.

Introduction

People vary along four layers of diversity: personality, internal dimensions, external dimensions, and organizational dimensions. Differences across these four layers are likely to influence interpersonal relationships and the ability or willingness to work with others. You will be asked to compare yourself with a group of other people you interact with and then to examine the quality of the relationships between yourself and these individuals. This enables you to gain a better understanding of how similarities and differences among people influence attitudes and behavior.

Instructions

Complete the diversity profile by first selecting five current or past co-workers/work associates or fellow students.[93] Alternatively, you can select five people you interact with in order to accomplish your personal goals (e.g., team members on a class project). Write their names on the diagonal lines at the top of the worksheet. Next, determine whether each person is similar to or different from you with respect to each diversity dimension. Mark an "S" if the person is the same or a "D" if the person is different from yourself. Finally, answer the questions for discussion.

Questions for Discussion

1. To whom are you most similar and different?

2. Which diversity dimensions have the greatest influence with respect to whom you are drawn to and whom you like the best?

3. Which dimensions of diversity seem relatively unimportant with respect to the quality of your interpersonal relationships?

4. Consider the individual that you have the most difficult time working with or getting along with. Which dimensions are similar and different? Which dimensions seem to be the source of your difficulty?

5. If you choose co-workers for this exercise, discuss the management actions, policies, and/or programs that could be used to increase inclusiveness, reduce turnover, and increase job satisfaction.

Diversity Worksheet

Work Associates

Diversity Dimensions					
Personality					
e.g., Loyalty					
Internal Dimensions					
Age					
Gender					
Sexual orientation					
Physical ability					
Ethnicity					
Race					
External Dimensions					
Geographic location					
Income					
Personal habits					
Recreational habits					
Religion					
Educational background					
Work experience					
Appearance					
Parental status					
Marital status					
Organizational Dimensions					
Functional level/classification					
Work content/field					
Division/department/unit/group					
Seniority					
Work location					
Union affiliation					
Management status					

Group Exercise

Managing Diversity-Related Interactions

Objectives

1. To improve your ability to manage diversity-related interactions more effectively.

2. To explore different approaches for handling diversity interactions.

Introduction

The interpersonal component of managing diversity can be awkward and uncomfortable. This is partly due to the fact that resolving diversity interactions requires us to deal with situations we may never have encountered before. The purpose of this exercise is to help you manage diversity-related interactions more effectively. To do so, you will be asked to read three scenarios and then decide how you will handle each situation.

Instructions

Presented here are three scenarios depicting diversity-related interactions. Please read the first scenario, and then answer the three questions that follow it. Follow the same procedure for the next two scenarios. Next, divide into groups of three. One at a time, each person should present his or her responses to the three questions for the first scenario. The groups should then discuss the various approaches that were proposed to resolve the diversity interaction and try to arrive at a consensus recommendation. Follow the same procedure for the next two scenarios.

Scenario 1

> Dave, who is one of your direct reports, comes to you and says that he and Scott are having a special commitment ceremony to celebrate the beginning of their lives together. He has invited you to the ceremony. Normally the department has a party and cake for special occasions. Mary, who is one of Dave's peers, has just walked into your office and asks you whether you intend to have a party for Dave.
>
> A. How would you respond?
> _____
> _____
> _____
>
> B. What is the potential impact of your response?
> _____
> _____
> _____
>
> C. If you choose not to respond, what is the potential impact of your behavior?
> _____
> _____
> _____

Scenario 2

> You have an open position for a supervisor, and your top two candidates are an African-American female and a white female. Both candidates are equally qualified. The position is responsible for five white team leaders. You hire the white female because the work group likes her. The team leaders said that they felt more comfortable with the white female. The vice president of human resources has just called you on the phone and asks you to explain why you hired the white female.
>
> A. How would you respond?
> _____
> _____
> _____
>
> B. What is the potential impact of not hiring the African-American?
> _____
> _____
> _____
>
> C. What is the potential impact of hiring the African-American?
> _____
> _____
> _____

Scenario 3

While attending an off-site business meeting, you are waiting in line with a group of team leaders to get your lunch at a buffet. Without any forewarning, one of your peers in the line loudly says, "Thank goodness Terry is at the end of the line. With his size and appetite there wouldn't be any food left for the rest of us." You believe Terry may have heard this comment, and you feel the comment was more of a "weight-related" slur than a joke.

A. How would you respond?

_____

_____

_____

B. What is the potential impact of your response?

_____

_____

_____

C. If you choose not to respond, what is the potential impact of your behavior?

_____

_____

_____

Questions for Discussion

1. What was the recommended response for each scenario?

2. Which scenario generated the most emotion and disagreement? Explain why this occurred.

3. What is the potential impact of a manager's lack of response to Scenarios 1 and 3? Explain.

Chapter Three

Organizational Culture and Ethics

Learning Objectives

When you finish studying the material in this chapter, you should be able to:

1. Discuss the difference between espoused and enacted values.

2. Explain the typology of organizational values.

3. Describe the manifestations of an organization's culture and the four functions of organizational culture.

4. Discuss the three general types of organizational culture and their associated normative beliefs.

5. Discuss the process of developing an adaptive culture.

6. Summarize the methods used by organizations to embed their cultures.

7. Describe the three phases in Feldman's model of organizational socialization.

8. Discuss the two basic functions of mentoring and summarize the phases of mentoring.

9. Describe how women and men respond to moral problems.

10. Specify at least four actions managers can take to improve an organization's ethical climate.

WorldCom Inc. CEO Bernard J Ebbers didn't waste any time in showing MCI Communications Corp.'s senior brass that the free-spending days of the second-largest, long-distance company were over. When he summoned MCI's top 20 executives to a powwow in Destin, [Florida,] last July—two months before the two companies merged—he gave them several weeks' notice. Why? He wanted the execs, who were accustomed to plush corporate jets and first-class comfort, to scrounge up discount airfares. When they got there, more surprises awaited: Instead of finding the usual company limos that would whisk them to their hotels, they had to elbow their way to the rental-car counter. No buffet was set up for their arrival. And they had to double up in hotel rooms.

Ebbers—known as "Bernie" throughout the industry—was just as welcoming. First on the meeting's agenda: He warned that anyone who left the room during the presentation couldn't return until the break. Then he told them that under the WorldCom regime, they would have to submit monthly revenue statements—or "monrevs"—so he personally could police their spending. "It was a tough change," says one MCI exec.

Since WorldCom completed its $37 billion acquisition of MCI, Ebbers has brought a new slim-fast management approach to the long-distance company. . . .

Buy 'n' Slash. Ebbers' secret to success is tried and true. Since the

Bernard J. Ebbers, WorldCom Inc., CEO
(AP/Wide World Photos)

former high school basketball coach got into the phone business in 1983 with the purchase of tiny long-distance reseller LDDS, he has bought 67 phone companies, changing their name to World-Com in 1995. After buying companies, he slashes expenses and consolidates all traffic on a single network. Small wonder that his first yacht was named Aquasitions.

Ebbers is applying the same bottom-line philosophy at MCI WorldCom. On September 27, the new company's top sales managers gathered at the America's Center in St. Louis. The folksy Ebbers told stories to help set the priorities for the new company. He said that one employee who is a single mother had been able to send her kids to college because of her WorldCom stock. Another woman had recently been able to buy a house in a better neighborhood thanks to her WorldCom shares. The point: Employees should focus on boosting shareholder returns. He then told them that everyone would receive stock options.[1]

FOR DISCUSSION
What type of organizational culture is Bernard Ebbers trying to create at MCI WorldCom? Explain.

The opening vignette highlights how the CEO of WorldCom is trying to influence the values and norms associated with cost cutting and efficiency at MCI. His efforts will surely affect MCI's organizational culture. Much has been written and said about organizational culture, values, and ethics in recent years. The results of this activity can be arranged on a continuum of academic rigor. At the low end of the continuum are simplistic typologies and exaggerated claims about the benefits of imitating Japanese-style corporate cultures and values. Here the term *corporate culture* is little more than a pop psychology buzzword. At the other end of the continuum is a growing body of theory and research with valuable insights but plagued by definitional and measurement inconsistencies.[2] By systematically sifting this diverse collection of material, we find that an understanding of organizational culture is central to learning how to manage people at work in both domestic and international operations.

This chapter will help you better understand how managers can use organizational culture as a competitive advantage. We discuss (1) the foundation of organizational culture, (2) the development of a high-performance culture, (3) the organization socialization process, (4) the role of mentoring in socialization, and (5) the importance of ethics in organizational behavior.

Foundation of Organizational Culture

Organizational culture

Shared values and beliefs that underlie a company's identity.

Organizational culture is "the set of shared, taken-for-granted implicit assumptions that a group holds and that determines how it perceives, thinks about, and reacts to its various environments."[3] This definition highlights three important characteristics of organizational culture. First, organizational culture is passed on to new employees through the process of socialization, a topic discussed later in this chapter. Second, organizational culture influences our behavior at work. Finally, organizational culture operates at two different levels. Each level varies in terms of outward visibility and resistance to change.[4]

At the more visible level, culture represents artifacts. Artifacts consist of the physical manifestation of an organization's culture. Organizational examples include acronyms, manner of dress, awards, myths and stories told about the organization, published lists of values, observable rituals and ceremonies, special parking spaces, decorations, and so on. This level also includes visible behaviors exhibited by people and groups. Consider the various artifacts displayed at PeopleSoft Inc.:

Even by the standards of Silicon Valley, PeopleSoft is famous for an aggressively informal and sensitive corporate culture. Its staff routinely worked 70-hour weeks, but for more than the stock options. There was a payoff in PeopleSoft's in-house jokes and clubby code words—in company lingo, employees are "PeoplePeople," they feast on company-funded "PeopleSnacks," which causes them to gain "PeoplePounds."[5]

Artifacts are easier to change than the less visible aspects of organizational culture. At the less visible level, culture reflects the values and beliefs shared among organizational members. These values tend to persist over time and are more resistant to change.

Each level of culture influences the other. For example, if a company truly values providing high-quality service, employees are more likely to adopt the behavior of responding faster to customer complaints. Similarly, causality can flow in the other direction. Employees can come to value high-quality service based on their experiences as they interact with customers.

To gain a better understanding of how organizational culture is formed and used by employees, this section begins by discussing organizational values, the foundation of organizational culture. We then review the manifestations of organizational culture, a model for interpreting organizational culture, the four functions of organizational culture, and the research on organizational cultures.

Organizational Values: The Foundation of Organizational Culture

Organizational values and beliefs constitute the foundation of an organization's culture. They also play a key role in influencing ethical behavior, a topic discussed later in this chapter. Values possess five key components. "**Values** (1) are concepts or beliefs, (2) pertain to desirable end-states or behaviors, (3) transcend situations, (4) guide selection or evaluation of behavior and events, and (5) are ordered by relative importance."[6] It is important to distinguish between values that are espoused versus those that are enacted.[7]

Espoused values represent the explicitly stated values and norms that are preferred by an organization. They are generally established by the founder of a new or small company and by the top management team in a larger organization. Gerald Levin, chairman of Time Warner Inc., for instance, is "putting groups of its most promising executives through an intensive two-day program designed to define and disseminate what the company calls its 'core values and guiding principles'—among them 'diversity,' 'respect,' and 'integrity.' "[8] Time Warner is sending 1,000 executives to these sessions. Because espoused values constitute aspirations that are explicitly communicated to employees, managers such as Levin hope that espoused values will directly influence employee behavior. Unfortunately, aspirations do not automatically produce the desired behaviors because people do not always "walk the talk."

Enacted values, on the other hand, represent the values and norms that actually are exhibited or converted into employee behavior. Let us consider the difference between these two types of values. A company might espouse that it values integrity. If employees display integrity by following through on their commitments, then the espoused value is enacted and individual behavior is being influenced by the value of integrity. In contrast, if employees do not follow through on their commitments, then the value of integrity is simply a "stated" aspiration that does not influence behavior. The gap between espoused and enacted values is important because it can significantly influence an organization's culture and employee attitudes. A recent study of 312 British Rail train drivers, supervisors, and senior managers revealed that the creation of a safety culture was negatively affected by large gaps between senior management's espoused and enacted values. Employees were more cynical about safety when they

Values
Enduring belief in a mode of conduct or end-state.

Espoused values
The stated values and norms that are preferred by an organization.

Enacted values
The values and norms that are exhibited by employees.

believed that senior managers' behaviors were inconsistent with the stated values regarding safety.[9]

It also is important to consider how an organization's value system influences organizational culture because companies subscribe to multiple values. An organization's **value system** reflects the patterns of conflict and compatibility among values, not the relative importance among values.[10] This definition highlights the point that organizations endorse a constellation of values that contain both conflicting and compatible values. For example, management scholars believe that organizations have two fundamental value systems that naturally conflict with each other. One system relates to the manner in which tasks are accomplished and the other includes values related to maintaining internal cohesion and solidarity. The central issue underlying this value conflict revolves around identifying the main goal being pursued by an organization. Is the organization predominantly interested in financial performance, relationships, or some combination of the two? To help you understand how organizational values influence organizational culture, we present a typology of organizational values and review relevant research.

Value system

Pattern of values within an organization.

Ethics at Work

Imagine, for instance, that you manage a company located in India that has been recently purchased by a large multinational corporation (MNC). Your company has long adopted a culturally accepted Indian practice of guaranteeing a job to at least one of each of your employees' children. This practice reflects a deep moral concern for employees' families. However, now that your company has been purchased by the MNC, you are expected to enforce a corporate nepotism policy prohibiting hiring based solely on personal or family relationships. Both the Indian employment practices and the MNC's anti-nepotism policy are based on moral values that are easily justified. The Indian hiring practice is linked to strong family values, while the corporate policy is based on moral values of fairness or equity.[11]

You Decide . . .
What would you do?

For an interpretation of the results, visit our Web site **www.mhhe.com/kreitner**

A Typology of Organizational Values   Figure 3–1 presents a typology of organizational values that is based on crossing organizational reward norms and organization power structures.[12] Organizational reward norms reflect a company's fundamental belief about how rewards should be allocated. According to the equitable reward norm, rewards should be proportionate to contributions. In contrast, an egalitarian-oriented value system calls for rewarding all employees' equally, regardless of their comparative contributions. Organization power structures reflect a company's basic belief about how power and authority should be shared and distributed. These beliefs range from an extreme of being completely unequal or centralized to equal or completely decentralized.

Figure 3–1 identifies four types of value systems: elite, meritocratic, leadership, and collegial. Each value system contains a set of values that are reinforced or endorsed by that type of value system and a set of values that are inconsistent or discouraged by that value system. For example, an elite value system endorses values related to acceptance of authority, high performance, and equitable rewards. This value system, however, does not encourage values related to teamwork, participation, commitment, or affiliation. In contrast, a collegial value system supports values associated with teamwork, participation, commitment, and affiliation while discouraging values of authority, high performance, and equitable rewards.

Practical Application of Research   Organizations subscribe to a constellation of values rather than to only one and can be profiled according to their values.[13] This, in turn, enables managers to determine whether an organization's values are consistent and supportive of its corporate goals and initiatives. Organizational change is unlikely to succeed if it is based on a set of values that is highly inconsistent with employees' individual values.[14] Finally, a study of 85 Australian organizations from 1986–1990 revealed four interesting trends about the typology of organizational values presented in Figure 3–1:[15]

Figure 3–1   *A Typology of Organizational Values*

Unequal or
Centralized Power

Equal or
Decentralized Power

Organization Power Structure

Organizational Reward Norms

Equitable
– *Contribution*

Elite		Meritocratic	
Endorsed Values	Discouraged Values	Endorsed Values	Discouraged Values
Authority	Teamwork	Performance	Authority
Performance	Participation	rewards	
rewards	Commitment	Teamwork	
	Affiliation	Participation	
		Commitment	
		Affiliation	

Egalitarian
– *equal*

Leadership		Collegial	
Endorsed Values	Discouraged Values	Endorsed Values	Discouraged Values
Authority	Participation	Teamwork	Authority
Performance		Participation	Performance
rewards		Commitment	rewards
Teamwork		Affiliation	
Commitment			
Affiliation			

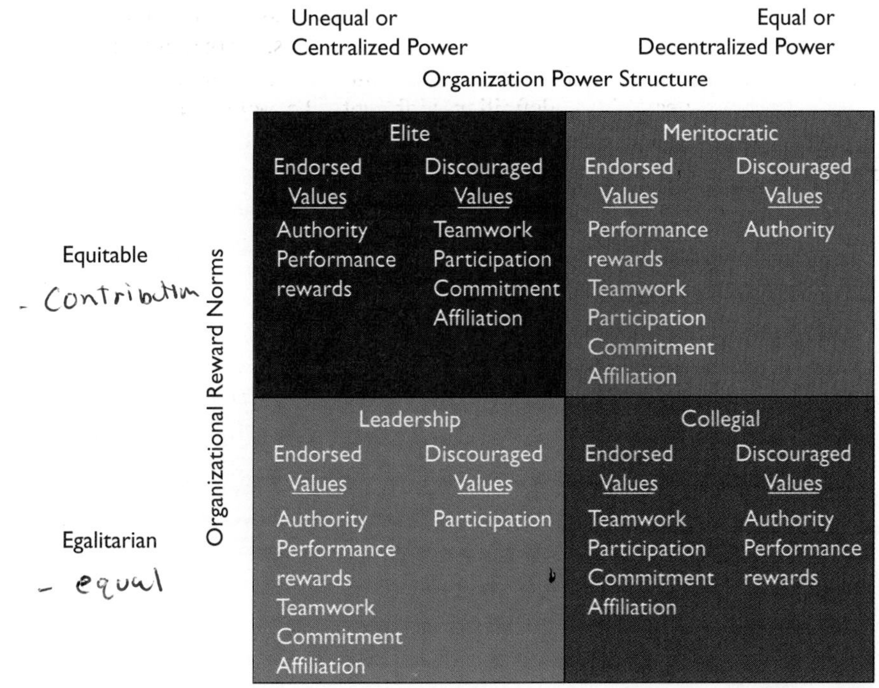

SOURCE: Adapted from B Kabanoff and J Holt, "Changes in the Espoused Values of Australian Organizations 1986–1990," *Journal of Organizational Behavior,* May 1996, pp 201–19.

1. Organizational values were quite stable over four years. This result supports the contention that values are relatively stable and resistant to change.

2. There was not a universal movement to one type of value system. The 85 organizations represented all four value systems. This finding reinforces the earlier conclusion that there is no one best organizational culture or value system.

3. Organizations with elite value systems experienced the greatest amount of change over the four-year period. Elite organizations tended to become more collegial. This finding is consistent with results from a national sample of 2,408 US workers. Two-thirds of the survey respondents indicated that they desired more influence or decision making in their jobs.[16]

4. There was an overall increase in the number of organizations that endorsed the individual value of employee commitment. This trend is consistent with the notion that organizational success is partly dependent on the extent to which employees are committed to their organizations.

Manifestations of Organizational Culture

When is an organization's culture most apparent? In addition to the physical artifacts of organizational culture that were previously discussed, cultural assumptions assert themselves through socialization of new employees, subculture clashes, and top management behavior. Consider these three situations, for example: A newcomer who shows up late for an important meeting is told a story about someone who was fired for repeated tardiness. Conflict between product design engineers who emphasize a product's function and

Figure 3–2   *A Model for Observing and Interpreting General Manifestations of Organizational Culture*

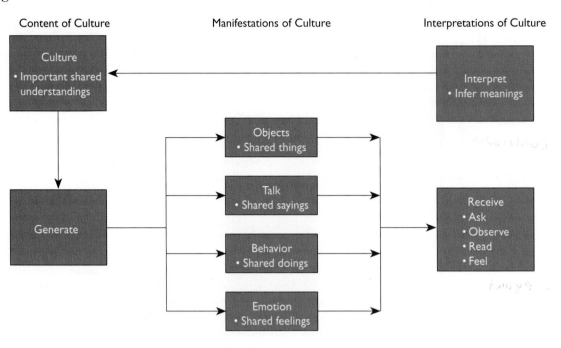

SOURCE: V Sathe, "Implications of Corporate Culture: A Manager's Guide to Action." Reprinted, by permission of publisher, from *Organizational Dynamics,* Autumn 1983. © 1983 American Management Association. Reprinted by permission of the American Management Association International, New York, NY. All rights reserved. http://www.amanet.org

marketing specialists who demand a more stylish product reveals an underlying clash of subculture values. Top managers, through the behavior they model and the administrative and reward systems they create, prompt a significant improvement in the quality of a company's products.

A Model for Interpreting Organizational Culture

A useful model for observing and interpreting organizational culture was developed by Vijay Sathe, a Harvard researcher (see Figure 3–2). Four general manifestations or evidence of organizational culture in his model are shared things (objects), shared sayings (talk), shared doings (behavior), and shared feelings (emotion). One can begin collecting cultural information within the organization by asking, observing, reading, and feeling.

The OB Exercise provides you with the opportunity to practice identifying the manifestations of organizational culture at the Ritz-Carlton and McDonald's by using the model presented in Figure 3–2. These examples highlight different manifestations of organizational culture.

Four Functions of Organizational Culture

As illustrated in Figure 3–3, an organization's culture fulfills four functions.[17] To help bring these four functions to life, let us consider how each of them has taken shape at 3M. 3M is a particularly instructive example because it has a long history of being an

OB Exercise · Manifestations of Organizational Culture at the Ritz-Carlton and McDonald's

Instructions

Read the following descriptions and answer the discussion questions. Answers can be found following the Notes at the end of the book.

Ritz-Carlton

The Ritz-Carlton has created "a climate and culture that allows them to succeed as an ever-expanding, upscale hotel chain in a very competitive market. At Ritz-Carlton, each hotel employee is part of a team whose members are empowered to do whatever it takes to satisfy a customer. These employees are guided by a credo, called the "Gold Standards," that specifies desired behaviors. More importantly, there are policies, practices, procedures, and routines designed to support and reward employees engaging in these desired behaviors. Ritz-Carlton makes every employee feel like a valued person. The employee motto is "We are ladies and gentlemen serving ladies and gentlemen." Guests and employees alike are treated the right way; there are no mixed messages in Ritz-Carlton's climate and culture.

McDonald's

McDonald's vision is to provide customers with quality, service, convenience, and value (QSCV). Ray Kroc, the founder, wanted a restaurant system known for its consistently high quality and uniform methods of preparation. He created Hamburger University, which offers a degree in Hamburgerology, to help create this culture. Franchisees, managers, and assistant managers are indoctrinated into McDonald's culture and associated policies and procedures at the University. McDonald's policies and procedures meticulously spell out desired employee behaviors and job responsibilities. For example, they specify how often the bathroom should be cleaned and what color of nail polish to wear. McDonald's culture is reinforced by using contests and ceremonies to reward those franchisees who best meet their goals. McDonald's recently implemented a set of business practices known as Franchising 2000. Two key components are as follows: franchisees must submit annual financial goals for approval, and a single pricing strategy is established for all products. Franchisees who fail to adhere to the policies and procedures risk losing their franchises when they expire. McDonald's likes to hire executives who have strong traditional values such as loyalty, dedication, and service.

Discussion Questions

1. Identify the shared things, sayings, doings, and feelings at both the Ritz-Carlton and McDonald's.
2. Which organization is based more on control and/or competition?

SOURCE: The Ritz-Carlton description was excerpted from B Schneider, A P Brief, and R A Guzzo, "Creating a Climate and Culture for Sustainable Organizational Change," *Organizational Dynamics,* Spring 1996, p 16. Material about McDonald's was obtained from R Gibson, "A Bit of Heartburn: Some Franchisees Say Moves by McDonald's Hurt Their Operations," *The Wall Street Journal,* April 17, 1996, pp A1, A8; and M A Salva-Ramirez, "McDonald's: A Prime Example of Corporate Culture," *Public Relations Quarterly,* Winter 1995/96, pp 30–31.

---

innovative company—the company was founded in 1902—and it was ranked as the 94th most admired company in the United States by *Fortune* in 1998, partly due to its strong and distinctive culture.[18]

1. *Give members an organizational identity.* 3M is known as being an innovative company that relentlessly pursues new-product development. One way of promoting innovation is to encourage the research and development of new products and services. For example, 3M regularly sets future sales targets based on the percentage of sales that must come from new products. In one year, the senior management decreed

Figure 3–3   *Four Functions of Organizational Culture*

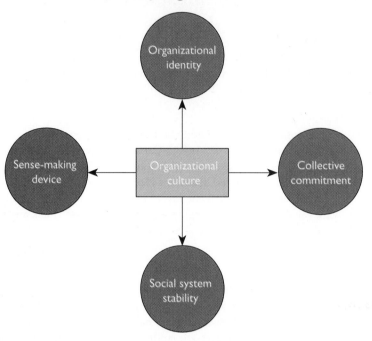

SOURCE: Adapted from discussion in L Smircich, "Concepts of Culture and Organizational Analysis," *Administrative Science Quarterly,* September 1983, pp 339–58. Reproduced by permission of John Wiley & Sons, Limited.

that 30% of its sales must come from products introduced within the past four years. The old standard was 25% in five years. This identity is reinforced by creating rewards that reinforce innovation. For example, "The 3M Corporation has its version of a Nobel Prize for innovative employees. The prize is the Golden Step award, whose trophy is a winged foot. Several Golden Steps are given out each year to employees whose new products have reached significant revenue and profit levels."[19]

2. *Facilitate collective commitment.* One of 3M's corporate values is to be "a company that employees are proud to be a part of." People who like 3M's culture tend to stay employed there for long periods of time. Approximately 24,000 of its employees have more than 15 years of tenure with the company while 19,600 have stayed more than 20 years. Consider the commitment and pride expressed by Kathleen Stanislawski, a staffing manager. "I'm a 27-year 3Mer because, quite frankly, there's no reason to leave. I've had great opportunities to do different jobs and to grow a career. It's just a great company."[20]

3. *Promote social system stability.* Social system stability reflects the extent to which the work environment is perceived as positive and reinforcing, and conflict and change are managed effectively. Consider how 3M dealt with its financial problems in 1998. "Even in tough times, which have now arrived because of the upheavals in Asia, 3M hasn't become a mean, miserly, or miserable place to work. It's shedding about 4,500 jobs, but slowly, and mostly by attrition."[21] This strategy helped to maintain a positive work environment in the face of adversity. The company also attempts to promote stability through a promote-from-within culture, a strategic hiring policy that ensures that capable college graduates are hired

in a timely manner, and a layoff policy that provides displaced workers six months to find another job at 3M before being terminated.

4. *Shape behavior by helping members make sense of their surroundings.* This function of culture helps employees understand why the organization does what it does and how it intends to accomplish its long-term goals. 3M sets expectations for innovation in a variety of ways. For example, the company employs an internship and co-op program. 3M also shapes expectations and behavior by providing detailed career feedback to its employees. New hires are measured and evaluated against a career growth standard during their first six months to three years of employment.

Types of Organizational Culture

Researchers have attempted to identify and measure various types of organizational culture in order to study the relationship between types of culture and organizational effectiveness. This pursuit was motivated by the possibility that certain cultures were more effective than others. Unfortunately, research has not uncovered a universal typology of cultural styles that everyone accepts.[22] Just the same, there is value in providing an example of various types of organizational culture. Table 3–1 is thus presented as an illustration rather than a definitive conclusion about the types of organizational culture that exist. Awareness of these types provides you with greater understanding about the manifestations of culture.

The Golden Step award is 3M's version of the Nobel Prize. Each year the company presents the award to several employees whose new products achieve significant revenue levels. Reward systems linked to target behaviors like innovativeness help establish strong corporate cultures.

Courtesy of 3M Corporation

Table 3–1 shows that there are three general types of organizational culture—constructive, passive–defensive, and aggressive–defensive—and that each type is associated with a different set of normative beliefs.[23] **Normative beliefs** represent an individual's thoughts and beliefs about how members of a particular group or organization are expected to approach their work and interact with others. A *constructive culture* is one in which employees are encouraged to interact with others and to work on tasks and projects in ways that will assist them in satisfying their needs to grow and develop. This type of culture endorses normative beliefs associated with achievement, self-actualizing, humanistic-encouraging, and affiliative. In contrast, a *passive–defensive culture* is characterized by an overriding belief that employees must interact with others in ways that do not threaten their own job security. This culture reinforces the normative beliefs associated with approval, conventional, dependent, and avoidance (see Table 3–1).

Normative beliefs
Thoughts and beliefs about expected behavior and modes of conduct.

Finally, companies with an *aggressive–defensive culture* encourage employees to approach tasks in forceful ways in order to protect their status and job security. This type of culture is more characteristic of normative beliefs reflecting oppositional, power, competitive, and perfectionist. Try to identify the characteristics associated with Intel Corp.'s aggressive–defensive culture in the following example involving James Meadlock, chief executive officer of Intergraph, in Huntsville, Alabama:

Mr. Meadlock showed up at a graphics-industry conference in August 1997 in Los Angeles with 40 computer workstations ready to display in Intel's booth, to show off the power of Intel's latest chips. But Intel representatives told him they wouldn't be showing Intergraph machines that day.

Table 3–1   *Types of Organizational Culture*

General Types of Culture	Normative Beliefs	Organizational Characteristics
Constructive	Achievement	Organizations that do things well and value members who set and accomplish their own goals. Members are expected to set challenging but realistic goals, establish plans to reach these goals, and pursue them with enthusiasm. (Pursuing a standard of excellence)
Constructive	Self-actualizing	Organizations that value creativity, quality over quantity, and both task accomplishment and individual growth. Members are encouraged to gain enjoyment from their work, develop themselves, and take on new and interesting activities. (Thinking in unique and independent ways)
Constructive	Humanistic-encouraging	Organizations that are managed in a participative and person-centered way. Members are expected to be supportive, constructive, and open to influence in their dealings with one another. (Helping others to grow and develop)
Constructive	Affiliative	Organizations that place a high priority on constructive interpersonal relationships. Members are expected to be friendly, open, and sensitive to the satisfaction of their work group. (Dealing with others in a friendly way)
Passive–defensive	Approval	Organizations in which conflicts are avoided and interpersonal relationships are pleasant—at least superficially. Members feel that they should agree with, gain the approval of, and be liked by others. ("Going along" with others)
Passive–defensive	Conventional	Organizations that are conservative, traditional, and bureaucratically controlled. Members are expected to conform, follow the rules, and make a good impression. (Always following policies and practices)
Passive–defensive	Dependent	Organizations that are hierarchically controlled and nonparticipative. Centralized decision making in such organizations leads members to do only what they are told and to clear all decisions with superiors. (Pleasing those in positions of authority)
Passive–defensive	Avoidance	Organizations that fail to reward success but nevertheless punish mistakes. This negative reward system leads members to shift responsibilities to others and avoid any possibility of being blamed for a mistake. (Waiting for others to act first)
Aggressive–defensive	Oppositional	Organizations in which confrontation and negativism are rewarded. Members gain status and influence by being critical and thus are reinforced to oppose the ideas of others. (Pointing out flaws)
Aggressive–defensive	Power	Nonparticipative organizations structured on the basis of the authority inherent in members' positions. Members believe they will be rewarded for taking charge, controlling subordinates and, at the same time, being responsive to the demands of superiors. (Building up one's power base)

(continued)

Table 3–1   *(Continued)*

General Types of Culture	Normative Beliefs	Organizational Characteristics
Aggressive–defensive	Competitive	Winning is valued and members are rewarded for outperforming one another. Members operate in a "win-lose" framework and believe they must work against (rather than with) their peers to be noticed. (Turning the job into a contest)
Aggressive–defensive	Perfectionistic	Organizations in which perfectionism, persistence, and hard work are valued. Members feel they must avoid any mistake, keep track of everything, and work long hours to attain narrowly defined objectives. (Doing things perfectly)

SOURCE: Reproduced with permission of authors and publisher from R A Cooke and J L Szumal, "Measuring Normative Beliefs and Shared Behavioral Expectations in Organizations: The Reliability and Validity of the Organizational Culture Inventory," *Psychological Reports,* 1993, 72, 1299–1330. © *Psychological Reports,* 1993.

Infuriated, Mr. Meadlock demanded to see the top Intel executive on site, a hard-charging vice president named Patrick Gelsinger. Things would get better for Intergraph, Mr. Gelsinger reportedly said, if Intergraph would just sign over its patents to Intel at no cost.

A week later, Intel formally asked Intergraph to return all confidential materials to Intel. Within a few months, the companies were in a state of legal warfare, with Intergraph alleging that Intel used its monopoly power to engage in a pattern of incidents like the encounter at the trade show in hopes of forcing Intergraph to give up its patents.[24]

Gelsinger declined to discuss this incident with a reporter from *The Wall Street Journal,* but he stated that Intel's business practices are honorable and that the company is aggressive and very competitive. The courts will have to determine the truth about these alleged aggressive–defensive tactics.

Although an organization may predominately represent one cultural type, it still can manifest normative beliefs and characteristics from the others. Research demonstrates that organizations can have functional subcultures, hierarchical subcultures based on one's level in the organization, geographical subcultures, occupational subcultures based on one's title or position, social subcultures derived from social activities such as a bowling or golf league and a reading club, and counter-cultures.[25] It is important for managers to be aware of the possibility that conflict between subgroups that form subcultures can undermine an organization's overall performance. Consider the effect of the counterculture that rose up against 3M CEO Livio DeSimone in 1998:

Last summer, after some managers began sending anonymous letters to the 3M board, directors began investigating complaints about DeSimone's management style and performance. The campaign began, executives say, with dissatisfied researchers and scientists in divisions such as pharmaceuticals and telecommunications, who were angered by what they saw as DeSimone's lack of commitment to research. It soon spread to other divisions such as industrial tape and abrasives, where compensation worries were high. Then, in August, 3M's operating committee—made up of the 10 executives who report to DeSimone—brought in a Harvard Business School professor, David A Garvin, to study management and strategy. Not long after, the board began discussing the 62-year-old's replacement.[26]

Research on Organizational Cultures

Because the concept of organizational culture is a relatively recent addition to OB, the research base is incomplete. Studies to date are characterized by inconsistent definitions and varied methodologies. Quantitative treatments are sparse because there is little agreement on how to measure cultural variables. As a matter of convenience, we review two streams of organizational culture research in this section. One stream has been reported in best-selling books and the other in research journal articles.[27]

Anecdotal Evidence from Best-Selling Books about Organizational Culture   Initial widespread interest in organizational cultures was stirred by William Ouchi's 1981 best-seller, *Theory Z: How American Business Can Meet the Japanese Challenge.* From a research standpoint, Ouchi's two main contributions were (1) focusing attention on internal culture as a key determinant of organizational effectiveness and (2) developing an instructive typology of organizations based in part on cultural variables.[28]

Close on the heels of Ouchi's book came two 1982 best-sellers: Deal and Kennedy's *Corporate Cultures: The Rites and Rituals of Corporate Life*[29] and Peters and Waterman's *In Search of Excellence.*[30] Both books drew upon interviews and the authors' consulting experience. Each team of authors relied on abundant anecdotal evidence to make the point that successful companies tend to have strong cultures. For example, Peters and Waterman observed:

> Without exception, the dominance and coherence of culture proved to be an essential quality of the excellent companies. Moreover, the stronger the culture and the more it was directed toward the marketplace, the less need was there for policy manuals, organization charts, or detailed procedures and rules. In these companies, people way down the line know what they are supposed to do in most situations because the handful of guiding values is crystal clear.[31]

These best-sellers generated excitement about cultural factors such as heroes and stories. They also generated the impression that organizations have one distinct culture. As previously discussed, few people accept this generic conclusion. Finally, these best-sellers failed to break any new ground in the measurement and evaluation of organizational cultures.

Evidence from Research Articles and Management Implications
Although there is not a uniformly agreed-upon method to assess culture, there are several cultural surveys and interviewing protocols that have been recommended.[32] So, what have we learned to date? First, financial performance was higher among companies that had adaptive and flexible cultures.[33] The explanation for this important relationship is discussed in the next section on developing high-performance cultures. Second, studies of mergers indicated that they frequently failed due to incompatible cultures.[34] For example, Jerry Dark, human resources vice president for E*Trade Group, concluded that cultural and communications issues were the major stumbling block when E*Trade acquired ShareData Inc. in 1998. He recommended that companies should define roles and responsibilities for key executives and middle managers at both companies during the initial stages of a merger in order to reduce these problems.[35] Due to the increasing number of corporate mergers around the world, and the conclusion that 7 out of 10 mergers and acquisitions failed

The Merger between Deutsche Bank and Bankers Trust Requires Cultural and Structural Change

Deutsche Bank is now run by a managing board, or *Vorstand,* in which a handful of executives make all the decisions by consensus. Responsibility is shared, and assigning blame is difficult. Deutsche Bank Chairman Rolf Breuer says that won't work following the merger with Bankers Trust. Instead, he is implementing what he calls "a virtual holding company" approach, meaning a structure where different divisions are run almost like separate entities, with their own bottom lines and management boards.

"I have said that there is now an end to Soviet Union behavior of the central committee, where everyone is present but no one is accountable," he says.

SOURCE: Excerpted from J L Hiday, A Raghavan, and J Sapsford, "Sizing Up: BNP Bid Raises Issue of How Large a Bank Can Get, or Should," *The Wall Street Journal,* March 11, 1999, p A6.

to meet their financial promise, managers within merged companies would be well advised to consider the role of organizational culture in creating a new organization.[36] The International OB provides an example of how the management structure and culture at Deutsche Bank changed after the company merged with Bankers Trust. How do you think the employees at Deutsche Bank will respond to Mr. Breuer's proposed changes?

Third, several studies demonstrated that organizational culture was significantly correlated with employee behavior and attitudes. For example, a constructive culture was positively related with job satisfaction, intentions to stay at the company, and innovation and was negatively associated with work avoidance. In contrast, passive–defensive and aggressive–defensive cultures were negatively correlated with job satisfaction and intentions to stay at the company.[37] These results suggest that employees seem to prefer organizations that encourage people to interact and work with others in ways that assist them in satisfying their needs to grow and develop. Finally, results from several studies revealed that the congruence between an individual's values and the organization's values was significantly associated with organizational commitment, job satisfaction, intention to quit, and turnover.[38]

These research results underscore the significance of organizational culture. They also reinforce the need to learn more about the process of cultivating and changing an organization's culture. An organization's culture is not determined by fate. It is formed and shaped by the combination and integration of everyone who works in the organization. As a case in point, a longitudinal study of 322 employees working in a governmental organization revealed that managerial intervention successfully shifted the organizational culture toward greater participation and employee involvement. This change in organizational culture was associated with improved job satisfaction and communication across all hierarchical levels.[39] This study further highlights the interplay between organizational culture and organizational change. Successful organizational change is highly dependent on an organization's culture.[40] A change-resistant culture, for instance, can undermine the effectiveness of any type of organizational change. Although it is not an easy task to change an organization's culture, the next section provides a preliminary overview of how this might be done.

Developing High-Performance Cultures

An organization's culture may be strong or weak, depending on variables such as cohesiveness, value consensus, and individual commitment to collective goals. Contrary to what one might suspect, a strong culture is not necessarily a good thing. The nature of the culture's central values is more important than its strength. For example, a strong but change-resistant culture may be worse, from the standpoint of profitability and competitiveness, than a weak but innovative culture. IBM is a prime example: Its strong culture, coupled with a dogged determination to continually pursue a strategic plan that was out of step with the market, led to its failure to maintain its leadership in the personal computer market. This strategy ultimately cost the company about $90 billion.[41] This section discusses the type of organizational cultures that enhance an organization's financial performance and the process by which cultures are embedded in an organization and learned by employees.

What Type of Cultures Enhance an Organization's Financial Performance?

Three perspectives have been proposed to explain the type of cultures that enhance an organization's economic performance. They are referred to as the strength, fit, and adaptive perspectives, respectively:

Strength perspective
Assumes that the strength of corporate culture is related to a firm's financial performance.

1. The **strength perspective** predicts a significant relationship between strength of corporate culture and long-term financial performance. The idea is that strong cultures create goal alignment, employee motivation, and needed structure and controls to improve organizational performance.[42] Critics of this perspective believe that companies with a strong culture can become arrogant, inwardly focused, and bureaucratic after they achieve financial success because financial success reinforces the strong culture. This reinforcement can blind senior managers to the need for new strategic plans and may result in a general resistance to change.

Fit perspective
Assumes that culture must align with its business or strategic context.

2. The **fit perspective** is based on the premise that an organization's culture must align with its business or strategic context. For example, a culture that promotes standardization and planning might work well in a slow-growing industry but be totally inappropriate for Internet companies that work in a highly volatile and changing environment. Consider how Ed Siciliano described the difference between working at Xerox and at Applied Theory, an internet-service provider based on Long Island, New York:

> "At Xerox, you're following a well-defined process for just about everything," he says. At Applied Theory, "you don't have time to haul out the guidebook." At Xerox, for example, he held monthly sales reviews with each salesperson. At his new job [at Applied Theory], "you grab people in the hallway, the lunch-room, or on the weekend and that's where you have your discussion of sales prospects," he says. He also dropped the lengthy, Xerox-style sales reports he prepared for superiors each month because nobody read them.[43]

Likewise, a culture in which individual performance is valued might help a sales organization but would undermine performance in an organization where people work in teams. Accordingly, there is no one best culture. A culture is predicted to facilitate economic performance only if it "fits" its context.[44]

Adaptive perspective
Assumes that adaptive cultures enhance a firm's financial performance.

3. The **adaptive perspective** assumes that the most effective cultures help organizations anticipate and adapt to environmental changes. A team of management experts defined this culture as follows:

Figure 3–4   *Developing and Preserving an Adaptive Culture*

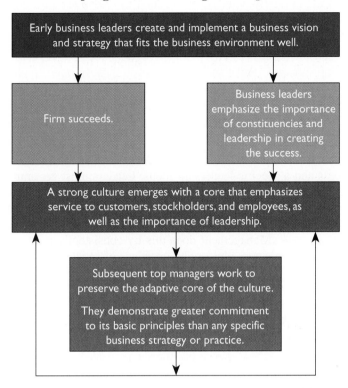

SOURCE: Adapted with permission of The Free Press, a division of Simon and Schuster, from *Corporate Culture and Performance* by J P Kotter and J L Heskett. Copyright © 1992 by Kotter Associates, Inc and James L. Heskett.

> An adaptive culture entails a risk-taking, trusting, and proactive approach to organizational as well as individual life. Members actively support one another's efforts to identify all problems and implement workable solutions. There is a shared feeling of confidence: The members believe, without a doubt, that they can effectively manage whatever new problems and opportunities will come their way. There is widespread enthusiasm, a spirit of doing whatever it takes to achieve organizational success. The members are receptive to change and innovation.[45]

This proactive adaptability is expected to enhance long-term financial performance.

A Test of the Three Perspectives   John Kotter and James Heskett tested the three perspectives on a sample of 207 companies from 22 industries for the period 1977 to 1988. After correlating results from a cultural survey and three different measures of financial performance, results partially supported the strength and fit perspectives. However, findings were completely consistent with the adaptive culture perspective. Long-term financial performance was highest for organizations with an adaptive culture.[46]

Developing an Adaptive Culture   Figure 3–4 illustrates the process of developing and preserving an adaptive culture. The process begins with leadership; that is, leaders must create and implement a business vision and associated strategies that fit the organizational context. A **vision** represents a long-term goal that describes "what"

Vision
Long-term goal describing "what" an organization wants to become.

an organization wants to become. Kevin Jenkins, former CEO of Canadian Airlines International Ltd., correctly noted, however, that the existence of a corporate vision does not guarantee organizational success:

> "A vision held only by its leadership is not enough to create any real change," indicated Jenkins. "To ensure success, management must continuously—and creatively—articulate the company's vision and goals. This is achieved through open communication systems that encourage employee feedback and facilitate a two-way flow of information. Because the company's ultimate goal must be to satisfy the customer, it is imperative that employees understand what is expected of them as well as their responsibility for achieving results."[47]

As noted by Jenkins, adaptiveness is promoted over time by a combination of organizational success and a specific leadership focus. Leaders must get employees to buy into a timeless philosophy or set of values that emphasizes service to the organization's key constituents—customers, stockholders, and employees—and also emphasizes the improvement of leadership. An infrastructure must then be created to preserve the organization's adaptiveness. Management does this by consistently reinforcing and supporting the organization's core philosophy or values of satisfying constituency needs and improving leadership. This is precisely what Herb Kelleher, CEO of Southwest Airlines, has done at Southwest Airlines.

Southwest Airlines has grown from a startup company in 1971 to the fourth largest and most consistently profitable airline in 1999 by creating a "strong" or widely shared belief in a constituency oriented culture:

> Long before "empowerment" became a management buzzword, Ms. Barrett [the No. 2 executive at Southwest] was giving employees freedom from centralized policies. She constantly reinforces the company's message that employees should be treated like customers and continually celebrates workers who go above and beyond the call of duty. And when she sensed the carrier was outgrowing its personality-kid-among-the-impersonal-giants image, she created a "culture committee" of employees charged with preserving Southwest's spirit . . .
>
> Southwest employees are well-paid compared with counterparts at other airlines. Celebrations are an important part of work, from spontaneous "fun sessions" to Christmas parties beginning in September to a lavish annual awards banquet, where the individual's contribution to the whole is glorified.
>
> At the same time, employees work like crazy between festivities. With that formula, the airline has avoided bureaucracy and mediocrity that infect other companies when they outgrow their entrepreneurial roots.[48]

How Cultures Are Embedded in Organizations

An organization's initial culture is an outgrowth of the founder's philosophy. For example, an achievement culture is likely to develop if the founder is an achievement-oriented individual driven by success. Over time, the original culture is either embedded as is or modified to fit the current environmental situation. Edgar Schein, a well-known OB scholar, notes that embedding a culture involves a teaching process. That is, organizational members teach each other about the organization's preferred values, beliefs, expectations, and behaviors. This is accomplished by using one or more of the following mechanisms:[49]

1. *Formal statements of organizational philosophy, mission, vision, values, and materials used for recruiting, selection, and socialization.* American Express, for example, publishes a list of six American Express corporate values. This list,

which is imparted during the socialization process for all new employees and is widely reinforced throughout the organization, includes the following corporate values: place the interests of clients and customers first; continuously strive for quality in everything; treat people with respect and dignity; use conduct that reflects the highest standards of integrity; promote teamwork; and be good citizens in the communities in which employees live and work.

2. *The design of physical space, work environments, and buildings.* Consider the use of a new alternative workplace design called "hoteling:"

> As in the other shared-office options, "hotel" work spaces are furnished, equipped, and supported with typical office services. Employees may have mobile cubbies, file cabinets, or lockers for personal storage; and a computer system routes phone calls and E-mail as necessary. But "hotel" work spaces are reserved by the hour, by the day, or by the week instead of being permanently assigned. In addition, a "concierge" may provide employees with travel and logistic support. At its most advanced, "hotel" work space is customized with individuals' personal photos and memorabilia, which are stored electronically, retrieved, and "placed" on occupants' desktops just before they arrive, and then removed as soon as they leave.[50]

This new alternative workplace is driven by the need to be adaptable and flexible to changing market conditions. Companies such as AT&T and IBM also have experienced significant cost savings by using a variety of alternative workplace arrangements. AT&T has improved cash flow by $550 million, and IBM is saving more than $100 million annually through the use of alternative workplace initiatives.[51]

3. *Slogans, language, acronyms, and sayings.* For example, Bank One promotes its desire to provide excellent client service through the slogan "whatever it takes." Employees are encouraged to do whatever it takes to exceed customer expectations.

4. *Deliberate role modeling, training programs, teaching, and coaching by managers and supervisors.*

5. *Explicit rewards, status symbols (e.g., titles), and promotion criteria.* For example, Herman-Miller Company developed a team-based reward system that encouraged team members to work together to satisfy customer needs.[52]

6. *Stories, legends, and myths about key people and events.* The stories in the International OB box, for instance, are used within Tesco PLC, a leading food retailer in England, Scotland, and Wales, to embed the value of providing outstanding customer service.

7. *The organizational activities, processes, or outcomes that leaders pay attention to, measure, and control.* Employees are much more likely to pay attention to the amount of on-time deliveries when senior management uses on-time deliveries as a measure of quality or customer service.

8. *Leader reactions to critical incidents and organizational crises.*

9. *The workflow and organizational structure.* Hierarchical structures are more likely to embed an orientation toward control and authority than a flatter organization.

10. *Organizational systems and procedures.* An organization can promote achievement and competition through the use of sales contests.

11. *Organizational goals and the associated criteria used for recruitment, selection, development, promotion, layoffs, and retirement of people.* PepsiCo reinforces a high-performance culture by setting challenging goals. Executives strive to achieve a 15% increase in revenue per year.[53]

The Organizational Socialization Process

Organizational socialization

Process by which employees learn an organization's values, norms, and required behaviors.

Organizational socialization is defined as "the process by which a person learns the values, norms, and required behaviors which permit him to participate as a member of the organization."[54] As previously discussed, organization socialization is a key mechanism used by organizations to embed their organizational cultures. In short, organizational socialization turns outsiders into fully functioning insiders by promoting and reinforcing the organization's core values and beliefs. Consider the socialization process at General Electric:

GE's socialization process demands that individuals continually hone their skills ... At GE, job security is only maintained as long as an individual remains the best person for his/her job. If the company acquires another business, or closes down a business, that has personnel who can perform the person's job better, s/he is replaced. Education is constant; managers continually experience state-of-the-art leadership development training. As a result of the socialization, GE's employees are strongly rooted in the corporate value system of competitiveness and self-reliance.[55]

GE's socialization process can certainly be anxiety producing; newcomers—called recruits, new hires, rookies, pledges, trainees, or apprentices—must adapt or fall by the wayside. This section introduces a three-phase model of organizational socialization and examines the practical application of socialization research.

A Three-Phase Model of Organizational Socialization

One's first year in a complex organization can be confusing. There is a constant swirl of new faces, strange jargon, conflicting expectations, and apparently unrelated events. Some organizations treat new members in a rather haphazard, sink-or-swim manner. More typically, though, the socialization process is characterized by a sequence of identifiable steps.[56]

Organizational behavior researcher Daniel Feldman has proposed a three-phase model of organizational socialization that promotes deeper understanding of this important process. As illustrated in Figure 3–5, the three phases are (1) anticipatory socialization, (2) encounter, and (3) change and acquisition. Each phase has its associated perceptual and social processes. Feldman's model also specifies behavioral and affective outcomes

Figure 3–5   *A Model of Organizational Socialization*

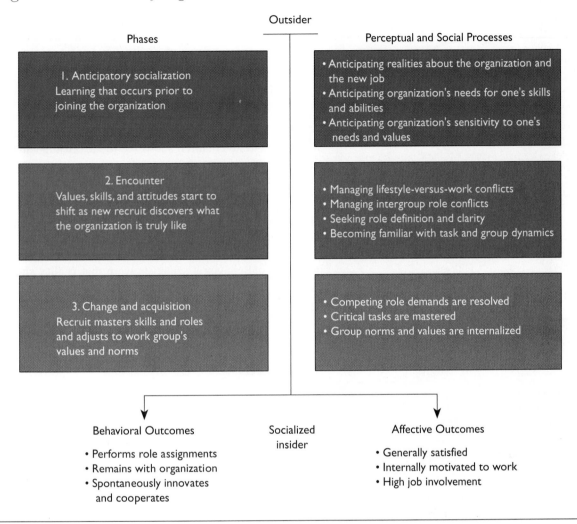

SOURCE: Adapted from material in D C Feldman, "The Multiple Socialization of Organization Members," *Academy of Management Review,* April 1981, pp 309–18.

that can be used to judge how well an individual has been socialized. The entire three-phase sequence may take from a few weeks to a year to complete, depending on individual differences and the complexity of the situation.

Phase I: Anticipatory Socialization   Organizational socialization begins *before* the individual actually joins the organization. Anticipatory socialization information comes from many sources. US Marine recruiting ads, for example, prepare future recruits for a rough-and-tumble experience. Widely circulated stories about the fast- and ever-changing environments within Internet companies probably deter those, who would prefer working in a more stable environment, from applying.

All of this information—whether formal or informal, accurate or inaccurate—helps the individual anticipate organizational realities. Unrealistic expectations about the nature of the work, pay, and promotions are often formulated during phase I.

How would you like to work for a company that encourages employees to have fun while working? Henry Quadracci, founder and CEO of Quad/Graphics, has created such a company by reducing status barriers, investing in employees' development, and by having fun at work himself.

Courtesy of Quad/Graphics

Because employees with unrealistic expectations are more likely to quit their jobs in the future, organizations may want to use realistic job previews.[57] A **realistic job preview** (RJP) involves giving recruits a realistic idea of what lies ahead by presenting both positive and negative aspects of the job. RJPs may be verbal, in booklet form, audiovisual, or hands-on. Research supports the practical benefits of using RJPs. A recent meta-analysis of 40 studies revealed that RJPs were related to higher performance and to lower attrition from the recruitment process. Results also demonstrated that RJPs lowered job applicants' initial expectations and led to lower turnover among those applicants who were hired.[58]

Phase 2: Encounter   This second phase begins when the employment contract has been signed. It is a time for surprise and making sense as the newcomer enters unfamiliar territory. Behavioral scientists warn that **reality shock** can occur during the encounter phase:

Becoming a member of an organization will upset the everyday order of even the most well-informed newcomer. Matters concerning such aspects as friendships, time, purpose, demeanor, competence, and the expectations the person holds of the immediate and distant future are suddenly made problematic. The newcomer's most pressing task is to build a set of guidelines and interpretations to explain and make meaningful the myriad of activities observed as going on in the organization.[59]

Many companies use a combination of orientation and training programs to socialize employees during the encounter phase. Consider the socialization tactics used by Harry Quadracci, founder and CEO of Quad/Graphics:

But here, the half-day class in Quad Culture and the nine-week Quad Technologies course aren't just for newbies; they're for anyone who wants to go.

Realistic job preview
Presents both positive and negative aspects of a job.

Reality shock
A newcomer's feeling of surprise after experiencing unexpected situations or events.

"Strictly speaking, 'orientation' is limited to the usual things—signing up for benefits, and teaching safety rules," says Claire Ho, Quad/Graphics' corporate-communications manager. "Our concern was, with such a strong corporate culture, how do we continue to demonstrate and communicate this when we're growing so fast and expanding across the country? So we emphasize perpetuating the culture through *actions*."

Unusual actions, too. Like the navy-blue uniforms—kind of like a gas station attendant's, Ho confesses—that everyone wears, . . . "The president wears a bow tie with his," Ho says. This custom, in place since 1993, emphasizes the commonality of employee goals: "The uniforms say we're all production workers, no matter what our job," she says. "It really breaks down walls."[60]

The encounter phase at Quad/Graphics clearly teaches employees that Harry Quadracci wants to create an organization where people can have fun and still work hard.

During the encounter phase, the individual is challenged to resolve any conflicts between the job and outside interests. If the hours prove too long, for example, family duties may require the individual to quit and find a more suitable work schedule. Also, as indicated in Figure 3–5, role conflict stemming from competing demands of different groups needs to be confronted and resolved.

Phase 3: Change and Acquisition   Mastery of important tasks and resolution of role conflict signals the beginning of this final phase of the socialization process. Those who do not make the transition to phase 3 leave voluntarily or involuntarily or become isolated from social networks within the organization. Senior executives frequently play a direct role in the change and acquisition phase.

Practical Application of Socialization Research

Past research suggests five practical guidelines for managing organizational socialization.[61]

1. Managers should avoid a haphazard, sink-or-swim approach to organizational socialization because formalized socialization tactics positively influence new hires. Formalized socialization enhanced the manner in which newcomers adjusted to their jobs over a 10-month period, and reduced role ambiguity, role conflict, stress symptoms, and intentions to quit while simultaneously increasing job satisfaction and organizational commitment for a sample of 295 recent college graduates.[62]

2. The encounter phase of socialization is particularly important. Studies of newly hired accountants demonstrated that the frequency and type of information obtained during their first six months of employment significantly affected their job performance, their role clarity, their understanding of the organizational culture, and the extent to which they were socially integrated.[63] Managers play a key role during the encounter phase. A recent study of 205 new college graduates further revealed that their manager's task- and relationship-oriented input during the socialization process significantly helped these newcomers to adjust to their new jobs.[64] In summary, managers need to help new hires integrate within the organizational culture.

3. Support for stage models is mixed. Although there are different stages of socialization, they are not identical in order, length, or content for all people or jobs.[65] Managers are advised to use a contingency approach toward organizational socialization. In other words, different techniques are appropriate for different people at different times.

4. The organization can benefit by training new employees to use proactive socialization behaviors. A study of 154 entry-level professionals showed that effectively using proactive socialization behaviors influenced the newcomers' general anxiety and stress during the first month of employment and their motivation and anxiety six months later.[66]

5. Managers should pay attention to the socialization of diverse employees. Research demonstrated that diverse employees, particularly those with disabilities, experienced different socialization activities than other newcomers. In turn, these different experiences affected their long-term success and job satisfaction.[67]

Mentoring
Process of forming and maintaining developmental relationships between a mentor and a junior person.

Socialization through Mentoring

Mentoring is defined as the process of forming and maintaining an intensive and lasting developmental relationship between a senior person (the mentor) and a junior person (the protégé, if male; or protégée, if female). The modern word *mentor* derives from Mentor, the name of a wise and trusted counselor in Greek mythology. Terms typically used in connection with mentoring are *teacher, coach, godfather,* and *sponsor.*

Figure 3–6   *The Career and Psychosocial Functions of Mentoring*

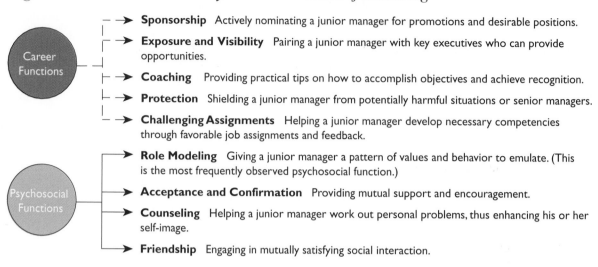

Sponsorship Actively nominating a junior manager for promotions and desirable positions.

Exposure and Visibility Pairing a junior manager with key executives who can provide opportunities.

Coaching Providing practical tips on how to accomplish objectives and achieve recognition.

Protection Shielding a junior manager from potentially harmful situations or senior managers.

Challenging Assignments Helping a junior manager develop necessary competencies through favorable job assignments and feedback.

Role Modeling Giving a junior manager a pattern of values and behavior to emulate. (This is the most frequently observed psychosocial function.)

Acceptance and Confirmation Providing mutual support and encouragement.

Counseling Helping a junior manager work out personal problems, thus enhancing his or her self-image.

Friendship Engaging in mutually satisfying social interaction.

SOURCE: Adapted from discussion in K E Kram, *Mentoring of Work: Developmental Relationships in Organizational Life* (Glenview, IL: Scott, Foresman, 1985), pp 22–39.

Mentoring is an important part of developing a high-performance culture for three reasons. First, mentoring contributes to creating a sense of oneness by promoting the acceptance of the organization's core values throughout the organization. Second, the socialization aspect of mentoring also promotes a sense of membership. Finally, mentoring increases interpersonal exchanges among organizational members.

Functions of Mentoring

Kathy Kram, a Boston University researcher, conducted in-depth interviews with both members of 18 pairs of senior and junior managers. As a by-product of this study, Kram identified two general functions—career and psychosocial—of the mentoring process (see Figure 3–6). Five *career functions* that enhanced career development were sponsorship, exposure-and-visibility, coaching, protection, and challenging assignments. Four *psychosocial functions* were role modeling, acceptance-and-confirmation, counseling, and friendship. The psychosocial functions clarified the participants' identities and enhanced their feelings of competence.[68]

Darryl Hartley-Leonard's experience at Hyatt Hotels exemplifies how important the career and psychosocial functions of mentoring can be to your career. Darryl started as a desk clerk at Hyatt in 1964 and rose to the position of CEO. In an interview with *The Wall Street Journal*, Hartley-Leonard indicated that his relationship with Pat Foley, the general manager who originally hired him, changed his life:

> The shy Englishman [Darryl] copied his gregarious boss's style and mannerisms. He learned how to treat employees from Mr. Foley, who washed dishes with the kitchen help and co-signed an $800 note for Mr. Hartley-Leonard's first car. "People would walk through walls for him," he says.
>
> As Mr. Foley's career prospered, so did Mr. Hartley-Leonard's. When Mr. Foley became the resident manager at Hyatt's first big hotel in Atlanta, he hired Mr. Hartley-Leonard as a front-office supervisor. Mr. Foley eventually became president and installed his protege as executive vice president.

Not surprisingly, Mr. Hartley-Leonard considers mentoring a critical element in his ascent. "If you get five people of equal ability, the one who gets mentoring will have the edge," he says.[69]

This example also highlights the fact that both members of the mentoring relationship can benefit from these career and psychosocial functions. Both of the authors of this text, for example, benefited from mentoring PhD students during their graduate education. Mentoring is not strictly a top-down proposition, as many mistakenly believe.

Phases of Mentoring

In addition to identifying the functions of mentoring, Kram's research revealed four phases of the mentoring process: (1) initiation, (2) cultivation, (3) separation, and (4) redefinition. As indicated in Table 3–2, the phases involve *variable* rather than fixed time periods. Telltale turning points signal the evolution from one phase to the next. For example, when a junior manager begins to resist guidance and strives to work more autonomously, the separation phase begins. The mentoring relationships in Kram's sample lasted an average of five years.

Research Evidence on Mentoring

Research findings uncovered both individual and organizational benefits of mentoring programs. Individuals with mentors received more promotions, were more mobile, had greater career satisfaction, and made more income than those without mentors.[70] The impact of mentoring on income was even more pronounced when employees were mentored by white men. For example, a study of 1,018 MBA graduates revealed that graduates who were mentored by white men obtained an average annual compensation advantage of $16,840 over those with mentors possessing other demographic characteristics.[71] The same trend was found for people of color. A sample of 170 male and female African-Americans who graduated with either an undergraduate or MBA degree revealed that graduates who subsequently established mentoring relationships with white males earned $9,794 more than those without mentoring relationships. On a positive note, there were no gender-based pay differences found among this sample.[72] Mentoring inconsistently affected performance. Research revealed that ability and past experience impacted performance more than career and psychosocial mentoring.[73]

Research also supports the organizational benefits of mentoring. In addition to the obvious benefit of employee development, mentoring enhances the effectiveness of organizational communication. Specifically, mentoring increases the amount of vertical communication both up and down an organization, and it provides a mechanism for modifying or reinforcing organizational culture. Consider the benefits derived by the approach used at Network Management, a $10 million health-care consultancy in Minneapolis:

> The company, which added 65 employees in 1998, urges all newcomers to lunch individually with each member of its 10-person management team. "When new hires meet the CEO and have a discussion about the company from his perspective, they can really get infected by that," says Scott Ofstead, director of human resources.[74]

These informal lunches sound like a good vehicle to increase vertical communication and to reinforce the organization's preferred values and beliefs.

Research also investigated the dynamics associated with the establishment of mentoring relationships. Two key findings were uncovered. First, mentoring relationships were

Table 3–2   *Phases of the Mentor Relationship*

Phase	Definition	Turning Points*
Initiation	A period of six months to a year during which time the relationship gets started and begins to have importance for both managers.	Fantasies become concrete expectations. Expectations are met; senior manager provides coaching, challenging work, visibility; junior manager provides technical assistance, respect, and desire to be coached. There are opportunities for interaction around work tasks.
Cultivation	A period of two to five years during which time the range of career and psychosocial functions provided expand to a maximum.	Both individuals continue to benefit from the relationship. Opportunities for meaningful and more frequent interaction increase. Emotional bond deepens and intimacy increases.
Separation	A period of six months to two years after a significant change in the structural role relationship and/or the emotional experience of the relationship.	Junior manager no longer wants guidance but rather the opportunity to work more autonomously. Senior manager faces midlife crisis and is less available to provide mentoring functions. Job rotation or promotion limits opportunities for continued interaction; career and psychosocial functions can no longer be provided. Blocked opportunity creates resentment and hostility that disrupts positive interaction.
Redefinition	An indefinite period after the separation phase, during which time the relationship is ended or takes on significantly different characteristics, making it a more peerlike friendship.	Stresses of separation diminish, and new relationships are formed. The mentor relationship is no longer needed in its previous form. Resentment and anger diminish; gratitude and appreciation increase. Peer status is achieved.

*Examples of the most frequently observed psychological and organizational factors that cause movement into the current relationship phase.

SOURCE: K E Kram, "Phases of the Mentor Relationship," *Academy of Management Journal,* December 1983, p 622. Used with permission.

more likely to form when the mentor and protégé/protégée possessed similar attitudes, philosophies, personalities, interests, background, and education.[75] This trend is consistent with a study that demonstrated that African-American and Hispanic MBA graduates were less likely to create mentoring relationships with white men than were their white peers.[76] Second, the most common cross-gender mentor relationship involved a male mentor and female protégée. This trend occurred for three reasons: (1) There is an underrepresentation of women in executive-level positions, (2) women perceived more negative drawbacks to becoming mentors than did men, and (3) there are a number of individual, group, and organizational barriers that inhibit mentoring relationships for diverse employees.[77]

Getting the Most Out of Mentoring

A team of mentoring experts offered the following guidelines for implementing effective organizational mentoring programs:[78]

1. Train mentors and protégés/protégées on how to best use career and psychosocial mentoring.

2. Use both formal and informal mentoring, but do not dictate mentoring relationships.

3. Diverse employees should be informed about the benefits and drawbacks associated with establishing mentoring relationships with individuals of similar and different gender and race.

4. Women should be encouraged to mentor others. Perceived barriers need to be addressed and eliminated for this to occur.

5. Increase the number of diverse mentors in high-ranking positions.

Ethics and Organizational Behavior

The issue of ethics and ethical behavior is receiving greater attention today. This interest is partly due to reported cases of questionable or potentially unethical behavior and the associated costs. For instance, US industries lose about $400 billion a year from unethical and criminal behavior. Another nationwide survey revealed that 20% of the respondents were asked to do something that violated their ethical standards: 41% complied.[79] Unethical behavior is a relevant issue for all employees. It occurs from the bottom to the top of an organization. For example, a recent survey of 1,000 senior-level executives revealed that as many as one-third lied on their resumes.[80] Maybe this result should not be surprising because there are more benefits to lying, such as a higher salary and stock options, and the competition for senior management positions is fierce. As you will learn, there are a variety of individual and organizational characteristics that contribute to unethical behavior. OB is an excellent vantage point for better understanding and improving workplace ethics. If OB can provide insights about managing human work behavior, then it can teach us something about avoiding *misbehavior.*

Ethics involves the study of moral issues and choices. It is concerned with right versus wrong, good versus bad, and the many shades of gray in supposedly black-and-white issues. Moral implications spring from virtually every decision, both on and off the job. Managers are challenged to have more imagination and the courage to do the right thing. Consider what occurred to male and female human resource management professionals as they attempted to ethically perform their jobs:

> "This was a lily-white organization when I joined it," he says. "The only diversity was in the lower-end jobs. I brought in two minority managers and, shortly thereafter, started receiving some pressure from the board along some stereotypical lines: 'We don't hire people like that. You're not from here. You don't understand.' They wanted me to fire them. I refused, and it ultimately cost me my job."
>
> Another HR professional lost her job . . . because, she says, she refused to sit back and do things she considered wrong. What kind of things? Allowing a pay inequity to persist between a male employee whose salary was more than double that of two female colleagues; testing new applicants for HIV and basing hiring decisions on the results; screening out female applicants in their 30s based on the boss's fear that they would miss a lot of work due to child-care issues.[81]

Are you amazed that these individuals were fired for making the decisions that they did? What do you think you would have done in these situations? To enhance your

Ethics
Study of moral issues and choices.

Figure 3–7   *A Model of Ethical Behavior in the Workplace*

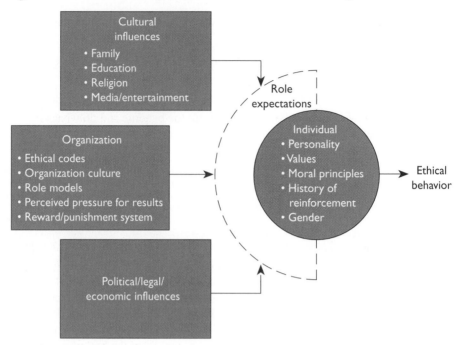

understanding about the causes of ethical and unethical behavior, we present a conceptual framework for making ethical decisions.

A Model of Ethical Behavior

Ethical and unethical conduct is the product of a complex combination of influences (see Figure 3–7). At the center of the model in Figure 3–7 is the individual decision maker. He or she has a unique combination of personality characteristics, values, and moral principles, leaning toward or away from ethical behavior. Personal experience with being rewarded or reinforced for certain behaviors and punished for others also shapes the individual's tendency to act ethically or unethically. Finally, gender plays an important role in explaining ethical behavior. Men and women have significantly different moral orientations toward organizational behavior.[82] This issue is discussed later in this section.

Next, Figure 3–7 illustrates three major sources of influence on one's role expectations. People play many roles in life, including those of employee or manager. One's expectations for how those roles should be played are shaped by cultural, organizational, and general environmental factors. The International OB describes the cultural differences between China and Western societies that influence role expectations and ethical behavior. This example illustrates how a single behavior such as hiring relatives can be viewed as both ethical and unethical by people with varying cultural backgrounds.

Focusing on one troublesome source of organizational influence, many studies have found a tendency among middle- and lower-level managers to act unethically in the face of perceived pressure for results. By fostering a pressure-cooker atmosphere for results, managers can unwittingly set the stage for unethical shortcuts by employees who seek to please and be loyal to the company. In contrast, consider

International OB — Religious and Cultural Differences between China and the West Influence Ethical Behavior

By Western standards, China is a secular society; most Chinese do not "belong" to a faith in the sense of being a Christian, a Jew, or a Muslim. Little thought is given to supreme beings, other than venerated ancestors, or to such matters as holiness or life after death. There is a dearth of universal ethical principles or moral absolutes other than maintaining the security and well-being of the family and living up to one's Confucian obligations. These remain the primary normative prescriptions for correct behavior. Because maintaining social harmony and order is the highest ideal, minimization of conflict is essential and absolutes are seen as sources of conflict ...

Confucianism makes no pretense as a religion. Rather, it is a system of values that govern interpersonal behavior with an eye toward building a civil society. It does not speak to humanity's relationship with any supreme being ...

Chinese religion has evolved in ways that support and advance the maintenance of social harmony. In contrast, Judaism and Christianity (and Islam as well) prescribe behavioral and ethical standards intended to allow the faithful an opportunity to please and prove their worthiness to their Creator and Supreme Being. While banning behavior detrimental to maintaining a civil society (though perhaps one not quite as well-mannered as China's), these religions also prescribe how the Supreme Being should be worshipped and require followers to hold certain beliefs, make certain expressions of faith, and participate in various rituals.

Secular authorities in the West, particularly the Romans building on the precedent set by the ancient Greeks, extended ecclesiastical law into a natural law that dealt with practices, abstract principles, and beliefs beyond the spiritual domain. From natural law, greatly elaborated during the Enlightenment, were derived such notions as liberty, justice, equity, fairness, the binding contract, and, ultimately, the social contract between people and their governments. These important social and political virtues, binding governments as well as citizens, acquired the force of principle as important to many—and perhaps more so to some—as the tenets of sacred scripture. Though Westerners might disagree on what is "fair" in any set of circumstances, few would argue against the worth of "fairness."

The Chinese, like most human beings, will recognize the evil of a wanton crime, but they will have trouble responding to the invocation of abstractions such as "fair trade." What is fair to the Chinese is whatever works, whatever action or manner of speech is necessary to execute a transaction satisfactorily for both parties. Westerners are taught to place the principle of honesty above the nicety of harmony; for them, constructive criticism is the "right" thing to do, even if painful. For the Chinese, this threat to harmony is antisocial. Likewise, most Westerners would be appalled that a manager could be so unprincipled as to show favoritism in hiring a relative. A Chinese would be equally appalled by any reluctance to do so.

SOURCE: Excerpted from J Scarborough, "Comparing Chinese and Western Cultural Roots: Why "East Is East and ...," *Business Horizons*, November–December 1998, pp 19–20. Reprinted with permission of *Business Horizons*. Copyright © 1998 by the Board of Trustees at Indiana University Kelley School of Business.

how the organizational culture at Timberland reinforces and encourages employees to engage in socially responsible behaviors:

> Everyone gets paid for 40 hours a year of volunteer work. On Timberland's 25th anniversary, the whole place shut down so that employees could work on community projects. One employee described the event as a "religious experience."[83]

This example also highlights that an organization's reward system can influence ethical behavior. Individuals are more likely to behave ethically/unethically when they are incented to do so.[84] Managers are encouraged to examine their reward systems to ensure that the preferred types of behavior are being reinforced.

Because ethical or unethical behavior is the result of person–situation interactions, we need to discuss both the decision maker's moral principles and the organization's ethical climate.[85]

These Timberland employees volunteered at a New Hampshire food bank as part of the company's commitment to support the communities in which it operates. Timberland is willing to pay its employees for participating in such programs.

(Brooks Kraft/Sygma)

Do Moral Principles Vary by Gender?

Yes, men and women view moral problems and situations differently. This is why research demonstrates that men and women reliably choose alternative solutions to the same moral problems or dilemmas.[86] Carol Gilligan, a well-known psychologist, identified one underlying cause of these gender differences. Her research revealed that men and women differed in terms of how they conceived moral problems. Males perceived moral problems in terms of a **justice perspective** while women relied on a **care perspective.** The two perspectives are described as follows:

Justice perspective
Based on the ideal of reciprocal rights and driven by rules and regulations.

Care perspective
Involves compassion and an ideal of attention and response to need.

> A justice perspective draws attention to problems of inequality and oppression and holds up an ideal of reciprocal rights and equal respect for individuals. A care perspective draws attention to problems of detachment or abandonment and holds up an ideal of attention and response to need. Two moral injunctions, not to treat others unfairly and not to turn away from someone in need, capture these different concerns.[87]

This description underscores the point that men tend to view moral problems in terms of rights, whereas women conceptualize moral problems as an issue of care involving empathy and compassion. In turn, the justice perspective leads males to focus on the "rules of the game." The female perspective, in contrast, is more situational and contextual and results in women focusing on the dynamics and expectations associated with the people involved in the situation at hand.[88]

Although some people believe that the care perspective is more appropriate than the justice approach or vice versa, we believe that men and women have equally valid approaches to ethical behavior. The key point is for all of us to be aware of these gender differences and to draw on the best from both perspectives when trying to resolve moral or ethical problems.

General Moral Principles

Management consultant and writer Kent Hodgson has helpfully taken managers a step closer to ethical decisions by identifying seven general moral principles (see Table 3–3). Hodgson calls them "the magnificent seven" to emphasize their timeless and worldwide relevance. Both the justice and care perspectives are clearly evident in the magnificent seven, which are more detailed and, hence, more practical. Importantly, according to Hodgson, there are no absolute ethical answers for decision makers. The goal for managers should be to rely on moral principles so their decisions are *principled, appropriate,* and *defensible.*[89] Managers require a supportive organizational climate that translates general moral principles into specific do's and don't's and fosters ethical decisions.

Table 3–3   *The Magnificent Seven: General Moral Principles for Managers*

1. *Dignity of human life: The lives of people are to be respected.* Human beings, by the fact of their existence, have value and dignity. We may not act in ways that directly intend to harm or kill an innocent person. Human beings have a right to live; we have an obligation to respect that right to life. Human life is to be preserved and treated as sacred.

2. *Autonomy: All persons are intrinsically valuable and have the right to self-determination.* We should act in ways that demonstrate each person's worth, dignity, and right to free choice. We have a right to act in ways that assert our own worth and legitimate needs. We should not use others as mere "things" or only as means to an end. Each person has an equal right to basic human liberty, compatible with a similar liberty for others.

3. *Honesty: The truth should be told to those who have a right to know it.* Honesty is also known as integrity, truth telling, and honor. One should speak and act so as to reflect the reality of the situation. Speaking and acting should mirror the way things really are. There are times when others have the right to hear the truth from us; there are times when they do not.

4. *Loyalty: Promises, contracts, and commitments should be honored.* Loyalty includes fidelity, promise keeping, keeping the public trust, good citizenship, excellence in quality of work, reliability, commitment, and honoring just laws, rules, and policies.

5. *Fairness: People should be treated justly.* One has the right to be treated fairly, impartially, and equitably. One has the obligation to treat others fairly and justly. All have the right to the necessities of life—especially those in deep need and the helpless. Justice includes equal, impartial, unbiased treatment. Fairness tolerates diversity and accepts differences in people and their ideas.

6. *Humaneness.* There are two parts: (1) *Our actions ought to accomplish good,* and (2) *we should avoid doing evil.* We should do good to others and to ourselves. We should have concern for the well-being of others; usually, we show this concern in the form of compassion, giving, kindness, serving, and caring.

7. *The common good: Actions should accomplish the "greatest good for the greatest number" of people.* One should act and speak in ways that benefit the welfare of the largest number of people, while trying to protect the rights of individuals.

SOURCE: A Rock and a Hard Place: How to Make Ethical Business Decisions When the Choices Are Tough, © 1992 Kent Hodgson, pp 69–73. Published by AMACOM, a division of the American Management Association. Used with permission.

How to Improve the Organization's Ethical Climate

A team of management researchers recommended the following actions for improving on-the-job ethics.[90]

- *Behave ethically yourself.* Managers are potent role models whose habits and actual behavior send clear signals about the importance of ethical conduct. Ethical behavior is a top-to-bottom proposition.

- *Screen potential employees.* Surprisingly, employers are generally lax when it comes to checking references, credentials, transcripts, and other information on applicant résumés. More diligent action in this area can screen out those given to fraud and misrepresentation. Integrity testing is fairly valid but is no panacea.[91]

- *Develop a meaningful code of ethics.* Codes of ethics can have a positive impact if they satisfy these four criteria:

  1. They are *distributed* to every employee.

  2. They are firmly *supported* by top management.

  3. They refer to *specific* practices and ethical dilemmas likely to be encountered by target employees (e.g., salespersons paying kickbacks, purchasing agents receiving payoffs, laboratory scientists doctoring data, or accountants "cooking the books").

  4. They are evenly *enforced* with rewards for compliance and strict penalties for noncompliance.

Honeywell Inc.'s code of ethics meets all four of these criteria:

> Honeywell Inc., based in Minneapolis, recently has translated its formal code of ethics into six foreign languages. Senior management regularly communicates the importance of ethics and compliance in newsletters, ethics presentations, and other periodic communications. For example, a recent newsletter for the Asia Pacific region included a letter from the president talking about bribery. He reiterated that bribery will not be tolerated at all and that the company will walk away from business rather than engage in bribery.[92]

- *Provide ethics training.* Employees can be trained to identify and deal with ethical issues during orientation and through seminar and video training sessions.

- *Reinforce ethical behavior.* Behavior that is reinforced tends to be repeated, whereas behavior that is not reinforced tends to disappear. Ethical conduct too often is punished while unethical behavior is rewarded.

- *Create positions, units, and other structural mechanisms to deal with ethics.* Ethics needs to be an everyday affair, not a one-time announcement of a new ethical code that gets filed away and forgotten. The Body Shop and Ben & Jerry's are both using a social or ethical audit to assess how well the company is living up to its ethical standards. Organizational changes are then made on the basis of the audit results.[93]

Summary of Key Concepts

1. *Discuss the difference between espoused and enacted values.* Espoused values represent the explicitly stated values and norms that are preferred by an organization. Enacted values, in contrast, reflect the values and norms that actually are exhibited or converted into employee behavior. Employees become cynical when management espouses one set of values and norms and then behaves in an inconsistent fashion.

2. *Explain the typology of organizational values.* The typology of organizational values identifies four types of organizational value systems. It is based on crossing organizational reward norms and organization power structures. The types of value systems include elite, meritocratic, leadership, and collegial. Each type of value system contains a set of values that are both consistent and inconsistent with the underlying value system.

3. *Describe the manifestations of an organization's culture and the four functions of organizational culture.* General manifestations of an organization's culture are shared objects, talk, behavior, and emotion. Four functions of organization culture are organizational identity, collective commitment, social system stability, and sense-making device.

4. *Discuss the three general types of organizational culture and their associated normative beliefs.* The three general types of organizational culture are constructive, passive–defensive, and aggressive–defensive. Each type is grounded in different normative beliefs. Normative beliefs represent an individual's thoughts and beliefs about how members of a particular group or organization are expected to approach their work and interact with others. A constructive culture is associated with the beliefs of achievement, self-actualizing, humanistic-encouraging, and affiliative. Passive–defensive organizations tend to endorse the beliefs of approval, conventional, dependent, and avoidance. Aggressive–defensive cultures tend to endorse the beliefs of oppositional, power, competitive, and perfectionistic.

5. *Discuss the process of developing an adaptive culture.* The process begins with charismatic leadership that creates a business vision and strategy. Over time, adaptiveness is created by a combination of organizational success and leaders' ability to get employees to buy into a philosophy or set of values of satisfying constituency needs and improving leadership. Finally, an infrastructure is created to preserve the organization's adaptiveness.

6. *Summarize the methods used by organizations to embed their cultures.* Embedding a culture amounts to teaching employees about the organization's preferred values, beliefs, expectations, and behaviors. This is accomplished by using one or more of the following 11 mechanisms: (a) formal statements of organizational philosophy, mission, vision, values, and materials used for recruiting, selection, and socialization; (b) the design of physical space, work environments, and buildings; (c) slogans, language, acronyms, and sayings; (d) deliberate role modeling, training programs, teaching, and coaching by managers and supervisors; (e) explicit rewards, status symbols, and promotion criteria; (f) stories, legends, and myths about key people and events; (g) the organizational activities, processes, or outcomes that leaders pay attention to, measure, and control; (h) leader reactions to critical incidents and organizational crises; (i) the workflow and organizational structure; (j) organizational systems and procedures; and (k) organizational goals and associated criteria used for recruitment, selection, development, promotion, layoffs, and retirement of people.

7. *Describe the three phases in Feldman's model of organizational culture.* The three phases of Feldman's model are anticipatory socialization, encounter, and change and acquisition. Anticipatory socialization begins before an individual actually joins the organization. The encounter phase begins when the employment contract has been signed. Phase 3 involves the period in which employees master important tasks and resolve any role conflicts.

8. *Discuss the two basic functions of mentoring and summarize the phases of mentoring.* Mentors help protégés in two basic functions: career and psychosocial functions. For career functions, mentors provide advice and support in regard to sponsorship, exposure and visibility, coaching, protection, and challenging assignments. Psychosocial functions entail role modeling, acceptance and confirmation, counseling, and friendship. There are four phases of the mentoring process: (a) initiation, (b) cultivation, (c) separation, and (d) redefinition. Each phase involves variable rather than fixed periods of time, and there are key activities that occur during each phase.

9. *Describe how women and men respond to moral problems.* Males and females respond to moral problems in terms of a justice and care perspective, respectively. A justice perspective is based on the ideal of reciprocal rights and is driven by rules and regulations. In contrast, the care perspective involves compassion and an ideal of attention and response to need. Men tend to focus on the "rules of the game" when responding to moral problems, whereas women pay attention to interpersonal dynamics and expectations among people.

10. *Specify at least four actions managers can take to improve an organization's ethical climate.* They can do so by (a) behaving ethically themselves, (b) screening potential employees, (c) developing a code of ethics, (d) providing ethics training, (e) reinforcing and rewarding ethical behavior, and (f) creating positions and structural mechanisms dealing with ethics.

Discussion Questions

1. How would you respond to someone who made the following statement? "Organizational cultures are not important as far as managers are concerned."

2. What type of organizational culture exists within your current or most recent employer? Explain.

3. Can you think of any organizational heroes who have influenced your work behavior? Describe them, and explain how they affected your behavior.

4. Do you know of any successful companies that do not have a positive adaptive culture? Why do you think they are successful?

5. Why is socialization essential to organizational success?

6. Have you ever had a mentor? Explain how things turned out.

7. What type of value system exists within your current classroom? Provide examples to support your evaluation.

8. Which particular source of influence in the left-hand side of Figure 3–7 do you think has had the greatest impact on your ethical behavior? Explain.

9. Which of the magnificent seven in Table 3–3 is the most important moral principle in your life? Explain. Will this help or hinder you as a manager?

10. What would you say to an individual who says that women are more ethical than men?

Internet Exercise

This chapter focused on the role of values and beliefs in forming an organization's culture. We also discussed how cultures are embedded and reinforced through socialization and mentoring. The topic of organizational culture is big business on the Internet. Many companies use their Web pages to describe their mission, vision, and corporate values and beliefs. There also are many consulting companies that advertise how they help organizations to change their cultures. The purpose of this exercise is for you to obtain information pertaining to the organizational culture for two different companies. You can go about this task by very simply searching on the key words "organizational culture" or "corporate vision and values." This search will identify numerous companies for you to use in answering the following questions. You may want to select a company for this exercise that you would like to work for in the future.

Questions

1. What are the organization's espoused values and beliefs?

2. Using Table 3–1 as a guide, how would you classify the organization's culture? Be sure to provide supporting evidence.

3. To what extent does the company engage in socially responsible actions?

OB in Action Case Study   www.kingston.com

Kingston Technology's Organizational Culture Promotes Financial Success[94]

Nowadays Kingston Technology, the private firm the two men still own [John Tu and David Sun], is the world's second-biggest maker of add-on memory modules for personal computers. Its profits remain secret, but in 1994 its 300 workers each accounted for about $2.7 million in sales—more than oil-rich Exxon ($1.3 million) and leaving such models of high-tech efficiency as Intel ($353,400) trailing in the dust.

These numbers, the cut-throat commodity nature of the computer business, and Kingston's location in the faceless suburb of Fountain Valley, south of Los Angeles, conjure up a picture of a silicon sweat shop. Not so. Mr. Sun, who was born in Taiwan, and Mr. Tu, who hails from Shanghai, decided from the outset that their employees, suppliers, and customers would be treated as members of their family. This meant instilling such Asian family values as trust, loyalty, and mutual support in an industry where screwing your customers—let alone your suppliers and employees—is second nature. Is there a method in their madness?

At first sight apparently not. The studious, bespectacled 54-year-old Mr. Tu still seems surprised at his success. The generally noisier Mr. Sun, who is 10 years younger, offers no more clues. Although some of the things they say ("we built this company to care for people") sound, on the face of it, pretty vapid, they appear to be sincere. The pair shun the trappings of office: Both sit in open cubicles in the middle of a chaotic office; neither has a secretary. Employees (two-thirds of them from ethnic minorities) are paid well above the industry average. Should the firm fail, each employee has been promised between one and two years' salary. Mr. Sun has offered to make payments on one employee's house until the end of the century.

Yet this generosity makes hard financial sense—as the sales-per-employee figure shows. Labor represents a tiny fraction of Kingston's total costs, which means it can afford to pay over the odds. And the firm's benevolence breeds extraordinary loyalty. Since Kingston was formed in 1987, only 2% of its workers have quit.

The duo bring the same family values to their relationships with outsiders—with similar tangible results. Astonishingly, most of the firm's multi-million-dollar deals are done on a handshake. Kingston never pressures suppliers on price, pays ahead of schedule if it can, and has never canceled an order. This civility (alongside the sheer size of its orders) pays off with suppliers—which include such brutes as Samsung, Hitachi, and Motorola. Not only does Kingston get the best deals on price; it also always gets its supplies—an important factor in a market that is prone to shortages.

Even more riskily, Kingston lets outsiders run a big portion of its business. Apart from design, some assembly, and final testing, it subcontracts everything to other firms. And it designs its products to be built with off-the-shelf memory chips from a variety of suppliers. Kingston usually has matching add-on memory modules ready for sale within a week of the launch of a new PC, and it fulfills customers' orders within a day. An efficient Japanese car-parts maker might turn over its stock of raw materials and work-in-progress 30 to 40 times a year; Kingston does it three times a day . . .

It is hard to argue with sales that have on average doubled every year for six years, hitting $802 million in 1994, or with a company whose overheads are the lowest in the business. For now, the basic Tu-Sun philosophy—that if you make your customers, workers, and suppliers happy, your business will prosper—is working. Sometimes Mr. Tu wraps this formula in unnecessary Confucian obfuscation. "The culture," he proclaims, "is the core competence of this company." What it really amounts to is that he and Mr. Sun have noticed earlier than others that supplying memory chips is as much a service business as it is a commodity business and that people and relationships can give you an edge in the marketplace.

Can this service culture be sustained? Not easily. As Kingston grows, job titles are already creeping in. Identity tags—those badges of corporate conformity—have been spotted. A mentoring program—"it's like brainwashing," jokes Mr. Tu—is used to indoctrinate new employees. And the firm is drafting its first mission statement. Kingston's culture may be hard to sustain as the firm continues to grow. It is also, however, a culture that is hard to copy. Imitators can mimic the firm's products or plagiarize its mission statement. The energetic paternalism of Messrs. Tu and Sun is not so easily replicated. Until Kingston's rivals find a way to clone a character, or the firm grows too big for them to control, Messrs. Tu and Sun are safe.

Since this case was written, John Tu and David Sun sold an 80% equity interest in the company to SOFTBANK Corporation in 1996. Kingston's co-founders retained the remaining 20% equity interest. SOFTBANK's leadership decided to let Kingston operate autonomously. John Tu and David Sun continue to run the company, and they were permitted to retain the company's current management and its operating philosophies. For example, Messers. Tu and Sun gave Kingston's 1,000 employees a $20 million bonus in 1998. This amounted to roughly $20,000 per employee. They had previously given a $38 million, or $69,000 per employee, bonus in 1997.[95]

Questions for Discussion

1. Using Figure 3–1, how would you categorize Kingston's core corporate values?

2. What are the shared things, sayings, doings, and feelings at Kingston Technology? Explain.

3. How would you describe the type of organizational culture that exists at Kingston Technology? Be sure to provide examples about the extent to which Kingston displays the 12 types of normative beliefs.

4. Use Figure 3–4 to describe how Kingston Technology is trying to develop an adaptive culture.

5. How do John Tu and David Sun practice socialization and mentoring? Explain.

6. Will Kingston Technology be able to maintain its current organizational culture as the company grows? Explain.

Personal Awareness and Growth Exercise

How Does Your Current Employer Socialize Employees?

Objectives

1. To promote deeper understanding of organizational socialization processes.

2. To provide you with a useful tool for analyzing and comparing organizations.

Introduction

Employees are socialized in many different ways in today's organizations. Some organizations, such as IBM, have made an exact science out of organizational socialization. Others leave things to chance in hopes that collective goals will somehow be achieved. The questionnaire[96] in this exercise is designed to help you gauge how widespread and systematic the socialization process is in a particular organization.

Instructions

If you are presently employed and have a good working knowledge of your organization, you can complete this questionnaire yourself. If not, identify a manager or professional (e.g., corporate lawyer, engineer, nurse), and have that individual complete the questionnaire for his or her organization.

Respond to the items below as they apply to the handling of professional employees (including managers). Upon completion, compute the total score by adding up your responses. For comparison, scores for a number of strong, intermediate, and weak culture firms are provided.

	Not True of This Company				Very True of This Company
1. Recruiters receive at least one week of intensive training.	1	2	3	4	5
2. Recruitment forms identify several key traits deemed crucial to the firm's success; traits are defined in concrete terms, and interviewer records specific evidence of each trait.	1	2	3	4	5
3. Recruits are subjected to at least four in-depth interviews.	1	2	3	4	5
4. Company actively facilitates deselection during the recruiting process by revealing minuses as well as pluses.	1	2	3	4	5

	Not True of This Company				Very True of This Company

5. New hires work long hours, are exposed to intensive training of considerable difficulty, and/or perform relatively menial tasks in the first months.   1   2   3   4   5

6. The intensity of entry-level experience builds cohesiveness among peers in each entering class.   1   2   3   4   5

7. All professional employees in a particular discipline begin in entry-level positions regardless of experience or advanced degrees.   1   2   3   4   5

8. Reward systems and promotion criteria require mastery of a core discipline as a precondition of advancement.   1   2   3   4   5

9. The career path for professional employees is relatively consistent over the first 6 to 10 years with the company.   1   2   3   4   5

10. Reward systems, performance incentives, promotion criteria and other primary measures of success reflect a high degree of congruence.   1   2   3   4   5

11. Virtually all professional employees can identify and articulate the firm's shared values (i.e., the purpose or mission that ties the firm to society, the customer, or its employees).   1   2   3   4   5

12. There are very few instances when actions of management appear to violate the firm's espoused values.   1   2   3   4   5

13. Employees frequently make personal sacrifices for the firm out of commitment to the firm's shared values.   1   2   3   4   5

	Not True of This Company				Very True of This Company

14. When confronted with trade-offs between systems measuring short-term results and doing what's best for the company in the long term, the firm usually decides in favor of the long term.   1   2   3   4   5

15. This organization fosters mentor-protégé relationships.   1   2   3   4   5

16. There is considerable similarity among high potential candidates in each particular discipline.   1   2   3   4   5

Total score = _____

For Comparative Purposes:

Scores

Strongly socialized firms	65–80	IBM, P&G, Morgan Guaranty
	55–64	AT&T, Morgan Stanley, Delta Airlines
	45–54	United Airlines, Coca-Cola
	35–44	General Foods, PepsiCo
Weakly socialized firms	25–34	United Technologies, ITT
	Below 25	Atari

Questions for Discussion

1. How strongly socialized is the organization in question? What implications does this degree of socialization have for satisfaction, commitment, and turnover?

2. In examining the 16 items in the preceding questionnaire, what evidence of realistic job previews and behavior modeling can you find? Explain.

3. What does this questionnaire say about how organizational norms are established and enforced? Frame your answer in terms of specific items in the questionnaire.

4. Using this questionnaire as a gauge, would you rather work for a strongly, moderately, or weakly socialized organization?

Group Exercise

Investigating the Difference in Moral Reasoning between Men and Women

Objectives

1. To determine if men and women resolve moral/ethical problems differently.

2. To determine if males and females use a justice and care perspective, respectively, to solve moral/ethical problems.

3. To improve your understanding about the moral reasoning used by men and women.

Introduction

Men and women view moral problems and situations dissimilarly. This is one reason men and women solve identical moral or ethical problems differently. Researchers believe that men rely on a justice perspective to solve moral problems whereas women are expected to use a care perspective. This exercise presents two scenarios that possess a moral/ethical issue. You will be asked to solve each problem and to discuss the logic behind your decision. The exercise provides you with the opportunity to hear the thought processes used by men and women to solve moral/ethical problems.

Instructions

Your instructor will divide the class into groups of four to six. (An interesting option is to use gender-based groups.) Each group member should first read the scenario alone and then make a decision about what to do. Once this is done, use the space provided to outline the rationale for your decision to this scenario. Next, read the second scenario and follow the same procedure: Make a decision and explain your rationale. Once all group members have completed their analyses for both scenarios, meet as a group to discuss the results. One at a time, each group member should present his or her final decision and the associated reasoning for the first scenario. Someone should keep a running tally of the decisions so that a summary can be turned in to the professor at the end of your discussion. Follow the same procedure for the second scenario.[97]

Scenario 1

You are the manager of a local toy store. The hottest Christmas toy of the year is the new "Peter Panda" stuffed animal. The toy is in great demand and almost impossible to find. You have received your one and only shipment of 12, and they are all promised to people who previously stopped in to place a deposit and reserve one. A woman comes by the store and pleads with you, saying that her six-year-old daughter is in the hospital very ill, and that "Peter Panda" is the one toy she has her heart set on. Would you sell her one, knowing that you will have to break your promise and refund the deposit to one of the other customers? (There is no way you will be able to get an extra toy in time.)

Your Decision: _____

	Would Sell	Would Not Sell	Unsure
Men			
Women			

Rationale for Your Decision:

Scenario 2

You sell corporate financial products, such as pension plans and group health insurance. You are currently negotiating with Paul Scott, treasurer of a *Fortune* 500 firm, for a sale that could be in the millions of dollars. You feel you are in a strong position to make the sale, but two competitors are also negotiating with Scott, and it could go either way. You have become friendly with Scott, and over lunch one day he confided in you that he has recently been under treatment for manic depression. It so happens that in your office there is a staff psychologist who does employee counseling. The thought has occurred to you that such a trained professional might be able to coach you on how to act with and relate to a personality such as Scott's, so as to persuade and influence him most effectively. Would you consult the psychologist?

Your Decision: _____

	Would Consult	Would Not Consult	Unsure
Men			
Women			

Rationale for Your Decision:

Questions for Discussion

1. Did males and females make different decisions in response to both scenarios? (Comparative norms can be found in Note 98.)

2. What was the moral reasoning used by women and men to solve the two scenarios?[99]

3. To what extent did males and females use a justice and care perspective, respectively?

4. What useful lessons did you learn from this exercise?

Chapter Four

International OB: Managing Across Cultures

Learning Objectives

When you finish studying the material in this chapter, you should be able to:

1   Explain how societal culture and organizational culture combine to influence on-the-job behavior.

2   Define *ethnocentrism,* and distinguish between high-context and low-context cultures.

3   Draw a distinction between individualistic cultures and collectivist cultures.

4   Explain the difference between monochronic and polychronic cultures.

5   Discuss the cultural implications of interpersonal space, language, and religion.

6   Describe the practical lessons from the Hofstede–Bond cross-cultural studies.

7   Explain what cross-cultural studies have found about leadership styles.

8   Specify why US managers have a comparatively high failure rate in foreign assignments, and identify skills needed by today's global managers.

9   Discuss the importance of cross-cultural training relative to the foreign assignment cycle.

Even the best-kept corporate secrets eventually break into the open. For Stefan Buchner, a 39-year-old purchasing director at Daimler-Benz headquarters in Stuttgart, the news came during an afternoon strategy meeting last May. That's when a colleague rushed in to say German radio had just reported that Daimler was on the verge of a $38 billion merger with Chrysler, America's third largest carmaker. Six time zones away at Chrysler headquarters, Louise Linder's phone rang. Her contacts at Chrysler's suppliers had heard the same news and wanted the inside scoop. "Hey, I know as much as you do," she told them. Late that afternoon Linder's vice president called her into his office. Assemble your staff in the auditorium, he said. Prepare for a big announcement.

Mergers are traditionally tallied in dollars, and the sum hit a record last year: corporate couplings totaled $2.5 trillion. But beneath those piles of money are several million people whose lives are often upended when two companies put themselves together. For top executives, mergers can bring incredible riches; for bottom-rung workers toiling in plants or behind counters, changes may be imperceptible. The folks in the middle face the biggest challenges. Midlevel managers are often axed to cut costs after deals; those who remain are taxed to find savings, work through culture clashes, and integrate two companies into one.

Alabama employees and the first Mercedes ever built outside Germany.
(M. Schwartz/The Image Works)

While chairmen Robert Eaton and Jürgen Schrempp make grand plans for the new DaimlerChrysler, it's up to managers like Buchner and Linder, who perform identical tasks on different sides of the Atlantic, to make the deal work. As the anniversary of their merger nears, *Newsweek* asked them to reconstruct their first year in the trenches together.

. . . for Linder and Buchner, there are reasons for optimism. They have big responsibilities. Each ranks one rung below vice president, and together they oversee 140 employees who buy seats, steering wheels and other interior components. But unlike top officers, they haven't had to battle to preserve power or joust for the upper hand as jobs consolidate. Says Linder: "I haven't felt any stress or anxiety about whether they're going to choose between Stefan or I." They also work in purchasing, an area where the companies share similar philosophies and are led by an American, limiting concerns—at least on the US side—of too much German control. Most important, their careers are still on the upswing, and both believe the merger puts their performance in the spotlight. "It's a huge chance to develop my career," Buchner says. Even if they're tempted to complain, they're probably too busy. Mergers breed countless committee assignments and brutally long days. Says Linder: "It almost feels like a second job". . . .

In the last year their teams have gotten well acquainted. The process began at a distance. Linder spent the early summer reading up on Daimler and quizzing suppliers who'd been through mergers. In August Buchner's team traveled to Detroit, where they discussed big-picture issues: how their departments are organized, how they work with suppliers to reduce prices. Until the deal was sealed in November, "the really interesting questions were taboo," Buchner says. "For example, what does an airbag cost here, what does it cost there?" Since then they've begun comparing and brainstorming ways to consolidate and save. Linder and her American colleagues praise their German counterparts' skill with English (though they try to cut out slang to simplify speech when the Germans are in town). To reciprocate, many Americans are taking German lessons. They can also tick off cultural eccentricities: the Germans eat hamburgers with knives and forks and call their cell phones "handies." At a Detroit piano bar one night last summer, Linder's team got its biggest surprise: the Germans know all the lyrics to rock-and-roll oldies.

Back in Stuttgart, the Germans have been experimenting with business casual dress. They've taken classes on cultural awareness (key points: Americans shake hands less and aren't allowed to compliment women). As they've begun meeting with Americans more often, they're learning to understand their different decision-making style. Americans favor fast-paced trial-and-error experimentation; Germans lay painstaking plans, and implement them precisely. The potential result: "The Americans think the Germans are stubborn militarists, and the Germans think the Americans are totally chaotic," says Edith Meissner, an executive at the Sindelfingen plant. To foster compromise, Americans are encouraged to make more specific plans, and Germans are urged to begin experimenting more quickly. Both sides surround workers with their sister culture. When DaimlerChrysler stock began trading on Nov. 17, German workers celebrated with American-style cheerleaders, a country-Western band called The Hillbillies, doughnuts, and corn on the cob.[1]

FOR DISCUSSION

Based on what you have read here (and perhaps elsewhere), do you think DaimlerChrysler will be able to blend its German and US units into a successful global competitor? Explain.

Globalization of the economy challenges virtually all employees to become more internationally aware and cross-culturally adept. The path to the top typically winds through one or more foreign assignments today. A prime example is Samir F Gibara, chief executive officer of Goodyear Tire & Rubber, who spent 27 of his 30 years with the company on foreign assignments in Canada, France, Morocco, and Belgium.[2] Even managers and employees who stay in their native country will find it hard to escape today's global economy. Many will be thrust into international relationships by working for foreign-owned companies or by dealing with foreign suppliers, customers, and co-workers. *Management Review* recently offered this helpful perspective:

> It's easy to think that people who have lived abroad or who are multilingual have global brains, while those who still live in their hometowns are parochial. But both notions are fallacies. Managers who have never left their home states can have global brains if they are interested in the greater world around them, make an effort to learn about other people's perspectives, and integrate those perspectives into their own way of thinking.[3]

The global economy is a rich mix of cultures, and the time to prepare to work in it is now.[4] Accordingly, the purpose of this chapter is to help you take a step in that direction by exploring the impacts of culture in today's increasingly internationalized organization. This chapter draws upon the area of cultural anthropology. We begin with a model that shows how societal culture and organizational culture (covered in Chapter 3) combine to influence work behavior, followed by a fundamental cultural distinction. Next, we examine key dimensions of international OB with the goal of enhancing cross-cultural awareness. Practical lessons from cross-cultural management research are then reviewed. The chapter concludes by exploring the challenge of accepting a foreign assignment.

Culture and Organizational Behavior

How would you, as a manager, interpret the following situations?

An Asian executive for a multinational company, transferred from Taiwan to the Midwest, appears aloof and autocratic to his peers.

A West Coast bank embarks on a "friendly teller" campaign, but its Filipino female tellers won't cooperate.

A white manager criticizes a black male employee's work. Instead of getting an explanation, the manager is met with silence and a firm stare.[5]

If you attribute the behavior in these situations to personalities, three descriptions come to mind: arrogant, unfriendly, and hostile. These are reasonable conclusions. Unfortunately, they are probably wrong, being based more on prejudice and stereotypes than on actual fact. However, if you attribute the behavioral outcomes to *cultural* differences, you stand a better chance of making the following more valid interpretations: "As it turns out, Asian culture encourages a more distant managing style, Filipinos associate overly friendly behavior in women with prostitution, and blacks as a group act more deliberately, studying visual cues, than most white men."[6] One cannot afford to overlook relevant cultural contexts when trying to understand and manage organizational behavior.

Culture Is Complex and Multilayered

While noting that cultures exist in social units of all sizes (from civilizations to countries to ethnic groups to organizations to work groups), Edgar Schein defined **culture** as follows:

Culture
Socially derived, taken-for-granted assumptions about how to think and act.

> A pattern of basic assumptions—invented, discovered, or developed by a given group as it learns to cope with its problems of external adaptation and internal integration—that has worked well enough to be considered valid and, therefore, to be taught to new members as the correct way to perceive, think, and feel in relation to those problems.[7]

The word *taught* needs to be interpreted carefully because it implies formal education or training. While cultural lessons may indeed be taught in schools, religious settings, and on the job, formal inculcation is secondary. Most cultural lessons are learned by observing and imitating role models as they go about their daily affairs or as observed in the media.[8]

Culture is difficult to grasp because it is multilayered. International management experts Fons Trompenaars (from the Netherlands) and Charles Hampden-Turner (from Britain) offer this instructive analogy in their landmark book, *Riding the Waves of Culture:*

> Culture comes in layers, like an onion. To understand it you have to unpeel it layer by layer.
>
> On the outer layer are the products of culture, like the soaring skyscrapers of Manhattan, pillars of private power, with congested public streets between them. These are expressions of deeper values and norms in a society that are not directly visible (values such as upward mobility, "the more-the-better," status, material success). The layers of values and norms are deeper within the "onion," and are more difficult to identify.[9]

Culture Is a Subtle but Pervasive Force

Culture generally remains below the threshold of conscious awareness because it involves *taken-for-granted assumptions* about how one should perceive, think, act, and feel. Cultural anthropologist Edward T Hall put it this way:

> Since much of culture operates outside our awareness, frequently we don't even know what we know. We pick . . . [expectations and assumptions] up in the cradle. We unconsciously learn what to notice and what not to notice, how to divide time and space, how to walk and talk and use our bodies, how to behave as men or women, how to relate to other people, how to handle responsibility, whether experience is seen as whole or fragmented. This applies to all people. The Chinese or the Japanese or the Arabs are as unaware of their assumptions as we are of our own. We each assume that they're part of human nature. What we think of as "mind" is really internalized culture.[10]

In sum, it has been said: "you are your culture, and your culture is you." As part of the growing sophistication of marketing practices in the global economy, companies are hiring anthropologists to decipher the cultural roots of customer needs and preferences (see the International OB, p 108).

A Model of Societal and Organizational Cultures

As illustrated in Figure 4–1, culture influences organizational behavior in two ways. Employees bring their societal culture to work with them in the form of customs and language. Organizational culture, a by-product of societal

We are immersed in cultural cues from the time of birth that influence us in subtle yet powerful ways. For instance, what do all these books tell this youngster about the value of reading and learning?

(Myrleen Ferguson/PhotoEdit)

Figure 4–1   *Cultural Influences on Organizational Behavior*

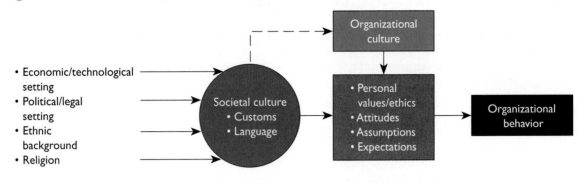

SOURCE: Adapted in part from B J Punnett and S Withane, "Hofstede's Value Survey Module: To Embrace or Abandon?" in *Advances in International Comparative Management,* vol 5, ed S B Prasad (Greenwich, CT: JAI Press, 1990), pp 69–89.

culture, in turn affects the individual's values/ethics, attitudes, assumptions, and expectations.[11] The term *societal* culture is used here instead of national culture because the boundaries of many modern nation-states were not drawn along cultural lines. The former Soviet Union, for example, included 15 republics and more than 100 ethnic nationalities, many with their own distinct language.[12] Meanwhile, English-speaking Canadians in Vancouver are culturally closer to Americans in Seattle than to their French-speaking compatriots in Quebec. Societal culture is shaped by the various environmental factors listed in the left-hand side of Figure 4–1.

Once inside the organization's sphere of influence, the individual is further affected by the *organization's* culture. Mixing of societal and organizational cultures can produce interesting dynamics in multinational companies. For example, with French and American employees working side by side at General Electric's medical imaging production facility in Waukesha, Wisconsin, unit head Claude Benchimol has witnessed some culture shock:

> The French are surprised the American parking lots empty out as early as 5 PM; the Americans are surprised the French don't start work at 8 AM. Benchimol feels the French are more talkative and candid. Americans have more of a sense of hierarchy and are less likely to criticize. But they may be growing closer to the French. Says Benchimol: "It's taken a year to get across the idea that we are all entitled to say what we don't like to become more productive and work better."[13]

Same company, same company culture, yet GE's French and American co-workers have different attitudes about time, hierarchy, and communication. They are the products of different societal cultures.[14]

When managing people at work, the individual's societal culture, the organizational culture, and any interaction between the two need to be taken into consideration. For example, American workers' cultural orientation toward quality improvement differs significantly from the Japanese cultural pattern.

> Unlike Japanese workers, Americans aren't interested in making small step-by-step improvements to increase quality. They want to achieve the breakthrough, the impossible dream. The way to motivate them: Ask for the big leap, rather than for tiny steps.[15]

International OB Anthropologists Help Adapt Products to World's Cultures

A year ago in a hot, dusty outdoor market in Baku, Azerbaijan, anthropologist Jean Canavan made her discovery.

She was watching vendors display their wares to discerning customers and praise their value and durability. But it was the customers' ability to read intricate origination codes on the merchandise that was the surprise.

"They'd flip the cell phone over, take the battery out and actually read the bar code on it to see where the phone was built," Canavan says.

She and two colleagues were doing fieldwork for their employer, Motorola, investigating how the company could best enter the emerging markets of Azerbaijan, Kazakhstan, and Uzbekistan.

They found that people in the Caspian Sea area have learned to read the numbers on bar codes to see where products were manufactured. The buyers believe that products from American companies are better if they were built in America.

"It created an awareness on the part of Motorola that this is an important purchasing criterion for people," Canavan says.

Think anthropologists spend their days hanging out in Pago Pago studying the local culture? Think again. Like everyone else, anthropologists and ethnographers increasingly are finding jobs with high-tech companies, using their highly developed skills as observers to study how people live, work, and use technology.

"This is not *Raiders of the Lost Ark*," says Susan Squires, incoming president of the 1,000-member National Association for the Practice of Anthropology, which has a Web site at www.ameranthassn.org/napa.htm.

"Anthropology developed methods to understand people who were so different from Europeans that you couldn't just go up and ask questions, so we came up with methods such as participant observation and fieldwork," says Squires, who also works at GVO Inc., a product development company in Palo Alto, California. . . .

The point of hiring anthropologists is to help companies understand their users and find new products and markets the engineers and marketers never dreamed of—such as Intel looking into designing a computer chip that can withstand a blast from a deck hose. . . .

That particular idea came from John Sherry, a member of the end user research group at Intel's Hillsboro offices. Sherry's undergraduate degree was in computer science, not an uncommon combination for techno-anthropologists. He did his doctoral anthropological fieldwork with Navajos, has worked for Microsoft's usability group and has been with Intel for 2½ years.

Sherry set out to find computers being used in extreme environments. He ended up on an Alaskan salmon boat.

The tender, who picks up the catch from the fisherman and carries it back to the cannery, has to keep a lot of records, from tickets issued for payments to reports filed for the fisheries board, all on a deck slippery with scales and blood. This particular tender, Sherry says, had duct-taped a notebook computer to the entryway of his cabin. "He told me, 'I need a computer that's so durable I can blast it with a deck hose and it will still work.' "

Back in his offices in Oregon, Sherry doesn't regret leaving the halls of academia. "This is a fantastic job," he says. "In my wildest dreams in graduate school I couldn't have imagined a job this great."

Colleague [Genevieve] Bell, in obvious agreement, just returned from a fact-finding mission to look into ways high-speed data communications could work in northern Italy. After weeks of eating, drinking, and spending hours at the dining room table with her Italian hosts, the answer was "not very well."

"It's hard to imagine how technology could improve that life," she says.

She found close-knit communities revolving around family and the table. Dinners are hours-long affairs, husbands come home for lunch, and the kitchen is the center of life. "In the United States, we talk about the computer competing with television," Bell says. "In Italy, it would be food."

But technology in other forms holds possibilities. In households where shoe boxes full of photos were pulled out to show Bell the family history and tell family stories, digital cameras proved interesting.

SOURCE: Excerpted from E Weise, "Companies Learn Value of Grass Roots," *USA Today*, May 26, 1999, p 4D. Copyright © 1999. *USA Today* Reprinted with permission.

Ethnocentrism: A Cultural Roadblock in the Global Economy

Ethnocentrism, the belief that one's native country, culture, language, and modes of behavior are superior to all others, has its roots in the dawn of civilization. First identified as a behavioral science concept in 1906, involving the tendency of groups to reject outsiders,[16] the term *ethnocentrism* generally has a more encompassing (national or societal) meaning today. Worldwide evidence of ethnocentrism is plentiful. For example, when a congressman said, "It is the English language which unites us,"[17] during a 1996 debate on an English-only bill for US federal agencies, charges of ethnocentrism were made by civil rights groups worried about the loss of bilingual ballots for non-English-speaking citizens. Meanwhile, ethnocentrism led to deadly "ethnic cleansing" in Bosnia and Kosovo and genocide in the African nations of Rwanda and Burundi.

Less dramatic, but still troublesome, is ethnocentrism within managerial and organizational contexts. Experts on the subject framed the problem this way:

> [Ethnocentric managers have] a preference for putting home-country people in key positions everywhere in the world and rewarding them more handsomely for work, along with a tendency to feel that this group is more intelligent, more capable, or more reliable.... Ethnocentrism is often not attributable to prejudice as much as to inexperience or lack of knowledge about foreign persons and situations. This is not too surprising, since most executives know far more about employees in their home environments. As one executive put it, "At least I understand why our own managers make mistakes. With our foreigners, I never know. The foreign managers may be better. But if I can't trust a person, should I hire him or her just to prove we're multinational?"[18]

Recent research suggests ethnocentrism is bad for business. A survey of 918 companies with home offices in the United States (272 companies), Japan (309), and Europe (337) found ethnocentric staffing and human resource policies to be associated with increased personnel problems. Those problems included recruiting difficulties, high turnover rates, and lawsuits over personnel policies. Among the three regional samples, Japanese companies had the most ethnocentric human resource practices and the most international human resource problems.[19]

Current and future managers can effectively deal with ethnocentrism through education, greater

Ethnocentrism
Belief that one's native country, culture, language, and behavior are superior.

Ethnocentrism turned deadly in 1999 for these ethnic Albanian refugees fleeing Serbian ethnic cleansing in Kosovo. Prejudice and bigotry need to be stamped out if societies and organizations are to progress.

(Reuters/Nikola Solic/Archive Photos)

cross-cultural awareness, international experience, and a conscious effort to value cultural diversity.

Ethics at Work

Anyone interested in doing business in Russia should clearly understand that the ethical rules and traditions are going to be different. For instance, what Americans often consider to be small bribes may be seen in Russia as a means of establishing a relationship. In fact, they may be the only way to establish a successful business relationship. To adapt, Westerners essentially have three choices: (1) choose not to do business in Russia at this time; (2) choose to have someone else conduct the transactions; or (3) decide that "while in Russia, do as the Russians do." If one chooses the latter course, it is important to consult current US law. Although outright bribery is illegal for American firms, tokens of friendship usually are not. Typically, such tokens are more important than monetary "gifts," although some "transaction fees" may be necessary to persuade bureaucrats to move paperwork forward.

SOURCE: Excerpted from W B Snavely, S Miassoedov, and K McNeilly, "Cross-Cultural Peculiarities of the Russian Entrepreneur: Adapting to the New Russia," *Business Horizons*, March–April 1998, p 10. For background reading, see D A Andelman, "Bribery: The New Global Outlaw," *Management Review*, April 1998, pp 49–51.

You Decide . . .

Which of the three choices would you make? Why? Is it ethnocentric to impose your ethical values on your hosts when doing business in a foreign country? Explain.

For an interpretation of this situation, visit our Web site **www.mhhe.com/kreitner.**

High-Context and Low-Context Societal Cultures

Cultural anthropologists believe interesting and valuable lessons can be learned by comparing one culture with another. Many models have been proposed for distinguishing among the world's rich variety of cultures. One general distinction contrasts high-context and low-context cultures[20] (see Figure 4–2). Managers in multicultural settings need to know the difference if they are to communicate and interact effectively.

Reading between the Lines in High-Context Cultures   People from **high-context cultures** rely heavily on situational cues for meaning when perceiving and communicating with another person. Nonverbal cues such as one's official position or status convey messages more powerfully than do spoken words. Thus, we come to better understand the ritual of exchanging *and reading* business cards in Japan. Japanese culture is relatively high-context. One's business card, listing employer and official position, conveys vital silent messages to members of Japan's homogeneous society. An intercultural communications authority explains:

Nearly all communication in Japan takes place within an elaborate and vertically organized social structure. Everyone has a distinct place within this framework. Rarely do people converse without knowing, or determining, who is above and who is below them. Associates are always older or younger, male or female, subordinate or superior. And these distinctions all carry implications for the form of address, choice of words, physical distance, and demeanor. As a result, conversation tends to reflect this formal hierarchy.[21]

Verbal and written communication in high-context cultures such as China, Korea, and Japan are secondary to taken-for-granted cultural assumptions about other people.[22]

High-context cultures

Primary meaning derived from nonverbal situational cues.

Reading the Fine Print in Low-Context Cultures   In **low-context cultures,** written and spoken words carry the burden of shared meaning. True, people in low-context cultures read nonverbal messages from body language, dress, status, and belongings. However, they tend to double-check their perceptions and assumptions verbally. To do so in China or Japan would be to gravely insult the other person, thus causing them to *lose face.*[23] Their positions on the continuum in Figure 4–2 indicate the German preoccupation with written rules for even the finest details of behavior and

Figure 4–2   *Contrasting High-Context and Low-Context Cultures*

High-Context
- Establish social trust first
- Value personal relations and goodwill
- Agreement by general trust
- Negotiations slow and ritualistic

Low-Context
- Get down to business first
- Value expertise and performance
- Agreement by specific, legalistic contract
- Negotiations as efficient as possible

SOURCE: M Munter, "Cross-Cultural Communication for Managers." Reprinted with permission from *Business Horizons,* May–June 1993, Figure 3, p 72. Copyright © 1993 by the Board of Trustees at Indiana University, Kelley School of Business.

the North American preoccupation with precise legal documents.[24] In high-context cultures, agreements tend to be made on the basis of someone's word or a handshake, after a rather prolonged trust-building period. European-Americans, who have been taught from birth not to take anything for granted, see the handshake as a prelude to demanding a signature on a detailed, lawyer-approved, iron-clad contract.

> **Low-context cultures**
> Primary meaning derived from written and spoken words.

Implications for a Diverse Workforce   High- and low-context cultural differences can be found in countries with heterogeneous populations such as the United States, Australia, and Canada. African-Americans, Asian-Americans, and Native Americans tend to be higher-context than Americans of European descent. This helps explain our earlier example of the white manager's frustration with the African-American employee's nonverbal response. Culture dictates how people communicate. The white manager's ignorance of (or insensitivity to) the African-American employee's cultural context blocked effective communication.

Toward Greater Cross-Cultural Awareness and Competence

Aside from being high- or low-context, cultures stand apart in other ways as well.[25] Let us briefly review the following basic factors that vary from culture to culture: individualism, time, interpersonal space, language and communication, and religion.[26] This list is intended to be indicative rather than exhaustive. Separately or together these factors can foster huge cross-cultural gaps. Effective multicultural management often depends on whether or not these gaps can be bridged.

A qualification needs to be offered at this juncture. It is important to view all of the cultural differences in this chapter and elsewhere as *tendencies* and *patterns,* rather than as absolutes. As soon as one falls into the trap of assuming *all* Germans are this, *all* British are that, and so on, potentially instructive generalizations become mindless stereotypes.[27] Well-founded cultural generalizations are fundamental to successfully doing business in other cultures. But one needs to be constantly alert to *individuals* who are exceptions to the local cultural rule. For instance, it is possible to encounter talkative and aggressive Japanese and quiet and deferential Americans who simply do not fit their respective cultural molds. Also, tipping the scale against clear cultural differences are space age transportation; global telecommunications, television, and computer networks; tourism; global marketing; and music and entertainment. These areas are homogenizing the peoples of the world. The result, according to experts on the subject, is an emerging "world culture" in which, someday, people may be more alike than different.[28]

Individualism versus Collectivism

Have you ever been torn between what you personally wanted and what the group, organization, or society expected of you? If so, you have firsthand experience with a fundamental and important cultural distinction: individualism versus collectivism. Awareness of this distinction, as we will soon see, can spell the difference between success and failure in cross-cultural business dealings.

Individualistic culture
Primary emphasis on personal freedom and choice.

Collectivist culture
Personal goals less important than community goals and interests.

Individualistic cultures, characterized as "I" and "me" cultures, give priority to individual freedom and choice. **Collectivist cultures,** oppositely called "we" and "us" cultures, rank shared goals higher than individual desires and goals. People in collectivist cultures are expected to subordinate their own wishes and goals to those of the relevant social unit. A worldwide survey of 30,000 managers by Trompenaars and Hampden-Turner, who prefer the term *communitarianism* to collectivism, found the highest degree of individualism in Israel, Romania, Nigeria, Canada, and the United States. Countries ranking lowest in individualism—thus qualifying as collectivist cultures—were Egypt, Nepal, Mexico, India, and Japan. Brazil, China, and France also ended up toward the collectivist end of the scale.[29]

A Business Success Factor　Of course, one can expect to encounter both individualists and collectivists in culturally diverse countries such as the United States. For example, imagine the frustration of Dave Murphy, a Boston-based mutual fund salesperson, when he recently tried to get Navajo Indians in Arizona interested in saving money for their retirement. After several fruitless meetings with groups of Navajo employees, he was given this cultural insight by a local official: "If you come to this environment, you have to understand that money is different. It's there to be spent. If you have some, you help your family."[30] To traditional Navajos, enculturated as collectivists, saving money is an unworthy act of selfishness. Subsequently, the sales pitch was tailored to emphasize the *family* benefits of individual retirement savings plans.

Allegiance to Whom?　The Navajo example brings up an important point about collectivist cultures. Specifically, which unit of society predominates? For the Navajos, family is the key reference group. But, as Trompenaars and Hampden-Turner observe, important differences exist among collectivist (or communitarian) cultures:

> For each single society, it is necessary to determine the group with which individuals have the closest identification. They could be keen to identify with their trade union, their family, their corporation, their religion, their profession, their nation, or the state apparatus. The French tend to identify with *la France, la famille, le cadre;* the Japanese with the corporation; the former eastern bloc with the Communist Party; and Ireland with the Roman Catholic Church. Communitarian goals may be good or bad for industry depending on the community concerned, its attitude and relevance to business development.[31]

Cultural Perceptions of Time

In North American and Northern European cultures, time seems to be a simple matter. It is linear, relentlessly marching forward, never backward, in standardized chunks. To the American who received a watch for his or her third birthday, time is like money. It is spent, saved, or wasted.[32] Americans are taught to show up 10 minutes early for appointments. When working across cultures, however, time becomes a very complex matter.[33] Imagine a New Yorker's chagrin when left in a waiting room for 45 minutes, only to find a Latin American government official dealing with three other people at once. The North American resents the lack of prompt and undivided attention. The Latin American official resents the North American's impatience and apparent self-centeredness.[34] This vicious cycle of resentment can be explained by the distinction between **monochronic time** and **polychronic time:**

> The former is revealed in the ordered, precise, schedule-driven use of public time that typifies and even caricatures efficient Northern Europeans and North Americans. The latter is seen in the multiple and cyclical activities and concurrent involvement with different people in Mediterranean, Latin American, and especially Arab cultures.[35]

A Matter of Degree   Monochronic and polychronic are relative rather than absolute concepts. Generally, the more things a person tends to do at once, the more polychronic that person is.[36] Thanks to computers and advanced telecommunications systems, highly polychronic managers can engage in "multitasking."[37] For instance, it is possible to talk on the telephone, read and respond to computer E-mail messages, print a report, check a pager message, *and* eat a stale sandwich all at the same time. Unfortunately, this extreme polychronic behavior too often is not as efficient as hoped and, as discussed in Chapter 18, can be very stressful.

Monochronic people prefer to do one thing at a time. What is your attitude toward time? (You can find out by completing the Polychronic Attitude Index in the OB Exercise, p 114).

Practical Implications   Low-context cultures, such as that of the United States, tend to run on monochronic time while high-context cultures, such as that of Mexico, tend to run on polychronic time. People in polychronic cultures view time as flexible, fluid, and multidimensional. The Germans and Swiss have made an exact science of monochronic time. In fact, a new radio-controlled watch made by a German company, Junghans, is "guaranteed to lose no more than one second in 1 million years."[38] Many a visitor has been a minute late for a Swiss train, only to see its taillights leaving the station. Time is more elastic in polychronic cultures. During the Islamic holy month of Ramadan in Middle Eastern nations, for example, the faithful fast during daylight hours, and the general pace of things markedly slows. Managers need to reset their mental clocks when doing business across cultures.

Interpersonal Space

Anthropologist Edward T Hall noticed a connection between culture and preferred interpersonal distance. People from high-context cultures were observed standing close when talking to someone. Low-context cultures appeared to dictate a greater amount of interpersonal space. Hall applied the term **proxemics** to the study of cultural expectations about interpersonal space.[39] He specified four interpersonal distance zones. Some call them space bubbles. They are *intimate* distance, *personal* distance, *social*

Monochronic time
Preference for doing one thing at a time because time is limited, precisely segmented, and schedule driven.

Polychronic time
Preference for doing more than one thing at a time because time is flexible and multidimensional.

Proxemics
Hall's term for the study of cultural expectations about interpersonal space.

OB Exercise   The Polychronic Attitude Index

Please consider how you feel about the following statements. Circle your choice on the scale provided: strongly agree, agree, neutral, disagree, or strongly disagree.

	Strongly Disagree	Disagree	Neutral	Agree	Strongly Agree
I do not like to juggle several activities at the same time.	5	4	3	2	1
People should not try to do many things at once.	5	4	3	2	1
When I sit down at my desk, I work on one project at a time.	5	4	3	2	1
I am comfortable doing several things at the same time.	1	2	3	4	5

Add up your points, and divide the total by 4. Then plot your score on the scale below.

1.0	1.5	2.0	2.5	3.0	3.5	4.0	4.5	5.0
Monochronic								Polychronic

The lower your score (below 3.0), the more monochronic your orientation; and the higher your score (above 3.0), the more polychronic.

SOURCE: A C Bluedorn, C F Kaufman, and P M Lane, "How Many Things Do You Like to Do at Once? An Introduction to Monochronic and Polychronic Time," *Academy of Management Executive*, November 1992, Exhibit 2, p 20.

distance, and *public* distance. Ranges for the four interpersonal distance zones are illustrated in Figure 4–3, along with selected cultural differences.

North American business conversations normally are conducted at about a three- to four-foot range, within the personal zone in Figure 4–3. A range of approximately one foot is common in Latin American and Asian cultures, uncomfortably close for Northern Europeans and North Americans. Arabs like to get even closer. Mismatches in culturally dictated interpersonal space zones can prove very distracting for the unprepared. Hall explains:

> Arabs tend to get very close and breathe on you. It's part of the high sensory involvement of a high-context culture...
>
> The American on the receiving end can't identify all the sources of his discomfort but feels that the Arab is pushy. The Arab comes close, the American backs up. The Arab follows, because he can only interact at certain distances. Once the American learns that Arabs handle space differently and that breathing on people is a form of communication, the situation can sometimes be redefined so the American relaxes.[40]

Asian and Middle-Eastern hosts grow weary of having to seemingly chase their low-context guests around at social gatherings to maintain what they feel is proper conversational range. Backing up all evening to keep conversational partners at a proper distance is an awkward experience as well. Awareness of cultural differences, along with skillful accommodation, are essential to productive intercultural business dealings.

Language and Cross-Cultural Communication

More than 3,000 different languages are spoken worldwide. What is the connection between these languages and information processing and behavior? There is an ongoing debate among anthropologists concerning the extent to which language influences perception and behavior. On one side of the argument, the *relativists* claim each language

Figure 4–3   *Interpersonal Distance Zones for Business Conversations Vary from Culture to Culture*

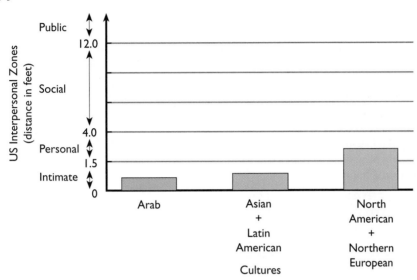

fosters unique perceptions. On the other side, *universalists* state that all languages share common elements and thus foster common thought processes and perceptions. A study involving subjects from eight countries attempted to resolve this debate. Subjects from the United States, Britain, Italy, Greece, former Yugoslavia, Pakistan, Hong Kong, and Vietnam were shown 15 flash cards, each printed with three pairs of words. Language experts certified the various translations as accurate. The idea was to see if adults from different cultures, speaking different languages, would perceive the same semantic elements in the paired words. Illustrative semantic elements, or basic language building blocks, are as follows: opposite = alive/dead; similar = furniture/bed. The researchers found "considerable cross-cultural agreement on the meaning and use of semantic relations."[41] Greatest agreement was found for semantic opposites (e.g., alive/dead). These findings tip the scale in favor of the universalists. We await additional research evidence for a definitive answer.

Three Cross-Cultural Communication Options Those attempting to communicate across cultures have three options: (1) stick to their own language, (2) rely on translators, or (3) learn

Need a place to stay tonight? Weary travelers can't help but get the good news from this multi-language sign. But dealing with different languages in complex business transactions is not so easy.

(Tony Freeman/PhotoEdit)

the local language. The first option, preferred by those who insist English has become the language of global business, are at a serious competitive disadvantage. Ignorance of the local language means missing subtle yet crucial meanings, risking unintended insult, and jeopardizing the business transaction. For example, according to one well-traveled business writer, "In Asia, a 'yes' answer to a question simply means the question is understood. It's the beginning of negotiations. In the Middle East, the response will probably be some version of 'God willing.' "[42] Live translations, translations of written documents and advertisements, and computer E-mail translations are helpful but plagued by accuracy problems.[43] Successful international managers tell us there is no adequate substitute for knowing the local language.[44]

General Guidelines for Effective Cross-Cultural Communication

Regardless of which cross-cultural communication option is used, four guidelines from international management scholars Philip R Harris and Robert T Moran are useful:

- *No matter how hard one tries, one cannot avoid communicating.* All behavior in human interaction has a message and communicates something. Body language communicates as well as our activity or inactivity, the color of our skin, the color of our clothes, or the gift we give. All behavior is communication because all behavior contains a message, whether intended or not.
- *Communication does not necessarily mean understanding.* Even when two individuals agree that they are communicating or talking to each other, it does not mean that they have understood each other. Understanding occurs when the two individuals have the same interpretation of the symbols being used in the communication process whether the symbols be words or gestures.
- *Communication is irreversible.* One cannot take back one's communication (although sometimes one wishes that he or she could). However, one can explain, clarify, or restate one's message. Once one has communicated, it is part of his or her experience, and it influences present and future meanings. Disagreeing with a Saudi Arabian in the presence of others is an "impoliteness" in the Arab world and may be difficult to remedy.
- *Communication occurs in a context.* One cannot ignore the context of communication that occurs at a certain time, in some place, using certain media. Such factors have message value and give meaning to the communicators. For example, a business conversation with a French manager in France during an evening meal may be inappropriate.[45]

Training magazine offers this blunt advice to American managers: "The lesson for those plying foreign markets or hosting business visitors is: *Slow down. Shut up. Listen.*"[46]

Religion

Religious beliefs and practices can have a profound effect on cross-cultural relations. A comprehensive treatment of different religions is beyond the scope of our current discussion. However, we can examine the relationship between religious affiliation and work-related values. A study of 484 international students at a midwestern US university uncovered wide variability. The following list gives the most important work-related value for each of five religious affiliations:

Catholic—Consideration ("Concern that employees be taken seriously, be kept informed, and that their judgments be used.")

Protestant—Employer effectiveness ("Desire to work for a company that is efficient, successful, and a technological leader.")

Buddhist—Social responsibility ("Concern that the employer be a responsible part of society.")

Muslim—Continuity ("Desire for stable environment, job longevity, reduction of uncertainty.")

No religious preference—Professional challenge ("Concern with having a job that provides learning opportunities and opportunities to use skills well.")[47]

Thus, there was virtually *no agreement* across religions about the primary work value. This led the researchers to conclude: "Employers might be wise to consider the impact that religious differences (and more broadly, cultural factors) appear to have on the values of employee groups."[48] Of course, in the United States and other selected countries, equal employment opportunity laws forbid managers from basing employment-related decisions on an applicant's religious preference.

Nancy Adler, an international OB specialist at Canada's McGill University, has offered the following introductory definition. "**Cross-cultural management** studies the behavior of people in organizations around the world and trains people to work in organizations with employee and client populations from several cultures."[49] Inherent in this definition are three steps: (1) understand cultural differences, (2) identify culturally appropriate management practices, and (3) teach cross-cultural management lessons. The cross-cultural studies discussed in this section contribute to all three.

Practical Insights from Cross-Cultural Management Research

The Hofstede–Bond Stream of Research

Instructive insights surfaced in the mid-1980s when the results of two very different cross-cultural management studies were merged. The first study was conducted under the guidance of Dutch researcher Geert Hofstede. Canadian Michael Harris Bond, at the Chinese University of Hong Kong, was a key researcher in the second study. What follows is a brief overview of each study, a discussion of the combined results, and a summary of important practical implications.

Cross-cultural management
Understanding and teaching behavioral patterns in different cultures.

The Two Studies   Hofstede's study is a classic in the annals of cross-cultural management research.[50] He drew his data for that study from a collection of 116,000 attitude surveys administered to IBM employees worldwide between 1967 and 1973. Respondents to the attitude survey, which also asked questions on cultural values and beliefs, included IBM employees from 72 countries. Fifty-three cultures eventually were analyzed and contrasted according to four cultural dimensions. Hofstede's database was unique, not only because of its large size, but also because it allowed him to isolate cultural effects. If his subjects had not performed *similar jobs* in *different countries* for the *same company,* no such control would have been possible. Cross-cultural comparisons were made along the first four dimensions listed in Table 4–1, power distance, individualism–collectivism, masculinity–femininity, and uncertainty avoidance.

Bond's study was much smaller, involving a survey of 100 (50% women) students from 22 countries and 5 continents. The survey instrument was the Chinese Value Survey (CVS), based on the Rokeach Value Survey.[51] The CVS also tapped four cultural dimensions. Three corresponded to Hofstede's first three in Table 4–1. Hofstede's fourth cultural dimension, uncertainty avoidance, was not measured by the CVS. Instead, Bond's study isolated the fifth cultural dimension in Table 4–1. It eventually

Table 4–1   *Key Cultural Dimensions in the Hofstede–Bond Studies*

Power distance: How much do people expect inequality in social institutions (e.g., family, work organizations, government)?

Individualism–collectivism: How loose or tight is the bond between individuals and societal groups?

Masculinity–femininity: To what extent do people embrace competitive masculine traits (e.g., success, assertiveness and performance) or nurturing feminine traits (e.g., solidarity, personal relationships, service, quality of life)?

Uncertainty avoidance: To what extent do people prefer structured versus unstructured situations?

Long-term versus short-term orientation (Confucian values): To what extent are people oriented toward the future by saving and being persistent versus being oriented toward the present and past by respecting tradition and meeting social obligations?

SOURCE: Adapted from discussion in G Hofstede, "Cultural Constraints in Management Theories," *Academy of Management Executive,* February 1993, pp 81–94.

was renamed *long-term versus short-term orientation* to reflect how strongly a person believes in the long-term thinking promoted by the teachings of the Chinese philosopher Confucius (551–479 BC). According to an update by Hofstede: "On the long-term side one finds values oriented towards the future, like thrift (saving) and persistence. On the short-term side one finds values rather oriented towards the past and present, like respect for tradition and fulfilling social obligations."[52] Importantly, one may embrace Confucian long-term values without knowing a thing about Confucius.[53]

East Meets West   By merging the two studies, a serious flaw in each was corrected. Namely, Hofstede's study had an inherent Anglo-European bias, and Bond's study had a built-in Asian bias. How would cultures compare if viewed through the overlapping lenses of the two studies? Hofstede and Bond were able to answer that question because 18 countries in Bond's study overlapped the 53 countries in Hofstede's sample.[54] Table 4–2 lists the countries scoring highest on each of the five cultural dimensions. (Countries earning between 67 and 100 points on a 0 to 100 relative ranking scale qualified as "high" for Table 4–2.) The United States scored the highest in individualism, moderate in power distance, masculinity, and uncertainty avoidance, and low in long-term orientation.

Practical Lessons   Individually, and together, the Hofstede and Bond studies yielded the following useful lessons for international managers:

1. Due to varying cultural values, management theories and practices need to be adapted to the local culture. This is particularly true for made-in-America management theories (e.g., Maslow's need hierarchy theory) and Japanese management practices.[55] *There is no one best way to manage across cultures.*

2. High long-term orientation was the only one of the five cultural dimensions to correlate positively with national economic growth. (Note how the four Asian countries listed under high long-term orientation in Table 4–2 have been among the world's economic growth leaders over the past 25 years, with the exception of the Asian currency crisis in 1997–1998.) In the long term, this correlation may not bode well for countries scoring lowest on this dimension: Pakistan, Philippines, Canada, Great Britain, and the United States.

Table 4–2   *Countries Scoring the Highest in the Hofstede–Bond Studies*

High Power Distance	High Individualism	High Masculinity	High Uncertainty Avoidance	High Long-Term Orientation*
Philippines	United States	Japan	Japan	Hong Kong***
India	Australia		Korea	Taiwan
Singapore	Great Britain		Brazil	Japan
Brazil	Netherlands		Pakistan	Korea
Hong Kong***	Canada		Taiwan	
	New Zealand			
	Sweden			
	Germany**			

*Originally called Confucian Dynamism.

**Former West Germany.

***Reunited with China.

SOURCE: Adapted from Exhibit 2 in G Hofstede and M H Bond, "The Confucius Connection: From Cultural Roots to Economic Growth," *Organizational Dynamics*, Spring 1988, pp 12–13.

3. Industrious cultural values are a necessary but insufficient condition for economic growth. Markets and a supportive political climate also are required to create the right mix.[56] (It remains to be seen if Hong Kong can achieve long-term economic vitality following the 1997 takeover by China and if Japan can pull out of its long recession.)

4. Cultural arrogance is a luxury individuals and nations can no longer afford in a global economy.

A Contingency Model for Cross-Cultural Leadership

If a manager has a favorite leadership style in his or her own culture, will that style be equally appropriate in another culture? According to a model that built upon Hofstede's work, the answer is "not necessarily."[57] Four leadership styles—directive, supportive, participative, and achievement—were matched with variations of three of Hofstede's cultural dimensions. The dimensions used were power distance, individualism–collectivism, and uncertainty avoidance.

By combining this model with Hofstede's and Bond's findings, we derived the useful contingency model for cross-cultural leadership in Table 4–3. Participative leadership turned out to be culturally appropriate for all 18 countries. Importantly, this does *not* mean that the participative style is necessarily the *best* style of leadership in cross-cultural management. It simply has broad applicability. One exception surfaced in a more recent study in Russia's largest textile mill. The researchers found that both rewarding good performance with American-made goods and motivating performance with feedback and positive reinforcement improved output. But an employee participation program actually made performance *worse*. This may have been due to the Russians' lack of faith in participative schemes, which were found to be untrustworthy in the past.[58]

Table 4–3   *A Contingency Model for Cross-Cultural Leadership*

Country	MOST CULTURALLY APPROPRIATE LEADERSHIP BEHAVIORS			
	Directive	Supportive	Participative	Achievement
Australia		X	X	X
Brazil	X		X	
Canada		X	X	X
France	X		X	
Germany*		X	X	X
Great Britain		X	X	X
Hong Kong**	X	X	X	X
India	X		X	X
Italy	X	X	X	
Japan	X	X	X	
Korea	X	X	X	
Netherlands		X	X	X
New Zealand			X	X
Pakistan	X	X	X	
Philippines	X	X	X	X
Sweden			X	X
Taiwan	X	X	X	
United States		X	X	X

*Former West Germany.

**Reunited with China.

SOURCES: Adapted in part from C A Rodrigues, "The Situation and National Culture as Contingencies for Leadership Behavior: Two Conceptual Models," in *Advances in International Comparative Management* vol. 5, ed S B Prasad (Greenwich, CT: JAI Press, 1990), pp 51–68; and G Hofstede and M H Bond, "The Confucius Connection: From Cultural Roots to Economic Growth," *Organizational Dynamics,* Spring 1988, pp 4–21.

Also of note, with the exception of France, the directive style appears to be culturally *inappropriate* in North America, Northern Europe, Australia, and New Zealand. Some locations, such as Hong Kong and the Philippines, require great leadership versatility. Leadership needs to be matched to the prevailing cultural climate. (We will discuss leadership further in Chapter 17.)

Preparing Employees for Successful Foreign Assignments

As the reach of global companies continues to grow, many opportunities for living and working in foreign countries will arise. Imagine, for example, the opportunities for foreign duty and cross-cultural experiences at Gillette, the maker of razors and other personal-care products. According to company calculations, an estimated 1.2 billion members of the world's population use a Gillette product on any given day.[59] Foreign business accounts for 70% of Gillette's annual sales of more than $10 billion. As discussed a bit later, Gillette and other global players need a vibrant and growing cadre of employees who are willing and able to do business across cultures. Thus, the purpose of this

When Gillette sells its personal care products in foreign countries, such as seen here in India, special care needs to be taken to accommodate and not offend local tastes and traditions. The byword for those who do business across cultures today is to "think globally, act locally."
(Pablo Bartholomew/The Liaison Agency)

final section is to help you prepare yourself and others to work successfully in foreign countries.

Why Do US Expatriates Fail On Foreign Assignments?

As we use the term here, **expatriate** refers to anyone living and/or working outside their home country. Hence, they are said to be *expatriated* when transferred to another country and *repatriated* when transferred back home. US expatriate managers usually are characterized as culturally inept and prone to failure on international assignments. Sadly, research supports this view. A pair of international management experts recently offered this assessment:

> Over the past decade, we have studied the management of expatriates at about 750 US, European, and Japanese companies. We asked both the expatriates themselves and the executives who sent them abroad to evaluate their experiences. In addition, we looked at what happened after expatriates returned home....
>
> Overall, the results of our research were alarming. We found that between 10% and 20% of all US managers sent abroad returned early because of job dissatisfaction or difficulties in adjusting to a foreign country. Of those who stayed for the duration, nearly one-third did not perform up to the expectations of their superiors. And perhaps most problematic, one-fourth of those who completed an assignment left their company, often to join a competitor, within one year after repatriation. That's a turnover rate double that of managers who did not go abroad.[60]

Because of the high cost of sending employees and their families to foreign countries for extended periods, significant improvement is needed.

Research has uncovered specific reasons for the failure of US expatriate managers. Listed in decreasing order of frequency, the seven most common reasons are as follows:

1. The manager's spouse cannot adjust to new physical or cultural surroundings.

2. The manager cannot adapt to new physical or cultural surroundings.

3. Family problems.

4. The manager is emotionally immature.

5. The manager cannot cope with foreign duties.

6. The manager is not technically competent.

7. The manager lacks the proper motivation for a foreign assignment.[61]

Expatriate
Anyone living or working in a foreign country.

Collectively, *family and personal adjustment problems,* not technical competence, are the main stumbling block for American managers working in foreign countries.

This conclusion is reinforced by the results of a survey that asked 72 human resource managers at multinational corporations to identify the most important success factor in a foreign assignment. "Nearly 35% said cultural adaptability: patience, flexibility, and tolerance for others' beliefs. Only 22% of them listed technical and management skills."[62] US multinational companies clearly need to do a better job of preparing employees and their families for foreign assignments.

A Bright Spot: North American Women on Foreign Assignments

Historically, a woman from the United States or Canada on a foreign assignment was a rarity. Things are changing, albeit slowly. A review of research evidence and anecdotal accounts uncovered these insights:

- The proportion of corporate women from North America on foreign assignments grew from about 3% in the early 1980s to between 11% and 15% in the late 1990s.
- Self-disqualification and management's assumption that women would not be welcome in foreign cultures—not foreign prejudice, itself—are the primary barriers for potential female expatriates.
- Expatriate North American women are viewed first and foremost by their hosts as being foreigners, and only secondarily as being female.
- North American women have a very high success rate on foreign assignments.[63]

Considering the rapidly growing demand for global managers today, self-disqualification by women and management's prejudicial policies are counterproductive.

The Global Manager

On any given day in today's global economy, a manager can interact with colleagues from several different countries or cultures. For instance, at PolyGram, the British music company, the top 33 managers are from 15 different countries.[64] If they are to be effective, managers in such multicultural situations need to develop *global* skills (see Table 4–4). Developing skilled managers who move comfortably from culture to culture takes time. Consider, for example, this comment by the head of Gillette, who wants twice as many global managers on the payroll. "We could try to hire the best and the brightest, but it's the experience with Gillette that we need. About half of our [expatriates] are now on their fourth country—that kind of experience. It takes 10 years to make the kind of Gillette manager I'm talking about."[65]

Importantly, these global skills will help managers in culturally diverse countries such as the United States and Canada do a more effective job on a day-to-day basis (See the International OB, p 124).

Avoiding OB Trouble Spots in Foreign Assignments

Finding the right person (often along with a supportive and adventurous family) for a foreign position is a complex, time-consuming, and costly process.[66] For our purposes, it is sufficient to narrow the focus to common OB trouble spots in the foreign assign-

Table 4–4   *Global Skills for Global Managers*

Skill	Description
Global perspective	Broaden focus from one or two countries to a global business perspective.
Cultural responsiveness	Become familiar with many cultures.
Appreciate cultural synergies	Learn the dynamics of multicultural situations.
Cultural adaptability	Be able to live and work effectively in many different cultures.
Cross-cultural communication	Engage in cross-cultural interaction every day, whether at home or in a foreign country.
Cross-cultural collaboration	Work effectively in multicultural teams where everyone is equal.
Acquire broad foreign experience	Move up the career ladder by going from one foreign country to another, instead of taking frequent home-country assignments.

SOURCE: Adapted from N J Adler and S Bartholomew, "Managing Globally Competent People," *Academy of Management Executive,* August 1992, Table 1, pp 52–65.

Figure 4–4   *The Foreign Assignment Cycle (with OB Trouble Spots)*

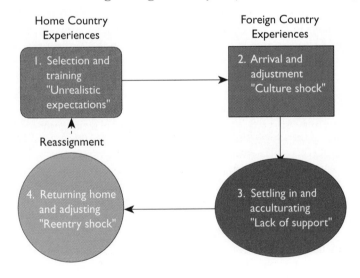

ment cycle. As illustrated in Figure 4–4, the first and last stages of the cycle occur at home. The middle two stages occur in the foreign or host country. Each stage hides an OB-related trouble spot that needs to be anticipated and neutralized. Otherwise, the bill for another failed foreign assignment will grow.

Avoiding Unrealistic Expectations with Cross-Cultural Training   Realistic job previews (RJPs) have proven effective at bringing people's unrealistic expectations about a pending job assignment down to earth by providing a realistic balance of

The Melting Pot Still Has a Few Lumps

BusinessWeek Sunwook Kong was a little anxious when he showed up at Purdue University's Krannert Graduate School of Management from Seoul, South Korea, last fall. A media planner with little business experience, he was uncomfortable with his English and desperately feared speaking out in class—a hallmark of the US B-school. "Koreans are accustomed to the kind of education that forces students to learn by heart," says Kong.

Thanks to his study team, he didn't have much of a choice. Kong's group—African-American Jevon Gordon; Jatuphat Tangkaravakoon, a Thai national; Chinese-American Steven H. Tsang; and Shawn A. Vij, an American born in India—forced Kong to do the writing and presentation part of a statistics project. The experience got Kong over his fear and helped galvanize the group. Now, they're not only effective study buddies, they're close pals. This Christmas, they're planning a trip to Asia to visit the homes of Tangkaravakoon and Kong. "They were friends outside of class," says Kong. "They showed me kindness."

"Abrasive." If only all foreign B-school students could say their experience had such a happy ending. Sure, nearly every B-school has gone global, hanging flags for each country represented, offering sushi and couscous nights, Latin dance parties, and study trips to Africa and China. But even as most have embraced classroom diversity as the best way to teach global management, deans at many B-schools have been negligent in making the reality live up to the promise for many students. Foreign students often still find themselves isolated academically and socially. Many also have trouble finding a job. And some domestic students, too, aren't getting the global interaction and deep cultural understanding they thought they paid for.

Start with the most obvious difficulty: The culture of most US business schools remains strongly American, both in the classroom and out. Many foreign students aren't used to a system that requires class participation and direct communication. "At the beginning, I found the more outgoing nature of people in the US abrasive," says Eammonn T. O'Sullivan, an Irish member of the class of 1998 at Dartmouth's Amos Tuck B-school. "I was uncomfortable being very up-front, saying, for example, I want to work with you in your study group." With team-based projects an increasingly important part of coursework—and of each student's grade—this reticence can be a problem.

Moreover, B-school places a huge premium on keg parties and ski trips to provide students the opportunity to make connections that will endure in the workplace. That's a very different idea of school than most non-Americans have. And it's not always clear that it's important to show up for happy hour; even if you're a teetotaler. Because many of the international students are married, any free moment is likely to be spent at home with one's spouse, particularly if that person is new to the country and doesn't have his or her own social network. "It wasn't impressed on [international students] that much of the MBA experience was a social aspect," says Sheung L Li, a recent graduate of Stanford University's B-school born in Hong Kong but raised in the [United States]. "There is a very aggressive social schedule here, and that's something most of the East Asian crowd stays out of." ...

There's a flip side to the international equation—the unmet expectations and growing frustration felt by American students. When students from abroad aren't encouraged to become active members of the class, Americans, too, are robbed of the window into other cultures that they've been told will be a key element of their education. "Domestic students made all the contributions to class discussion," says Tessa J Jackson, a recent graduate of the University of California, Berkeley's Haas School. "So you don't know how business is conducted in Europe or the Pacific Rim."

SOURCE: Excerpted from J Reingold, "The Melting Pot Still Has a Few Lumps," *Business Week*, October 19, 1998, pp 104, 108.

good and bad news. People with realistic expectations tend to quit less often and be more satisfied than those with unrealistic expectations. RJPs are a must for future expatriates. In addition, cross-cultural training is required.

Cross-cultural training
Structured experiences to help people adjust to a new culture/country.

Cross-cultural training is any type of structured experience designed to help departing employees adjust to a foreign culture. As documented in the case at the end of the chapter, the trend is toward more such training. Although costly, companies believe cross-cultural training is less expensive than failed foreign assignments. Programs vary widely in type and also in rigor.[67] Of course, the greater the difficulty, the greater the time and expense:

- *Easiest.* Predeparture training is limited to informational materials, including books, lectures, films, videos, and internet searches.
- *Moderately difficult.* Experiential training is conducted through case studies, role playing, assimilators (simulated intercultural incidents), and introductory language instruction.
- *Most difficult.* Departing employees are given some combination of the preceding methods plus comprehensive language instruction and field experience in the target culture. As an example of the latter, PepsiCo Inc. transfers "about 25 young foreign managers a year to the US for one-year assignments in bottling plants."[68]

Which approach is the best? Research to date does not offer a final answer. One study involving US employees in South Korea led the researcher to recommend a *combination* of informational and experiential predeparture training.[69] As a general rule of thumb, the more rigorous the cross-cultural training, the better. Our personal experience with teaching OB to foreign students both in the United States and abroad reminds us that there really is no substitute for an intimate knowledge of the local language and culture.[70]

Avoiding Culture Shock   Have you ever been in a totally unfamiliar situation and felt disoriented and perhaps a bit frightened? If so, you already know something about culture shock. According to anthropologists, **culture shock** involves anxiety and doubt caused by an overload of unfamiliar expectations and social cues.[71] College freshmen often experience a variation of culture shock. An expatriate manager, or family member, may be thrown off balance by an avalanche of strange sights, sounds, and behaviors. Among them may be unreadable road signs, strange-tasting food, inability to use your left hand for social activities (in Islamic countries, the left hand is the toilet hand), or failure to get a laugh with your sure-fire joke. For the expatriate manager trying to concentrate on the fine details of a business negotiation, culture shock is more than an embarrassing inconvenience. It is a disaster! Like the confused college freshman who quits and goes home, culture-shocked employees often panic and go home early.

The best defense against culture shock is comprehensive cross-cultural training, including intensive language study. Once again, the only way to pick up subtle—yet important—social cues is via the local language. Quantum, the Milpitas, California, maker of computer hard-disk drives has close ties to its manufacturing partner in Japan, Matsushita-Kotobuki Electronics (MKE):

> MKE is constantly proposing changes in design that make new disk drives easier to manufacture. When the product is ready for production, 8 to 10 Quantum engineers descend on MKE's plant in western Japan for at least a month. To smooth teamwork, Quantum is offering courses in Japanese language and culture, down to mastering etiquette at a tea ceremony.[72]

This type of program reduces culture shock by taking the anxiety-producing mystery out of an unfamiliar culture.[73]

Support During the Foreign Assignment   Especially during the first six months, when everything is so new to the expatriate, a support system needs to be in place.[74] *Host-country sponsors,* assigned to individual managers or families, are recommended because they serve as "cultural seeing-eye dogs." In a foreign country, where even the smallest errand can turn into an utterly exhausting production, sponsors can get things done quickly because they know the cultural and geographical territory.

Culture shock
Anxiety and doubt caused by an overload of new expectations and cues.

Honda's Ohio employees, for example, enjoyed the help of family sponsors when training in Japan:

> Honda smoothed the way with Japanese wives who once lived in the US. They handled emergencies such as when Diana Jett's daughter Ashley needed stitches in her chin. When Task Force Senior Manager Kim Smalley's daughter, desperate to fit in at elementary school, had to have a precisely shaped bag for her harmonica, a Japanese volunteer stayed up late to make it.[75]

Avoiding Reentry Shock   Strange as it may seem, many otherwise successful expatriate managers encounter their first major difficulty only after their foreign assignment is over. Why? Returning to one's native culture is taken for granted because it seems so routine and ordinary. But having adjusted to another country's way of doing things for an extended period of time can put one's own culture and surroundings in a strange new light. Three areas for potential reentry shock are work, social activities, and general environment (e.g., politics, climate, transportation, food). Ira Caplan's return to New York City exemplifies reentry shock:

> During the past 12 years, living mostly in Japan, he and his wife had spent their vacations cruising the Nile or trekking in Nepal. They hadn't seen much of the US. They are getting an eyeful now...
>
> Prices astonish him. The obsession with crime unnerves him. What unsettles Mr. Caplan more, though, is how much of himself he has left behind.
>
> In a syndrome of return no less stressful than that of departure, he feels displaced, disregarded, and diminished...
>
> In an Italian restaurant, crowded at lunchtime, the waiter sets a bowl of linguine in front of him. Mr. Caplan stares at it. "In Asia, we have smaller portions and smaller people," he says.
>
> Asia is on his mind. He has spent years cultivating an expertise in a region of huge importance. So what? This is New York.[76]

Work-related adjustments were found to be a major problem for samples of repatriated Finnish, Japanese, and American employees.[77] Upon being repatriated, a 12-year veteran of one US company said: "Our organizational culture was turned upside down. We now have a different strategic focus, different 'tools' to get the job done, and different buzzwords to make it happen. I had to learn a whole new corporate 'language.' "[78] Reentry shock can be reduced through employee career counseling and home-country sponsors. Simply being aware of the problem of reentry shock is a big step toward effectively dealing with it.[79]

Overall, the key to a successful foreign assignment is making it a well-integrated link in a career chain rather than treating it as an isolated adventure.

Summary of Key Concepts

1. *Explain how societal culture and organizational culture combine to influence on-the-job behavior.* Culture involves the taken-for-granted assumptions collections of people have about how they should think, act, and feel. Key aspects of societal culture, such as customs and language, are brought to work by the individual. Working together, societal and organizational culture influence the person's values, ethics, attitudes, and expectations.

2. *Define* ethnocentrism, *and distinguish between high-context and low-context cultures.* Ethnocentrism is the belief that one's native culture, language, and ways of doing things are superior to all others. People from low-context cultures infer relatively less from situational cues and extract more meaning from spoken and written words. In high-context cultures such as China and Japan, managers prefer slow negotiations and trust-building meetings, which tends to

frustrate low-context Northern Europeans and North Americans who prefer to get right down to business.

3. *Draw a distinction between individualistic cultures and collectivist cultures.* People in individualistic cultures think primarily in terms of "I" and "me" and place a high value on freedom and personal choice. Collectivist cultures teach people to be "we" and "us" oriented and to subordinate personal wishes and goals to the interests of the relevant social unit (such as family, group, organization, or society).

4. *Explain the difference between monochronic and polychronic cultures.* People in monochronic cultures are schedule driven and prefer to do one thing at a time. To them, time is like money; it is spent wisely or wasted. In polychronic cultures, there is a tendency to do many things at once and to perceive time as flexible and multidimensional. Polychronic people view monochronic people as being too preoccupied with time.

5. *Discuss the cultural implications of interpersonal space, language, and religion.* Anthropologist Edward Hall coined the term *proxemics* to refer to the study of cultural expectations about interpersonal space. Asians and Latin Americans like to stand close (6 inches to 1 foot) during business conversations, while North Americans and Northern Europeans prefer a larger interpersonal distance (3 to 4 feet). Conflicting expectations about proper interpersonal distance can create awkward cross-cultural situations. Research uncovered a high degree of agreement about semantic elements across eight cultures. Another study found no agreement about the primary work value across five different religious preference groups.

6. *Describe the practical lessons from the Hofstede–Bond cross-cultural studies.* According to the Hofstede–Bond cross-cultural management studies, caution needs to be exercised when transplanting management theories and practices from one culture to another. Also, long-term orientation was the only one of five cultural dimensions in the Hofstede–Bond studies to correlate positively with national economic growth.

7. *Explain what cross-cultural studies have found about leadership styles.* One cross-cultural management study suggests the need to vary leadership styles from one culture to another. The participative style turned out to be the only leadership style applicable in all 18 countries studied. Still, the participative style has its limitations and is not universally effective.

8. *Specify why US managers have a comparatively high failure rate in foreign assignments, and identify skills needed by today's global managers.* American expatriates are troubled by family and personal adjustment problems. Experts say global managers need the following skills: global perspective, cultural responsiveness, appreciation of cultural synergies, cultural adaptability, cross-cultural communication, cross-cultural collaboration, and broad foreign experience.

9. *Discuss the importance of cross-cultural training relative to the foreign assignment cycle.* The foreign assignment cycle has four stages: selection and training, arrival and adjustment, settling in and acculturating, and returning home and adjusting. Cross-cultural training, preferably combining informational and experiential predeparture sessions, can help expatriates avoid two OB trouble spots: unrealistic expectations and culture shock. There are no adequate substitutes for knowing the local language and culture.

Discussion Questions

1. Regarding your cultural awareness, how would you describe the prevailing culture in your country to a stranger from another land?

2. What are your personal experiences with ethnocentrism and cross-cultural dealings? What lessons have you learned?

3. Why are people from high-context cultures such as China and Japan likely to be misunderstood by low-context Westerners?

4. Culturally speaking, are you individualistic or collectivist? How does that cultural orientation affect how you run your personal and/or business affairs?

5. Based on your score on the Polychronic Attitude Index, are you relatively monochronic or polychronic? What difficulties do you encounter because of this cultural tendency?

6. In your view, what is the most important lesson for global managers from the Hofstede–Bond studies? Explain.

7. Based on your personal experience with one or more of the countries listed in Table 4–3, do you agree or disagree with the leadership profiles? Explain.

8. What needs to be done to improve the success rate of US managers in foreign assignments?

9. Which of the global manager skills in Table 4–4 do you need to develop? Explain.

10. What is your personal experience with culture shock? Which of the OB trouble spots in Figure 4–4 do you believe is the greatest threat to expatriate employee success? Explain.

Internet Exercise

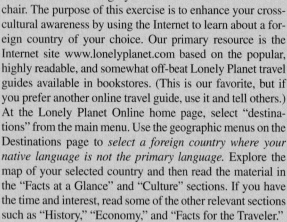

Thanks to the power of the Internet, you can take a trip to a far-flung corner of the world without ever leaving your chair. The purpose of this exercise is to enhance your cross-cultural awareness by using the Internet to learn about a foreign country of your choice. Our primary resource is the Internet site www.lonelyplanet.com based on the popular, highly readable, and somewhat off-beat Lonely Planet travel guides available in bookstores. (This is our favorite, but if you prefer another online travel guide, use it and tell others.) At the Lonely Planet Online home page, select "destinations" from the main menu. Use the geographic menus on the Destinations page to *select a foreign country where your native language is not the primary language.* Explore the map of your selected country and then read the material in the "Facts at a Glance" and "Culture" sections. If you have the time and interest, read some of the other relevant sections such as "History," "Economy," and "Facts for the Traveler."

A second important stop on your Internet trip is www.travlang.com to start building your language skills

for your selected country. At the home page, follow steps 1 and 2. Next, select "Basic Words" from the language page you picked in step 2. Practice essential words such as "Hello," "Yes," "No," "Thank you," and any others you deem necessary. Take the language *quiz* if you have time.

Questions

1. How strong is your interest in taking a foreign assignment in your selected country? Explain.

2. Culturally, does your focus country seem to be high-context or low-context, individualistic or collectivist, and monochronic or polychronic? Cite specific clues from your Internet research.

3. How do you say "Hello" and "Thank you" in the primary language of your chosen country? (Perhaps you have a classmate who can help you with your pronunciation.)

4. What is the likelihood of experiencing "culture shock" in this country? How could you avoid or minimize it?

OB in Action Case Study

Pack Your Bags, You've Been Transferred to Kenya[80]

Dale Pilger, General Motors Corp.'s new managing director for Kenya, wonders if he can keep his Kenyan employees from interrupting his paperwork by raising his index finger.

"The finger itself will offend," warns Noah Midamba, a Kenyan. He urges that Mr. Pilger instead greet a worker with an effusive welcome, offer a chair, and request that he wait. It can be even trickier to fire a Kenyan, Mr. Midamba says. The government asked one German auto executive to leave Kenya after he dismissed a man—whose brother was the East African country's vice president.

Mr. Pilger, his adventurous wife, and their two teenagers, miserable about moving, have come to this Rocky Mountain college town [Boulder, Colorado] for three days of cross-cultural training. The Cortland, Ohio, family learns to cope with being strangers in a strange land as consultants Moran, Stahl & Boyer International give them a crash immersion in African political history, business practices, social customs, and nonverbal gestures. The training enables managers to grasp cultural differences and handle culture-shock symptoms such as self-pity.

Cross-cultural training is on the rise everywhere because more global-minded corporations moving fast-track executives overseas want to curb the cost of failed expatriate stints. . .

But as cross-cultural training gains popularity, it attracts growing criticism. A lot of the training is garbage, argues

Robert Bontempo, assistant professor of international business at Columbia University. Even customized family training offered by companies like Prudential Insurance Co. of America's Moran Stahl—which typically costs $6,000 for three days—hasn't been scientifically tested. "They charge a huge amount of money, and there's no evidence that these firms do any good" in lowering foreign-transfer flops, Prof. Bontempo contends.

"You don't need research" to prove that cross-cultural training works because so much money has been wasted on failed overseas assignments, counters Gary Wederspahn, director of design and development at Moran Stahl.

General Motors agrees. Despite massive cost cutting lately, the auto giant still spends nearly $500,000 a year on cross-cultural training for about 150 Americans and their families headed abroad. "We think this substantially contributes to the low [premature] return rate" of less than 1% among GM expatriates, says Richard Rachner, GM general director of international personnel. That compares with a 25% rate at concerns that don't properly select and coach expatriates, he adds.

The Pilgers' experience reveals the benefits and drawbacks of such training. Mr. Pilger, a 38-year-old engineer employed by GM for 20 years, sought an overseas post but never lived abroad before. He finds the sessions "worthwhile" in readying him to run a vehicle-assembly plant that is 51% owned by Kenya's government. But he finds the training "horribly empty . . . in helping us prepare for the personal side of the move."

Dale and Nancy Pilger have just spent a week in Nairobi. But the executive's scant knowledge of Africa becomes clear when trainer Jackson Wolfe, a former Peace Corps official, mentions Nigeria. "Is that where Idi Amin was from?" Mr. Pilger asks. The dictator ruled Uganda. With a sheepish smile, Mr. Pilger admits: "We don't know a lot about the world."

The couple's instructors don't always know everything about preparing expatriates for Kenyan culture, either. Mr. Midamba, an adjunct international-relations professor at Kent State University and son of a Kenyan political leader, concedes that he neglected to caution Mr. Pilger's predecessor against holding business dinners at Nairobi restaurants.

As a result, the American manager "got his key people to the restaurant and expected their wives to be there," Mr. Midamba recalls. But "the wives didn't show up." Married women in Kenya view restaurants "as places where you find prostitutes and loose morals," notes Mungai Kimani, another Kenyan trainer.

The blunder partly explains why Mr. Midamba goes to great lengths to teach the Pilgers the art of entertaining at home. Among his tips: Don't be surprised if guests arrive an hour early, an hour late, or announce their departure four times.

The Moran Stahl program also zeros in on the family's adjustment (though not to Mr. Pilger's satisfaction). A family's poor adjustment causes more foreign-transfer failures than a manager's work performance. That is the Pilger's greatest fear because 14-year-old Christy and 16-year-old Eric bitterly oppose the move. The lanky, boyish-looking Mr. Pilger remembers Eric's tearful reaction as: " 'You'll have to arrest me if you think you're going to take me to Africa.' "

While distressed by his children's hostility, Mr. Pilger still believes living abroad will be a great growth experience for them. But he says he promised Eric that if "he's miserable" in Kenya, he can return to Ohio for his last year of high school next year.

To ease their adjustment, Christy and Eric receive separate training from their parents. The teens' activities include sampling Indian food (popular in Kenya) as well as learning how to ride Nairobi public buses, speak a little Swahili, and juggle, of all things.

By the training's last day, both youngsters grudgingly accept being uprooted from friends, her swim team, and his brand-new car. Going to Kenya "no longer seems like a death sentence," Christy says. Eric mumbles that he may volunteer at a wild-game reserve.

But their usually upbeat mother has become increasingly upset as she hears more about a country troubled by drought, poverty, and political unrest—where foreigners live behind walled fortresses. Now, at an international parenting session, she clashes with youth trainer Amy Kaplan over whether her offspring can safely ride Nairobi's public buses, even with Mrs. Pilger initially accompanying them.

"All the advice we've gotten is that it's deadly" to ride buses there, Mrs. Pilger frets. Ms. Kaplan retorts: "It's going to be hard" to let teenagers do their own thing in Kenya, but then they'll be less likely to rebel. The remark fails to quell Mrs. Pilger's fears that she can't handle life abroad. "I'm going to let a lot of people down if I blow this," she adds, her voice quavering with emotion.

Questions for Discussion

1. What would you like to tell General Motors' employees in Kenya about working effectively with Americans?

2. Has General Motors done a good job of preparing the Pilger family for an assignment in Kenya? Explain.

3. If you were a cross-cultural consultant, what advice would you give General Motors about preparing employees and their families for foreign assignments?

4. Putting yourself in Dale Pilger's place, would you accept the transfer to Kenya? Explain. Putting yourself in Nancy Pilger's place, would you agree to moving the family to Kenya? Explain.

Personal Awareness and Growth Exercise

How Do Your Work Goals Compare Internationally?

Objectives

1. To increase your cross-cultural awareness.

2. To see how your own work goals compare internationally.

Introduction

In today's multicultural global economy, it is a mistake to assume everyone wants the same things from the job as you do. This exercise provides a "window" on the world of work goals.

Instructions

Below is a list of 11 goals potentially attainable in the workplace. In terms of your own personal preferences, rank the goals from 1 to 11 (1 = Most important; 11 = Least important). After you have ranked all 11 work goals, compare your list with the national samples under the heading *Survey Results*. These national samples represent cross sections of employees from all levels and all major occupational groups. (Please complete your ranking now, before looking at the national samples.)

How important are the following in your work life?

Rank	Work Goals
_____	A lot of opportunity to *learn* new things
_____	Good *interpersonal relations* (supervisors, co-workers)
_____	Good opportunity for upgrading or *promotion*
_____	*Convenient* work *hours*
_____	A lot of *variety*
_____	*Interesting* work (work that you really like)
_____	Good *job security*
_____	A good *match* between your job requirements and your abilities and experience
_____	Good *pay*
_____	Good physical working *conditions* (such as light, temperature, cleanliness, low noise level)
_____	A lot of *autonomy* (you decide how to do your work)[81]

Questions for Discussion

1. Which national profile of work goals most closely matches your own? Is this what you expected, or not?

2. Are you surprised by any of the rankings in the four national samples? Explain.

3. What sorts of motivational/leadership adjustments would a manager have to make when moving among the four countries?

Survey Results[82]

Ranking of Work Goals by Country

(1 = MOST IMPORTANT; 11 = LEAST IMPORTANT)

Work Goals	United States	Britain	Germany*	Japan
Interesting work	1	1	3	2
Pay	2	2	1	5
Job security	3	3	2	4
Match between person and job	4	6	5	1
Opportunity to learn	5	8	9	7
Variety	6	7	6**	9
Interpersonal relations	7	4	4	6
Autonomy	8	10	8	3
Convenient work hours	9	5	6**	8
Opportunity for promotion	10	11	10	11
Working conditions	11	9	11	10

*Former West Germany.
**Tie.

Group Exercise

Looking into a Cultural Mirror

Objectives

1. To generate group discussion about the impact of societal culture on managerial style.

2. To increase your cultural awareness.

3. To discuss the idea of a distinct American style of management.

4. To explore the pros and cons of the American style of management.

Introduction

A time-tested creativity technique involves "taking something familiar and making it strange." This technique can yield useful insights by forcing us to take a close look at things we tend to take for granted. In the case of this group exercise, the focus of your attention will be mainstream cultural tendencies in the United States (or any other country you or your instructor may select) and management. A 15-minute, small-group session will be followed by brief oral presentations and a general class discussion. Total time required is about 35 to 45 minutes.

Instructions

Your instructor will divide your class randomly into small groups of five to eight. Half of the teams will be designated "red" teams, and half will be "green" teams. Each team will assign someone the role of recorder/presenter, examine the cultural traits listed below, and develop a cultural profile of the "American management style." Members of each red team will explain the *positive* implications of each trait in their cultural profile. Green team members will explain the *negative* implications of the traits in their profiles.

During the brief oral presentations by the various teams, the instructor may jot down on the board or flip chart a composite cultural profile of American managers. A general class discussion of positive and negative implications will follow. Note: Special effort should be made to solicit comments and observations from foreign students and students who have traveled and/or worked in other countries.

Discussion needs to focus on the appropriateness or inappropriateness of the American cultural style of management in other countries and cultures.

As "seed" for group discussion, here is a list of American cultural traits identified by researchers[83] (feel free to supplement this short list):

- Individualistic.
- Independent.
- Aggressive/assertive/blunt.
- Competitive.
- Informal.
- Pragmatic/practical.
- Impatient.

- Materialistic.
- Unemotional/rational/objective.
- Hard working.

Questions for Discussion

1. Are you surprised by anything you have just heard? Explain.

2. Is there a distinct American management style? Explain.

3. Can the American management style be exported easily? If it needs to be modified, how?

4. What do American managers need to do to be more effective at home and in foreign countries?

Part Two

Individual Behavior in Organizations

Chapter Five

Individual Differences: Personality, Attitudes, Abilities, and Emotions

Learning Objectives

When you finish studying the material in this chapter, you should be able to:

1 Explain the nature and determinants of organization-based self-esteem.

2 Define self-efficacy, and explain its sources.

3 Contrast high and low self-monitoring individuals, and describe resulting problems each may have.

4 Identify and describe the Big Five personality dimensions, and specify which one is correlated most strongly with job performance.

5 Explain the difference between an internal and an external locus of control.

6 Explain how attitudes influence behavior in terms of the Fishbein and Ajzen model of behavioral intentions.

7 Describe Carl Jung's cognitive styles typology.

8 Distinguish between positive and negative emotions, and explain how they can be judged.

When Marlene Krauss gave birth to twins 14 months ago at the age of 53—after working at her venture-capital firm until her delivery date—some acquaintances couldn't believe it. "Others thought I was crazy," she says. And some, aware that she has always been a pioneer, weren't surprised at all.

In 1965, when she was 20, Ms. Krauss was among the first trickle of women admitted to Harvard Business School, one of 11 females in a class of several hundred men. She spent eight years working in investment banking on Wall Street, then switched careers at 30, enrolling in Harvard Medical School and becoming an eye surgeon.

She married at 39, had a daughter at 44, and then launched KBL Healthcare Venture, a New York venture capital company, with her husband. Yearning for more children, she also kept trying to get pregnant, ignoring those who said she was too old and ultimately proving them wrong. "I haven't wanted to miss anything," she says.

Her willingness to take risks to pursue her dreams provides a lesson to others seeking new careers or life adventures. "When someone tells me, 'You can't do that,' that's a challenge to me," says Ms. Krauss, the only child of immigrant parents from Hungary. They raised her "to be a girl and a boy, a

Confidence and self-esteem can boost one's credibility when communicating.
(© Leo Snider/The Image Works)

housewife and career person," and to succeed at each. Typically, Ms. Krauss undertakes new challenges without thinking too much about the hurdles ahead until she's halfway there. "That's when I suddenly ask myself, 'What have I done?' and start worrying," she says.

She acknowledges that it is "highly stressful" to change and take risks, and always requires a lot of hard work. "But still I say go for what you want most and stay flexible. Lots of people get paralyzed trying to decide what they want to be, out of fear they can never change their minds again," she says. "A career choice doesn't have to be the ultimate decision for the rest of your life."[1]

FOR DISCUSSION

What can parents, teachers, and managers do to build self-esteem and an I-can-do-it attitude in young people (characteristics so clearly exhibited by Marlene Krauss)?

What makes you *you?* What characteristics do you share with others? Which ones set you apart? Perhaps you have a dynamic personality and dress accordingly, while a low-key friend dresses conservatively and avoids crowds. People's attitudes, abilities, and emotions also vary. Some computer buffs would rather surf the Internet than eat; other people suffer from computer phobia. Sometimes students who skim their reading assignments at the last moment get higher grades than those who study for days. People standing patiently in a long line watch an angry customer shout at a store clerk. One employee consistently does more than asked while another equally skilled employee barely does the job. Thanks to a vast array of individual differences such as these, modern organizations have a rich and interesting human texture. On the other hand, individual differences make the manager's job endlessly challenging. In fact, according to research, "variability among workers is substantial at all levels but increases dramatically with job complexity. In life insurance sales, for example, variability in performance is around six times as great as in routine clerical jobs."[2]

Growing workforce diversity compels managers to view individual differences in a fresh new way. The case for this new perspective was presented in Britain's *Journal of Managerial Psychology:*

> For many years America's businesses sought homogeneity—a work force that believed in, supported, and presented a particular image. The notion of the company man dressed for success in the banker's blue or corporation's grey flannel suit was *de riguer.* Those able to move into leadership positions succeeded to the extent they behaved and dressed according to a rather narrowly defined standard.
>
> To compete today, and in preparation for the work force of tomorrow, successful businesses and organisations are adapting to both internal and external changes. New operational styles, language, customs, values, and even dress, are a real part of this adaptation. We now hear leaders talking about "valuing differences," and learning to "manage diversity."[3]

So rather than limiting diversity, as in the past, today's managers need to better understand and accommodate employee diversity and individual differences.[4]

This chapter explores the following important dimensions of individual differences: (1) self-concept, (2) personality traits, (3) attitudes, (4) abilities, and (5) emotions. Figure 5–1 is a conceptual model showing the relationship between self-concept (how you view yourself), personality (how you appear to others), and key forms of self-expression. Considered as an integrated package, these factors provide a foundation for better understanding each organizational contributor as a unique and special individual.

Figure 5–1   *A Conceptual Model for the Study of Individual Differences in OB*

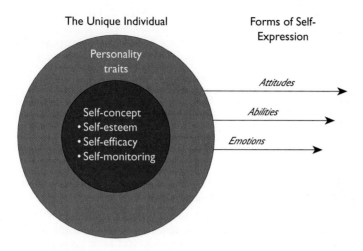

The Unique Individual   Forms of Self-Expression

Self is the core of one's conscious existence. Awareness of self is referred to as one's self-concept. Sociologist Viktor Gecas defines **self-concept** as "the concept the individual has of himself as a physical, social, and spiritual or moral being."[5] In other words, because you have a self-concept, you recognize yourself as a distinct human being. A self-concept would be impossible without the capacity to think. This brings us to the role of cognitions. **Cognitions** represent "any knowledge, opinion, or belief about the environment, about oneself, or about one's behavior."[6] Among many different types of cognitions, those involving anticipation, planning, goal setting, evaluating, and setting personal standards are particularly relevant to OB.[7] Several cognition-based topics are discussed in later chapters. Differing cognitive styles are introduced in this chapter. Cognitions play a central role in social perception, as will be discussed in Chapter 6. Also, as we will see in Chapters 7 and 8, modern motivation theories and techniques are powered by cognitions. Successful self-management, covered in Chapter 10, requires cognitive support.

Importantly, ideas of self and self-concept vary from one historical era to another, from one socioeconomic class to another, and from culture to culture.[8] How well one detects and adjusts to different cultural notions of self can spell the difference between success and failure in international dealings. For example, as detailed in the International OB (p 138), Japanese–US communication and understanding is often hindered by significantly different degrees of self-disclosure. With a comparatively large public self, Americans pride themselves in being open, honest, candid, and to the point. Meanwhile, Japanese, who culturally discourage self-disclosure, typically view Americans as blunt, prying, and insensitive to formalities. For their part, Americans tend to see Japanese as distant, cold, and evasive.[9] One culture is not right and the other wrong. They are just different, and a key difference involves culturally rooted conceptions of self and self-disclosure.

Keeping this cultural qualification in mind, let us explore three topics invariably mentioned when behavioral scientists discuss self-concept. They are self-esteem, self-efficacy, and self-monitoring. We also consider the ethical implications of organizational identification, a social aspect of self. Each of these areas deserves a closer look by those who want to better understand and effectively manage people at work.

Self-Concept: The I and Me in OB

Self-concept
Person's self-perception as a physical, social, spiritual being.

Cognitions
A person's knowledge, opinions, or beliefs.

International OB   Culture Dictates the Degree of Self-Disclosure in Japan and the United States

Japanese Public and Private Self

American Public and Private Self

Private self (the self not revealed to others)
Public self (the self made accessible to others)

Survey research in Japan and the United States uncovered the following *distinct contrasts* in Japanese versus American self-disclosure:

- Americans disclosed nearly as much to strangers as the Japanese did to their own fathers.
- Americans reported two to three times greater physical contact with parents and twice greater contact with friends than the Japanese.
- The Japanese may be frightened at the prospect of being communicatively invaded (because of the unexpected spontaneity and bluntness of the American); the American is annoyed at the prospect of endless formalities and tangential replies.
- American emphasis on self-assertion and talkativeness cultivates a communicator who is highly self-oriented and expressive; the Japanese emphasis on "reserve" and "sensitivity" cultivates a communicator who is other-oriented and receptive.

SOURCE: Adapted from D C Barnlund, "Public and Private Self in Communicating with Japan," *Business Horizons*, March–April 1989, pp 32–40.

Self-Esteem: A Controversial Topic

Self-esteem
One's overall self-evaluation.

Self-esteem is a belief about one's own self-worth based on an overall self-evaluation.[10] Self-esteem is measured by having survey respondents indicate their agreement or disagreement with both positive and negative statements. A positive statement on one general self-esteem survey is: "I feel I am a person of worth, the equal of other people."[11] Among the negative items is: "I feel I do not have much to be proud of."[12] Those who agree with the positive statements and disagree with the negative statements have high self-esteem. They see themselves as worthwhile, capable, and acceptable. People with low self-esteem view themselves in negative terms. They do not feel good about themselves and are hampered by self-doubts.[13]

The Battle Over Self-Esteem The subject of self-esteem has generated a good deal of controversy in recent years, particularly among educators and those seeking to help the disadvantaged.[14] While both sides generally agree that positive self-esteem is a good thing for students and youngsters, disagreement rages over how to improve self-esteem. Consider, for example, how the battle lines have been drawn in one Boston school:

> The students at Mather School in Boston start the day with a pledge: They'll work hard and learn from their mistakes. They don't chant "I am special because I'm me" mantras. Weaknesses have to be faced, praise has to be earned.
>
> Their pledge is in stark contrast to the principles of the "self-esteem movement," which tries to build kids' self-worth through lots of praise, love-yourself maxims, and easy-to-achieve goals.
>
> Kim Marshall, principal of Mather, never bought into that movement. And though the concept has been embraced by parents and become firmly entrenched in school curricula, he doesn't think kids ever really bought it, either. "Praise (from teachers) needs to be specific, genuine, and believable," he says. "When you talk to kids in a phony way, they see right through it."[15]

Feelings of self-esteem are, in fact, shaped by our circumstances and how others treat us. Researchers who tracked 654 young adults (192 male, 462 female) for eight years found higher self-esteem among those in school or working full-time than among those with part-time jobs or unemployed.[16]

Surprising Research Insights   Is high self-esteem always a good thing? Research evidence provides both expected and surprising answers. A pair of recent studies confirmed that people with high self-esteem (HSE) handle failure better than those with low self-esteem (LSE). Specifically, when confronted with failure, HSEs drew upon their strengths and emphasized the positive whereas LSEs focused on their weaknesses and had primarily negative thoughts.[17] But in another study, HSEs tended to become egotistical and boastful when faced with pressure situations.[18] Other researchers found high levels of self-esteem associated with aggressive and even violent behavior. Indeed, contrary to the common belief that low self-esteem and criminality go hand in hand, youth gang members and criminals often score highly on self-esteem and become violent when their inflated egos are threatened.[19] Our conclusion is that high self-esteem *can* be a good thing, but only *if*—like many other human characteristics such as creativity, intelligence, and persistence—it is nurtured and channeled in constructive and ethical ways. Otherwise, it can become antisocial and destructive.[20]

Self-Esteem across Cultures   What are the cross-cultural implications for self-esteem, a concept that has been called uniquely Western? In a survey of 13,118 students from 31 countries worldwide, a moderate positive correlation was found between self-esteem and life satisfaction. But the relationship was stronger in individualistic cultures (e.g., United States, Canada, New Zealand, Netherlands) than in collectivist cultures (e.g., Korea, Kenya, Japan). The researchers concluded that individualistic cultures socialize people to focus more on themselves, while people in collectivist cultures "are socialized to fit into the community and to do their duty. Thus, how a collectivist feels about him- or herself is less relevant to . . . life satisfaction."[21] Global managers need to remember to deemphasize self-esteem when doing business in collectivist ("we") cultures, as opposed to emphasizing it in individualistic ("me") cultures.

Can General Self-Esteem Be Improved?   The short answer is *yes*. More detailed answers come from research. In one study, youth-league baseball coaches who were trained in supportive teaching techniques had a positive effect on the self-esteem

Instructions

Relative to your present (or last) job, how strongly do you agree or disagree with each of the following statements? Arbitrary norms for comparison purposes are: Low OBSE = 10–20; Moderate OBSE = 21–39; High OBSE = 40–50.

	Strongly Disagree	Strongly Agree		Strongly Disagree	Strongly Agree
1. I count around here.	1—2—3—4—5		6. I can make a difference around here.	1—2—3—4—5	
2. I am taken seriously around here.	1—2—3—4—5		7. I am valuable around here.	1—2—3—4—5	
3. I am important around here.	1—2—3—4—5		8. I am helpful around here.	1—2—3—4—5	
4. I am trusted around here.	1—2—3—4—5		9. I am efficient around here.	1—2—3—4—5	
5. There is faith in me around here.	1—2—3—4—5		10. I am cooperative around here.	1—2—3—4—5	
	Total score = _____			Total score = _____	

SOURCE: Adapted from discussion in J L Pierce, D G Gardner, L L Cummings, and R B Dunham, "Organization-Based Self-Esteem: Construct Definition, Measurement, and Validation," *Academy of Management Journal,* September 1989, pp 622–48.

of young boys. A control group of untrained coaches had no such positive effect.[22] Another study led to this conclusion: "Low self-esteem can be raised more by having the person think of *desirable* characteristics *possessed* rather than of undesirable characteristics from which he or she is free."[23] This approach can help neutralize the self-defeating negative thoughts of LSEs, discussed earlier. (See our related discussions of the self-fulfilling prophecy in Chapter 6 and self-talk in Chapter 10.)

Organization-based self-esteem

An organization member's self-perceived value.

Organization-Based Self-Esteem The self-esteem just discussed is a global belief about oneself. But what about self-esteem in organizations, a more restricted context of greater importance to managers? A model of organization-based self-esteem was developed and validated with seven studies involving 2,444 teachers, students, managers, and employees. The researchers defined **organization-based self-esteem (OBSE)** as the "self-perceived value that individuals have of themselves as organization members acting within an organizational context."[24] Those scoring high on OBSE tend to view themselves as important, worthwhile, effectual, and meaningful within the context of their employing organization. Take a moment to complete the brief OBSE questionnaire in the OB Exercise. This exercise will help you better understand the concept of organization-based self-esteem, as well as assessing the supportiveness of your work setting.

A basic model of OBSE is displayed in Figure 5–2. On the left side of the model are three primary determinants of organization-based self-esteem. OBSE tends to increase when employees believe their supervisors have a genuine concern for employees' welfare. Flexible, organic organization structures generate higher OBSE than do mechanistic (rigid bureaucratic) structures (the organic–mechanistic distinction is discussed in Chapter 19). Complex and challenging jobs foster higher OBSE than do simple, repetitious, and boring jobs. Significantly, these same factors also are associated with greater task motivation.

Figure 5–2   *The Determinants and Consequences of Organization-Based Self-Esteem (OBSE)*

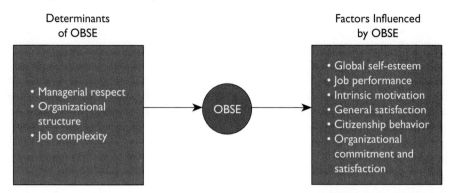

Determinants
of OBSE

• Managerial respect
• Organizational
  structure
• Job complexity

OBSE

Factors Influenced
by OBSE

• Global self-esteem
• Job performance
• Intrinsic motivation
• General satisfaction
• Citizenship behavior
• Organizational
  commitment and
  satisfaction

Factors positively influenced by high OBSE and negatively impacted by low OBSE are listed in the right side of Figure 5–2. Intrinsic motivation refers to personal feelings of accomplishment. *Citizenship behavior* involves doing things beneficial for the organization itself. The other consequences of OBSE are self-explanatory. In sum, active enhancement of organization-based self-esteem promises to build a very important cognitive bridge to greater productivity and satisfaction.[25]

Practical Tips for Building On-the-Job Self-Esteem   According to a study by the Society for Human Resource Management, managers can build employee self-esteem in four ways:

1. Be supportive by showing concern for personal problems, interests, status, and contributions.

2. Offer work involving variety, autonomy, and challenges that suit the individual's values, skills, and abilities.

3. Strive for management–employee cohesiveness and build trust. (Trust, an important teamwork element, is discussed in Chapter 13.)

4. Have faith in each employee's self-management ability (see Chapter 10). Reward successes.[26]

Self-Efficacy

Have you noticed how those who are confident about their ability tend to succeed, while those who are preoccupied with failing tend to fail? Perhaps that

When accepting awards for her unique contributions in the entertainment field, Whoopi Goldberg should be sure to say "Thanks, Mom." Her mother helped build her self-efficacy, an I-can-do-it approach to life.

(Benainous-Duclos/The Liaison Agency)

explains the comparative golfing performance of your authors! One consistently stays in the fairways and hits the greens. The other spends the day thrashing through the underbrush, wading in water hazards, and blasting out of sand traps. At the heart of this performance mismatch is a specific dimension of self-esteem called self-efficacy. **Self-efficacy** is a person's belief about his or her chances of successfully accomplishing a specific task. According to one OB writer, "Self-efficacy arises from the gradual acquisition of complex cognitive, social, linguistic, and/or physical skills through experience."[27] Childhood experiences have a powerful effect on a person's self-efficacy. Whoopi Goldberg, for example, attributes much of her success as a performing artist to her mother's guidance. Says Goldberg, who grew up in New York City as Caryn Johnson,

> My mom encouraged me to explore the city, get on the bus and go watch Leonard Bernstein conduct the young people's concerts, go to the museums and planetarium, Central Park and Coney Island. There were always things for me to investigate, and she encouraged me to ask a lot of questions.
>
>   As kids, my mom instilled in both my brother [Clyde] and me an ideal of what life could and should be, and how we could participate in it. It was never intimated to me that I couldn't be exactly what I wanted to be.[28]

The relationship between self-efficacy and performance is a cyclical one. Efficacy→ performance cycles can spiral upward toward success or downward toward failure.[29] Researchers have documented a strong linkage between high self-efficacy expectations and success in widely varied physical and mental tasks, anxiety reduction, addiction control, pain tolerance, illness recovery, and avoidance of seasickness in naval cadets.[30] Oppositely, those with low self-efficacy expectations tend to have low success rates. Chronically low self-efficacy is associated with a condition called **learned helplessness,** the severely debilitating belief that one has no control over one's environment.[31] Although self-efficacy sounds like some sort of mental magic, it operates in a very straightforward manner, as a model will show.

What Are the Mechanisms of Self-Efficacy?

A basic model of self-efficacy is displayed in Figure 5–3. It draws upon the work of Stanford psychologist Albert Bandura. Let us explore this model with a simple illustrative task. Imagine you have been told to prepare and deliver a 10-minute talk to an OB class of 50 students on the workings of the self-efficacy model in Figure 5–3. Your self-efficacy calculation would involve cognitive appraisal of the interaction between your perceived capability and situational opportunities and obstacles.

As you begin to prepare for your presentation, the four sources of self-efficacy beliefs would come into play. Because prior experience is the most potent source, according to Bandura, it is listed first and connected to self-efficacy beliefs with a solid line.[32] Past success in public speaking would boost your self-efficacy. But bad experiences with delivering speeches would foster low self-efficacy. Regarding behavior models as a source of self-efficacy beliefs, you would be influenced by the success or failure of your classmates in delivering similar talks. Their successes would tend to bolster you (or perhaps their failure would if you were very competitive and had high self-esteem). Likewise, any supportive persuasion from your classmates that you will do a good job would enhance your self-efficacy. Physical and emotional factors also might affect your self-confidence. A sudden case of laryngitis or a bout of stage fright could cause your self-efficacy expectations to plunge. Your cognitive evaluation of the situation then would yield a self-efficacy belief—ranging

Self-efficacy
Belief in one's ability to do a task.

Learned helplessness
Debilitating lack of faith in one's ability to control the situation.

Figure 5–3   *A Model of How Self-Efficacy Beliefs Can Pave the Way for Success or Failure*

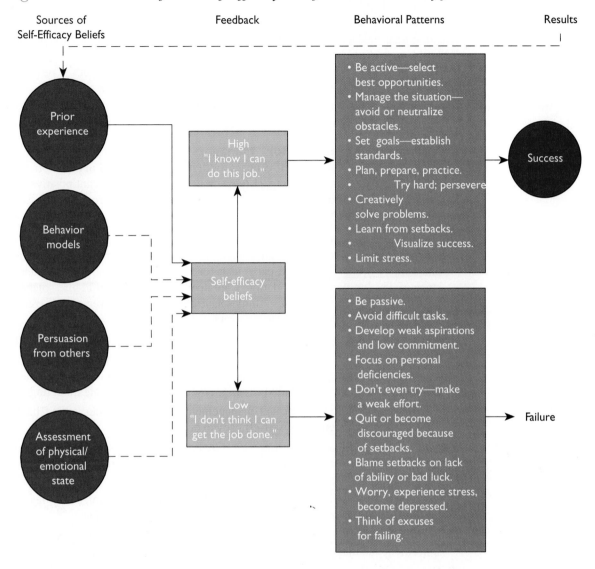

SOURCES: Adapted from discussion in A Bandura, "Regulation of Cognitive Processes through Perceived Self-Efficacy," *Developmental Psychology,* September 1989, pp 729–35; and R Wood and A Bandura, "Social Cognitive Theory of Organizational Management," *Academy of Management Review,* July 1989, pp 361–84.

from high to low expectations for success. Importantly, self-efficacy beliefs are not merely boastful statements based on bravado; they are deep convictions supported by experience.

Moving to the *behavioral patterns* portion of Figure 5–3, we see how self-efficacy beliefs are acted out. In short, if you have high self-efficacy about giving your 10-minute speech you will work harder, more creatively, and longer when preparing for your talk than will your low-self-efficacy classmates. The results would then take shape accordingly. People program themselves for success or failure by enacting their self-efficacy expectations. Positive or negative results subsequently become feedback for one's base of personal experience. Bob Schmonsees, a software entrepreneur, is an inspiring example of the success pathway through Figure 5–3:

> A contender in mixed-doubles tennis and a former football star, Mr. Schmonsees was standing near a ski lift when an out-of-control skier rammed him. His legs were paralyzed. He would spend the rest of his life in a wheelchair.
>
> Fortunately, he discovered a formula for his different world: Figure out the new rules for any activity, then take as many small steps as necessary to master those rules. After learning the physics of a tennis swing on wheels and the geometry of playing a second bounce (standard rules), he became the world's top wheelchair player over age 40.[33]

Self-Efficacy Implications for Managers   On-the-job research evidence encourages managers to nurture self-efficacy, both in themselves and in others. In fact, a recent meta-analysis encompassing 21,616 subjects found a significant positive correlation between self-efficacy and job performance.[34] Self-efficacy requires constructive action in each of the following managerial areas:

1. *Recruiting/selection/job assignments.* Interview questions can be designed to probe job applicants' general self-efficacy as a basis for determining orientation and training needs. Pencil-and-paper tests for self-efficacy are not in an advanced stage of development and validation. Care needs to be taken not to hire solely on the basis of self-efficacy because studies have detected below-average self-esteem and self-efficacy among women and protected minorities.[35]

2. *Job design.* Complex, challenging, and autonomous jobs tend to enhance perceived self-efficacy.[36] Boring, tedious jobs generally do the opposite.

3. *Training and development.* Employees' self-efficacy expectations for key tasks can be improved through guided experiences, mentoring, and role modeling.[37]

4. *Self-management.* Systematic self-management training, as discussed in Chapter 10, involves enhancement of self-efficacy expectations.[38]

5. *Goal setting and quality improvement.* Goal difficulty needs to match the individual's perceived self-efficacy.[39] As self-efficacy and performance improve, goals and quality standards can be made more challenging.

6. *Coaching.* Those with low self-efficacy and employees victimized by learned helplessness need lots of constructive pointers and positive feedback.[40]

7. *Leadership.* Needed leadership talent surfaces when top management gives high self-efficacy managers a chance to prove themselves under pressure.

8. *Rewards.* Small successes need to be rewarded as stepping-stones to a stronger self-image and greater achievements.

Self-Monitoring

Consider these contrasting scenarios:

1. You are rushing to an important meeting when a co-worker pulls you aside and starts to discuss a personal problem. You want to break off the conversation, so you glance at your watch. He keeps talking. You say, "I'm late for a big meeting." He continues. You turn and start to walk away. The person keeps talking as if they never received any of your verbal and nonverbal signals that the conversation was over.

2. Same situation. Only this time, when you glance at your watch, the person immediately says, "I know, you've got to go. Sorry. We'll talk later."

In the first all-too-familiar scenario, you are talking to a "low self-monitor." The second scenario involves a "high self-monitor." But more is involved here than an irritating situation. A significant and measurable individual difference in self-expression behavior, called self-monitoring, is highlighted. **Self-monitoring** is the extent to which a person observes their own self-expressive behavior and adapts it to the demands of the situation. Experts on the subject offer this explanation:

> Individuals high in self-monitoring are thought to regulate their expressive self-presentation for the sake of desired public appearances, and thus be highly responsive to social and interpersonal cues of situationally appropriate performances. Individuals low in self-monitoring are thought to lack either the ability or the motivation to so regulate their expressive self-presentations. Their expressive behaviors, instead, are thought to functionally reflect their own enduring and momentary inner states, including their attitudes, traits, and feelings.[41]

In organizational life, both high and low monitors are subject to criticism. High self-monitors are sometimes called *chameleons,* who readily adapt their self-presentation to their surroundings. Low self-monitors, on the other hand, often are criticized for being on their own planet and insensitive to others. Former US Housing Secretary and 1996 vice presidential candidate, Jack Kemp, frustrated his political handlers with his low self-monitoring ways:

> Bush Administration veterans recall windy lectures on US urban policy during cabinet meetings, and friends say Kemp will debate anything with anyone, any time. "We used to laugh at him for going to Iowa, where he'd wind up talking the gold standard with two farmers, three hogs, and two dogs," a former staffer says. "Everyone else had left."[42]

Importantly, within an OB context, self-monitoring is like any other individual difference—not a matter of right or wrong or good versus bad, but rather a source of diversity that needs to be adequately understood by present and future managers.

A Matter of Degree   Self-monitoring is not an either-or proposition. It is a matter of degree; a matter of being relatively high or low in terms of related patterns of self-expression. The OB Exercise on p 147 is a self-assessment of your self-monitoring tendencies. It can help you better understand your*self.* Take a short break from your reading to complete the 10-item survey. Does your score surprise you in any way? Are you unhappy with the way you present yourself to others? What are the ethical implications of your score (particularly with regard to items 9 and 10)?

Research Findings and Practical Recommendations   According to field research, there is a positive relationship between high self-monitoring and career success. Among 139 MBA graduates who were tracked for five years, high self-monitors enjoyed more internal and external promotions than did their low self-monitoring classmates.[43] Another study of 147 managers and professionals found that high self-monitors had a better record of acquiring a mentor (someone to act as a personal career coach and professional sponsor).[44] These results mesh well with an earlier study that found managerial success (in terms of speed of promotions) tied to political savvy (knowing how to socialize, network, and engage in organizational politics).[45]

The foregoing evidence and practical experience lead us to make these practical recommendations:

> *For high, moderate, and low self-monitors:* Become more consciously aware of your self-image and how it affects others (the OB Exercise is a good start).[46]

Self-monitoring
Observing one's own behavior and adapting it to the situation.

For high self-monitors: Don't overdo it by turning from a successful chameleon into someone who is widely perceived as insincere, dishonest, phoney, and untrustworthy. You cannot be everything to everyone.

For low self-monitors: You can bend without breaking, so try to be a bit more accommodating while being true to your basic beliefs. Don't wear out your welcome when communicating. Practice reading and adjusting to nonverbal cues in various public situations. If your conversation partner is bored or distracted, stop—because they are not really listening.

Organizational Identification: A *Social* Aspect of Self-Concept with Ethical Implications

Organizational identification
Organizational values or beliefs become part of one's self-identity.

The dividing line between self and others is not a neat and precise one. A certain amount of blurring occurs, for example, when an employee comes to define him- or herself with a *specific* organization—a psychological process called *organizational identification.* According to an expert on this emerging OB topic, "**organizational identification** occurs when one comes to integrate beliefs about one's organization into one's identity."[47] Organizational identification goes to the heart of organizational culture and socialization (recall our discussion in Chapter 3).

Managers put a good deal of emphasis today on organizational mission, philosophy, and values with the express intent of integrating the company into each employee's self-identity. Hopefully, as the logic goes, employees who identify closely with the organization will be more loyal, more committed, and harder working.[48] As an extreme case in point, organizational identification among employees at Harley-Davidson's motorcycle factories is so strong many have had the company logo tattooed on their bodies.[49] Working at Harley is not just a job, it is a lifestyle. (Somehow, your authors have a hard time imagining an employee with a Pepsi or Burger King tattoo!)

A company tattoo may be a bit extreme, but the ethical implications of encouraging employees to identify closely with the organization are profound. As discussed in Chapter 1, the new employment contract calls for a *fair* exchange between employee and employer. Therefore, it is fine for employers to strive for greater organizational identification—as long as they nurture employees as valuable human resources and not treat them as expendable goods.

We now turn our attention to how the self is expressed through personality traits.

Talk about organizational identification! How willing are you to paint your personal vehicle purple and adorn its hood with a giant company logo? Amazing what people will do when they own a big chunk of stock options in a young, fast-growing company.

(Mark Richards/PhotoEdit)

Individuals have their own way of thinking and acting, their own unique style or *personality*. **Personality** is defined as the combination of stable physical and mental characteristics that give the individual his or her identity.[50] These characteristics or traits—including how one looks, thinks, acts, and feels—are the product of interacting genetic and environmental influences. In this section, we introduce the Big Five personality dimensions, issue some cautions about workplace personality testing, and examine an important personality factor called locus of control.

Personality: Dimensions, Insights, and Issues

Personality
Stable physical and mental characteristics responsible for a person's identity.

The Big Five Personality Dimensions

Long and confusing lists of personality dimensions have been distilled in recent years to the Big Five.[51] They are extraversion, agreeableness, conscientiousness, emotional stability, and openness to experience (see Table 5–1 for descriptions). Standardized personality tests determine how positively or negatively a person scores on each of the Big Five. For example, someone scoring negatively on extraversion would be an introverted person

Table 5–1   *The Big Five Personality Dimensions*

Personality Dimension	Characteristics of a Person Scoring Positively on the Dimension
1. Extraversion	Outgoing, talkative, sociable, assertive
2. Agreeableness	Trusting, good natured, cooperative, soft hearted
3. Conscientiousness	Dependable, responsible, achievement oriented, persistent
4. Emotional stability	Relaxed, secure, unworried
5. Openness to experience	Intellectual, imaginative, curious, broad minded

SOURCE: Adapted from M R Barrick and M K Mount, "Autonomy as a Moderator of the Relationships between the Big Five Personality Dimensions and Job Performance," *Journal of Applied Psychology*, February 1993, pp 111–18.

prone to shy and withdrawn behavior.[52] Someone scoring negatively on emotional security would be nervous, tense, angry, and worried. A person's scores on the Big Five reveal a personality profile as unique as his or her fingerprints. Yet one important question lingers: Are personality models ethnocentric or unique to the culture in which they were developed? At least as far as the Big Five model goes, recent cross-cultural research evidence points in the direction of "no." Specifically, the Big Five personality structure held up very well in a study of women and men from Russia, Canada, Hong Kong, Poland, Germany, and Finland.[53]

Personality and Job Performance   Those interested in OB want to know the connection between the Big Five and job performance. Ideally, Big Five personality dimensions that correlate positively and strongly with job performance would be helpful in the selection, training, and appraisal of employees. A meta-analysis of 117 studies involving 23,994 subjects from many professions offers guidance.[54] Among the Big Five, *conscientiousness* had the strongest positive correlation with job performance and training performance. According to the researchers, "those individuals who exhibit traits associated with a strong sense of purpose, obligation, and persistence generally perform better than those who do not."[55] Another expected finding: Extraversion (an outgoing personality) was associated with success for managers and salespeople. Also, extraversion was a stronger predictor of job performance than agreeableness, across all professions. The researchers concluded, "It appears that being courteous, trusting, straightforward, and soft-hearted has a smaller impact on job performance than being talkative, active, and assertive."[56]

Issue: Is There an "Ideal" Employee Personality Profile?   Given the complexity of today's work environments, the diversity of today's workforce, and recent research evidence,[57] the quest for an ideal employee personality profile is sheer folly. Just as one shoe does not fit all people, one personality profile does not fit all job situations.

Issue: What about Personality Testing in the Workplace?   Personality testing as a tool for making decisions about hiring, training, and promotion is questionable for two main reasons. First is the issue of *predictive validity*. Can personality tests actually predict job performance? In the Big Five meta-analysis discussed earlier, conscientiousness may have been the best predictor of job performance, but it was *not a*

Table 5–2   *Words of Caution about Personality Testing in the Workplace*

- Rely on reputable, licensed psychologists for selecting and overseeing the administration, scoring, and interpretation of personality and psychological tests.
- Do not make employment-related decisions strictly on the basis of personality test results. Supplement any personality test data with information from reference checks, personal interviews, ability tests, and job performance records.
- Avoid hiring people on the basis of specified personality profiles. As a case in point, there is no distinct "managerial personality." One study found the combination of mental ability and personality to be responsible for only 21% of the variation in managerial success.*
- Regularly assess any possible adverse impact on women and minorities.
- Be wary of slickly packaged gimmicks claiming to accurately assess personalities. A prime example is *graphology,* whereby handwriting "experts" infer personality traits and aptitudes from samples of one's penmanship. This European transplant has enjoyed zealous growth in the United States. But judging from research evidence, graphology is an inappropriate hiring tool and probably an open invitation to discrimination lawsuits. In a meta-analysis of 17 studies, 63 graphologists did a slightly *worse* job of predicting future performance than did a control group of 51 nongraphologists. Indeed, psychologists with no graphology experience consistently outperformed the graphologists.†
- The rapidly growing use of *integrity* tests to screen out dishonest job applicants seems to be justified by recent research evidence. Dishonest people reportedly have a general lack of conscientiousness that is difficult for them to fake, even on a paper-and-pencil test.‡

SOURCES: *For details, see J S Schippmann and E P Prien, "An Assessment of the Contributions of General Mental Ability and Personality Characteristics to Managerial Success," *Journal of Business and Psychology,* Summer 1989, pp 423–37; †Data from E Neter and G Ben-Shakhar, "The Predictive Validity of Graphological Inferences: A Meta-Analytic Approach," *Personality and Individual Differences,* no. 7, 1989, pp 737–45; ‡See D S Ones, C Viswesvaran, and F L Schmidt, "Comprehensive Meta-Analysis of Integrity Test Validities: Findings and Implications for Personnel Selection and Theories of Job Performance," *Journal of Applied Psychology,* August 1993, pp 679–703; and D S Ones and C Viswesvaran, "Gender, Age, and Race Differences on Overt Integrity Tests: Results across Four Large-Scale Job Applicant Data Sets," *Journal of Applied Psychology,* February 1998, pp 35–42.

strong predictor. Moreover, the most widely used personality test, the Minnesota Multiphasic Personality Inventory (MMPI), does not directly measure conscientiousness. No surprise that the MMPI and other popular personality tests historically have been poor predictors of job performance.[58]

Second is the issue of *differential validity,* relative to race. Do personality tests measure whites and minority races differently? We still do not have a definitive answer to this important and difficult question. Respected Big Five researchers recently concluded, "To date, the evidence indicates that differential validity is not typically associated with personality measures. Caution is required in interpreting this conclusion, however, in light of the small number of studies available."[59] Meanwhile, personality testing remains a lightening rod for controversy on the job. In police departments, where psychological testing is routinely used supposedly to weed out racists, critics claim the opposite actually occurs. According to *The Wall Street Journal,* ". . . many black police officers in particular remain skeptical, contending that the psychological evaluations are so subjective that they have been used to discriminate against minorities."[60]

The practical tips in Table 5–2 can help managers avoid abuses and costly discrimination lawsuits when using personality and psychological testing for employment-related decisions.[61] Another alternative for employers is to eliminate personality testing altogether. At Microsoft, where 12,000 résumés stream in every month, recruits are screened with challenging interviews, but no psychological tests. When *Fortune* magazine asked David Pritchard, Microsoft's director of recruiting, about the standard practice of screening recruits with psychological tests, Pritchard replied, "It doesn't really interest me much. In the end, you end up with a bunch of people who answer the questions correctly, and that's not always what you want. How can a multiple-choice test tell whether someone is creative or not?"[62] The growing practice of job-related skills testing is another alternative to personality testing.[63]

Issue: Why Not Just Forget about Personality?

Personality testing problems and unethical applications do not automatically cancel out the underlying concepts. Present and future managers need to know about personality traits and characteristics, despite the controversy over personality testing. Rightly or wrongly, the term *personality* is routinely encountered both on and off the job.[64] Knowledge of the Big Five encourages more precise understanding of the rich diversity among today's employees. Good management involves taking the time to get to know *each* employee's *unique combination* of personality, abilities, and potential and then creating a productive and satisfying person-job fit.

Let us take a look at locus of control, another important job-related personality factor.

Ethics at Work

Several years ago I visited an AlliedSignal factory in Virginia where managers wore name badges color-coded to reveal how they had scored on a test of personality type. The idea was that people could communicate better if they understood their . . . [co-workers'] characters.

Source: Excerpted from T A Stewart, "Escape from the Cult of Personality Tests," *Fortune,* March 16, 1998, p 80.

You Decide . . .

Is this an ethical management practice? Why or why not?

For an interpretation of this situation, visit our Web site **www.mhhe.com/kreitner**

Locus of Control: Self or Environment?

Individuals vary in terms of how much personal responsibility they take for their behavior and its consequences. Julian Rotter, a personality researcher, identified a dimension of personality he labeled *locus of control* to explain these differences. He proposed that people tend to attribute the causes of their behavior primarily to either themselves or environmental factors.[65] This personality trait produces distinctly different behavior patterns.

Internal locus of control

Attributing outcomes to one's own actions.

People who believe they control the events and consequences that affect their lives are said to possess an **internal locus of control.** For example, such a person tends to attribute positive outcomes, such as getting a passing grade on an exam, to her or his own abilities. Similarly, an "internal" tends to blame negative events, such as failing an exam, on personal shortcomings—not studying hard enough, perhaps. Many entrepreneurs eventually succeed because their *internal* locus of control helps them overcome setbacks and disappointments. They see themselves as masters of their own fate and not simply lucky. But, as *Fortune*'s Jaclyn Fierman humorously noted, luck is a matter of interpretation and not always a bad thing:

> For those of us who believe we are the masters of our fate, the captains of our soul, the notion that a career might hinge on random events is unthinkable. Self-made men and women are especially touchy on this subject. If they get all the breaks, it's because they're smarter and harder working than everyone else. If they know the right people, it's because they network the nights away. Luck? Many successful people think it diminishes them.
>
> Hard workers do get ahead, no doubt about it. . . . But then there are folks like Ringo Starr. One day he was an obscure drummer of limited talent from Liverpool; the next day he was a Beatle.

Nobody demonstrates better than Ringo that true luck is accidental, not inevitable.[66]

On the other side of this personality dimension are those who believe their performance is the product of circumstances beyond their immediate control. These individuals are said to possess an **external locus of control** and tend to attribute outcomes to environmental causes, such as luck or fate. Unlike someone with an internal locus of control, an "external" would attribute a passing grade on an exam to something external (an easy test or a good day) and attribute a failing grade to an unfair test or problems at home. A shortened version of an instrument Rotter developed to measure one's locus of control is presented in the OB Exercise on p 152. Where is your locus of control: internal, external, or a combination?

External locus of control
Attributing outcomes to circumstances beyond one's control.

Research Findings on Locus of Control
Researchers have found important behavioral differences between internals and externals:

- Internals display greater work motivation.
- Internals have stronger expectations that effort leads to performance.
- Internals exhibit higher performance on tasks involving learning or problem solving, when performance leads to valued rewards.
- There is a stronger relationship between job satisfaction and performance for internals than externals.
- Internals obtain higher salaries and greater salary increases than externals.
- Externals tend to be more anxious than internals.[67]

essay

Implications of Locus of Control Differences for Managers
The preceding summary of research findings on locus of control has important implications for managing people at work. Let us examine two of them.

First, since internals have a tendency to believe they control the work environment through their behavior, they will attempt to exert control over the work setting. This can be done by trying to influence work procedures, working conditions, task assignments, or relationships with peers and supervisors. As these possibilities imply, internals may resist a manager's attempts to closely supervise their work. Therefore, management may want to place internals in jobs requiring high initiative and low compliance. Externals, on the other hand, might be more amenable to highly structured jobs requiring greater compliance. Direct participation also can bolster the attitudes and performance of externals. This conclusion comes from a field study of 85 computer system users in a wide variety of business and government organizations. Externals who had been significantly involved in designing their organization's computer information system had more favorable attitudes toward the system than their external-locus co-workers who had not participated.[68]

Second, locus of control has implications for reward systems. Given that internals have a greater belief that their effort leads to performance, internals likely would prefer and respond more productively to incentives such as merit pay or sales commissions.[69]

Hardly a day goes by without the popular media reporting the results of another attitude survey. The idea is to take the pulse of public opinion. What do we think about candidate X, the war on drugs, gun control, or abortion? In the workplace, meanwhile, managers conduct attitude surveys to monitor such things as job and pay satisfaction.[70] All this attention to attitudes is

Attitudes and Behavior

OB Exercise   Where Is Your Locus of Control?

Circle one letter for each pair of items, in accordance with your beliefs:

1. A. Many of the unhappy things in people's lives are partly due to bad luck.
   B. People's misfortunes result from the mistakes they make.
2. A. Unfortunately, an individual's worth often passes unrecognized no matter how hard he tries.
   B. In the long run, people get the respect they deserve.
3. A. Without the right breaks one cannot be an effective leader.
   B. Capable people who fail to become leaders have not taken advantage of their opportunities.
4. A. I have often found that what is going to happen will happen.
   B. Trusting to fate has never turned out as well for me as making a decision to take a definite course of action.
5. A. Most people don't realize the extent to which their lives are controlled by accidental happenings.
   B. There really is no such thing as "luck."
6. A. In the long run, the bad things that happen to us are balanced by the good ones.
   B. Most misfortunes are the result of lack of ability, ignorance, laziness, or all three.
7. A. Many times I feel I have little influence over the things that happen to me.
   B. It is impossible for me to believe that chance or luck plays an important role in my life.

Note: In determining your score, A = 0 and B = 1.

Arbitrary norms for this shortened version are: External locus of control = 1–3; Balanced internal and external locus of control = 4; Internal locus of control = 5–7.

SOURCE: Excerpted from J B Rotter, "Generalized Expectancies for Internal versus External Control of Reinforcement," *Psychological Monographs*, vol. 80 (Whole no. 609, 1966), pp 11–12. Copyright © 1966 by the American Psychological Association. Reprinted with permission.

based on the assumption that attitudes somehow influence behavior such as voting for someone, working hard, or quitting one's job. In this section, we will examine the connection between attitudes and behavior.

Attitudes versus Values

Attitude

Learned predisposition toward a given object.

Something specific

An **attitude** is defined as "a learned predisposition to respond in a consistently favorable or unfavorable manner with respect to a given object."[71] Attitudes affect behavior at a different level than do values. While values represent global beliefs that influence behavior across *all* situations, attitudes relate only to behavior directed toward *specific* objects, persons, or situations.[72] Values and attitudes generally, but not always, are in harmony. A manager who strongly values helpful behavior may have a negative attitude toward helping an unethical co-worker.

How Stable Are Attitudes?

In one landmark study, researchers found the *job* attitudes of 5,000 middle-aged male employees to be very stable over a five-year period. Positive job attitudes remained positive; negative ones remained negative. Even those who changed jobs or occupations tended to maintain their prior job attitudes.[73] More recent research suggests the foregoing study may have overstated the stability of attitudes because it was restricted to a middle-aged sample. This time, researchers asked: What happens to attitudes over the entire span of adulthood? *General* attitudes were found to be more susceptible to

Figure 5–4   *A Model of Behavioral Intention*

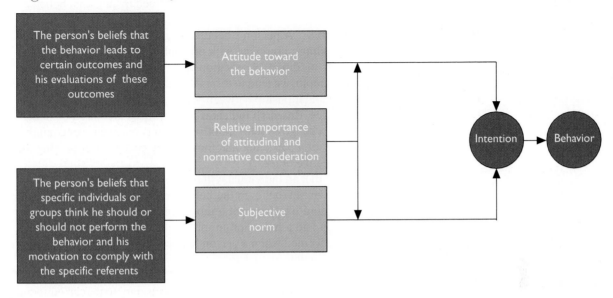

Note: Arrows indicate the direction of influence.
SOURCE: Icek Ajzen and Martin Fishbein, *Understanding Attitudes and Predicting Social Behavior*, © 1980, p 8. Reprinted by permission of Prentice Hall, Upper Saddle River, NJ.

change during early and late adulthood than during middle adulthood. Three factors accounted for middle-age attitude stability: (1) greater personal certainty, (2) perceived abundance of knowledge, and (3) a need for strong attitudes. Thus, the conventional notion that general attitudes become less likely to change as the person ages was rejected. Elderly people, along with young adults, can and do change their general attitudes because they are more open and less self-assured.[74]

Because our cultural backgrounds and experiences vary, our attitudes and behavior vary. Attitudes are translated into behavior via behavioral intentions. Let us examine an established model of this important process.

Attitudes and Behavioral Intentions

Behavioral scientists Martin Fishbein and Icek Ajzen developed a comprehensive model of behavioral intentions used widely to explain attitude—behavior relationships.[75] As depicted in Figure 5–4, an individual's intention to engage in a given behavior is the best predictor of that behavior. For example, the quickest and possibly most accurate way of determining whether an individual will quit his or her job is to have an objective third party ask if he or she intends to quit. A meta-analysis of 34 studies of employee turnover involving more than 83,000 employees validated this direct approach. The researchers found stated behavioral intentions to be a better predictor of employee turnover than job satisfaction, satisfaction with the work itself, or organizational commitment.[76]

Although asking about intentions enables one to predict who will quit, it does not help explain *why* an individual would want to quit. Thus, to better understand why employees exhibit certain behaviors, such as quitting their jobs, one needs to consider their relevant attitudes. As shown in Figure 5–4, behavioral intentions are influenced both by one's attitude toward the behavior and by perceived norms about exhibiting the behavior. In turn, attitudes and subjective norms are determined by personal beliefs.

Beliefs Influence Attitudes   A person's belief system is a mental representation of his or her relevant surroundings, complete with probable cause-and-effect relationships. Beliefs are the result of direct observation and inferences from previously learned relationships. For example, we tend to infer that a laughing co-worker is happy. In terms of the strength of the relationship between beliefs and attitudes, beliefs do not have equal impacts on attitudes. Research indicates that attitudes are based on salient or important beliefs that may change as relevant information is received. For example, your beliefs about the quality of a particular automobile may change after hearing the car has been recalled for defective brakes.

In Figure 5–4, you can see that an individual will have positive attitudes toward performing a behavior when he or she believes the behavior is associated with positive outcomes. An individual is more likely to quit a job when he or she believes quitting will result in a better position and a reduction in job stress. In contrast, negative attitudes toward quitting will be formed when a person believes quitting leads to negative outcomes, such as the loss of money and status.

Beliefs Influence Subjective Norms   Subjective norms refer to perceived social pressure to perform a specific behavior. As noted by Ajzen and Fishbein, "Subjective norms are also a function of beliefs, but beliefs of a different kind, namely the person's beliefs that specific individuals or groups think he should or should not perform the behavior."[77] Subjective norms can exert a powerful influence on the behavioral intentions of those who are sensitive to the opinions of respected role models. This effect was observed in a laboratory study of students' intentions to apply for a job at companies that reportedly tested employees for drugs. The students generally had a negative attitude about companies that tested for drugs. But positive statements from influential persons about the need for drug testing tended to strengthen intentions to apply at companies engaged in drug testing.[78]

Thus, as diagrammed in Figure 5–4, both attitudes and subjective norms shape behavioral intentions.

Attitudinal Research and Application

Research has demonstrated that Fishbein and Ajzen's model accurately predicted intentions to buy consumer products, have children, and choose a career versus becoming a homemaker. Weight loss intentions and behavior, voting for political candidates, attending on-the-job training sessions, and reenlisting in the National Guard also have been predicted successfully by the model.[79] In fact, the model correctly identified 82% of the 225 National Guard personnel in the study who actually reenlisted.[80]

From a practical management standpoint, the behavioral intention model we have just reviewed has important implications. First, managers need to appreciate the dynamic relationships between beliefs, attitudes, subjective norms, and behavioral intentions when attempting to foster productive behavior. For example, the negative attitudes among 349 Florida college students toward affirmative action plans often were based on incorrect beliefs.[81] Although attitudes often are resistant to change, they can be influenced *indirectly* through education and training experiences that change underlying beliefs. A case in point is a recent study documenting how men's beliefs about gender differences can be reduced by taking a women's studies course.[82] Another tactic involves redirecting subjective norms through clear and credible communication, organizational culture values, and role models. Finally, regular employee-attitude surveys can let managers know if their ideas and changes go with or against the grain of popular sentiment.[83]

Abilities and Performance

Individual differences in abilities and accompanying skills are a central concern for managers because nothing can be accomplished without appropriately skilled personnel. An **ability** represents a broad and stable characteristic responsible for a person's maximum—as opposed to typical—performance on mental and physical tasks. A **skill,** on the other hand, is the specific capacity to physically manipulate objects. Consider this difference as you imagine yourself being the only passenger on a small commuter airplane in which the pilot has just passed out. As the plane nose-dives, your effort and abilities will not be enough to save yourself and the pilot if you do not possess flying skills. As shown in Figure 5–5, successful performance (be it landing an airplane or performing any other job) depends on the right combination of effort, ability, and skill.

Ability
Stable characteristic responsible for a person's maximum physical or mental performance.

Skill
Specific capacity to manipulate objects.

Abilities and skills are getting a good deal of attention in management circles these days. The more encompassing term *competencies* is typically used. According to the head of a New Jersey consulting firm,

> In the past decade, thousands of organizations throughout the world have joined the quest for competencies. Often, they spend a year or more conducting competency studies—identifying "clusters" of knowledge, attitudes, and skills needed to perform various jobs. The competencies turned up by these studies become the basis for decisions about hiring, training, promotions, and other human resource issues.[84]

Among the many desirable competencies are oral communication, initiative, decisiveness, tolerance, problem solving, and adaptability. Importantly, our earlier cautions about on-the-job personality testing extend to ability, intelligence, and competency testing and certification.

Before moving on, we need to say something about a modern-day threat to abilities, skills, and general competence. That threat, according to public health officials, is *sleep deprivation* (take a short break for the OB Exercise on p 156). If you are routinely short-changing your basic sleep needs, you are likely to be less effective and more stressed (see Chapter 18) than you should be.

Figure 5–5   *Performance Depends on the Right Combination of Effort, Ability, and Skill*

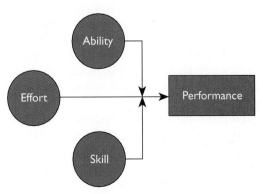

Wake Up! Are Your Abilities and Skills Being Eroded by a Lack of Sleep?

Background

During the past three decades, Americans have put in longer hours at the office and packed ever more into their pre-bedtime hours: working at home on laptop computers, surfing the Internet and E-mailing friends, flipping among ever-expanding choices on television.

The result: Nearly two-thirds of adults get less than the eight hours of sleep a night during the week that the average American adult requires. . . . And nearly one-third of Americans make due with 6½ hours or less sleep a night during the work week. . .

The upshot of this mass sleep deprivation? Many Americans are yawning their way through life. According to . . . [sleep experts;] about 62% of adults have driven while drowsy during the past year and 27% have, alarmingly, dozed off behind the wheel. About 40% of adults are so sleepy during the day that it interferes with their jobs, family duties and other daily activities.*

Instructions

Realizing that the optimum amount of sleep is a very individualized thing, rate your daily sleep needs and habits with the following unscientific index. Are you compromising your health, potential, and effectiveness with lack of adequate sleep?

I feel refreshed and up to my full potential after _____ hours of sleep.
My performance starts to decline with less than _____ hours of sleep.
My performance seriously declines with less than _____ hours of sleep.
I can go for _____ days without getting adequate sleep before I "crash."
I am a complete "zombie" when I get less than _____ hours of sleep.
During the last month, I have averaged _____ hours of sleep per 24-hour period.
I view quality sleep as a resource that I carefully manage. True? False?

SOURCE: *Excerpted from N A Jeffrey, "Sleep: The New Status Symbol," *The Wall Street Journal,* April 2, 1999, pp W1, W12.

The balance of this section explores important abilities and cognitive styles related to job performance.

Intelligence and Cognitive Abilities

Intelligence
Capacity for constructive thinking, reasoning, problem solving.

Although experts do not agree on a specific definition, **intelligence** represents an individual's capacity for constructive thinking, reasoning, and problem solving.[85] Historically, intelligence was believed to be an innate capacity, passed genetically from one generation to the next. Research since has shown, however, that intelligence (like personality) also is a function of environmental influences.[86] Organic factors have more recently been added to the formula as a result of mounting evidence of the connection between alcohol and drug abuse by pregnant women and intellectual development problems in their children.[87]

Researchers have produced some interesting findings about abilities and intelligence in recent years. A unique five-year study documented the tendency of people to "gravitate into jobs commensurate with their abilities."[88] This prompts the vision of the labor market acting as a giant sorting or sifting machine, with employees tumbling into various ability bins. Meanwhile, a steady and significant rise in average intelligence among those in

Table 5–3   *Mental Abilities Underlying Performance*

Ability	Description
1. Verbal comprehension	The ability to understand what words mean and to readily comprehend what is read.
2. Word fluency	The ability to produce isolated words that fulfill specific symbolic or structural requirements (such as all words that begin with the letter *b* and have two vowels).
3. Numerical	The ability to make quick and accurate arithmetic computations such as adding and subtracting.
4. Spatial	Being able to perceive spatial patterns and to visualize how geometric shapes would look if transformed in shape or position.
5. Memory	Having good rote memory for paired words, symbols, lists of numbers, or other associated items.
6. Perceptual speed	The ability to perceive figures, identify similarities and differences, and carry out tasks involving visual perception.
7. Inductive reasoning	The ability to reason from specifics to general conclusions.

SOURCE: Adapted from M D Dunnette, "Aptitudes, Abilities, and Skills," in *Handbook of Industrial and Organizational Psychology*, ed M D Dunnette (Skokie, IL: Rand McNally, 1976), pp 478–83.

developed countries has been observed over the last 70 years. Why? Experts at a recent American Psychological Association conference concluded, "Some combination of better schooling, improved socioeconomic status, healthier nutrition, and a more technologically complex society might account for the gains in IQ scores."[89] So if you think you're smarter than your parents and your teachers, you're probably right!

Two Types of Abilities   Human intelligence has been studied predominantly through the empirical approach. By examining the relationships between measures of mental abilities and behavior, researchers have statistically isolated major components of intelligence. Using this empirical procedure, pioneering psychologist Charles Spearman proposed in 1927 that all cognitive performance is determined by two types of abilities. The first can be characterized as a general mental ability needed for *all* cognitive tasks. The second is unique to the task at hand.[90] For example, an individual's ability to complete crossword puzzles is a function of his or her broad mental abilities as well as the specific ability to perceive patterns in partially completed words.

Seven Major Mental Abilities   Through the years, much research has been devoted to developing and expanding Spearman's ideas on the relationship between cognitive abilities and intelligence. One research psychologist listed 120 distinct mental abilities. Table 5–3 contains definitions of the seven most frequently cited mental abilities. Of the seven abilities, personnel selection researchers have found verbal ability, numerical ability, spatial ability, and inductive reasoning to be valid predictors of job performance for both minority and majority applicants.[91]

What About Emotional Intelligence?   In 1995, Daniel Goleman, a psychologist turned journalist, created a stir in education and management circles with the publication of his book *Emotional Intelligence.* Hence, an obscure topic among psychologists became mainstream. According to Goleman, traditional models of intelligence (IQ) are too narrow. His approach to *emotional intelligence* includes

> …abilities such as being able to motivate oneself and persist in the face of frustrations; to control impulse and delay gratification; to regulate one's moods and keep distress from swamping the ability to think; to empathize and to hope. Unlike IQ, with its nearly one-hundred-year history of research with hundreds of thousands of people, emotional intelligence is a new concept. No one can yet say exactly how much of the variability from person to person in life's course it accounts for. But what data exist suggest it can be as powerful, and at times more powerful, than IQ.[92]

Self-assessment instruments supposedly measuring emotional intelligence have appeared in the popular management literature. Sample questions include: "I believe I can stay on top of tough situations,"[93] and "I am able to admit my own mistakes."[94] Recent research, however, casts serious doubt on the reliability and validity of such instruments.[95] Even Goleman concedes, "It's very tough to measure our own emotional intelligence, because most of us don't have a very clear sense of how we come across to other people. . . ."[96] Honest feedback from others is necessary. Still, the area of emotional intelligence is useful for teachers and organizational trainers because, unlike IQ, social problem solving and the ability to control one's emotions can be taught and learned. Scores on emotional intelligence tests definitely should *not* be used for making hiring and promotion decisions until valid measuring tools are developed.

Jung's Cognitive Styles Typology

Cognitive style

A perceptual and judgmental tendency, according to Jung's typology.

Within the context of Jung's theory, the term **cognitive style** refers to mental processes associated with how people perceive and make judgments from information. Although the landmark work on cognitive styles was completed in the 1920s by the noted Swiss psychoanalyst Carl Jung, his ideas did not catch on in the United States until the 1940s. That was when the mother–daughter team of Katharine C Briggs and Isabel Briggs Myers developed the Myers-Briggs Type Indicator (MBTI), an instrument for measuring Jung's cognitive styles. Today, the MBTI is a widely used (and abused) personal growth and development tool in schools and businesses.[97]

Four Different Cognitive Styles   According to Jung, two dimensions influence perception and two others affect individual judgment. Perception is based on either *sensation,* using one's physical senses to interpret situations, or *intuition,* relying on past experience. In turn, judgments are made by either *thinking* or *feeling.* Finally, Jung proposed that an individual's cognitive style is determined by the pairing of one's perception and judgment tendencies. The resulting four cognitive styles are as follows:

- Sensation/thinking (ST).
- Intuition/thinking (NT).
- Sensation/feeling (SF).
- Intuition/feeling (NF).

Characteristics of each style are presented in Figure 5–6.[98] (The Personal Awareness and Growth Exercise at the end of this chapter, patterned after the MBTI, will help you determine your cognitive style.)

An individual with an ST style uses senses for perception and rational thinking for judgment. The ST-style person uses facts and impersonal analysis and develops greater

Figure 5–6　*People Have Different Cognitive Styles and Corresponding Characteristics*

	Decision Style			
	ST Sensation/Thinking	NT Intuition/Thinking	SF Sensation/Feeling	NF Intuition/Feeling
Focus of attention	Facts	Possibilities	Facts	Possibilities
Method of handling things	Impersonal analysis	Impersonal analysis	Personal warmth	Personal warmth
Tendency to become	Practical and matter-of-fact	Logical and ingenious	Sympathetic and friendly	Enthusiastic and insightful
Expression of abilities	Technical skills with facts and objects	Theoretical and technical developments	Practical help and services for people	Understanding and communicating with people
Representative occupation	Technician	Planner	Teacher	Artist
		Manager		

SOURCE: W Taggart and D Robey, "Minds and Managers: On the Dual Nature of Human Information Processing and Management," *Academy of Management Review*, April 1981, p 190. Used with permission.

abilities in technical areas involving facts and objects. A successful engineer could be expected to exhibit this cognitive style. In contrast, a person with an NT style focuses on possibilities rather than facts and displays abilities in areas involving theoretical or technical development. This style would enhance the performance of a research scientist. Although an SF person likely is interested in gathering facts, he or she tends to treat others with personal warmth, sympathy, and friendliness. Successful counselors or teachers probably use this style. Finally, an individual with an NF style tends to exhibit artistic flair while relying heavily on personal insights rather than objective facts (see Figure 5–6).

Practical Research Findings　If Jung's cognitive styles typology is valid, then individuals with different cognitive styles should seek different kinds of information when making a decision. A study of 50 MBA students found that those with different cognitive styles did in fact use qualitatively different information while working on a strategic planning problem.[99] Research also has shown that people with different cognitive styles prefer different careers. For example, people who rely on intuition prefer careers in psychology, advertising, teaching, and the arts.

Findings have further shown that individuals who make judgments based on the "thinking" approach have higher work motivation and quality of work life than those who take a "feeling" approach. In addition, individuals with a sensation mode of perception have higher job satisfaction than those relying on intuition.[100] Small business owner/managers with a "thinking" style made more money than their "feeling" counterparts. But no correlation was found between the four Jungian styles and small business owner/manager success.[101] The following conclusion from a recent exhaustive review of management-oriented MBTI studies makes us cautious about these findings: "It is clear that efforts to detect simplistic linkages between type preferences and managerial effectiveness have been disappointing. Indeed, given the mixed quality of research and the inconsistent findings, no definitive conclusions regarding these relationships can be drawn."[102] On balance, we believe Jung's cognitive styles typology and the MBTI are useful for diversity training and management development purposes,[103] but inappropriate for making personnel decisions such as hiring and promotions.

Emotions: An Emerging OB Topic

In the ideal world of management theory, employees pursue organizational goals in a logical and rational manner. Emotional behavior seldom is factored into the equation. Yet day-to-day organizational life shows us how prevalent and powerful emotions can be. Anger and jealousy, both potent emotions, often push aside logic and rationality in the workplace. Managers use fear and other emotions to both motivate and intimidate. For example, consider Microsoft CEO Steve Ballmer's management style prior to his recent efforts to become a kinder, gentler leader (see the case study following Chapter 1):

> Ballmer shouts when he gets excited or angry—his voice rising so suddenly that it's like an electric shock. . . By the early 1990s, Ballmer had to have throat surgery to fix problems brought on by shouting.[104]

Less noisy, but still emotion laden, is Intel Chairman Andy Grove's use of Grove's Law to keep a competitive edge in the global computer chip market. According to Grove's Law, "Only the paranoid survive."[105] A combination of curiosity and fear is said to drive Barry Diller, CEO of USA Networks, and one of the media world's legendary dealmakers. Says Diller: "I and my friends succeeded because we were scared to death of failing."[106] These admired corporate leaders would not have achieved what they have without the ability to be logical and rational decision makers *and* be emotionally charged. Too much emotion, however, could have spelled career and organizational disaster for any one of them.

In this final section, our examination of individual differences turns to defining emotions, reviewing a typology of 10 positive and negative emotions, and focusing on the management of anger, a potentially destructive and dangerous emotion.

Positive and Negative Emotions

Emotions

Complex human reactions to personal achievements and setbacks that may be felt and displayed.

Richard S Lazarus, a leading authority on the subject, defines **emotions** as "complex, patterned, organismic reactions to how we think we are doing in our lifelong efforts to survive and flourish and to achieve what we wish for ourselves."[107] The word *organismic* is appropriate because emotions involve the *whole* person—biological, psychological, and social. Importantly, psychologists draw a distinction between *felt* and *displayed* emotions.[108] For example, referring back to our earlier discussion, Goleman would say a person with high emotional intelligence might feel angry (felt emotion) at a rude co-worker but not make a nasty remark in return (displayed emotion). As discussed in Chapter 18, emotions play roles in both causing and adapting to stress and its associated biological and psychological problems. The destructive effect of emotional behavior on social relationships is all too obvious in daily life.

Lazarus's definition of emotions centers on a person's goals. Accordingly, his distinction between positive and negative emotions is goal oriented. Some emotions are triggered by frustration and failure when pursuing one's goals. Lazarus calls these *neg-*

Figure 5–7   *Positive and Negative Emotions*

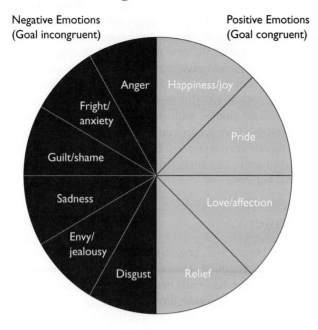

SOURCE: Adapted from discussion in R S Lazarus, *Emotion and Adaptation* (New York: Oxford University Press, 1991), Chs 6, 7.

ative emotions. They are said to be goal incongruent. For example, which of the six negative emotions in Figure 5–7 are you likely to experience if you fail the final exam in a required course? Failing the exam would be incongruent with your goal of graduating on time. On the other hand, which of the four *positive* emotions in Figure 5–7 would you probably experience if you graduated on time and with honors? The emotions you would experience in this situation are positive because they are congruent (or consistent) with an important lifetime goal. The individual's goals, it is important to note, may or may not be socially acceptable. Thus, a positive emotion, such as love/affection, may be undesirable if associated with sexual harassment. Oppositely, slight pangs of guilt, anxiety, and envy can motivate extra effort. On balance, the constructive or destructive nature of a particular emotion must be judged in terms of both its intensity and the person's relevant goal.

More Attention Needed

Emotional behavior receives less than its fair share of attention in the general business and management literature. Often, as with the executives discussed in the introduction to this section, emotions are mentioned only in passing or as a side issue. For example, when Jessica M Bibliowicz took a top job at the Wall Street firm of Smith Barney Inc., *Business Week* reported that she had to work extra hard to avoid co-worker envy and jealousy because her father headed Smith Barney's parent company.[109] Other recent articles have mentioned how emotions can override reason, how leaders need to acknowledge and deal with both their own and others' emotions, and the role of fear in team-building activities.[110]

The OB research literature is even more sparse. Emotional behavior typically is not covered as a central variable but rather as a subfactor in discussions of organizational politics, conflict, and stress. Here are some recent insights. According to a British organizational psychologist, we need to do a better job of dealing with emotions in career management programs.[111] Under the new employment contract, job-hunting skills are not enough. Emotional skills are needed to handle frequent and often difficult career transitions. A pair of laboratory studies with US college students as subjects found no gender difference in *felt* emotions. But the women were more emotionally *expressive* than the men.[112] Two field studies with nurses and accountants as subjects found a strong linkage between the work group's collective mood and the individual's mood.[113] The bad news: Foul moods are contagious. But so are good moods. Go spread the cheer!

We look forward to more comprehensive OB research on the causes and consequences of emotional behavior.

Managing Anger

Of all the emotions in Figure 5–7, anger is the one most likely to be downright dangerous. It deserves special attention. Unchecked anger could be a key contributing factor to what one team of researchers calls *organization-motivated aggression.*[114] Worse, uncontrolled anger certainly is a contributor to workplace violence. The US workplace has become increasingly dangerous, as these statistics indicate: "Three people are murdered in the workplace every day in the United States, while an estimated 1 million workers—18,000 a week—are assaulted each year."[115] Anger-management training for all employees, based on the self-control tactics in Table 5–4, could make a positive contribution to reducing workplace violence and improving the general quality of work life. The US Postal Service, stung by a reputation for workplace violence, has become a model for constructive action:

> In a year's time, 61,000 supervisors, managers, craft and union officials—representing 500,000 person-hours—went through eight hours of violence awareness training. Additionally, the USPS' 250 employee-assistance program (EAP) counselors provided one-hour anger-management training to thousands of employees through health and wellness seminars.[116]

In summary, if the most troublesome emotion—anger—can be managed through learned self-control, then all the emotions can be managed. (See the behavioral self-management model and related techniques in Chapter 10.) Meantime, the workplace remains an emotionally charged environment where too much of either positive or negative emotions is counterproductive.

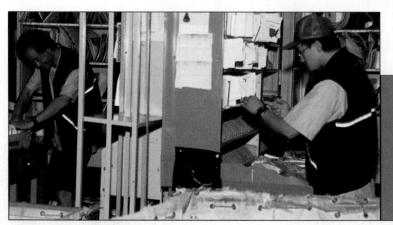

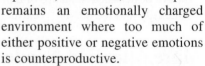

Overload and tedious, schedule-driven work at the US Postal Service have caused some employees to snap. Comprehensive anger-management training has helped the 900,000-employee organization to improve its reputation for workplace violence.

(Mary Kate Denny/PhotoEdit)

Table 5–4　*How to Manage Anger in Yourself and Others*

Reducing Chronic Anger [in Yourself]	Responding to Angry Provocation
Guides for Action	**Guides for Action**
• Appreciate the potentially valuable lessons from anger.	• Expect angry people to exaggerate.
• Use mistakes and slights to learn.	• Recognize the other's frustrations and pressures.
• Recognize that you and others can do well enough without being perfect.	• Use the provocation to develop your abilities.
• Trust that most people want to be caring, helpful family members and colleagues.	• Allow the other to let off steam.
• Forgive others and yourself.	• Begin to problem solve when the anger is at moderate levels.
• Confront unrealistic, blame-oriented assumptions.	• Congratulate yourself on turning an outburst into an opportunity to find solutions.
• Adopt constructive, learning-oriented assumptions.	• Share successes with partners.
Pitfalls to Avoid	**Pitfalls to Avoid**
• Assume every slight is a painful wound.	• Take every word literally.
• Equate not getting what you want with catastrophe.	• Denounce the most extreme statements and ignore more moderate ones.
• See every mistake and slip as a transgression that must be corrected immediately.	• Doubt yourself because the other does.
• Attack someone for your getting angry.	• Attack because you have been attacked.
• Attack yourself for getting angry.	• Forget the experience without learning from it.
• Try to be and have things perfect.	
• Suspect people's motives unless you have incontestable evidence that people can be trusted.	
• Assume any attempt to change yourself is an admission of failure.	
• Never forgive.	

SOURCE: Reprinted with permission from D Tjosvold, *Learning to Manage Conflict: Getting People to Work Together Productively*, pp 127–29. Copyright © 1993 Dean Tjosvold. First published by Lexington Books. All rights reserved.

Summary of Key Concepts

1. *Explain the nature and determinants of organization-based self-esteem.* Organization-based self-esteem (OBSE) is an employee's self-perceived value as an organizational member. People high in OBSE see themselves as important and meaningful within the organization. Three primary determinants of high OBSE are managerial respect and concern, flexible organization structure, and complex and challenging jobs.

2. *Define self-efficacy, and explain its sources.* Self-efficacy involves one's belief about his/her ability to accomplish specific tasks. Those extremely low in self-efficacy suffer

from learned helplessness. Four sources of self-efficacy beliefs are prior experience, behavior models, persuasion from others, and assessment of one's physical and emotional states. High self-efficacy beliefs foster constructive and goal-oriented action, whereas low self-efficacy fosters passive, failure-prone activities and emotions.

3. *Contrast high and low self-monitoring individuals, and describe resulting problems each may have.* A high self-monitor strives to make a good public impression by closely monitoring his or her behavior and adapting it to the situation. Very high self-monitoring can create a "chameleon" who is seen as insincere and dishonest. Low self-monitors do the opposite by acting out their momentary feelings, regardless of their surroundings. Very low self-monitoring can lead to a one-way communicator who seems to ignore verbal and nonverbal cues from others.

4. *Identify and describe the Big Five personality dimensions, and specify which one is correlated most strongly with job performance.* The Big Five personality dimensions are extraversion (social and talkative), agreeableness (trusting and cooperative), conscientiousness (responsible and persistent), emotional stability (relaxed and unworried), and openness to experience (intellectual and curious). Conscientiousness is the best predictor of job performance.

5. *Explain the difference between an internal and external locus of control.* People with an *internal* locus of control, such as

entrepreneurs, believe they are masters of their own fate. Those with an *external* locus of control attribute their behavior and its results to situational forces.

6. *Explain how attitudes influence behavior in terms of the Fishbein and Ajzen model of behavioral intentions.* According to Fishbein and Ajzen's model, beliefs about behavior-outcome relationships and how one should act influence attitudes and subjective norms. Depending on their relative importance, attitudes and norms together foster a behavioral intention, the best predictor of actual behavior.

7. *Describe Carl Jung's cognitive styles typology.* By combining two dimensions of perception (sensation and intuition) with two dimensions of judgment (thinking and feeling), Carl Jung identified four cognitive styles. They are sensation/thinking (practical and matter-of-fact), intuition/thinking (logical and ingenious), sensation/feeling (sympathetic and friendly), and intuition/feeling (enthusiastic and insightful).

8. *Distinguish between positive and negative emotions, and explain how they can be judged.* Positive emotions—happiness/joy, pride, love/affection, and relief—are personal reactions to circumstances congruent with one's goals. Negative emotions—anger, fright/anxiety, guilt/shame, sadness, envy/jealousy, and disgust—are personal reactions to circumstances incongruent with one's goals. Both types of emotions need to be judged in terms of intensity and the appropriateness of the person's relevant goal.

Discussion Questions

1. How should the reality of a more diverse workforce affect management's approach to dealing with individual differences?

2. What is your personal experience with organization-based self-esteem?

3. How is someone you know with low self-efficacy, relative to a specified task, "programming themselves for failure?" What could be done to help that individual develop high self-efficacy?

4. What are the career implications of your self-monitoring score in the second OB Exercise?

5. Why is organizational identification both a good and bad thing in today's workplace?

6. On scales of Low = 1 to High = 10, how would you rate yourself on the Big Five personality dimensions? Is your personality profile suitable for a managerial position?

7. How would you respond to the following statement? "Whenever possible, managers should hire people with an external locus of control."

8. How would you respond to a manager who made this statement? "I'm only interested in behavior. I've never seen an attitude, so why be concerned with attitudes?"

9. According to Jung's typology, which cognitive style do you exhibit? How can you tell? Is it an advantage or a disadvantage?

10. What are your personal experiences with negative emotions being positive and positive emotions being negative?

Internet Exercise   **www.iqtest.com/welcometest.html**

Lots of interactive questionnaires can be found on the
Internet to help you learn
more about yourself. *Note:
These self-tests are for instructional and entertainment
purposes only.* They are not intended to replace rigorously
validated and properly administered psychometric tests and
should not be used to establish qualifications or make personnel decisions. Still, they can provide useful insights and
stimulate discussion. The purpose of this exercise is to
learn more about general intelligence (IQ) and emotional
intelligence (EQ), two topics discussed in this chapter.

A Free Online Interactive Intelligence (IQ) Test

Go to Self Discovery Workshop's home page on the Internet (www.iqtest.com/welcometest.html). For instructive
background, select and read the first two menu items,
"What is an IQ score?" and "History of this intelligence
test." Then proceed to the third menu item, "Let me take
this intelligence test now." Follow the prompts. You will be
given some instructions, a sample three-item pretest, and
then you will be asked to provide some personal data. *Note:
As specified in the instructions, you do not have to fill out
the name, address, etc. section to take the free IQ test.* Simply skip ahead to the test, making sure to read the instructions very carefully because you will be given only 13
minutes to complete the 38 true/false test items. Only one
pass through the IQ test is appropriate if the results are to
have any meaning at all. The test is scored automatically
and you will be given both your IQ score and comparative
norms. (Note: We recommend that you take this test when
you are rested, refreshed, and have a clear mind. Also, people who do not respond well to time pressure may want to
skip it to avoid unnecessary stress.)

A Free Online Interactive Emotional Intelligence (EQ) Test

Go to *Fortune* magazine's Internet site (www.pathfinder.
com/fortune/) and select "Careers" from the main menu. At
the Career Resource Center page, scroll down the middle
column to the subheading "Quizzes," and select "How
High Is Your Work EQ?" Read the instructions and complete the 25 test items. (Note: This is a very quick-and-easy
test.) Follow the prompt to submit your answers to automatic scoring. You may want to explore some of *Fortune's*
other career resources while you are there, or bookmark the
site for later reference.

Questions

1. Do you believe this sort of so-called pencil-and-paper
   psychological testing has any merit? Explain your
   rationale.

2. Could self-serving bias, discussed at the end of Chapter
   6, influence the way people evaluate intelligence tests?
   Briefly, self-serving bias involves taking personal
   responsibility for your successes and blaming your failures on other factors. For example, "I scored high, so I
   think it's a good test." "I scored low, so it's an unfair or
   invalid test." Explain.

3. Do you agree with psychologist Daniel Goleman that EQ
   can be more important and more powerful than IQ?
   Explain.

OB in Action Case Study   **http://cnnfn.com (search: Michael Milken)**

Michael Milken: Bad Guy, Good Guy, or Both?

BusinessWeek   Having just finished up his yoga routine,
Milken shows his meditation technique:
He sits cross-legged, his elbows resting on his knees, hands
extended, eyes closed. Yet even as he relaxes, the ultracompet-
itive Milken seems to be setting goals. "You know, if you are
really good," he says, half-smiling, "you can stop breathing."

The miracle about Michael R Milken is that he is breathing at all. Diagnosed with terminal prostate cancer in 1993,
Milken was told by his doctors that he had 12 to 18 months
to live. Rather than give up, Milken counterattacked. He
learned everything about his disease, took up yoga and
meditation to reduce stress, and became a strict vegetarian,
abandoning his diet of burgers and fries for steamed broc-
coli and soy shakes. So far, Milken has proven his doctors
wrong: His cancer is in full remission.

Had Milken not beaten the odds, cancer would have
taken one of the most storied, vilified business figures of
our time. From his X-shaped trading desk, Mike Milken, as

everyone knows, launched a revolution that transformed the financial system forever. But he also overreached. And when he became ensnared in a federal crackdown on insider trading, Milken's world crumbled. In the public's mind, Milken was the iconic white-collar criminal, a symbol of everything wrong with Wall Street.

It has been eight years since Milken went to jail, but the debate over who Mike Milken is and how bad his crimes were goes on. Junk-bond villain or brilliant financial innovator? There are plenty who think Milken got sandbagged with trumped up, politicized charges, and plenty more who think he simply got what he deserved. And long after many of the less reputable characters he financed have been forgotten, Milken remains controversial. . . .

All that is certain is that Mike Milken has moved on. As far as Milken is concerned, he has paid his penalties—a total of $1.1 billion—and done his time. But that doesn't mean he has faded from the scene. Far from it. For the past six years, Milken has used every waking moment to rebuild his life and his reputation. First, he became a major cancer philanthropist, raising some $75 million for research and appearing regularly on such TV programs as *Larry King Live* and *The Charlie Rose Show* to push efforts to cure prostate cancer. And since 1996, he's moved back into business in a big way, founding Knowledge Universe (KU), a new venture that he hopes to build into a huge presence in the $800 billion educational-services industry. Together, his twin pursuits have given Milken a new platform from which, on his own terms, he is once again a player.

To have risen so high, to have crashed so hard, and then, to just pick up the pieces and move on. That could not have been easy. . .

Cancer doesn't seem to have slowed him. The man works—really works—15 hours a day, seven days a week. He seems almost too focused, lacking the little flaws and weaknesses that make the rest of us fallible, susceptible to distraction, and in a word, human. He doesn't touch coffee, alcohol, or even soda. He never swears. His jokes are always hopelessly wholesome and corny. Even as a kid, he never rebelled. When he married his wife, Lori, at the age of 22 in 1968, the pair had been dating since the ninth grade.

Some of his friends and those who've worked closely with Milken say his drive for perfection is both inspiring and maddening. "In so many ways, he is who you hope your kids become. He is diligent, loyal, a great listener, grounded, persistent, optimistic, generous to a fault," says Joseph Costello, who was hired by Milken in 1997 to run KU, only to quit months later after a disagreement over strategy. "But something is missing. He never seems completely relaxed. There is always a point, a purpose. If he could just lose it, let go, he would be easier to relate to.". . .

Despite all his frenetic activity, ask Milken what he wants his legacy to be and the answer will not be curing cancer or revolutionizing capital or education. Instead, his response seems to jump right out of a 1950s black-and-white TV sitcom. "I'll take 'great dad,' " he says without hesitation. "I love being a dad, a husband, a son. Relationships make life worth living. That is what got me through the legal storm.". . .

Milken, of course, isn't just making up for years lost in the past. He's also making up for the near certainty of years lost in the future. Although his cancer is in remission, he knows it could strike again at any time. Says Milken: "My hope is there will be a breakthrough." But that might take a while. And unless new treatments are found, Milken "is living with a ticking time bomb," says [his] oncologist [Dr Stuart] Holden.[117]

Questions for Discussion

1. How do you suppose Milken maintains his self-esteem when so many people despise him as a very wealthy white-collar criminal?

2. How would you rate Milken on self-monitoring? Explain your reasoning.

3. On scales of Low = 1 to High = 10, how would you score Milken on each of the Big Five personality dimensions in Table 5–1? How does the personality profile you have constructed for Milken explain his incredible comeback after prison and cancer?

4. Does Milken have an internal or external locus of control, and has this tendency helped or hindered him?

5. How would you rate Milken's emotional intelligence? Explain.

6. What role do *your* emotions play in your conclusion that, all things considered, Milken is a bad guy, a good guy, or both?

Personal Awareness and Growth Exercise

What Is Your Cognitive Style?

Objectives

1. To identify your cognitive style, according to Carl Jung's typology.[118]

2. To consider the managerial implications of your cognitive style.

Instructions

Please respond to the next 16 items. There are no right or wrong answers. After you have completed all the items, refer to the scoring key, and follow its directions.

Questionnaire

Part I. Circle the response that comes closest to how you usually feel or act.

1. Are you more careful about:
   A. People's feelings
   B. Their rights

2. Do you usually get along better with:
   A. Imaginative people
   B. Realistic people

3. Which of these two is the higher compliment:
   A. A person has real feeling
   B. A person is consistently reasonable

4. In doing something with many other people, does it appeal more to you:
   A. To do it in the accepted way
   B. To invent a way of your own

5. Do you get more annoyed at:
   A. Fancy theories
   B. People who don't like theories

6. It is higher praise to call someone:
   A. A person of vision
   B. A person of common sense

7. Do you more often let:
   A. Your heart rule your head
   B. Your head rule your heart

8. Do you think it is worse:
   A. To show too much warmth
   B. To be unsympathetic

9. If you were a teacher, would you rather teach:
   A. Courses involving theory
   B. Fact courses

Part II. Which word in each of the following pairs appeals to you more? Circle A or B.

10. A. Compassion
    B. Foresight

11. A. Justice
    B. Mercy

12. A. Production
    B. Design

13. A. Gentle
    B. Firm

14. A. Uncritical
    B. Critical

15. A. Literal
    B. Figurative

16. A. Imaginative
    B. Matter of fact

Scoring Key

To categorize your responses to the questionnaire, count one point for each response on the following four scales, and total the number of points recorded in each column. Instructions for classifying your scores are indicated below.

Sensation	Intuition	Thinking	Feeling
2 B _____	2 A _____	1 B _____	1 A _____
4 A _____	4 B _____	3 B _____	3 A _____
5 A _____	5 B _____	7 B _____	7 A _____
6 B _____	6 A _____	8 A _____	8 B _____
9 B _____	9 A _____	10 B _____	10 A _____
12 A _____	12 B _____	11 A _____	11 B _____
15 A _____	15 B _____	13 B _____	13 A _____
16 B _____	16 A _____	14 B _____	14 A _____
Totals = _____	_____	_____	_____

Classifying Total Scores

Write *intuitive* if your intuition score is equal to or greater than your sensation score.
Write *sensation* if sensation is greater than intuition.
Write *feeling* if feeling is greater than thinking.
Write *thinking* if thinking is greater than feeling.
When *thinking* equals feeling, you should write feeling if a male and thinking if a female.

Questions for Discussion

1. What is your cognitive style?
   Sensation/thinking (ST) _____
   Intuition/thinking (NT) _____
   Sensation/feeling (SF) _____
   Intuition/feeling (NF) _____

2. Do you agree with this assessment? Why or why not?

3. Will your cognitive style, as determined in this exercise, help you achieve your career goal(s)?

4. Would your style be an asset or liability for a managerial position involving getting things done through others?

Group Exercise

Anger Control Role Play

Objectives

1. To demonstrate that emotions can be managed.
2. To develop your interpersonal skills for managing both your own and someone else's anger.

Introduction

Personal experience and research tell us that anger begets anger. People do not make their best decisions when angry. Angry outbursts often inflict unintentional interpersonal damage by triggering other emotions (e.g., disgust in observers and subsequent guilt and shame in the angry person). Effective managers know how to break the cycle of negative emotions by defusing anger in themselves and others. This is a role-playing exercise for groups of four. You will have a chance to play two different roles. All the roles are generic, so they can be played as either a woman or a man.

Instructions

Your instructor will divide the class into groups of four. Everyone should read all five roles described. Members of each foursome will decide among themselves who will play which roles. All told, you will participate in two rounds of role playing (each round lasting no longer than eight minutes). In round one, one person will play Role 1 and another will play Role 3; the remaining two group members will play Role 5. In round two, those who played Role 5 in the first round will play Roles 2 and 4. The other two will switch to Role 5.

ROLE 1: THE ANGRY (OUT-OF-CONTROL) SHIFT SUPERVISOR

You work for a leading electronics company that makes computer chips and other computer-related equipment. Your factory is responsible for assembling and testing the company's most profitable line of computer microprocessors. Business has been good, so your factory is working three shifts. The day shift, which you are now on, is the most desirable one. The night shift, from 11 P.M. to 7:30 A.M. is the least desirable and least productive. In fact, the night shift is such a mess that your boss, the factory manager, wants you to move to the night shift next week. Your boss just broke this bad news as the two of you are having lunch in the company cafeteria. You are shocked and angered because you are one of the most senior and highly rated shift supervisors in the factory. Thanks to your leadership, your shift has

broken all production records during the past year. As the divorced single parent of a 10-year-old child, the radical schedule change would be a major lifestyle burden. Questions swirl through your head. "Why me?" "What kind of reliable child-care will be available when I sleep during the day and work at night?" "Why should I be 'punished' for being a top supervisor?" "Why don't they hire someone for the position?" Your boss asks what you think.

When playing this role, be as realistic as possible without getting so loud that you disrupt the other groups. Also, if anyone in your group would be offended by foul language, please refrain from cursing during your angry outburst.

ROLE 2: THE ANGRY (UNDER-CONTROL) SHIFT SUPERVISOR

Same situation as in Role 1. But this role will require you to read and act according to the tips for reducing chronic anger in the left side of Table 5–4. You have plenty of reason to be frustrated and angry, but you realize the importance of maintaining a good working relationship with the factory manager.

ROLE 3: THE (HARD-DRIVING) FACTORY MANAGER

You have a reputation for having a "short fuse." When someone gets angry with you, you attack. When playing this role, be as realistic as possible. Remember, you are responsible for the entire factory with its 1,200 employees and hundreds of millions of dollars of electronics products. A hiring freeze is in place, so you have to move one of your current supervisors. You have chosen your best supervisor because the night shift is your biggest threat to profitable operations. The night-shift supervisor gets a 10% pay premium. Ideally, the move will only be for six months.

ROLE 4: THE (MELLOW) FACTORY MANAGER

Same general situation as in Role 3. However, this role will require you to read and act according to the tips for responding to angry provocation in the right side of Table 5–4. You have a reputation for being results-oriented but reasonable. You are good at taking a broad, strategic view of problems and are a good negotiator.

ROLE 5: SILENT OBSERVER

Follow the exchange between the shift supervisor and the factory manager without talking or getting actively involved. Jot down some notes (for later class discussion) as you observe whether the factory manager did a good job of managing the supervisor's anger.

Questions for Discussion

1. Why is uncontrolled anger a sure road to failure?
2. Is it possible to express anger without insulting others? Explain.
3. Which is more difficult, controlling anger in yourself or defusing someone else's anger? Why?
4. What useful lessons did you learn from this role-playing exercise?

Chapter Six

Social Perception and Attributions

Learning Objectives

When you finish studying the material in this chapter, you should be able to:

1 Describe perception in terms of the social information processing model.

2 Identify and briefly explain four managerial implications of social perception.

3 Discuss stereotypes and the process of stereotype formation.

4 Summarize the managerial challenges and recommendations of sex-role, age, race, and disability stereotypes.

5 Discuss how the self-fulfilling prophecy is created and how it can be used to improve individual and group productivity.

6 Explain, according to Kelley's model, how external and internal causal attributions are formulated.

7 Review Weiner's model of attribution.

8 Contrast the fundamental attribution bias and the self-serving bias.

BusinessWeek Are you starting to notice. . . . A name or fact is on the tip of your tongue, but you can't remember it, and your conversations are increasingly studded with, "You know, what's-his-name?"

Don't panic. You're not losing your mind. Many people experience slight memory problems as they age. But if you've been jogging all these years to keep physically fit, you may wonder if there's a way to keep mentally fit as well. Would nutritional supplements and memory-improvement classes make a difference? Recent research suggests supplements, such as ginkgo biloba, and the right mental exercises could help.

Regardless of age, mnemonic abilities vary from one person to the next. Some people have always been forgetful, others have extraordinary recall well into old age. In general, though, there is "a certain amount of slowing of synaptic neural transmissions with age" that can start as early as your 30s, says Patricia Tun, associate director of

the memory and cognition lab at Brandeis University. In other words, it takes longer to retrieve information such as names and dates. Tun's research also shows people grow more distractible with age and find it harder to block out certain background noise.

Why memory slows with age is unknown. "There may be some loss of nerve cells and accumulation of intercellular sludge, and it's thought that the parts are wearing out," says Dr Barry Gordon, director of the memory clinic

Can't remember what you had for breakfast? Maybe you didn't eat the right foods.
(Markova/The Stock Market)

at Johns Hopkins Medical Institutes in Baltimore. To understand what could go wrong and what might help, it's useful to review how memory works.

Contrary to popular belief, memory is not located in a distinct part of the brain or stored in brain cells. Rather it is a network of thoughts that's created as chemicals called neurotransmitters—acetylcholine, in particular—and electrical impulses trace pathways through the brain. As we learn new information, the interconnections, or synapses, between brain cells increase, creating a more complex network of associations. Orchestrating this process is the hippocampus, a part of the brain that determines what information goes into long-term memory. Unless new input has special meaning for you or is frequently repeated, you quickly forget it....

Vitamin E is well-recognized as an antioxidant and in daily doses of 800 to 2,000 mg can have blood-thinning properties. Two other nutrients that may sharpen the mind are the omega-3 fatty acids docosahexaenoic acid (DHA) and phosphotidyl serine (PS). Brain cells are made largely of fatty acids, and these supplements may keep them supple.

Before you rush to the health-food store, note that you can get a similar benefit by eating lots of fruit, vegetables, and fish. "Fruits and vegetables are found more and more to have important antioxidant effects in the body," says the National Institute of Mental Health's Cott. Salmon, tuna, sardines, and canola and flaxseed oil are all rich sources of omega-3 fatty acids.

Downtime. Other considerations affect memory as well. Stress and depression often appear to impair memory because they sap mental energy. And many people think they are becoming forgetful when in fact they're too busy to keep track of everything they have to do. "A common misconception is that you're having memory problems when you're not really paying attention," says Tun. "For people in middle age, it can be important to have some downtime to relax." ...

Physical exercise is equally important. Brain cells need oxygen and regular blood flow, and aerobic exercise helps prevent cardiac conditions that can lead to dementia. It all boils down to the maxim that what is healthy for the body is healthy for the mind.[1]

FOR DISCUSSION

How can you enhance your memory about the contents of this chapter for your next test?

The opening news story reveals that our memories are influenced by what we eat, how we feel, how much we sleep, and whether or not we exercise. This is important to remember as you read this chapter because we use information contained in memory to interpret the world around us, and memory influences our performance on a variety of tasks.[2] As human beings, we constantly strive to make sense of our surroundings. The resulting knowledge influences our behavior and helps us navigate our way through life. Think of the perceptual process that occurs when meeting someone for the first time. Your attention is drawn to the individual's physical appearance, mannerisms, actions, and reactions to what you say and do. You ultimately arrive at conclusions based on your perceptions of this social interaction. The brown-haired, green-eyed individual turns out to be friendly and fond of outdoor activities. You further conclude that you like this person and then ask him or her to go to a concert, calling the person by the name you stored in memory.

This reciprocal process of perception, interpretation, and behavioral response also applies at work. A field study illustrates this relationship. Researchers wanted to know whether employees' perceptions of how much an organization valued them affected their behavior and attitudes. The researchers asked samples of high school teachers, brokerage-firm clerks, manufacturing workers, insurance representatives, and police officers to indicate their perception of the extent to which their organization valued their contributions and their well-being. Employees who perceived that their organization cared about them reciprocated with reduced absenteeism, increased performance, innovation, and positive work attitudes.[3] This study illustrates the importance of employees' perceptions. Let us now begin our exploration of the perceptual process and its associated outcomes.

In this chapter we focus on (1) a social information processing model of perception, (2) stereotypes, (3) the self-fulfilling prophecy, and (4) how causal attributions are used to interpret behavior.

A Social Information Processing Model of Perception

Perception is a cognitive process that enables us to interpret and understand our surroundings. Recognition of objects is one of this process's major functions. For example, both people and animals recognize familiar objects in their environments. You would recognize a picture of your best friend; dogs and cats can recognize their food dishes or a favorite toy. Reading involves recognition of visual patterns representing letters in the alphabet. People must recognize objects to meaningfully interact with their environment. But since OB's principal focus is on people, the following discussion emphasizes *social* perception rather than object perception.

The study of how people perceive one another has been labeled *social cognition* and *social information processing.* In contrast to the perception of objects,

> Social cognition is the study of how people make sense of other people and themselves. It focuses on how ordinary people think about people and how they think they think about people....
>
> Research on social cognition also goes beyond naive psychology. The study of social cognition entails a fine-grained analysis of how people think about themselves and others, and it leans heavily on the theory and methods of cognitive psychology.[4]

Moreover, while general theories of perception date back many years, the study of social perception is relatively new, having originated about 1976.

Perception
Process of interpreting one's environment.

Four-Stage Sequence and a Working Example

Social perception involves a four-stage information processing sequence (hence, the label "social information processing"). Figure 6–1 illustrates a basic social information processing model. Three of the stages in this model—selective attention/comprehension, encoding and simplification, and storage and retention—describe how specific social information is observed and stored in memory. The fourth and final stage, retrieval and response, involves turning mental representations into real-world judgments and decisions.

Figure 6–1   *Social Perception: A Social Information Processing Model*

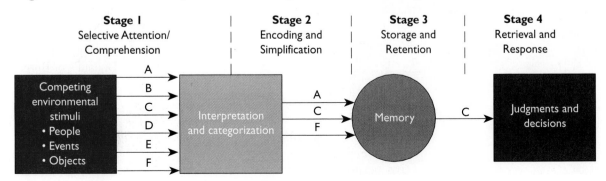

Keep the following everyday example in mind as we look at the four stages of social perception. Suppose you were thinking of taking a course in, say, personal finance. Three professors teach the same course, using different types of instruction and testing procedures. Through personal experience, you have come to prefer good professors who rely on the case method of instruction and essay tests. According to social perception theory, you would likely arrive at a decision regarding which professor to take as follows:

Stage 1: Selective Attention/Comprehension

People are constantly bombarded by physical and social stimuli in the environment. Since they do not have the mental capacity to fully comprehend all this information, they selectively perceive subsets of environmental stimuli. This is where attention plays a role. **Attention** is the process of becoming consciously aware of something or someone. Attention can be focused on information either from the environment or from memory. Regarding the latter situation, if you sometimes find yourself thinking about totally unrelated events or people while reading a textbook, your memory is the focus of your attention. Research has shown that people tend to pay attention to salient stimuli.

Attention
Being consciously aware of something or someone.

Salient Stimuli   Something is *salient* when it stands out from its context. For example, a 250-pound man would certainly be salient in a women's aerobics class but not at a meeting of the National Football League Players' Association. Social salience is determined by several factors, including

- Being novel (the only person in a group of that race, gender, hair color, or age).

- Being bright (wearing a yellow shirt).

- Being unusual for that person (behaving in an unexpected way, such as a person with a fear of heights climbing a steep mountain).

- Being unusual for a person's social category (such as a company president driving a motorcycle to work).

- Being unusual for people in general (driving 20 miles per hour in a 55-mph speed zone).

- Being extremely positive (a noted celebrity) or negative (the victim of a bad traffic accident).

- Being dominant in the visual field (sitting at the head of the table).[5]

One's needs and goals often dictate which stimuli are salient. For a driver whose gas gauge is on empty, an Exxon or Mobil sign is more salient than a McDonald's or Burger

What's the first thing that caught your attention on this page? People tend to pay attention to unusual or extraordinary stimuli.

(Markel/The Liaison Agency)

King sign. The reverse would be true for a hungry driver with a full gas tank. More-over, research shows that people have a tendency to pay more attention to negative than positive information. This leads to a negativity bias.[6] This bias helps explain the gawk-ing factor that slows traffic to a crawl following a car accident.

Back to Our Example   You begin your search for the "right" personal finance professor by asking friends who have taken classes from the three professors. You also may interview the various professors who teach the class to gather still more relevant information. Returning to Figure 6–1, all the information you obtain represents com-peting environmental stimuli labeled A through F. Because you are concerned about the method of instruction (e.g., line A in Figure 6–1), testing procedures (e.g., line C), and past grade distributions (e.g., line F), information in those areas is particularly salient to you. Figure 6–1 shows that these three salient pieces of information thus are per-ceived, and you then progress to the second stage of information processing. Mean-while, competing stimuli represented by lines B, D, and E in Figure 6–1 fail to get your attention and are discarded from further consideration.

Stage 2: Encoding and Simplification

Observed information is not stored in memory in its original form. Encoding is required; raw information is interpreted or translated into mental representations. To accomplish this, perceivers assign pieces of information to **cognitive categories.** "By *category* we mean a number of objects that are considered equivalent. Categories are generally designated by names, e.g., *dog, animal.*"[7] People, events, and objects are interpreted and evaluated by comparing their characteristics with information con-tained in schemata (or schema in singular form).

Schemata   According to social information processing theory, a **schema** represents a person's mental picture or summary of a particular event or type of stimulus.[8] For example, your restaurant schema probably is quite similar to the description provided in Table 6–1.

Cognitive-category labels are needed to make schemata meaningful. The OB Exercise on p 177, illustrates this by having you rate the comprehensiveness of a schema both with-out and with its associated category label. Take a moment now to complete this exercise.

Encoding Outcomes   We use the encoding process to interpret and evaluate our environment. Interestingly, this process can result in differing interpretations and eval-uations of the same person or event. The International OB on p 178, for example, explains how countries with universalist and particularist cultures encode and interpret events oppositely. Varying interpretations of what we observe occur for many reasons. First, people possess different information in the schemata used for interpretation. For instance, male CEOs and female executives disagree in their assessment of barriers pre-venting women from advancing to positions of corporate leadership. Women and men also have different ideas about what types of behavior constitute sexual harassment.[9] Second, our moods and emotions influence our focus of attention and evaluations.[10] Third, people tend to apply recently used cognitive categories during encoding. For example, you are more likely to interpret a neutral behavior exhibited by a professor as positive if you were recently thinking about positive categories and events.[11] Fourth, individual differences influence encoding. Pessimistic or depressed individuals, for instance, tend to interpret their surroundings more negatively than optimistic and happy

Cognitive categories
Mental depositories for storing information.

Schema
Mental picture of an event or object.

Table 6–1   *Restaurant Schema*

Schema: Restaurant.

Characters: Customers, hostess, waiter, chef, cashier.

Scene 1: Entering.
   Customer goes into restaurant.
   Customer finds a place to sit.
      He may find it himself.
      He may be seated by a hostess.
         He asks the hostess for a table.
         She gives him permission to go to the table.

Scene 2: Ordering.
   Customer receives a menu.
   Customer reads it.
   Customer decides what to order.
   Waiter takes the order.
      Waiter sees the customer.
      Waiter goes to the customer.
      Customer orders what he wants.
   Chef cooks the meal.

Scene 3: Eating.
   After some time the waiter brings the meal from the chef.
   Customer eats the meal.

Scene 4: Exiting.
   Customer asks the waiter for the check.
   Waiter gives the check to the customer.
   Customer leaves a tip.
      The size of the tip depends on the goodness of the service.
   Customer pays the cashier.
   Customer leaves the restaurant.

SOURCE: From D. Rumelhart, *Introduction to Human Information Processing* (New York: John Wiley & Sons, Inc., 1977. Reprinted by permission of John Wiley & Sons, Inc.

people.[12] The point is that we should not be surprised when people interpret and evaluate the same situation or event differently. Researchers are currently trying to identify the host of factors that influence the encoding process.

Back to Our Example   Having collected relevant information about the three personal finance professors and their approaches, you compare this information with other details contained in schemata. This leads you to form an impression and evaluation of what it would be like to take a course from each professor. In turn, the relevant information contained on paths A, C, and F in Figure 6–1 are passed along to the third stage of information processing.

Stage 3: Storage and Retention

This phase involves storage of information in long-term memory. Long-term memory is like an apartment complex consisting of separate units connected to one another. Although different people live in each apartment, they sometimes interact. In addition,

OB Exercise Does a Schema Improve the Comprehension of Written Material?

Instructions

The purpose of this exercise is to demonstrate the role of schema in encoding. First read the passage shown below. Once done, rate the comprehensiveness of what you read using the scale provided. Next, examine the schema label presented in Reference 8 in the Notes section at the end of the book. With this label in mind, reread the passage, and rate its comprehensiveness. Now think about the explanation for why your ratings changed. You just experienced the impact of schema in encoding.

Read This Passage

The procedure is actually quite simple. First you arrange things into different groups. Of course, one pile may be sufficient depending on how much there is to do. If you have to go somewhere else due to lack of facilities, that is the next step; otherwise you are pretty well set. It is important not to overdo things. That is, it is better to do too few things at once than too many. In the short run this may not seem important, but complications can easily arise. A mistake can be expensive as well. At first the whole procedure will seem complicated. Soon, however, it will become just another facet of life. It is difficult to foresee any end to the necessity for this task in the immediate future, but then you never can tell. After the procedure is completed, you arrange the materials into different groups again. Then they can be put into their appropriate places. Eventually they will be used once more, and the whole cycle will then have to be repeated. However, that is part of life.

Comprehensive Scale

Very		**Neither**		**Very**
Uncomprehensive		1 — 2 — 3 — 4 — 5		**Comprehensive**

SOURCE: J D Bransford and M K Johnson, "Contextual Prerequisite for Understanding: Some Investigations of Comprehension and Recall," *Journal of Verbal Learning and Verbal Behavior*, December 1972, p 722. Copyright © 1972 by Academic Press. Reproduced by permission of the publisher.

large apartment complexes have different wings (such as A, B, and C). Long-term memory similarly consists of separate but related categories. Like the individual apartments inhabited by unique residents, the connected categories contain different types of information. Information also passes among these categories. Finally, long-term memory is made up of three compartments (or wings) containing categories of information about events, semantic materials, and people.[13]

Event Memory   This compartment is composed of categories containing information about both specific and general events. These memories describe appropriate sequences of events in well-known situations, such as going to a restaurant (refer back to Table 6–1), going on a job interview, going to a food store, or going to a movie.

Semantic Memory   Semantic memory refers to general knowledge about the world. In so doing, it functions as a mental dictionary of concepts. Each concept contains a definition (e.g., a good leader) and associated traits (outgoing), emotional states (happy), physical characteristics (tall), and behaviors (works hard). Just as there are schemata for general events, concepts in semantic memory are stored as schemata. Given our previous discussion of managing diversity in Chapter 2 and International OB in Chapter 4, it should come as no surprise that there are cultural differences in the type of information stored in semantic memory.

International OB   Perception and Culture: Universalist (Rule-Based) versus Particularist (Relationship-Based) Cultures

There are two "pure" yet alternative types of judgment. At one extreme we encounter an obligation to adhere to standards which are universally agreed to by the culture in which we live. "Do not lie. Do not steal. Do unto others as you would have them do unto you" (the Golden Rule), and so on. At the other extreme we encounter particular obligations to people we know. "X is my dear friend, so obviously I would not lie to him or steal from him. It would hurt us both to show less than kindness to one another."

Universalist, or rule-based, behavior tends to be abstract. Try crossing the street when the light is red in a very rule-based society like Switzerland or Germany. Even if there is no traffic, you will still be frowned at. It also tends to imply equality in the sense that all persons falling under the rule should be treated the same. But situations are ordered by categories. For example, if "others" to whom you "do unto" are not categorized as human, the rules may not apply. Finally, rule-based conduct has a tendency to resist exceptions that might weaken that rule. There is a fear that once you start to make exceptions for illegal conduct the system will collapse.

Particularist judgments focus on the exceptional nature of present circumstances. This person is not "a citizen" but my friend, brother, husband, child, or person of unique importance to me, with special claims on my love or my hatred. I must therefore sustain, protect, or discount this person no matter what the rules say. [Particularist cultures are found in Russia, China, India, and Mexico.]

Business people from both societies will tend to think each other corrupt. A universalist will say of particularists, "they cannot be trusted because they will always help their friends" and a particularist, conversely, will say of universalists, "you cannot trust them; they would not even help a friend."

In practice we use both kinds of judgment, and in most situations we encounter they reinforce each other. If an employee is harassed in the workplace we would disapprove of this because "harassment is immoral and against company rules" and/or because "it was a terrible experience for Jennifer and really upset her." The universalist's chief objection, though, will be the breach of rules: "employees should not have to deal with harassment in the workplace; it is wrong." The particularist is likely to be more disapproving of the fact that it caused distress to poor Jennifer.

SOURCE: Excerpted from F Trompenaars and C Hampden-Turner, *Riding the Waves of Culture* (New York: McGraw-Hill, 1998), pp 31–32. © 1998. Reproduced with permission of the McGraw-Hill Companies.

Person Memory   Categories within this compartment contain information about a single individual (your supervisor) or groups of people (managers).

Back to Our Example   As the time draws near for you to decide which personal finance professor to take, your schemata of them are stored in the three categories of long-term memory. These schemata are available for immediate comparison and/or retrieval.

Stage 4: Retrieval and Response

People retrieve information from memory when they make judgments and decisions. Our ultimate judgments and decisions are either based on the process of drawing on, interpreting, and integrating categorical information stored in long-term memory or on retrieving a summary judgment that was already made.[14]

Concluding our example, it is registration day and you have to choose which professor to take for personal finance. After retrieving from memory your schemata-based impressions of the three professors, you select a good one who uses the case method and gives essay tests (line C in Figure 6–1). In contrast, you may choose your preferred professor by simply recalling the decision you made two weeks ago.

Managerial Implications

Social cognition is the window through which we all observe, interpret, and prepare our responses to people and events. A wide variety of managerial activities, organizational processes, and quality-of-life issues are thus affected by perception. Consider, for example, the following implications.

Hiring   Interviewers make hiring decisions based on their impression of how an applicant fits the perceived requirements of a job. Inaccurate impressions in either direction produce poor hiring decisions. Moreover, interviewers with racist or sexist schemata can undermine the accuracy and legality of hiring decisions. Those invalid schemata need to be confronted and improved through coaching and training. Failure to do so can lead to poor hiring decisions. For example, a study of 46 male and 66 female financial-institution managers revealed that their hiring decisions were biased by the physical attractiveness of applicants. More attractive men and women were hired over less attractive applicants with equal qualifications.[15] On the positive side, however, a recent study demonstrated that interviewer training can reduce the use of invalid schema. Training improved interviewers' ability to obtain high-quality, job-related information and to stay focused on the interview task. Trained interviewers provided more balanced judgments about applicants than did nontrained interviewers.[16]

Performance Appraisal   Faulty schemata about what constitutes good versus poor performance can lead to inaccurate performance appraisals, which erode work motivation, commitment, and loyalty. For example, a recent study of 166 production employees indicated that they had greater trust in management when they perceived that the performance appraisal process provided accurate evaluations of their performance.[17] Therefore, it is important for managers to accurately identify the behavioral characteristics and results indicative of good performance at the beginning of a performance review cycle. These characteristics then can serve as the benchmarks for evaluating employee performance. The importance of using objective rather than subjective measures of employee performance was highlighted in a meta-analysis involving 50 studies and 8,341 individuals. Results revealed that objective and subjective measures of employee performance were only moderately related. The researchers concluded that objective and subjective measures of performance are not interchangeable.[18] Managers are thus advised to use more objectively based measures of performance as much as possible because subjective indicators are prone to bias and inaccuracy. In those cases where the job does not possess objective measures of performance, however, managers should still use subjective evaluations. Furthermore, because memory for specific instances of employee performance deteriorates over time, managers need a mechanism for accurately recalling employee behavior.[19] Research reveals that individuals can be trained to be more accurate raters of performance.[20]

Leadership   Research demonstrates that employees' evaluations of leader effectiveness are influenced strongly by their schemata of good and poor leaders. A leader will have a difficult time influencing employees when he or she exhibits behaviors contained in employees' schemata of poor leaders. A team of researchers investigated the behaviors contained in our schemata of good and poor leaders. Good leaders were perceived as exhibiting the following behaviors: (1) assigning specific tasks to group members, (2) telling others that they had done well, (3) setting specific goals for the group, (4) letting other group members make decisions, (5) trying to get the group to work as a team, and (6) maintaining definite standards of performance. In contrast, poor leaders were perceived to exhibit these behaviors: (1) telling others that they had performed poorly, (2) insisting on having their own way, (3) doing things without explaining themselves, (4) expressing worry over the group members' suggestions, (5) frequently changing plans, and (6) letting the details of the task become overwhelming.[21]

Communication Managers need to remember that social perception is a screening process that can distort communication, both coming and going. Messages are interpreted and categorized according to schemata developed through past experiences and influenced by one's age, gender, and ethnic, geographic, and cultural orientations. Effective communicators try to tailor their messages to the receiver's perceptual schemata. This requires well-developed listening and observation skills and cross-cultural sensitivity.

Stereotypes: Perceptions about Groups of People

While it is often true that beauty is in the eye of the beholder, perception does result in some predictable outcomes. Managers aware of the perception process and its outcomes enjoy a competitive edge. The Walt Disney Company, for instance, takes full advantage of perceptual tendencies to influence customers' reactions to waiting in long lines at its theme parks:

> In order to make the experience less psychologically wearing, the waiting times posted by each attraction are generously overestimated, so that one comes away mysteriously grateful for having hung around 20 minutes for a 58-second twirl in the Alice in Wonderland teacups. ("I used the same trick when I was trying to sell sitcoms to the networks," says [Chairman and CEO Michael D.] Eisner. "I showed them a 23-minute 'Happy Days' pilot and told them it was a half hour. They thought it was the fastest-paced show they'd ever seen.")
> The lines, moreover, are always moving, even if what looks like the end is actually the start of a second set of switchbacks leading to—oh, no!—a pre-ride waiting area. Those little tricks of the theme park mean a lot.[22]

Likewise, managers can use knowledge of perceptual outcomes to help them interact more effectively with employees. For example, Table 6–2 describes five common perceptual errors. Since these perceptual errors often distort the evaluation of job applicants and of employee performance, managers need to guard against them. This section examines one of the most important and potentially harmful perceptual outcomes associated with person perception: stereotypes. After exploring the process of stereotype formation and maintenance, we discuss sex-role stereotypes, age stereotypes, race stereotypes, disability stereotypes, and the managerial challenge to avoid stereotypical biases.

Stereotype Formation and Maintenance

Stereotype

Beliefs about the characteristics of a group.

"A **stereotype** is an individual's set of beliefs about the characteristics or attributes of a group."[23] Stereotypes are not always negative. For example, the belief that engineers are good at math is certainly part of a stereotype. Stereotypes may or may not be accurate. Engineers may in fact be better at math than the general population. In general, stereotypic characteristics are used to differentiate a particular group of people from other groups.[24]

Table 6–2   *Commonly Found Perceptual Errors*

Perceptual Error	Description	Example
Halo	A rater forms a overall impression about an object and then uses that impression to bias ratings about the object.	Rating a professor high on the teaching dimensions of ability to motivate students, knowledge, and communication because we like him or her.
Leniency	A personal characteristic that leads an individual to consistently evaluate other people or objects in an extremely positive fashion.	Rating a professor high on all dimensions of performance regardless of his or her actual performance. The rater who hates to say negative things about others.
Central tendency	The tendency to avoid all extreme judgments and rate people and objects as average or neutral.	Rating a professor average on all dimensions of performance regardless of his or her actual performance.
Recency effects	The tendency to remember recent information. If the recent information is negative, the person or object is evaluated negatively.	Although a professor has given good lectures for 12 to 15 weeks, he or she is evaluated negatively because lectures over the last 3 weeks were done poorly.
Contrast effects	The tendency to evaluate people or objects by comparing them with characteristics of recently observed people or objects.	Rating a good professor as average because you compared his or her performance with three of the best professors you have ever had in college. You are currently taking courses from the three excellent professors.

Consider walking into a business meeting with 10 people situated around a conference table. You notice a male at the head of the table and a woman seated immediately to his right, taking notes. Due to ingrained stereotypes, you might assume that the man is the top-ranking person in the room and the woman, his administrative assistant. This example highlights how people use stereotypes to interpret their environment and to make judgments about others.

Unfortunately, stereotypes can lead to poor decisions, can create barriers for women, older individuals, people of color, and people with disabilities, and can undermine loyalty and job satisfaction. For example, a recent study of 280 minority executives revealed that 40% believed that they had been denied well-deserved promotions because of discrimination. Another sample of 2,958 workers indicated that women and people of color perceived lower chances of advancement than whites. Finally, respondents who saw little opportunity for advancement tended to be less loyal, less committed, and less satisfied with their jobs.[25]

Stereotyping is a four-step process. It begins by categorizing people into groups according to various criteria, such as gender, age, race, and occupation. Next, we infer that all people within a particular category possess the same traits or characteristics (e.g., all women are nurturing, older people have more job-related accidents, all African-Americans are good athletes, all professors are absentminded). Then, we form expectations of others and interpret their behavior according to our stereotypes. Finally, stereotypes are maintained by (1) overestimating the frequency of stereotypic behaviors exhibited by others, (2) incorrectly explaining expected and unexpected behaviors, and (3) differentiating minority individuals from oneself.[26] Although these steps are self-reinforcing, there are ways to break the chain of stereotyping.

Research shows that the use of stereotypes is influenced by the amount and type of information available to an individual and his or her motivation to accurately process information.[27] People are less apt to use stereotypes to judge others when they encounter salient information that is highly inconsistent with a stereotype. For instance, you are unlikely to assign stereotypic "professor" traits to a new professor you have this semester if he or she rides a Harley-Davidson, wears leather pants to class, and has a pierced nose. People also are less likely to rely on stereotypes when they are motivated to avoid using them. That is, accurate information processing requires mental effort. Stereotyping is generally viewed as a less effortful strategy of information processing. Let us now take a look at different types of stereotypes and consider additional methods for reducing their biasing effects.

Sex-Role Stereotypes

Sex-role stereotype
Beliefs about appropriate roles for men and women.

A **sex-role stereotype** is the belief that differing traits and abilities make men and women particularly well suited to different roles. For example, gender stereotypes view women as more expressive, less independent, more emotional, less logical, less quantitatively oriented, and more participative than men. Men, on the other hand, are more often perceived as lacking interpersonal sensitivity and warmth, less expressive, less apt to ask for directions, more quantitatively oriented, and more autocratic and directive than women.[28] Although research demonstrates that men and women do not systematically differ in the manner suggested by traditional stereotypes,[29] these stereotypes still persist. A study compared sex-role stereotypes held by men and women from five countries: China, Japan, Germany, the United Kingdom, and the United States. Males in all five countries perceived that successful managers possessed characteristics and traits more commonly ascribed to men in general than to women in general. Among the females, the same pattern of managerial sex typing was found in all countries except the United States. US females perceived that males and females were equally likely to possess traits necessary for managerial success.[30] The key question now becomes whether these stereotypes influence the hiring, evaluation, and promotion of people at work.

A meta-analysis of 19 studies comprising 1,842 individuals found no significant relationships between applicant gender and hiring recommendations.[31] A second meta-analysis of 24 experimental studies revealed that men and women received similar performance ratings for the same level of task performance. Stated differently, there was no pro-male bias. These experimental results were further supported in a field study of female and male professors.[32] Unfortunately, results pertaining to promotion decisions are not as promising. A field study of 682 employees in a multinational *Fortune* 500 company revealed that gender was significantly related to promotion potential ratings. Men received more favorable evaluations than women in spite of controlling for age, education, organizational tenure, salary grade, and type of job.[33] Another recent study of 100 male and female U.S. Army commissioned officers at the rank of captain unfortunately produced similar results. Men were consistently judged to be better leaders than women.[34] The existence of sex-role stereotypes may partially explain this finding.

Age Stereotypes

Age stereotypes reinforce age discrimination because of their negative orientation. For example, long-standing age stereotypes depict older workers as less satisfied, not as involved with their work, less motivated, not as committed, less productive than their younger co-workers, and more apt to be absent from work. Older employees are also perceived as being more accident prone. As with sex-role stereotypes, these age stereotypes are more fiction than fact.

OB researcher Susan Rhodes sought to determine whether age stereotypes were supported by data from 185 different studies. She discovered that as age increases so do employees' job satisfaction, job involvement, internal work motivation, and organizational commitment. Moreover, older workers were not more accident prone. A recent report by the Bureau of Labor Statistics supports this last finding. The Bureau found that employees 55 and over were one-third less likely than younger workers to be injured enough at work to take time off.[35]

Results are not as clear cut regarding job performance. A meta-analysis of 96 studies representing 38,983 people and a cross section of jobs revealed that age and job performance were unrelated.[36] Some OB researchers, however, believe that this finding does not reflect the true relationship between age and performance. They propose that the relationship between age and performance changes as people grow older.[37] This idea was tested on data obtained from 24,219 individuals. In support of this hypothesis, results revealed that age was positively related to performance for younger employees (25 to 30 years of age) and then plateaued: Older employees were not less productive. Age and experience also predicted performance better for more complex jobs than other jobs, and job experience had a stronger relationship with performance than age.[38] Another recent study examined memory, reasoning, spatial relations, and dual tasking for 1,000 doctors, ages 25 to 92, and 600 other adults. The researchers concluded "that a large proportion of older individuals scored as well or better on aptitude tests as those in the prime of life. We call these intellectually vigorous individuals 'optimal agers' "[39]

What about turnover and absenteeism? A meta-analysis containing 29 samples and a total of 12,356 individuals revealed that age and turnover were negatively related. That is, older employees quit less often than younger employees did. Similarly, another meta-analysis of 34 studies encompassing 7,772 workers indicated that age was inversely related to both voluntary (a day at the beach) and involuntary (sick day) absenteeism.[40] Contrary to stereotypes, older workers are ready and able to meet their job requirements. Moreover, results from the meta-analysis suggest managers should focus more attention on the turnover and absenteeism among younger workers than among older workers.

Race Stereotypes

There are many different racial stereotypes that exist. For instance, African-Americans have been viewed as athletic and aggressive; Asians as quiet, introverted, smarter, and more quantitatively oriented; and Hispanics as family oriented and religious.[41]

Unfortunately, negative stereotypes such as some of those just listed are still apparent in many organizations. Consider the evidence presented in the following paragraphs.

There is not a large percentage of African-American, Hispanic, and Asian managers in the United States. African-Americans and Hispanics held 7% and 4.5%, respectively, of all managerial and professional jobs in 1996. Further, African-Americans and Hispanics together accounted for less than 2% of senior executive positions in the United States in 1999.[42] Negative racial stereotypes are one of several potential explanations for this state of affairs. Furthermore, a study examined the relationship of race to employee attitudes across 814 African-American managers and 814 white managers. Results demonstrated that African-Americans, when compared with whites, felt less accepted by peers, perceived lower managerial discretion on their jobs, reached career plateaus more frequently, noted lower levels of career satisfaction, and received lower performance ratings.[43] Negative findings such as these prompted researchers to investigate if race stereotypes actually bias hiring decisions, performance ratings, and promotion decisions.

A meta-analysis of interview decisions from 31 studies with total samples of 4,169 African-Americans and 6,307 whites revealed that whites received higher interviewer evaluations. Another study of 2,805 interviews uncovered a same-race bias for Hispanics and African-Americans, but not for whites. That is, Hispanics and African-American interviewers evaluated applicants of their own race more favorably than applicants of other races. White interviewers did not exhibit any such bias.[44] Performance ratings were found to be unbiased in two studies that used large samples of 21,547 and 39,537 rater-ratee pairs of African-American and white employees, respectively, from throughout the United States. These findings revealed that African-American and white managers did not differentially evaluate their employees based on race.[45] Finally, a study of 153 police officers' promotion decisions by panel interviews indicated a same-race rating effect. That is, candidates received higher evaluations when they were racially similar to the interviewers.[46] Given the increasing number of people of color that will enter the workforce over the next 10 years (recall our discussion in Chapter 2), employers should focus on nurturing and developing women and people of color as well as increasing managers' sensitivities to invalid racial stereotypes.

Disability Stereotypes

People with disabilities not only face negative stereotypes that affect their employability, but they also can be stigmatized by the general population. Consider Paul Stephen Miller's experience after he graduated from Harvard Law School near the top of his class:

> He looked forward to a future full of possibilities, having graduated from arguably the top law school in the country, a virtual guarantee of a high-paying job in an elite law firm. While his classmates snared those prestigious jobs, over 40 firms with whom he interviewed rejected him. Miller is a dwarf. He prefers to call himself "short stature." Most employers simply explained that there were other "more qualified" candidates. A Philadelphia firm explained, however, that while impressed with his credentials, they feared their clients might see Miller in the hallway and "think we were running some sort of circus freak show."[47]

Unfortunately, Mr Miller's experience is not atypical. Although two out of three individuals with disabilities can and want to work, only 28% are employed.[48] In addition, disabled employees make less money on average than their peers. For instance, men without disabilities, with moderate disabilities, and with severe disabilities earned $2,633, $2,244, and $1,663, respectively, in 1994.[49] Moreover, people with disabilities face stereotypes that depict them as more likely to miss work, more costly to employ, more difficult to manage, and defective. So what do we know about the performance and costs of employing people with disabilities?

A Harris poll in 1987 found that almost 90% of disabled workers received "good" or "excellent" performance ratings. They also were found to perform their jobs just as well as employees without disabilities, and they were not more difficult to manage. A 1995 Harris poll indicated that employers supported policies to increase the employment of disabled people because they were so pleased with the performance of their disabled employees. DuPont, for example, found that disabled employees had higher safety ratings than their nondisabled counterparts. The stereotypes about disabled employees being expensive to accommodate also is untrue. Nearly 20% of accommodations cost nothing, and 50% cost less than $500.[50]

Managerial Challenges and Recommendations

The key managerial challenge is to make decisions that are blind to gender, age, race, and disabilities. To do so, organizations first need to educate themselves about the problem of stereotyping through employee training. Training also can be used to equip managers with the skills needed to handle unique situations associated with managing employees with mental disabilities. The next step entails engaging in a broad effort to reduce stereotypes throughout the organization. The International OB on p 186, discusses how the Bank of Montreal tried to accomplish this recommendation. Social scientists believe that "quality" interpersonal contact among mixed groups is the best way to reduce stereotypes because it provides people with more accurate data about the characteristics of other groups of people. As such, organizations should create opportunities for diverse employees to meet and work together in cooperative groups of equal status.

Another recommendation is for managers to identify valid individual differences (discussed in Chapter 5) that differentiate between successful and unsuccessful performers. As previously discussed, for instance, research reveals experience is a better predictor of performance than age. Research also shows that managers can be trained to use these valid criteria when hiring applicants and evaluating employee performance.[51]

Removing promotional barriers for men and women, people of color, and for persons with disabilities is another viable solution to alleviating the stereotyping problem. This can be accomplished by minimizing the differences in job experience across groups of people. Similar experience, coupled with the accurate evaluation of performance, helps managers to make decisions that are blind to gender, age, race, and disability.

Ethics at Work

Imagine that you are a postal inspector faced with the following situation: In the summer of 1997, US Postal Service officials in a North Carolina district office were scrambling to resolve a personnel problem that was on the verge of exploding into violence. A postal employee had threatened his co-workers and was removed from the workplace. He applied for a mental disability retirement, but his application was stalled. As the delay increased, he became more and more irate. Postal officials believed the employee was capable of returning to work to carry out his previous threats, so they contacted postal inspectors.

SOURCE: Excerpted from D Bencivenga, "Dealing with the Dark Side," *HR Magazine*, January 1999, p 54.

You Decide . . .
What would you do? Explain the pros and cons of your solution.

For an interpretation of this situation, visit our Web site **www.mhhe.com/kreitner.**

There are several recommendations that can be pursued based on the documented relationship between age and performance:

1. Because performance plateaus with age for noncomplex jobs, organizations may use the variety of job design techniques discussed in Chapter 7 to increase employees' intrinsic motivation.

2. Organizations may need to consider using incentives to motivate employees to upgrade their skills and abilities. This will help avoid unnecessary plateaus.[52]

3. It may be advisable to hire older people in order to acquire their accumulated experience. This is especially useful for highly complex jobs. Moreover, hiring older workers is a good solution for reducing turnover, providing role models for younger employees, and coping with the current shortage of qualified entry-level workers.

It is important to obtain top management's commitment and support to eliminate the organizational practices that support or reinforce stereotyping and discriminatory decisions. Research clearly demonstrates that top management support is essential to successful implementation of the types of organizational changes being recommended.[53]

Self-Fulfilling Prophecy: The Pygmalion Effect

Self-fulfilling prophecy
People's expectations determine behavior and performance.

Historical roots of the self-fulfilling prophecy are found in Greek mythology. According to mythology, Pygmalion was a sculptor who hated women yet fell in love with an ivory statue he carved of a beautiful woman. He became so infatuated with the statue that he prayed to the goddess Aphrodite to bring her to life. The goddess heard his prayer, granted his wish, and Pygmalion's statue came to life. The essence of the **self-fulfilling prophecy,** or Pygmalion effect, is that people's expectations or beliefs determine their behavior and performance, thus serving to make their expectations come true. In other words, we strive to validate our *perceptions* of reality, no matter how faulty they may be. Thus, the self-fulfilling prophecy is an important perceptual outcome we need to better understand.

Research and an Explanatory Model

The self-fulfilling prophecy was first demonstrated in an academic environment. After giving a bogus test of academic potential to students from grades 1 to 6, researchers informed teachers that certain students had high potential for achievement. In reality, students were randomly assigned to the "high potential" and "control" (normal potential) groups. Results showed that children designated as having high potential obtained significantly greater increases in both IQ scores and reading ability than did the control students.[54] The teachers of the supposedly high potential group got better results because their high expectations caused them to give harder assignments, more feedback, and more recognition of achievement. Students in the normal potential group did not excel because their teachers did not expect outstanding results.

Research similarly has shown that by raising instructors' and managers' expectations for individuals performing a wide variety of tasks, higher levels of achievement/productivity can be obtained.[55] Subjects in these field studies included airmen at the United States Air Force Academy Preparatory School, disadvantaged people in job-training programs, electronics assemblers, trainees in a military command course, US naval personnel, and cadets in a naval officer course in the Israel Defense Forces. There is an interesting trend inherent in research supporting the Pygmalion effect. All studies exclusively involved men.

To overcome this limitation, a recent team of researchers conducted two experimental studies on samples of women and men cadets in the Israel Defense Forces. Results revealed that the Pygmalion effect was produced for both women and men cadets, but only when the leader was a male. Female leaders did not produce a significant Pygmalion effect. This finding must be considered in light of the fact that women were rated as better leaders than men in the Israel Defense Forces. The researchers concluded that the Pygmalion effect clearly works on both women and men when the leader is male, but not when the leader is female.[56] Future research is obviously needed to uncover the cause of these gender-based differences.

Figure 6–2 presents a model of the self-fulfilling prophecy that helps explain these results. This model attempts to outline how supervisory expectations affect employee performance. As indicated, high supervisory expectancy produces better leadership (linkage 1), which subsequently leads employees to develop higher self-expectations (linkage 2). Higher expectations motivate workers to exert more effort (linkage 3), ultimately increasing performance (linkage 4) and supervisory expectancies (linkage 5). Successful performance also improves an employee's self-expectancy for achievement (linkage 6). A team of researchers recently coined the term the "set-up-to-fail syndrome" to represent the negative side of the performance enhancing process depicted in Figure 6–2.[57] Let us consider how it works.

Say that an employee makes a mistake such as losing notes during a meeting or exhibits poor performance on a task—turning in a report a day late. A manager then begins to wonder if this person has what it takes to be successful in the organization. This doubt leads the manager to watch this person more carefully. The employee of course notices this doubt and begins to sense a loss of trust. The suspect employee then responds in one of two ways. He or she may doubt his or her own judgment and competence. This in turn leads the individual to become more risk averse and to decrease the amount of ideas and suggestions for the manager's critical review. The manager notices this behavior and interprets it as an example of less initiative. Oppositely, the employee may take on more and more responsibility so that he or she can demonstrate his or her competence and worth. This is likely to cause the employee to screw up on something, which in turn reinforces the manager's suspicions.[58] You can see that this process results in a destructive relationship

Figure 6–2   *A Model of the Self-Fulfilling Prophecy*

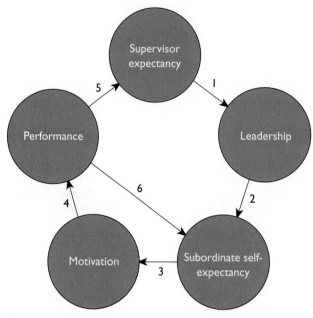

SOURCE: D Eden, "Self-Fulfilling Prophecy as a Management Tool: Harnessing Pygmalion," *Academy of Management Review*, January 1984, p 67. Used with permission.

that is fueled by negative expectations. The point to remember is that the self-fulfilling prophecy works in both directions. The next section discusses ideas for enhancing the Pygmalion effect and reducing the set-up-to-fail syndrome.

Putting the Self-Fulfilling Prophecy to Work

Largely due to the Pygmalion effect, managerial expectations powerfully influence employee behavior and performance. Consequently, managers need to harness the Pygmalion effect by building a hierarchical framework that reinforces positive performance expectations throughout the organization.

Employees' self-expectations are the foundation of this framework. In turn, positive self-expectations improve interpersonal expectations by encouraging people to work toward common goals. This cooperation enhances group-level productivity and promotes positive performance expectations within the work group. At Microsoft Corporation, for example, employees routinely put in 75-hour weeks, especially when work groups are trying to meet shipment deadlines for new products. Because Microsoft is known for meeting its deadlines, positive group-level expectations help create and reinforce an organizational culture of high expectancy for success. This process then excites people about working for the organization, thereby reducing turnover.[59]

Because positive self-expectations are the foundation for creating an organization-wide Pygmalion effect, let us consider how managers can create positive performance expectations. This task may be accomplished by using various combinations of the following:

1. Recognize that everyone has the potential to increase his or her performance.

2. Instill confidence in your staff.

3. Set high performance goals.

4. Positively reinforce employees for a job well done.

5. Provide constructive feedback when necessary.

6. Help employees advance through the organization.

7. Introduce new employees as if they have outstanding potential.

8. Become aware of your personal prejudices and nonverbal messages that may discourage others.

9. Encourage employees to visualize the successful execution of tasks.

10. Help employees master key skills and tasks.[60]

Causal Attributions

Attribution theory is based on the premise that people attempt to infer causes for observed behavior. Rightly or wrongly, we constantly formulate cause-and-effect explanations for our own and others' behavior. Attributional statements such as the following are common: "Joe drinks too much because he has no willpower; but I need a couple of drinks after work because I'm under a lot of pressure." Formally defined, **causal attributions** are suspected or inferred causes of behavior. Even though our causal attributions tend to be self-serving and are often invalid, it is important to understand how people formulate attributions because they profoundly affect organizational behavior. For example, a supervisor who attributes an employee's poor performance to a lack of effort might reprimand that individual. However, training might be deemed necessary if the supervisor attributes the poor performance to a lack of ability.

Causal attributions
Suspected or inferred causes of behavior.

Generally speaking, people formulate causal attributions by considering the events preceding an observed behavior. This section introduces and explores two different widely cited attribution models proposed by Harold Kelley and Bernard Weiner. Attributional tendencies, research, and related managerial implications also are discussed.

Kelley's Model of Attribution

Current models of attribution, such as Kelley's, are based on the pioneering work of the late Fritz Heider. Heider, the founder of attribution theory, proposed that behavior can be attributed either to **internal factors** within a person (such as ability) or to **external factors** within the environment (such as a difficult task). This line of thought parallels the idea of an internal versus external locus of control, as discussed in Chapter 5. Building on Heider's work, Kelley attempted to pinpoint major antecedents of internal and external attributions. Kelley hypothesized that people make causal attributions after gathering information about three dimensions of behavior: consensus, distinctiveness, and consistency.[61] These dimensions vary independently, thus forming various combinations and leading to differing attributions.

Internal factors
Personal characteristics that cause behavior.

External factors
Environmental characteristics that cause behavior.

Figure 6–3 presents performance charts showing low versus high consensus, distinctiveness, and consistency. These charts are now used to help develop a working knowledge of all three dimensions in Kelley's model.

- *Consensus* involves a comparison of an individual's behavior with that of his or her peers. There is high consensus when one acts like the rest of the group and low consensus when one acts differently. As shown in Figure 6–3, high consensus is indicated when persons A, B, C, D, and E obtain similar levels of individual performance. In contrast, person C's performance is low in consensus because it significantly varies from the performance of persons A, B, D, and E.

Figure 6–3   *Performance Charts Showing Low and High Consensus, Distinctiveness, and Consistency Information*

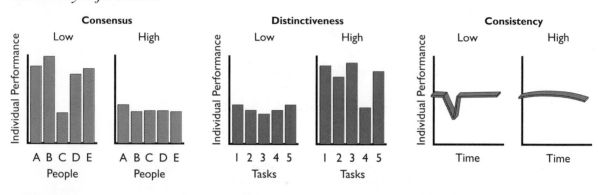

SOURCE: K A Brown, "Explaining Group Poor Performance: An Attributional Analysis," *Academy of Management Review,* January 1984, p 56. Used with permission.

- *Distinctiveness* is determined by comparing a person's behavior on one task with his or her behavior on other tasks. High distinctiveness means the individual has performed the task in question in a significantly different manner than he or she has performed other tasks. Low distinctiveness means stable performance or quality from one task to another. Figure 6–3 reveals that the employee's performance on task 4 is highly distinctive because it significantly varies from his or her performance on tasks 1, 2, 3, and 5.

- *Consistency* is determined by judging if the individual's performance on a given task is consistent over time. High consistency implies that a person performs a certain task the same, time after time. Unstable performance of a given task over time would mean low consistency. The downward spike in performance depicted in the consistency graph of Figure 6–3 represents low consistency. In this case, the employee's performance on a given task varied over time.

It is important to remember that consensus relates to other *people,* distinctiveness relates to other *tasks,* and consistency relates to *time.* The question now is: How does information about these three dimensions of behavior lead to internal or external attributions?

Kelley hypothesized that people attribute behavior to *external* causes (environmental factors) when they perceive high consensus, high distinctiveness, and low consistency. *Internal* attributions (personal factors) tend to be made when observed behavior is characterized by low consensus, low distinctiveness, and high consistency. So, for example, when all employees are performing poorly (high consensus), when the poor performance occurs on only one of several tasks (high distinctiveness), and the poor performance occurs during only one time period (low consistency), a supervisor will probably attribute an employee's poor performance to an external source such as peer pressure or an overly difficult task. In contrast, performance will be attributed to an employee's personal characteristics (an internal attribution) when only the individual in question is performing poorly (low consensus), when the inferior performance is found across several tasks (low distinctiveness), and when the low performance has persisted over time (high consistency). Many studies supported this predicted pattern of attributions.[62]

Figure 6–4   *A Modified Version of Weiner's Attribution Model*

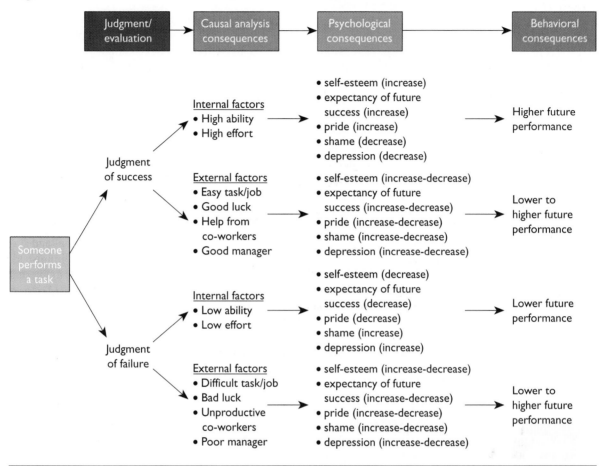

SOURCE: Based in part on B Weiner, "An Attributional Theory of Achievement Motivation and Emotion," *Psychological Review,* October 1985, pp 548–73; and T S Bateman, G R Ferris, and S Strasser, "The 'Why' behind Individual Work Performance," *Management Review,* October 1984, p 71.

Weiner's Model of Attribution

Bernard Weiner, a noted motivation theorist, developed an attribution model to explain achievement behavior and to predict subsequent changes in motivation and performance. Figure 6–4 presents a modified version of his model. Weiner believes that the attribution process begins after an individual performs a task. A person's performance leads him or her to judge whether it was successful or unsuccessful. This evaluation then produces a causal analysis to determine if the performance was due to internal or external factors. Figure 6–4 shows that ability and effort are the primary internal causes of performance and task difficulty, luck, and help from others the key external causes. These attributions for success and failure then influence how individuals feel about themselves. For instance, a meta-analysis of 104 studies involving almost 15,000 subjects found that people who attributed failure to their lack of ability (as opposed to bad luck) experienced psychological depression. The exact opposite attributions (to good luck rather than to high ability) tended to trigger depression in people experiencing positive events. In short, perceived bad luck took the sting out of a negative outcome, but perceived good luck reduced the joy associated with success.[63]

Returning to Figure 6–4, note that the psychological consequences can either increase or decrease depending on the causes of performance. For example, your self-esteem is likely to increase after achieving an "A" on your next exam if you believe that your performance was due to your ability or effort. In contrast, this same grade can either increase or decrease your self-esteem if you believe that the test was easy. Finally, the feelings that people have about their past performance influences future performance. Figure 6–4 reveals that future performance is higher when individuals attribute success to internal causes and lower when failure is attributed to external factors. Future performance is more uncertain when individuals attribute either their success or failure to external causes.

In further support of Weiner's model, a study of 130 male salespeople in the United Kingdom revealed that positive, internal attributions for success were associated with higher sales and performance ratings.[64] A second study examined the attributional processes of 126 employees who were permanently displaced by a plant closing. Consistent with the model, as the explanation for job loss was attributed to internal and stable causes, life satisfaction, self-esteem, and expectations for reemployment diminished. Furthermore, research also shows that when individuals attribute their success to internal rather than external factors, they (1) have higher expectations for future success, (2) report a greater desire for achievement, and (3) set higher performance goals.[65]

Attributional Tendencies

Researchers have uncovered two attributional tendencies that distort one's interpretation of observed behavior—*fundamental attribution bias* and *self-serving bias.*

Fundamental attribution bias
Ignoring environmental factors that affect behavior.

Fundamental Attribution Bias   The **fundamental attribution bias** reflects one's tendency to attribute another person's behavior to his or her personal characteristics, as opposed to situational factors. This bias causes perceivers to ignore important environmental forces that often significantly affect behavior. For example, a study of 1,420 employees of a large utility company demonstrated that supervisors tended to make more internal attributions about worker accidents than did the workers. Interestingly, research also shows that people from Westernized cultures tend to exhibit the fundamental attribution bias more than individuals from East Asia.[66]

Two types of attributional tendencies distort our ability to interpret observed behavior—fundamental attribution bias and self-serving bias. When students attribute their good grades to ability or hard work, and bad grades to unfair tests or unclear lectures, they are exhibiting a self-serving bias.

(Tom Stewart/The Stock Market)

Self-Serving Bias   The **self-serving bias** represents one's tendency to take more personal responsibility for success than for failure. Referring again to Figure 6–4, employees tend to attribute their successes to internal factors (high ability and/or hard work) and their failures to uncontrollable external factors (tough job, bad luck, unproductive co-workers, or an unsympathetic boss).[67] This self-serving bias is evident in how students typically analyze their performance on exams. "A" students are likely to attribute their grade to high ability or hard work. "D" students, meanwhile, tend to pin the blame on factors like an unfair test, bad luck, or unclear lectures. Because of self-serving bias, it is very difficult to pin down personal responsibility for mistakes in today's complex organizations.

Self-serving bias
Taking more personal responsibility for success than failure.

Managerial Application and Implications

Attribution models can be used to explain how managers handle poorly performing employees. One study revealed that managers gave employees more immediate, frequent, and negative feedback when they attributed their performance to low effort. This reaction was even more pronounced when the manager's success was dependent on an employee's performance. A second study indicated that managers tended to transfer employees whose poor performance was attributed to a lack of ability. These same managers also decided to take no immediate action when poor performance was attributed to external factors beyond an individual's control.[68]

The preceding situations have several important implications for managers. First, managers tend to disproportionately attribute behavior to *internal* causes.[69] This can result in inaccurate evaluations of performance, leading to reduced employee motivation. No one likes to be blamed because of factors they perceive to be beyond their control. Further, because managers' responses to employee performance vary according to their attributions, attributional biases may lead to inappropriate managerial actions, including promotions, transfers, layoffs, and so forth. This can dampen motivation and performance. Attributional training sessions for managers are in order. Basic attributional processes can be explained, and managers can be taught to detect and avoid attributional biases. Finally, an employee's attributions for his or her own performance have dramatic effects on subsequent motivation, performance, and personal attitudes such as self-esteem. For instance, people tend to give up, develop lower expectations for future success, and experience decreased self-esteem when they attribute failure to a lack of ability. Fortunately, attributional retraining can improve both motivation and performance. Research shows that employees can be taught to attribute their failures to a lack of effort rather than to a lack of ability.[70] This attributional realignment paves the way for improved motivation and performance.

In summary, managers need to keep a finger on the pulse of employee attributions if they are to make full use of the motivation concepts in the next two chapters.

Summary of Key Concepts

1. *Describe perception in terms of the social information processing model.* Perception is a mental and cognitive process that enables us to interpret and understand our surroundings. Social perception, also known as social cognition and social information processing, is a four-stage process. The four stages are selective attention/comprehension, encoding and simplification, storage and retention, and retrieval and response. During social cognition, salient stimuli are matched with schemata, assigned to cognitive categories, and stored in long-term memory for events, semantic materials, or people.

2. *Identify and briefly explain four managerial implications of social perception.* Social perception affects hiring decisions, performance appraisals, leadership perceptions, and communication processes. Inaccurate schemata or racist and sexist schemata may be used to evaluate job applicants. Similarly, faulty schemata about what constitutes good versus poor performance can lead to inaccurate performance appraisals. Invalid schemata need to be identified and replaced with appropriate schemata through coaching and training. Further, managers are advised to use objective rather than subjective measures of performance. With respect to leadership, a leader will have a difficult time influencing employees when he or she exhibits behaviors contained in employees' schemata of poor leaders. Finally, communication is influenced by schemata used to interpret any message. Effective communicators try to tailor their messages to the receiver's perceptual schemata.

3. *Discuss stereotypes and the process of stereotype formation.* Stereotypes represent grossly oversimplified beliefs or expectations about groups of people. Stereotyping is a four-step process that begins by categorizing people into groups according to various criteria. Next, we infer that all people within a particular group possess the same traits or characteristics. Then, we form expectations of others and interpret their behavior according to our stereotypes. Finally, stereotypes are maintained by (*a*) overestimating the frequency of stereotypic behaviors exhibited by others, (*b*) incorrectly explaining expected and unexpected behaviors, and (*c*) differentiating minority individuals from oneself. The use of stereotypes is influenced by the amount and type of information available to an individual and his or her motivation to accurately process information.

4. *Summarize the managerial challenges and recommendations of sex-role, age, race, and disability stereotypes.* The key managerial challenge is to make decisions that are blind to gender, age, race, and disabilities. Training can be used to educate employees about the problem of stereotyping and to equip managers with the skills needed to handle unique situations associated with managing employees with mental disabilities. Because mixed-group contact reduces stereotyping, organizations should create opportunities for diverse employees to meet and work together in cooperative groups of equal status. Hiring decisions should be based on valid individual differences, and managers can be trained to use valid criteria when evaluating employee performance. Minimizing differences in job opportunities and experiences across groups of people can help alleviate promotional barriers. Job design techniques can be used to reduce performance plateaus associated with age. Organizations also may need to use incentives to motivate employees to upgrade their skills and abilities, and hiring older workers has many potential organizational benefits. It is critical to obtain top management's commitment and support to eliminate stereotyping and discriminatory decisions.

5. *Discuss how the self-fulfilling prophecy is created and how it can be used to improve individual and group productivity.* The self-fulfilling prophecy, also known as the Pygmalion effect, describes how people behave so their expectations come true. High managerial expectations foster high employee self-expectations. These, in turn, lead to greater effort and better performance, and yet higher expectations. Conversely, the set-up-to-fail syndrome represents the negative side of the self-fulfilling prophecy. Managers are encouraged to harness the Pygmalion effect by building a hierarchical framework that reinforces positive performance expectations throughout the organization.

6. *Explain, according to Kelley's model, how external and internal causal attributions are formulated.* Attribution theory attempts to describe how people infer causes for observed behavior. According to Kelley's model of causal attribution, external attributions tend to be made when consensus and distinctiveness are high and consistency is low. Internal (personal responsibility) attributions tend to be made when consensus and distinctiveness are low and consistency is high.

7. *Review Weiner's model of attribution.* Weiner's model of attribution predicts achievement behavior in terms of causal attributions. Attributions of ability, effort, task difficulty, luck, and help from others affect how individuals feel about themselves. In turn, these feelings directly influence subsequent achievement-related performance.

8. *Contrast the fundamental attribution bias and the self-serving bias.* Fundamental attribution bias involves emphasizing personal factors more than situational factors while formulating causal attributions for the behavior of others. Self-serving bias involves personalizing the causes of one's successes and externalizing the causes of one's failures.

Discussion Questions

1. Why is it important for managers to have a working knowledge of perception and attribution?

2. When you are sitting in class, what stimuli are salient? What is your schema for classroom activity?

3. Have you ever been stereotyped by someone else? Discuss.

4. Which type of stereotype (sex-role, age, race, or disability) do you believe is more pervasive in organizations? Why?

5. What evidence of self-fulfilling prophecies have you seen lately?

6. How might your professor use the process outlined in Figure 6–2 to improve the overall performance of the students in your class?

7. How would you formulate an attribution, according to Kelley's model, for the behavior of a classmate who starts arguing in class with your professor?

8. In what situations do you tend to attribute your successes/failures to luck? How well does Weiner's

attributional model in Figure 6–4 explain your answers? Explain.

9. Are poor people victimized by a fundamental attribution bias? Explain.

10. What evidence of the self-serving bias have you observed lately?

Internet Exercise

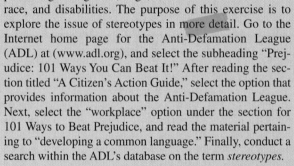

www.adl.org

This chapter examined the process of stereotype formation and discussed stereotypes pertaining to gender, age, race, and disabilities. The purpose of this exercise is to explore the issue of stereotypes in more detail. Go to the Internet home page for the Anti-Defamation League (ADL) at (www.adl.org), and select the subheading "Prejudice: 101 Ways You Can Beat It!" After reading the section titled "A Citizen's Action Guide," select the option that provides information about the Anti-Defamation League. Next, select the "workplace" option under the section for 101 Ways to Beat Prejudice, and read the material pertaining to "developing a common language." Finally, conduct a search within the ADL's database on the term *stereotypes*.

Questions

1. Who founded the ADL? What is the purpose of the ADL and how has it evolved?

2. What are the differences among stereotypes, prejudice, discrimination, and scapegoating?

3. How prevalent are anti-Semitic views? Who is most likely to hold anti-Semitic views?

4. How can organizations reduce the use of stereotypes and prejudice at work?

OB In Action Case Study

Do the Skills That Come with Age Count for Less and Less in Today's Organizations?[71]

America is no place to age gracefully. Of course, basketball players, dancers, and fashion models are finished young; mathematicians and chess players peak early too. So do construction workers and coal miners. Once you're 55, it's almost impossible to find a job in business. But a new trend is emerging: In corporate America, 40 is starting to look and feel old.

Since the early 1980s big companies have been getting rid of people. For a long time, though, seniority mattered. Hierarchy was respected too. If people had to be fired, the younger, junior people were usually the first to go. That's no longer true. The working world has changed. It has become faster and more efficient and, for many people, crueler. The unemployment rate hovers at 30-year lows; even so, companies announced the elimination of some 600,000 US jobs last year, according to Challenger Gray & Christmas, an outplacement firm that tracks such depressing data. There's no way to tell how many of those people are over 40, but this

much is sure: Companies today have less and less tolerance for people they believe are earning more than their output warrants. Such intolerance, or pragmatism, hits older workers hardest. The older an employee, the more likely it is he can be replaced by someone younger who earns half as much. "For my salary the company could hire two twenty-somethings," says a 41-year-old we spoke to. "I'm good at what I do. But am I better than two people? Even I know that's not true." Today, for many people, the longer you've been at one company, the more disposable you are. . . .

Perhaps technology is to blame. Maybe in this "new" economy, the old ways of doing business are indeed anachronistic—if the economy is new, who needs experience? Whatever the reason, in America today the skills that come with age and experience appear to count for less and less. It's hard to demonstrate with numbers, but a lot of people over 40 sense it: Youth, with its native optimism, is what companies want now. . . .

That so many workers are over 40 compounds the problem. In just four years, for the first time ever, there will be more workers over 40 than there are workers under 40. . . . All those people—the 78 million baby-boomers—are competing for a limited number of top jobs. For those who have made it (status, money, fan mail, a title, a corner office), there's no problem; but for the millions who are just decent, everyday performers, it's another story. These people are squeezed: They can't rise to the top (there's no room), and right behind, ready to overtake them, is another generation. In years gone by, executives in this position spoke of reaching a plateau— if their path no longer led upward, at least they were in a stable, safe place. Now the plateau is a narrow ledge. Suddenly, at an age when they expected to be at the peak of their careers, growing numbers of fortysomethings are slipping backward.

Debbie Brown is a software engineer who recently lost her job after 14 years at Northrop Grumman. Since last June, when Brown first knew she'd lose her job, she has sent out about 300 résumés. Her yield so far: four phone interviews, one in-person interview, and not a single job offer. Brown is 44. She earned a master's degree in software engineering from the University of California at Irvine in 1983 and has 23 years of industry experience. According to headhunters, however, she's obsolete—not because she's worked in the defense business (although that probably doesn't help), but largely because she moved into management in an era when fortysomething middle managers are a dime a dozen. As for her technical skills, well, people half her age are better qualified. To get a job offer, she must be prepared to cut her $88,500 salary in half, headhunters advise. Either that or go back to school. "I came to Northrop thinking that I'd retire here," she says. "And now here I am, at 44, out of work and useless."

It's not only high-tech firms that are slamming the door on people over 40. In older industries, too, as the lives of products get shorter and as the speed of change gets faster, it can be awfully hard to keep up unless you have the stamina of a 25-year-old. . . .

There are advantages to age. Older employees have more experience than younger workers; they also have better judgment, have a greater commitment to quality, are more likely to show up on time, and are less likely to quit—that's what a recent study commissioned by the American Association of Retired Persons found. Younger workers, by contrast (in this case defined as under 50), were found to be more flexible, more adaptable, more accepting of new technology, and better at learning new skills. It may seem that there are as many advantages in hiring older workers as in hiring younger ones. But as the AARP study discovered, increasingly what matters to companies is potential, not experience; street smarts, not wisdom. "The traits most commonly desired for the new world of work are flexibility, acceptance of change, and the ability to solve problems independently—performance attributes on which managers generally did not rate older workers highly," notes the AARP study. "The message is consistent: Managers generally view older workers as less suitable for the future work environment than other segments of the work force."

To discover, after years of being promoted, that all of a sudden you are "less suitable" for your job than people younger than you is not easy. On Jan. 6, 1998, FedEx delivered letters to the homes of 389 Gerber Products salespeople telling them they were out of work. Of those 389 employees, nearly 70% were over 40. One of them was Tom Johnson. He had been selling Gerber baby food for 27 years; he started with the company when he was 21. Shouldn't he have known he was vulnerable? "Right up until D-day, I was convinced I wouldn't be hit, what with me calling on national accounts and all," Johnson says.

It's human nature that causes us to be blind-sided: No matter how often we hear stories of corporate ruthlessness, of 45-year-olds being replaced by 28-year-olds, we believe it won't happen to us. Sitting in his living room in Mesquite, Texas, in his La-Z-Boy, Johnson opened up that FedEx letter and felt sick. "I sat in my chair and read it eight times and couldn't believe it, I just couldn't believe it. It was like someone grabbed me and hit me as hard as they could right in the stomach. I thought, 'God, all I've done and all I've worked, and it doesn't mean a thing.'" His unemployment insurance checks, at $476 every two weeks, ran out months ago. When we last spoke to him, he had sent out about 400 résumés, and still he hadn't found a job. If truth be told, his chance of finding anything that comes close to paying what he earned at Gerber is probably zero. . . .

"The market is so fast moving that for some reason it's reduced the premium these [older] guys have," notes a New Yorker who runs a hedge fund. Callously, but realistically, he explains his preference for younger employees this way (and for obvious reasons he won't let his name be used): "The way I look at it, for $40,000 or $50,000, I can get a smart, raw kid right out of undergrad who's going to work seven days a week for me for the next two years. I'll train him the way I want him, he'll grow with me, and I'll pay him long-term options so I own him, for lack of a better word. He'll do exactly what I want—and if he doesn't, I'll fire him. . . . The alternative is to pay twice as much for some 40-year-old who does half the amount of work, has been trained improperly, and doesn't listen to what I say." . . .

What unnerves these fortysomethings is that in a world increasingly dominated by information technology, people in their 20s and early 30s (Generation X) are more technically savvy than most baby-boomers. Even more, many Gen Xers work 60 or 70 hours a week, mostly because their job is their whole life. But so what? From the perspective of an employer, such single-mindedness, such devotion to the company, makes Gen Xers all the more valuable. It also makes for unflattering comparisons to the fortysomething employee who leaves the office right at 6 P.M. to pick up the children from day care. As one highly placed human resources manager put it, "The attitude is, Why not hire someone who's young and idealistic and will work 80 hours a week?" . . .

In an economy where the rules seem to shift every day, it's the risk takers, the people who believe they can do anything, who are being rewarded. And after all, who's more likely to take risks—a 46-year-old with a mortgage and two kids in college, or a 30-year-old with nothing to lose? (Freedom may be just another word for not having a mortgage.) Robert Michlewicz is the president of one of Consolidated Graphics' biggest plants, Houston-based Chas P Young Co., with sales of $20 million. He's 30, oversees a staff of 150 people, and works 70 hours a week. When he started with the company, just out of Texas A&M, Michlewicz wouldn't be constrained by the printing industry's traditional ways of doing business. "When I got into sales here, there was this rule of thumb that once you sold $1 million worth of printing, you were an established, veteran salesperson," he explains. "I did $500,000 in my first year, $1.5 million in my second year, and $6.1 million in 1995. . . . I had no preconceived notions. That million-dollar threshold didn't mean anything to me."

The harder Gen Xers work, the more they tend to resent all those 44-year-olds who put in half as many hours and earn more money. "A large percentage [of us] have decided not to buy into a corporate system clogged with entrenched boomers who won't make way for people who are more efficient and have better ideas," writes 28-year-old "Delsyn" in an Internet posting on the Boomer Board chat room. Younger generations may have always felt thus; what's different now is that Delsyn, or someone like her, may be your next boss.

"You have to do more for young people because they are likely to turn over more quickly than older workers. Consequently, a lot of companies are putting young people on the fast track, so you have 28-year-olds running entire departments that 20 years ago were run by 55-year-olds," explains Joe Gibbons, a human resources consultant at William M Mercer. "That's a big change—it's a sea change." . . .

Older employees don't just earn more. Granting more vacation time costs money. The costs of medical benefits and insurance, too, rise with age. And the older an employee, and the longer he's been with the firm, the more expensive it becomes to support his pension plan. If length of work experience really counted for something, these extra costs wouldn't be an issue; but several studies have shown that differences in job performance between someone with 20 years' experience and someone with just five years are often negligible. That is to say that a 28-year-old with six years on the job may perform as well as a 48-year-old with 26 years on the job. The 28-year-old, however, earns $45,000, while the 48-year-old makes $120,000 (assuming a 5% raise every year). . . .

If companies discard older workers because they're earning more than they deserve, then perhaps the solution is to change the way people are being paid: Pay them what they're worth. It's self-evident, but it's rarely the way companies compensate people. "The solution is to develop compensation plans that pay for ideas, not tenure; that pay for contribution, not hierarchy," declares George Bailey, who until recently was head of Watson Wyatt's human-capital group.

Implementing performance-based compensation plans isn't easy. The key is figuring out how to value the performance of every employee ("If you can't find a way to measure [a job's value], you can probably eliminate it," declares Bailey). How many new ideas did she think up this year? How much money did she save? What did she do to help meet our goals? Did she accomplish the goals we set for her? It's a lot of work, but it beats rewarding people just because they've been with the firm for a long time.

Questions for Discussion

1. Do the skills that come with age and experience count for less in today's organizations? Explain.

2. What examples of age stereotypes did you observe in the case? Discuss.

3. To what extent is Debbie Brown being influenced by the self-fulfilling prophecy?

4. Use Weiner's model to assess how Debbie Brown and Tom Johnson are reacting to being laid off by their respective companies. Be sure to identify the perceived causes of the layoff and the associated psychological and behavioral consequences that are apparent in the case.

5. Do you agree with the theme that organizations are better off to replace forty-somethings with younger employees? Explain your rationale.

6. What advice would you give to people who are either twenty-something or forty-something based on this case?

Personal Awareness and Growth Exercise

How Do Diversity Assumptions Influence Team Member Interactions?

Objectives

1. To identify diversity assumptions.
2. To consider how diversity assumptions impact team members' interactions.

Introduction

Assumptions can be so ingrained that we do not even know that we are using them. Negative assumptions can limit our relationships with others because they influence how we perceive and respond to those we encounter in our daily lives. This exercise is designed to help identify the assumptions that you have about groups of people. Although this exercise may make you uncomfortable because it asks you to identify stereotypical assumptions, it is a positive first step at facing and examining the assumptions we make about other people. This awareness can lead to positive behavioral change.

Instructions

Complete the diversity assumptions worksheet.[72] The first column contains various dimensions of diversity. For each dimension, the second column asks you to identify the assumptions held by the general public about people with this characteristic. Use the third column to determine how each assumption might limit team members' ability to effectively interact with each other. Finally, answer the questions for discussion.

Questions for Discussion

1. Where do our assumptions about others come from?
2. Is it possible to eliminate negative assumptions about others? How might this be done?
3. What most surprised you about your answers to the diversity assumption worksheet?

Diversity Assumption Worksheet[73]

Dimension of Diversity	Assumption That Might Be Made	Impact on Team Members' Interactions
Age	Example: You can't teach an old dog new tricks. Older people are closed to new ideas. Example: Younger people haven't had the proper experience to come up with good solutions.	Example: Older people are considered to be resistant to change. Example: Input from younger employees is not solicited.
Ethnicity (e.g., Mexican)		
Gender		
Race		
Physical ability (e.g., hard of hearing)		
Sexual orientation		
Marital/parental status (e.g., single parent with children)		
Religion (e.g., Buddhist)		
Recreational habits (e.g., hikes on weekends)		
Educational background (e.g., college education)		
Work experience (e.g., union)		
Appearance (e.g., overweight)		
Geographic location (e.g., rural)		
Personal habits (e.g., smoking)		
Income (e.g., well-to-do)		

Group Exercise

Using Attribution Theory to Resolve Performance Problems

Objectives

1. To gain experience determining the causes of performance.

2. To decide on corrective action for employee performance.

Introduction

Attributions are typically made to internal and external factors. Perceivers arrive at their assessments by using various informational cues or antecedents. To determine the types of antecedents people use, we have developed a case containing various informational cues about an individual's performance. You will be asked to read the case and make attributions about the causes of performance. To assess the impact of attributions on managerial behavior, you will also be asked to recommend corrective action.

Instructions

Presented on the following page is a case that depicts the performance of Mary Martin, a computer programmer. Please read the case to the right and then identify the causes of her behavior by answering the questions following the case. Then determine whether you made an internal or external attribution. After completing this task, decide on the appropriateness of various forms of corrective action. A list of potential recommendations has been developed. The list is divided into four categories. Read each action, and evaluate its appropriateness by using the scale provided. Next, compute a total score for each of the four categories.

Causes of Performance

To what extent was each of the following a cause of Mary's performance? Use the following scale:

Very Little   **Very Much**

1 ——— 2 ——— 3 ——— 4 ——— 5

a. High ability	1	2	3	4	5
b. Low ability	1	2	3	4	5
c. Low effort	1	2	3	4	5
d. Difficult job	1	2	3	4	5
e. Unproductive co-workers	1	2	3	4	5
f. Bad luck	1	2	3	4	5

Internal attribution (total score for causes a, b, and c) _____

External attribution (total score for causes d, e, and f) _____

THE CASE OF MARY MARTIN

Mary Martin, 30, received her baccalaureate degree in computer science from a reputable state school in the Midwest. She also graduated with above-average grades. Mary is currently working in the computer support/analysis department as a programmer for a nationally based firm. During the past year, Mary has missed 10 days of work. She seems unmotivated and rarely has her assignments completed on time. Mary is usually given the harder programs to work on.

Past records indicate Mary, on the average, completes programs classified as "routine" in about 45 hours. Her co-workers, on the other hand, complete "routine" programs in an average time of 32 hours. Further, Mary finishes programs considered "major problems," on the average, in about 115 hours. Her co-workers, however, finish these same "major problem" assignments, on the average, in about 100 hours. When Mary has worked in programming teams, her peer performance reviews are generally average to negative. Her male peers have noted she is not creative in attacking problems and she is difficult to work with.

The computer department recently sent a questionnaire to all users of its services to evaluate the usefulness and accuracy of data received. The results indicate many departments are not using computer output because they cannot understand the reports. It was also determined that the users of output generated from Mary's programs found the output chaotic and not useful for managerial decision making.

Appropriateness of Corrective Action

Evaluate the following courses of action by using the scale below:

| Very Inappropriate | | | | Very Appropriate |

1 ——— 2 ——— 3 ——— 4 ——— 5

Coercive Actions

	1	2	3	4	5
a. Reprimand Mary for her performance	1	2	3	4	5
b. Threaten to fire Mary if her performance does not improve	1	2	3	4	5

Change Job

	1	2	3	4	5
c. Transfer Mary to another job	1	2	3	4	5
d. Demote Mary to a less demanding job	1	2	3	4	5

Nonpunitive Actions

	1	2	3	4	5
e. Work with Mary to help her do the job better	1	2	3	4	5
f. Offer Mary encouragement to help her improve	1	2	3	4	5

No Immediate Actions

	1	2	3	4	5
g. Do nothing	1	2	3	4	5
h. Promise Mary a pay raise if she improves	1	2	3	4	5

Compute a score for the four categories:[69]

Coercive actions = a + b =

Change job = c + d =

Nonpunitive actions = e + f =

No immediate actions = g + h =

Questions for Discussion

1. How would you evaluate Mary's performance in terms of consensus, distinctiveness, and consistency?

2. Is Mary's performance due to internal or external causes?

3. What did you identify as the top two causes of Mary's performance? Are your choices consistent with Weiner's classification of internal and external factors? Explain.

4. Which of the four types of corrective action do you think is most appropriate? Explain. Can you identify any negative consequences of this choice?

Chapter Seven

Motivation through Needs, Job Design, and Satisfaction

Learning Objectives

When you finish studying the material in this chapter, you should be able to:

1 Define the term *motivation*.

2 Discuss the job performance model of motivation.

3 Review the historical roots of modern motivation theories.

4 Contrast Maslow's and McClelland's need theories.

5 Demonstrate your familiarity with scientific management, job enlargement, job rotation, and job enrichment.

6 Explain the practical significance of Herzberg's distinction between motivators and hygiene factors.

7 Describe how internal work motivation is increased by using the job characteristics model.

8 Discuss the causes and consequences of job satisfaction.

9 Critique the three hypotheses that explain the nature of work-family relationships.

BusinessWeek For all the country's New Economy ways, most jobs are still modeled on the clock-punching culture of the industrial past. Like wired-up assembly-line drones, people are expected to show up Monday through Friday and do their work in eight-, nine-, or ten-hour chunks of time. This rusty arrangement is exactly what IBM's vice-president of global workforce diversity, Ted Childs, wants to smash to pieces. Sounding like a corporate General Patton, Childs warns: "We're going to grab that old model by the throat and choke it to death."

That's strong talk for a human resources executive. But Childs is waging a difficult campaign. So far, most of Corporate America's response to the skin-tight labor market has been to lather job candidates with juicy options packages and perks. But there's fresh evidence that those companies are missing the boat. New studies, including one from the Boston College Center for Work & Family, find that most workers' No. 1 concern has nothing to do with getting free flying lessons or health insurance for their pets. It doesn't even have to do with chopping the hours they work or fattening their paychecks. Rather, employees' top priority is getting the flexibility to control their own time and when, how, and where they do their jobs—giving them the freedom to finesse their own work-life balance.

IBM's Joanna Dapkevich working from home.
(Will & Deni McIntyre)

Spooked Shareholders. Sounds easy. But that requires no less than rethinking and reengineering people's jobs. Called "work redesign," these projects often involve clipboard-toting consultants who nose around in every department, sometimes tearing apart people's routines for months . . .

Today at IBM, the company that was once so rigid that it banned floral ties, managers are allowed to work part-time—and from home—so they can better juggle the demands of their children and their jobs. From a den in the family colonial, Joanna Dapkevich manages 50 software customer-service representatives at IBM's office park in Raleigh, NC, 10 miles away.

After Dapkevich got pregnant in 1997, she asked her boss if she could work part-time from home but still keep her job. Accommodations had to be made. Since Dapkevich would only be working part-time, a third of her business had to be spun off to two other managers itching for more responsibility. And Dapkevich had to retrain her people to not think they were bothering her every time they phoned her at home.

Since her new schedule went into effect, Dapkevich's customer-satisfaction ratings have risen sharply, from 80% to 85%. Her team's morale is also the highest of the four that make up her division. Says Dapkevich: "This way, I can give 120% to IBM and 120% to my newborn, and this nets out to zero guilt for me."

Guilt-Free. Working parents at Merck & Co. are feeling a lot less guilty, too. A year ago, the Whitehouse Station (NJ)-based company embarked on a massive work-redesign effort, asking employees what maddened them most about their jobs. People in the payroll department made big noises about the mounds of overtime that had become as habitual as coffee breaks. The pharmaceutical giant realized how much of the department's work wasn't computerized, and how the 9-to-5 workday didn't match the cyclical pileup of work. Automation and new schedules helped sink department overtime 50% and allowed the number of people with flexible work arrangements to double, to 45%.

The benefits of work redesign have even shown up in some unlikely places—like the bedroom. After moving 200 bankers from pricey downtown Boston office space to cheaper digs in Framingham, Mass., Fleet Financial Group got pounded with a raft of complaints about longer commutes, smaller support staff, and a focus on pumping out as many loans as possible instead of providing quality and customer service. With the help of researchers from Radcliffe's Public Policy Institute, telecommuting options were offered. A new backlog manager was hired to handle the overload, and officers were allowed to swap loans with each other. It didn't take long for the bad feelings to die down. The number of employees who reported struggling with insomnia dropped by 35%.

The upsides aren't surprising, considering a recent poll by Los Angeles-based Flexible Resources Inc., in which 56% of managers say employees with flexible schedules are more productive per hour. That kind of positive buzz is what has driven work redesign successes at such places as Ernst & Young, Hewlett-Packard, Bank of America, and Lucent Technologies.[1]

FOR DISCUSSION
Why are companies increasingly using job design? Explain.

Effective employee motivation has long been one of management's most difficult and important duties. Success in this endeavor is becoming more challenging in light of organizational trends to downsize and reengineer and the demands associated with managing a diverse workforce. As revealed in the chapter-opening vignette, IBM, Merck, and Fleet Financial implemented a variety of work redesign techniques to meet this challenge. These companies found that employees were more motivated, productive, and satisfied when their work environments were positively redesigned. The purpose of this chapter, as well as the next, is to provide you with a foundation for understanding the complexities of employee motivation.

Specifically, this chapter provides a definitional and theoretical foundation for the topic of motivation so that a rich variety of motivation theories and techniques can be introduced and discussed. Coverage of employee motivation extends to Chapter 8.

After providing a conceptual model for understanding motivation, this chapter focuse on (1) need theories of motivation, (2) an overview of job design methods used to mo vate employees, (3) a job characteristics approach to job design, and (4) job satisfa tion and work-family relationships. In the next chapter, attention turns to equi expectancy, and goal-setting.

What Does Motivation Involve?

Motivation
Psychological processes that arouse and direct goal-directed behavior.

A Job Performance Model of Motivation

Terence Mitchell, a well-known OB researcher, proposed a broad conceptual model that explains how motivation influences job behaviors and performance. This model, which is shown in Figure 7–1, integrates elements from several of the theories we discuss in this book. It identifies the causes and consequences of motivation.[3]

Figure 7–1   *A Job Performance Model of Motivation*

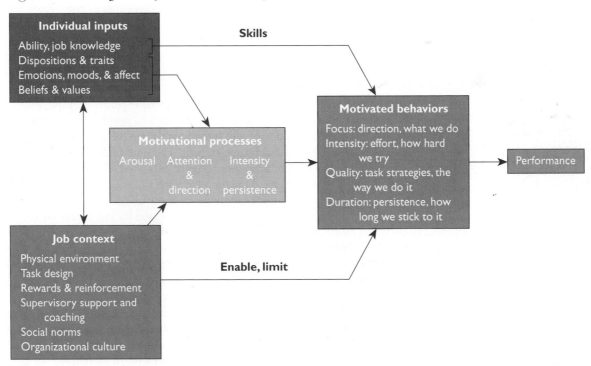

SOURCE: Adapted from T R Mitchell, "Matching Motivational Strategies with Organizational Contexts," in *Research in Organizational Behavior* (vol 19), eds L L Cummings and B M Staw (Greenwich, CT: JAI Press, 1997), p 63.

Figure 7–1 shows that individual inputs and job context are the two key categories of factors that influence motivation. As discussed in Chapter 5, employees bring ability, job knowledge, dispositions and traits, emotions, moods, beliefs, and values to the work setting. The job context includes the physical environment, the tasks one completes, the organization's approach to recognition and rewards, the adequacy of supervisory support and coaching, and the organization's culture (recall our discussion in Chapter 3). These two categories of factors influence each other as well as the motivational processes of arousal, direction, and persistence. Consider the motivational implications associated with the job contexts at Systems Group Inc, American Group Inc, and ACNielsen:

> When Robyn Feigenbaum, president of Systems Group, Inc., technology consultants in St. Louis, asked one of her high-performing employees to look up Orlando, Fla., in a travel guidebook, he found two round-trip tickets to Disney World in his name. American Group Inc., a Boca Raton, Fla., peatmoss company, this year begins giving employees their wedding anniversary off. Mike Connors, who runs the Asia-Pacific business of ACNielsen, a Stamford, Conn., market-research firm, had his head shaved last month at a global management meeting. He was making good on a pledge to go bald if William Pulver, the company's new Japan-group chief executive, turned that unit's losses into a $1 million profit.[4]

These examples suggest that employees are more likely to be motivated when they believe that their performance will be recognized and rewarded with outcomes they value.

Figure 7–1 further reveals that *motivated behaviors* are directly affected by an individual's ability and job knowledge (skills), motivation, and a combination of enabling and limiting job context factors. For instance, it would be difficult to persist on a project if you were working with defective raw materials or broken equipment. In contrast, motivated behaviors are likely to be enhanced when managers supply employees with adequate resources to get the job done and provide effective coaching. This coaching might entail furnishing employees with successful role models, showing employees how to complete complex tasks, and helping them maintain high self-efficacy and self-esteem (recall the discussion in Chapter 5). Performance is, in turn, influenced by motivated behavior.

There are four important conclusions to remember about Figure 7–1. First, motivation is different from behavior. Motivation involves a host of psychological processes that culminate in an individual's desire and intentions to behave in a particular way. Behavior reflects something that we can see or hear. The outcomes of motivation are generally assessed in terms of the behaviors actually exhibited, the amount of effort exerted, or the choice of strategies used to complete a job or task. Actual effort or persistence are the most direct behavioral outcomes of motivation. Second, behavior is influenced by more than just motivation. Behavior is affected by individual inputs, job context factors, and motivation. For example, the amount of time you spend studying for your next exam (behavior) is influenced by your motivation in combination with your ability and personal goals (individual inputs) and the quality of your lecture notes (enabling/limiting job context variable). This example illustrates that behavior is due to a combination of factors rather than simply to just motivation.

Third, behavior is different from performance. Performance represents an accumulation of behaviors that occur over time and across contexts and people. Performance also reflects an external standard that is typically set by the organization and assessed by an employee's manager. Consider the final grade a student might receive for accumulating a final course average of 88%. While this average is based on behaviors exhibited over an entire class, the student's final grade or performance might range from an A to a B. The final grade depends on the specific professor's standards and the grade distribution of the class under consideration. Fourth, motivation is a necessary but insufficient contributor to job performance. This conclusion reveals that performance problems are due to a combination of individual inputs, job context factors, motivation, and appropriate motivated behaviors. Drawing a distinction between motivation and performance has its advantages. According to one motivation expert,

> The implication is that there probably are some jobs for which trying to influence motivation will be irrelevant for performance. These circumstances can occur in a variety of ways. There may be situations in which ability factors or role expectation factors are simply more important than motivation. For example, the best predictor of high school grades typically is intellectual endowment, not hours spent studying . . .
>
> Another circumstance may occur in which performance is controlled by technological factors. For example, on an assembly line, given that minimally competent and attentive people are there to do the job, performance may not vary from individual to individual. Exerting effort may be irrelevant for performance.[5]

Managers are better able to identify and correct performance problems when they recognize that poor performance is not due solely to inadequate motivation. This awareness can foster better interpersonal relations in the workplace.

Historical Roots of Modern Motivation Theories

Five methods of explaining behavior—needs, reinforcement, cognition, job characteristics, and feelings/emotions—underlie the evolution of modern theories of human motivation. As we proceed through this review, remember the objective of each alternative motivation theory is to explain and predict purposeful or goal-directed behavior. As will become apparent, the differences between theoretical perspectives lie in the causal mechanisms used to explain behavior.

Needs   Needs theories are based on the premise that individuals are motivated by unsatisfied needs. Dissatisfaction with your social life, for example, should motivate you to participate in more social activities. Henry Murray, a 1930s psychologist, was the first behavioral scientist to propose a list of needs thought to underlie goal-directed behavior. From Murray's work sprang a wide variety of need theories, some of which remain influential today. Recognized need theories of motivation are explored in the next section of this chapter.

Reinforcement   Reinforcement theorists, such as Edward L Thorndike and B F Skinner, proposed that behavior is controlled by its consequences, not by the result of hypothetical internal states such as instincts, drives, or needs. This proposition is based on research data demonstrating that people repeat behaviors followed by favorable consequences and avoid behaviors resulting in unfavorable consequences. Few would argue with the statement that organizational rewards have a motivational impact on job behavior. However, behaviorists and cognitive theorists do disagree over the role of internal states and processes in motivation.

Cognitions   Uncomfortable with the idea that behavior is shaped completely by environmental consequences, cognitive motivation theorists contend that behavior is a function of beliefs, expectations, values, and other mental cognitions. Behavior is therefore viewed as the result of rational and conscious choices among alternative courses of action. In Chapter 8, we discuss cognitive motivation theories involving equity, expectancies, and goal setting.

Job Characteristics   This theoretical approach is based on the idea that the task itself is the key to employee motivation. Specifically, a boring and monotonous job stifles motivation to perform well, whereas a challenging job enhances motivation. Three ingredients of a more challenging job are variety, autonomy, and decision authority. Two popular ways of adding variety and challenge to routine jobs are job enrichment (or job redesign) and job rotation. These techniques are discussed later in this chapter.

Feelings/Emotions   This most recent addition to the evolution of motivation theory is based on the idea that workers are whole people who pursue goals outside of becoming a high performer.[6] For example, you may want to be an A student, a loving boyfriend or girlfriend, a caring parent, a good friend, a responsible citizen, or a happy person. Work motivation is thus thought to be a function of your feelings and emotions toward the multitude of interests and goals that you have. You are likely to study long and hard if your only interest in life is to enter graduate school and become a doctor. In contrast, a highly motivated professor is likely to quit lecturing and dismiss class upon receiving a message that his or her child was seriously hurt in an accident.

A Motivational Puzzle   Motivation theory presents managers with a psychological puzzle composed of alternative explanations and recommendations. There is not any one motivation theory that is appropriate in all situations. Rather, managers need to use a contingency framework to pick and choose the motivational techniques best suited to the people and situation involved. The matrix in Figure 7–2 was created to help managers make these decisions.

Because managers face a variety of motivational problems that can be solved with different theories of motivation, the matrix crosses outcomes of interest with six major motivation theories.[7] Entries in the matrix indicate which theories are best suited for explaining each outcome. For instance, each motivation theory can help managers determine how to increase employee effort. In contrast, need, equity, and job characteristics theories are most helpful in developing programs aimed at increasing employees' job satisfaction. Managers faced with high turnover are advised to use the reinforcement, equity, expectancy, or job characteristics theory to correct the problem.

You will be better able to apply this matrix after reading the material in this chapter and Chapters 8 and 10. This chapter covers theories related to needs and job characteristics, Chapter 8 focuses on equity, expectancy, and goal setting, and reinforcement theory is reviewed in Chapter 10.

Figure 7–2   *Motivation Theories and Workplace Outcomes: A Contingency Approach*

| | Motivation Theories | | | | | |
Outcome of Interest	Need	Reinforcement	Equity	Expectancy	Goal Setting	Job Characteristics
• Choice to pursue a course of action				X		
• Effort	X	X	X	X	X	X
• Performance		X	X		X	X
• Satisfaction	X		X			X
• Absenteeism		X	X			X
• Turnover		X	X	X		X

SOURCE: Adapted and extended from F J Landy and W S Becker, "Motivation Theory Reconsidered," in L L Cummings and B M Staw (eds), *Research in Organizational Behavior* (Greenwich, CT: JAI Press, 1987), vol. 9, p 33.

Need theories attempt to pinpoint internal facto[r...]
Needs are physiological or psychological deficier[...]
They can be strong or weak and are influenced [...]
Thus, human needs vary over time and place. Two [...]
discussed in this section: Maslow's need hierarch[y...]
need theory.

Maslow's Need Hierarchy Theo[ry]

In 1943, psychologist Abraham Maslow published h[...]
ory of motivation. Although the theory was based o[...]
neurotic individuals, it has subsequently been used [...]
human behavior. Maslow proposed that motivation [...]
physiological, safety, love, esteem, and self-actuali[...]

Maslow said these five need categories are arr[a...]
other words, he believed human needs generally eme[...]
ion. Accordingly, when one's physiological needs a[...]
needs emerge, and so on up the need hierarchy, one step at a time. Once a need is satisfied it activates the next higher need in the hierarchy. This process continues until the
need for self-actualization is activated.[8]

Part Two   Individu[al]

Research Findin[gs]

theory because r[...]
A well-know[n...]

In balan[...]
orga[...]
c[...]

210

Figure 7–3   *Maslow's Need Hierarchy*

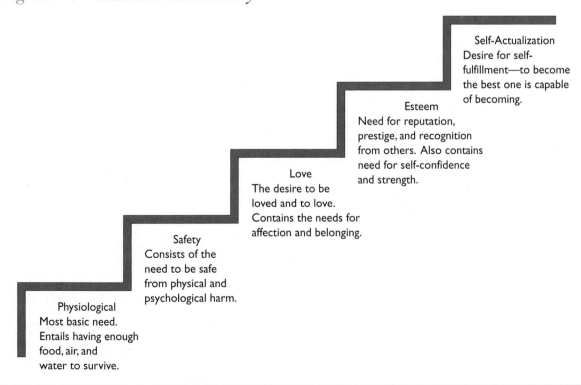

Self-Actualization
Desire for self-
fulfillment—to become
the best one is capable
of becoming.

Esteem
Need for reputation,
prestige, and recognition
from others. Also contains
need for self-confidence
and strength.

Love
The desire to be
loved and to love.
Contains the needs for
affection and belonging.

Safety
Consists of the
need to be safe
from physical and
psychological harm.

Physiological
Most basic need.
Entails having enough
food, air, and
water to survive.

SOURCE: Adapted from descriptions provided by A H Maslow, "A Theory of Human Motivation," *Psychological Review*, July 1943, pp 370–96.

gs on Maslow's Theory   Research does not clearly support this
sults from studies testing the need hierarchy are difficult to interpret.
motivation scholar summarized the research evidence as follows:

> ce, Maslow's theory remains very popular among managers and students of
> izational behavior, although there are still very few studies that can legitimately
> nfirm (or refute) it . . . It may be that the dynamics implied by Maslow's theory of
> needs are too complex to be operationalized and confirmed by scientific research. If
> this is the case, we may never be able to determine how valid the theory is, or—more
> precisely—which aspects of the theory are valid and which are not.[9]

Managerial Implications of Maslow's Theory   A satisfied need may lose its
motivational potential. Therefore, managers are advised to motivate employees by
devising programs or practices aimed at satisfying emerging or unmet needs. Dan
Logan, president of Boston-based Trinity Communications, followed this recommendation. He administered a survey to find out what motivates his younger or "Generation X" employees. Here is what Trinity did in response to the results:

> Trinity changed many of its policies and added some new programs. For instance, the
> company changed 401(k) providers, added more-aggressive mutual funds, reduced the
> time before a new hire could join the plan from 18 months to 6 months, and made
> vesting instantaneous. The company also altered its vacation policy and now offers
> everyone an annual six-week time-off bank for vacation, personal days, sick days, and
> holidays. Lunchtime diversity programs were added, and Trinity has begun participat-
> ing in three minority-based internship programs. Logan also decided to supply all
> employees with home computers, Internet accounts, and training in new media. The
> total price tag: about $175,000.[10]

The same recommendation applies to the context of motivating customers to purchase
specific products.

The Ritz-Carlton, for example, believes that customer loyalty and satisfaction are
based on satisfying customer needs. The organization attempts to motivate us to stay at
its hotels by first gathering detailed information on customer preferences and needs from
a variety of sources. This information is then entered into an on-line, nationwide computer system. The Ritz-Carlton then uses this information to satisfy customer needs:

> When a repeat customer calls the central reservations number to book a room, the
> agent can retrieve the individual's preference information directly from the on-line sys-
> tem. This information is sent to the specific Ritz location where the room is reserved.
> The hotel then outputs the data in a daily guest recognition and preference report,
> which is circulated to all staff. With this system, hotel staff can anticipate a particular
> guest's breakfast habits, newspaper choices, and room preferences.

(DILBERT reprinted by permission of United Feature Syndicate, Inc.)

The Ritz's employees are well trained to ensure they are able to respond to the customers' needs. A customer management system ensures that the first employee who becomes aware of a customer complaint becomes responsible for resolving the problem quickly and completely. Each employee can reverse a transaction up to $2,000, without prior approval—if necessary—to keep a customer satisfied.[11]

Need theory offers another recommendation for companies undergoing downsizing or large scale layoffs: 1,746,655 people were laid off within the United States in 1998 and 376,728 during the first three months of 1999.[12] Because layoffs create stress and feelings of job insecurity, organizations can implement support programs and severance payments to help employees cope with their feelings, emotions, and financial concerns.[13] Elo TouchSystems Inc., for example, was able to increase productivity, customer satisfaction, and quality during the 14-month period in which it was closing a plant in Oak Ridge, Tennessee, by following these guidelines.[14]

McClelland's Need Theory

David McClelland, a well-known psychologist, has been studying the relationship between needs and behavior since the late 1940s. Although he is most recognized for his research on the need for achievement, he also investigated the needs for affiliation and power. Before discussing each of these needs, let us consider the typical approach used to measure the strength of an individual's needs.

Ethics at Work

Tom Kilroy of North Olmsted [Ohio] learned Feb. 10 [1999] that his employer of 14 years would close and that he would lose his $42,000-a-year-job. But instead of looking for a new job right away, the Builders Square assistant manager decided to wait because the home-improvement chain promised to pay him $18,000 in severance and accrued vacation if he stayed until the stores closed in June. The reward for his loyalty? Zilch. As the stores were shutting their doors last month, Builders Square told Kilroy and some 3,000 other employees to kiss the promised payments goodbye because the company had filed for bankruptcy.

SOURCE: Excerpted from T D Murray, "Many Workers Have Lost Trust as Firms Close Unexpectedly," *The Plain Dealer*, July 11, 1999, p 1D.

You Decide . . .

Do you think that the management at Builders Square acted ethically?

For an interpretation of this situation, visit our Web site **www.mhhe.com/kreitner**

Measuring Need Strength   The Thematic Apperception Test (TAT) is frequently used to measure an individual's motivation to satisfy various needs. In completing the TAT, people are asked to write stories about ambiguous pictures. These descriptions are then scored for the extent to which they contain achievement, power, and affiliation imagery. A meta-analysis of 105 studies demonstrated that the TAT is a valid measure of the need for achievement.[15] At this time, we would like you to examine the picture in the OB Exercise on p 212, and then write a brief description of what you think is happening to the people in the picture and what you think will happen to them in the future. Use the scoring guide to determine your need strength. What is your most important need?

The Need for Achievement   Achievement theories propose that motivation and performance vary according to the strength of one's need for achievement. For example, a field study of 222 life insurance brokers found a positive correlation between the number of policies sold and the brokers' need for achievement. McClelland's research supported an analogous relationship for societies as a whole. His results revealed that a country's level of economic development was positively

OB Exercise   Assess Your Need Strength with a Thematic Apperception Test (TAT)

Instructions

The purpose of this exercise is to help you identify motivational themes expressed in the picture shown below. There are two steps. First, look at the picture briefly (10 to 20 seconds), and write the story it suggests by answering the following questions: (1) What is happening? Who are the people? (2) What past events led to this situation? (3) What is wanted by whom? and (4) What will happen? What will be done? Next, score your story for achievement, power, and affiliation motivation by using the scoring guide and scales shown below. Score the motives from 1 (low) to 5 (high). The scoring guide identifies the types of story descriptions/words that are indicative of high motives. Give yourself a low score if you fail to describe the story with words and phrases contained in the scoring guidelines. A moderate score indicates that you used some of the phrases identified in the scoring guide to describe your story. Do not read the scoring guidelines until you have written your story.

Scoring Guidelines

Score _achievement_ motivation high if:
- A goal, objective, or standard of excellence is mentioned.
- Words such as good, better, or best are used to evaluate performance.
- Someone in your story is striving for a unique accomplishment.
- Reference is made to career status or being a success in life.

Score _power_ motivation high if:
- There is emotional concern for influencing someone else.
- Someone is actively striving to gain or keep control over others by ordering, arguing, demanding, convincing, threatening, or punishing.
- Clear reference is made to a superior–subordinate relationship and the superior is taking steps to gain or keep control over the subordinate.

Score _affiliation_ motivation high if:
- Someone is concerned about establishing or maintaining a friendly relationship with another.
- Someone expresses the desire to be liked by someone else.
- There are references to family ties, friendly discussions, visits, reunions, parties, or informal get-togethers.

	LOW	MODERATE	HIGH
• Achievement motivation	1——2——3——4——5		
• Power motivation	1——2——3——4——5		
• Affiliation motivation	1——2——3——4——5		

Need for achievement

Desire to accomplish something difficult.

related to its overall achievement motivation.[16] The **need for achievement** is defined by the following desires:

> To accomplish something difficult. To master, manipulate, or organize physical objects, human beings, or ideas. To do this as rapidly and as independently as possible. To overcome obstacles and attain a high standard. To excel one's self. To rival and surpass others. To increase self-regard by the successful exercise of talent.[17]

This definition reveals that the need for achievement overlaps Maslow's higher order needs of esteem and self-actualization. K Y Ho is a good example of someone with a high need for achievement (see the International OB on p 214). Not only does Mr. Ho display the need for achievement, but his story highlights the point that achievement needs display themselves in all walks of life. One does not have to be a famous athlete, executive, or personality to display high achievement. Let us now consider the characteristics of high achievers.

Characteristics of High Achievers   Achievement-motivated people share three common characteristics. One is a preference for working on tasks of *moderate* difficulty. For example, when high achievers are asked to stand wherever they like while tossing rings at a peg on the floor, they tend to stand about 10 to 20 feet from the peg. This distance presents the ring tosser with a challenging but not impossible task. People with a low need for achievement, in contrast, tend to either walk up to the peg and drop the rings on or gamble on a lucky shot from far away. The high achiever's preference for moderately difficult tasks reinforces achievement behavior by reducing the frequency of failure and increasing the satisfaction associated with successfully completing challenging tasks.

Achievers also like situations in which their performance is due to their own efforts rather than to other factors, such as luck. A third identifying characteristic of high achievers is that they desire more feedback on their successes and failures than do low achievers.[18] Given these characteristics, McClelland proposed that high achievers are more likely to be successful entrepreneurs. A recent review of research on the "entrepreneurial" personality supported this conclusion. Entrepreneurs were found to have a higher need for achievement than nonentrepreneurs.[19]

The Need for Affiliation   Researchers believe that people possess a basic desire to form and maintain a few lasting, positive, and important interpersonal relationships. A recent summary of research supported this premise. In addition, the researchers noted that both psychological and physical health problems are higher among people who lack social attachments.[20] Just the same, not everyone has a high need to affiliate. People with a high **need for affiliation** prefer to spend more time maintaining social relationships, joining groups, and wanting to be loved. Individuals high in this need are not the most effective managers or leaders because they have a hard time making difficult decisions without worrying about being disliked.

Need for affiliation
Desire to spend time in social relationships and activities.

The Need for Power   The **need for power** reflects an individual's desire to influence, coach, teach, or encourage others to achieve. People with a high need for power like to work and are concerned with discipline and self-respect. There is a positive and negative side to this need. The negative face of power is characterized by an "if I win, you lose" mentality. In contrast, people with a positive orientation to power focus on accomplishing group goals and helping employees obtain the feeling of competence. More is said about the two faces of power in Chapter 16.

Need for power
Desire to influence, coach, teach, or encourage others to achieve.

Because effective managers must positively influence others, McClelland proposes that top managers should have a high need for power coupled with a low need for affiliation. He also believes that individuals with high achievement motivation are *not* best suited for top management positions. Several studies support these propositions.[21]

Managerial Implications   Given that adults can be trained to increase their achievement motivation,[22] organizations should consider the benefits of providing achievement training for employees. Moreover, achievement, affiliation, and power

International OB K Y Ho Displays a High Need for Achievement

BusinessWeek For K Y Ho, growing up in mainland China in the 1950s meant hunger and ragged clothes. To help out his mother, Ho, the youngest of three brothers and a sister, peddled vegetables from the family garden. His father, laboring in Hong Kong for most of Ho's childhood, sent back what he could. Later, after the family reunited in Hong Kong, life in a crammed one-room flat was scarcely better. Says Ho: "We always worried about money, money, money."

No longer. Now the 48-year-old Ho, living in Canada since 1983, is one of that country's most successful high-tech entrepreneurs. Today, Ho is worth about $143 million, thanks to his 4.4% stake in ATI Technologies Inc., which he started with two friends shortly after arriving in Canada. ATI makes graphics accelerators, the specialized 3-D chips that give popular video games such as *Tomb Raider* and *Quake III* their realistic look ...

Despite his early poverty, Ho hails from a highly educated, upper-class family. His maternal grandfather was a prosperous landowner who fell on hard times after the Japanese invasion in 1937. His paternal grandfather was a book dealer and teacher. After the communists came to power in 1949, both grandparents lost most of their property. Ho's father, also a teacher, was unable to find work and left his wife and young children for a series of factory jobs in Hong Kong when Ho was still an infant. Twelve long years later, Ho and his mother joined Ho's father and an older brother. Ho's other brother and sister were forced by the government to stay behind.

Later, Ho earned a spot at a top Taiwanese college, National Cheng Kung University, where he studied electrical engineering. Away from home and the watchful eyes of his parents, Ho didn't hit the books much. Friends remember him as an average student. "He spent a lot of time outside the library," recalls K D Au, a classmate who now owns the computer-peripherals wholesaler Althon Micro Inc. in Los Angeles.

But once in the job market, Ho thrived. After graduating from university in 1974, he raced through several electronics-industry jobs at big-name corporations in Hong Kong, including Control Data Systems Inc. and Philips Electronics. Ho learned all about video games in 1981 when he went to work for Wong's Electronics Co. Ltd., a leading Hong Kong manufacturer that dealt regularly with hotshot game makers Atari and Coleco. "He learned everything very, very fast," recalls Benedict C M Wong, the company's president.

Entrepreneurs such as K Y Ho, cofounder of ATI Technologies Inc., tend to have a high need for achievement. Mr. Ho's need for achievement surely contributed to his rise from poverty in mainland China to one of Canada's most successful high-tech entrepreneurs.

Courtesy of ATI Technologies

Affable and quick with a smile, Ho nonetheless often disagreed with his superiors. "He's so straightforward that he could hardly get along with the boss," recalls Patrick Hung, a classmate who later worked with Ho at Wong's. In 1983, Ho left for Canada, where many Hong Kong Chinese went looking for a fresh start. Ho's first impression: "A lot of open space and lots of opportunity."

SOURCE: Excerpted from J Weber and A Reinhardt, "From Rags to 3-D Chips," *Business Week*, June 21, 1999, pp 86, 90.

needs can be considered during the selection process, for better placement. For example, a study revealed that individuals' need for achievement affected their preference to work in different companies. People with a high need for achievement were more attracted to companies that had a pay-for-performance environment than were those with a low achievement motivation.[23] Finally, managers should create challenging task assignments or goals because the need for achievement is positively correlated with goal commitment, which, in turn, influences performance.[24] Moreover, challenging goals should be accompanied with a more autonomous work environment and employee empowerment to capitalize on the characteristics of high achievers.

Historical Approaches to Job Design

Job design, also referred to as job redesign, "refers to any set of activities that involve the alteration of specific jobs or interdependent systems of jobs with the intent of improving the quality of employee job experience and their on-the-job productivity."[25] There are two very different routes, one traditional and one modern, that can be taken when deciding how to design jobs. Each is based on a different assumption about people.

Job design
Changing the content and/or process of a specific job to increase job satisfaction and performance.

The first route entails *fitting people to jobs.* It is based on the assumption that people will gradually adjust and adapt to any work situation. Thus, employee attitudes toward the job are ignored, and jobs are designed to produce maximum economic and technological efficiency. This approach uses the principles of scientific management and work simplification. In contrast, the second route involves *fitting jobs to people.* It assumes that people are underutilized at work and that they desire more challenges and responsibility. This philosophy is part of the driving force behind the widespread implementation of work teams across the United States. Techniques such as job enlargement, job rotation, job enrichment, and job characteristics are used when designing jobs according to this second alternative.

The remainder of this section discusses the first four methods of job design to be widely used in industry. They are scientific management, job enlargement, job rotation, and job enrichment. The next section explores the job characteristics approach to job design.

Scientific Management

Developed by Frederick Taylor, scientific management relied on research and experimentation to determine the most efficient way to perform jobs. He used time and task studies to determine the most efficient and safe manner to perform a job. Jobs are highly specialized and standardized when they are designed according to the principles of scientific management. This technique was the impetus for the development of assembly line technology and currently is used in many manufacturing and production-oriented firms throughout the United States.

Designing jobs according to the principles of scientific management has both positive and negative consequences. Positively, employee efficiency and productivity are increased. On the other hand, research reveals that simplified, repetitive jobs also lead to job dissatisfaction, poor mental health, higher levels of stress, and low sense of accomplishment and personal growth.[26] Further, the principles of scientific management do not apply to professional "knowledge" workers, and they are not consistent with the trend to empower both employees and work teams. These negative consequences paved the way for the development of other job designs. Newer approaches attempt to design intrinsically satisfying jobs.

Job Enlargement

Job enlargement
Putting more variety into a job.

This technique was first used in the late 1940s in response to complaints about tedious and overspecialized jobs. **Job enlargement** involves putting more variety into a worker's job by combining specialized tasks of comparable difficulty. Some call this *horizontally loading* the job. Consider how Westinghouse Air Brake Company in Chicago enlarged Jeffrey Byrom's job:

> In traditional factories, workers often are assigned to run single machines, churning out huge batches of parts. But this is no traditional plant. Mr Byrom's job requires him to juggle the operation of three different machines simultaneously while also checking regularly for defects in finished items … Mr Byrom works on a line that produces "slack adjusters," big pogo-stick-like devices used to keep the distance steady between the brakes and wheels on trains, and his job is an elaborate juggling act. Operating in a tight U-shaped area known as a "cell," he first uses a big blue metal-cutting device to shape both ends of a long bar, which he then puts into a second machine that cuts a threading into one end. From there, he places the bar in a third machine that welds a metal ring onto it.[27]

Although Byrom's job is hectic and a bit stressful, he says that he enjoys the pace because it makes the day go by faster. Westinghouse also reports that Byrom's line now produces 10 times more per day than in 1991.[28]

Proponents of job enlargement claim it can improve employee satisfaction, motivation, and quality of production. Unfortunately, research reveals that job enlargement, by itself, does not have a significant and lasting positive impact on job performance. Researchers recommend using job enlargement as part of a broader approach that uses multiple job design techniques.[29]

Job Rotation

Job rotation
Moving employees from one specialized job to another.

As with job enlargement, job rotation's purpose is to give employees greater variety in their work. **Job rotation** calls for moving employees from one specialized job to another. Rather than performing only one job, workers are trained and given the opportunity to perform two or more separate jobs on a rotating basis. By rotating employees from job to job, managers believe they can stimulate interest and motivation while providing employees with a broader perspective of the organization.

Other proposed advantages of job rotation include increased worker flexibility and easier scheduling because employees are cross trained to perform different jobs. In turn, this cross training requires employees to learn new skills, which can assist them in upward or lateral mobility. For example, the New York City-based Metropolitan Transportation Authority (MTA) implemented a job rotation program as part of its Future Managers Program (FMP). The FMP is designed to develop managerial candidates across all five of its agencies:

> Sherry Herrington, assistant superintendent of transportation at Metro-North Commuter Railroad, and technical adviser to the FMP, says that very specific steps are involved in designing a rotation schedule. "The first thing we do is look at what position they're going for and what they need to learn to fulfill that position. With that overall picture in mind, we design rotations into different areas of the department, so that the participant gets some understanding of various job responsibilities. We'll pick an expert—who the person rotates with—and we'll design a rotation form that addresses the learning needs we expect that future manager to come away with in that specific rotation." …

Herrington designed the rotation schedule for Gus Meyers, a future manager in training for a transportation department position as train master with Metro-North. (A train master manages movement of a specific line.) Prior to the program, Meyers was an iron worker who built bridges for the railroad. "It can be hectic and demanding, but I'm learning a lot," Meyers said about the job rotations. "When you've been working in one department, you tend to have tunnel vision. The rotations give you a broader perspective on how one department affects another. Plus, when we're in class, we meet our counterparts at other agencies and we see how they solve problems. The contacts and the people you meet are the best part of this program."[30]

Although this example supports the use of job rotation, the promised benefits associated with job rotation programs have not been adequately researched.[31] It is thus difficult to draw any empirical conclusions about their effectiveness.

Job Enrichment

Job enrichment is the practical application of Frederick Herzberg's motivator–hygiene theory of job satisfaction.[32] After reviewing the foundation of Herzberg's theory, we will discuss its application through job enrichment.

The Legacy of Herzberg's Motivator–Hygiene Theory   Herzberg's theory is based on a landmark study in which he interviewed 203 accountants and engineers. These interviews sought to determine the factors responsible for job satisfaction and dissatisfaction. Herzberg found separate and distinct clusters of factors associated with job satisfaction and dissatisfaction. Job satisfaction was more frequently associated with achievement, recognition, characteristics of the work, responsibility, and advancement. These factors were all related to outcomes associated with the *content* of the task being performed. Herzberg labeled these factors **motivators** because each was associated with strong effort and good performance. He hypothesized that motivators cause a person to move from a state of no satisfaction to satisfaction (see Figure 7–4). Therefore, Herzberg's theory predicts managers can motivate individuals by incorporating "motivators" into an individual's job.

> **Motivators**
> Job characteristics associated with job satisfaction.

Herzberg found job *dissatisfaction* to be associated primarily with factors in the work *context* or environment. Specifically, company policy and administration, technical supervision, salary, interpersonal relations with one's supervisor, and working conditions were most frequently mentioned by employees expressing job dissatisfaction. Herzberg labeled this second cluster of factors **hygiene factors.** He further proposed that they were not motivational. At best, according to Herzberg's interpretation, an individual will experience no job dissatisfaction when he or she has no grievances about hygiene factors (refer to Figure 7–4).[33]

> **Hygiene factors**
> Job characteristics associated with job dissatisfaction.

A Zero Midpoint   The key to adequately understanding Herzberg's motivator–hygiene theory is recognizing that he believes that satisfaction is not the opposite of dissatisfaction. Herzberg concludes that "the opposite of job satisfaction is not job dissatisfaction, but rather no job satisfaction; and similarly, the opposite of job dissatisfaction is not job satisfaction, but no dissatisfaction."[34] Herzberg thus asserts that the dissatisfaction–satisfaction continuum contains a zero midpoint at which dissatisfaction and satisfaction are absent. Conceivably, an organization member who has good supervision, pay, and working conditions but a tedious and unchallenging task with little chance of advancement would be at the zero midpoint. That person would have no dissatisfaction (because of good hygiene factors) and no satisfaction (because of a lack of motivators).

Figure 7–4 *Herzberg's Motivator–Hygiene Model*

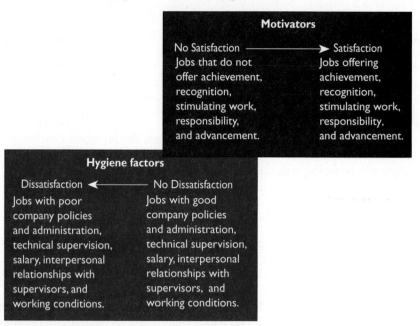

SOURCE: Adapted in part from D A Whitsett and E K Winslow, "An Analysis of Studies Critical of the Motivator–Hygiene Theory," *Personnel Psychology*, Winter 1967, pp 391–415.

Consequently, Herzberg warns managers that it takes more than good pay and good working conditions to motivate today's employees. It takes an "enriched job" that offers the individual opportunity for achievement and recognition, stimulation, responsibility, and advancement. Unfortunately, a study of 600 managers and 900 workers indicated that organizations may not be heeding Herzberg's advice. Results revealed that only 33% felt that their managers knew what motivated them, and 60% concluded that they did not receive any sort of recognition or rewards for their work.[35]

Research on the Motivator–Hygiene Theory   Herzberg's theory generated a great deal of research and controversy. The controversy revolved around whether studies supporting the theory were flawed, and thus invalid.[36] A motivation scholar attempted to sort out the controversy by concluding:

> In balance, when we combine all of the evidence with all of the allegations that the theory has been misinterpreted, and that its major concepts have not been assessed properly, one is left, more than twenty years later, not really knowing whether to take the theory seriously, let alone whether it should be put into practice in organizational settings ... There is support for many of the implications the theory has for enriching jobs to make them more motivating. But the two-factor aspect of the theory—the feature that makes it unique—is not really a necessary element in the use of the theory for designing jobs, per se.[37]

Job enrichment
Building achievement, recognition, stimulating work, responsibility, and advancement into a job.

Applying Herzberg's Model through Vertical Loading   Job enrichment is based on the application of Herzberg's ideas. Specifically, **job enrichment** entails modifying a job such that an employee has the opportunity to experience achievement,

Table 7–1   *Principles of Vertically Loading a Job*

Principle	Motivators Involved
A. Removing some controls while retaining accountability	Responsibility and personal achievement
B. Increasing the accountability of individuals for their own work	Responsibility and recognition
C. Giving a person a complete natural unit of work (module, division, area, and so on)	Responsibility, achievement, and recognition
D. Granting additional authority to an employee in his activity; job freedom	Responsibility, achievement, and recognition
E. Making periodic reports directly available to the worker himself rather than to the supervisor	Internal recognition
F. Introducing new and more difficult tasks not previously handled	Growth and learning
G. Assigning individuals specific or specialized tasks, enabling them to become experts	Responsibility, growth, and advancement

SOURCE: Reprinted by permission of the *Harvard Business Review*. An exhibit from "One More Time: How Do You Motivate Employees?" by F Herzberg (January/February 1968). Copyright © 1968 by the President and Fellows of Harvard College; all rights reserved.

recognition, stimulating work, responsibility, and advancement. These characteristics are incorporated into a job through vertical loading.

Rather than giving employees additional tasks of similar difficulty (horizontal loading), *vertical loading* consists of giving workers more responsibility. In other words, employees take on chores normally performed by their supervisors. Managers are advised to follow seven principles when vertically loading jobs (see Table 7–1).

Job Characteristics Approach to Job Design

The job characteristics model is a more recent approach to job design. It is a direct outgrowth of job enrichment and attempts to pinpoint those situations and those individuals for which job design is most effective. In this regard, the job characteristics model represents a contingency approach.

Overview of the Job Characteristics Model

Two OB researchers, J Richard Hackman and Greg Oldham, played a central role in developing the job characteristics approach. These researchers tried to determine how work can be structured so that employees are internally (or intrinsically) motivated. **Internal motivation** occurs when an individual is "turned on to one's work because of the positive internal feelings that are generated by doing well, rather than being dependent on external factors (such as incentive pay or compliments from the boss) for the motivation to work effectively."[38] These positive feelings power a self-perpetuating cycle of motivation. As shown in Figure 7–5, internal work motivation is determined by three psychological states. In turn, these psychological states are fostered by the presence of five core job dimensions. As you can see in Figure 7–5, the object of this approach is to promote high internal motivation by designing jobs that possess the five

Internal motivation
Motivation caused by positive internal feelings.

Figure 7–5   *The Job Characteristics Model*

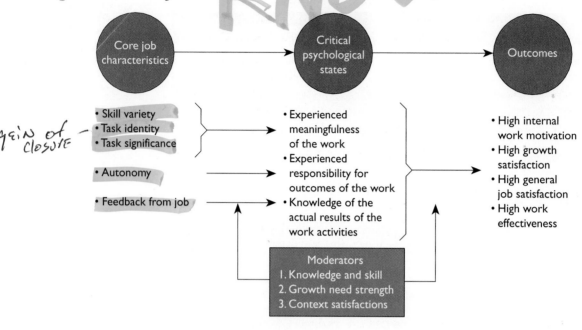

gain of closure

SOURCE: J R Hackman and G R Oldham, *Work Redesign,* © 1980, Addison-Wesley Publishing Co., Reading, MA, p 90. Reprinted with permission.

core job characteristics. Let us examine the major components of this model to see how it works.

Critical Psychological States   A group of management experts described the conditions under which individuals experienced the three critical psychological states. They are:

Experienced meaningfulness
Feeling that one's job is important and worthwhile.

1. **Experienced meaningfulness.** The individual must perceive her work as worthwhile or important by some system of value she accepts.

Experienced responsibility
Believing that one is accountable for work outcomes.

2. **Experienced responsibility.** He must believe that he personally is accountable for the outcomes of his efforts.

Knowledge of results
Feedback about work outcomes.

3. **Knowledge of results.** She must be able to determine, on some fairly regular basis, whether or not the outcomes of her work are satisfactory.[39]

These psychological states generate internal work motivation. Moreover, they encourage job satisfaction and perseverance because they are self-reinforcing.

If one of the three psychological states is shortchanged, motivation diminishes. Consider, for example, Joyce Roché's decision to quit her job as vice president of global marketing at Avon:

> The decision to ditch a plum, six-figure position in a major corporation where one is highly regarded might strike most people as insane. But Roché's decision grew out of her realization that despite the great title and income (she had a six-figure salary with substantial bonus potential), her job did not hold the level of autonomy or responsibility she initially thought it had.[40]

Joyce Roché's internal motivation was diminished by not feeling the psychological state of "experienced responsibility."

Core Job Dimensions   In general terms, **core job dimensions** are common characteristics found to a varying degree in all jobs. Once again, five core job characteristics elicit the three psychological states (see Figure 7–5). Three of those job characteristics combine to determine experienced meaningfulness of work. They are

- *Skill variety.* The extent to which the job requires an individual to perform a variety of tasks that require him or her to use different skills and abilities.
- *Task identity.* The extent to which the job requires an individual to perform a whole or completely identifiable piece of work. In other words, task identity is high when a person works on a product or project from beginning to end and sees a tangible result.
- *Task significance.* The extent to which the job affects the lives of other people within or outside the organization.

Experienced responsibility is elicited by the job characteristic of autonomy, defined as follows:

- *Autonomy.* The extent to which the job enables an individual to experience freedom, independence, and discretion in both scheduling and determining the procedures used in completing the job.

Finally, knowledge of results is fostered by the job characteristic of feedback, defined as follows:

- *Feedback.* The extent to which an individual receives direct and clear information about how effectively he or she is performing the job.[41]

Motivating Potential of a Job   Hackman and Oldham devised a self-report instrument to assess the extent to which a specific job possesses the five core job characteristics. With this instrument, which is discussed in the next section, it is possible to calculate a motivating potential score for a job. The **motivating potential score** (MPS) is a summary index that represents the extent to which the job characteristics foster internal work motivation. Low scores indicate that an individual will not experience high internal work motivation from the job. Such a job is a prime candidate for job redesign. High scores reveal that the job is capable of stimulating internal motivation. The MPS is computed as follows:

$$\text{MPS} = \frac{\begin{array}{c}\text{Skill} \\ \text{variety}\end{array} + \begin{array}{c}\text{Task} \\ \text{identity}\end{array} + \begin{array}{c}\text{Task} \\ \text{significance}\end{array}}{3} \times \text{Autonomy} \times \text{Feedback}$$

Judging from this equation, which core job characteristic do you think is relatively more important in determining the motivational potential of a job? Because autonomy and feedback are not divisible by another number, low amounts of autonomy and feedback have a greater chance of lowering MPS than the job characteristics of skill variety, task identity, and task significance.

Does the Theory Work for Everyone?   As previously discussed, not all people may want enriched work. Hackman and Oldham incorporated this conclusion into their model by identifying three attributes that affect how individuals respond to jobs with a high MPS. These attributes are concerned with the individual's knowledge and skill, growth need strength (representing the desire to grow and develop as an individual), and context satisfactions (see Figure 7–5). Context satisfactions represent the extent to which employees are satisfied with various aspects of their job, such as satisfaction with pay, co-workers, or supervision.

Hackman and Oldham proposed that people will respond positively to jobs with a high MPS when (1) they have the knowledge and skills necessary to do the job, (2) they have high growth needs, and (3) they are satisfied with various aspects of the work context, such as pay and co-workers. Although these recommendations make sense, several studies did not support the moderating influence of an employee's growth needs and context satisfaction.[42] The model worked equally well for employees with high and low growth needs and context satisfaction. Future research needs to examine whether an employee's knowledge and skills are an important moderator of the model's effectiveness.

Applying the Job Characteristics Model

There are three major steps to follow when applying Hackman and Oldham's model. Since the model seeks to increase employee motivation and satisfaction, the first step consists of diagnosing the work environment to determine if a problem exists. Hackman and Oldham developed a self-report instrument for managers to use called the *job diagnostic survey* (JDS).

Diagnosis begins by determining if motivation and satisfaction are lower than desired. If they are, a manager then assesses the MPS of the jobs being examined. National norms are used to determine whether the MPS is low or high.[43] National norms represent the average scores for the MPS and the individual job characteristics based on administering the JDS to numerous samples throughout the United States. If the MPS is low, an attempt is made to determine which of the core job characteristics is causing the problem. If the MPS is high, managers need to look for other factors eroding motivation and satisfaction. (You can calculate your own MPS in the group exercise at the end of this chapter.) Potential factors may be identified by considering other motivation theories discussed in this book.

Step two consists of determining whether job redesign is appropriate for a given group of employees. Job redesign is most likely to work in a participative environment in which employees have the necessary knowledge and skills. The owners of TBM Consulting, a North Carolina–based firm of manufacturing specialists, adhered to this advice after they purchased Alexander Doll Co. and redesigned its factory. The owners began the redesign by soliciting the input of the company's 470 workers. This input resulted in the following work design:

Instead of individually producing parts, the workers were organized in seven- or eight-person teams, each of which is responsible for completing about 300 doll or wardrobe assemblies a

Making dolls is harder than you think. Workers at Alexander Doll Company previously used more than 30 production steps to produce a doll. During that time, boxes of doll parts like the one shown here were often stacked to the ceiling, making parts hard to find and preventing orders from being filled. The application of job redesign significantly increased quality and reduced the time it took to produce a doll.

(Alexander Doll Co.)

Suzanne Opton

day. The amount of work in progress has been cut by 96%, and orders can now be filled in one or two weeks instead of two months.[44]

In the third step, managers need to consider how to redesign the job. The focus of this effort is to increase those core job characteristics that are lower than national norms. Managers are advised to gain employees' input during this step.

Practical Implications of the Job Characteristics Model

Managers may want to use this model to increase employee job satisfaction. Research overwhelmingly demonstrates a moderately strong relationship between job characteristics and satisfaction.[45] A recent study of 459 employees from a glass manufacturing company also indirectly supported the job characteristics model. The company redesigned the work environment by increasing employees' autonomy and participation in decision making and then measured employees' self-efficacy to carry out a broader and more proactive role 18 months later. Job redesign resulted in higher self-efficacy.[46] Unfortunately, job redesign appears to reduce the quantity of output just as often as it has a positive impact. Caution and situational appropriateness are advised. For example, one study demonstrated that job redesign works better in less complex organizations (small plants or companies).[47] Nonetheless, managers are likely to find noticeable increases in the quality of performance after a job redesign program. Results from 21 experimental studies revealed that job redesign resulted in a median increase of 28% in the quality of performance.[48] Moreover, two separate meta-analyses support the practice of using the job characteristics model to help managers reduce absenteeism and turnover,[49] and job characteristics were found to predict absenteeism over a six-year period.[50] This later result is very encouraging because it suggests that job redesign can have long-lasting positive effects on employee behavior.

Job characteristics research also underscores an additional implication for companies undergoing reengineering. Reengineering potentially leads to negative work outcomes because it increases job characteristics beyond reasonable levels. This occurs for two reasons: (1) reengineering requires employees to use a wider variety of skills to perform their jobs, and (2) reengineering typically results in downsizing and short-term periods of understaffing.[51] The unfortunate catch is that understaffing was found to produce lower levels of group performance, and jobs with either overly low or high levels of job characteristics were associated with higher stress.[52] Managers are advised to carefully consider the level of perceived job characteristics when implementing reengineering initiatives.

In conclusion, managers need to realize that job redesign is not a panacea for all their employee satisfaction and motivation problems. To enhance their chances of success with this approach, managers need to remember that a change in one job or department can create problems of perceived inequity in related areas or systems within the organization. Managers need to take an open systems perspective when implementing job redesign, as was suggested by Hackman and Oldham. They wrote:

> Our observations of work redesign programs suggest that attempts to change jobs frequently run into—and sometimes get run over by—other organizational systems and practices, leading to a diminution (or even a reversal) of anticipated outcomes ...
>
> The "small change" effect, for example, often develops as managers begin to realize that radical changes in work design will necessitate major changes in other organizational systems as well.[53]

Job Satisfaction and Work-Family Relationships

An individual's work motivation is related to his or her job satisfaction and work-family relationships. Motivation is not independent of an employee's work environment or personal life. For example, your desire to study for your next OB test is jointly affected by how much you like the course and the state of your health at the time you are studying. It is very hard to study when you have a bad cold or the flu. Consider Warren Buffett's feelings about this issue. Buffett is the founder and chairman and CEO of Berkshire Hathaway, an investment firm located in Omaha, Nebraska, and is one of the wealthiest individuals in the United States. This is what he said to a group of students at the University of Washington:

> I can certainly define happiness, because happy is what I am … I get to do what I like to do every single day of the year. I get to do it with people I like, and I don't have to associate with anybody who causes my stomach to churn. I tapdance to work … I'd advise you that when you go to work, work for an organization of people you admire, because it will turn you on. I always worry about people who say, "I'm going to do this for 10 years; I really don't like it very well. And then I'll do this …" That's a little like saving up sex for your old age. Not a very good idea. I have turned down business deals that were otherwise decent deals because I didn't like the people I would have to work with. I didn't see any sense in pretending.[54]

Job satisfaction
An affective or emotional response to one's job.

Buffett is clearly motivated by his job and work environment. Because of the dynamic relationships between motivation, job satisfaction, and work-family relationships, we conclude this chapter by discussing the causes and consequences of job satisfaction and work-family relationships. This information will increase your understanding about how to motivate others as well as yourself.

The Causes of Job Satisfaction

Job satisfaction is an affective or emotional response toward various facets of one's job. This definition means job satisfaction is not a unitary concept. Rather, a person can be relatively satisfied with one aspect of his or her job and dissatisfied with one or more other aspects. For example, researchers at Cornell University developed the Job Descriptive Index (JDI) to assess one's satisfaction with the following job dimensions: work, pay, promotions, co-workers, and supervision.[55] Researchers at the University of Minnesota concluded there are 20 different dimensions underlying job satisfaction. Selected Minnesota Satisfaction Questionnaire (MSQ) items measuring

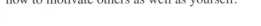

Warren Buffet, founder, chairman, and CEO of Berkshire Hathaway, believes that people will make more money and be happier when their work entails doing something they enjoy. His passion for investing has made him one of the wealthiest people in the United States.

(Jodi Buren/Woodfin Camp & Associates)

OB Exercise   How Satisfied Are You with Your Present Job?

	Very Dissatisfied				Very Satisfied
1. The way I am noticed when I do a good job	1 ——	2 ——	3 ——	4 ——	5
2. The recognition I get for the work I do	1 ——	2 ——	3 ——	4 ——	5
3. The praise I get for doing a good job	1 ——	2 ——	3 ——	4 ——	5
4. How my pay compares with that for similar jobs in other companies	1 ——	2 ——	3 ——	4 ——	5
5. My pay and the amount of work I do	1 ——	2 ——	3 ——	4 ——	5
6. How my pay compares with that of other workers	1 ——	2 ——	3 ——	4 ——	5
7. The way my boss handles employees	1 ——	2 ——	3 ——	4 ——	5
8. The way my boss takes care of complaints brought to him/her by employees	1 ——	2 ——	3 ——	4 ——	5
9. The personal relationship between my boss and his/her employees	1 ——	2 ——	3 ——	4 ——	5

Total score for satisfaction with recognition (add questions 1–3), compensation (add questions 4–6), and supervision (add questions 7–9).
Comparative norms for each dimension of job satisfaction are: Total score of 3–6 = Low job satisfaction; 7–11 = Moderate satisfaction; 12 and above = High satisfaction.

SOURCE: Adapted from D J Weiss, R V Dawis, G W England, and L H Lofquist, *Manual for the Minnesota Satisfaction Questionnaire*, (Minneapolis: Industrial Relations Center, University of Minnesota, 1967). Used with permission.

satisfaction with recognition, compensation, and supervision are listed in the OB Exercise. Please take a moment now to determine how satisfied you are with these three aspects of your present or most recent job, and then use the norms to compare your score.[56] How do you feel about your job?

Five predominant models of job satisfaction specify its causes. They are need fulfillment, discrepancy, value attainment, equity, and dispositional/genetic components. A brief review of these models will provide insight into the complexity of this seemingly simple concept.[57]

Need Fulfillment   These models propose that satisfaction is determined by the extent to which the characteristics of a job allow an individual to fulfill his or her needs. For example, a recent survey of 30 Massachusetts law-firms revealed that 35% to 50% of law-firm associates left their employers within three years of starting because the firms did not accommodate family needs. This example illustrates that unmet needs can affect both satisfaction and turnover.[58] Although these models generated a great degree of controversy, it is generally accepted that need fulfillment is correlated with job satisfaction.[59]

Discrepancies   These models propose that satisfaction is a result of met expectations. **Met expectations** represent the difference between what an individual expects to receive from a job, such as good pay and promotional opportunities, and what he or she actually receives. When expectations are greater than what is received, a person will

Met expectations
The extent to which one receives what he or she expects from a job.

be dissatisfied. In contrast, this model predicts the individual will be satisfied when he or she attains outcomes above and beyond expectations. A meta-analysis of 31 studies that included 17,241 people demonstrated that met expectations were significantly related to job satisfaction.[60]

Value attainment
The extent to which a job allows fulfillment of one's work values.

Value Attainment   The idea underlying **value attainment** is that satisfaction results from the perception that a job allows for fulfillment of an individual's important work values.[61] In general, research consistently supports the prediction that value fulfillment is positively related to job satisfaction.[62] Managers can thus enhance employee satisfaction by structuring the work environment and its associated rewards and recognition to reinforce employees' values.

Equity   In this model, satisfaction is a function of how "fairly" an individual is treated at work. Satisfaction results from one's perception that work outcomes, relative to inputs, compare favorably with a significant other's outcomes/inputs. A meta-analysis involving data from 30 different organizations and 12,979 people supported this model. Employees perceived fairness of pay and promotions were significantly correlated with job satisfaction.[63] Chapter 8 explores this promising model in more detail.

Dispositional/Genetic Components   Have you ever noticed that some of your co-workers or friends appear to be satisfied across a variety of job circumstances, whereas others always seem dissatisfied? This model of satisfaction attempts to explain this pattern.[64] Specifically, the dispositional/genetic model is based on the belief that job satisfaction is partly a function of both personal traits and genetic factors. As such, this model implies that stable individual differences are just as important in explaining job satisfaction as are characteristics of the work environment. Although only a few studies have tested these propositions, results support a positive, significant relationship between personal traits and job satisfaction over time periods ranging from 2 to 50 years.[65] Genetic factors also were found to significantly predict life satisfaction, well-being, and general job satisfaction.[66] Additional research is needed to test this new model of job satisfaction.

The Consequences of Job Satisfaction

This area has significant managerial implications because thousands of studies have examined the relationship between job satisfaction and other organizational variables. Because it is impossible to examine them all, we will consider a subset of the more important variables from the standpoint of managerial relevance.

Table 7–2 summarizes the pattern of results. The relationship between job satisfaction and these other variables is either positive or negative. The strength of the relationship ranges from weak (very little relationship) to strong. Strong relationships imply that managers can significantly influence the variable of interest by increasing job satisfaction. Let us now consider several of the key correlates of job satisfaction.

Motivation   A recent meta-analysis of nine studies and 2,237 workers revealed a significant positive relationship between motivation and job satisfaction. Because satisfaction with supervision also was significantly correlated with motivation, managers are advised to consider how their behavior affects employee satisfaction.[67] Managers can potentially enhance employees' motivation through various attempts to increase job satisfaction.

Table 7-2   *Correlates of Job Satisfaction*

Variables Related with Satisfaction	Direction of Relationship	Strength of Relationship
Motivation	Positive	Moderate
Job involvement	Positive	Moderate
Organizational citizenship behavior	Positive	Moderate
Organizational commitment	Positive	Strong
Absenteeism	Negative	Weak
Tardiness	Negative	Weak
Turnover	Negative	Moderate
Heart disease	Negative	Moderate
Perceived stress	Negative	Strong
Pro-union voting	Negative	Moderate
Job performance	Positive	Weak
Life satisfaction	Positive	Moderate
Mental health	Positive	Moderate

Job Involvement   Job involvement represents the extent to which an individual is personally involved with his or her work role. A meta-analysis involving 27,925 individuals from 87 different studies demonstrated that job involvement was moderately related with job satisfaction.[68] Managers are thus encouraged to foster satisfying work environments in order to fuel employees' job involvement.

Organizational Citizenship Behavior   Organizational citizenship behaviors consist of employee behaviors that are beyond the call of duty. Examples include "such gestures as constructive statements about the department, expression of personal interest in the work of others, suggestions for improvement, training new people, respect for the spirit as well as the letter of housekeeping rules, care for organizational property, and punctuality and attendance well beyond standard or enforceable levels."[69] Managers certainly would like employees to exhibit these behaviors. A meta-analysis covering 6,746 people and 28 separate studies revealed a significant and moderately positive correlation between organizational citizenship behaviors and job satisfaction.[70] Moreover, additional research demonstrated that employees' citizenship behaviors were determined more by leadership and characteristics of the work environment than by an employee's personality.[71] It thus appears that managerial behavior significantly influences an employee's willingness to exhibit citizenship behaviors. This relationship is important to recognize because organizational citizenship behaviors were positively correlated with performance ratings.[72]

Organizational Commitment   Organizational commitment reflects the extent to which an individual identifies with an organization and is committed to its goals. A meta-analysis of 68 studies and 35,282 individuals uncovered a significant and strong relationship between organizational commitment and satisfaction.[73] Managers are advised to increase job satisfaction in order to elicit higher levels of commitment. In turn, higher commitment can facilitate higher productivity.[74]

Absenteeism   Absenteeism is costly, and managers are constantly on the lookout for ways to reduce it. One recommendation has been to increase job satisfaction. If this is a valid recommendation, there should be a strong negative relationship (or negative correlation) between satisfaction and absenteeism. In other words, as satisfaction increases, absenteeism should decrease. A researcher tracked this prediction by synthesizing three separate meta-analyses containing a total of 74 studies. Results revealed a weak negative relationship between satisfaction and absenteeism.[75] It is unlikely, therefore, that managers will realize any significant decrease in absenteeism by increasing job satisfaction.

Turnover   Turnover is important to managers because it both disrupts organizational continuity and is very costly. A meta-analysis of 78 studies covering 27,543 people demonstrated a moderate negative relationship between satisfaction and turnover.[76] (See Table 7–2.) Given the strength of this relationship, managers would be well advised to try to reduce turnover by increasing employee job satisfaction.

Perceived Stress   Stress can have very negative effects on organizational behavior and an individual's health. Stress is positively related to absenteeism, turnover, coronary heart disease, and viral infections.[77] According to Linda Rosenstock, director of the National Institute for Occupational Safety and Health, stress at work has been increasing because of the widespread downsizing of corporate America in recent years. She believes that 25% to 33% of the workforce is under high stress and is drained and used up by the end of a workday. In addition, people are working more hours. For example, the average number of hours Americans work (47 hours per week) has increased by 8% between 1998 and 1999—20% of the workforce works at least 49 hours per week.[78] Based on a meta-analysis of seven studies covering 2,659 individuals, Table 7–2 reveals that perceived stress has a strong, negative relationship with job satisfaction.[79] It is hoped that managers would attempt to reduce the negative effects of stress by improving job satisfaction.

Job Performance   One of the biggest controversies within organizational research centers on the relationship between satisfaction and job performance. Some, such as Herzberg, argue that satisfaction leads to higher performance while others contend that high performance leads to satisfaction. In an attempt to resolve this controversy, a meta-analysis accumulated results from 74 studies. Overall, the relationship between job satisfaction and job performance was examined for 12,192

Conflict between our personal life and work life affects our performance at work and the overall quality of our lives. Some companies such as Synovus recognize their interdependency and attempt to help employees cope with these competing demands. Synovus's "Right Choice" benefit program enables employees to take time off to spend with their children at school.

Courtesy of Synovus Financial Corporation

people. It was discovered that there was a small positive relationship between satisfaction and performance.[80]

Researchers have identified two key reasons this result is misleading and understates the true relationship between satisfaction and performance. First, job satisfaction is not theoretically expected to have a strong influence on behavior (e.g., performance and turnover). Rather, satisfaction is hypothesized to indirectly affect performance through an employee's intentions or effort.[81] Figure 7–1 shows this relationship. Returning to Figure 7–1, note how job satisfaction, which is represented by the term "affect" in the individual input box, is at the far left of the model and that performance is on the far right. Performance is expected to be more strongly influenced by the boxes in between individual inputs and performance, namely, motivational processes and motivated behaviors. A recent meta-analysis supported this conclusion.[82] The second reason revolves around the accuracy of measuring an individual's performance. If performance ratings do not reflect the actual interactions and interdependencies at work, weak meta-analytic results are partially due to incomplete measures of individual-level performance.[83] Examining the relationship between *aggregate* measures of job satisfaction and organizational performance is one solution to correct this problem. In support of these ideas, a recent study found a significant, positive correlation between organizational performance and employee satisfaction for data collected from 298 schools and 13,808 teachers.[84] Thus, it appears that managers can positively affect performance by increasing employee job satisfaction.

Work-Family Relationships

The relationship between an individual's work life and personal life is becoming increasingly important in light of the demographic trends occurring within the United States. For example, the increased number of women in the workforce (particularly those with children), the growth in dual-career couples, and an aging population are pressuring employees to more effectively balance work and family issues. Consider the sentiments expressed by Rand Pearsall, president of Oasis Advertising, in a letter written to *The Wall Street Journal:*

> I am the president of a successful and growing advertising agency. My wife is the director of consumer promotion at Nabisco. We have four children and a day doesn't go by that doesn't force us to use our management skills to keep our family and household running.
>
> While we're thankful for an excellent income, the demands of career and family can be overwhelming. We each face constant doubts about whether this income is actually making our lives better. I'm beginning to think that a workday in which you can actually forget to eat or go to the bathroom is probably not very healthy.
>
> We have learned to be more efficient. Like a corporation, we have "re-engineered" our lives to keep the focus on the children and careers …And there is no leisure time for us as adults, either separately or together.[85]

This example dramatically illustrates the interplay between an individual's work and personal lives. Let us now consider three rival hypotheses to explain the dynamic interaction between work-family relationships and one's subsequent job and life satisfaction. We conclude by discussing organizational responses to this issue.

Hypotheses Regarding Work-Family Relationships   The first hypothesis, called the *compensation effect,* suggests that job and life satisfaction are negatively related. That is, we compensate for low job or life satisfaction by seeking satisfying activities in the other domains. A meta-analysis of 34 studies covering 19,811 people failed to support this prediction. Results revealed a significant and positive correlation between job and life satisfaction.[86] The *segmentation hypothesis* proposes that job satisfaction and life satisfaction are independent—one supposedly does not influence the other. Research also did not confirm this model. Recent research supports the third hypothesis, which is called the *spillover model.*

Spillover model
Describes the reciprocal relationship between job and life satisfaction.

The **spillover model** hypothesizes that job satisfaction or dissatisfaction spills over into one's personal life and vice versa. In other words, each affects the other both positively and negatively on an ongoing basis.[87] A spillover relationship suggests that individuals experience both conflict and support as they manage the interplay between responsibilities at work and home.[88] As indicated in the previous quote by Rand Pearsall, managing this conflict can be quite stressful.

Organizational Response to Work-Family Issues   Organizations are increasingly implementing a variety of "family-friendly" programs and services aimed at helping employees to manage the interplay between their work and personal lives. They can include providing child-care services, flexible work schedules, cafeteria benefit plans, telecommuting (nearly 18 million Americans telecommute), dry-cleaning services, ATMs at work, and stress reduction programs.[89] Organizations hope that such programs will enhance employees' satisfaction and productivity. Consider the following examples:

> More companies tailor benefits to solve conflicts involving children or elderly parents. In Omaha, Neb., ConAgra Inc. sends a visiting nurse to an employee's house to take care of a sick child or elder for up to 12 hours. Lincoln National Corp., a Fort Wayne, Ind., financial-services company, launches a "homework-assistance helpline" staffed with teachers for children of employees. "It takes a load off parents who haven't been around a trigonometry lesson in a while," a spokesman says.
>
> The moves can help reduce turnover in low-wage industries. Marriott Corp. unveiled a toll-free hotline this year to give employees references for day care, legal help, or personal-finance advice . . . Brookdale Plastics Inc., Plymouth, Minn., buys eyeglasses and clothing for some workers unable to buy their own.[90]

First Tennessee Bank is a good example of a strong proponent of family-friendly programs. The organization experienced higher customer retention, reduced employee turnover, and increased productivity after implementing several work-family initiatives.[91] Although these results are quite promising, researchers have only recently begun to conduct rigorous evaluations of family-friendly programs.[92] Nonetheless, it seems reasonable to conclude that organizations will continue to search for ways to help employees cope with the potentially conflicting demands within their personal and work lives given the dynamics of modern-day life. We believe that this recommendation is a win-win solution that helps individuals and organizations alike.

Summary of Key Concepts

1. *Define the term* motivation. Motivation is defined as those psychological processes that cause the arousal, direction, and persistence of voluntary, goal-oriented actions. Managers need to understand these psychological processes if they are to successfully guide employees toward accomplishing organizational objectives.

2. *Discuss the job performance model of motivation.* Individual inputs and job context variables are the two key categories of factors that influence motivation. In turn, motivation leads to motivated behaviors, which then affect performance. The model highlights four key issues: (a) Motivation is different from behavior. (b) Behavior is influenced by more than just motivation. (c) Behavior is different from performance. (d) Motivation is a necessary but insufficient contributor to job performance.

3. *Review the historical roots of modern motivation theories.* Five ways of explaining behavior—needs, reinforcement, cognition, job characteristics, and feelings/emotions—underlie the evolution of modern theories of human motivation. Some theories of motivation focus on internal energizers of behavior such as needs, satisfaction, and feelings/emotions. Other motivation theories, which deal in terms of reinforcement, cognitions, and job characteristics, focus on more complex person-environment interactions. There is no single, universally accepted theory of motivation.

4. *Contrast Maslow's and McClelland's need theories.* Two well-known need theories of motivation are Maslow's need hierarchy and McClelland's need theory. Maslow's notion of a prepotent or stair-step hierarchy of five levels of needs has not stood up well under research. McClelland believes that motivation and performance vary according to the strength of an individual's need for achievement. High achievers prefer moderate risks and situations where they can control their own destiny. Top managers should have a high need for power coupled with a low need for affiliation.

5. *Demonstrate your familiarity with scientific management, job enlargement, job rotation, and job enrichment.* Each of these techniques is used in the process of job design. Job design involves altering jobs with the intent of increasing employee job satisfaction and productivity. Scientific management designs jobs by using research and experimentation to identify the most efficient way to perform tasks. Jobs are horizontally loaded in job enlargement by giving workers more than one specialized task to complete. Job rotation increases workplace variety by moving employees from one specialized job to another. Job enrichment vertically loads a job by giving employees administrative duties normally performed by their superiors.

6. *Explain the practical significance of Herzberg's distinction between motivators and hygiene factors.* Herzberg believes job satisfaction motivates better job performance. His *hygiene* factors, such as policies, supervision, and salary, erase sources of dissatisfaction. On the other hand, his *motivators,* such as achievement, responsibility, and recognition, foster job satisfaction. Although Herzberg's motivator–hygiene theory of job satisfaction has been criticized on methodological grounds, it has practical significance for job enrichment.

7. *Describe how internal work motivation is increased by using the job characteristics model.* The psychological states of experienced meaningfulness, experienced responsibility, and knowledge of results produce internal work motivation. These psychological states are fostered by the presence of five core job characteristics. People respond positively to jobs containing these core job characteristics when they have the knowledge and skills necessary to perform the job, high growth needs, and high context satisfactions.

8. *Discuss the causes and consequences of job satisfaction.* Job satisfaction is an affective or emotional response toward various facets of one's job. Five models of job satisfaction specify its causes. They are need fulfillment, discrepancy, value attainment, equity, and trait/genetic components. Job satisfaction has been correlated with hundreds of consequences. Table 7–2 summarizes the pattern of results found for a subset of the more important variables.

9. *Critique the three hypotheses that explain the nature of work-family relationships.* The compensation effect predicts that job and life satisfaction are negatively related, and the segmentation hypothesis proposes that job satisfaction and life satisfaction are independent. Neither of these hypotheses are supported by research. The spillover hypothesis, which is confirmed by research, predicts that job satisfaction and life satisfaction affect each other both positively and negatively on an ongoing basis.

Discussion Questions

1. Why should the average manager be well versed in the various motivation theories?

2. From a practical standpoint, what is a major drawback of theories of motivation based on internal factors such as needs, satisfaction, and feelings/emotions?

3. Are you a high achiever? How can you tell? How will this help or hinder your path to top management?

4. How have hygiene factors and motivators affected your job satisfaction and performance?

5. How might the job characteristics model be used to increase your internal motivation to study?

6. Do you know anyone who would not respond positively to an enriched job? Describe this person.

7. Do you believe that job satisfaction is partly a function of both personal traits and genetic factors? Explain.

8. Do you think job satisfaction leads directly to better job performance? Explain.

9. What are the three most valuable lessons about employee motivation that you have learned from this chapter?

10. How would you respond to a manager who said, "Work-life balance is a personal problem that does not belong in the workplace. If you want to get ahead, be prepared to work a lot of hours and don't complain."

Internet Exercise

This chapter discussed a variety of approaches for motivating employees. We noted that there is not one best theory of motivation and that managers can use different theories to solve various types of performance problems. The purpose of this exercise is for you to identify motivational techniques or programs that are being used at different companies. Begin by visiting the Web site for The Foundation for Enterprise Development at http://www.fed.org/library/index.html. The Foundation is a non-profit organization that helps managers to implement equity-based compensation and broad-based participation programs aimed at improving corporate performance. To begin your search, select the resource library and follow up by choosing to view the library by subject. You will be given a variety of categories to choose from. Use the categories of "case studies of private companies" or "case studies of public companies," and then pick two companies that you would like to analyze.

Questions

1. In what ways are these companies using the theories and models discussed in this chapter?

2. To what extent is employee motivation related to these organizations' cultures?

3. What motivational methods are these companies using that were not discussed in this chapter?

OB in Action Case Study

Fast-Growing Companies Use a Variety of Motivation Techniques[93]

Chances are, Prospect Associates Ltd. won't ever offer Drew Melton a corner office and his pick of the company art collection; he started out as a copy-machine operator three years ago, and that's exactly what he is today.

A dead-end job? In a different company, maybe. Two weeks after he was hired at the Rockville, Md., health-communications-policy consultancy, Melton went to its president, Laura Henderson, and told her how he could run document production better and faster. "I think in terms of efficiency," says Melton. So does Henderson, who gave Melton carte blanche to do things his way. "They're listening to my ideas, and that's where I'm making changes and contributing to the company," says Melton. Today he runs a virtual Xerox fiefdom, dispensing advice to Prospect's harried consultants, who rely on his painstaking attention to detail to give their proposals a professional look.

Has Melton advanced? You bet. He hasn't climbed a corporate ladder, but he has increased his contribution to the company by honing his skills and expanding the scope of his job. His salary has increased by more than 40%, he's respected by the company's professional staff, and there's no pressure on him to "move up." . . .

Like most "best company" CEOs, Henderson took into account the nature of her business and the needs of her employees and created a system of "advancement" that makes sense for both. As a player in the highly competitive government-consulting business, Prospect relies on all employees not only to generate ideas but to market them, too. Marisa Arbona, for example, has been given the freedom to parlay her special interest—communications about Native American health issues—into new business for Prospect, something she wasn't allowed to do by her former employer. "As long as I can present my ideas and make them work, I don't think there are any limitations for me here," says Arbona, who won a National Cancer Institute Recognition Award last year. "That was very fulfilling," she says. "It wouldn't have come if I hadn't been working at Prospect." . . .

Nowhere are the opportunities for advancement as dramatic as in fast-growing companies. "There's no ladder to climb," says Jon Goodman, director of the Entrepreneur Program at the University of Southern California in Los Angeles. "They're building the ladder as they grow." So the challenge is to hire the kinds of employees that will help build the ladder. "You don't want to advance—you want to enlarge," adds Goodman. "Your technical skills become greater; you build your résumé in terms of span of control and responsibility."

Such is the case in Stonyfield Farm Inc., in Londonderry, N.H., which has seen annual sales growth average over 60% for the past three years. "A year ago we had 9 supervisors," says Stonyfield CEO Gary Hirshberg. "Now we have 22, and only 3 of those were new hires." In other words, 10 Stonyfield employees have been promoted to supervisor level. That's what happened to former limo driver Edward Souza, who knew nothing about the dairy business when he applied for a job at Stonyfield, five years ago. "But they emphasized that there was plenty of room to advance for people willing to learn as much as they could," he says. Souza started as a yogurt checker but soon learned how to clean equipment and process milk. A year later he became head processor, and six months after that he was promoted to production supervisor and then to production manager. Souza, who now supervises 40 people, has helped grow production capacity from 9,000 to 60,000 cases a week in only three and a half years . . .

But even at Phoenix [St. Louis's Phoenix Textile Corp.], which, says [Pam] Reynolds [CEO], "has a very structured system where people have specific jobs," there is plenty of room for "horizontal" advancement. Kim Roussin, for example, ran Phoenix's data-processing division for several years before she finally concluded that she wouldn't succeed if she stayed in that position. Roussin expressed an interest in sales, so the company moved her into sales support. "That might sound like a demotion, but to me it was a different form of advancing," she says.

David Kelley would agree. In fact, he founded IDEO Product Development, in Palo Alto, Calif., on that principle. "I set out to make a company that was a great place for my friends to work," says Kelley. He had worked for big companies, but, he says, they took the spark out of his life. So he decided to start his own product-design company, eschewing the hierarchy he so disdained. At IDEO, no one has a title, or a "boss," for that matter. Designers form teams around specific projects; each of those teams has a leader whose authority lasts only as long as the project, so today's manager may be tomorrow's subordinate.

So what's the measure of success in such an unstructured environment? "We're talking about climbing the self-fulfillment ladder," says Kelley. "For some employees here,

self-fulfillment comes from how technical they are. For others, it means climbing a ladder based on how big a project you run, or how many you can run." Employees get a fix on their progress with regular peer reviews. They select their own reviewers; most choose someone who they know is especially critical, because that person's praise is valued more.

Questions for Discussion

1. Using the job performance model of motivation shown in Figure 7–1, why do you think the motivational programs at Prospect, Stonyfield Farm, Phoenix Textile, and IDEO are working?

2. Using need theories, what is likely to happen to the motivation of Drew Melton at Prospect, Edward Souza at Stonyfield Farms, Kim Roussin at Phoenix Textile, and employees at IDEO?

3. How did the top executives from each company use the principles of job enrichment?

4. Using the job characteristics model in Figure 7–5, describe how the different companies fostered intrinsic motivation by increasing the three critical psychological states.

5. Which of the relationships outlined in Table 7–2 are supported by information in the case? Provide detailed examples to support your conclusions.

6. Would the same motivational techniques used at Prospect, Stonyfield Farm, Phoenix Textile, and IDEO work in larger organizations? Explain.

Personal Awareness and Growth Exercise

What Is Your Work Ethic?

Objectives

1. To measure your work ethic.
2. To determine how well your work ethic score predicts your work habits.

Introduction

The work ethic reflects the extent to which an individual values work. A strong work ethic involves the belief that hard work is the key to success and happiness. In recent years, there has been concern that the work ethic is dead or dying. This worry is based on findings from observational studies and employee attitude surveys.

People differ in terms of how much they believe in the work ethic. These differences influence a variety of behavioral outcomes. What better way to gain insight into the work ethic than by measuring your own work ethic and seeing how well it predicts your everyday work habits?

Instructions

To assess your work ethic, complete the eight-item instrument developed by a respected behavioral scientist.[94] Being honest with yourself, circle your responses on the rating scales following each of the eight items. There are no right or wrong answers. Add up your total score for the eight items, and record it in the space provided. *The higher your total score, the stronger your work ethic.*

Following the work ethic scale is a short personal-work-habits questionnaire. Your responses to this questionnaire will help you determine whether your work ethic score is a good predictor of your work habits.

Work Ethic Scale

1. When the workday is finished, people should forget their jobs and enjoy themselves.

   Agree completely   1—2—3—4—5   Disagree completely

2. Hard work does not make an individual a better person.
   Agree completely   1—2—3—4—5   Disagree completely

3. The principal purpose of a job is to provide a person with the means for enjoying his or her free time.
   Agree completely   1—2—3—4—5   Disagree completely

4. Wasting time is not as bad as wasting money.
   Agree completely   1—2—3—4—5   Disagree completely

5. Whenever possible, a person should relax and accept life as it is, rather than always striving for unreachable goals.
   Agree completely   1—2—3—4—5   Disagree completely

6. A person's worth should not be based on how well he or she performs a job.
   Agree completely   1—2—3—4—5   Disagree completely

7. People who do things the easy way are the smart ones.
   Agree completely   1—2—3—4—5   Disagree completely

8. If all other things are equal, it is better to have a job with little responsibility than one with a lot of responsibility.
   Agree completely   1—2—3—4—5   Disagree completely

Total = _____

Personal Work Habits Questionnaire

1. How many unexcused absences from classes did you have last semester or quarter?
   _____ absences

2. How many credit hours are you taking this semester or quarter?
   _____ hours

3. What is your overall grade point average?
   _____ GPA

4. What percentage of your school expenses are you earning through full- or part-time employment?
   _____ %

5. In terms of percent, how much effort do you typically put forth at school and/or work?
   School = _____%   Work = _____%

Questions for Discussion

1. How strong is your work ethic?
   Weak = 8–18   Moderate = 19–29
   Strong = 30–40

2. How would you rate your work habits/results?
   Below average _____   Average _____
   Above average _____

3. How well does your work ethic score predict your work habits or work results?
   Poorly _____ Moderately well_____
   Very well _____

Group Exercise

Applying the Job Characteristics Model

Objectives

1. To assess the motivating potential score (MPS) of several jobs.

2. To determine which core job characteristics need to be changed for each job.

3. To explore how you might redesign one of the jobs.

Introduction

The first step in calculating the MPS of a job is to complete the job diagnostic survey (JDS). Since the JDS is a long questionnaire, we would like you to complete a subset of the instrument. This will enable you to calculate the MPS and to identify deficient job characteristics.

Instructions

Your instructor will divide the class into groups of four to six. Each group member will first assess the MPS of his or her current job and then will identify which core job characteristics need to be changed. Once each group member completes these tasks, the group will identify the job with the lowest MPS and devise a plan for redesigning it. The following steps should be used.

You should first complete the 12 items from the JDS. For each item, indicate whether it is an accurate or inaccurate description of your current or most recent job by selecting one number from the scale provided. Write your response in the space provided next to each item. After completing the JDS, use the scoring key to compute a total score for each of the core job characteristics.

1 = Very inaccurate   5 = Slightly accurate
2 = Mostly inaccurate   6 = Mostly accurate
3 = Slightly inaccurate   7 = Very accurate
4 = Uncertain

_____ 1. Supervisors often let me know how well they think I am performing the job.

_____ 2. The job requires me to use a number of complex or high-level skills.

_____ 3. The job is arranged so that I have the chance to do an entire piece of work from beginning to end.

_____ 4. Just doing the work required by the job provides many chances for me to figure out how well I am doing.

_____ 5. The job is not simple and repetitive.

_____ 6. This job is one where a lot of other people can be affected by how well the work gets done.

_____ 7. The job does not deny me the chance to use my personal initiative or judgment in carrying out the work.

_____ 8. The job provides me the chance to completely finish the pieces of work I begin.

_____ 9. The job itself provides plenty of clues about whether or not I am performing well.

_____ 10. The job gives me considerable opportunity for independence and freedom in how I do the work.

_____ 11. The job itself is very significant or important in the broader scheme of things.

_____ 12. The supervisors and co-workers on this job almost always give me "feedback" about how well I am doing in my work.

Scoring Key

Compute the *average* of the two items that measure each job characteristic.

Skill variety (2 and 5)   _____
Task identity (3 and 8)   _____
Task significance (6 and 11)   _____
Autonomy (7 and 10)   _____
Feedback from job itself (4 and 9)   _____
Feedback from others (1 and 12)   _____

Now you are ready to calculate the MPS. First, you need to compute a total score for the feedback job characteristic. This is done by computing the average of the job characteristics entitled "feedback from job itself" and "feedback from others." Second, use the MPS formula presented earlier in this chapter to compute the MPS. Finally, use the JDS norms provided to interpret the relative status of the MPS and each individual job characteristic.[95]

Once all group members have finished these activities, convene as a group to complete the exercise. Each group member should present his or her results and interpretations of the strengths and deficiencies of the job characteristics. Next, pick the job within the group that has the lowest MPS. Prior to redesigning this job, however, each group member needs more background information. The individual who works in the lowest MPS job should thus provide a thorough description of the job, including its associated tasks, responsibilities, and reporting relationships. A brief overview of the general working environment is also useful. With this information in hand, the group should now devise a detailed plan for how it would redesign the job.

Norms

	TYPE OF JOB			
	Professional/ Technical	Clerical	Sales	Service
Skill variety	5.4	4.0	4.8	5.0
Task identity	5.1	4.7	4.4	4.7
Task significance	5.6	5.3	5.5	5.7
Autonomy	5.4	4.5	4.8	5.0
Feedback from job itself	5.1	4.6	5.4	5.1
Feedback from others	4.2	4.0	3.6	3.8
MPS	135	90	106	114

Questions for Discussion

1. Using the norms, which job characteristics are high, average, or low for the job being redesigned?

2. Which job characteristics did you change? Why?

3. How would you specifically redesign the job under consideration?

4. What would be the difficulties in implementing the job characteristics model in a large organization?

Chapter Eight

Motivation through Equity, Expectancy, and Goal Setting

Learning Objectives

When you finish studying the material in this chapter, you should be able to:

1 Discuss the role of perceived inequity in employee motivation.

2 Explain the differences among distributive, procedural, and interactional justice.

3 Describe the practical lessons derived from equity theory.

4 Explain Vroom's expectancy theory.

5 Discuss Porter and Lawler's expectancy theory of motivation.

6 Describe the practical implications of expectancy theory of motivation.

7 Explain how goal setting motivates an individual.

8 Identify five practical lessons to be learned from goal-setting research.

9 Specify issues that should be addressed before implementing a motivational program.

Annoyed by carry-on restrictions, disgruntled by ever-more-cramped quarters and enraged by being held on the tarmac for hours, air travelers are filing complaints against carriers at the highest rate since 1991. And now some members of Congress are responding to the rising ire with proposed new legislation to protect passengers' rights.

According to newly released figures from the U.S. Department of Transportation, the number of passenger complaints per 100,000 passenger boardings was 26% higher in 1998 than the year before. "Tensions are running high," says David S Stempler, president of Air Travelers Association, a consumer group in Washington. "You're being squashed into tighter planes without a lot of service. It's a tough environment to function in."

While airlines don't dispute the surge in the rate of gripes, they point out that the actual number of complaints filed with the Department of Transportation—nearly 6,000—is relatively low considering the nation's 500 million passenger boardings last year. Plus, "we expect our numbers will go down," says a spokeswoman for Northwest Airlines, which led the industry last year in complaints.

The bulk of last year's complaints focused on late flights, cancellations, and "customer service." Eight of the nation's 10 largest carriers experienced complaint increases last year, including

Tired and frustrated from long waits and poor service, air travelers fight back.
(J. Greenberg/The Image Works)

a 35% jump at UAL Corp.'s United Airlines and 32% at Continental Airlines. Northwest, which struggled with a two-week-long pilots' strike in September, was the target of over one-sixth of all complaints.

Only two carriers saw a drop in complaints: Alaska Airlines and Southwest Airlines. "We treat our passengers like human beings as opposed to dictating to them," says a spokeswoman for Southwest, which had just 0.25 complaints per 100,000 passenger boardings, lowest in the industry. . . .

According to Department of Transportation figures, complaints about flight delays and cancellations jumped 35% last year, while complaints about frequent-flier programs were up 8%. Last year, several carriers began raising mileage requirements for earning free trips, or creating more blackout days restricting their usage. The result: 15% to 45% fewer frequent-flier tickets were issued last year than three years before, according to Paul Hudson of the Aviation Consumer Action Project.

Last week, Democratic Sen. Ron Wyden of Oregon and Republican Sen. John McCain of Arizona introduced a bill aimed at guaranteeing more passengers rights. The "Air Traveler's Bill of Rights" would require airlines to do everything from refunding tickets within 48 hours of purchase to telling passengers the real reason for a flight delay or cancellation.

"We're not mandating fluffy pillows here," Sen. Wyden says. "But we think airlines ought to comply with the same rules as the corner grocery store or the local movie theater."

Passengers aren't just waiting for Congress to act, either. After Northwest passengers were held on the tarmac of Detroit Metropolitan Airport for as long as 11 hours last month, a suit seeking class-action status was filed in Michigan's Wayne County Circuit Court against Northwest, the Detroit airport and Wayne County, which owns the airport. Northwest calls the suit unwarranted. Whatever the outcome, the events underlying the suit have sparked a wave of fresh criticism that airlines fail to treat their customers with the respect of other industries.[1]

> FOR DISCUSSION
> What is motivating airline passengers to complain and file suit against Northwest Airlines? Have you been unfairly treated by an airline? What did you do about it?

The concept of motivation applies to all of our behavior, not just to performance. The opening vignette highlights this point by describing how airline passengers were motivated to complain about customer service. The vignette also illustrates that the motivation to file a lawsuit against Northwest, the Detroit airport, and Wayne County was partially motivated by passengers' perceptions of being treated unjustly or unfairly. The equity theory of motivation provides a good explanation for why passengers behaved the way they did in this case.

This chapter explores three cognitive theories of work motivation: equity, expectancy, and goal setting. Each theory is based on the premise that employees' cognitions are the key to understanding their motivation. To help you apply what you have learned, we conclude the chapter by highlighting the prerequisites of successful motivational programs.

Equity theory

Holds that motivation is a function of fairness in social exchanges.

Adams's Equity Theory of Motivation

Defined generally, **equity theory** is a model of motivation that explains how people strive for *fairness* and *justice* in social exchanges or give-and-take relationships. Equity theory is based on cognitive dissonance theory, developed by social psychologist Leon Festinger in the 1950s.[2]

According to Festinger's theory, people are motivated to maintain consistency between their cognitive beliefs and their behavior. Perceived inconsistencies create cognitive dissonance (or psychological discomfort), which, in turn, motivates corrective action. For example, a cigarette smoker who sees a heavy-

238

smoking relative die of lung cancer probably would be motivated to quit smoking if he or she attributes the death to smoking. Accordingly, when victimized by unfair social exchanges, our resulting cognitive dissonance prompts us to correct the situation. Corrective action may range from a slight change in attitude or behavior to stealing to the extreme case of trying to harm someone. For example, researchers have demonstrated that people attempt to "get even" for perceived injustices by using either direct (e.g., theft or sabotage) or indirect (e.g., intentionally working slowly, giving a co-worker the silent treatment) retaliation.[3] Consider the various forms of retaliation that may occur at America West Airlines:

> America West baggage handlers say luggage problems may soar after an announcement this week that they won't be getting last year's bonus pay because they voted for a union in January. . . . "We feel like we earned this money," baggage handler Jon Davis said, adding that the 2,200 fleet service workers met their service goals. . . . [Pat] Rezler [a baggage handler] and Davis say the workers are so angry about being denied the bonus pay that they may retaliate by misdirecting baggage or just taking their time unloading luggage.[4]

Psychologist J Stacy Adams pioneered application of the equity principle to the workplace. Central to understanding Adams's equity theory of motivation is an awareness of key components of the individual–organization exchange relationship. This relationship is pivotal in the formation of employees' perceptions of equity and inequity.

The Individual–Organization Exchange Relationship

Adams points out that two primary components are involved in the employee–employer exchange, *inputs* and *outcomes.* An employee's inputs, for which he or she expects a just return, include education, experience, skills, and effort. On the outcome side of the exchange, the organization provides such things as pay, fringe benefits, and recognition. These outcomes vary widely, depending on one's organization and rank. Table 8–1 presents a list of on-the-job inputs and outcomes employees consider when making equity comparisons.

Negative and Positive Inequity

On the job, feelings of inequity revolve around a person's evaluation of whether he or she receives adequate rewards to compensate for his or her contributive inputs. People perform these evaluations by comparing the perceived fairness of their employment exchange to that of relevant others. This comparative process, which is based on an equity norm, was found to generalize across countries.[5] People tend to compare themselves to other individuals with whom they have close interpersonal ties—such as friends—and/or to similar others—such as people performing the same job or individuals of the same gender or educational level—rather than dissimilar others.[6]

Three different equity relationships are illustrated in Figure 8–1: equity, negative inequity, and positive inequity. Assume the two people in each of the equity relationships in Figure 8–1 have equivalent backgrounds (equal education, seniority, and so forth) and perform identical tasks. Only their hourly pay rates differ. Equity exists for an individual when his or her ratio of perceived outcomes to inputs is equal to the ratio of outcomes to inputs for a relevant co-worker (see part A in Figure 8–1). Since equity is based on comparing *ratios* of outcomes to inputs, inequity will not necessarily be

Table 8–1   *Factors Considered When Making Equity Comparisons*

Inputs	Outcomes
Time	Pay/bonuses
Education/training	Fringe benefits
Experience	Challenging assignments
Skills	Job security
Creativity	Career advancement/promotions
Seniority	Status symbols
Loyalty to organization	Pleasant/safe working environment
Age	Opportunity for personal growth/development
Personality traits	Supportive supervision
Effort expended	Recognition
Personal appearance	Participation in important decisions

SOURCE: Based in part on J S Adams, "Toward an Understanding of Inequity," *Journal of Abnormal and Social Psychology*, November 1963, pp 422–36.

Figure 8–1   *Negative and Positive Inequity*

A. An Equitable Situation

B. Negative Inequity

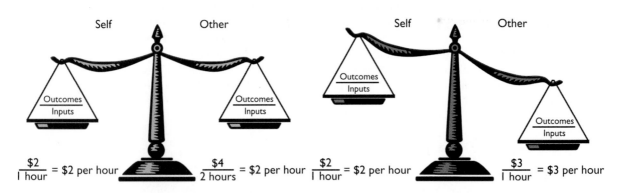

C. Positive inequity

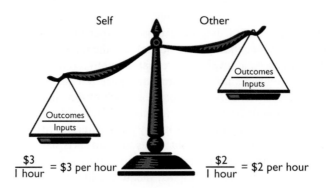

Derek Jeter of the World Series-winning N.Y. Yankees puts the tag on an opponent. Whether on the field or in the office, top players like Jeter and GE's Jack Welch get paid top dollars, creating large pay gaps between upper and lower levels in organizations.

(Reuters/Mike Blake/Archive Photos)

perceived just because someone else receives greater rewards. If the other person's additional outcomes are due to his or her greater inputs, a sense of equity may still exist. However, if the comparison person enjoys greater outcomes for similar inputs, **negative inequity** will be perceived (see part B in Figure 8–1). On the other hand, a person will experience **positive inequity** when his or her outcome to input ratio is greater than that of a relevant co-worker (see part C in Figure 8–1).

Let us consider the type of equity associated with the pay gap between chief executive officers and workers:

> CEO pay again outpaced the stock market in 1998, rising 36%....That 36% raise compares to 2.7% for the average blue-collar worker, one-tenth of a percentage point above last year's boost. White-collar workers got 3.9%, according to the Bureau of Labor Statistics' Employment Cost Index. This year [1999], the boss earned 419 times the average wage of a blue-collar worker. Although such constantly levitating numbers can be hard to truly grasp, consider this: The AFL-CIO calculates that a worker making $25,000 in 1994 would now make $138,350 this year if his pay grew at the same speed as the average CEO.[7]

How do you think the typical employee would interpret this situation? Workers are likely to interpret this situation as negative inequity in spite of the increased stress and responsibility associated with being a CEO. In contrast, CEOs such as Jack Welch, from General Electric, and Eastman Kodak's George Fisher believe that compensation is fair. When *The Wall Street Journal* asked Welch about his $22 million compensation in 1995, he replied, "This is a market. It's a free market and people have choices." Similarly, George Fisher concluded, "We all should be compensated based on competitive issues. If you want a world-class shortstop, you pay. The good news is that many CEOs are getting well compensated for really good performances."[8]

Negative inequity
Comparison in which another person receives greater outcomes for similar inputs.

Positive inequity
Comparison in which another person receives lesser outcomes for similar inputs.

International OB Pay Equity Is an International Issue

BusinessWeek France's Alcatel learned a hard lesson last month in how costly it can be to keep up with US pay. It paid $350 million for Assured Access Technology Inc. in Milpitas, Calif., which provides plumbing for the Internet. Included in the price: $60 million to keep Assured's 55 engineers from bolting at the prospect of a low-paying French employer.

The Alcatel experience shows how pressure is mounting on Europeans to boost pay. Globalizing outfits such as DaimlerChrysler and Deutsche Bank say they can't compete in the United States or hire top international people without offering US pay. But it's not just about grabbing talent abroad: Once companies do that, they find homegrown employees clamoring for more, too. Meanwhile, a new focus on shareholder interests is breaking down barriers to stock options and incentive-pay packages.

To be sure, salaries in Europe remain below those in America. In Britain, for example, companies offer base salaries for chief executives from the United States that are 30% more than their British counterparts get, according to consultants Monks Partnership. Bonuses for US executives are even more generous—twice the British level. The difference reflects a recognition by companies that, if they want to hire a top American manager, they have to pay a premium. That also explains why the CEO of drugmaker SmithKline Beecham PLC, Jan Leschly—a Dane who spent most of his career in the United States—just won a $143 million package, Britain's highest ever. Still, shareholders remained conspicuously silent—which shows how perceptions have changed.

Elsewhere in egalitarian Europe, though, big pay remains controversial. When Finnish papers reported last spring that Chairman Jorma Ollila of Nokia Corp. had accumulated $15 million worth of company stock under an incentive-pay program, it caused a scandal. Ollila's response: Nokia needed a stock-option program to attract top talent. "It's no easy job recruiting people to live in Helsinki," he says. . . .

When Daimler-Benz took over Chrysler Corp. last year, CEO Jürgen E Schrempp had to confront the fact that Chrysler CEO Robert Eaton—who earned over $11 million in 1997, including exercised options—appears to have made more than the rest of Daimler's management board members put together. Worse, Daimler had to pay $395 million—primarily in stock—to Chrysler's top 30 executives to cash out their options. Since cutting the pay of the Chrysler people would be tough, Daimler was forced to boost its own compensation. Deutsche Bank faces similar pressures. Burned by defections from its US operations last year, it agreed to pay $187 million to retain five top execs at Bankers Trust Co. after its takeover of the US bank is done. Not bad, considering CEO Rolf Breuer is estimated to make no more than about $1.5 million a year.

SOURCE: Excerpted from J Ewing, S Baker, W Echikson, and K Capell, "Eager Europeans Press Their Noses to the Glass," *Business Week*, April 19, 1999, p 91.

The issue of pay equity also applies in Europe. The International OB, for example, highlights how compensation practices affect companies that have operations in both the United States and Europe or international companies that want to hire American managers.

Dynamics of Perceived Inequity

Managers can derive practical benefits from Adams's equity theory by recognizing that (1) negative inequity is less tolerable than positive inequity and (2) inequity can be reduced in a variety of ways.

Thresholds of Inequity People have a lower tolerance for negative inequity than they do for positive inequity. Those who are shortchanged are more powerfully motivated to correct the situation than those who are excessively rewarded. For example, if you have ever been overworked and underpaid, you know how negative inequity can erode your job satisfaction and performance. Perhaps you put forth less effort or quit the job to escape the negative inequity. Hence, it takes much more positive than nega-

Table 8–2   *Eight Ways to Reduce Inequity*

Methods	Examples
1. Person can increase his or her inputs.	Work harder; attend school or a specialized training program.
2. Person can decrease his or her inputs.	Don't work as hard; take longer breaks.
3. Person can attempt to increase his or her outcomes.	Ask for a raise; ask for a new title; seek outside intervention.
4. Person can decrease his or her outcomes.	Ask for less pay.
5. Leave the field.	Absenteeism and turnover.
6. Person can psychologically distort his or her inputs and outcomes.	Convince self that certain inputs are not important; convince self that he or she has a boring and monotonous job.
7. Person can psychologically distort the inputs or outcomes of comparison other.	Conclude that other has more experience or works harder; conclude that other has a more important title.
8. Change comparison other.	Pick a new comparison person; compare self to previous job.

SOURCE: Adapted from J S Adams, "Toward an Understanding of Inequity," *Journal of Abnormal and Social Psychology*, November 1963, pp 422–36.

tive inequity to produce the same degree of motivation. Moreover, a meta-analysis of 12,979 people demonstrated that males and females had equal reactions to negative inequity. There were no gender differences in response to perceived inequity.[9]

Reducing Inequity   Table 8–2 lists eight possible ways to reduce inequity. It is important to note that equity can be restored by altering one's equity ratios behaviorally and/or cognitively. The chapter opening vignette is a good illustration of method 3 shown in Table 8–2. Recall that passenger complaints led to the introduction of the "Air Traveler's Bill of Rights" in the US Senate—an outside intervention—while other passengers attempted to increase their outcomes by filing suit against Northwest, the Detroit airport, and Wayne County.

Expanding the Concept of Equity

Beginning in the 1980s, researchers began to expand the role of equity theory in explaining employee attitudes and behavior. This led to a domain of research called *organizational justice*. Organizational justice reflects the extent to which people perceive that they are treated fairly at work. This, in turn, led to the identification of three different components of organizational justice: distributive, procedural, and interactional. **Distributive justice** reflects the perceived fairness of how resources and rewards are distributed or allocated. **Procedural justice** is defined as the perceived fairness of the process and procedures used to make allocation decisions. Research shows that positive perceptions of distributive and procedural justice are enhanced by giving employees a "voice" in decisions that affect them.[10] Voice represents the extent to which employees who are affected by a decision can present relevant information about the decision to others. Voice is analogous to asking employees for their input into the decision-making process.

Distributive justice
The perceived fairness of how resources and rewards are distributed.

Procedural justice
The perceived fairness of the process and procedures used to make allocation decisions.

Interactional justice
The perceived fairness of the decision maker's behavior in the process of decision making.

The last justice component pertains to the interpersonal side of how employees are treated at work. Specifically, **interactional justice** "refers to the interpersonal side of decision making, specifically to the fairness of the decision maker's behavior in the process of decision making. Decision makers behave in an interactionally fair manner when they treat those affected by the decision properly and enact the decision policy or procedure properly."[11] Fair interpersonal treatment necessitates that managers communicate truthfully and treat people with courtesy and respect. Fair enactment of procedures further requires that managers suppress personal biases, consistently apply decision-making criteria, provide timely feedback, and justify decisions.[12]

Equity Research Findings

Different managerial insights have been gained from laboratory and field studies.

Insights from Laboratory Studies   The basic approach used in laboratory studies is to pay an experimental subject more (overpayment) or less (underpayment) than the standard rate for completing a task. People are paid on either an hourly or piece-rate basis. Research findings supported equity theory. Overpaid subjects on a piece-rate system lowered the quantity of their performance and increased the quality of their performance. In contrast, underpaid subjects increased the quantity and decreased the quality of their performance.[13] A study extended this stream of research by examining the effect of underpayment inequity on ethical behavior. A total of 102 undergraduate students were either equitably paid or underpaid for performing a clerical task. Results indicated that underpaid students stole money to compensate for their negative inequity.[14]

Insights from Field Studies   Field studies of organizational justice are on the rise. Overall, results support predictions derived from equity theory. For example, perceptions of distributive justice and procedural justice were positively related to pay and benefit satisfaction, job satisfaction, organizational commitment, trust in management, and commitment to support a decision[15] and negatively associated with retaliatory behaviors, absenteeism, intentions to quit, and turnover.[16] It thus appears beneficial for managers to equitably distribute monetary rewards and promotions by using a fair and equitable decision-making process. Interactional justice also was positively correlated with job satisfaction and reactions to performance appraisals and negatively related with work withdrawal and experiences of sexual harassment.[17] These findings further suggest that the perceived fairness of interpersonal interactions between employees and decision makers can significantly influence important organizational outcomes.

Practical Lessons from Equity Theory

Equity theory has at least eight important practical implications. First, equity theory provides managers with yet another explanation of how beliefs and attitudes affect job performance. According to this line of thinking, the best way to manage job behavior is to adequately understand underlying cognitive processes. Indeed, we are motivated powerfully to correct the situation when our ideas of fairness and justice are offended.

Second, research on equity theory emphasizes the need for managers to pay attention to employees' perceptions of what is fair and equitable. No matter how fair management thinks the organization's policies, procedures, and reward system are, each employee's *perception* of the equity of those factors is what counts. People respond negatively when they perceive organizational and interpersonal injustices. Managers thus are encouraged to make hiring and promotion decisions on merit-based, job-related information. Moreover, because justice perceptions are influenced by the extent to which managers explain their decisions, managers are encouraged to explain the rationale behind their decisions.[18]

Third, managers benefit by allowing employees to participate in making decisions about important work outcomes. For example, employees were more satisfied with their performance appraisals and resultant outcomes when they had a "voice" during the appraisal review.[19] Fourth, employees should be given the opportunity to appeal decisions that affect their welfare. Being able to appeal a decision promotes the belief that management treats employees fairly. In turn, perceptions of fair treatment promote job satisfaction and organizational commitment and help reduce absenteeism and turnover.

Fifth, employees are more likely to accept and support organizational change when they believe it is implemented fairly and when it produces equitable outcomes.[20]

Sixth, managers can promote cooperation and teamwork among group members by treating them equitably. Research reveals that people are just as concerned with fairness in group settings as they are with their own personal interests.[21] Seventh, treating employees inequitably can lead to litigation and costly court settlements. Employees denied justice at work are more likely to turn to arbitration and the courts.[22] Finally, managers need to pay attention to the organization's climate for justice. For example, an organization's climate for justice was found to significantly influence employees' job satisfaction.[23] Researchers also believe that a climate of justice can significantly influence the type of customer service provided by employees. In turn, this level of service is likely to influence customers' perceptions of "fair service" and their subsequent loyalty and satisfaction.[24]

Managers can attempt to follow these practical implications by monitoring equity and justice perceptions through informal conversations, interviews, or attitude surveys. For example, researchers have developed and validated a host of surveys that can be used for this purpose. Please take a moment now to complete the OB Exercise on p 246. It contains part of a survey that was developed to measure employees' perceptions of fair interpersonal treatment. If you perceive your work organization as interpersonally unfair, you are probably dissatisfied and have contemplated quitting. In contrast, your organizational loyalty and attachment are likely greater if you believe you are treated fairly at work.

Expectancy Theory of Motivation

Expectancy theory holds that people are motivated to behave in ways that produce desired combinations of expected outcomes. Perception plays a central role in expectancy theory because it emphasizes cognitive ability to anticipate likely consequences of behavior. Embedded in expectancy theory is the principle of hedonism. Hedonistic people strive to maximize their pleasure and minimize their pain. Generally, expectancy theory can be used to predict behavior in any situation in which a choice between two or more alternatives must be made. For example, it can be used to predict whether to quit or stay at a job; whether to exert substantial or minimal effort at a task; and whether to major in management, computer science, accounting, marketing, psychology, or communication.

> **Expectancy theory**
> Holds that people are motivated to behave in ways that produce valued outcomes.

This section introduces and explores two expectancy theories of motivation: Vroom's expectancy theory and Porter and Lawler's expectancy theory. Understanding these cognitive process theories can help managers develop organizational policies and practices that enhance rather than inhibit employee motivation.

OB Exercise Measuring Perceived Fair Interpersonal Treatment

Instructions
Indicate the extent to which you agree or disagree with each of the following statements by considering what your organization is like most of the time. Then compare your overall score with the arbitrary norms that are presented.

	Strongly Disagree	Disagree	Neither	Agree	Strongly Agree
1. Employees are praised for good work.	1	2	3	4	5
2. Supervisors do not yell at employees.	1	2	3	4	5
3. Employees are trusted.	1	2	3	4	5
4. Employees' complaints are dealt with effectively.	1	2	3	4	5
5. Employees are treated with respect.	1	2	3	4	5
6. Employees' questions and problems are responded to quickly.	1	2	3	4	5
7. Employees are treated fairly.	1	2	3	4	5
8. Employees' hard work is appreciated.	1	2	3	4	5
9. Employees' suggestions are used.	1	2	3	4	5
10. Employees are told the truth.	1	2	3	4	5

Total score = _____

Arbitrary Norms
Very fair organization = 38–50
Moderately fair organization = 24–37
Unfair organization = 10–23

SOURCE: Adapted in part from M A Donovan, F Drasgow, and L J Munson, "The Perceptions of Fair Interpersonal Treatment Scale: Development and Validation of a Measure of Interpersonal Treatment in the Workplace," *Journal of Applied Psychology*, October 1998, pp 683–92.

Vroom's Expectancy Theory

Victor Vroom formulated a mathematical model of expectancy theory in his 1964 book *Work and Motivation*.[25] Vroom's theory has been summarized as follows:

> The strength of a tendency to act in a certain way depends on the strength of an expectancy that the act will be followed by a given consequence (or outcome) and on the value or attractiveness of that consequence (or outcome) to the actor.[26]

Motivation, according to Vroom, boils down to the decision of how much effort to exert in a specific task situation. This choice is based on a two-stage sequence of expectations (effort→performance and performance→outcome). First, motivation is affected by an individual's expectation that a certain level of effort will produce the intended performance goal. For example, if you do not believe increasing the amount of time you spend studying will significantly raise your grade on an exam, you probably will not study any harder than usual. Motivation also is influenced by the employee's perceived chances of getting various outcomes as a result of accomplishing his or her performance goal. Finally, individuals are motivated to the extent that they value the outcomes received. Consider the motivation and behavior of Ross Mandell:

> "This is not fun and games," Mr. Mandell barked at the stockbrokers . . . "You can have fun when you work, but for me, this is the pursuit of cash. I want to be wealthy." . . .
>
> His quest for cash has led to 14 investigator complaints, four job terminations for alleged misconduct, and a New York Stock Exchange investigation of his sales practices, according to industry and regulatory records.
>
> Last year, the exchange concluded that Mr. Mandell repeatedly traded stocks in customers' accounts without their knowledge or permission. Its penalty: a six-week suspension and a written "censure." The exchange levied no fine, and Mr. Mandell is now back in business.[27]

Based on expectancy theory, we would expect Mandell to continue his current behavior because he highly values money and there are no major consequences for his questionable conduct.

Vroom used a mathematical equation to integrate these concepts into a predictive model of motivational force or strength. For our purposes, however, it is sufficient to define and explain the three key concepts within Vroom's model—*expectancy, instrumentality,* and *valence.*

Expectancy An **expectancy,** according to Vroom's terminology, represents an individual's belief that a particular degree of effort will be followed by a particular level of performance. In other words, it is an effort→ performance expectation. Expectancies take the form of subjective probabilities. As you may recall from a course in statistics, probabilities range from zero to one. An expectancy of zero indicates effort has no anticipated impact on performance.

For example, suppose you do not know how to use a typewriter. No matter how much effort you exert, your perceived probability of typing 30 error-free words per minute likely would be zero. An expectancy of one suggests that performance is totally dependent on effort. If you decided to take a typing course as well as practice a couple of hours a day for a few weeks (high effort), you should be able to type 30 words per minute without any errors. In contrast, if you do not take a typing course and only practice an hour or two per week (low effort), there is a very low probability (say, a 20% chance) of being able to type 30 words per minute without any errors.

The following factors influence an employee's expectancy perceptions:

- Self-esteem.
- Self-efficacy.
- Previous success at the task.
- Help received from a supervisor and subordinates.
- Information necessary to complete the task.
- Good materials and equipment to work with.[28]

Instrumentality An **instrumentality** is a performance→ outcome perception. It represents a person's belief that a particular outcome is contingent on accomplishing a specific level of performance. Performance is instrumental when it leads to something else. For example, passing exams is instrumental to graduating from college.

Instrumentalities range from −1.0 to 1.0. An instrumentality of 1.0 indicates attainment of a particular outcome is totally dependent on task performance. An instrumentality of

Expectancy
Belief that effort leads to a specific level of performance.

Instrumentality
A performance→ outcome perception.

zero indicates there is no relationship between performance and outcome. For example, most companies link the number of vacation days to seniority, not job performance. Finally, an instrumentality of -1.0 reveals that high performance reduces the chance of obtaining an outcome while low performance increases the chance. For example, the more time you spend studying to get an A on an exam (high performance), the less time you will have for enjoying leisure activities. Similarly, as you lower the amount of time spent studying (low performance), you increase the amount of time that may be devoted to leisure activities.

The concept of instrumentality can be seen in practice by considering the travel incentive program used by Frank Parsons Paper Company. Executive Vice President Michael Eaton described the program in a recent interview:

> "When you have someone who's making a good income, money's not always the best motivator," says Eaton. "We've found that travel really excites our sales force." Eaton operates a number of incentive programs for the 53 Frank Parsons salespeople. . . . A common denominator in most of the incentive programs is the Marriott Resort gift certificate. "The Marriott certificates are one of the top motivators," says Eaton. . . . To earn the certificates, employees have to meet overall sales goals set by the company. In addition, product suppliers like paper company Union Camp or office product supply company Sony will conduct cooperative incentive programs with Eaton. "We can get very specific about brand and product goals for each salesperson," he says. Eaton keeps the sales force posted every month on where they stand on their goals.[29]

The incentive program clearly makes performance instrumental for receiving travel gift certificates.

Valence
The value of a reward or outcome.

Valence   As Vroom used the term, **valence** refers to the positive or negative value people place on outcomes. Valence mirrors our personal preferences.[30] For example, most employees have a positive valence for receiving additional money or recognition. In contrast, job stress and being laid off would likely be negatively valent for most individuals. In Vroom's expectancy model, *outcomes* refer to different consequences that are contingent on performance, such as pay, promotions, or recognition. An outcome's valence depends on an individual's needs and can be measured for research purposes with scales ranging from a negative value to a positive value. For example, an individual's valence toward more recognition can be assessed on a scale ranging from -2 (very undesirable) to 0 (neutral) to $+2$ (very desirable).

Vroom's Expectancy Theory in Action   Vroom's expectancy model of motivation can be used to analyze a real-life motivation program. Consider the following performance problem described by Frederick W Smith, founder and chief executive officer of Federal Express Corporation:

> . . . we were having a helluva problem keeping things running on time. The airplanes would come in, and everything would get backed up. We tried every kind of control mechanism that you could think of, and none of them worked. Finally, it became obvious that the underlying problem was that it was in the interest of the employees at the cargo terminal—they were college kids, mostly—to run late, because it meant that they made more money. So what we did was give them all a minimum guarantee and say, "Look, if you get through before a certain time, just go home, and you will have beat the system." Well, it was unbelievable. I mean, in the space of about 45 days, the place was way ahead of schedule. And I don't even think it was a conscious thing on their part.[31]

Figure 8–2   *Porter and Lawler's Expectancy Model*

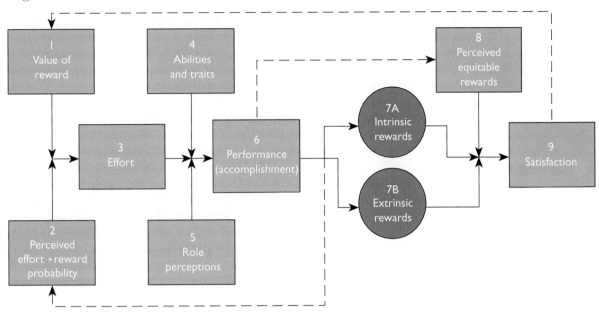

SOURCE: L W Porter and E E Lawler III, *Managerial Attitudes and Performance* (Homewood, IL: Richard D. Irwin, 1968), p 165.

How did Federal Express get its college-age cargo handlers to switch from low effort to high effort? According to Vroom's model, the student workers originally exerted low effort because they were paid on the basis of time, not output. It was in their best interest to work slowly and accumulate as many hours as possible. By offering to let the student workers *go home early if and when they completed their assigned duties,* Federal Express prompted high effort. This new arrangement created two positively valued outcomes: guaranteed pay plus the opportunity to leave early. The motivation to exert high effort became greater than the motivation to exert low effort.

Judging from the impressive results, the student workers had both high effort→performance expectancies and positive performance→outcome instrumentalities. Moreover, the guaranteed pay and early departure opportunity evidently had strongly positive valences for the student workers.

Porter and Lawler's Extension

Two OB researchers, Lyman Porter and Edward Lawler III, developed an expectancy model of motivation that extended Vroom's work. This model attempted to (1) identify the source of people's valences and expectancies and (2) link effort with performance and job satisfaction. The model is presented in Figure 8–2.[32]

Predictors of Effort   Effort is a function of the perceived value of a reward (box 1 in Figure 8–2), which represents the reward's valence, and the perceived effort→ reward probability (box 2, which reflects an expectancy). Employees should exhibit more effort when they believe they will receive valued rewards for task accomplishment.

Predictors of Performance   Performance is determined by more than effort. Figure 8–2 indicates that the relationship between effort and performance is contingent on an employee's abilities and traits (box 4) and role perceptions (box 5). That is, employees with higher abilities attain higher performance for a given level of effort than employees with less ability. Similarly, effort results in higher performance when employees clearly understand and are comfortable with their roles. This occurs because effort is channeled into the most important job activities or tasks.

Predictors of Satisfaction   Employees receive both intrinsic (circle 7A in Figure 8–2) and extrinsic (circle 7B) rewards for performance. Intrinsic rewards are self-granted and consist of intangibles such as a sense of accomplishment and achievement. Extrinsic rewards are tangible outcomes such as pay and public recognition. In turn, job satisfaction is determined by employees' perceptions of the equity of the rewards received (box 8 in Figure 8–2). Employees are more satisfied when they feel equitably rewarded. Figure 8–2 further shows that job satisfaction affects employees' subsequent valence of rewards. Finally, employees' future effort→ reward probabilities are influenced by past experience with performance and rewards.

Research on Expectancy Theory and Managerial Implications

Many researchers have tested expectancy theory. In support of the theory, a meta-analysis of 77 studies indicated that expectancy theory significantly predicted performance, effort, intentions, preferences, and choice.[33] Another summary of 16 studies revealed that expectancy theory correctly predicted occupational or organizational choice 63.4% of the time; this was significantly better than chance predictions.[34] Further, components of expectancy theory accurately predicted task persistence, achievement, employment status of previously unemployed people, job satisfaction, decisions to retire (80% accuracy), voting behavior in union representation elections (over 75% accuracy), reenlistment in the National Guard (66% accuracy), and the frequency of drinking alcohol.[35]

Nonetheless, expectancy theory has been criticized for a variety of reasons. For example, the theory is difficult to test, and the measures used to assess expectancy, instrumentality, and valence have questionable validity.[36] In the final analysis, however, expectancy theory has important practical implications for individual managers and organizations as a whole (see Table 8–3).

Managers are advised to enhance effort→performance expectancies by helping employees accomplish their performance goals. Managers can do this by providing support and coaching and by increasing employees' self-efficacy. A management expert suggests that managers can effectively coach for success by (1) establishing both individual and team goals, (2) holding individuals and team members accountable for goals, (3) showing employees how to complete difficult assignments and tasks, (4) advising employees on how to overcome performance roadblocks, (5) verbally expressing support, (6) listening to employees and fostering two-way communication, and (7) sharing and recognizing progress.[37]

It also is important for managers to influence employees' instrumentalities and to monitor valences for various rewards. This raises the issue of whether organizations should use monetary rewards as the primary method to reinforce performance. Although money is certainly a positively valent reward for most people, there are three

Table 8–3   *Managerial and Organizational Implications of Expectancy Theory*

Implications for Managers	Implications for Organizations
Determine the outcomes employees value.	Reward people for desired performance, and do not keep pay decisions secret.
Identify good performance so appropriate behaviors can be rewarded.	Design challenging jobs.
Make sure employees can achieve targeted performance levels.	Tie some rewards to group accomplishments to build teamwork and encourage cooperation.
Link desired outcomes to targeted levels of performance.	Reward managers for creating, monitoring, and maintaining expectancies, instrumentalities, and outcomes that lead to high effort and goal attainment.
Make sure changes in outcomes are large enough to motivate high effort.	Monitor employee motivation through interviews or anonymous questionnaires.
Monitor the reward system for inequities.	Accommodate individual differences by building flexibility into the motivation program.

(DILBERT reprinted by permission of United Feature Syndicate, Inc.)

issues to consider when deciding on the relative balance between monetary and non-monetary rewards. First, some research shows that workers value interesting work and recognition more than money.[38] Second, extrinsic rewards can lose their motivating properties over time and may undermine intrinsic motivation.[39] This conclusion, however, must be balanced by the fact that performance is related to the receipt of financial incentives. A recent meta-analysis of 39 studies involving 2,773 people showed that financial incentives were positively related to performance quantity but not to performance quality. Another recent study showed that the promise of a financial reward increased children's creativity when they knew that there was an explicit positive relationship between creative performance and rewards.[40] Third, monetary rewards must be large enough to generate motivation. For example, Steven Kerr, chief learning officer at General Electric, estimates that monetary awards must be at least 12% to 15% above employees' base pay to truly motivate people.[41] Unfortunately, this percentage is well above the typical salary increase received by employees. In summary, there is no one best type of reward. Individual differences and need theories tell us that people are motivated by different rewards. Managers should therefore focus on linking employee performance to valued rewards regardless of the type of reward used to enhance motivation.

There are four prerequisites to linking performance and rewards:

1. Managers need to develop and communicate performance standards to employees. For instance, a survey of 487 managers indicated that they were not held accountable for increasing quality. In turn, these managers did not set or enforce high performance standards among their employees.[42] Without question, increased motivation will not result in higher performance unless employees know how and where to direct their efforts.

2. Managers need valid and accurate performance ratings with which to compare employees. Inaccurate ratings create perceptions of inequity and thereby erode motivation.

3. Managers need to determine the relative mix of individual versus team contribution to performance and then reward accordingly. If an employee is truly an independent contributor, then recognition and rewards should be based solely on his or her performance. In contrast, many organizations believe that individual performance is partly due to team-level efforts and productivity. For example, team-based rewards among mid-sized and large US employers grew from 12% in 1993 to 24% in 1999. More specifically, Viking Freight Inc. uses a team-based incentive to reward all employees who work at one of its many terminals. Monetary incentives at a particular terminal are based on how well that terminal does at achieving pre-set objectives.[43]

4. Managers should use the performance ratings to differentially allocate rewards among employees. That is, it is critical that managers allocate significantly different amounts of rewards for various levels of performance.

Ethics at Work

General Electric uses a forced-distribution rating system to evaluate its managers on a curve. Each manager receives a rating from 1 to five. This is how Jack Welch, chairman and chief executive officer of General Electric, described the process of evaluating employees and how these evaluations affect the receipt of stock options:

> 1's are the top 10%. These are the top people. 2's are the next-strongest 15%. 3's are the middle 50%. The ones in the middle have a real future. Then 4's are the caution 15%. They can move to the left. 5's are the least effective 10%. We've got to get rid of them. We don't want to see these people again. On every performance appraisal they are being told you are at 1, 2, 3, 4, or 5. So no one will ever come in with any chance to say, "I was always told I was great. And now you are telling me I am not great." …All the 1's will get [stock] options. About 90%-plus of the 2's will get options. About half of the 3's will get options. And the 4's get no stock options.

SOURCE: Excerpted from C Hymowitz and M Murray, "Raises and Praise or Out the Door: How GE's Chief Rates and Spurs His Employees," *The Wall Street Journal*, June 21, 1999, p. B4.

You Decide . . .

Is it ethical to use a forced-distribution rating system that results in 10% of the employees being dismissed? Explain.

For an interpretation of this situation, visit our Web site **www.mhhe.com**

Motivation through Goal Setting

Regardless of the nature of their specific achievements, successful people tend to have one thing in common. Their lives are goal oriented. This is as true for politicians seeking votes as it is for rocket scientists probing outer space. In Lewis Carroll's delightful tale of *Alice's Adventures in Wonderland,* the smiling Cheshire cat advised the bewildered Alice, "If you don't know where you're going, any road will take you there." Goal-oriented managers tend to find the right road because they know where they are going. Within the context of employee motivation, this section explores the theory, research, and practice of goal setting.

Goals: Definition and Background

Edwin Locke, a leading authority on goal setting, and his colleagues define a **goal** as "what an individual is trying to accomplish; it is the object or aim of an action."[44] Expanding this definition, they add:

> The concept is similar in meaning to the concepts of purpose and intent.... Other frequently used concepts that are also similar in meaning to that of goal include performance standard (a measuring rod for evaluating performance), quota (a minimum amount of work or production), work norm (a standard of acceptable behavior defined by a work group), task (a piece of work to be accomplished), objective (the ultimate aim of an action or series of actions), deadline (a time limit for completing a task), and budget (a spending goal or limit).[45]

The motivational impact of performance goals and goal-based reward plans has been recognized for a long time. At the turn of the century, Frederick Taylor attempted to scientifically establish how much work of a specified quality an individual should be assigned each day. He proposed that bonuses be based on accomplishing those output standards. More recently, goal setting has been promoted through a widely used management technique called management by objectives (MBO). **Management by objectives** is a management system that incorporates participation in decision making, goal setting, and objective feedback.[46] A meta-analysis of MBO programs showed productivity gains in 68 of 70 different organizations. Specifically, results uncovered an average gain in productivity of 56% when top-management commitment was high. The average gain was only 6% when commitment was low. A second meta-analysis of 18 studies further demonstrated that employees' job satisfaction was significantly related to top management's commitment to an MBO implementation.[47] These impressive results highlight the positive benefits of implementing MBO and setting goals. To further understand how MBO programs can increase both productivity and satisfaction, let us examine the process by which goal setting works.

How Does Goal Setting Work?

Despite abundant goal-setting research and practice, goal-setting theories are surprisingly scarce. An instructive model was formulated by Locke and his associates (see Figure 8–3). According to Locke's model, goal setting has four motivational mechanisms.

Goals Direct Attention   Goals that are personally meaningful tend to focus one's attention on what is relevant and important. If, for example, you have a term project due in a few days, your thoughts tend to revolve around completing that project. Similarly, the members of a home appliance salesforce who are told they can win a trip to Hawaii for selling the most refrigerators will tend to steer customers toward the refrigerator display.

Goals Regulate Effort   Not only do goals make us selectively perceptive, they also motivate us to act. The instructor's deadline for turning in your term project would prompt you to complete it, as opposed to going out with friends, watching television, or studying for another course. Generally, the level of effort expended is proportionate to the difficulty of the goal.

Goals Increase Persistence   Within the context of goal setting, **persistence** represents the effort expended on a task over an extended period of time. It takes effort to run 100 meters; it takes persistence to run a 26-mile marathon. Persistent people tend

Goal
What an individual is trying to accomplish.

Management by objectives
Management system incorporating participation in decision making, goal setting, and feedback.

Persistence
Extent to which effort is expended on a task over time.

Figure 8–3   *Locke's Model of Goal Setting*

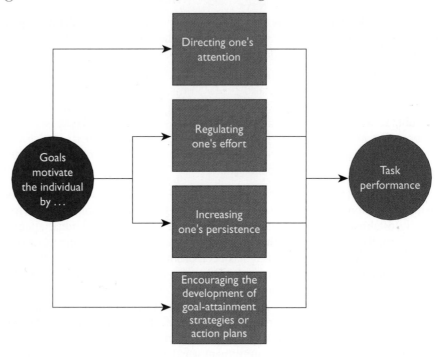

SOURCE: Adapted *A Theory of Goal Setting & Task Performance* by Locke/Latham, © 1990. Adapted by permission of Prentice-Hall, Inc., Upper Saddle River, N.J. (Englewood Cliffs, NJ: Prentice-Hall, 1990). Reprinted by permission of Prentice-Hall, Inc.

to see obstacles as challenges to be overcome rather than as reasons to fail. A difficult goal that is important to an individual is a constant reminder to keep exerting effort in the appropriate direction. Steven Spielberg is a great example of someone who persisted at his goal to be a filmmaker:

> As the most popular and successful filmmaker ever, the 52-year-old Spielberg has directed nine of the 50 top-grossing films of all time. All totaled, films he has directed have brought in more than $5 billion worldwide, and films he's produced have brought in another $4 billion . . . Spielberg identified his dream early in life and tenaciously pursued it. He allowed himself to imagine and trusted his imagination in his art. . . . Spielberg started making movies at age 11 when he learned how to use his father's eight-millimeter windup camera. . . . Having defined his ambition to direct movies from a young age, Spielberg suffered a setback when the prestigious UCLA and USC film schools rejected him because of low high school grades. Instead, because it was near Hollywood, he enrolled as an English major at California State University at Long Beach.
>
> The summer before college, Spielberg took the Universal Studios Tour, and when the tour guides weren't watching, he broke away from the group to wander the giant movie-making factory.
>
> "I went back there every day for three months," says Spielberg in Frank Sanello's *Spielberg: The Man, the Movies, the Mythology.* "I walked past the guard every day, waved at him and he waved back. I always wore a suit and carried a briefcase, and he assumed I was some kid related to some mogul."
>
> He took over an unused office and put his name in the building directory with plastic letters: Steven Spielberg, room 23C. He immersed himself in film production at the

Steven Spielberg is a great example of someone who persisted at his goal to be a filmmaker. Spielberg identified his dream early in life and tenaciously pursued it, overcoming several obstacles along the way, such as being rejected by the UCLA and USC film schools because of low high school grades. Ironically, Spielberg went on to become the most popular and successful filmmaker ever.

(Westenberger/The Liaison Agency)

industry's epicenter, wandering the Universal property to watch directors at work, and once got to see one of his heroes, Alfred Hitchcock, direct scenes for *Tom Curtain.*

Hanging out with directors, writers, and editors, Spielberg learned that to get the attention of studio executives he had to demonstrate his directing ability on the professional film width of 35 millimeters. A friend who wished to become a producer fronted $15,000 for Spielberg to make the short film *Amblin,* which caught the eye of Universal executive Sid Sheinberg, who offered Spielberg a contract to direct television shows. Still several months short of graduating from college, Spielberg hesitated. In a now famous retort, Sheinberg shot back, "Kid, do you want to go to college or do you want to direct?" Spielberg dropped out and took the job.[48]

Goals Foster Strategies and Action Plans   If you are here and your goal is out there somewhere, you face the problem of getting from here to there. For example, the person who has resolved to lose 20 pounds must develop a plan for getting from "here" (his or her present weight) to "there" (20 pounds lighter). Goals can help because they encourage people to develop strategies and action plans that enable them to achieve their goals.[49] By virtue of setting a weight-reduction goal, the dieter may choose a strategy of exercising more, eating less, or some combination of the two. For a work-related example, consider the strategies and plans used by Barbara Smith to develop and grow a new restaurant. Smith was a previous cabaret singer, play producer, author, actress, television spokesperson, and the first African-American on the cover of Mademoiselle:

"When I returned to the [United States] from Vienna I decided to really go for it, so I wrote down my goals and figured out exactly how I was going to get there."

Unlike some celebrity restaurateurs who show up for opening night only to follow the paparazzi to the next media event, Smith has been hands-on from the outset. To begin with she talked a prospective partner into letting her work at another restaurant from pre-opening day through its first year of business. Starting out as a hostess, she studied every aspect of running the restaurant, eventually working her way up to being floor manager. At the end of the year Smith had so impressed the prospective boosters with her cost-consciousness, attention to detail, and aptitude for building a customer base that she received the go-ahead to find an appropriate space to locate B Smith's.[50]

Barbara Smith's strategies and plans paid good dividends. Her New York restaurant celebrated its 10th anniversary in 1996, and she has since opened a second restaurant in Washington D.C.

Figure 8–4   *Relationship between Goal Difficulty and Performance*

A Performance of committed individuals with adequate ability
B Performance of committed individuals who are working at capacity
C Performance of individuals who lack commitment to high goals

SOURCE: *A Theory of Goal Setting and Task Performance,* by Locke/Latham, © 1990. Adapted by permission of Prentice-Hall, Upper Saddle River, N.J. Reprinted by permission of Prentice-Hall, Inc., Englewood Cliffs, NJ.

Insights from Goal-Setting Research

Research consistently has supported goal setting as a motivational technique. Setting performance goals increases individual, group, and organizational performance. Further, the positive effects of goal setting were found in six other countries or regions: Australia, Canada, the Caribbean, England, West Germany, and Japan. Goal setting works in different cultures. Reviews of the many goal-setting studies conducted over the last couple of decades have given managers five practical insights:

Goal difficulty
The amount of effort required to meet a goal.

1. *Difficult goals lead to higher performance.* **Goal difficulty** reflects the amount of effort required to meet a goal. It is more difficult to sell nine cars a month than it is to sell three cars a month. A meta-analysis spanning 4,000 people and 65 separate studies revealed that goal difficulty was positively related to performance.[51] As illustrated in Figure 8–4, however, the positive relationship between goal difficulty and performance breaks down when goals are perceived to be impossible. Figure 8–4 reveals that performance goes up when employees are given hard goals as opposed to easy or moderate goals (section A). Performance then plateaus (section B) and drops (section C) as the difficulty of a goal goes from challenging to impossible.[52]

Goal specificity
Quantifiability of a goal.

2. *Specific, difficult goals lead to higher performance for simple rather than complex tasks.* **Goal specificity** pertains to the quantifiability of a goal. For example, a goal of selling nine cars a month is more specific than telling a salesperson to do his or her best. In an early review of goal-setting research, 99 of 110 studies (90%) found that specific, hard goals led to better performance than did easy, medium, do-your-best, or no goals. This result was confirmed in a meta-analysis of 70 studies conducted between 1966 and 1984, involving 7,407 people.[53]

In contrast to these positive effects, several recent studies demonstrated that setting specific, difficult goals leads to poorer performance under certain circumstances. For example, a meta-analysis of 125 studies indicated that goal-setting effects were strongest for easy tasks and weakest for complex tasks.[54] There are two explanations for this finding. First, employees are not likely to put forth increased effort to achieve complex goals unless they "buy-in" or support them.[55] Thus, it is important for managers to obtain employee buy-in to the goal-setting process. Second, novel and complex tasks take employees longer to complete. This occurs because employees spend more time thinking about how to approach and solve these tasks. In contrast, employees do not have to spend much time thinking about solutions for easy tasks. Specific difficult goals thus impair performance on novel, complex tasks when employees do not have clear strategies for solving these types of problems. On a positive note, however, a recent study demonstrated that goal setting led to gradual improvements in performance on complex tasks when people were encouraged to explicitly solve the problem at hand.[56]

Finally, positive effects of goal setting also were reduced when people worked on interdependent tasks.[57] Managers need to encourage cooperation and efficient work flow in these situations.

3. *Feedback enhances the effect of specific, difficult goals.* Feedback plays a key role in all of our lives. For example, consider the role of feedback in bowling. Imagine going to the bowling lanes only to find that someone had hung a sheet from the ceiling to the floor in front of the pins. How likely is it that you would reach your goal score or typical bowling average? Not likely, given your inability to see the pins. Regardless of your goal, you would have to guess where to throw your second ball if you did not get a strike on your first shot. The same principles apply at work.

Feedback lets people know if they are headed toward their goals or if they are off course and need to redirect their efforts. Goals plus feedback is the recommended approach.[58] Goals inform people about performance standards and expectations so that they can channel their energies accordingly. In turn, feedback provides the information needed to adjust direction, effort, and strategies for goal accomplishment.

4. *Participative goals, assigned goals, and self-set goals are equally effective.* Both managers and researchers are interested in identifying the best way to set goals. Should goals be participatively set, assigned, or set by the employee him- or herself? A summary of goal-setting research indicated that no single approach was consistently more effective than others in increasing performance.[59]

Managers are advised to use a contingency approach by picking a method that seems best suited for the individual and situation at hand. For example, employees' preferences for participation should be considered. Some employees desire to participate in the process of setting goals, whereas others do not. Employees are also more likely to respond positively to the opportunity to participate in goal setting when they have greater task information, higher levels of experience and training, and greater levels of task involvement. Finally, a participative approach helps reduce employees' resistance to goal setting.

5. *Goal commitment and monetary incentives affect goal-setting outcomes.* **Goal commitment** is the extent to which an individual is personally committed to achieving a goal. In general, an individual is expected to persist in attempts to accomplish a goal when he or she is committed to it. Researchers believe that goal commitment moderates the relationship between the difficulty of a goal and performance. That is, difficult goals lead to higher performance only when employees are committed to their goals. Conversely, difficult goals are hypothesized to lead to lower

Goal commitment
Amount of commitment to achieving a goal.

OB Exercise   Is Your Commitment to Achieving Your Performance Goal for This Course Related to Your Behavior?

Instructions

Begin by identifying your performance goal (desired grade) for this class. My desired grade is _____ . Next, use the rating scale shown below to circle the answer that best represents how you feel about each of the following statements. After computing a total score for the goal commitment items, answer the questions related to your study habits for this course.

1 = Strongly disagree
2 = Disagree
3 = Neither agree nor disagree
4 = Agree
5 = Strongly agree

1. I am trying hard to reach my performance goal.	1	2	3	4	5
2. I am exerting my maximum effort (100%) in pursuit of my performance goal.	1	2	3	4	5
3. I am committed to my performance goal.	1	2	3	4	5
4. I am determined to reach my performance goal.	1	2	3	4	5
5. I am enthusiastic about attempting to achieve my performance goal.	1	2	3	4	5
6. I am striving to attain my performance goal.	1	2	3	4	5

Total score _____

Arbitrary Norms:

Low goal commitment = 6–15
Moderate goal commitment = 15–23
High goal commitment = 24–30

Study Habits:

How many hours have you spent studying for this class? _____ hours
What is your grade at this point in the course? _____
How many times have you missed class? _____ absences

SOURCE: Items were adapted from those presented in R W Renn, C Danehower, P M Swiercz, and M L Icenogle, "Further Examination of the Measurement Properties of Leifer & McGannon's (1986) Goal Acceptance and Goal Commitment Scales," *Journal of Occupational and Organizational Psychology*, March 1999, pp 107–13.

performance when people are not committed to their goals. A meta-analysis of 21 studies based on 2,360 people supported these predictions.[60] Take a moment now to complete the goal commitment scale and the study habits questions contained in the OB Exercise. Is your goal commitment related to the behaviors associated with your study habits? If not, what is the cause of the discrepancy?

Like goal setting, the use of monetary incentives to motivate employees is seldom questioned. Unfortunately, recent research uncovered some negative consequences when goal achievement is linked to individual incentives. Case studies, for example, reveal that pay should not be linked to goal achievement unless (*a*) performance goals are under the employees' control; (*b*) goals are quantitative and measurable; and (*c*) frequent, relatively large payments are made for performance achievement.[61] Goal-based incentive systems are more likely to produce undesirable effects if these three conditions are not satisfied.

Moreover, empirical studies demonstrated that goal-based bonus incentives produced higher commitment to easy goals and lower commitment to difficult goals. People were reluctant to commit to difficult goals that were tied to monetary incentives. People with high goal commitment also offered less help to their co-workers when they received goal-based bonus incentives to accomplish difficult individual goals. Individuals neglected aspects of the job that were not covered in the performance goals.[62] For example, a sales consultant who works for a national retail store and is paid an hourly rate plus a commission tied to achieving sales goals indicates that the salespeople who make the most sales and receive the greatest commissions are those who focus on their own self-interests. So, rather than engaging in behaviors that promote outstanding customer service (e.g., keeping the floor straightened up and clean, taking the time to ring up small dollar sales, writing up sales for salespeople who are missing from the floor, following up with customers to ensure that they received their merchandise in a timely manner, and sending thank-you notes), these individuals focus on maximizing their personal monetary sales at the expense of customer service for the store at large. As another case in point, several studies revealed that quality suffered when employees were given quantity goals.[63]

These findings underscore some of the dangers of using goal-based incentives, particularly for employees in complex, interdependent jobs requiring cooperation. Managers need to consider the advantages, disadvantages, and dilemmas of goal-based incentives prior to implementation.

Practical Application of Goal Setting

There are three general steps to follow when implementing a goal-setting program. Serious deficiencies in one step cannot make up for strength in the other two. The three steps need to be implemented in a systematic fashion.

Step 1: Set Goals   A number of sources can be used as input during this goal-setting stage. Time and motion studies are one source. Goals also may be based on the average past performance of job holders. Third, the employee and his or her manager may set the goal participatively, through give-and-take negotiation. Fourth, goals can be set by conducting external or internal benchmarking. Benchmarking is used when an organization wants to compare its performance or internal work processes to those of other organizations (external benchmarking) or to other internal units, branches, departments, or divisions within the organization (internal benchmarking).[64] For example, a company might set a goal to surpass the customer service levels or profit of a benchmarked competitor. Finally, the overall strategy of a company (e.g., become the lowest-cost producer) may affect the goals set by employees at various levels in the organization.

In accordance with available research evidence, goals should be "SMART." SMART is an acronym that stands for specific, measurable, attainable, results oriented, and time bound. Table 8–4 contains a set of guidelines for writing SMART goals. There are two additional recommendations to consider when setting goals. First, for complex tasks, managers should train employees in problem-solving techniques and encourage them to develop a performance action plan. Action plans specify the strategies or tactics to be used in order to accomplish a goal.

Table 8–4   *Guidelines for Writing SMART Goals*

Specific	Goals should be stated in precise rather than vague terms. For example, a goal that provides for 20 hours of technical training for each employee is more specific than stating that a manager should send as many people as possible to training classes. Goals should be quantified when possible.
Measurable	A measurement device is needed to assess the extent to which a goal is accomplished. Goals thus need to be measurable. It also is critical to consider the quality aspect of the goal when establishing measurement criteria. For example, if the goal is to complete a managerial study of methods to increase productivity, one must consider how to measure the quality of this effort. Goals should not be set without considering the interplay between quantity and quality of output.
Attainable	Goals should be realistic, challenging, and attainable. Impossible goals reduce motivation because people do not like to fail. Remember, people have different levels of ability and skill.
Results oriented	Corporate goals should focus on desired end-results that support the organization's vision. In turn, an individual's goals should directly support the accomplishment of corporate goals. Activities support the achievement of goals and are outlined in action plans. To focus goals on desired end-results, goals should start with the word "to," followed by verbs such as complete, acquire, produce, increase, and decrease. Verbs such as develop, conduct, implement, or monitor imply activities and should not be used in a goal statement.
Time bound	Goals specify target dates for completion.

SOURCE: A J Kinicki, *Performance Management Systems*, (Superstition Mt., AZ: Kinicki and Associates Inc., 1992), pp 2–9. Reprinted with permission; all rights reserved.

Second, because of individual differences (recall our discussion in Chapter 5), it may be necessary to establish different goals for employees performing the same job. For example, a study of 103 undergraduate business students revealed that individuals high in conscientiousness had higher motivation, had a greater goal commitment, and obtained higher grades than students low in conscientiousness.[65] An individual's goal orientation is another important individual difference to consider when setting goals. There are two types of goal orientations: a learning goal orientation and a performance goal orientation. A team of researchers described the differences and implications for goal setting in the following way:

> Individuals with a learning goal orientation are primarily concerned with developing their skills and ability. Given this focus, a difficult goal should be of interest because it provides a challenging opportunity that can lead to personal growth. In contrast, individuals with a performance goal orientation are concerned with obtaining positive evaluations about their ability. Given this focus, a difficult goal should be of lower interest because it provides a greater potential for failure. As goal difficulty increases, the probability of obtaining a positive evaluation through goal attainment decreases.[66]

A series of studies demonstrated that people set higher goals, exerted more effort, and achieved higher performance when they possessed a learning orientation toward goal setting rather than a performance orientation.[67] In conclusion, managers should consider individual differences when setting goals.

Step 2: Promote Goal Commitment Obtaining goal commitment is important because employees are more motivated to pursue goals they view as reasonable, obtainable, and fair. Goal commitment may be increased by using one or more of the following techniques:

1. Provide an explanation for why the organization is implementing a goal-setting program.

2. Present the corporate goals, and explain how and why an individual's personal goals support them.

3. Have employees establish their own goals and action plans. Encourage them to set challenging, stretch goals. Goals should not be impossible.

4. Train managers in how to conduct participative goal-setting sessions, and train employees in how to develop effective action plans.

5. Be supportive, and do not use goals to threaten employees.

6. Set goals that are under the employees' control, and provide them with the necessary resources.

7. Provide monetary incentives or other rewards for accomplishing goals.

Step 3: Provide Support and Feedback Step 3 calls for providing employees with the necessary support elements or resources to get the job done. This includes ensuring that each employee has the necessary abilities and information to reach his or her goals. As a pair of goal-setting experts succinctly stated, "Motivation without knowledge is useless."[68] Training often is required to help employees achieve difficult goals. Moreover, managers should pay attention to employees' perceptions of effort→ performance expectancies, self-efficacy, and valence of rewards. Finally, as we discuss in detail in Chapter 9 employees should be provided with timely, specific feedback (knowledge of results) on how they are doing.

Successfully designing and implementing motivational programs is not easy. Managers cannot simply take one of the theories discussed in this book and apply it word for word. Dynamics within organizations interfere with applying motivation theories in "pure" form. According to management scholar Terence Mitchell,	**Putting Motivational Theories to Work**

> There are situations and settings that make it exceptionally difficult for a motivational system to work. These circumstances may involve the kinds of jobs or people present, the technology, the presence of a union, and so on. The factors that hinder the application of motivational theory have not been articulated either frequently or systematically.[69]

With Mitchell's cautionary statement in mind, this section uses Figure 7–1 (see page 205 in Chapter 7) to raise issues that need to be addressed before implementing a motivational program. Our intent is not to discuss all relevant considerations but rather to highlight a few important ones.

Assuming a motivational program is being considered to improve productivity, quality, or customer satisfaction, the first issue revolves around the difference between motivation and performance. As pointed out in Chapter 7, motivation and performance are not one and the same. Motivation is only one of several factors that influence performance. For example, poor performance may be more a function of outdated or inefficient materials and machinery, not having goals to direct one's attention, a monotonous job, feelings of inequity, a negative work environment characterized by political behavior and conflict, poor supervisory support and coaching, or poor work flow. Motivation cannot make up for a deficient job context (see Figure 7–1). For example, employees are unlikely to identify safety issues if they feel punished for doing so. Consider the case of Glenda Kay Miller:

> When security engineer Glenda Kay Miller questioned the reliability of a proposed employee-identification system at the Browns Ferry nuclear plant near Decatur, Ala., she says, the plant's operator sent her to company psychologists.
>
> The psychological sessions, which Mrs Miller recalls as a series of hostile interviews, began in February 1995. She says she was questioned about her church attendance, how much she missed her husband when he traveled, and whether she had ever had more than $100 of unpaid parking tickets. . . .
>
> Mrs Miller says further: "I'm a pretty normal person. But they were trying to portray me as a terrorist."[70]

Glenda Kay Miller was ultimately fired. Do you think that this incident motivated Miller or her peers to expose future safety concerns? Probably not. The point is that it only takes a single demotivating incident to dampen employee motivation. Managers, therefore, need to carefully consider the causes of poor performance and employee misbehavior.

Importantly, managers should not ignore the individual inputs identified in Figure 7–1. As discussed in this chapter as well as Chapters 5 and 7, individual differences are an important input that influence motivation and motivated behavior. Managers are advised to develop employees so that they have the ability and job knowledge to effectively perform their jobs. In addition, attempts should be made to nurture positive employee characteristics, such as self-esteem, self-efficacy, positive emotions, a learning goal orientation, and need for achievement.

Because motivation is goal directed, the process of developing and setting goals should be consistent with our previous discussion. Moreover, the method used to evaluate performance also needs to be considered. Without a valid performance appraisal system, it is difficult, if not impossible, to accurately distinguish good and poor performers. Managers need to keep in mind that both equity and expectancy theory suggest that employee motivation is squelched by inaccurate performance ratings. Inaccurate ratings also make it difficult to evaluate the effectiveness of any motivational program, so it is beneficial for managers to assess the accuracy and validity of their appraisal systems.

Consistent with expectancy theory and the principles of behavior modification discussed in Chapter 10 managers should make rewards contingent on performance.[71] In doing so, it is important that managers consider the accuracy and fairness of the reward system. As discussed under expectancy theory, the promise of increased rewards will not prompt higher effort and good performance unless those rewards are clearly tied to performance and they are large enough to gain employees' interest or attention.

Consider the practices used by Hyde Manufacturing and Cigna Corporation:

> Hyde Manufacturing Co., Southbridge, Mass., maker of putty knives, wallpaper scrapers, and animal-hoof cleaners, last year began quarterly bonus payouts to workers when certain profit levels are reached, on top of other performance rewards the company says have produced record sales. . . . In a program begun in late 1997 by Cigna Corp.'s health-care unit in Bloomfield, Conn., about 35% of eligible employees, such as claims processors, are boosting pay, with monthly bonuses, as much as 50% over their

base salary—and lifting productivity, too—by increasing the number of calls they handle, for example.[72]

Moreover, equity theory tells us that motivation is influenced by employee perceptions about the fairness of reward allocations. Motivation is decreased when employees believe rewards are inequitably allocated. Rewards also need to be integrated appropriately into the appraisal system. If performance is measured at the individual level, individual achievements need to be rewarded. On the other hand, when performance is the result of group effort, rewards should be allocated to the group.

Feedback also should be linked with performance. Feedback provides the information and direction needed to keep employees focused on relevant tasks, activities, and goals. Managers should strive to provide specific, timely, and accurate feedback to employees.

Rhino Foods is a good example of a company that instituted several of the recommendations discussed in the chapter. After identifying several outputs it wanted to encourage, the company instituted a feedback and incentive program to reinforce the desired outputs and behaviors:

> Just as Rhino shares information with employees, it shares success. In fact, the company has not one, not two, but three profit-sharing programs. They're designed to recognize the workforce as a whole for performance, the workforce as a whole by seniority, as well as employees for individual performance.
>
> The first program, around for the past six years, is playfully called *The Game*. Every day Rhino posts key information that shows where the company stands financially—its "score" for the day. For instance, on Tuesday, the score may indicate that if operations continue smoothly, each employee will receive $26 at month's end. On Wednesday, the score may be down to $10 or $1. But all the information is posted to inform employees what happened on Tuesday to cause the drop—maybe a lot of product had to be scrapped. The point is, employees always know where they stand and what they have to do to keep their bonuses, which are given once a month in equal amounts to all employees.
>
> To also acknowledge employees' contributions to the company over time, a six-month profit sharing is distributed to people based on seniority. "If we make money, the people here for one year would get a small amount," says Dailey [Director of Human Resources]. "The people who participated in the growth of the company over a longer period of time would get a lot. It doesn't matter if they're making $8 an hour, they'll get a heck of a lot more than I will [Dailey's been at Rhino four years]."
>
> Finally, a pool of extra profits can be distributed to individuals based on their performance. "These programs keep employees tuned into the bottom line," says Dailey. Castle [president and owner] himself names the profit-sharing initiatives among Rhino's proudest accomplishments. . . .
>
> At some organizations, you can always spy the employee who has goofed up. The poor, errant worker is generally huddled in a corner of the cubicle, waiting for the boom to drop. Rhino is not one of those organizations. It's not a blame-based type of company. It's a "let's identify the problem and figure out the solution together" kind of company.[73]

Finally, we end this chapter by noting that an organization's culture significantly influences employee motivation and behavior. A positive self-enhancing culture such as that at Rhino Foods, for example, is more likely to engender higher motivation and commitment than a culture dominated by suspicion, fault finding, and blame.

Summary of Key Concepts

1. *Discuss the role of perceived inequity in employee motivation.* Equity theory is a model of motivation that explains how people strive for fairness and justice in social exchanges. On the job, feelings of inequity revolve around a person's evaluation of whether he or she receives adequate rewards to compensate for his or her contributive inputs. People perform these evaluations by comparing the perceived fairness of their employment exchange with that of relevant others. Perceived inequity creates motivation to restore equity.

2. *Explain the differences among distributive, procedural, and interactional justice.* Distributive, procedural, and interactional justice are the three key components underlying organizational justice. Distributive justice reflects the perceived fairness of how resources and rewards are distributed. Procedural justice represents the perceived fairness of the process and procedures used to make allocation decisions. Interactional justice entails the perceived fairness of a decision maker's behavior in the process of decision making.

3. *Describe the practical lessons derived from equity theory.* Equity theory has at least eight practical implications. First, because people are motivated to resolve perceptions of inequity, managers should not discount employees' feelings and perceptions when trying to motivate workers. Second, managers should pay attention to employees' *perceptions* of what is fair and equitable. It is the employee's view of reality that counts when trying to motivate someone, according to equity theory. Third, employees should be given a voice in decisions that affect them. Fourth, employees should be given the opportunity to appeal decisions that affect their welfare. Fifth, employees are more likely to accept and support organizational change when they believe it is implemented fairly and when it produces equitable outcomes. Sixth, managers can promote cooperation and teamwork among group members by treating them equitably. Seventh, treating employees inequitably can lead to litigation and costly court settlements. Finally, managers need to pay attention to the organization's climate for justice because it influences employee attitudes and behavior.

4. *Explain Vroom's expectancy theory.* Expectancy theory assumes motivation is determined by one's perceived chances of achieving valued outcomes. Vroom's expectancy model of motivation reveals how effort→performance expectancies and performance→outcome instrumentalities influence the degree of effort expended to achieve desired (positively valent) outcomes.

5. *Discuss Porter and Lawler's expectancy theory of motivation.* Porter and Lawler developed a model of expectancy that expanded upon the theory proposed by Vroom. This model specifies (*a*) the source of people's valences and expectancies and (*b*) the relationship between performance and satisfaction.

6. *Describe the practical implications of expectancy theory of motivation.* Managers are advised to enhance effort→performance expectancies by helping employees accomplish their performance goals. With respect to instrumentalities and valences, managers should attempt to link employee performance and valued rewards. There are four prerequisites to linking performance and rewards: (*a*) Managers need to develop and communicate performance standards to employees, (*b*) managers need valid and accurate performance ratings, (*c*) managers need to determine the relative mix of individual versus team contribution to performance and then reward accordingly, and (*d*) managers should use performance ratings to differentially allocate rewards among employees.

7. *Explain how goal setting motivates an individual.* Four motivational mechanisms of goal setting are as follows: (*a*) Goals direct one's attention, (*b*) goals regulate effort, (*c*) goals increase one's persistence, and (*d*) goals encourage development of goal-attainment strategies and action plans.

8. *Identify five practical lessons to be learned from goal-setting research.* Difficult goals lead to higher performance than easy or moderate goals: goals should not be impossible to achieve. Specific, difficult goals lead to higher performance for simple rather than complex tasks. Third, feedback enhances the effect of specific, difficult goals. Fourth, participative goals, assigned goals, and self-set goals are equally effective. Fifth, goal commitment and monetary incentives affect goal-setting outcomes.

9. *Specify issues that should be addressed before implementing a motivational program.* Managers need to consider the variety of causes of poor performance and employee misbehavior. Undesirable employee performance and behavior may be due to a host of deficient individual inputs (e.g., ability, dispositions, emotions, and beliefs) or job context factors (e.g., materials and machinery, job characteristics, reward systems, supervisory support and coaching, and social norms). The method used to evaluate performance as well as the link between performance and rewards must be examined. Performance must be accurately evaluated and rewards should be equitably distributed. Managers should also recognize that employee motivation and behavior are influenced by organizational culture.

Discussion Questions

1. Have you experienced positive or negative inequity at work? Describe the circumstances in terms of the inputs and outcomes of the comparison person and yourself.

2. Could a manager's attempt to treat his or her employees equally lead to perceptions of inequity? Explain.

3. What work outcomes (refer to Table 8–1) are most important to you? Do you think different age groups value different outcomes? What are the implications for managers who seek to be equitable?

4. Relative to Table 8–2, what techniques have you relied on recently to reduce either positive or negative inequity?

5. What is your definition of studying hard? What is your expectancy for earning an A on the next exam in this course? What is the basis of this expectancy?

6. If someone who reported to you at work had a low expectancy for successful performance, what could you do to increase this person's expectancy?

7. Do goals play an important role in your life? Explain.

8. How would you respond to a manager who said, "Goals must be participatively set?"

9. Goal-setting research suggests that people should be given difficult goals. How does this prescription mesh with expectancy theory? Explain.

10. How could a professor use equity, expectancy, and goal-setting theory to motivate students?

Internet Exercise

www.ge.com/index.htm

This chapter discussed how employee motivation is influenced by goal setting and the relationship between performance and rewards. We also reviewed the variety of issues that managers should consider when implementing motivational programs. The purpose of this exercise is for you to examine the motivational techniques used by General Electric (GE). GE is one of the most successful companies in the world. The company is well known for establishing clear corporate goals and then creating the infrastructure (e.g., rewards) to achieve them. Begin by visiting GE's home page at http://www.ge.com/index.htm. Begin your search by locating GE's corporate values and corporate goals. Then expand your search by looking for information that discusses the different incentives GE uses to motivate its employees.

Questions

1. How will the values influence goal-setting and motivation?

2. Based on the values and goals, what type of behavior is the organization trying to motivate?

3. What rewards does GE use to reinforce desired behavior and performance?

4. To what extent are GE's practices consistent with the material covered in this chapter?

OB in Action Case Study

www.cypress.com

Cypress Semiconductor Corporation Uses a Computerized Management System to Monitor and Motivate Employees[74]

T J Rodgers, CEO, says: "Most companies don't fail for lack of talent or strategic vision. They fail for lack of execution—the mundane blocking and tackling that the great companies consistently do well and strive to do better.

At Cypress, our management systems track corporate, departmental, and individual performance so regularly and in such detail that no manager, including me, can plausibly claim to be in the dark about critical problems. . . .

All of Cypress's 1,400 employees have goals, which, in theory, makes them no different from employees at most other companies. What does make our people different is that every week they set their own goals, commit to achieving them by a specific date, enter them into a database, and report whether or not they completed prior goals. Cypress's computerized goal system is an important part of our managerial infrastructure. It is a detailed guide to the future and an objective record of the past. In any given week, some 6,000 goals in the database come due. Our ability to meet those goals ultimately determines our success or failure.

Most of the work in our company is organized by project rather than along strict functional lines. Members of a project team may be (and usually are) from different parts of the organization. Project managers need not be (and often aren't) the highest ranking member of the group. Likewise, the goal system is organized by project and function. In Monday project meetings, employees set short-term goals and rank them in priority order. Short-term goals take from one to six weeks to complete, and different employees have different numbers of goals. At the beginning of a typical week, for example, a member of our production-control staff initiated seven new goals in connection with three different projects. He said he would, among other things, report on progress with certain mini-computer problems (two weeks), monitor and report on quality rejection rates for certain products (three weeks), update killer software for the assembly department (two weeks), and assist a marketing executive with a forecasting software enhancement (four weeks).

On Monday night, the project goals are fed back into a central computer. On Tuesday mornings, functional managers receive a printout of their direct reports' new and pending project goals. These printouts are the basis of Tuesday afternoon meetings in which managers work with their people to anticipate overload and conflicting goals, sort out priorities, organize work, and make mutual commitments about what's going to get done. This is a critical step. The failure mode in our company (and I suspect in most growing companies) is that people overcommit themselves rather than establish unchallenging goals. By 5 PM Tuesday, the revised schedule is fed back into the central database.

This 'two pass' system generates the work program that coordinates the mostly self-imposed activities of every Cypress employee. It allows the organization to be project driven, which helps us emphasize speed and agility, as well as functionally accurate, which works against burnout and failure to execute. On Wednesday morning, our eight vice presidents receive goal printouts for their people and the people below them—another conflict-resolution mechanism. . . .

On Wednesday afternoons at my weekly staff meeting, I review various database reports with my vice presidents. We talk about what's going wrong and how to help managers who are running into problems. The following reports typically serve as the basis for discussion: progress with goals on critical projects; percentage of delinquent goals sorted by managers (their goals plus those of their subordinates); percentage of delinquent goals sorted by vice president (the percentage of pending goals that are delinquent for all people reporting up the chain of command to each vice president); all employees without goals (something I do not tolerate); all goals five or more weeks delinquent; and all employees with two or more delinquent goals, sorted by manager.

As we've refined the goal system and used it more extensively, I've developed some general principles. First, people are going to have goals they don't achieve on time; the key is to sense when a vice president or a manager is losing control of the operation. My rule of thumb is that vice presidents should not have delinquency rates above 20% and managers should not let more than 30% of their goals become delinquent. When managers do have a delinquency problem, I usually intervene with a short note: 'Your delinquency rate is running at 35%, what can I do to help?' I often get back requests for specific assistance. Part of my role is to hold people accountable. But it is also to identify problems before they become crises and to provide help in getting them fixed.

Second, people need positive feedback. Every month we issue a Completed Goal Report for every person in the company. The report lists all goals completed over the past four weeks as well as those that have yet to come due. 'Individual Monthly Goal Report,' an excerpt from a monthly report for a production-control staffer, lists all goals completed in workweek 45 of last year. The entire report consists of 49 goals, 28 of which were completed on time, 4 of which were completed late, and 17 of which were pending—an outstanding record.

The completed goal report is also a valuable tool for performance evaluation. . . . At Cypress, the completed goal report triggers a performance minireview; each month managers read through their people's printouts and prepare brief, factual evaluations. At year end, managers have a dozen such objective reviews to refresh their memories and fight the proximity effect.

Managers shouldn't expect outstanding performance unless they're prepared to reward outstanding performers. Yet evaluation and reward systems remain an organizational black hole for three reasons.

First, managers aren't very scientific about rating their people. They may be able to identify the real stars and the worst laggards, but the vast majority of people (who must still be ranked) get lost somewhere in the middle. Second, even if they evaluate people correctly, managers like to spread raises around evenly to keep the troops happy. This is a deadly policy that saps the morale of standouts who deserve more and sends the wrong signal to weak performers. Third, managers are totally incapable of distinguishing between 'merit' and 'equity' when awarding increases. Merit refers to that portion of a raise awarded for the quality of past performance. Equity refers to adjustments in that raise to more closely align salaries of equally ranked peers. Merit and equity both have a place in the incentive mix, but confusing the two makes for mushy logic, counterproductive results, and dissatisfied people. . . .

As with all our resource-allocation systems, the focal-review system starts with policies at the top and forces middle management decisions to be consistent with that thinking. Senior management and the board of directors review our annual revenue forecasts, survey compensation trends among our competitors, and settle on a total corporate allowance for raises. The 'raise budget' is not negotiable, and it drives raises throughout the company. If the corporate budget is 8%, then every department must meet a weighted-average salary increase of 8%. It's up to managers to distribute the 8% pool, which is where the focal-review system comes in. . . .

Only after they have awarded percentage increases based strictly on merit can managers make adjustments for salary inequities created by personal circumstances and historical accidents."

Update on Cypress's Goal-Tracking System[75]

A number of problems emerged with Cypress's computerized goal-setting system over the years. For example, employees found ways to override the software and trick the system in order to change the dates that their goals were due. This enabled people to create the impression that they never fell behind in meeting their goals. Employees also became resistant to entering their goals into the system because it took too much time. T J Rodgers ultimately concluded that 100% adherence to the system led employees to engage in counterproductive behaviors. People began to hide potential problems rather than admitting that a particular goal had not been met. This led Rodgers in 1997 to conclude that the use of the goals system was optional rather than mandatory. Half of the company's managers used the system in 1998.

Questions for Discussion

1. Does Cypress treat its employees equitably? Explain.

2. To what extent is Cypress's management system consistent with expectancy theory?

3. How does Cypress use goal setting to motivate employees?

4. Which of the five insights from goal-setting research is Cypress following?

5. What are the drawbacks associated with Cypress's goal-setting and tracking system? Discuss.

6. Would you like to work at Cypress? Explain.

Personal Awareness and Growth Exercise

What Outcomes Motivate Employees?

Objectives

1. To determine how accurately you perceive the outcomes that motivate nonmanagerial employees.

2. To examine the managerial implications of inaccurately assessing employee motivators.

Introduction

One thousand employees were given a list of 10 outcomes people want from their work. They were asked to rank these items from most important to least important.[76] We are going to have you estimate how you think these workers ranked the various outcomes. This will enable you to compare your perceptions with the average rankings documented by a researcher. The survey results are presented in Note 77 at the end of this book. Please do not read them until indicated.

Instructions

Below is a list of 10 outcomes people want from their work. Read the list, and then rank each item according to how you think the typical nonmanagerial employee would rank them. Rank the outcomes from 1 to 10; 1 = Most important and 10 = Least important. (Please do this now before reading the rest of these instructions.) After you have completed your ranking, calculate the discrepancy between your perceptions and the actual results. Take the absolute value of the difference between your ranking and the actual ranking for each item, and then add them to get a total discrepancy score. For example, if you gave job security a ranking of 1, your discrepancy score would be 3 because the actual ranking was 4. The lower your discrepancy score, the more accurate your perception of the typical employee's needs. The actual rankings are shown in Note 77.

How do you believe the typical nonmanagerial employee would rank these outcomes?

_____ Full appreciation of work done
_____ Job security
_____ Good working conditions
_____ Feeling of being in on things
_____ Good wages
_____ Tactful discipline
_____ Personal loyalty to employees
_____ Interesting work
_____ Sympathetic help with personal problems
_____ Promotion and growth in the organization

Questions for Discussion

1. Were your perceptions accurate? Why or why not?

2. What would Vroom's expectancy theory suggest you should do?

3. Based on the size of your discrepancy, what does Porter and Lawler's expectancy model suggest will happen to satisfaction?

4. Would you generalize the actual survey results to all nonmanagerial employees? Why or why not?

Group Exercise

The Case of the Missing Form

Objectives

1. To give you practice at diagnosing the causes of a performance problem by using the job performance model of motivation presented in Figure 7–1.
2. To apply one of the motivation models discussed in Chapters 7 and 8 in order to solve a performance problem.

Introduction

Managers frequently encounter performance problems. These problems might represent incidents such as missed deadlines, poor quality, inadequate levels of performance, excessive time off, cynical or negative behavior, and lack of cooperation with team members. As we discussed in both this chapter and Chapter 7, motivation is only one factor in these types of performance problems. As such, managers must learn how to diagnose the cause(s) of performance problems prior to trying to solve them. The following case provides you this opportunity. After diagnosing the cause(s) of the performance problem, you will be asked to solve it. The models of motivation presented in Chapters 7 and 8 provide useful frameworks for generating solutions.

Instructions

Your instructor will divide the class into groups of four to six. You should first read the case provided. Once all group members are finished, meet as a group to discuss the case. Begin your discussion by brainstorming a list of potential causes of the performance problem. Use the job performance model of motivation presented in Figure 7–1 to conduct this brainstorming activity. Be sure to consider whether each and every individual input and job context factor are possible causes of the problem. Once the group has identified the causes of the performance problem, the group should answer the discussion questions that follow the case.

THE CASE OF THE MISSING FORM[78]

S	M	T	W	T	F	S		S	M	T	W	T	F	S
			MAY								JUNE			
		1	2	3	4									1
5	6	7	8	9	10	11		2	3	4	5	6	7	8
12	13	14	15	16	17	18		9	10	11	12	13	14	15
19	20	21	22	23	24	25		16	17	18	19	20	21	22
26	27	28	29	30	31			23	24	25	26	27	28	29
								30						

Ann Anders has been manager of Training and Development at TYCO Financial Services for 3 years.

(Ann has been with TYCO 21 years.) She has 10 professional level training employees reporting to her.

Her boss, Joyce Davis, Director of Training, asked Ann to put together a new cost benefit analysis package on a project Ann had completed. This was not a requirement for Ann by her previous boss; training has never been measured in terms of dollars and cents.

Joyce explained that she wanted Ann to document the savings that the "Customer Dispute Resolution" training program had produced so she could share it with her peers in the other divisions of TYCO. She wanted to formalize the practice of preparing a cost benefit analysis (CBA) format because this was something no one else had done. She directed Ann to further research the numbers to validate the findings and put it into a form (Joyce's idea of a form was a page with lines and boxes). It was Wednesday, May 15th; Joyce was leaving for a meeting in New York at 8:00 AM Monday, May 20th. She wanted to take this assignment with her. Joyce asked Ann to see her Friday with her progress.

On Thursday, Ann met with the Performance Engineering department at TYCO and shared with Joyce a format they were currently using on their projects. Ann agreed to apply that process to her training project. Joyce was pleased with the progress.

Ann returned to Joyce on Friday, May 17th, with the formula for the training CBA typed on a plain white page. Joyce acknowledged the work to prepare the calculations and again asked if Ann could create a form. Joyce had to catch her airplane first thing Monday morning and knew she would not have time to review a second document. Joyce took the work Ann had completed; however, she decided to stall until the next monthly meeting in June to present the idea.

The following week, on May 27th, Joyce explained to Ann that there was not enough time to discuss her CBA so she would do it next month. Joyce asked Ann for additional information that needed to be gathered to effectively document the project and set a new completion date, June 10th: only one week prior to the June 17th meeting.

Ann returned on June 10th with more calculations that were thoroughly documented. Joyce was happy to see the additional research. However, she was disappointed because the format had not yet been put into a professional "form." Joyce then took out a piece of paper and wrote the sections for Ann so she could better understand what she wanted.

Joyce felt confident that Ann understood what she wanted. Joyce, in order to give Ann the maximum time to get it right this time, said she needed the document no later than the end of the day Friday, June 14th.

The end of the day Friday, June 14th, Ann walked into Joyce's office proudly displaying this neatly typed document. However, there were no lines or boxes as you would see on a traditional business form. Joyce said "This is not in a form! I'll take it home over the weekend and bring you the revision Monday morning, you can then fax me the changes at the meeting."

Joyce then took 15 to 20 minutes Sunday to draw out the lines and reformat the information for ease of reading and to create a professional image for the product. On Monday morning Joyce stopped by and gave the changes to her secretary to finish. Ann faxed the changes. Joyce presented "the form" at the meeting, and it had the positive impact she expected.

After the meeting, Joyce reflected on Ann's problem. After 21 years with this company and 3 years as a manager, why couldn't Ann create something as simple as a business form? Joyce is trying to determine the root cause(s) of Ann's poor performance.

Questions for Discussion

1. What are the causes of Ann's poor performance? Explain your rationale.

2. Based on the causes you identified, how would you keep the problem from happening again?

3. Which of the motivation models discussed in Chapters 7 and 8 are most relevant for solving this problem? Why?

4. How would you use the model identified in question 3 to improve Ann's future performance? Be sure to specifically discuss how you would apply the model.

Chapter Nine

Improving Job Performance with Feedback and Rewards

Learning Objectives

When you finish studying the material in this chapter, you should be able to:

1 Specify the two basic functions of feedback and three sources of feedback.

2 Discuss how the recipient's characteristics, perceptions, and cognitive evaluations affect how the individual processes feedback.

3 List at least three practical lessons from feedback research.

4 Define upward feedback and 360-degree feedback, and summarize the general tips for giving good feedback.

5 Briefly explain the four different organizational reward norms.

6 Summarize the reasons rewards often fail to motivate employees.

7 Distinguish among profit sharing, gainsharing, and team-based pay.

8 Discuss how managers can generally improve pay-for-performance plans.

Many people, including his wife, thought he was crazy. A few actually believed he was evil. All Rob Rodin knew for sure was that he was worried. He was about to do something extremely radical for the CEO of a large distribution company: He was going to wipe out all—truly *all*—individual incentives for his sales force. No commissions. No bonuses. No Alaskan cruises or Acapulco vacations or Hawaiian pig roasts or color TVs or plaques. Just a base salary plus the opportunity for profit sharing, which would be the same percent of salary for everyone, based on the whole company's performance.

In a few days Rodin will celebrate the sixth anniversary of that decision, and he hasn't looked back. He's CEO of Marshall Industries, a big distributor of electronic components based in El Monte, Calif. (1997 sales: $1.2 billion), and I asked him how his heretical move is working out. Pretty well, it seems: Productivity per person has almost tripled, he says, "and the system is

more right today than it was six years ago." He loves how the new system gets rid of distortions that used to mask real results—people shipping early to meet quotas, pushing costs from one quarter into the next to make budget, beating one another up over allocating the costs of computer systems, and a million others. Plus, he says, "look at the trust that develops when everyone's on profit sharing." Some doubters still tell him he's crazy;

Rob Rodin, the unconventional CEO of Marshall Industries.
Courtesy of Marshall Industries

they insist salespeople just won't perform without incentives. But Rodin isn't changing the rules. "How do you design an incentive system robust enough to accommodate every change in every customer and every product and every market every day? You *can't*—you'd be designing it the rest of your life." The doubters will never stop, but Rodin realizes they are now just part of his life. "I have to explain this system to somebody every day," he says. "Except customers—they get it right away."[1]

FOR DISCUSSION

What are the positives and negatives of this unconventional approach to employee compensation?

Productivity and total quality experts tell us we need to work smarter, not harder. While it is true that a sound education and appropriate skill training are needed if one is to work smarter, the process does not end there. Today's employees need instructive and supportive feedback and desired rewards if they are to translate their knowledge into improved productivity and superior quality. This point was reinforced by a recent survey of 612 employees in the United States. When asked about the changes top management needs to make to attract and keep good people, these two items headed the list: "improving salaries and benefits" (72%) and "recognizing and rewarding good employee performance" (69%).[2] Figure 9–1 illustrates a learning- and development-focused cycle in which feedback enhances ability, encourages effort, and acknowledges results. Rewards, meanwhile, motivate effort and compensate results. Learning and personal development, according to the authors of the book, *Working Wisdom,* are the key to success at all levels:

> . . . work can be an enriching experience, a way of developing mastery in the world, a source of valued relationships, and for some—however high-minded this may sound—a path to self-realization. Combining work and learning to promote personal development, as well as a profitable enterprise, is the key. As the pace of change quickens, individuals, companies, and countries that fail to continually learn and adapt to change will be left behind.[3]

Properly administered feedback and rewards can guide, teach, and motivate people in the direction of positive change.

This chapter continues our discussion of individual behavior by discussing the effect of feedback and rewards on behavior and by integrating those insights with what you have learned about individual differences, perception, and various motivational tools such as goal setting.

Understanding the Feedback Process

Numerous surveys tell us employees have a hearty appetite for feedback.[4] So also do achievement-oriented students. Following a difficult exam, for instance, students want to know two things: how they did and how their peers did. By letting students know how their work measures up to grading and competitive standards, an instructor's feedback permits the students to adjust their study habits so they can reach their goals. Likewise, managers in well-run organizations follow up goal setting with a feedback program to provide a rational basis for adjustment and improvement. For example, consider these two diverse feedback examples:

IBM's Raleigh, North Carolina, personal computer factory: "Every day, managers see a fresh . . . number on their screens, telling them how many PCs have been

Figure 9–1   *Feedback and Rewards Are Important Links in the Job Performance Cycle*

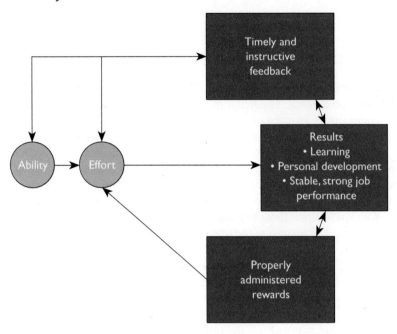

shipped so far this year . . . every model is broken out so managers can see what's moving and what's not."[5]

A 55,000-employee copper mine in Zambia, Africa: "As largely uneducated workers march into the front entrance, they can't help but spot a 50-foot-high scoreboard that lists monthly and year-to-date financials, from 'copper revenue' to 'corporate depreciation.' "[6]

Although this sort of *open book management* is becoming popular, feedback too often gets shortchanged. In fact, "poor or insufficient feedback" was the leading cause of deficient performance in a survey of US and European companies.[7]

As the term is used here, **feedback** is objective information about individual or collective performance. Subjective assessments such as, "You're doing a poor job," "You're too lazy," or "We really appreciate your hard work" do not qualify as objective feedback. But hard data such as units sold, days absent, dollars saved, projects completed, customers satisfied, and quality rejects are all candidates for objective feedback programs. Management consultants Chip Bell and Ron Zemke offered this perspective of feedback:

> Feedback is, quite simply, any information that answers those "How am I doing?" questions. *Good* feedback answers them truthfully and productively. It's information people can use either to confirm or correct their performance.
>
> Feedback comes in many forms and from a variety of sources. Some is easy to get and requires hardly any effort to understand. The charts and graphs tracking group and individual performance that are fixtures in many workplaces are an example of this variety. Performance feedback—the numerical type at least—is at the heart of most approaches to total quality management.

Feedback
Objective information about performance.

Some feedback is less accessible. It's tucked away in the heads of customers and managers. But no matter how well-hidden the feedback, if people need it to keep their performance on track, we need to get it to them—preferably while it's still fresh enough to make an impact.[8]

Two Functions of Feedback

Experts say feedback serves two functions for those who receive it, one is *instructional* and the other *motivational*. Feedback instructs when it clarifies roles or teaches new behavior. For example, an assistant accountant might be advised to handle a certain entry as a capital item rather than as an expense item. On the other hand, feedback motivates when it serves as a reward or promises a reward.[9] Having the boss tell you that a grueling project you worked on earlier has just been completed can be a rewarding piece of news. As documented in one study, the motivational function of feedback can be significantly enhanced by pairing *specific,* challenging goals with *specific* feedback about results.[10] We expand upon these two functions in this section by analyzing a cognitive model of feedback, and reviewing the practical implications of recent feedback research.

A Cognitive-Processing Model of Performance Feedback

Giving and receiving feedback on the job are popular ideas today. Conventional wisdom says the more feedback organizational members get, the better. An underlying assumption is that feedback works automatically. Managers simply need to be motivated to give it. According to a recent meta-analysis of 23,663 feedback incidents, however, feedback is far from automatically effective. While feedback did, in fact, have a generally positive impact on performance, performance actually *declined* in more than 38% of the feedback incidents.[11] Feedback also can be warped by nontask factors, such as race. A recent laboratory study at Stanford University focused on cross-race feedback on the content (subjective feedback) and writing mechanics (objective feedback) of written essays. White students gave African-American students *less* critical *subjective* feedback than they did to white students. This positive racial bias disappeared with objective feedback.[12] These results are a bright caution light for those interested in improving job performance with feedback. Subjective feedback is easily contaminated by situational factors. Moreover, if objective feedback is to work as intended, managers need to understand the interaction between feedback recipients and their environment.[13] A fuller understanding of how employees cognitively or mentally process feedback is an important first step in the right direction. This complex process is illustrated in Figure 9–2. Immediately obvious is the fact that feedback must successfully clear many hurdles if the desired behavioral outcomes are to be achieved.

A lighthearted case in point is Scott Adams, the former telephone company employee who draws the popular cartoon strip, Dilbert. According to *The Wall Street Journal,*

> . . . he can thank feedback from his readers, who flooded him with comments—about 200 a day—after he published his e-mail address in 1993. They persuaded him to concentrate on workplace issues, which had been a smaller part of the strip, and Dilbert's popularity soared. "There was this huge vein of discontent and nobody was talking about it from the employees' perspective," he says.
>
> Thanks to his experiences in the trenches, and his e-mail army, Mr Adams has become a walking database of workplace foibles and career frustrations.[14]

Figure 9–2   *A Cognitive-Processing Model of Feedback*

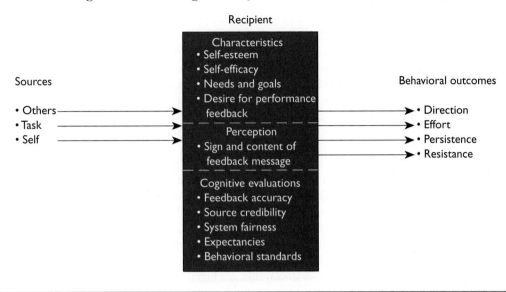

SOURCES: Based in part on discussion in M S Taylor, C D Fisher, and D R Ilgen, "Individuals' Reactions to Performance Feedback in Organizations: A Control Theory Perspective," in *Research in Personnel and Human Resources Management,* vol. 2, eds K M Rowland and G R Ferris (Greenwich, CT: JAI Press, 1984), pp 81–124; and A N Kluger and A DeNisi, "The Effects of Feedback Interventions on Performance: A Historical Review, a Meta-Analysis, and a Preliminary Feedback Intervention Theory," *Psychological Bulletin,* March 1996, pp 254–84.

If you've ever gotten a good laugh from a Dilbert cartoon, you can thank the feedback process. Feedback—from customers, in this case—was effective because cartoonist Adams (1) wanted feedback, (2) actively sought feedback, and (3) acted on the feedback. A step-by-step exploration of the model in Figure 9–2 can help us better understand this sort of feedback-performance relationship.

Sources of Feedback

It almost goes without saying that employees receive objective feedback from others such as peers, supervisors, subordinates, and outsiders. Perhaps less obvious is the fact that the task itself is a ready source of objective feedback.[15] Anyone who has spent hours on a "quick" Internet search can appreciate the power of task-provided feedback. Similarly, skilled tasks such as computer programming or landing a jet airplane provide a steady stream of feedback about how well or poorly one is doing. A third source of feedback is oneself, but self-serving bias and other perceptual problems can contaminate this source. Those high in self-confidence tend to rely on personal feedback more than those with low self-confidence. Although circumstances vary, an employee can be bombarded by feedback from all three sources simultaneously. This is where the gatekeeping functions of perception and cognitive evaluation are needed to help sort things out.

The Recipient of Feedback

Listed in the center portion of Figure 9–2 are three aspects of the recipient requiring our attention. They are the individual's characteristics, perceptions, and cognitive evaluations. As characterized earlier, each recipient variable is a hurdle intended feedback must clear if it is to be effective. Knowing about these recipient hurdles is a big step in the right direction.

The Recipient's Characteristics   Personality characteristics such as self-esteem and self-efficacy can help or hinder one's readiness for feedback.[16] Those having low self-esteem and low self-efficacy generally do not actively seek feedback that, unfortunately, would tend to confirm those problems. Needs and goals also influence one's openness to feedback. In a laboratory study, Japanese psychology students who scored high on need for achievement responded more favorably to feedback than did their classmates who had low need for achievement.[17] This particular relationship likely exists in Western cultures as well. For example, 331 employees in the marketing department of a large public utility in the United States were found to seek feedback on important issues or when faced with uncertain situations. Long-tenured employees from this sample also were less likely to seek feedback than employees with little time on the job.[18] High self-monitors, those chameleonlike people we discussed in Chapter 5, are also more open to feedback because it helps them adapt their behavior to the situation. Recall from Chapter 5 that high self-monitoring employees were found to be better at initiating relationships with mentors (who typically provide feedback).[19] Low self-monitoring people, in contrast, are tuned into their own internal feelings more than they are to external cues. For example, someone observed that talking to media kingpin Ted Turner, a very low self-monitor, was like having a conversation with a radio!

Researchers have started to focus more directly on the recipient's actual desire for feedback, as opposed to indirectly on personality characteristics, needs, and goals. Everyday experience tells us that not everyone really wants the performance feedback they supposedly seek. Restaurant servers who ask, "How was everything?" while presenting the bill, typically are not interested in a detailed reply. A study of 498 supervisors yielded an instrument for measuring desire for performance feedback[20] (see the OB Exercise on p 277, for a shortened version). Such desire involves *self-reliance* (items 1–3), *self-assessment ability* (items 4–6), and a *preference for external information* (items 7–10). The general contingency approach to management would require different strategies for giving feedback to employees scoring low versus high on the OB Exercise.

The Recipient's Perception of Feedback   The *sign* of feedback refers to whether it is positive or negative. Generally, people tend to perceive and recall positive feedback more accurately than they do negative feedback.[21] But feedback with a negative sign (e.g., being told your performance is below average) can have a *positive* motivational impact. In fact, in one study, those who were told they were below average on a creativity test subsequently outperformed those who were led to believe their results were above average. The subjects apparently took the negative feedback as a challenge and set and pursued higher goals. Those receiving positive feedback apparently were less motivated to do better.[22] Nonetheless, feedback with a negative sign or threatening content needs to be administered carefully to avoid creating insecurity and defensiveness. Self-efficacy also can be damaged by negative feedback, as discovered in a pair of experiments with business students. The researchers concluded, "To facilitate the development of strong efficacy beliefs, managers should be careful about the provision of negative feedback. Destructive criticism by managers which attributes the cause of poor performance to internal factors reduces both the beliefs of self-efficacy and the self-set goals of recipients."[23]

The Recipient's Cognitive Evaluation of Feedback   Upon receiving feedback, people cognitively evaluate factors such as its accuracy, the credibility of the source, the fairness of the system (e.g., performance appraisal system), their performance-reward

OB Exercise — How Strong Is Your Desire for Performance Feedback?

Instructions

Circle one number indicating the strength of your agreement or disagreement with each statement. Total your responses, and compare your score with our arbitrary norms.

	Disagree			Agree

1. As long as I think that I have done something well, I am not too concerned about how other people think I have done.   5 — 4 — 3 — 2 — 1

2. How other people view my work is not as important as how I view my own work.   5 — 4 — 3 — 2 — 1

3. It is usually better not to put much faith in what others say about your work, regardless of whether it is complimentary or not.   5 — 4 — 3 — 2 — 1

4. If I have done something well, I know it without other people telling me so.   5 — 4 — 3 — 2 — 1

5. I usually have a clear idea of what I am trying to do and how well I am proceeding toward my goal.   5 — 4 — 3 — 2 — 1

6. I find that I am usually a pretty good judge of my own performance.   5 — 4 — 3 — 2 — 1

7. It is very important to me to know what people think of my work.   1 — 2 — 3 — 4 — 5

8. It is a good idea to get someone to check on your work before it's too late to make changes.   1 — 2 — 3 — 4 — 5

9. Even though I may think I have done a good job, I feel a lot more confident of it after someone else tells me so.   1 — 2 — 3 — 4 — 5

10. Since one cannot be objective about their own performance, it is best to listen to the feedback provided by others.   1 — 2 — 3 — 4 — 5

Total score = _____

Arbitrary Norms

10–23 = Low desire for feedback   24–36 = Moderate desire for feedback   37–50 = High desire for feedback

SOURCE: Excerpted and adapted from D M Herold, C K Parsons, and R B Rensvold, "Individual Differences in the Generation and Processing of Performance Feedback," *Educational and Psychological Measurement*, February 1996, Table 1, p 9. Copyright © 1996 by Sage Publications. Reprinted by permission of Sage Publications, Inc.

expectancies, and the reasonableness of the standards. Any feedback that fails to clear one or more of these cognitive hurdles will be rejected or downplayed. Personal experience largely dictates how these factors are weighed. For instance, you would probably discount feedback from someone who exaggerates or from someone who performed poorly on the same task you have just successfully completed. In view of the "trust gap," discussed in Chapter 13, managerial credibility is an ethical matter of central importance today. According to the authors of the book *Credibility: How Leaders Gain and Lose It, Why People Demand It,* "without a solid foundation of personal credibility, leaders can have no hope of enlisting others in a common vision."[24] Managers who have proven untrustworthy and not credible have a hard time improving job performance through feedback.[25]

Feedback from a source who apparently shows favoritism or relies on unreasonable behavior standards would be suspect.[26] Also, as predicted by expectancy motivation theory, feedback must foster high effort→performance expectancies and performance→reward instrumentalities if it is to motivate desired behavior. For example, many growing children have been cheated out of the rewards of athletic competition because they were told by respected adults that they were too small, too short, too slow, too clumsy, and so forth. Feedback can have a profound and lasting impact on behavior.

Behavioral Outcomes of Feedback

In Chapter 8, we discussed how goal setting gives behavior direction, increases expended effort, and fosters persistence. Because feedback is intimately related to the goal-setting process, it involves the same behavioral outcomes: direction, effort, and persistence. However, while the fourth outcome of goal setting involves formulating goal-attainment strategies, the fourth possible outcome of feedback is *resistance*. Feedback schemes, that smack of manipulation or fail one or more of the perceptual and cognitive evaluation tests just discussed, breed resistance.[27] Steve Jobs, the cofounder of Apple Computer (and once again its CEO), left the firm amid controversy in 1985 partly because his uneven and heavy-handed feedback bred resistance:

> According to several insiders, Jobs, a devout believer that new technology should supersede the old, couldn't abide the success of the venerable Apple II. Nor did he hide his feelings. He once addressed the Apple II marketing staff as members of the "dull and boring product division." As chairman and largest stockholder, with an 11.3 percent block, Jobs was a disproportionately powerful general manager. And he had disproportionate enthusiasm for the [Macintosh] staff. Says one of them: "He was so protective of us that whenever we complained about somebody outside the division, it was like unleashing a Doberman. Steve would get on the telephone and chew the guy out so fast your head would spin."[28]

Practical Lessons from Feedback Research

After reviewing dozens of laboratory and field studies of feedback, a trio of OB researchers cited the following practical implications for managers:

- The acceptance of feedback should not be treated as a given; it is often misperceived or rejected. This is especially true in intercultural situations.
- Managers can enhance their credibility as sources of feedback by developing their expertise and creating a climate of trust.
- Negative feedback is typically misperceived or rejected.
- Although very frequent feedback may erode one's sense of personal control and initiative, feedback is too *infrequent* in most work organizations.
- Feedback needs to be tailored to the recipient.
- While average and below-average performers need extrinsic rewards for performance, high performers respond to feedback that enhances their feelings of competence and personal control.[29]

More recent research insights about feedback include the following:

- Computer-based performance feedback leads to greater improvements in performance when it is received directly from the computer system rather than via an immediate supervisor.[30]
- Recipients of feedback perceive it to be more accurate when they actively participate in the feedback session versus passively receiving feedback.[31]

Table 9–1   *Six Common Trouble Signs for Organizational Feedback Systems*

1. Feedback is used to punish, embarrass, or put down employees.
2. Those receiving the feedback see it as irrelevant to their work.
3. Feedback information is provided too late to do any good.
4. People receiving feedback believe it relates to matters beyond their control.
5. Employees complain about wasting too much time collecting and recording feedback data.
6. Feedback recipients complain about feedback being too complex or difficult to understand.

SOURCE: Adapted from C Bell and R Zemke, "On-Target Feedback," *Training*, June 1992, pp 36–44.

- Destructive criticism tends to cause conflict and reduce motivation.[32]
- "The higher one rises in an organization the less likely one is to receive quality feedback about job performance."[33]

Managers who act on these research implications and the trouble signs in Table 9–1 can build credible and effective feedback systems.[34]

Our discussion to this point has focused on traditional downward feedback. Let us explore a couple of new and interesting approaches to feedback in the workplace.

Nontraditional Feedback: Upward and 360-Degree

Traditional top-down feedback programs have given way to some interesting variations in recent years. Two newer approaches, discussed in this section, are upward feedback and so-called 360-degree feedback. Aside from breaking away from a strict superior-to-subordinate feedback loop, these newer approaches are different because they typically involve *multiple sources* of feedback. Instead of getting feedback from one boss, often during an annual performance appraisal, more and more managers are getting structured feedback from superiors, subordinates, peers, and even outsiders such as customers. Nontraditional feedback is growing in popularity for at least six reasons:

1. Traditional performance appraisal systems have created widespread dissatisfaction.
2. Team-based organization structures are replacing traditional hierarchies. This trend requires managers to have good interpersonal skills that are best evaluated by team members.
3. Multiple-rater systems are said to make feedback more valid than single-source feedback.[35]
4. Advanced computer network technology (the Internet and company intranets) greatly facilitates multiple-rater systems.[36]
5. Bottom-up feedback meshes nicely with the trend toward participative management and employee empowerment.
6. Co-workers and subordinates are said to know more about a manager's strengths and limitations than the boss.[37]

Together, these factors make a compelling case for looking at better ways to give and receive performance feedback.

Upward Feedback

Upward feedback
Subordinates evaluate their boss.

Upward feedback stands the traditional approach on its head by having subordinates provide feedback on a manager's style and performance. This type of feedback is generally anonymous. Most students are familiar with upward feedback programs from years of filling out anonymous teacher evaluation surveys. Early adopters of upward evaluations include AT&T, General Mills, Motorola, and Procter & Gamble.[38]

Managers typically resist upward feedback programs because they believe it erodes their authority. Other critics say anonymous upward feedback can become little more than a personality contest or, worse, be manipulated by managers who make promises or threats. What does the research literature tell us about upward feedback?

Research Insights   Studies with diverse samples have given us these useful insights:

- The question of whether upward feedback should be *anonymous* was addressed by a study at a large US insurance company. All told, 183 employees rated the skills and effectiveness of 38 managers. Managers who received anonymous upward feedback received *lower* ratings and liked the process *less* than did those receiving feedback from identifiable employees. This finding confirmed the criticism that employees will tend to go easier on their boss when not protected by confidentiality.[39]

(DILBERT reprinted by permision of United Feature Syndicate, Inc.)

SOURCE: S Adams, *The Dilbert Principle* (New York: HarperBusiness, 1996), p 108.

- In another study, 83 supervisors employed by a US government agency were divided into three feedback groups: (1) feedback from both superiors and subordinates, (2) feedback from superiors only, and (3) feedback from subordinates only. Group 1 was most satisfied with the overall evaluation process and responded more positively to upward feedback. "Group 3 expressed more concern that subordinate appraisals would undermine supervisors' authority and that supervisors would focus on pleasing subordinates."[40]

- A large-scale study at the US Naval Academy, where student leaders and followers live together day and night, discovered a positive impact of upward feedback on leader behavior.[41]

- In a field study of 238 corporate managers, upward feedback had a positive impact on the performance of low to moderate performers.[42]

General Recommendations for Using Upward Feedback   These research findings suggest the practical value of *anonymous* upward feedback used in *combination* with other sources of performance feedback and evaluation. Because of managerial resistance and potential manipulation, using upward feedback as the primary determinant for promotions and pay decisions is *not* recommended. Carefully collected upward feedback is useful for management development programs.

360-Degree Feedback

The concept of giving a manager collective feedback from different levels and categories of co-workers is not new. Training and development specialists have used multirater, multilevel feedback for more than 20 years. Aggressively marketed 360-degree feedback software programs have mushroomed in recent years. A 1999 product review identified 30 different 360-degree packages for sale.[43] Consequently, according to *HRMagazine,* "An estimated 90 percent of *Fortune* 1000 firms use some form of multi-source assessment."[44] Whether 360-degree feedback goes down in history as just another passing fad or an established practice remains to be seen.[45] An unfortunate by-product of sudden popularity is that enthusiastic sellers of 360-degree feedback systems are more interested in advocacy than objective evaluation.[46] Importantly, our goal here is not to provide cookbook instructions in how to administer complex 360-degree reviews. Rather, our purpose is to see if the concept is sound and deserves managerial time and money.

The concept of **360-degree feedback** involves letting individuals compare their own perceived performance with behaviorally specific (and usually anonymous) performance information from their manager, subordinates, and peers. Even outsiders may be involved in what is sometimes called full-circle feedback (see Figure 9–3). *Fortune* offered this humorous yet instructive explanation:

360-degree feedback
Comparison of anonymous feedback from one's superior, subordinates, and peers with self-perceptions.

Figure 9–3   *Sources and Types of Feedback in the 360-Degree Approach*

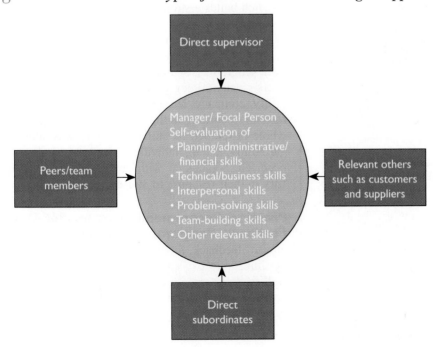

Here's how it works. Everyone from the office screwup to your boss, including your crackerjack assistant and your rival across the hall, will fill out lengthy, anonymous questionnaires about you. You'll complete one too. Are you crisp, clear, and articulate? Abrasive? Spreading yourself too thin? Trustworthy? Off-the-cuff remarks may be gathered too. A week or two later you'll get the results, all crunched and graphed by a computer. Ideally, all this will be explained by someone from your human-resources department or the company that handled the questionnaires, a person who can break bad news gently. You get to see how your opinion of yourself differs from those of the group of subordinates who participated, your peer group, and the boss.[47]

The idea is to let the individual know how their behavior affects others, with the goal of motivating change. In a 360-degree feedback program, a given manager will play different roles, including focal person, superior, subordinate, and peer. Of course, the focal person role is played only once. The other roles are played more than once for various other focal persons.[48]

Relevant Research Evidence   Because upward feedback is a part of 360-degree feedback programs, the evidence reviewed earlier applies here as well. As with upward feedback, peer- and self-evaluations, central to 360-degree feedback programs, also are a significant affront to tradition. But advocates say co-workers and managers themselves are appropriate performance evaluators because they are closest to the action. Generally, research builds a stronger case for peer appraisals than for self-appraisals.[49] Self-serving bias, discussed in Chapter 6, is a problem.

Rigorous research evidence of 360-degree feedback programs is scarce. A two-year study of 48 managers given 360-degree feedback in a large US public utility company led to these somewhat promising results. According to the researchers, "The group as a whole developed its skills, but there was substantial variability among individuals in how much change occurred."[50] Thus, as with any feedback, individuals vary in their response to 360-degree feedback.

Practical Recommendations for 360-Degree Feedback Programs   Our recommendations for upward feedback, *favoring* anonymity and *discouraging* linkage to pay and promotion decisions, apply as well to 360-degree feedback programs. According to one expert, *trust* is the issue:

Trust is at the core of using 360-degree feedback to enhance productivity. Trust determines how much an

---

Ethics at Work

If you've ever wondered whether building an intranet is worthwhile, then consider the example of Motley Fool, an on-line investor-education company based in Alexandria, Va. Last November, in an intranet-based program called "Stop, Start, Continue," the company's 125 employees were asked to use an intranet board to assess one another's job performance and comment on the work habits of coworkers. Tom Conner, a Web developer at the company, says using the intranet encouraged more honesty—especially when it came to offering constructive criticism to superiors he might otherwise have been reluctant to confront. "It feels good to formally tell people things you wouldn't say face-to-face," he says.

Here's how it worked: Employees clicked on a coworker's name in a particular section of the company's intranet, then wrote suggestions regarding specific habits that person should stop, start, or continue. The comments were forwarded verbatim to department coordinators, who were instructed to keep all complaints anonymous. Because it's not that big a company, however, "most people could tell from the writing style" who wrote the comment, says information-technology coordinator Dwight Gibbs.

The company plans to use the system again, possibly doing three rounds of evaluations a year. For now the intranet "suggestion box" will be used independent of the company's official annual review process, through which promotions are decided and awarded. The idea is to help employees improve their performance by bonus time.

SOURCE: Excerpted from I Mochari, "How Motley Fools Talk Back," *Inc.*, June 1999, p 108.

You Decide . . .

Is this an ethical application of the 360-degree feedback concept? Explain. Should the company make 360-degree input part of the annual performance review process? Explain, from an ethical standpoint.

For an interpretation of this situation, visit our Web site **www.mhhe.com/kreitner**

individual is willing to contribute for an employer. Using 360 confidentially, for developmental purposes, builds trust; using it to trigger pay and personnel decisions puts trust at risk.[51]

We agree that 360-degree feedback has a place in the development of managerial skills, especially in today's team-based organizations. However, it is important to remember that this complex feedback process is only as strong as its various components:

- Process design and planning.
- Instrument development.
- Instrument design.
- Administration.
- Feedback processing and reporting.
- Action planning as a result of feedback.[52]

It is not a quick-and-easy fix, as some advocates would have us believe.

Some Concluding Tips for Giving Good Feedback

Managers need to keep the following tips in mind when giving feedback:

- Relate feedback to existing performance *goals* and clear *expectations.*
- Give *specific* feedback tied to observable behavior or measurable results.
- Channel feedback toward *key result areas.*
- Give feedback as *soon* as possible.[53]
- Give positive feedback for *improvement,* not just final results.
- Focus feedback on *performance,* not personalities.
- Base feedback on *accurate* and *credible* information.

Organizational Reward Systems

Rewards are an ever-present and always controversial feature of organizational life.[54] Some employees see their jobs as the source of a paycheck and little else. Others derive great pleasure from their jobs and association with co-workers. Even volunteers who donate their time to charitable organizations, such as the Red Cross, walk away with rewards in the form of social recognition and pride of having given unselfishly of their time. Hence, the subject of organizational rewards includes, but goes far beyond, monetary compensation.[55] This section examines key components of organizational reward systems to provide a conceptual background for discussing the timely topics of pay for performance and team-based pay.

Despite the fact that reward systems vary widely, it is possible to identify and interrelate some common components. The model in Figure 9–4 focuses on four important components: (1) types of rewards, (2) reward norms, (3) distribution criteria, and (4) desired outcomes. Let us examine these components.

Types of Rewards

Including the usual paycheck, the variety and magnitude of organizational rewards boggles the mind—from subsidized day care to college tuition reimbursement to stock

Figure 9–4   *A General Model of Organizational Reward Systems*

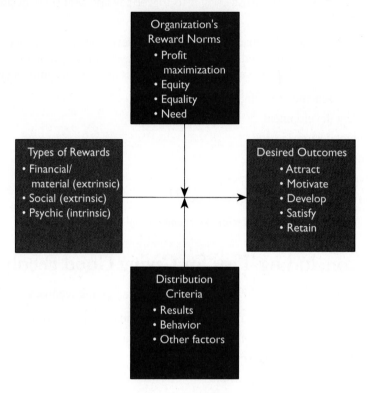

options.[56] A US Bureau of Labor Statistics economist offered the following historical perspective of employee compensation:

> One of the more striking developments ... over the past 75 years has been the growing complexity of employee compensation. Limited at the outbreak of World War I largely to straight-time pay for hours worked, compensation now includes a variety of employer-financed benefits, such as health and life insurance, retirement income, and paid time off. Although the details of each vary widely, these benefits are today standard components of the compensation package, and workers generally have come to expect them.[57]

Today, it is common for nonwage benefits to be 50% or more of total compensation.

In addition to the obvious pay and benefits, there are less obvious social and psychic rewards. Social rewards include praise and recognition from others both inside and outside the organization. Psychic rewards come from personal feelings of self-esteem, self-satisfaction, and accomplishment.

Extrinsic rewards
Financial, material, or social rewards from the environment.

Intrinsic rewards
Self-granted, psychic rewards.

An alternative typology for organizational rewards is the distinction between extrinsic and intrinsic rewards. Financial, material, and social rewards qualify as **extrinsic rewards** because they come from the environment. Psychic rewards, however, are **intrinsic rewards** because they are self-granted. An employee who works to obtain extrinsic rewards, such as money or praise, is said to be extrinsically motivated. One who derives pleasure from the task itself or experiences a sense of competence or self-determination is said to be intrinsically motivated.[58] The relative importance of extrinsic and intrinsic rewards is a matter of culture and personal tastes (See the International OB on p 285).

International OB

Foreign Employers Rely on Unique Extrinsic and Intrinsic Rewards in China

In spite of all the complications for foreign employers, one advantage they do have is that the Chinese like working for them because it gives the workers status. As one individual reported: "I work for a joint venture and I report to a foreign boss—this is cool." Also, it usually means that they get to practice their English and learn about life and cultures outside China. I was told of good employees quitting when they have been assigned to a local Chinese boss.

For foreign firms, the other big attraction that can keep mainland Chinese anchored to the desk for some time is the chance to travel abroad, particularly for training. Although it is not always easy to get people exit permits, at least for any length of time, it is an increasing trend. Typically, Chinese nationals are being trained in Singapore, Australia, New Zealand, and the [United States]. The main advantage of training employees abroad is that it buys some time, and companies usually link overseas development assignments to an agreement for individuals to stay with the company for two to three years after they return.

An example of this is Johnson & Johnson's executive MBA program with the University of Singapore. Twenty of its own staff and ten from its distributors take part in a three-year program that costs upwards of $20,000 per person. This kind of investment gives foreign companies a good reputation (which means local talent will be quick to join you), and in China, good news travels fast around the cadre of highly qualified personnel.

SOURCE: Excerpted from M Johnson, "Beyond Pay: What Rewards Work Best When Doing Business in China," *Compensation & Benefits Review*, November–December 1998, p 54.

Organizational Reward Norms

As discussed in Chapter 8 under the heading of equity theory, the employer–employee linkage can be viewed as an exchange relationship. Employees exchange their time and talent for rewards. Ideally, four alternative norms dictate the nature of this exchange. In pure form, each would lead to a significantly different reward distribution system. They are as follows:

- *Profit maximization.* The objective of each party is to maximize its net gain, regardless of how the other party fares. A profit-maximizing company would attempt to pay the least amount of wages for maximum effort. Conversely, a profit-maximizing employee would seek maximum rewards, regardless of the organization's financial well-being, and leave the organization for a better deal.

- *Equity.* According to the **reward equity norm,** rewards should be allocated proportionate to contributions. Those who contribute the most should be rewarded the most. A cross-cultural study of American, Japanese, and Korean college students led the researchers to the following conclusion: "Equity is probably a phenomenon common to most cultures, but its strength will vary."[59] Basic principles of fairness and justice, evident in most cultures, drive the equity norm. However, pay equity between women and men in the United States remains an unresolved issue.[60]

Reward equity norm
Rewards should be tied to contributions.

- *Equality.* The **reward equality norm** calls for rewarding all parties equally, regardless of their comparative contributions. Because absolute equality does not exist in today's hierarchical organizations, researchers recently explored the impact of pay *inequality*. They looked at *pay dispersion* (the pay gap between high-level and low-level employees). Result: The smaller the pay gap, the better the individual and organizational performance.[61] Thus, the outlandish compensation

Reward equality norm
Everyone should get the same rewards.

packages for many of today's top executives is not only a widely debated moral issue, it is a productivity issue as well.[62]

• *Need.* This norm calls for distributing rewards according to employees' needs, rather than their contributions.[63]

A pair of researchers concluded that these contradictory norms are typically intertwined:

> We propose that employer–employee exchanges are governed by the contradictory norms of profit maximization, equity, equality, and need. These norms can coexist; what varies is the extent to which the rules for correct application of a norm are clear and the relative emphasis different managements will give to certain norms in particular allocations.[64]

Conflict and ethical debates often arise over the perceived fairness of reward allocations because of disagreement about reward norms.[65] Stockholders might prefer a profit-maximization norm, while technical specialists would like an equity norm, and unionized hourly workers would argue for a pay system based on equality. A reward norm anchored to need might prevail in a family owned and operated business. Effective reward systems are based on clear and consensual exchange norms.

Reward Distribution Criteria

According to one expert on organizational reward systems, three general criteria for the distribution of rewards are as follows:

• *Performance: results.* Tangible outcomes such as individual, group, or organization performance; quantity and quality of performance.

• *Performance: actions and behaviors.* Such as teamwork, cooperation, risk taking, creativity.

• *Nonperformance considerations.* Customary or contractual, where the type of job, nature of the work, equity, tenure, level in hierarchy, etc., are rewarded.[66]

As illustrated in the following example, the trend today is toward *performance* criteria and away from nonperformance criteria:

Del Wallick wears his pride under his sleeve. A handshake reveals his prized wristwatch, given to mark his 25th anniversary with Timken Co. "I only take it off to shower and sleep," he says.

The hallways of Mr. Wallick's home in Canton, Ohio, are filled with an array of certificates marking

Extrinsic rewards such as a handsome wall plaque or an appreciative call from the boss and intrinsic rewards such as a feeling of accomplishment after a big project can boost motivation and productivity.

(Jim Cambon/Tony Stone Images)

the milestones in his 31-year career as a Timken steel-mill worker. Down in his rec room, a mantel clock that he and his wife picked out from a Timken gift catalog rests atop the family television.

But these days, once-paternal companies like Timken are trying to move away from rewarding employees for long service. Many are reducing service-award programs—and a few are eliminating them entirely. Besides wanting to save money, these companies hope to tilt recognition more toward performance and away from years of loyal service.[67]

This is all part of the new employment contract we discussed in Chapter 1.

Desired Outcomes of the Reward System

As listed in Figure 9–4, a good reward system should attract talented people and motivate and satisfy them once they have joined the organization.[68] Further, a good reward system should foster personal growth and development and keep talented people from leaving. A prime example is Herman Miller Inc., the profitable office-furniture maker. Not only does the firm maintain a much lower than average ratio between top management and shop-floor pay levels, Herman Miller shares generous productivity bonuses with its employees as well. The net results: low turnover, a strong supportive culture, and excellent employee–management working relationships.[69]

Why Do Rewards Fail to Motivate?

Despite huge investments of time and money for organizational reward systems, the desired motivational impact often is not achieved. A management consultant/writer recently offered these eight reasons:

1. Too much emphasis on monetary rewards.
2. Rewards lack an "appreciation effect."
3. Extensive benefits become entitlements.
4. Counterproductive behavior is rewarded. (For example, "a pizza delivery company focused its rewards on the on-time performance of its drivers, only to discover that it was inadvertently rewarding reckless driving."[70])
5. Too long a delay between performance and rewards.
6. Too many one-size-fits-all rewards.
7. Use of one-shot rewards with a short-lived motivational impact.
8. Continued use of demotivating practices such as layoffs, across-the-board raises and cuts, and excessive executive compensation.[71]

These stubborn problems have fostered a growing interest in more effective reward and compensation practices. Although we cannot engage in a comprehensive discussion of modern compensation practices in the balance of this chapter, a subject requiring an entire book,[72] we can explore general approaches to boosting the motivational impact of monetary rewards. This is where pay for performance—including profit sharing, gainsharing, and team-based pay—enters the picture.

Our discussion of organizational rewards would not be complete without more closely considering the role of *money* (see the OB Exercise, p 288). In today's workplace, despite lots of complaints about pay, money remains the central organizational reward. Consequently, we need to address this important underlying OB

Pay for Performance

question: How can managers increase the incentive effect of monetary compensation? Managers who adequately comprehend this issue are in a better position to make decisions about specific compensation plans.

Pay for Performance: The Concept

Pay for performance
Monetary incentives tied to one's results or accomplishments.

Pay for performance is the popular term for monetary incentives linking at least some portion of the paycheck directly to results or accomplishments. Many refer to it simply as *incentive pay,* while others call it *variable pay.*[73] The general idea behind pay-for-performance schemes—including but not limited to merit pay, bonuses, and profit sharing—is to give employees an incentive for working harder and/or smarter. Pay for performance is something extra, compensation above and beyond basic wages and salaries. Proponents of incentive compensation say something extra is needed because hourly wages and fixed salaries do little more than motivate people to show up at work and put in the required hours.[74] The most basic form of pay for performance is the traditional piece rate plan, whereby the employee is paid a specified amount of money for each unit of work. For example, a drill press operator gets 25 cents for every gasket drilled in four places. Sales commissions, whereby a salesperson receives a specified amount of money for each unit sold, is another longstanding example of pay for performance. Today's service economy is forcing management to creatively adapt and go beyond piece rate and sales commission plans to accommodate greater emphasis on product and service quality, interdependence, and teamwork. Dell Computer Corp., the leader in direct-to-the-customer sales, is a prime example. As *Business Week* noted in late 1998:

> Dell has tied bonuses and profit-sharing to service improvements of at least 15% this year. Success will be measured by shipping deadlines, fixing machines on the first try, and getting repair people to customers within 24 hours.[75]

Many jobs in the high-tech sector, such as this one being performed by an employee at Dell Computer, are rather tedious and monotonous. Motivation and output can suffer. Some believe pay-for-performance plans are the answer. But mixed results have cast a shadow over the idea of pay-for-performance.

Courtesy of Dell Computer Company

For Dell's employees, the path to being an industry leader in customer service is paved with financial incentives.

Pay for Performance: The Evidence

Does pay for performance work as promised? According to available expert opinion and research results, pay for performance too often falls short of its goal of improved job performance. "Experts say that roughly half the incentive plans they see don't work, victims of poor design and administration."[76] In fact, one recent study documented how incentive pay had a *negative* effect on the performance of 150,000 managers from 500 financially distressed companies.[77] A recent meta-analysis of 39 studies found only a modest positive correlation between financial incentives and performance *quantity* and no impact on performance *quality*.[78] Other researchers have found only a weak statistical link between large executive bonuses paid out in good years and subsequent improvement in corporate profitability.[79] Also, in a survey of small business owners, more than half said their commission plans failed to motivate extra effort from their salespeople.[80] Linking teachers' merit pay to student performance, an exciting school reform idea, turned out to be a big disappointment: "The bottom line is that despite high hopes, none of the 13 districts studied was able to use teacher pay incentives to achieve significant, lasting gains in student performance."[81] Clearly, the pay-for-performance trend could stall if constructive steps are not taken. Could profit sharing and gainsharing help?

Profit Sharing versus Gainsharing

The terms *profit sharing* and *gainsharing* sometimes are used interchangeably. That is not only a conceptual mistake, but a major disservice to gainsharing as well. These two general approaches to pay for performance differ significantly in both method and results.

Profit Sharing   Most of today's corporate pay-for-performance plans are profit-sharing schemes. **Profit sharing** occurs when individual employees or work groups are granted a specified portion of any economic profits earned by the business as a whole. These internally distributed profits may be apportioned according to the equality or equity norms discussed earlier. Equity distributions supposedly occur when performance appraisal results are used to gauge who gets how much in the way of merit pay or profit-sharing bonuses. Profit-sharing bonuses may be paid in cash, deferred until

Profit sharing
Portion of bottom-line economic profits given to employees.

Table 9–2   *Profit-Sharing and Gainsharing Plans*

Types of Profit-Sharing Plans

Deferred plan—Credit individuals with periodic earnings, delaying actual distribution until their disability, retirement, or death.

Distribution plan—Fully distributes each period's earned benefits as soon as the profit-sharing pool can be calculated.

Combination plan—Allows employees to receive a portion of each period's earnings in cash, while the remainder awaits future distribution.

Types of Gainsharing Plans

Improshare plans—Based on employees' ability to complete assignments in less time than would be expected given the historical productivity base ratio. Work-hours saved are divided between the firm and plan participants according to a set percentage, such as 50 percent. Individuals receive a corresponding percentage increase in gross pay. Although no structural barriers exist, these plans generally do not provide formal participation in decision making.

Rucker plan—Generally limits decision-making participation to a single screening committee or the interface of a production and a screening committee. The Rucker formula assesses the relationship between the value added to produced goods as they pass through the manufacturing process and total labor costs. Unlike the typical Scanlon ratio, this formula enables workers to benefit from savings in production-related materials, supplies, and services. Bonuses result when the current ratio is better than that for the base period. A reserve pool is established to offset bad months. The reserves left over at the end of the year are paid out to employees as an additional bonus.

Scanlon plan—Uses a dual-committee system to foster companywide participation in decision making. Draws upon a historical productivity base ratio relating adjusted sales to total payroll. A bonus pool is created whenever actual output, as measured by adjusted sales, requires lower labor costs than would be expected using the base ratio. Each month, a percentage of the bonus pool is held in reserve to offset deficit months. The remaining funds are divided between the firm and employees. All of the retained funds remaining at year's end are proportionately shared by the parties.

SOURCE: "Analyzing Group Incentive Plans," by Gary W. Florkowski, January 1990. Reprinted with permission of *HRMagazine,* published by the Society for Human Resource Management, Alexandria, VA.

retirement or death, or some combination of both (see the top section of Table 9–2). According to a 20-year study of 500 US companies, "Productivity increases 3.5% to 5% on average after companies adopt profit-sharing programs. . . . Profit sharing lifts productivity more in smaller companies [ones with 775 or fewer employees]."[82]

Gainsharing   Perhaps because it tends to be used in smaller companies with 500 or fewer employees, gainsharing is not as popularly known as profit sharing. In fact, only 9 out of 279 large US companies surveyed in 1993 reportedly used gainsharing for half or more of their employees. The figures for a parallel study in 1990 were 3 out of 313.[83]

Gainsharing
Bonuses tied to measurable productivity increases.

"**Gainsharing** involves a measurement of productivity combined with the calculation of a bonus designed to offer employees a mutual share of any increases in total organizational productivity. Usually all those responsible for the increase receive the bonus."[84] Gainsharing has been around for more than a half century and typically goes by one of the following names: Improshare,® Rucker® plan, or Scanlon plan (see the bottom section of Table 9–2 for details). Distinguishing characteristics of gainsharing include the following:

- An organizational culture based on labor–management cooperation, trust, free-flowing information, and extensive participation.
- Built-in employee involvement structures such as suggestion systems or quality circles.
- Precise measurement and tracking of cost and/or productivity data for comparison purposes.
- The sharing with managerial and nonmanagerial employees of the proceeds from any productivity gains.[85]

Ideally, a self-perpetuating cycle develops. Communication and participation generate creative suggestions which foster productivity gains that yield bonuses which build motivation and trust.[86]

How Do Profit Sharing and Gainsharing Measure Up?   Profound differences mark these two general approaches to pay for performance. Gainsharing, by definition, is anchored to hard productivity data; profit sharing typically is more loosely linked to performance appraisal results. Thus profit-sharing determinations, like performance appraisals, are readily plagued by bias and misperception. Another significant problem with profit sharing is that bottom-line profits are influenced by many factors beyond the average employee's control. Those factors include strategy, pricing, competition, and fluctuating interest rates, to name just a few. Profit sharing's principal weaknesses are effectively neutralized by gainsharing's major strength, namely, a quantified performance-pay formula.

Critics of profit sharing admit it is generous to share the good times with employees, but they fear profit-sharing bonuses are perceived as a reward for past performance, not as an incentive to work harder in the future. Moreover, gainsharing rewards participation and teamwork while profit sharing generally does not. On the other hand, gainsharing formulas are complex and require extensive communication and training commitments.[87]

So, on balance, which is better? Judging by available research evidence, much of which is subjective, the vote goes to gainsharing. One study of 71 managers and professionals in a metals processing company found no significant correlation between individual performance and profit-sharing bonuses.[88] Another study of 1,746 manufacturing employees, at seven firms with Scanlon plans and two control firms without Scanlon plans, found higher job satisfaction and commitment among the Scanlon employees. Additionally, participation was a significantly stronger cultural norm in the Scanlon organizations. Scanlon participants quickly passed this norm along to new employees.[89] (Gainsharing seems to work best when it becomes embedded in the organization's culture.[90]) Positive results, in

Thanks to videoconferencing technology, these Sun Microsystems engineers can make progress despite being physically dispersed. Teams, both face-to-face and virtual, are a hallmark of modern organizations. However, when it comes to team-based rewards, things remain rather primitive.

(Cindy Charles/PhotoEdit)

terms of lower costs, improved quality, and improved health and safety conditions, were documented in a study of four companies with Scanlon-type plans in force for four or more years.[91] Meanwhile, AmeriSteel, with four mini-mills in the southeastern United States, credits gainsharing for an 8% annual productivity growth rate during the late 1990s. Management believes having a gainsharing plan for each steel mill, rather than a companywide plan, gives employees a tighter linkage between their job and the bottom line. AmeriSteel's employees reportedly get a motivational boost by receiving their generous gainsharing bonuses *weekly*.[92]

Team-Based Pay

One very clear trend in today's workplace is the move toward teams (see Chapter 13). There are permanent work teams and temporary project teams. There are cross-functional teams with specialists from different areas such as engineering, production, marketing, and finance. There are self-managed teams, where employees take turns handling traditional managerial tasks including staffing, scheduling, training, and recordkeeping. Most recently, there are *virtual* teams where people from different geographic locations collaborate via computer networks, often with little or no face-to-face contact. While the move toward team structure certainly is a promising one, there are many loose ends, a major one being how to reward team members and teamwork. *Training* magazine's Beverly Geber puts things into context by noting:

> It's a struggle trying to persuade many employees that working cooperatively with others is in their best interest. It's an epic battle teaching them *how* to collaborate, especially when it means they must resist a lifetime of seeking personal glory. And it's truly exasperating trying to get nonteamed parts of the organization, as well as customers and suppliers, to work harmoniously with the teams.
>
> Unfortunately, there's another bugaboo waiting just around the corner. It is the issue of compensation. To wit: Now that people are working closely together to produce a product jointly, how do you pay them in a way that encourages collaboration and spurs the team to produce its utmost, but does not ignore the individual's innate desire for personal recognition?[93]

Team-based pay
Linking pay to teamwork behavior and/or team results.

Team-based pay is defined as incentive compensation that rewards individuals for teamwork and/or rewards teams for collective results. This definition highlights an important distinction between individual *behavior* and team *results*. Stated another way, it takes team players to get team results. Any team-oriented pay plan that ignores this distinction almost certainly will fail.

Team-based rewards plans among mid-sized and large US companies reportedly grew from 12% in 1993 to 24% in 1999. "Another 23% of the 2,000 respondents are now considering introducing team-based arrangements."[94]

Problems   The biggest single barrier to effective team-based pay is *cultural,* especially in highly individualistic cultures such as the United States, Canada, Norway, and Australia.[95] Individual competition for pay and pay raises has long been the norm in the United States. Entrenched grading schemes in schools and colleges, focused on individual competition and not group achievement, are a good preview of the traditional American workplace. Team-based pay is a direct assault on the cultural tradition of putting the individual above the group. Indeed, a recent scientific poll of nearly 1,500 full-time employees across the United States found little support for team-based rewards and a strong preference for permanent pay increases for individual performance. This led the researchers to conclude: "Workers' lack of interest in team pay implies that employers are simply not rewarding teams as effectively as they could."[96]

Another culturally rooted problem is a general *lack of teamwork skills.* Members of high-performance teams are skilled communicators, conflict handlers, and negotiators; they are flexible, adaptable, and open to change. Employees accustomed to being paid for personal achievements tend to resent having their pay dependent upon others' performance and problems. The combination of poor interpersonal skills and an individualistic work ethic can breed conflict and excessive peer pressure, as Levi Strauss & Co. learned at its El Paso, Texas, pants factory. The El Paso plant was one of 27 sewing operations in the United States, where Levi's switched from traditional assembly lines to 20- to 30-worker multitask teams responsible for complete batches of pants, from start to finish. Eighteen months into the new team structure, orders were being processed in only three days, as opposed to a seven-day turnaround under the old system. But Levi's got more than improved productivity:

> Under the team system, a worker's incentive pay is tied to team performance. A poor performer or absent worker affects everybody's paycheck. When someone is perceived to be faking sick days or lollygagging on a sewing machine, tempers flare. Says [team member Salvador] Salas: "Somebody's fooling around, and somebody else calls attention to that, and the first guy will just flip him off." Supervisor Gracie Cortez says that "it gets tough out there." She finds herself intervening to prevent "big fights." Says plant manager Edward Alvarez: "Peer pressure can be vicious and brutal."[97]

Levi's officials eventually realized that only two weeks of "group dynamics" training for plant workers, prior to the shift to teams, was insufficient.

Research Evidence   Research evidence to date is not encouraging. A recent comprehensive review of studies that examined team-based rewards in the workplace led to this conclusion: "The field-based empirical evidence is limited and inconclusive."[98]

Recommendations   The state of the art in team-based pay is very primitive today. Given the many different types of teams, we can be certain there is no single best approach. However, based on anecdotal evidence from the general management literature and case studies,[99] we can make these five recommendations:

- *Prepare employees* for team-based systems with as much interpersonal skills training as possible. This ongoing effort should include diversity training and skill training in communication, conflict resolution, trust building, group problem solving, and negotiating.
- *Establish teams* and get them running smoothly before introducing team-based pay incentives to avoid overload and frustration.
- Create a pay plan that *blends* individual achievement and team incentives.
- Begin by rewarding teamwork *behaviors* (such as mutual support, cooperation, and group problem solving), and then phase in pay incentives for team *results.*
- When paying for team results, make sure individual team members see a clear connection between their own work and team results. Compensation specialists call this *a clear line of sight.*

Making Pay for Performance Work

From a practical "so what" perspective, the real issue is not profit sharing versus gainsharing versus team-based pay. Rather, the issue is this: How can managers improve the motivational impact of their current pay-for-performance plan? The fact is, most such plans are not pure types. They are hybrids. They combine features of profit sharing, gainsharing, and team approaches.[100] One option is to hire consultants to establish one of the trademarked gainsharing plans or the Scanlon plan. A second, more broadly applicable, option is to build the best characteristics of profit sharing, gainsharing, and team pay plans into the organization's pay-for-performance plan. The following practical recommendations can help in this regard:

- Make pay for performance an integral part of the organization's basic strategy (e.g., pursuit of best-in-the-industry product or service quality).
- Base incentive determinations on objective performance data.
- Have all employees actively participate in the development, implementation, and revision of the performance-pay formulas.
- Encourage two-way communication so problems with the pay-for-performance plan will be detected early.
- Build the pay-for-performance plan around participative structures such as suggestion systems or quality circles.
- Reward teamwork and cooperation whenever possible.
- Actively sell the plan to supervisors and middle managers who may view employee participation as a threat to their traditional notion of authority.
- If annual cash bonuses are granted, pay them in a lump sum to maximize their motivational impact.
- Remember that money motivates when it comes in significant amounts, not occasional nickels and dimes.

A stunning role model for this last point is California's Kingston Technology Co. As *The Wall Street Journal* reported in mid-1999:

> Company co-founders John Tu and David Sun have decided to give Kingston's 1,000 employees another $20 million bonus, or roughly $20,000 a piece. (Actual amounts are based on tenure and performance.) This largesse comes after the company paid $38 million, or $69,000 an employee, in 1997 and $20 million, or $28,000 each, in 1998. The founders say the payments—a rare form of compensation for a small, closely held company—are an expression of Kingston's "we're in it together" family culture.[101]

Now that's teamwork!

Summary of Key Concepts

1. *Specify the two basic functions of feedback and three sources of feedback.* Feedback, in the form of *objective* information about performance, both instructs and motivates. According to the cognitive-processing model, individuals receive feedback from others, the task, and from themselves.

2. *Discuss how the recipient's characteristics, perceptions, and cognitive evaluations affect how the individual processes feedback.* The recipient's openness to feedback is determined by one's self-esteem, self-efficacy, needs and goals, and desire for feedback. One's perception determines if feedback is viewed positively or negatively. Cognitively,

the recipient will tend to act on feedback that is seen as accurate, from a credible source, based on a fair system, and tied to reasonable expectations and behavioral standards.

3. *List at least three practical lessons from feedback research.* Feedback is not automatically accepted as intended, especially negative feedback. Managerial credibility can be enhanced through expertise and a climate of trust. Feedback must not be too frequent or too scarce and must be tailored to the individual. Feedback directly from computers is effective. Active participation in the feedback session

helps people perceive feedback as more accurate. The quality of feedback received decreases as one moves up the organizational hierarchy.

4. *Define upward feedback and 360-degree feedback, and summarize the general tips for giving good feedback.* Lower-level employees provide upward feedback (usually anonymous) to their managers. A focal person receives 360-degree feedback from subordinates, the manager, peers, and selected others such as customers or suppliers. Good feedback is tied to performance *goals* and clear *expectations,* linked with *specific* behavior and/or results, reserved for *key result areas,* given as *soon* as possible, provided for *improvement* as well as for final results, focused on *performance* rather than on personalities, and based on *accurate* and *credible* information.

5. *Briefly explain the four different organizational reward norms.* Maximizing individual gain is the object of the *profit maximization* reward norm. The *equity* norm calls for distributing rewards proportionate to contributions (those who contribute the most should earn the most). Everyone is rewarded equally when the *equality* reward norm is in force. The *need* reward norm involves distributing rewards based on employees' needs.

6. *Summarize the reasons rewards often fail to motivate employees.* Reward systems can fail to motivate employees for these reasons: overemphasis on money, no appreciation effect, benefits become entitlements, wrong behavior is rewarded, rewards are delayed too long, use of one-size-fits-all rewards, one-shot rewards with temporary impact, and demotivating practices such as layoffs.

7. *Distinguish among profit sharing, gainsharing, and team-based pay.* Profit-sharing plans give employees a specified portion of the business's economic profits. Gainsharing ties bonuses to documented productivity increases. Team-based pay is incentive pay for engaging in teamwork *behaviors* and/or for team *results.*

8. *Discuss how managers can generally improve pay-for-performance plans.* They need to be strategically anchored, based on quantified performance data, highly participative, actively sold to supervisors and middle managers, and teamwork oriented. Annual bonuses of significant size are helpful.

Discussion Questions

1. How can feedback and rewards *combine* to improve job performance?

2. How has feedback instructed and/or motivated you lately?

3. Relative to your school work, which of the three sources of feedback—others, task, self—has the greatest impact on your performance? If you have a job, which source of feedback is most potent in that situation?

4. Which of the five cognitive evaluation criteria for feedback—feedback accuracy, source credibility, system fairness, expectancies, behavioral standards—do you think ranks as most important? Explain.

5. What is the most valuable lesson feedback research teaches us? Explain.

6. How would you summarize the practical benefits and drawbacks of 360-degree feedback?

7. Which of the four organizational reward norms do you prefer? Why?

8. What is your personal experience with failed organizational reward systems and practices?

9. As a modern manager, which pay-for-performance approach do you like better: profit sharing, gainsharing, or team-based pay?

10. How would you respond to a manager who said, "Employees cannot be motivated with money"?

Internet Exercise

www.panoramicfeedback.com

As discussed in this chapter, 360-degree feedback is getting a good deal of attention these days. Our purpose here is to introduce you to a sample 360-degree evaluation from an innovative Internet-based program marketed by Panoramic Feedback. (Note: Our use of this sample is for instructional purposes only and does not constitute an endorsement of the program, that may or may not suit your needs.)

Go to the Internet home page (www.panoramicfeed back.com), and select "Sample Questionnaire" from the main menu. The sample evaluation is for a hypothetical supervisor named Leslie Jones. For our purposes, substitute the name of *your manager* from your present or past job. The idea is to do an *upward* evaluation of someone you actually know. Read the brief background piece, and proceed to Part One of the Questionnaire. Read and follow the instructions for the eight performance dimensions. All responses you click and any comments you type into the two boxes in Part One will show up on your printed copy, if you choose to make one. Move to Part Two and type your personal evaluations of your manager in the box provided. These comments also will be on any printed copy you may make.

Questions

1. How would you rate the eight performance dimensions in this brief sample? Relevant? Important? Good basis for constructive feedback?

2. If you were to expand this evaluation, what other performance scales would you add?

3. Is this a *fair* evaluation, as far as it goes? Explain.

4. How comfortable would you be evaluating the following people with this type of *anonymous* 360-degree instrument: Boss? Peers? Self? People reporting directly to you?

5. Would you like to be the focal person in a 360-degree review? Under what circumstances? Explain.

6. Results of anonymous 360-degree reviews should be used for which of the following purposes: Promotions? Pay raises? Job assignments? Feedback for personal growth and development? Explain.

OB in Action Case Study

www.lincolnelectric.com

A Model Incentive Plan Gets Caught in a Vise at Lincoln Electric[102]

BusinessWeek In recent years, Corporate America has rushed to embrace the idea of motivating employees by linking pay to performance. Nearly half of large companies have tilted their pay systems in this direction, surveys show, and many say they're eager to push the notion further. To learn more, thousands of managers flock to Cleveland-based Lincoln Electric Co. each year to look at one of the country's oldest and most radical pay-for-performance systems.

Unfortunately, the Lincoln model isn't quite the smashing success it once was. After management stumbles forced the family-controlled manufacturer of welding equipment and supplies to sell more shares to the public last year, Lincoln increasingly resembles a typical public company. With institutional shareholders and new, independent board members in place, worker bonuses are getting more of a gimlet eye. At the same time, management is readying itself for an expansion drive to remain globally competitive, putting more pressure on the balance sheet. All that has crimped bonuses, even though Lincoln is posting record sales and earnings. For workers who expect high bonuses if they deliver in output, the shift has hurt morale.

So Lincoln is taking its one-of-a-kind pay system in for an overhaul. The company is by no means ready to ditch the incentive plan, which once paid employees up to 100% of their wages in annual performance-linked bonuses. But executives are now considering ways to move toward a more traditional pay scheme and away from the flat percentage-bonus formula. "The bonus is a good program, and it has worked well, but it's got to be modified some," says Director David C Lincoln, whose father John C Lincoln founded the

company in 1895. Adds Edward E Lawler, who heads the University of Southern California's Center for Effective Organizations: "One of the issues with Lincoln is how [its pay plan] can survive rapid growth and globalization."

Plans such as Lincoln's may be getting a lot of attention these days, but they date back to the 19th-century piecework system. Each of Lincoln's 3,400 US employees is supposed to be a self-managing entrepreneur. There's minimal supervision. They get paid when they work—no sick or holiday pay. "How much money you make is in your own hands," says Thomas Gadomski, a painting-crew leader.

Each employee is accountable for the quality of his or her own work and is rated twice a year on quality, output, dependability, cooperation, and ideas. The ratings determine how much of the total corporate bonus pool each worker will get, which comes on top of his or her hourly wage. . . .

The average Lincoln factory hand earns $16.54 an hour, vs. the $14.25 average manufacturing wage in the Cleveland area. With a 56% average bonus in 1995—the lowest in years—production employees came out ahead of workers elsewhere even after paying for health-care benefits employers typically pick up. But unlike at other companies, Lincoln has huge variations in production-worker pay: from roughly $32,000 to more than $100,000 for the most hard-driving.

There's tremendous pressure to produce, but an employee advisory board meets regularly with top management to air workers' concerns. And Lincoln guarantees work to employees with three years' experience. No one has been laid off since 1948, and turnover is less than 4% among those with at least 180 days on the job. "There isn't any other place to work like Lincoln Electric," says Kathleen Hoenigman, an 18-year veteran. "They take care of you." Indeed, Lincoln went so far as to borrow more than $100 million in 1992 and 1993 to pay US bonuses, even though it lost a total of $84 million in those years, in part because of an ill-conceived foreign-acquisition spree. Says CEO Donald F Hastings: "I had to go to the board and say: 'We can't break our trust with this group because of management mistakes and recession elsewhere.'"

Still, it gets harder and harder to live up to the old deal. Even though the company has come roaring back after stumbling abroad, the red ink it spewed left Lincoln financially weakened. To make better acquisitions and expand further, Lincoln made its first public offering last July, pushing outsiders' stake to 40%. It also slashed total debt by nearly 40%, to $130 million, and paid a lower bonus per person, though the total bonus kitty was a record $64 million. . . .

The slimmer bonuses represent a sea change for employees. It didn't help that last year, Lincoln's centennial, was its first with $1 billion in sales. In November, some employees protested outside headquarters after they learned of the bonus size. "Everyone was upset," says one worker. Blue-collar workers had already been disgruntled with management when it set up a lower wage scale in 1993, at 75% of pay, for 700 new employees hired to meet demand and staff an expanded motor operation. Turnover among the new hires was high, and the disparate pay disturbed veterans. "If an individual shows he can handle the workload, he should be rewarded" with full pay, says Joseph Tuck, an inspector with 18 years at Lincoln. Because of the protests, Hastings eliminated the two-tier wage on Dec. 1.

To revamp the pay scheme without stirring up resentment, the company has set up a committee to study the bonus program. It has told employees that a new formula is in the works, and it has hired Price Waterhouse to study productivity. Although Hastings pledges that the incentive system will remain, over time, he wants employees to focus more on their overall earnings, not just the percentage bonus they receive. Already, he has started raising base pay—with a likely reduction of bonuses later—for engineering, sales, and other office staff.

Even after the changes, Lincoln's pay system is likely to remain more innovative than most. But as it tries to hire more outsiders, expand further abroad, and modernize, "we're getting to be a more normal company," says Director Frank L Steingass. That may not be quite what eager visitors expect to hear. But if Lincoln can adapt to new times without sacrificing employee goodwill, another model pay plan may yet emerge.

Questions for Discussion

1. Relative to Figure 9–4, which organizational reward norm has long been in effect at Lincoln Electric? How can you tell?

2. Should Lincoln Electric switch to another organizational reward norm? If no, why? If yes, which one?

3. Why have Lincoln Electric's traditionally huge annual cash bonuses motivated strong effort when critics say bonuses reward *past* performance?

4. Is Lincoln Electric's organizational culture suitable for installing team-based pay? Explain.

5. Regarding the recommendations for making pay for performance work (at the end of the chapter), what advice would you offer the company's compensation review committee?

Personal Awareness and Growth Exercise

What Kind of Feedback Are You Getting?

Objectives

1. To provide actual examples of on-the-job feedback from three primary sources: organization/supervisor, coworkers, and self/task.

2. To provide a handy instrument for evaluating the comparative strength of positive feedback from these three sources.

Introduction

A pair of researchers from Georgia Tech developed and tested a 63-item feedback questionnaire to demonstrate the importance of both the sign and content of feedback messages.[103] Although their instrument contains both positive and negative feedback items, we have extracted 18 positive items for this self-awareness exercise.

Instructions

Thinking of your current job (or your most recent job), circle one number for each of the 18 items. Alternatively, you could ask one or more other employed individuals to complete the questionnaire. Once the questionnaire has been completed, calculate subtotal and total scores by adding the circled numbers. Then try to answer the discussion questions.

Instrument

How frequently do you experience each of the following outcomes in your present (or past) job?

ORGANIZATIONAL/SUPERVISORY FEEDBACK

	Rarely	Occasionally	Very Frequently

1. My supervisor complimenting me on something I have done. 1——2——3——4——5

2. My supervisor increasing my responsibilities. 1——2——3——4——5

3. The company expressing pleasure with my performance. 1——2——3——4——5

4. The company giving me a raise. 1——2——3——4——5

5. My supervisor recommending me for a promotion or raise. 1——2——3——4——5

6. The company providing me with favorable data concerning my performance. 1——2——3——4——5

Subscore = _____

CO-WORKER FEEDBACK

7. My co-workers coming to me for advice. 1——2——3——4——5

8. My co-workers expressing approval of my work. 1——2——3——4——5

9. My co-workers liking to work with me. 1——2——3——4——5

10. My co-workers telling me that I am doing a good job. 1——2——3——4——5

11. My co-workers commenting favorably on something I have done. 1——2——3——4——5

12. Receiving a compliment from my co-workers. 1——2——3——4——5

Subscore = _____

SELF/TASK FEEDBACK

13. Knowing that the way I go about my duties is superior to most others. 1——2——3——4——5

14. Feeling I am accomplishing more than I used to. 1——2——3——4——5

15. Knowing that I can now perform or do things which previously were difficult for me. 1——2——3——4——5

16. Finding that I am satisfying my own standards for "good work." 1——2——3——4——5

17. Knowing that what I am doing "feels right." 1——2——3——4——5

18. Feeling confident of being able to handle all aspects of my job.

Subscore = _____

Total Score = _____

Questions for Discussion

1. Which items on this questionnaire would you rate as primarily instructional in function? Are all of the remaining items primarily motivational? Explain.

2. In terms of your own feedback profile, which of the three types is the strongest (has the highest subscore)? Which is the weakest (has the lowest subscore)? How well does your feedback profile explain your job performance and/or satisfaction?

3. How does your feedback profile measure up against those of your classmates? (Arbitrary norms, for comparative purposes, are as follows: Deficient feedback = 18–42; Moderate feedback = 43–65; Abundant feedback = 66–90.)

4. Which of the three sources of feedback is most critical to your successful job performance and/or job satisfaction? Explain.

Group Exercise

Rewards, Rewards, Rewards

Objectives

1. To tap the class's collective knowledge of organizational rewards.

2. To appreciate the vast array of potential rewards.

3. To contrast individual and group perceptions of rewards.

4. To practice your group creativity skills.

Introduction

Rewards are a centerpiece of organizational life. Both extrinsic and intrinsic rewards motivate us to join and continue contributing to organized effort. But not all rewards have the same impact on work motivation. Individuals have their own personal preferences for rewards. The best way to discover people's reward preferences is to ask them, both individually and collectively. This group brainstorming and class discussion exercise requires about 20 to 30 minutes.

Instructions

Your instructor will divide your class randomly into teams of five to eight people. Each team will go through the following four-step process:

1. Each team will have a six-minute brainstorming session, with one person acting as recorder. The objective of this brainstorming session is to list as many different organizational rewards as the group can think of. Your team might find it helpful to think of rewards by category (such as rewards from the work itself, rewards you can spend, rewards you can eat and drink, rewards you can feel, rewards you can wear, rewards you can share, rewards you cannot see, etc.). Remember, good brainstorming calls for withholding judgments about whether ideas are good or not. Quantity is wanted. Building upon other people's ideas also is encouraged.

2. Next, each individual will take four minutes to write down, in decreasing order of importance, 10 rewards they want from the job. Note: These are your *personal* preferences; your "top 10" rewards that will motivate you to do your best.

3. Each team will then take five minutes to generate a list of "today's 10 most powerful rewards." List them in decreasing order of their power to motivate job performance. Voting may be necessary.

4. A general class discussion of the questions listed below will conclude the exercise.

Questions for Discussion

1. How did your personal "top 10" list compare with your group's "top 10" list? If there is a serious mismatch, how would it affect your motivation? (To promote discussion, the instructor may have several volunteers read their personal "top 10" lists to the class.)

2. Which team had the most productive brainstorming session? (The instructor may request each team to read its brainstormed list of potential rewards and "top 10" list to the class.)

3. Were you surprised to hear certain rewards getting so much attention? Why?

4. How can managers improve the incentive effect of the rewards most frequently mentioned in class?

5. What is the likely future of organizational reward plans? Which of today's compensation trends will probably thrive, and which are probably passing fads?

Learning Module B
Performance Appraisal

P erformance appraisal, when done properly and fairly, can be an energizing experience for everyone involved. Consider this situation, for example:

In the spring of 1998, with Hewlett-Packard Co. stuck in one of the deepest funks of its 60-year history, the company's top executives agreed to put themselves through a so-called 360-degree evaluation in which they would open themselves up to criticism from employees, peers, and board members. That's when Ann M Livermore, then head of HP's $5 billion software and services business, discovered something about herself. "I learned that I'm a very, very well-controlled executive, but that my employees like when I go off the handle every once in a while—you know, show my human side," says Livermore. "It reinforced that leadership means touching people's hearts as well as their brains—so since then I haven't worried so much about keeping my lid on."[1]

Livermore's "new approach" helped HP become a serious contender on the Internet, after some fragmented attempts by others. (Recall our discussion of 360-degree feedback in Chapter 9.) Unfortunately, performance appraisal often does not have this sort of happy ending. Too often, performance appraisal is a tedious and demoralizing ritual for all involved. In fact, 75% of the managers responding to one survey expressed significant dissatisfaction with their company's performance appraisal system.[2] Legal problems can surface, as well.

The purpose of this module is to explore the foundation concepts of fair and effective performance appraisals. Complete books are devoted to performance appraisal theory, research, and practice. Our more restricted goal in this module is to give you a basic set of tools for understanding and evaluating the diverse array of appraisal techniques you will encounter in the years ahead. Those techniques, some of which do not even exist today, no doubt will range from excellent to bizarre.

Definition and Components

Performance appraisal

Judgmental evaluation of one's traits, behavior, or accomplishments as basis for personnel decisions and development plans.

In everyday life, it is hard to escape being on the receiving end of some sort of performance appraisal. There are report cards all through school, win-loss records in organized sports, and periodic meetings with one's boss. For managers, who are in the position of both giving and receiving them, performance appraisals are an especially important consideration. As used here, **performance appraisal** involves the judgmental evaluation of a jobholder's traits, behavior, or accomplishments as a basis for making important personnel decisions and development plans. A survey of 106 industrial psychologists identified the top 10 uses for performance appraisal data. In diminishing order of importance, they are used for

1. Salary administration.
2. Performance feedback.
3. Identifying individual strengths and weaknesses.
4. Documenting personnel decisions.

5. Recognition of individual performance.

6. Identifying poor performance.

7. Assisting in goal identification.

8. Promotion decisions.

9. Retention or termination of personnel.

10. Evaluating goal achievement.

Also, performance appraisal information was typically used for *multiple* purposes, rather than for a single purpose.[3] Economic efficiency, the principle of fairness, and applicable laws dictate that these decisions be made on the basis of valid and reliable evidence, rather than as the result of prejudice and guesswork.

Components of the Performance Appraisal Process

Although formal performance appraisals are practically universal in the managerial ranks (91% according to one study),[4] few express satisfaction with them, as mentioned above.[5] Appraisers and appraisees alike are unhappy with the process. Much of the problem stems from the complexity of the appraisal process. One writer has captured this issue with the following example:

> If you wonder why evaluating an employee's performance can be so difficult, consider a simpler appraisal: one made by the barroom fan who concludes that his team's quarterback is a bum because several of his passes have been intercepted. An objective appraisal would raise the following questions: Were the passes really that bad, or did the receivers run the wrong patterns? Did the offensive line give the quarterback adequate protection? Did he call those plays himself, or were they sent in by the coach? Was the quarterback recovering from an injury?
>
> And what about the fan? Has he ever played football himself? How good is his vision? Did he have a good view of the TV set through the barroom's smoky haze? Was he talking to his friends at the bar during the game? How many beers did he down during the game?[6]

Further complicating things are Equal Employment Opportunity laws and guidelines that constrain managers' actions during the appraisal process.[7] Let us begin to sort out the complex appraisal process by examining its key components. Four key components, as shown in Figure B–1, are the appraiser, the appraisee, the appraisal method, and the outcomes.

The Appraiser

Managers generally express discomfort with playing the role of performance appraiser. After finding that 95% of the mid- to lower-level management performance appraisals at 293 US companies were conducted by immediate supervisors, researchers concluded that "most supervisors dislike 'playing God' and that many try to avoid responsibility for providing subordinates with feedback of unflattering appraisal information."[8]

Charges of racism, sexism, and perceptual distortion also have been leveled at appraisers. In a survey of 267 corporations, 62% of the respondents reported that leniency was their number one appraisal problem.[9] Everyday experience and research evidence show how stereotyping and bias can contaminate the appraisal process. For example, combined evidence from a laboratory study and a field study documented how women professors tended to get lower ratings from students with traditional

Figure B–1   *Components of the Performance Appraisal Process.*

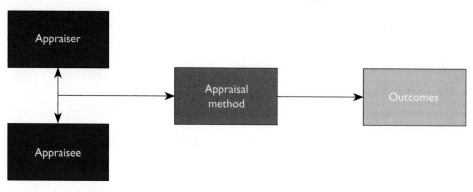

stereotypes of women.[10] Another study monitored the fates of 173 unionized employees who had filed grievances against their supervisors over an eight-year period. Those who had filed grievances tended to receive lower performance ratings from their supervisors than did their co-workers who had not filed grievances. This was especially true when the grievances had been settled in favor of the employee.[11] Thus, in this study at least, supervisors were shown to use performance appraisals as a weapon to get even with disliked subordinates. The ethical implications of this practice are obvious. Moreover, because performance appraisers engage in social perception (see Chapter 6), problems can occur in comprehending, encoding, retaining, or retrieving performance-related information.

Finally, managers typically lack the necessary performance appraisal skills. In fact, according to one study, only 25% of the managers doing performance appraisals had actually been trained for the task. The researchers added: "When there is training it often goes little further than to explain how to use the form, administrative procedures, and deadlines for submitting and getting the forms approved."[12] Experts on the subject have specified four criteria for a willing and able performance appraiser:

> The person doing the assessment must: (1) be in a position to observe the behavior and performance of the individual of interest; (2) be knowledgeable about the dimensions or features of performance; (3) have an understanding of the scale format and the instrument itself; and (4) must be motivated to do a conscientious job of rating.[13]

Managers need to ensure that all four criteria are satisfied if performance appraisals are to be conducted properly.

The Appraisee

Employees play a characteristically passive listening and watching role when their own performance is being appraised. This experience can be demeaning and often threatening. According to a pair of human resource consultants:

> Whatever method is used, performance appraisals are always manager-driven. Managers are in charge of the schedule, the agenda, and the results, and managers are the ones that receive any training and/or rewards concerning performance appraisals. Subordinates generally are given no responsibility or particular preparation for their roles in the process beyond attending the appraisal meetings.[14]

Table B-1   *Proactive Appraisee Roles during Performance Appraisal*

Role	Description
Analyzer	Performs self-assessment of goal achievement.
	Identifies performance strengths and weaknesses.
	Makes suggestions for performance improvement.
	Takes personal responsibility for solving performance problems.
Influencer	Improves communication skills (e.g., negotiations, advocating, providing information, advising, soliciting feedback, listening).
	Questions old assumptions and organizational roadblocks.
	Strives for collaborative relationship with boss.
Planner	Develops a clear vision of why his or her job exists.
	Identifies quality-of-service goals relative to "customers" or "clients."
	Understands what his or her job contributes (or does not contribute) to the organization.
Protégé	Learns from high-performing role models without compromising personal uniqueness.
	Learns through personal initiative rather than by waiting for instructions from others.

SOURCE: Adapted from B Jacobson and B L Kaye, "Career Development and Performance Appraisal: It Takes Two to Tango," *Personnel*, January 1986, pp 26–32.

Consequently, these consultants recommend four *proactive* roles (see Table B–1) for appraisees. They suggest formal *appraisee* training so analyzer, influencer, planner, and protégé roles can be performed skillfully. This represents a marked departure from the usual practice of training appraisers only. The goal of this promising approach is to marry performance appraisal and career development through enhanced communication and greater personal commitment.

The Appraisal Method

Three distinct approaches to appraising job performance have emerged over the years—the trait approach, the behavioral approach, and the results approach. Figure B–2 displays examples of these three approaches. Controversy surrounds the question of which of these three approaches (and a suggested contingency approach) is best.

- *Trait approach*—This approach involves rating an individual's personal traits or characteristics. Commonly assessed traits are initiative, decisiveness, and dependability. Although the trait approach is widely used by managers, it is generally considered by experts to be the weakest. Trait ratings are deficient because they are ambiguous relative to actual performance. For instance, rating someone low on initiative tells him or her nothing about how to improve job performance. Also, employees tend to react defensively to feedback about their personality (who or what they are).[15]

Figure B–2   *Three Basic Approaches to Appraising Job Performance*

The Trait Approach

	Indecisive		Moderately decisive		Very decisive

How decisive is the individual?

```
        |         |         |         |         |
        1         2         3         4         5
```

The Behavioral Approach

Teamwork (Check the box that best describes this individual's behavior)

☐ Works alone on all projects

☐ Works alone on most projects

☐ Works alone about half the time

☐ Teams up with others on most major projects

☐ Teams up with others on all major projects

The Results Approach

Key result area:____Unit sales_____

12-month goal:____12,000 units_____

Actual results:____10,500 units_____

Comments:_____

_____

_____

- *Behavioral approach*—How the person actually behaves, rather than his or her personality, matters in the behavioral approach.[16] As indicated in Figure B–3, the legal defensibility (in the United States) of performance appraisals is enhanced when performance ratings are supported with behavioral examples of performance.

- *Results approach*—Whereas the trait approach focuses on the "person" and the behavioral approach focuses on the "process," the results approach focuses on the "product" of one's efforts. In other words, what has the individual accomplished? *Management by objectives* (MBO) is the most common format for the results approach.[17]

- *Contingency approach*—A pair of performance appraisal experts has called the trait-behavioral-results controversy a "pseudo issue."[18] They contend that each approach has its appropriate use, depending on the demands of the situation. Thus, they recommend a contingency approach (see Table B–2). Note how the poorly regarded trait approach is appropriate when a promotion decision needs to be made for candidates with dissimilar jobs. Although it has widespread applicability, the results approach is limited by its failure to specify why the appraisee's objectives have not been met. Overall, the behavioral approach emerges as the strongest. But it too is subject to situational limitations, such as when employees with dissimilar jobs are being evaluated for a promotion.

Figure B–3   *Six Criteria of Legally Defensible Performance Appraisal Systems*

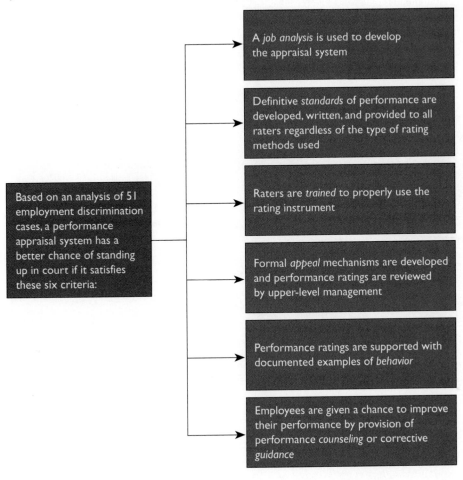

SOURCE: Adapted from G V Barret and M C Kernan, "Performance Appraisal and Terminations: A Review of Court Decisions since *Brito v. Zia* with implications for Personnel Practice," *Personnel Psychology,* Autumn 1987, pp 489–503.

Outcomes of the Appraisal

According to a researcher from the Center for Creative Leadership, there are three indicators of a useful performance appraisal:

- Timely feedback on performance.
- Input for key personnel decisions.
- Individual and organizational planning tool.[19]

To this list, we would add "human resource development tool." These four appraisal outcomes cannot be left to chance. They need to be forethoughts rather than afterthoughts.

Table B–2 *A Contingency Approach to Performance Appraisals*

Function of Appraisal	Appraisal Method	Comments
Promotion decisions	Trait	Appropriate when competing appraisees have *dissimilar* jobs.
	Behavioral	Appropriate when competing appraisees have *similar* jobs.
	Results	Same as above.
Development decisions	Trait	Tends to cause defensiveness among low self-esteem employees.
	Behavioral	Pinpoints specific performance improvement needs.
	Results	Identifies deficient results, but does not tell why.
Pay decisions	Trait	Weak performance-reward linkage.
	Behavioral	Enhances performance-reward linkage.
	Results	Same as above.
Layoff decisions	Trait	Inappropriate, potentially discriminatory.
	Behavioral	Weighted combination of behaviors, results, and seniority is recommended.
	Results	Same as above.

SOURCE: Adapted from K N Wexley and R Klimoski, "Performance Appraisal: An Update," in *Research in Personnel and Human Resources Management*, vol. 2, eds K M Rowland and G R Ferris (Greenwich, CT: JAI Press, 1984), pp 35–79.

Performance Appraisal Research Insights and Practical Implications

Researchers have probed many facets of the appraisal process. Resulting insights include the following:

- Appraisers typically rate same-race appraisees higher. A meta-analysis of 74 studies and 17,159 individuals revealed that white superiors tended to favor white subordinates. Similarly, African-American superiors tended to favor African-American subordinates in a meta-analysis of 14 studies and 2,248 people.[20]

- A recent field study found a higher degree of trust for management when employees approved of the performance appraisal system.[21]

- In a meta-analysis of 32 field samples, researchers discovered the more employees participated in the design and implementation of the appraisal process, the more satisfied they were.[22]

- In two studies involving university administrators and state government managers, managers who saw themselves as victims of unfair discrimination during performance appraisal tended to react favorably to a "procedurally just system." The researchers concluded: "Organizations may gain a great deal by providing vivid examples of system unfairness and its results both during training and afterward."[23]

- Although a great deal of effort has been devoted to creating more precise rating formats, formats account for very little difference (4% to 8%) in ratings.

- Performance appraisers tend to give poor performers significantly higher ratings when they have to give the appraisees face-to-face feedback as opposed to anonymous written feedback or no feedback.
- More experienced appraisers tend to render higher quality appraisals. This finding suggests that comprehensive appraiser training and practice can reduce rater errors.[24]

These research insights, along with evidence of rater bias discussed earlier, constitute a bad news–good news situation for management. The *bad* news: Performance appraisals can be contaminated by racism, sexism, personal bias, and fear of conflict. The *good* news: Managers can be sensitized to discrimination and trained to improve their performance appraisal skills.[25]

Chapter Ten

Behavior Modification and Self-Management

Learning Objectives

When you finish studying the material in this chapter, you should be able to:

1 State Thorndike's "law of effect" and explain Skinner's distinction between respondent and operant behavior.

2 Define the term *behavior modification* and explain the A→B→C model.

3 Demonstrate your knowledge of positive reinforcement, negative reinforcement, punishment, and extinction.

4 Distinguish between continuous and intermittent schedules of reinforcement, and specify which schedules are most resistant to extinction.

5 Demonstrate your knowledge of behavior shaping.

6 Identify and briefly explain each step in the four-step B Mod process.

7 Specify the six guidelines for managing consequences during B Mod.

8 Explain the social learning model of self-management.

Businessman Roger Rieger noticed in the early 1990s that the teen-agers he knew often were more motivated and worked harder at their summer jobs than they did at school.

He asked himself, "Why not pay kids to go to school? . . . It's a simple idea."

That idea has blossomed into a program that is part of Rieger's continuing effort to help at-risk students in Seattle's public schools.

Every other Wednesday for the past four years, Rieger has met quietly with 12-18 students at Nathan Hale High School.

He chats with students individually in the school library, checks attendance on a computer printout, reviews students' grades, and discusses everything from homework to sports.

If they're performing up to the standards he sets, he pays them. If not, there's no paycheck, and if they don't improve in later weeks, he "fires" them.

The program, one of a half-dozen that Rieger and his wife, Annette, have financed over the years, is called the "R Team."

Each student gets $5 a day for perfect attendance. "I'm very strict with them. No absences, no tardy slips, no excuses." After each five-week grading period, each earns $125 for maintaining straight Cs or better.

Good work pays off: Participating students can earn up to $175 during

Imagine a world in which students eagerly ran *into* high school.
(Superstock)

Tips: Be sure to rearrange antecedents and consequences for each target behavior (making realistic assumptions about existing A→B→C relationships). Use behavior charts whenever possible. Assign one team member the job of summarizing and reporting the team's B Mod strategies to the class.

Here are some things to keep in mind during step 3. Don't forget the common practice in B Mod of reinforcing a positive behavior (e.g., good attendance) rather than punishing its reciprocal deviant behavior (e.g., absenteeism). Of course, some of the deviant behaviors in the typology are so bad that termination of employment will be necessary. Your job as a human resource problem-solving team is to decide which behaviors warrant swift and sure punishment and which can be turned around with positive or negative reinforcement or extinction strategies.

Typology of Deviant Workplace Behavior[79]

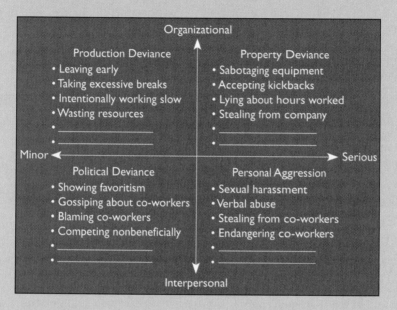

Questions for Discussion

1. Did your team do a good job of interpreting deviant behaviors as reinforceable productive behaviors (e.g., blaming co-workers versus owning up to one's mistakes)? Explain.

2. How difficult was it for your team to agree to fire someone for serious misconduct? Explain.

3. How realistic are the various B Mod strategies shared in class? Explain.

4. What situations were encountered where an approach other than B Mod would be best? Which approach?

Part Three

Group and Social Processes

Chapter Eleven

Individual and Group Decision Making

Learning Objectives

When you finish studying the material in this chapter, you should be able to:

1 Compare and contrast the rational model of decision making, Simon's normative model, and the garbage can model.

2 Discuss the contingency relationships that influence the three primary strategies used to select solutions.

3 Explain the model of decision-making styles.

4 Describe the model of escalation of commitment.

5 Summarize the pros and cons of involving groups in the decision-making process.

6 Explain how participative management affects performance.

7 Review Vroom and Jago's decision-making model.

8 Contrast brainstorming, the nominal group technique, the Delphi technique, and computer-aided decision making.

9 Describe the stages of the creative process.

10 Explain the model of organizational creativity and innovation.

BusinessWeek When Motorola Inc. executives dreamed up a globe-girdling satellite communications system to connect wireless telephone users anywhere on earth, it seemed like a grand idea. Motorola's engineers built a 66-satellite orbital network with technology so complex that Motorola CEO Christopher B Galvin has called it "the eighth wonder of the world."

More than a decade—and a billion dollars—later, the wonder is whether the project will fly. Since it was launched in November, Iridium has signed only 20,000 subscribers, far below the pace needed to nab 500,000 by yearend. Revenues have fallen short of the $30 million promised to bankers, putting Iridium in default on an $800 million line of credit. Now lead investor Motorola, with its 18% stake, is under pressure to pony up more money.

That's the last thing Motorola should do. It could exit now with hardly a blemish on its income statement. And bailing out would enable executives to continue the turnaround in the company's core products: digital telephones and chips.

Vain Hope. But Galvin is signaling support for the ill-starred project as it comes under intense financial pressure. Chase Manhattan Corp. wants Motorola to put up $300 million to guarantee the $800 million loan. That's on top of a $750 million loan Motorola has already guaranteed. And with a $90 million interest payment due on Aug. 15,

The demand for cellular phones is growing around the world.
(Bill Lai/The Image Works)

bondholders are looking to Motorola, too. Will Galvin dig into his pocket again? "We believe in the business model," he says. "We hope we will find a way to get through this."

Galvin argues that wireless naysayers were skeptical when Motorola entered the cellular phone business back in 1983. Critics predicted consumers wouldn't abandon their regular phones, but the number of wireless subscribers will hit 539 million worldwide in 2000. "This is like déjà vu all over again," Galvin insists.

Not necessarily. While industrial customers working in such remote places as deserts may want Iridium, it needs a broader range of customers to be profitable. But Iridium's birds can't handle more than 1,100 simultaneous calls each. That means Iridium can't achieve economies of scale needed to offer prices attractive to larger numbers of users.

What's worse, competition can only be expected to heat up. Globalstar is slated to start service in September. Teledesic, Lockheed Martin, and Boeing want to launch services. Rivals will offer cheaper packages than the $1,500 Iridium charges for phone gear and its $3-a-minute calls.

All of this is making investors anxious. Though Motorola is coming off second-quarter earnings of $273 million, up 44-fold from last year, its shares dropped 6% in the past month as Iridium's troubles mounted. "Investors are worried Motorola is going to hang on," says Mark McKechnie, a wireless-telecommunications analyst for Bank of America Securities.

If the company doesn't, it could emerge relatively unscathed. Its financial exposure is $1.3 billion, including bank guarantees, bonds it owns, and $400 million in vendor financing. While that shrinks Motorola's balance sheet, any loss wouldn't count against earnings.[1]

> **FOR DISCUSSION**
> Should Motorola continue to invest in the Iridium project? Explain your rationale.

ecision making is one of the primary responsibilities of being a manager. The quality of a manager's decisions is important for two principal reasons. First, the quality of a manager's decisions directly affects his or her career opportunities, rewards, and job satisfaction. Second, managerial decisions contribute to the success or failure of an organization.

In Part Two, we studied individual and personal factors within organizational settings. Now, in Part Three, our attention turns to the collective or social dimensions of organizational behavior. We begin this new focus by examining individual and group decision making.

The chapter opening vignette is a good illustration of why decision making is so important to an organization's profitability. Motorola has the potential to substantially increase its earnings if Chris Galvin decides to invest additional money into the Iridium project and if the technology is a market success. In contrast, Motorola can potentially lose $600 million if the company bails out of the project now. The losses will be much higher if Galvin decides to continue to invest in Iridium and the technology is not a viable product in the marketplace.

Decision making

Identifying and choosing solutions that lead to a desired end result.

Decision making is a means to an end. It entails identifying and choosing alternative solutions that lead to a desired state of affairs. The process begins with a problem and ends when a solution has been chosen. To gain an understanding of how managers can make better decisions, this chapter focuses on (1) models of decision making, (2) the dynamics of decision making, (3) group decision making, and (4) creativity.

There are several models of decision making. Each is based on a different set of assumptions and offers unique insight into the decision-making process. This section reviews three key historical models of decision making. They are (1) the rational model, (2) Simon's normative model, and (3) the garbage can model. Each successive model assumes that the decision-making process is less and less rational. Let us begin with the most orderly or rational explanation of managerial decision making.

Models of Decision Making

The Rational Model

The **rational model** proposes that managers use a rational, four-step sequence when making decisions: (1) identifying the problem, (2) generating alternative solutions, (3) selecting a solution, and (4) implementing and evaluating the solution. According to this model, managers are completely objective and possess complete information to make a decision. Despite criticism for being unrealistic, the rational model is instructive because it analytically breaks down the decision-making process and serves as a conceptual anchor for newer models.[2] Let us now consider each of these four steps.

Rational model
Logical four-step approach to decision making.

Identifying the Problem   A **problem** exists when the actual situation and the desired situation differ. For example, a problem exists when you have to pay rent at the end of the month and don't have enough money. Your problem is not that you have to pay rent. Your problem is obtaining the needed funds. Consider the situation faced by General Motors Corporation as it attempts to slash more than $1 billion from its annual warranty repair expenses.

Problem
Gap between an actual and desired situation.

> GM manufactures about 25,000 cars and trucks a day, which means little glitches can rapidly become epidemics. And behind every sick car is an unhappy customer. GM handles 22.5 million warranty claims a year, ranging from minor tweaks most customers barely notice to catastrophes such as engine failure. GM has made it a top priority for the entire company, from designers to dealers, to reduce warranty repairs with improved design and quality and early detection of problems. The goal is to eliminate some nine million claims and to save $1.6 billion in costs by 2001. Detecting problems early also is critical to avoiding costly recalls like the one of about a million trucks that GM announced last month, in which it will foot the bill to fix a switch miswired during manufacturing.[3]

General Motors' problem is the amount of warranty expenses the company is incurring: The company is spending far too much on repairing cars that are under warranty. Potential causes of the problem include poor design, defective parts, and manufacturing glitches.

How do companies like General Motors know when a problem exists or is going to occur in the near future? One expert proposed that managers use one of three methods to identify problems: historical cues, planning, and other people's perceptions:[4]

1. Using historical cues to identify problems assumes that the recent past is the best estimate of the future. Thus, managers rely on past experience to identify discrepancies (problems) from expected trends. For example, a sales manager may conclude that a problem exists because the first-quarter sales are less than they were a year ago. This method is prone to error because it is highly subjective.

2. A planning approach is more systematic and can lead to more accurate results. This method consists of using projections or scenarios to estimate what is

Scenario technique
Speculative forecasting method.

expected to occur in the future. A time period of one or more years is generally used. The **scenario technique** is a speculative, conjectural forecast tool used to identify future states, given a certain set of environmental conditions. Once different scenarios are developed, companies devise alternative strategies to survive in the various situations. This process helps to create contingency plans far into the future. Companies such as Royal Dutch/Shell, Fleet Financial Group, IBM, and Pfizer are increasingly using the scenario technique as a planning tool.[5]

3. A final approach to identifying problems is to rely on the perceptions of others. A restaurant manager may realize that his or her restaurant provides poor service when a large number of customers complain about how long it takes to receive food after placing an order. In other words, customers' comments signal that a problem exists. Interestingly, companies frequently compound their problems by ignoring customer complaints or feedback.

Generating Solutions   After identifying a problem, the next logical step is generating alternative solutions. For repetitive and routine decisions such as deciding when to send customers a bill, alternatives are readily available through decision rules. For example, a company might routinely bill customers three days after shipping a product. This is not the case for novel and unstructured decisions. Because there are no cut-and-dried procedures for dealing with novel problems, managers must creatively generate alternative solutions. Managers can use a number of techniques to stimulate creativity. Techniques to increase creativity are discussed later in this chapter.

Selecting a Solution   Optimally, decision makers want to choose the alternative with the greatest value. Decision theorists refer to this as maximizing the expected utility of an outcome. This is no easy task. First, assigning values to alternatives is complicated and prone to error. Not only are values subjective, but they also vary according to the preferences of the decision maker. Research demonstrates that people vary in their preferences for safety or risk when making decisions.[6] For example, a recent meta-analysis summarizing 150 studies revealed that males displayed more risk taking than females.[7] Further, evaluating alternatives assumes they can be judged according to some standards or criteria. This further assumes that (1) valid criteria exist, (2) each alternative can be compared against these criteria, and (3) the decision maker actually uses the criteria. As you know from making your own key life decisions, people frequently violate these assumptions.

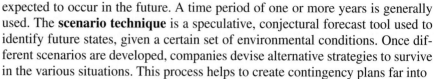

Ethics at Work

All of a sudden, Coke is under siege. The soft-drink giant is struggling to contain mushrooming alarm over the safety of its products in Belgium, France, Luxembourg, and the Netherlands. What started out last week as an isolated incident of several dozen Belgian schoolchildren getting nauseous has turned into an international health scare and public-relations nightmare. The government of France has asked Coke to stop shipping all canned products from its Dunkirk plant. Belgium has banned all Coca-Cola products.... There were even reports that Saudi Arabia and Germany had banned imports of all Coke beverages produced in Belgium and that the Spanish government had stopped a shipment of Belgian-bottled Coke and other brands for fear of contamination.... Even fierce rivals sympathized with Coke in its hour of despair, realizing the shoe could easily be on the other foot. Officials from PepsiCo Inc. have called their counterparts at Coke to offer assistance. And yesterday, Wayne Mailloux, Pepsi's European chief, sent an email to employees saying, "I would like to emphasize that this is not a situation which we should treat opportunistically or seek to take advantage of in any way." Pepsi has 2.2% market share in Belgium and 6.8% in France vs. 64% and 55% for Coca-Cola, respectively, according to Beverage Digest, an industry publication.

Source: Excerpted from J R Hagerty and N Deogun, "Coke Scrambles to Contain a Scare in Europe," *The Wall Street Journal,* June 17, 1999, p B1, B4.

You Decide . . .

What do you think of Wayne Mailloux's decision not to use Coke's problems as a market opportunity for Pepsi? Explain.

For an interpretation of this situation, visit our Web site **www.mhhe.com/kreitner**

Implementing and Evaluating the Solution   Once a solution is chosen, it needs to be implemented. Before implementing a solution, though, managers need to do their homework. For example, three ineffective managerial tendencies have been observed frequently during the initial stages of implementation (see Table 11–1). Skillful managers try to avoid these tendencies. Table 11–1 indicates that to promote necessary understanding, acceptance, and motivation, managers should involve implementators in the choice-making step.

After the solution is implemented, the evaluation phase assesses its effectiveness. If the solution is effective, it should reduce the difference between the actual and desired states that created the problem. If the gap is not closed, the implementation was not successful, and one of the following is true: Either the problem was incorrectly identified, or the solution was inappropriate. Assuming the implementation was unsuccessful, management can return to the first step, problem identification. If the problem was correctly identified, management should consider implementing one of the previously identified, but untried, solutions. This process can continue until all feasible solutions have been tried or the problem has changed.[8]

Summarizing the Rational Model   The rational model is based on the premise that managers optimize when they make decisions. **Optimizing** involves solving problems by producing the best possible solution. This assumes that managers

- Have knowledge of all possible alternatives.
- Have complete knowledge about the consequences that follow each alternative.
- Have a well-organized and stable set of preferences for these consequences.
- Have the computational ability to compare consequences and to determine which one is preferred.[9]

Optimizing
Choosing the best possible solution.

As noted by Herbert Simon, a decision theorist who in 1978 earned the Nobel Prize for his work on decision making, "The assumptions of perfect rationality are contrary to

Table 11–1   *Three Managerial Tendencies Reduce the Effectiveness of Implementation*

Managerial Tendency	Recommended Solution
The tendency not to ensure that people understand what needs to be done.	Involve the implementators in the choice-making step. When this is not possible, a strong and explicit attempt should be made to identify any misunderstanding, perhaps by having the implementor explain what he or she thinks needs to be done and why.
The tendency not to ensure the acceptance or motivation for what needs to be done.	Once again, involve the implementators in the choice-making step. Attempts should also be made to demonstrate the payoffs for effective implementation and to show how completion of various tasks will lead to successful implementation.
The tendency not to provide appropriate resources for what needs to be done.	Many implementations are less effective than they could be because adequate resources, such as time, staff, or information, were not provided. In particular, the allocations of such resources across departments and tasks are assumed to be appropriate because they were appropriate for implementing the previous plan. These assumptions should be checked.

SOURCE: Modified from G P Huber, *Managerial Decision Making* (Glenview, IL: Scott, Foresman, 1980), p 19.

Figure 11–2   *A Contingency Model for Selecting a Solution*

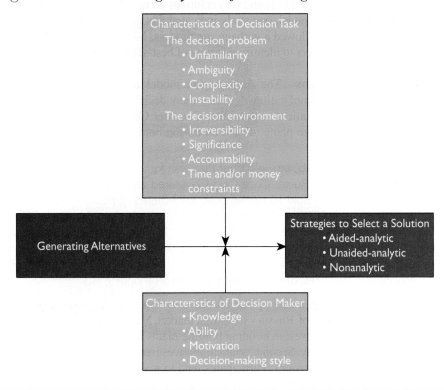

SOURCE: Based on L R Beach and T R Mitchell, "A Contingency Model for the Selection of Decision Strategies," *Academy of Management Review,* July 1978, pp 439–44.

Weather forecasters, astronomers, and insurance analysts are good examples of people who make their decisions by using an aided-analytic strategy. These types of professionals tend to make decisions by analyzing data with complex computer models.[21] In addition to using decision-making tools, organizations may create a decision-making team or hire consultants to conduct a formal study of the problem at hand. Consider the approach used by General Motors Corp. as it attempted to determine the companies that should get contracts to perform tool and die work for its US operations.

> Eleven executives and senior engineers, armed with clipboards and detailed questionnaires, boarded planes here and in Asia and converged on Thailand, Taiwan, South Korea, and Japan. Their mission: to evaluate 12 tool makers in 12 days as potential sources of stamping dies, the superhard steel molds used to shape sheet metal into fenders, hoods, and other parts of a vehicle's body.... Weeks before the planned four-nation purchasing mission, Mrs Nagle's [the executive in charge of the 711 people who buy GM's manufacturing equipment and supplies] staff asked GM engineers and purchasing personnel in the four countries to develop a list of top die makers. They then got each concern to fill out a 14-page questionnaire describing its structure, size, quality controls, areas of expertise, financial stability, and other qualifications.... Back home, the purchasing team threw itself into two weeks of rating the die shops. They narrowed the list to four or five and invited them to bid on specific tooling.[22]

GM ultimately decided to give the contracts to two vendors based on the analysis conducted by the purchasing team.

The quality of a decision can be the difference between success and failure. Unfortunately, decision makers can not always get input from others or rely on decision-making tools to arrive at a choice. Playing chess is a prime example of using an unaided-analytic strategy in which decisions are based solely on information that is processed in an individual's mind.

(Bob Thomas/Tony Stone Images)

In contrast, decision makers rely on the confines of their minds when using an **unaided-analytic** strategy. In other words, the decision maker systematically compares alternatives, but the analysis is limited to evaluating information that can be directly processed in his or her head. Decision-making tools such as a personal computer are not used. Chess masters and counselors use this strategy in the course of their work. Finally, a **nonanalytic** strategy consists of using a simple preformulated rule to make a decision. Examples are flipping a coin, habit, normal convention ("we've always done it that way"), using a conservative approach ("better safe than sorry"), or following procedures offered in instruction manuals. Both the cost and level of sophistication decrease as one moves from an aided-analytic to a nonanalytic strategy.

Determining which approach to use depends on two sets of contingency factors: characteristics of the decision task and characteristics of the decision maker (refer again to Figure 11–2).

Characteristics of the Decision Task   This set of contingency factors reflects the demands and constraints a decision maker faces. These characteristics are divided into two components: those pertaining to the specific problem and those related to the general decision environment. In general, the greater the demands and constraints encountered by a decision maker, the higher the probability that an aided-analytic approach will be used. This conclusion is consistent with results from two recent studies.

The first study conducted a series of experiments with undergraduate students. Findings revealed that the students made less consistent decisions in less predictable and unstable situations. Aided-analytic methods could have helped these individuals make more consistent decisions. The second study examined the strategic decision-making process within 24 organizations with annual sales ranging from $1.5 million to more than $3 billion. Results demonstrated that more effective decisions were made by managers who collected information and used analytical techniques than by managers who did not.[23]

The environment also restricts the type of analysis used. For instance, a study of 75 MBA students revealed that they purchased and used less information for decision making as the cost of information increased. In contrast, they purchased and used more information when they were rewarded for making good decisions. These results suggest that both the cost of information and one's accountability for a decision affect the type of

Unaided-analytic
Analysis is limited to processing information in one's mind.

Nonanalytic
Using preformulated rules to make decisions.

Table 11–2   *Contingency Relationships in Decision Making*

1. Analytic strategies are used when the decision problem is unfamiliar, ambiguous, complex, or unstable.

2. Nonanalytic methods are employed when the problem is familiar, straightforward, or stable.

3. Assuming there are no monetary or time constraints, analytic approaches are used when the solution is irreversible and significant and when the decision maker is accountable.

4. Nonanalytic strategies are used when the decision can be reversed and is not very significant or when the decision maker is not held accountable.

5. As the probability of making a correct decision goes down, analytic strategies are used.

6. As the probability of making a correct decision goes up, nonanalytic strategies are employed.

7. Time and money constraints automatically exclude some strategies from being used.

8. Analytic strategies are more frequently used by experienced and educated decision makers.

9. Nonanalytic approaches are used when the decision maker lacks knowledge, ability, or motivation to make a good decision.

SOURCE: Adapted from L R Beach and T R Mitchell, "A Contingency Model for the Selection of Decision Strategies," *Academy of Management Review,* July 1978, pp 439–44.

analysis used to solve a problem.[24] Moreover, time constraints influence selection of a solution. Poorer decisions are bound to be made in the face of severe time pressure.

Characteristics of the Decision Maker   Chapter 5 highlighted a variety of individual differences that affect employee behavior and performance. In the present context, knowledge, ability, and motivation affect the type of analytical procedure used by a decision maker. In general, research supports the prediction that aided-analytic strategies are more likely to be used by competent and motivated individuals.[25]

Contingency Relationships   There are many ways in which characteristics of the decision task and decision maker can interact to influence the strategy used to select a solution. In choosing a strategy, decision makers compromise between their desire to make correct decisions and the amount of time and effort they put into the decision-making process. Table 11–2 lists contingency relationships that help reconcile these competing demands. As shown in this table, analytic strategies are more likely to be used when the problem is unfamiliar and irreversible. In contrast, nonanalytic methods are employed on familiar problems or problems in which the decision can be reversed.

General Decision-Making Styles

The previous section highlighted that individual differences or characteristics of a decision maker influence the decision-making process. This section expands on this discussion by focusing on how an individual's decision-making style affects his or her approach to decision making.

Decision-making style
A combination of how individuals perceive and respond to information.

A **decision-making style** reflects the combination of how an individual perceives and comprehends stimuli and the general manner in which he or she chooses to respond to such information.[26] A team of researchers developed a model of decision-making

Figure 11–3   *Decision-Making Styles*

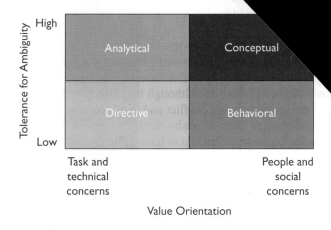

SOURCE: Based on discussion contained in A J Rowe and R O Mason, *Managing with Style: A Guide to Understanding, Assessing, and Improving Decision Making* (San Francisco: Jossey-Bass, 1987), pp 1–17.

styles that is based on the idea that styles vary along two different dimensions: value orientation and tolerance for ambiguity.[27] *Value orientation* reflects the extent to which an individual focuses on either task and technical concerns or people and social concerns when making decisions. Some people, for instance, are very task focused at work and do not pay much attention to people issues, whereas others are just the opposite. The second dimension pertains to a person's *tolerance for ambiguity.* This individual difference indicates the extent to which a person has a high need for structure or control in his or her life. Some people desire a lot of structure in their lives (a low tolerance for ambiguity) and find ambiguous situations stressful and psychologically uncomfortable. In contrast, others do not have a high need for structure and can thrive in uncertain situations (a high tolerance for ambiguity). Ambiguous situations can energize people with a high tolerance for ambiguity. When the dimensions of value orientation and tolerance for ambiguity are combined, they form four styles of decision making (see Figure 11–3): directive, analytical, conceptual, and behavioral.

Directive   People with a *directive* style have a low tolerance for ambiguity and are oriented toward task and technical concerns when making decisions. They are efficient, logical, practical, and systematic in their approach to solving problems. People with this style are action oriented and decisive and like to focus on facts. In their pursuit of speed and results, however, these individuals tend to be autocratic, exercise power and control, and focus on the short run.

Analytical   This style has a much higher tolerance for ambiguity and is characterized by the tendency to overanalyze a situation. People with this style like to consider more information and alternatives than do directives. Analytic individuals are careful decision makers who take longer to make decisions but who also respond well to new or uncertain situations. They can often be autocratic.

Conceptual   People with a conceptual style have a high tolerance for ambiguity and tend to focus on the people or social aspects of a work situation. They take a broad perspective to problem solving and like to consider many options and future possibilities. Conceptual types adopt a long-term perspective and rely on intuition and discussions

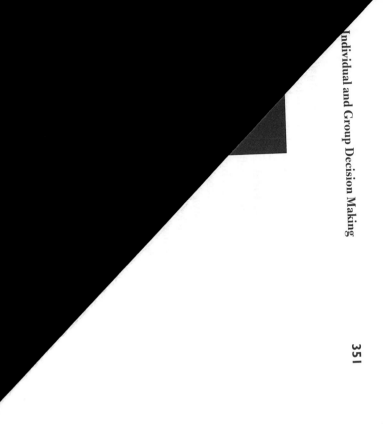

re willing to take risks and are good at
downside, however, a conceptual style
to decision making.

nted of the four styles. People with this
eractions in which opinions are openly
ptive to suggestions, show warmth, and
hey like to hold meetings, people with
to be too concerned about others. This
ıy" approach to decision making and to
difficulty making difficult decisions.

Research shows that very few people
Rather, most managers have charac-
also show that decision-making styles
[28] You can use knowledge of decision-
styles helps you to understand your-
ifying your strengths and weaknesses
or self-improvement. (You can assess
ersonal Awareness and Growth Exer-
you can increase your ability to influ-
, if you are dealing with an analytical
is possible to support your ideas. This

same approach is more likely to frustrate a directive type. Finally, knowledge of styles
gives you an awareness of how people can take the same information and yet arrive at
different decisions by using a variety of decision making strategies. Different decision-
making styles represent one likely source of interpersonal conflict at work (conflict is
thoroughly discussed in Chapter 14). It is important to conclude with the caveat that
there is not a best decision-making style that applies in all situations.

Escalation of Commitment

Escalation situations involve circumstances in which things have gone wrong but
where the situation can possibly be turned around by investing additional time, money,
or effort.[29] The International OB box on p 353, provides an example of escalation of
commitment at Daewoo Motor Company. Another classical example is illustrated by
the situation faced by Lyndon Johnson during the early stages of the Vietnam War.
Johnson received the following memo from George Ball, then undersecretary of state:

> The decision you face now is crucial. Once large numbers of US troops are committed
> to direct combat, they will begin to take heavy casualties in a war they are ill-equipped
> to fight in a noncooperative if not downright hostile countryside. Once we suffer large
> casualties, we will have started a well-nigh irreversible process. Our involvement will be
> so great that we cannot—without national humiliation—stop short of achieving our
> complete objectives. Of the two possibilities I think humiliation will be more likely than
> the achievement of our objectives—even after we have paid terrible costs.[30]

Escalation of commitment
Sticking to an ineffective course of action too long.

Unfortunately, President Johnson's increased commitment to the war helped make
George Ball's prediction come true.

As evidenced by Lyndon Johnson, **escalation of commitment** refers to the tendency
to stick to an ineffective course of action when it is unlikely that the bad situation can
be reversed. Personal examples include investing more money into an old or broken car,

International OB — Daewoo Motor Company Falls Prey to Escalation of Commitment

BusinessWeek

Kim Woo Choong thought he'd scored quite a coup in 1993. That year, his Daewoo Motor Co. got the green light to assemble cars in Vietnam. Then the economy stalled, and demand for cars plunged by one-third, to just 5,200 units annually. Daewoo's sales shriveled to 423 vehicles in 1998. Undaunted, Daewoo launched a new car, the Matiz, for $8,800. Sales in Vietnam may now double this year. But rivals doubt Daewoo's total $33 million investment is paying off. "There's no way they could make money at this price," says a foreign auto executive in Hanoi.

The Vietnam quagmire helps explain why Korea's Daewoo Group is in such a mess that creditors are now trying to force its breakup—and why it is negotiating with General Motors Corp. to sell pieces of its car company. From the United States to India, Chairman Kim is stumbling in his quest to build a car giant. In most places, the reasons are similar: plunging into dicey countries, selling at a loss to gain share, and refusing to retreat when the cause is hopeless.

Daewoo's Global Headaches

Korea	United States	Western Europe	India	Vietnam
Car sales plunged by 56% in 1998, to 234,000 units, as Daewoo was adding capacity.	The goal to sell 100,000 cars in its first year is unlikely to be met. Daewoo is offering steep rebates.	Sales have risen in Britain, Germany, and Italy. But analysts don't expect the gains to last.	Analysts estimate Daewoo is losing more than $30 million annually by offering $2,500 discounts.	Its hopes of hitting it big by arriving early have been dashed by rivals and a decline in demand.

SOURCE: Excerpted from J Veale, L Armstrong, and J Muller, "How Daewoo Ran Itself Off the Road," *Business Week,* August 30, 1999, p 48.

waiting an extremely long time for a bus to take you somewhere that you could have walked just as easily, or trying to save a disruptive interpersonal relationship that has lasted 10 years. Case studies also indicate that escalation of commitment is partially responsible for some of the worst financial losses experienced by organizations. For example, from 1966 to 1989 the Long Island Lighting Company's investment in the Shoreham nuclear power plant escalated from $65 million to $5 billion, despite a steady flow of negative feedback. The plant was never opened.[31]

OB Researchers Jerry Ross and Barry Staw identified four reasons for escalation of commitment (see Figure 11–4). They involve psychological and social determinants, organizational determinants, project characteristics, and contextual determinants.[32]

Psychological and Social Determinants Ego defense and individual motivations are the key psychological contributors to escalation of commitment. Individuals "throw good money after bad" because they tend to (1) bias facts so that they support previous decisions, (2) take more risks when a decision is stated in negative terms (to recover losses) rather than positive ones (to achieve gains), and (3) get too ego-involved with the project. Because failure threatens an individual's self-esteem or ego, people tend to ignore negative signs and push forward.[33]

Social pressures can make it difficult for a manager to reverse a course of action. For instance, peer pressure makes it difficult for an individual to drop a course of action when he or she publicly supported it in the past. Further, managers may continue to support bad decisions because they don't want their mistakes exposed to others. For example, a recent study involving 102 students working on a computer-simulated

Figure 11–4   *A Model of Escalation of Commitment*

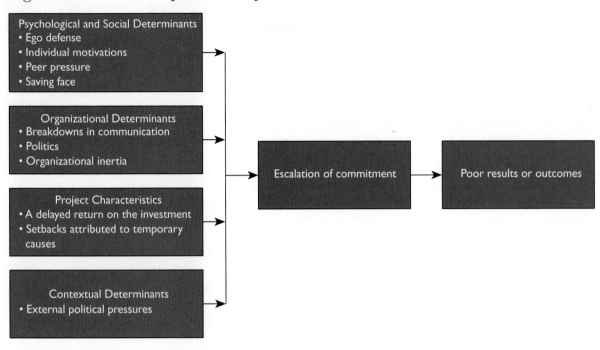

SOURCE: Based on discussion in J Ross and B M Staw, "Organizational Escalation and Exit: Lessons from the Shoreham Nuclear Power Plant," *Academy of Management Journal,* August 1993, pp 701–32.

competition revealed that they engaged in less escalation of commitment when their performance was being monitored.[34]

Organizational Determinants   Breakdowns in communication, workplace politics, and organizational inertia cause organizations to maintain bad courses of action.

Project Characteristics   Project characteristics involve the objective features of a project. They have the greatest impact on escalation decisions. For example, because most projects do not reap benefits until some delayed time period, decision makers are motivated to stay with the project until the end. Thus, there is a tendency to attribute setbacks to temporary causes that are correctable with additional expenditures. Moreover, escalation is related to whether the project has clearly defined goals and whether people receive clear feedback about performance. A recent study, for instance, revealed that escalation was fueled by ambiguous performance feedback and the lack of performance standards.[35]

Contextual Determinants   These causes of escalation are due to external political forces outside an organization's control. For instance, the continuance of the previously discussed Shoreham nuclear power plant was partially influenced by pressures from other public utilities interested in nuclear power, representatives of the nuclear power industry, and people in the federal government pushing for the development of nuclear power.[36]

Reducing Escalation of Commitment   It is important to reduce escalation of commitment because it leads to poor decision making for both individuals and groups.[37] Barry Staw and Jerry Ross, the researchers who originally identified the phenomenon of escalation, recommended several ways to reduce it:

- Set minimum targets for performance, and have decision makers compare their performance with these targets.
- Have different individuals make the initial and subsequent decisions about a project.
- Encourage decision makers to become less ego-involved with a project.
- Provide more frequent feedback about project completion and costs.
- Reduce the risk or penalties of failure.
- Make decision makers aware of the costs of persistence.[38]

Group Decision Making

Groups such as committees, task forces, or review panels often play a key role in the decision-making process. Are two or more heads always better than one? Do all employees desire to have a say in the decision-making process? When and how should a manager use group decision making? This section provides the background for answering these questions, essential for gaining maximum benefits from group decision making. We discuss (1) advantages and disadvantages of group-aided decision making, (2) participative management, (3) when to use groups in decision making, and (4) group problem-solving techniques. A broader examination of group dynamics is provided in Chapter 12.

Advantages and Disadvantages of Group-Aided Decision Making

Including groups in the decision-making process has both pros and cons (see Table 11–3). On the positive side, groups contain a greater pool of knowledge, provide more varied perspectives, create more comprehension of decisions, increase decision acceptance, and create a training ground for inexperienced employees. These advantages must be balanced, however, with the disadvantages listed in Table 11–3. In doing so, managers need to determine the extent to which the advantages and disadvantages apply to the decision situation. The following three guidelines may then be applied to help decide whether groups should be included in the decision-making process:

1. If additional information would increase the quality of the decision, managers should involve those people who can provide the needed information.
2. If acceptance is important, managers need to involve those individuals whose acceptance and commitment are important.
3. If people can be developed through their participation, managers may want to involve those whose development is most important.[39]

Group versus Individual Performance Before recommending that managers involve groups in decision making, it is important to examine whether groups perform better or worse than individuals. After reviewing 61 years of relevant research, a decision-making expert concluded that "Group performance was generally qualitatively and quantitatively superior to the performance of the average individual."[40] Although subsequent research of small-group decision making generally supported this conclusion, there are five important issues to consider when using groups to make decisions:

1. Groups were less efficient than individuals. This suggests that time constraints are an important consideration in determining whether to involve groups in decision making.

Table 11–3   *Advantages and Disadvantages of Group-Aided Decision Making*

Advantages	Disadvantages
1. *Greater pool of knowledge.* A group can bring much more information and experience to bear on a decision or problem than can an individual acting alone.	1. *Social pressure.* Unwillingness to "rock the boat" and pressure to conform may combine to stifle the creativity of individual contributors.
2. *Different perspectives.* Individuals with varied experience and interests help the group see decision situations and problems from different angles.	2. *Domination by a vocal few.* Sometimes the quality of group action is reduced when the group gives in to those who talk the loudest and longest.
3. *Greater comprehension.* Those who personally experience the give-and-take of group discussion about alternative courses of action tend to understand the rationale behind the final decision.	3. *Logrolling.* Political wheeling and dealing can displace sound thinking when an individual's pet project or vested interest is at stake.
4. *Increased acceptance.* Those who play an active role in group decision making and problem solving tend to view the outcome as "ours" rather than "theirs."	4. *Goal displacement.* Sometimes secondary considerations such as winning an argument, making a point, or getting back at a rival displace the primary task of making a sound decision or solving a problem.
5. *Training ground.* Less experienced participants in group action learn how to cope with group dynamics by actually being involved.	5. *"Groupthink."* Sometimes cohesive "in groups" let the desire for unanimity override sound judgment when generating and evaluating alternative courses of action. (Groupthink is discussed in Chapter 12.)

SOURCE: R Kreitner, *Management,* 7th ed (Boston: Houghton Mifflin, 1998), p 234.

2. Groups were more confident about their judgments and choices than individuals. Because group confidence is not a surrogate for group decision quality, this overconfidence can fuel groupthink—groupthink is discussed in Chapter 12—and a resistance to consider alternative solutions proposed by individuals outside the group.

3. Group size affected decision outcomes. Decision quality was negatively related to group size.[41]

4. Decision making accuracy was higher when (*a*) groups knew a great deal about the issues at hand and (*b*) group leaders possessed the ability to effectively evaluate the group members' opinions and judgments. Groups need to give more weight to relevant and accurate judgments while downplaying irrelevant or inaccurate judgments made by its members.[42]

5. The composition of a group affects its decision-making processes and ultimately performance. For example, groups of familiar people are more likely to make better decisions when members share a lot of unique information. In contrast, unacquainted group members should outperform groups of friends when most group members possess common knowledge.[43]

Additional research suggests that managers should use a contingency approach when determining whether to include others in the decision-making process. Let us now consider these contingency recommendations.

Practical Contingency Recommendations   If the
such as deciding on promotions or who qualifies for a loa.
tend to produce more consistent decisions than do individua
let the most competent individual, rather than a group, make
of environmental threats such as time pressure and potential
sion, groups use less information and fewer communication c
the probability of a bad decision.[44] This conclusion underscore
dation that managers should keep in mind: Because the qual,
strongly affects a group's productivity, on complex tasks it is esse
anisms to enhance communication effectiveness.

Participative Management

An organization needs to maximize its workers' potential if it wants
compete in the global economy. As noted by Jack Welch, CEO of G
"Only the most productive companies are going to win. If you can't s   ..op-qual-
ity product at the world's lowest price, you're going to be out of the game. In that
environment, 6% annual improvement in productivity may not be good enough anymore; you may need 8% to 9%."[45] Participative management and employee empowerment, which is discussed in Chapter 16, are highly touted methods for meeting this
productivity challenge. Interestingly, employees also seem to desire or recognize the
need for participative management. A nationwide survey of 2,408 employees, for
example, revealed that almost 66% desired more influence or decision-making power
in their jobs.[46]

Confusion exists about the exact meaning of participative management (PM). One
management expert clarified this situation by defining **participative management** as
the process whereby employees play a direct role in (1) setting goals, (2) making decisions, (3) solving problems, and (4) making changes in the organization. Without question, participative management entails much more than simply asking employees for
their ideas or opinions.

Advocates of PM claim employee participation increases employee satisfaction,
commitment, and performance. To get a fuller understanding of how and when
participative management works, we begin by discussing a model of participative
management.

A Model of Participative Management   Consistent with both Maslow's need
theory and the job characteristics model of job design (see Chapter 7), participative
management is predicted to increase motivation because it helps employees fulfill three
basic needs: (1) autonomy, (2) meaningfulness of work, and (3) interpersonal contact.
Satisfaction of these needs enhances feelings of acceptance and commitment, security,
challenge, and satisfaction. In turn, these positive feelings supposedly lead to increased
innovation and performance.[47]

Participative management does not work in all situations. The design of work, the
level of trust between management and employees, and the employees' competence
and readiness to participate represent three factors that influence the effectiveness of
PM. With respect to the design of work, individual participation is counterproductive
when employees are highly interdependent on each other, as on an assembly line. The
problem with individual participation in this case is that interdependent employees

**Participative
management**
Involving employees in
various forms of
decision making.

not have a broad understanding of the entire production process. Partici-
management also is less likely to succeed when employees do not trust man-
ent. Finally, PM is more effective when employees are competent, prepared, and
interested in participating.[48]

Research and Practical Suggestions for Managers   Participative management can significantly increase employee job involvement, organizational commitment, creativity, and perceptions of procedural justice and personal control.[49] Two
additional meta-analyses provided additional support for the value of participative
management. Results from a meta-analysis involving 27 studies and 6,732 individuals
revealed that employee participation in the performance appraisal process was positively related to an employee's satisfaction with his or her performance review, perceived value of the appraisal, motivation to improve performance following a
performance review, and perceived fairness of the appraisal process.[50] A second meta-
analysis of 86 studies involving 18,872 people further demonstrated that participation
had a small but significant effect on job performance and a moderate relationship with
job satisfaction.[51] This later finding questions the widespread conclusion that participative management should be used to increase employee performance.

So what is a manager to do? We believe that PM is not a quick-fix solution for low productivity and motivation, as some enthusiastic supporters claim. Nonetheless, because
participative management is effective in certain situations, managers can increase their
chances of obtaining positive results by using once again a contingency approach.[52] For
example, the effectiveness of participation depends on the type of interactions between
managers and employees as they jointly solve problems. Effective participation requires
a constructive interaction that fosters cooperation and respect, as opposed to competition
and defensiveness.[53] Managers are advised not to use participative programs when they
have destructive interpersonal interactions with their employees.

Experiences of companies implementing participative management programs suggest
three additional practical recommendations. First, supervisors and middle managers tend
to resist participative management because it reduces their power and authority. It is
important to gain the support and commitment from employees who have managerial
responsibility. Second, a longitudinal study of *Fortune* 1000 firms in 1987, 1990, and
1993 indicated that employee involvement was more effective when it was implemented
as part of a broader total quality management program.[54] This study suggests that organizations should use participative management and employee involvement as vehicles to
help them meet their strategic and operational goals as opposed to using these techniques
as ends in and of themselves. Third, the process of implementing participative management must be monitored and managed by top management.[55]

When to Have Groups Participate in Decision Making: The Vroom/Yetton/Jago Model

Victor Vroom and Philip Yetton developed a model in 1973 to help managers determine
the degree of group involvement in the decision-making process. It was later expanded
by Vroom and Arthur Jago.[56] The model is prescriptive in that it specifies decision-
making styles that should be effective in different situations.

Vroom and Jago's model is represented as a decision tree. The manager's task is to
move from left to right along the various branches of the tree. A specific decision-making
style is prescribed at the end point of each branch. Before we apply the model, however, it

Table 11–4   *Management Decision Styles*

AI	You solve the problem or make the decision yourself, using information available to you at that time.
AII	You obtain the necessary information from your subordinate(s), then decide on the solution to the problem yourself. You may or may not tell your subordinates what the problem is in getting the information from them. The role played by your subordinates in making the decision is clearly one of providing the necessary information to you rather than generating or evaluating solutions.
CI	You share the problem with relevant subordinates individually, getting their ideas and suggestions without bringing them together as a group. Then you make the decision that may or may not reflect your subordinates' influence.
CII	You share the problem with your subordinates as a group, collectively obtaining their ideas and suggestions. Then you make the decision that may or may not reflect your subordinates' influence.
GII	You share a problem with your subordinates as a group. Together you generate and evaluate alternatives and attempt to reach agreement (consensus) on a solution. Your role is much like that of a chairman. You do not try to influence the group to adopt "your" solution, and you are willing to accept and implement any solution that has the support of the entire group.

SOURCE: "A New Look at Managerial Decision Making" by V H Vroom. Reprinted from *Organizational Dynamics*, Spring 1973, p 67, © 1973 American Management Association International. Reprinted by permission of American Management Association International, New York, NY. All rights reserved. http://www.amanet.org.

is necessary to consider the different decision styles managers ultimately choose from and an approach for diagnosing the problem situation.

Five Decision-Making Styles   Vroom and Yetton identified five distinct decision-making styles. In Table 11–4, each style is represented by a letter. The letter indicates the basic thrust of the style. For example, A stands for *autocratic,* C for *consultive,* and G for *group.* There are several important issues to consider as one moves from an AI style to a GII style:

• The problem or decision is discussed with more people.

• Group involvement moves from merely providing data to recommending solutions.

• Group "ownership" and commitment to the solution increases.

• As group commitment increases, so does the time needed to arrive at a decision.

Style choice depends on the type of problem situation.

Matching the Situation to Decision-Making Style   Vroom and Jago developed eight problem attributes that managers can use to diagnose a situation. They are shown at the top of the decision tree presented in Figure 11–5 and are expressed as questions. Answers to these questions lead managers along different branches, pointing the way to potentially effective decision-making styles.

Applying the Model   Because Vroom and Jago developed four decision trees, the first step is to choose one of the trees. Each tree represents a generic type of problem that managers frequently encounter. They are (1) an individual-level problem with time

Figure 11–5   *Vroom and Jago's Decision-Making Model*

QR	Quality Requirement	How important is the technical quality of this decision?
CR	Commitment Requirement	How important is subordinate commitment to the decision?
LI	Leader's Information	Do you have sufficient information to make a high-quality decision?
ST	Problem Structure	Is the problem well structured?
CP	Commitment Probability	If you were to make the decision by yourself, is it reasonably certain that your subordinate(s) would be committed to the decision?
GC	Goal Congruence	Do subordinates share the organizational goals to be attained in solving this problem?
CO	Subordinate Conflict	Is conflict among subordinates over preferred solutions likely?
SI	Subordinate Information	Do subordinates have sufficient information to make a high-quality decision?

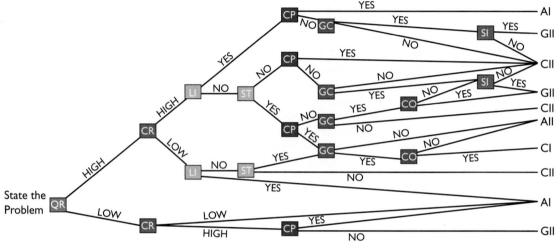

SOURCE: Reprinted from *The New Leadership: Managing Participation in Organizations* by Victor H Vroom and Arthur G Jago 1988, Englewood Cliffs, NJ: Prentice-Hall. © 1987 by V H Vroom and A G Jago. Used with permission of the authors.

constraints, (2) an individual-level problem in which the manager wants to develop an employee's decision-making abilities, (3) a group-level problem in which the manager wants to develop employees' decision-making abilities, and (4) a time-driven group problem[57] (illustrated in Figure 11–5).

To use the model in Figure 11–5, start at the left side and move toward the right by asking yourself the questions associated with each decision point (represented by a box in the figure) encountered. A decision-making style is prescribed at the end of each branch.

Let us track a simple example through Figure 11–5. Suppose you have to determine the work schedule for a group of part-time workers who report to you. The first question is "How important is the technical quality of this decision?" It seems rather low. This leads us to the second question: "How important is subordinate commitment to the decision?" Assuming acceptance is important, this takes us along the branch leading to the question about commitment probability (CP). If you were to make the decision by yourself, is it reasonably certain that your subordinate(s) would be committed to the decision? A yes answer suggests you should use an AI decision-making style (see Table 11–4) and a GII style if you answered no. The Group Exercise at the end of this chapter provides you the opportunity to apply this model. You will receive feedback on the accuracy of your analysis.

Research Insights and Managerial Implications   Very little research has tested the predictive accuracy of this model. Nonetheless, a study containing three different samples of managers supported the Vroom-Jago decision-making model. Decisions were more effective when managers used decision-making styles consistent with the model.[58] Managers thus are advised to use different decision-making styles to suit situational demands.

Also, the model can help managers determine when, and to what extent, they should involve employees in decision making. By simply being aware of the eight diagnostic questions, managers can enhance their ability to structure ambiguous problems. This should ultimately enhance the quality of managerial decisions.

Group Problem-Solving Techniques

Using groups to make decisions generally requires that they reach a consensus. According to a decision-making expert, a **consensus** "is reached when all members can say they either agree with the decision or have had their 'day in court' and were unable to convince the others of their viewpoint. In the final analysis, everyone agrees to support the outcome."[59] This definition indicates that consensus does not require unanimous agreement because group members may still disagree with the final decision but are willing to work toward its success.

Groups can experience roadblocks when trying to arrive at a consensus decision. For one, groups may not generate all relevant alternatives to a problem because an individual dominates or intimidates other group members. This is both overt and/or subtle. For instance, group members who possess power and authority, such as a CEO, can be intimidating, regardless of interpersonal style, simply by being present in the room. Moreover, shyness inhibits the generation of alternatives. Shy or socially anxious individuals may withhold their input for fear of embarrassment or lack of confidence.[60] Satisficing is another hurdle to effective group decision making. As previously noted, groups satisfice due to limited time, information, or ability to handle large amounts of information.[61] A management expert offered the following "do's" and "don'ts" for successfully achieving consensus: Groups should use active listening skills, involve as many members as possible, seek out the reasons behind arguments, and dig for the facts. At the same time, groups should not horse trade (I'll support you on this decision because you supported me on the last one), vote, or agree just to avoid "rocking the boat."[62] Voting is not encouraged because it can split the group into winners and losers.

Decision-making experts have developed three group problem-solving techniques— brainstorming, the nominal group technique, and the Delphi technique—to reduce the above roadblocks. Knowledge of these techniques can help current and future managers to more effectively use group-aided decision making. Further, the advent of computer-aided decision making enables managers to use these techniques to solve complex problems with large groups of people.

Brainstorming   Brainstorming was developed by A F Osborn, an advertising executive, to increase creativity.[63] **Brainstorming** is used to help groups generate multiple ideas and alternatives for solving problems. This technique is effective because it helps reduce interference caused by critical and judgmental reactions to one's ideas from other group members.

When brainstorming, a group is convened, and the problem at hand is reviewed. Individual members then are asked to silently generate ideas/alternatives for solving the problem. Silent idea generation is recommended over the practice of having group

Consensus
Presenting opinions and gaining agreement to support a decision.

Brainstorming
Process to generate a quantity of ideas.

members randomly shout out their ideas because it leads to a greater number of unique ideas. Next, these ideas/alternatives are solicited and written on a board or flip chart. A recent study suggests that managers or team leaders may want to collect the brainstormed ideas anonymously. Results demonstrated that more controversial ideas and more nonredundant ideas were generated by anonymous than nonanonymous brainstorming groups.[64] Finally, a second session is used to critique and evaluate the alternatives. Managers are advised to follow four rules for brainstorming:[65]

1. Stress quantity over quality. Managers should try to generate and write down as many ideas as possible. Encouraging quantity encourages people to think beyond their pet ideas.

2. Freewheeling should be encouraged; do not set limits. Group members are advised to offer any and all ideas they have. The wilder and more outrageous, the better.

3. Suspend judgment. Don't criticize during the initial stage of idea generation. Phrases such as "we've never done it that way," "it won't work," "it's too expensive," and "the boss will never agree" should not be used.

4. Ignore seniority. People are reluctant to freewheel when they are trying to impress the boss or when their ideas are politically motivated. The facilitator of a brainstorming session should emphasize that everyone has the same rank. No one is given "veto power" when brainstorming.

Brainstorming is an effective technique for generating new ideas/alternatives. It is not appropriate for evaluating alternatives or selecting solutions.

The Nominal Group Technique   The **nominal group technique** (NGT) helps groups generate ideas and evaluate and select solutions. NGT is a structured group meeting that follows this format:[66]

A group is convened to discuss a particular problem or issue. After the problem is understood, individuals silently generate ideas in writing. Each individual, in round-robin fashion, then offers one idea from his or her list. Ideas are recorded on a blackboard or flip chart; they are not discussed at this stage of the process. Once all ideas are elicited, the group discusses them. Anyone may criticize or defend any item. During this step, clarification is provided as well as general agreement or disagreement with the idea. The "30-second soap box" technique, which entails giving each participant a maximum of 30 seconds to argue for or against any of the ideas under consideration, can be used to facilitate this discussion. Finally, group members anonymously vote for their top choices with a weighted voting procedure (e.g., 1st choice = 3 points; 2nd choice = 2 points; 3rd choice = 1 point). The group leader then adds the votes to determine the group's choice. Prior to making a final decision, the group may decide to discuss the top ranked items and conduct a second round of voting.

The nominal group technique reduces the roadblocks to group decision making by (1) separating brainstorming from evaluation, (2) promoting balanced participation among group members, and (3) incorporating mathematical voting techniques in order to reach consensus. NGT has been successfully used in many different decision-making situations.

The Delphi Technique   This problem-solving method was originally developed by the Rand Corporation for technological forecasting.[67] It now is used as a multipurpose planning tool. The **Delphi technique** is a group process that anonymously generates ideas or judgments from physically dispersed experts. Unlike the NGT, experts' ideas are obtained from questionnaires or via the internet as opposed to face-to-face group discussions.

Nominal group technique
Process to generate ideas and evaluate solutions.

Delphi technique
Process to generate ideas from physically dispersed experts.

A manager begins the Delphi process by identifying the issue(s) he or she wants to investigate. For example, a manager might want to inquire about customer demand, customers' future preferences, or the effect of locating a plant in a certain region of the country. Next, participants are identified and a questionnaire is developed. The questionnaire is sent to participants and returned to the manager. In today's computer-networked environments, this often means that the questionnaires are E-mailed to participants. The manager then summarizes the responses and sends feedback to the participants. At this stage, participants are asked to (1) review the feedback, (2) prioritize the issues being considered, and (3) return the survey within a specified time period. This cycle repeats until the manager obtains the necessary information.

The Delphi technique is useful when face-to-face discussions are impractical, when disagreements and conflict are likely to impair communication, when certain individuals might severely dominate group discussion, and when groupthink is a probable outcome of the group process.[68]

Computer-Aided Decision Making   The purpose of computer-aided decision making is to reduce consensus roadblocks while collecting more information in a shorter period of time. There are two types of computer-aided decision making systems: chauffeur driven and group driven.[69] Chauffeur-driven systems ask participants to answer predetermined questions on electronic keypads or dials. Live television audiences on shows such as "Who Wants to Be a Millionaire" and "Whose Line Is It Anyway?" are frequently polled with this system. The computer system tabulates participants' responses in a matter of seconds.

Group-driven meetings are conducted in special facilities equipped with individual computer workstations that are networked to each other. Instead of talking, participants type their input, ideas, comments, reactions, or evaluations on their keyboards. The input simultaneously appears on a large projector screen at the front of the room, thereby enabling all participants to see all input. This computer-driven process reduces consensus roadblocks because input is anonymous, everyone gets a chance to contribute, and no one can dominate the process. Research demonstrated that computer-aided decision making produced greater quality and quantity of ideas than either traditional brainstorming or the nominal group technique for large groups of people. There were no significant advantages to group-aided decision making with groups of four to six.[70] Moreover, a recent study demonstrated that computer-aided decision making produced more ideas as group size increased from 5 to 10 members. The positive benefits of larger groups, however, were more pronounced for heterogeneous as opposed to homogeneous groups.[71]

Creativity

In light of today's need for fast-paced decisions, an organization's ability to stimulate the creativity and innovation of its employees is becoming increasingly important. Some organizations believe that creativity and innovation are the seeds of success. Consider Scitor, a systems-engineering consulting firm in Sunnyvale, California. The company was ranked as the fifth best company to work for in America by *Fortune* in 1999 "in part because it tells its managers their overriding mission is 'not to make money' but 'to capitalize on the creativity of the individual.'"[72]

To gain further insight into managing the creative process, we begin by defining creativity and highlighting the stages underlying individual creativity. This section then presents a model of organizational creativity and innovation.

If you want to enter the Specialized Bicycles website, you'll have to click on one of these alternatives. Which would you choose? Specialized Bicycle, an international leader in designing and manufacturing high-end bicycle equipment, has built its business by capitalizing on employee innovation. Employee "lunch time rides"—a long-standing tradition at Specialized—have been the source of some of the company's most exciting product innovations. The King Cobra helmet, for example, with its many air vents, was the result of employees' wish for a more stylish, well-ventilated helmet.

(Don Tracy/The Liaison Agency)

Definition and Stages

Creativity

Process of developing something new or unique.

Although many definitions have been proposed, **creativity** is defined here as the process of using imagination and skill to develop a new or unique product, object, process, or thought.[73] It can be as simple as locating a new place to hang your car keys or as complex as developing a pocket-size microcomputer. This definition highlights three broad types of creativity. One can create something new (creation), one can combine or synthesize things (synthesis), or one can improve or change things (modification).

Early approaches to explaining creativity were based on differences between the left and right hemispheres of the brain. Researchers thought the right side of the brain was responsible for creativity. More recently, however, researchers have questioned this explanation:

> "The left brain/right brain dichotomy is simplified and misleading," says Dr John C Mazziotta, a researcher at the University of California at Los Angeles School of Medicine.
>
> What scientists have found instead is that creativity is a feat of mental gymnastics engaging the conscious and subconscious parts of the brain. It draws on everything from knowledge, logic, imagination, and intuition to the ability to see connections and distinctions between ideas and things.[74]

Let us now examine the stages underlying the creativity process.

Researchers are not absolutely certain how creativity takes place. Nonetheless, we do know that creativity involves "making remote associations" between unconnected events,

Figure 11–6   *Stages of the Creative Process*

ideas, information stored in memory (recall our discussion in Chapter 6), or physical objects. Consider how remote associations led to a creative idea that ultimately increased revenue for Japan Railways (JR) East, the largest rail carrier in the world:

> While JR East was building a new bullet-train line, water began to cause problems in the tunnel being dug through Mount Tanigawa. As engineers drew up plans to drain it away, some of the workers had found a use for the water—they were drinking it. A maintenance worker, whose job was to check the safety of the tunneling equipment, thought it tasted so good that he proposed that JR East should bottle and market it as premium mineral water. This past year, "Oshimizu" water generated some $60 million of sales for JR East.[75]

The maintenance worker obviously associated the tunnel water with bottled water, and this led to the idea of marketing the water as a commercial product. Figure 11–6 depicts five stages underlying the creative process.[76]

The *preparation* stage reflects the notion that creativity starts from a base of knowledge. Experts suggest that creativity involves a convergence between tacit or implied knowledge and explicit knowledge. Notice how these two forms of knowledge converged to help create a new product at Matsushita Electric (see the International OB, p 366).

During the *concentration* stage, an individual focuses on the problem at hand. Interestingly, Japanese companies are noted for encouraging this stage as part of a quality improvement process more than American companies. For example, the average number of suggestions per employee for improving quality and productivity is significantly lower in the typical US company than in comparable Japanese firms.[77]

Incubation is done unconsciously. During this stage, people engage in daily activities while their minds simultaneously mull over information and make remote associations. These associations ultimately are generated in the *illumination* stage. Finally, *verification* entails going through the entire process to verify, modify, or try out the new idea.

Let us examine the stages of creativity to determine why Japanese organizations propose and implement more ideas than do American companies. To address this issue, a creativity expert visited and extensively interviewed employees from five major Japanese companies. He observed that Japanese firms have created a management infrastructure that encourages and reinforces creativity. People were taught to identify problems (discontents) on their first day of employment. In turn, discontents were referred to as "golden eggs" to reinforce the notion that it is good to identify problems.

These organizations also promoted the stages of incubation, illumination, and verification through teamwork and incentives. For example, some companies posted the golden eggs on large wall posters in the work area; employees were then encouraged to interact with each other to execute the final three stages of the creative process. Employees eventually received monetary awards for any suggestions that passed all five phases of this process.[78] This research underscores the conclusion that creativity can be enhanced by effectively managing the creativity process. Hallmark cards does a good job of managing the creativity process:

> It takes 740 creative people to produce 18,000 new Hallmark greeting cards each year. To manage that creative energy, CEO Irv Hockaday says, "We have the largest creative staff in the world. If you mismanage, it's like a sack full of cats. You have to strike a

International OB — Matsushita Electric Creates Breadmaker by Combining Tacit and Explicit Knowledge

Don Tracy/The Liaison Agency

In Japan, Matsushita Electric used to be known as *maneshita,* which means "copycat." Big and successful but not an innovator. That changed dramatically with the introduction of the Home Bakery, the first automatic breadmaker. A software engineer, a woman named Tanaka,

recognized that with Westernization, the time had come for a breadmaker in Japan. But she knew almost nothing about baking. So she apprenticed herself to a master baker. He had all the knowledge in his fingertips, but it was very hard for him to verbalize. After watching him for two or three weeks, she went back to Matsushita to write up a set of specifications for the machine, translating his tacit knowledge into something explicit.

They made a prototype, but the bread tasted terrible. So Tanaka-san brought a group of her peers to observe the baker again. Finally, they realized that what the machine lacked was the twisting motion the baker used when kneading his dough. Incorporating that understanding enabled them to develop a hugely successful product.

The breadmaker changed the corporate culture at Matsushita. People in other divisions said, "Why can't we do that?"

SOURCE: S Sherman, "Hot Products from Hot Tubs, or How Middle Managers Innovate," *Fortune,* April 29, 1996, pp 165–66. © 1996 Time Inc. All rights reserved.

balance between defining for them generally what you want and then giving them a lot of running room to try ways to respond to it. You don't overmanage, but you anchor them in well-articulated consumer needs. Then allow them exposure to all kinds of trends going on. We encourage them to travel and we support their traveling. They follow fashion trends, go to museums, look at what the automotive industry is doing in terms of design and color pallets. We have a wonderful pastoral environment, a retreat where they can go and reflect."[79]

A Model of Organizational Creativity and Innovation

Organizational creativity and innovation are relatively unexplored topics within the field of OB despite their importance for organizational success. Rather than focus on group and organizational creativity, researchers historically examined the predictors of individual creativity. This final section examines a process model of organizational creativity. Knowledge of its linkages can help you to facilitate and contribute to organizational creativity.

Figure 11–7 illustrates the process underlying organizational creativity and innovation. It shows that organizational creativity is directly influenced by organizational characteristics and the amount of creative behavior that occurs within work groups. In turn, a group's creative behavior is influenced by group characteristics and the individual creative behavior/performance of its members. Individual creative behavior is directly affected by a variety of individual characteristics. The double-headed arrows

Figure 11–7   *A Model of Organizational Creativity and Innovation*

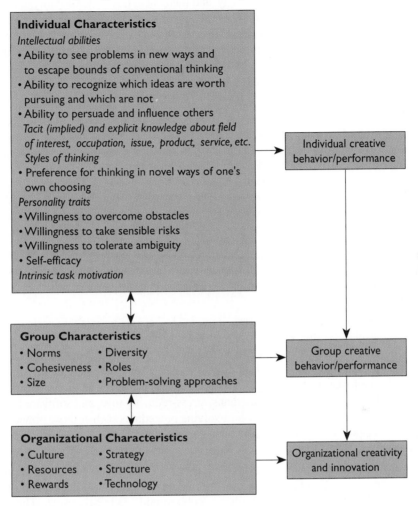

SOURCES: Based on discussion in R J Sternberg and R I Lubart, "Investing in Creativity," *American Psychologist*, July 1996, pp 677–88; and R W Woodman, J E Sawyer, and R W Griffin, "Toward a Theory of Organizational Creativity," *Academy of Management Review*, April 1993, pp 293–321.

between individual and group and between group and organizational characteristics indicate that the various characteristics all influence each other. Let us now consider the model's major components.

Individual Characteristics[80]   Creative people typically march to the beat of a different drummer. They are highly motivated individuals who spend considerable time developing both tacit (implied) and explicit knowledge about their field of interest or occupation. But contrary to stereotypes, creative people are not necessarily geniuses or introverted nerds. In addition, they are not *adaptors.* "Adaptors are those who . . . prefer to resolve difficulties or make decisions in such a way as to have the least impact upon the assumptions, procedures, and values of the organization. . . ."[81] In contrast, creative individuals are dissatisfied with the status quo. They look for new and exciting solutions to problems. Because of this, creative organizational members can be perceived as disruptive and hard to get along with. Further, research indicates that male and female managers do not differ in levels of creativity, and there are a host of personality characteristics that are associated with creativity. These characteristics include, but are not limited to, those shown in Figure 11–7. This discussion comes to life by considering the following example.

The Post-it Notes story represents a good illustration of how the individual characteristics shown in Figure 11–7 promote creative behavior/performance. Post-it Notes are a $200 million-a-year product for 3M Corporation:

> The idea originated with Art Fry, a 3M employee who used bits of paper to mark hymns when he sat in his church choir. These markers kept falling out of the hymn books. He decided that he needed an adhesive-backed paper that would stick as long as necessary but could be removed easily. He soon found what he wanted in the 3M laboratory, and the Post-it Note was born.
>
> Fry saw the market potential of his invention, but others did not. Market-survey results were negative; major office-supply distributors were skeptical. So he began giving samples to 3M executives and their secretaries. Once they actually used the little pieces of adhesive paper, they were hooked. Having sold 3M on the project, Fry used the same approach with other executives throughout the United States.[82]

Notice how Fry had to influence others to try out his idea. Figure 11–7 shows that creative people have the ability to persuade and influence others.

Group Characteristics   Figure 11–7 also lists six characteristics that influence the level of creative behavior/performance exhibited by a work group. In general, group creativity is fueled by a cohesive environment that supports open interactions, diverse viewpoints, and playful surroundings.[83] Kodak, for example, created a humor room where employees can relax and have creative brainstorming sessions. The room contains joke books, videotapes of comedians, stress-reducing toys, and software for creative decision making.[84] Structured problem-solving procedures such as those previously discussed and supportive supervision also enhance creativity.[85]

Organizational Characteristics   Research and corporate examples clearly support the importance of organizational characteristics in generating organizational creativity. Organizations such as Rubbermaid, 3M, Microsoft, The Body Shop, and DuPont are all known as innovative companies that encourage creativity via the organizational characteristics shown in Figure 11–7. DuPont, for example, created the Center for Creativity and Innovation in 1991. Its mission is to encourage creativity throughout the organization:

> Although the center is staffed by only three full-time employees, it has the support of 10 facilitators—creativity-training "volunteers" who hold full-time DuPont jobs outside the center. In this way, DuPont conducts creativity training in-house. This has two important advantages: First, the company has fewer security concerns; and second, training costs are lower.
>
> Top management support for the center is visible and continuous. A senior manager sponsors each creative problem-solving workshop and attends as a full participant, not just an observer. The company's support for creativity training is expressed by Edgar Woolard, chairman: "We intend to provide hero status to those who show us how to get products to the marketplace more promptly and more creatively."[86]

This example illustrates the point that organizational creativity requires resources, commitment, and a reinforcing organizational culture. Table 11–5 presents a number of suggestions that may be used to help create this culture.

Table 11–5   *Suggestions for Improving Employee Creativity*

Develop an environment that supports creative behavior.
Try to avoid using an autocratic style of leadership.
Encourage employees to be more open to new ideas and experiences.
Keep in mind that people use different strategies, like walking around or listening to music, to foster their creativity.
Provide employees with stimulating work that creates a sense of personal growth.
Allow employees to have fun and play around.
Encourage an open environment that is free from defensive behavior.
Treat errors and mistakes as opportunities for learning.
Let employees occasionally try out their pet ideas. Provide a margin of error.
Avoid using a negative mind-set when an employee approaches you with a new idea.
Reward creative behavior.

SOURCE: Adapted from discussion in E Raudsepp, "101 Ways to Spark Your Employees' Creative Potential," *Office Administration and Automation*, September 1985, pp 38, 39–43, 56.

Summary of Key Concepts

1. *Compare and contrast the rational model of decision making, Simon's normative model, and the garbage can model.* The rational decision-making model consists of identifying the problem, generating alternative solutions, evaluating and selecting a solution, and implementing and evaluating the solution. Research indicates that decision makers do not follow the series of steps outlined in the rational model.

   Simon's normative model is guided by a decision maker's bounded rationality. Bounded rationality means that decision makers are bounded or restricted by a variety of constraints when making decisions. The normative model suggests that decision making is characterized by (a) limited information processing, (b) the use of judgmental heuristics, and (c) satisficing.

   The garbage can model of decision making assumes that decision making does not follow an orderly series of steps. In a garbage can process, decisions result from the interaction among four independent streams of events: problems, solutions, participants, and choice opportunities.

2. *Discuss the contingency relationships that influence the three primary strategies used to select solutions.* Decision makers use either an aided-analytic, unaided-analytic, or nonanalytic strategy when selecting a solution. The choice of a strategy depends on the characteristics of the decision task and the characteristics of the decision maker. In general, the greater the demands and constraints faced by a decision maker, the higher the probability that an aided-analytic approach will be used. Aided-analytic strategies are more

likely to be used by competent and motivated individuals. Ultimately, decision makers compromise between their desire to make correct decisions and the amount of time and effort they put into the decision-making process.

3. *Explain the model of decision-making styles.* The model of decision-making styles is based on the idea that styles vary along two different dimensions: value orientation and tolerance for ambiguity. When these two dimensions are combined, they form four styles of decision making: directive, analytical, conceptual, and behavioral. People with a directive style have a low tolerance for ambiguity and are oriented toward task and technical concerns. Analytics have a higher tolerance for ambiguity and are characterized by a tendency to overanalyze a situation. People with a conceptual style have a high threshold for ambiguity and tend to focus on people or social aspects of a work situation. This behavioral style is the most people oriented of the four styles.

4. *Describe the model of escalation of commitment.* Escalation of commitment refers to the tendency to stick to an ineffective course of action when it is unlikely that a bad situation can be reversed. Psychological and social determinants, organizational determinants, project characteristics, and contextual determinants cause managers to exhibit this decision-making error.

5. *Summarize the pros and cons of involving groups in the decision-making process.* There are both pros and cons to

involving groups in the decision-making process. Although research shows that groups typically outperform the average individual, there are five important issues to consider when using groups to make decisions. (*a*) Groups are less efficient than individuals. (*b*) A group's overconfidence can fuel groupthink. (*c*) Decision quality is negatively related to group size. (*d*) Groups are more accurate when they know a great deal about the issues at hand and when the leader possesses the ability to effectively evaluate the group members' opinions and judgments. (*e*) The composition of a group affects its decision-making processes and performance. In the final analysis, managers are encouraged to use a contingency approach when determining whether to include others in the decision-making process.

6. *Explain how participative management affects performance.* Participative management reflects the extent to which employees participate in setting goals, making decisions, solving problems, and making changes in the organization. Participative management is expected to increase motivation because it helps employees fulfill three basic needs: (*a*) autonomy, (*b*) meaningfulness of work, and (*c*) interpersonal contact. Participative management does not work in all situations. The design of work and the level of trust between management and employees influence the effectiveness of participative management.

7. *Review Vroom and Jago's decision-making model.* Vroom, Yetton, and Jago developed a model to help managers determine the extent to which they should include groups in the decision-making process. Through the use of decision trees, the model identifies appropriate decision-making styles for various types of managerial problems. The styles range from autocratic to highly participative.

8. *Contrast brainstorming, the nominal group technique, the Delphi technique, and computer-aided decision making.* Group problem-solving techniques facilitate better decision making within groups. Brainstorming is used to help groups generate multiple ideas and alternatives for solving problems. The nominal group technique assists groups both to generate ideas and to evaluate and select solutions. The Delphi technique is a group process that anonymously generates ideas or judgments from physically dispersed experts. The purpose of computer-aided decision making is to reduce consensus roadblocks while collecting more information in a shorter period of time.

9. *Describe the stages of the creative process.* Creativity is defined as the process of using imagination and skill to develop a new or unique product, object, process, or thought. It is not adequately explained by differences between the left and right hemispheres of the brain. There are five stages of the creative process: preparation, concentration, incubation, illumination, and verification.

10. *Explain the model of organizational creativity and innovation.* Organizational creativity is directly influenced by organizational characteristics and the creative behavior that occurs within work groups. In turn, a group's creative behavior is influenced by group characteristics and the individual creative behavior/performance of its members. Individual creative behavior is directly affected by a variety of individual characteristics. Finally, individual, group, and organizational characteristics all influence each other within this process.

Discussion Questions

1. What role do emotions play in decision making?

2. Do you think people are rational when they make decisions? Under what circumstances would an individual tend to follow a rational process?

3. Describe a situation in which you satisficed when making a decision. Why did you satisfice instead of optimize?

4. Do you think the garbage can model is a realistic representation of organizational decision making? Explain your rationale.

5. Why would decision-making styles be a source of interpersonal conflict?

6. Describe a situation in which you exhibited escalation of commitment. Why did you escalate a losing situation?

7. Do you prefer to solve problems in groups or by yourself? Why?

8. Given the intuitive appeal of participative management, why do you think it fails as often as it succeeds? Explain.

9. Do you think you are creative? Why or why not?

10. What advice would you offer a manager who was attempting to improve the creativity of his or her employees? Explain.

Internet Exercise

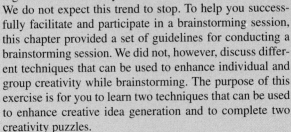

There are countless brainstorming sessions conducted by individuals and groups within organizations on a daily basis. We do not expect this trend to stop. To help you successfully facilitate and participate in a brainstorming session, this chapter provided a set of guidelines for conducting a brainstorming session. We did not, however, discuss different techniques that can be used to enhance individual and group creativity while brainstorming. The purpose of this exercise is for you to learn two techniques that can be used to enhance creative idea generation and to complete two creativity puzzles.

Begin the exercise by going to the following Internet site: www.brainstorming.co.uk. Then select their home page. Once at the home page, click on the option for "training on creative techniques." After a brief discussion about creativity, you will be given the option to learn more about a variety of different techniques that can be used to enhance

creativity. Choose any two techniques and then answer questions 1 and 2 below.

Now return to the home page, and select the option for creativity puzzles. Follow the instructions and attempt to complete two puzzles. Don't peek ahead to see the answers until you have tried to finish the activity. Based on your experience with these creativity puzzles, answer questions 3, 4, and 5.

Questions

1. How might you use these techniques in a class project?
2. Should different techniques be used in different situations? Explain.
3. To what extent were the puzzles hard to complete?
4. Why do these puzzles help people to think outside of the box?
5. How might these puzzles be used during a brainstorming session?

OB in Action Case Study

SmithKline Beecham Uses a Three-Step Process to Make Resource-Allocation Decisions[87]

In 1993, SmithKline Beecham was spending more than half a billion dollars per year on R&D, the lifeblood of any pharmaceuticals company. Ever since the 1989 merger that created the company, however, SB believed that it had been spending too much time arguing about how to value its R&D projects—and not enough time figuring out how to make them more valuable. . . .

Major resource-allocation decisions are never easy. For a company like SB, the problem is this: How do you make good decisions in a high-risk, technically complex business when the information you need to make those decisions comes largely from the project champions who are competing against one another for resources? A critical company process can become politicized when strong-willed, charismatic project leaders beat out their less competitive colleagues for resources. That in turn leads to the cynical view that your project is as good as the performance you can put on at funding time. . . .

Most organizations think of decision making as an event, not a process. They attach great importance to key decision meetings. But in most cases, and SB is no exception, the real problems occur before those meetings ever take place. And so the process that SB designed—a three-phase dialogue between the project teams and the com-

pany's decision makers—focused on the inputs to the resource-allocation decision and the role of the organization in preparing those inputs.

Phase I: Generating Alternatives

One of the major weaknesses of most resource-allocation processes is that project advocates tend to take an all-or-nothing approach to budget requests. At SB, that meant that project leaders would develop a single plan of action and present it as the *only* viable approach. Project teams rarely took the time to consider meaningful alternatives—especially if they suspected that doing so might mean a cutback in funding.

And so we insisted that each team develop at least four alternatives: the *current plan* (the team would follow the existing plan of activity), a *"buy-up" option* (the team would be given more to spend on the project), a *"buy-down" option* (the team would be given less to spend on the project), and a *minimal plan* (the team would abandon the project while preserving as much of the value earned to date as possible). Working with a facilitator, a team would begin by describing a project's objective, which usually was to develop a particular chemical entity targeted at one or more diseases. Then it would brainstorm about what it would do under each of the four funding alternatives. . . .

Near the end of this phase, the project alternatives were presented to a peer review board for guidance before any significant evaluation of the alternatives had been performed. Members of the review board, who were managers from key functions and major product groups within the pharmaceuticals organization, tested the fundamental assumptions of each alternative by asking probing questions: In the buy-down alternative, which trial should we eliminate? Should a once-a-day formulation be part of our buy-up alternative? Couldn't we do better by including Japan earlier in the current plan? The discussion session improved the overall quality of the project alternatives and helped build consensus about their feasibility and completeness.

The project teams then revised their alternatives where appropriate and submitted them again for review, this time to the group of senior managers who would, at a later point in the process, make the final investment decisions on all the projects. . . .

Phase II: Valuing Alternatives

Once we had engineered the process that took us through phase I, we needed a consistent methodology to value each one of the project alternatives. We chose to use decision analysis because of its transparency and its ability to capture the technical uncertainties and commercial risks of drug development. For each alternative, we constructed a decision tree, using the most knowledgeable experts to help structure the tree and assess the major uncertainties facing each project. . . .

We developed six requirements for achieving credibility and buy-in to the valuation of each alternative:

• First, the same information set must be provided for every project. . . .

• Second, the information must come from reliable sources. . . .

• Third, the sources of information must be clearly documented. . . .

• Fourth, the assessments must undergo peer review by experienced managers across functions and therapeutic areas. . . .

• Fifth, the valuations must be compared with those done by external industry observers and market analysts to establish that the numbers are realistic.

• Sixth, the impact of each variable on the project's expected value must be identified. . . .

We increased transparency and consistency in yet another way by having a specially designated group of analysts process the valuation information and draw preliminary insights. Having this work done by a neutral group was a relief to many project team members, who were rarely satisfied with the previous approaches to valuation, as well as to the top management group, who were tired of trying to make sense of widely disparate types of analysis.

As the company's CFO for pharmaceuticals put it, "Inconsistent valuations are worse than none."

Once the alternatives had been valued, a second peer-review meeting was held to make sure that all the participants had a chance to question and understand the results. This step was designed to ensure that no surprises would emerge when the decisions were being made. And again, the peer review was followed by a senior management review that provided an opportunity to challenge, modify, and agree on the underlying assumptions driving the valuations. During the meeting, however, the senior managers were explicitly asked *not* to begin discussing which alternatives to invest in; instead, they were asked only to confirm that they understood and believed the valuations. And if they didn't, why not? What seemed out of line? . . .

Phase III: Creating a Portfolio and Allocating Resources

The goal of this phase was to create the highest-value portfolio based on all the project alternatives that had been developed. This was no easy task: with 20 major projects—each of which had four well-conceived alternatives—the number of possible configurations was enormous. We appointed a neutral analytic team, rather than the project advocates, to carry out a systematic approach to identifying the highest-value portfolio based on return on investment.

The portfolio could then be examined along a number of strategic dimensions, including stability under different scenarios, balance across therapeutic areas and stages in the development pipeline, and feasibility of success given SB's technical and commercial resources. Because the senior managers had already agreed—and vigorously debated—the underlying project descriptions (phase I) and valuations (phase II) for each alternative, they now focused their complete attention on the portfolio decisions. . . .

The first 14 project decisions, which involved increasing or maintaining funding levels, were made without controversy. However, when it came time to discuss the first project whose funding would be cut, the manager of the relevant therapeutic area challenged the decision. The meeting's chairman listened to his case for maintaining the current funding and then asked whether that case was reflected in the project valuations. The manager agreed that it was, but repeated the argument that SB would lose value by terminating the project. The chairman agreed that value would be lost but pointed out that the funds originally scheduled for the project would create more value when applied elsewhere. That ended a potentially explosive discussion.

The new process not only reduced the controversy in the resource-allocation process, it also led the company to change its investment strategy. Although top management had set out to cut back on the company's development budget, they now saw their investment decision in a new light: they believed the new portfolio to be 30% more valuable than the old one—without any additional investment.

Furthermore, the marginal return on additional investment had tripled from 5:1 to 15:1. To exploit this opportunity, the company ultimately decided to increase development spending by more than 50%.

Questions for Discussion

1. Is SmithKline Beecham's resource-allocation decision-making process more characteristics of the rational, normative, or garbage can models of decision making? Discuss your rationale.

2. How does SmithKline's approach attempt to control for escalation of commitment?

3. To what extent is SmithKline's decision making process consistent with the contingency recommendations presented in Table 11–2? Explain.

4. To what extent does SmithKline Beecham promote organizational creativity and innovation? Explain your answer by applying Figure 11–7 to the case.

5. Why do you think the three-step decision-making process has been such a success? Discuss your rationale.

Personal Awareness and Growth Exercise

What Is Your Decision-Making Style?

Objectives

1. To assess your decision-making style.
2. To consider the managerial implications of your decision-making style.

Introduction

Earlier in the chapter we discussed a model of decision-making styles that is based on the idea that styles vary along the dimensions of an individual's value orientation and tolerance for ambiguity. In turn, these dimensions combine to form four styles of decision making (see Figure 11–3): directive, analytical, conceptual, and behavioral. Alan Rowe, an OB researcher, developed an instrument called the Decision Style Inventory to measure these four styles. This exercise provides you the opportunity to assess and interpret your decision-making style using this measurement device.

Instructions

The Decision Style Inventory consists of 20 questions, each with four responses.[88] You must consider each possible response for a question and then rank them according to how much you prefer each response. There are no right or wrong answers, so respond with what first comes to mind. Because many of the questions are anchored to how individuals make decisions at work, you can feel free to use your student role as a frame of reference to answer the questions. For each question, use the space on the survey to rank the four responses with either a 1, 2, 4, or 8. Use the number 8 for the responses that are **most** like you, a 4 for those that are **moderately** like you, a 2 for those that are **slightly** like you, and a 1 for the responses that are **least** like you. For instance, a question could be answered as follows: [8], [4], [2], [1]. Notice that each number was used only once to answer a question. Do not repeat any number when answering a given question. These numbers are placed in the boxes next to each of the answers. Once all of the responses for the 20 questions have been ranked, total the scores in each of the four columns. The total score for column one represents your score for the directive style, column two your analytical style, column three your conceptual style, and column four your behavioral style.

Questions for Discussion

1. In terms of your decision-making profile, which of the four styles best represents your decision-making style (has the highest subscore)? Which is the least reflective of your style (has the lowest subscore)?

2. Do you agree with this assessment? Explain.

3. How do your scores compare with the following norms: directive (75), analytical (90), conceptual (80), and behavioral (55)? What do the differences between your scores and the survey norms suggest about your decision-making style?

4. What are the advantages and disadvantages of your decision-making profile?

5. Which of the other decision-making styles is most inconsistent with your style? How would this difference affect your ability to work with someone who has this style?

1. My prime objective in life is:	to have a position with status		be the best in whatever I do		be recognized for my work		feel secure in my job
2. I enjoy work that:	is clear and well defined		is varied and challenging		lets me act independently		involves people
3. I expect people to be:	productive		capable		committed		responsive
4. My work lets me:	get things done		find workable approaches		apply new ideas		be truly satisfied
5. I communicate best by:	talking with others		putting things in writing		being open with others		having a group meeting
6. My planning focuses on:	current problems		how best to meet goals		future opportunities		needs of people in the organization
7. I prefer to solve problems by:	applying rules		using careful analysis		being creative		relying on my feelings
8. I prefer information:	that is simple and direct		that is complete		that is broad and informative		that is easily understood
9. When I'm not sure what to do:	I rely on my intuition		I search for alternatives		I try to find a compromise		avoid making a decision
10. Whenever possible, I avoid:	long debates		incomplete work		technical problems		conflict with others
11. I am really good at:	remembering details		finding answers		seeing many options		working with people
12. When time is important, I:	decide and act quickly		apply proven approaches		look for what will work		refuse to be pressured
13. In social settings, I:	speak with many people		observe what others are doing		contribute to the conversation		want to be part of the discussion
14. I always remember:	people's names		places I have been		people's faces		people's personalities
15. I prefer jobs where I:	receive high rewards		have challenging assignments		can reach my personal goals		am accepted by the group
16. I work best with people who:	are energetic and ambitious		are very competent		are open minded		are polite and understanding
17. When I am under stress, I:	speak quickly		try to concentrate on the problem		become frustrated		worry about what I should do
18. Others consider me:	aggressive		disciplined		imaginative		supportive
19. My decisions are generally:	realistic and direct		systematic and logical		broad and flexible		sensitive to the other's needs
20. I dislike:	losing control		boring work		following rules		being rejected
Total score						

Group Exercise

Applying the Vroom/Yetton/Jago Decision-Making Model

Introduction

Vroom and Jago extended an earlier model by Vroom and Yetton to help managers determine the extent to which they should include groups in the decision-making process. To enhance your understanding of this model, we would like you to use it to analyze a brief case. You will be asked to read the case and use the information to determine an appropriate decision-making style. This will enable you to compare your solution with that recommended by Vroom and Jago. Their analysis is presented in end-note number 90 and you will be instructed when to examine it for feedback.

Instructions

Your instructor will divide the class into groups of four to six. Once the group is assembled, each member should read the case presented. It depicts a situation faced by the manufacturing manager of an electronics plant.[89] The group should then use Vroom and Jago's model (refer to Figure 11–5 and Table 11–4) to arrive at a solution. At this point, it might be helpful for the group to reread the material that explains how to apply the model. Keep in mind that you move toward a solution by asking yourself the questions (at the top of Figure 11–4) associated with each relevant decision point. After the group completes its analysis, compare your solution with the one offered by Vroom and Jago.

LEADERSHIP CASE

You are a manufacturing manager in a large electronics plant. The company's management has recently installed new machines and put in a new simplified work system, but to the surprise of everyone, yourself included, the expected increase in productivity was not realized. In fact, production has begun to drop, quality has fallen off, and the number of employee separations has risen.

You do not believe that there is anything wrong with the machines. You have had reports from other companies that are using them, and they confirm this opinion. You have also had representatives from the firm that built the machines go over them, and they report that they are operating at peak efficiency.

You suspect that some parts of the new work system may be responsible for the change, but this view is not widely shared among your immediate subordinates, who are four first-line supervisors, each in charge of a section, and your supply manager. The drop in production has been variously attributed to poor training of the operators, lack of an adequate system of financial incentives, and poor morale. Clearly, this is an issue about which there is considerable depth of feeling within individuals and potential disagreement among your subordinates.

This morning you received a phone call from your division manager. He had just received your production figures for the last six months and was calling to express his concern. He indicated that the problem was yours to solve in any way that you think best, but that he would like to know within a week what steps you plan to take.

You share your division manager's concern with the falling productivity and know that your [people] are also concerned. The problem is to decide what steps to take to rectify the situation.

Questions for Discussion

1. What decision-making style from Table 11–4 do you recommend?

2. Did you arrive at the same solution as Vroom and Jago (their analysis is presented in endnote number 90)? If not, what do you think caused the difference?

3. Based on this experience, what problems would a manager encounter in trying to apply this model?

Chapter Twelve

Group Dynamics

Learning Objectives

When you finish studying the material in this chapter, you should be able to:

1 Identify the four criteria of a group from a sociological perspective.

2 Describe the five stages in Tuckman's theory of group development, and discuss the threat of group decay.

3 Distinguish between role conflict and role ambiguity.

4 Contrast roles and norms, and specify four reasons norms are enforced in organizations.

5 Distinguish between task and maintenance functions in groups.

6 Summarize the practical contingency management implications for group size and group member ability.

7 Discuss why managers need to carefully handle mixed-gender task groups.

8 Describe groupthink, and identify at least four of its symptoms.

9 Define social loafing, and explain how managers can prevent it.

BusinessWeek **"Small World" Theory:** John Guare's play and then 1993 movie *Six Degrees of Separation* popularized the notion that we are all connected to each other by a chain of six people or less.... As the song at the Disneyland exhibit puts it, "It's a small world after all." ...

But there is a serious side to the six-degree phenomenon. Two Cornell University researchers have come up with a mathematical model that shows in far more sophisticated terms what a small world this really is. The model is essentially a recipe for turning any large network of components into a "small world."

This is more than an intellectual exercise: The small-world model could be used to improve the operational efficiency of corporate giants like General Motors Corp....

The key to turning a large world into a smaller, more efficient one is short-cuts: well-connected individuals or components that can cut across traditional boundaries in an organization. Duncan J Watts, a postdoctoral fellow at Columbia University, and Steven H Strogatz, a mathematics professor at Cornell, theorized that just a few well-placed individuals could dramatically speed up the flow of information in a company, acting as emissaries among floors and departments. When Watts and Strogatz did the mathematics, they discovered that it takes only a very few random

The six-degree phenomenon, Hollywood style. (The Everett Collection)

connections, or shortcuts, to make a small world out of a large one. Once that world has been transformed, adding additional connections has little effect. "The key is to link well-connected people from each level," says Boston University professor James J Collins. . . .

The Internet and the availability of cheap, worldwide communication through E-mail is making our small world even smaller. Playwright John Guare hopes the process will continue. "May all our degrees of separation be in single digits" and "may we always be able to find the right six people," he says. And Watts and Strogatz have given the office gossip a new image—all that schmoozing just might be good for the whole organization.[1]

"Small World" Application:[2]

Strasburg, VA.—A chance conversation over lunch launched one of the biggest cost-saving accomplishments at Lear's auto supplier plant here.

A nine-member team of workers, the Eliminators, had been looking for ways to reduce the number of parts rejected for poor paint quality.

The plant builds interior parts for General Motors, Ford Motor, Chrysler and Nissan vehicles. Specifically, the Eliminators sought to improve the performance of the No. 2 paint line, where workers paint about 3.5 million door-pulls a year.

The problem: how to keep water that catches paint-gun overspray from leaving spots on parts.

Too many spots and the part must be repainted or rejected. Lear was repainting more than 35,000 parts a year.

Different paint nozzles, brighter lights, employee training and other potential solutions helped, but none solved the problem.

To visualize the problem, imagine a worker standing in front of a moving rack of parts that looks similar to the overhead clothes rack found in most dry cleaners. The worker uses a paint gun to blast each part with paint.

Behind the rack is a waterfall. The water catches the overspray from the paint gun, keeping potentially harmful fumes from entering the atmosphere. But after months of research, meetings and frustration, the team was hitting a dead end. Then one day during a lunch break, team members asked paint technician Rick Edge, who worked on another paint line, whether he had similar problems.

"I said no," Edge says. "I don't have a waterfall."

Edge's paint line, which handles armrests in a building across the street from the No. 2 paint line—uses vacuum air to suck the overspray onto a carboardlike filter that is burned. . . .

After a few glitches (initially, the air filters clogged every hour), the team came up with a plan that lowered the plant's scrap rate by 16% and defects by 25%, while improving productivity by 33% and saving Lear $112,000 this year.[2]

> **FOR DISCUSSION**
> How can managers take fuller advantage of this "small world" phenomenon?

Because the management of organizational behavior is above all else a social endeavor, managers need a strong working knowledge of *interpersonal* behavior.[3] Research consistently reveals the importance of social skills for both individual and organizational success. An ongoing study by the Center for Creative Leadership (involving diverse samplings from Belgium, France, Germany, Italy, the United Kingdom, the United States, and Spain) found four stumbling blocks that tend to derail executives' careers. According to the researchers, "A derailed executive is one who, having reached the general manager level, finds that there is little chance of future advancement due to a misfit between job requirements and personal skills."[4] The four stumbling blocks, consistent across the cultures studied, are as follows:

1. Problems with interpersonal relationships.
2. Failure to meet business objectives.
3. Failure to build and lead a team.
4. Inability to change or adapt during a transition.[5]

Notice how both the first and third career stumbling blocks involve interpersonal skills—the ability to get along and work effectively with others. Managers with interpersonal problems typically were described as manipulative and insensitive. Interestingly, two-thirds of the derailed European managers studied had problems with interpersonal relationships. That same problem reportedly plagued one-third of the derailed US executives.[6] Management, as defined in Chapter 1, involves getting things done with and through others. The job is simply too big to do it alone.

Let us begin by defining the term *group* as a prelude to examining types of groups, functions of group members, and the group development process. Our attention then turns to group roles and norms, the basic building blocks of group dynamics. Effects of group structure and member characteristics on group outcomes are explored next. Finally, three serious threats to group effectiveness are discussed. (This chapter serves as a foundation for our discussion of teams and teamwork in the following chapter.)

Groups: Definitions, Types, and Functions

Groups and teams are inescapable features of modern life.[7] College students are often teamed with their peers for class projects. Parents serve on community advisory boards at their local high school. Managers find themselves on product planning committees and productivity task forces. Productive organizations simply cannot function without gathering individuals into groups and teams.[8] But, as personal experience shows, group effort can bring out both the best and the worst in people. A marketing department meeting, where several people excitedly brainstorm and refine a creative new advertising campaign, can yield results beyond the capabilities of individual contributors. Conversely, committees have become the butt of jokes (e.g., a committee is a place where they take minutes and waste hours; a camel is a horse designed by a committee) because they all too often are plagued by lack of direction and by conflict. Modern managers need a solid understanding of groups and group processes so as to both avoid their pitfalls and tap their vast potential. Moreover, the huge and growing presence of the Internet—with its own unique network of informal and formal social relationships—is a major challenge for profit-minded business managers (see the International OB, p 380).

Although other definitions of groups exist, we draw from the field of sociology and define a **group** as two or more freely interacting individuals who share collective norms and goals and have a common identity.[9] Figure 12–1 illustrates how the four criteria in this definition combine to form a conceptual whole. Organizational psychologist Edgar Schein shed additional light on this concept by drawing instructive distinctions between a group, a crowd, and an organization:

> The size of a group is thus limited by the possibilities of mutual interaction and mutual awareness. Mere aggregates of people do not fit this definition because they do not interact and do not perceive themselves to be a group even if they are aware of each other as, for instance, a crowd on a street corner watching some event. A total department, a union, or a whole organization would not be a group in spite of thinking of themselves as "we," because they generally do not all interact and are not all aware of each other. However, work teams, committees, subparts of departments, cliques, and various other informal associations among organizational members would fit this definition of a group.[10]

Group
Two or more freely interacting people with shared norms and goals and a common identity.

Take a moment now to think of various groups of which you are a member. Does each of your "groups" satisfy the four criteria in Figure 12–1?

International OB Marketers Try to Profit from Global Online Communities

BusinessWeek Executives at Warner Brothers Online were fed up. For years, they had looked on as fans of Bugs Bunny, Batman, the Tazmanian Devil, and other characters banded together and hoisted brand images and sound clips onto personal home pages in *cybercommunities such as GeoCities and Tripod.* What really grated was the way the site operators were selling ad space on those pages. "They were underwriting the cost of copyright infringement," fumes Warner Online President Jim Moloshok.

Warner wasn't about to sue its own fans. Instead, in January [1999], Moloshok formed a joint venture with FortuneCity, a fast-growing online community based in London. Together, they created a site called ACMEcity as a beacon for fans around the world. The site has built home pages for 150,000 registered members in two months—luring many of them away from GeoCities and Tripod with giveaways.

Companies like Warner are finding much to love about online communities. *Once the frontier towns of the Net, these sites have blossomed into digital metropolises.* Their combined membership probably exceeds 25 million, if you count some 16 million subscribers to America Online Inc. Few of the sites are profitable as businesses. But companies are racing to partner with online communities—or build their own—in hopes of solving two of the toughest challenges on the Net: Reaching customers all over the planet and understanding who they are.

Like the Internet itself, online communities are often global from Day One. As Net-based communications obliterate national boundaries, these sites draw together like-minded individuals who would never converge in the real world. A unit of AOL called ICQ, for example, provides instant messaging to hip young members scattered from Fresno to Finland, and provides space for their home pages. Jupiter Communications figures 45% of new home pages at community sites are now going up outside the [United States].

Just as important to businesses, communities thrive on experimentation. First, they popularized online chat and "buddies" networks. Today, these neighborhoods are incubators for trends in E-business. "We've built massive Web sites with millions of relationships to consumers," says Bo Peabody, president and CEO of Tripod, a trendy community owned by Internet portal Lycos. "Now, we're finding ways to make those relationships profitable."

SOURCE: Excerpted from N Gross, "Building Global Communities," *Business Week* **E.BIZ**, March 22, 1999, pp EB 42–EB 43.

Formal and Informal Groups

Formal group
Formed by the organization.

Informal group
Formed by friends.

Individuals join groups, or are assigned to groups, to accomplish various purposes. If the group is formed by a manager to help the organization accomplish its goals, then it qualifies as a **formal group.** Formal groups typically wear such labels as work group, team, committee, quality circle, or task force. An **informal group** exists when the members' overriding purpose of getting together is friendship.[11] Although formal and informal groups often overlap, such as a team of corporate auditors heading for the tennis courts after work, some employees are not friends with their co-workers. The desirability of overlapping formal and informal groups is problematic. Some managers firmly believe personal friendship fosters productive teamwork on the job while others view workplace "bull sessions" as a serious threat to productivity. Both situations are common, and it is the manager's job to strike a workable balance, based on the maturity and goals of the people involved.

Functions of Formal Groups

Researchers point out that formal groups fulfill two basic functions: *organizational* and *individual.*[12] The various functions are listed in Table 12–1. Complex combinations of these functions can be found in formal groups at any given time.

Figure 12–1   *Four Sociological Criteria of a Group*

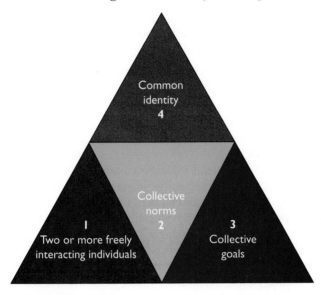

Table 12–1   *Formal Groups Fulfill Organizational and Individual Functions*

Organizational Functions	Individual Functions
1. Accomplish complex, interdependent tasks that are beyond the capabilities of individuals.	1. Satisfy the individual's need for affiliation.
2. Generate new or creative ideas and solutions.	2. Develop, enhance, and confirm the individual's self-esteem and sense of identity.
3. Coordinate interdepartmental efforts.	3. Give individuals an opportunity to test and share their perceptions of social reality.
4. Provide a problem-solving mechanism for complex problems requiring varied information and assessments.	4. Reduce the individual's anxieties and feelings of insecurity and powerlessness.
5. Implement complex decisions.	5. Provide a problem-solving mechanism for personal and interpersonal problems.
6. Socialize and train newcomers.	

SOURCE: Adapted from E H Schein, *Organizational Psychology*, 3rd ed (Englewood Cliffs, NJ: Prentice-Hall, 1980), pp 149–51.

For example, consider what Mazda's new American employees experienced when they spent a month working in Japan before the opening of the firm's Flat Rock, Michigan, plant:

> After a month of training in Mazda's factory methods, whipping their new Japanese buddies at softball and sampling local watering holes, the Americans were fired up….[A maintenance manager] even faintly praised the Japanese practice of holding group calisthenics at the start of each working day: "I didn't think I'd like doing exercises every morning, but I kind of like it."[13]

While Mazda pursued the organizational functions it wanted—interdependent team-work, creativity, coordination, problem solving, and training—the American workers benefited from the individual functions of formal groups. Among those benefits were affiliation with new friends, enhanced self-esteem, exposure to the Japanese social reality, and reduction of anxieties about working for a foreign-owned company. In short, Mazda created a workable blend of organizational and individual group functions by training its newly hired American employees in Japan.

The Group Development Process

Groups and teams in the workplace go through a maturation process, such as one would find in any life-cycle situation (e.g., humans, organizations, products). While there is general agreement among theorists that the group development process occurs in identifiable stages, they disagree about the exact number, sequence, length, and nature of those stages.[14] One oft-cited model is the one proposed in 1965 by educational psychologist Bruce W Tuckman. His original model involved only four stages (forming, storming, norming, and performing). The five-stage model in Figure 12–2 evolved when Tuckman and a doctoral student added "adjourning" in 1977.[15] A word of caution is in order. Somewhat akin to Maslow's need hierarchy theory, Tuckman's theory has been repeated and taught so often and for so long that many have come to view it as documented fact, not merely a theory. Even today, it is good to remember Tuckman's own caution that his group development model was derived more from group therapy sessions than from natural-life groups. Still, many in the OB field like Tuckman's five-stage model of group development because of its easy-to-remember labels and common-sense appeal.[16]

Five Stages

Let us briefly examine each of the five stages in Tuckman's model. Notice in Figure 12–2 how individuals give up a measure of their independence when they join and participate in a group. Also, the various stages are not necessarily of the same duration or intensity. For instance, the storming stage may be practically nonexistent or painfully long, depending on the goal clarity and the commitment and maturity of the members. You can make this process come to life by relating the various stages to your own experiences with work groups, committees, athletic teams, social or religious groups, or class project teams. Some group happenings that surprised you when they occurred may now make sense or strike you as inevitable when seen as part of a natural development process.

Stage 1: Forming   During this "ice-breaking" stage, group members tend to be uncertain and anxious about such things as their roles, who is in charge, and the group's goals. Mutual trust is low, and there is a good deal of holding back to see who takes charge and how. If the formal leader (e.g., a supervisor) does not assert his or her authority, an emergent leader will eventually step in to fulfill the group's need for leadership and direction. Leaders typically mistake this honeymoon period as a mandate for permanent control. But later problems may force a leadership change.

Stage 2: Storming   This is a time of testing. Individuals test the leader's policies and assumptions as they try to determine how they fit into the power structure.[17] Subgroups take shape, and subtle forms of rebellion, such as procrastination, occur. Many groups stall in stage 2 because power politics erupts into open rebellion.

Figure 12–2   *Tuckman's Five-Stage Theory of Group Development*

	Forming	Storming	Norming	Performing	Adjourning
Individual issues	"How do I fit in?"	"What's my role here?"	"What do the others expect me to do?"	"How can I best perform my role?"	"What's next?"
Group issues	"Why are we here?"	"Why are we fighting over who is in charge and who does what ?"	"Can we agree on roles and work as a team?"	"Can we do the job properly?"	"Can we help members transition out?"

Stage 3: Norming   Groups that make it through stage 2 generally do so because a respected member, other than the leader, challenges the group to resolve its power struggles so something can be accomplished. Questions about authority and power are resolved through unemotional, matter-of-fact group discussion. A feeling of team spirit is experienced because members believe they have found their proper roles. **Group cohesiveness,** defined as the "we feeling" that binds members of a group together, is the principal by-product of stage 3.[18]

Group cohesiveness
A "we feeling" binding group members together.

Stage 4: Performing   Activity during this vital stage is focused on solving task problems. As members of a mature group, contributors get their work done without hampering others. (See the Personal Awareness and Growth Exercise at the end of this chapter for a way to measure group maturity.) There is a climate of open communication, strong cooperation, and lots of helping behavior. Conflicts and job boundary disputes are handled constructively and efficiently. Cohesiveness and personal commitment to group goals help the group achieve more than could any one individual acting alone. According to a pair of group development experts,

> . . . the group structure can become flexible and adjust to fit the requirements of the situation without causing problems for the members. Influence can shift depending on who has the particular expertise or skills required for the group task or activity. Subgroups can work on special problems or subproblems without posing threats to the authority or cohesiveness of the rest of the group.[19]

Stage 5: Adjourning   The work is done; it is time to move on to other things. Having worked so hard to get along and get something done, many members feel a compelling sense of loss. The return to independence can be eased by rituals celebrating "the end" and "new beginnings." Parties, award ceremonies, graduations, or mock funerals can provide the needed punctuation at the end of a significant group project. Leaders need to emphasize valuable lessons learned in group dynamics to prepare everyone for future group and team efforts.

Group Development: Research and Practical Implications

A growing body of group development research provides managers with some practical insights.

Extending the Tuckman Model: Group Decay   An interesting new study of 10 software development teams, ranging in size from 5 to 16 members, enhanced the practical significance of Tuckman's model.[20] Unlike Tuckman's laboratory groups who worked together only briefly, the teams of software engineers worked on projects lasting *years*. Consequently, the researchers discovered more than simply a five-stage group development process. Groups were observed actually shifting into reverse once Tuckman's "performing" stage was reached, in what the researchers called *group decay*. In keeping with Tuckman's terminology, the three observed stages of group decay were labeled "de-norming," "de-storming," and "de-forming." These additional stages take shape as follows:

- *De-norming.* As the project evolves, there is a natural erosion of standards of conduct. Group members drift in different directions as their interests and expectations change.
- *De-storming.* This stage of group decay is a mirror opposite of the storming stage. Whereas disagreements and conflicts arise rather suddenly during the storming stage, an undercurrent of discontent slowly comes to the surface during the de-storming stage. Individual resistance increases and cohesiveness declines.
- *De-forming.* The work group literally falls apart as subgroups battle for control. Those pieces of the project that are not claimed by individuals or subgroups are abandoned. "Group members begin isolating themselves from each other and from their leaders. Performance declines rapidly because the whole job is no longer being done and group members little care what happens beyond their self-imposed borders."[21]

The primary management lesson from this study is that group leaders should not become complacent upon reaching the performing stage. According to the researchers: "The performing stage is a knife edge or saddle point, not a point of static equilibrium."[22] Awareness is the first line of defense. Beyond that, constructive steps need to be taken to reinforce norms, bolster cohesiveness, and reaffirm the common goal— *even when work groups seem to be doing their best.*

Feedback   Another fruitful study was carried out by a pair of Dutch social psychologists. They hypothesized that interpersonal feedback would vary systematically during the group development process. "The unit of feedback measured was a verbal message directed from one participant to another in which some aspect of behavior was addressed."[23] After collecting and categorizing 1,600 instances of feedback from four different eight-person groups, they concluded the following:

- Interpersonal feedback increases as the group develops through successive stages.

- As the group develops, positive feedback increases and negative feedback decreases.

- Interpersonal feedback becomes more specific as the group develops.

- The credibility of peer feedback increases as the group develops.[24]

These findings hold important lessons for managers. The content and delivery of interpersonal feedback among work group or committee members can be used as a gauge of whether the group is developing properly. For example, the onset of stage 2 (storming) will be signaled by a noticeable increase in *negative* feedback. Effort can then be directed at generating specific, positive feedback among the members so the group's development will not stall. The feedback model discussed in Chapter 9 is helpful in this regard.

Deadlines   Field and laboratory studies found uncertainty about deadlines to be a major disruptive force in both group development and intergroup relations. The practical implications of this finding were summed up by the researcher as follows:

> Uncertain or shifting deadlines are a fact of life in many organizations. Interdependent organizational units and groups may keep each other waiting, may suddenly move deadlines forward or back, or may create deadlines that are known to be earlier than is necessary in efforts to control erratic workflows. The current research suggests that the consequences of such uncertainty may involve more than stress, wasted time, overtime work, and intergroup conflicts. Synchrony in group members' expectations about deadlines may be critical to groups' abilities to accomplish successful transitions in their work.[25]

Thus, effective group management involves clarifying not only tasks and goals, but deadlines as well. When group members accurately perceive important deadlines, the pacing of work and timing of interdependent tasks tend to be more efficient.

Leadership Styles   Along a somewhat different line, experts in the area of leadership contend that different leadership styles are needed as work groups develop.

> In general, it has been documented that leadership behavior that is active, aggressive, directive, structured, and task-oriented seems to have favorable results early in the group's history. However, when those behaviors are maintained throughout the life of the group, they seem to have a negative impact on cohesiveness and quality of work. Conversely, leadership behavior that is supportive, democratic, decentralized, and participative seems to be related to poorer functioning in the early group development stages. However, when these behaviors are maintained throughout the life of the group, more productivity, satisfaction, and creativity result.[26]

The practical punch line here is that managers are advised to shift from a directive and structured leadership style to a participative and supportive style as the group develops.[27]

Roles and Norms: Social Building Blocks for Group and Organizational Behavior

Work groups transform individuals into functioning organizational members through subtle yet powerful social forces.[28] These social forces, in effect, turn "I" into "we" and "me" into "us." Group influence weaves individuals into the organization's social fabric by communicating and enforcing both role expectations and norms. We need to understand roles and norms if we are to effectively manage group and organizational behavior.

Roles

Four centuries have passed since William Shakespeare had his character Jaques speak the following memorable lines in Act II of *As You Like It:* "All the world's a stage, And all the men and women merely players; They have their exits and their entrances; And one man in his time plays many parts. . . ." This intriguing notion of all people as actors in a universal play was not lost on 20th-century sociologists who developed a complex theory of human interaction based on roles. According to an OB scholar, "**roles** are sets of behaviors that persons expect of occupants of a position."[29] Role theory attempts to explain how these social expectations influence employee behavior. This section explores role theory by analyzing a role episode and defining the terms *role overload, role conflict,* and *role ambiguity.*

Roles
Expected behaviors for a given position.

Role Episodes   A role episode, as illustrated in Figure 12–3, consists of a snapshot of the ongoing interaction between two people. In any given role episode, there is a role sender and a focal person who is expected to act out the role. Within a broader context, one may be simultaneously a role sender and a focal person. For the sake of social analysis, however, it is instructive to deal with separate role episodes.

Role episodes begin with the role sender's perception of the relevant organization's or group's behavioral requirements. Those requirements serve as a standard for formulating expectations for the focal person's behavior. The role sender then cognitively evaluates the focal person's actual behavior against those expectations. Appropriate verbal and behavioral messages are then sent to the focal person to pressure him or her into behaving as expected.[30] Consider how Westinghouse used a carrot-and-stick approach to communicate role expectations:

Figure 12–3   *A Role Episode*

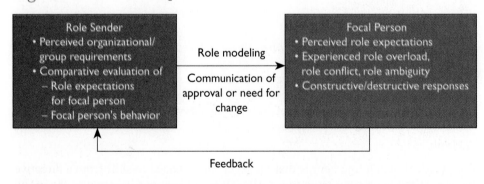

SOURCE: Adapted in part from R L Kohn, D M Wolfe, R P Quinn, and J D Snoek, *Organizational Stress: Studies in Role Conflict and Ambiguity,* 1981 edition (Malabar, FL: Robert E Krieger Publishing, 1964), p 26.

The carrot is a plan, that . . . rewarded 134 managers with options to buy 764,000 shares of stock for boosting the company's financial performance.

The stick is quarterly meetings that are used to rank managers by how much their operations contribute to earnings per share. The soft-spoken . . . [chairman of the board] doesn't scold. He just charts in green the results of the sectors that have met their goals and charts the laggards in red. Peer pressure does the rest. Shame "is a powerful tool," says one executive.[31]

On the receiving end of the role episode, the focal person accurately or inaccurately perceives the communicated role expectations and modeled behavior. Various combinations of role overload, role conflict, and role ambiguity are then experienced. (These three outcomes are defined and discussed in the following sections.) The focal person then responds constructively by engaging in problem solving, for example, or destructively because of undue tension, stress, and strain.[32]

Role Overload   According to organizational psychologist Edgar Schein, **role overload** occurs when "the sum total of what role senders expect of the focal person far exceeds what he or she is able to do."[33] Students who attempt to handle a full course load and maintain a decent social life while working 30 or more hours a week know full well the consequences of role overload. As the individual tries to do more and more in less and less time, stress mounts and personal effectiveness slips.

Role overload
Others' expectations exceed one's ability.

Role Conflict   Have you ever felt like you were being torn apart by the conflicting demands of those around you? If so, you were a victim of role conflict. **Role conflict** is experienced when "different members of the role set expect different things of the focal person."[34] Managers often face conflicting demands between work and family, for example.[35] Women experience greater role conflict between work and family than

Role conflict
Others have conflicting or inconsistent expectations.

Employees debate new product ideas at a software development firm in Taiwan, a country that has relatively high collectivism scores. People in collectivist cultures tend to have a clearer idea of others' expectations, i.e., less role ambiguity, according to one research study.

(J. Marshall/The Image Works)

men because women continue to perform the majority of the household duties and child-care responsibilities.[36] Employees in single-person households have their own version of role conflict between work and outside interests. This is the situation Liz Dolan faced prior to quitting her job as Nike's global marketing chief and becoming a part-time consultant:

> It's hard to admit that your work life is out of control. I loved my job at Nike, but it was all-consuming. I had no life. My housekeeper was spending more time at my house than I was. I reached a point where I could not remember the last time I had slept in my own bed. I love summers in Oregon, but I was never there long enough to enjoy one. But the real indicator that my life was out of whack came when I got a call from my brother, Brendan. He'd been trying to reach me for several weeks. I was always too "busy" to call him back. When we finally connected, he told me that he'd had to do a Lexis-Nexis search on me to figure out where I was that week. I was being Lexis-Nexised by my own brother! That really made me stop and think.[37]

Role conflict also may be experienced when internalized values, ethics, or personal standards collide with others' expectations. For instance, an otherwise ethical production supervisor may be told by a superior to "fudge a little" on the quality control reports so an important deadline will be met. The resulting role conflict forces the supervisor to choose between being loyal but unethical or ethical but disloyal. Tough ethical choices such as this mean personal turmoil, interpersonal conflict, and even resignation.[38] Consequently, experts say business schools should do a better job of weaving ethics training into their course requirements.

Role Ambiguity   Those who experience role conflict may have trouble complying with role demands, but they at least know what is expected of them. Such is not the case with **role ambiguity,** which occurs when "members of the role set fail to communicate to the focal person expectations they have or information needed to perform the role, either because they do not have the information or because they deliberately withhold it."[39] In short, people experience role ambiguity when they do not know what is expected of them. Organizational newcomers often complain about unclear job descriptions and vague promotion criteria. According to role theory, prolonged role ambiguity can foster job dissatisfaction, erode self-confidence, and hamper job performance.

As might be expected, role ambiguity varies across cultures. In a 21-nation study, people in individualistic cultures were found to have higher role ambiguity than peo-

---

Ethics at Work

A recent study by researchers from Canada and the United States of 187 work group members from 20 different organizations uncovered a "monkey see, monkey do" effect relative to antisocial behavior. In other words, employees who observed their co-workers engaging in antisocial conduct at work tended to exhibit the same bad behavior. Antisocial behavior, as measured in the study, included the following acts:

- Damaging company property.
- Saying hurtful things to co-workers.
- Doing poor work; working slowly.
- Complaining with co-workers.
- Bending or breaking rules.
- Criticizing co-workers.
- Doing something harmful to boss or employer.
- Starting an argument with a co-worker.
- Saying rude things about the boss or organization.

According to the researchers:

The message for managers seems clear—antisocial groups encourage antisocial individual behavior. It is crucial to nip behaviors deemed harmful in the bud so as to avoid a social influence effect. Managers who expect that isolating or ignoring antisocial groups will encourage them to change are probably mistaken.

SOURCE: Quoted and adapted from S L Robinson and A M O'Leary-Kelly, "Monkey See, Monkey Do: The Influence of Work Groups on the Antisocial Behavior of Employees," *Academy of Management Journal,* December 1998, pp 658–72.

You Decide . . .

As a manager, how would you handle these unethical acts in your work groups?

For an interpretation of this situation, visit our Web site **www.mhhe.com/kreitner.**

Role ambiguity

Others' expectations are unknown.

OB Exercise   Measuring Role Conflict and Role Ambiguity

Instructions

Step 1. While thinking of your current (or last) job, circle one response for each of the following statements. Please consider each statement carefully because some are worded positively and some negatively.

Step 2. In the space in the far right column, label each statement with either a "C" for role conflict or an "A" for role ambiguity. (See Ch. 12 footnote 42 for a correct categorization.)

Step 3. Calculate separate totals for role conflict and role ambiguity, and compare them with these arbitrary norms: 5–14 = low; 15–25 = moderate; 26–35 = high.

		Very False							Very True	
1.	I feel certain about how much authority I have.	7 — 6 — 5 — 4 — 3 — 2 — 1								_____
2.	I have to do things that should be done differently.	1 — 2 — 3 — 4 — 5 — 6 — 7								_____
3.	I know that I have divided my time properly.	7 — 6 — 5 — 4 — 3 — 2 — 1								_____
4.	I know what my responsibilities are.	7 — 6 — 5 — 4 — 3 — 2 — 1								_____
5.	I have to buck a rule or policy in order to carry out an assignment.	1 — 2 — 3 — 4 — 5 — 6 — 7								_____
6.	I feel certain how I will be evaluated for a raise or promotion.	7 — 6 — 5 — 4 — 3 — 2 — 1								_____
7.	I work with two or more groups who operate quite differently.	1 — 2 — 3 — 4 — 5 — 6 — 7								_____
8.	I know exactly what is expected of me.	7 — 6 — 5 — 4 — 3 — 2 — 1								_____
9.	I do things that are apt to be accepted by one person and not accepted by others.	1 — 2 — 3 — 4 — 5 — 6 — 7								_____
10.	I work on unnecessary things.	1 — 2 — 3 — 4 — 5 — 6 — 7								_____

Role conflict score   = _____

Role ambiguity score = _____

SOURCE: Adapted from J R Rizzo, R J House, and S I Lirtzman, "Role Conflict and Ambiguity in Complex Organizations," *Administrative Science Quarterly,* June 1970, p 156.

ple in collectivist cultures.[40] In other words, people in collectivist or "we" cultures had a clearer idea of others' expectations. Collectivist cultures make sure everyone knows their proper place in society. People in individualistic "me" cultures, such as the United States, may enjoy more individual discretion, but comparatively less input from others has its price—namely, greater role ambiguity.

As mentioned earlier, these role outcomes typically are experienced in some combination, usually to the detriment of the individual and the organization. In fact, a recent study in Israel documented lower job performance when employees experienced a combination of role conflict and role ambiguity.[41.]

Take a moment now to complete the self-assessment exercise in the OB Exercise. See if you can distinguish between sources of role conflict and sources of role ambiguity, as they affect your working life.

Norms

Norm
Shared attitudes, opinions, feelings, or actions that guide social behavior.

Norms are more encompassing than roles. While roles involve behavioral expectations for specific positions, norms help organizational members determine right from wrong and good from bad. According to one respected team of management consultants: "A **norm** is an attitude, opinion, feeling, or action—shared by two or more people—that guides their behavior."[43] Although norms are typically unwritten and seldom discussed openly, they have a powerful influence on group and organizational behavior.[44] PepsiCo Inc., for instance, has evolved a norm that equates corporate competitiveness with physical fitness. According to observers,

> Leanness and nimbleness are qualities that pervade the company. When Pepsi's brash young managers take a few minutes away from the office, they often head straight for the company's physical fitness center or for a jog around the museum-quality sculptures outside of PepsiCo's Purchase, New York, headquarters.[45]

Ostracism
Rejection by other group members.

At PepsiCo and elsewhere, group members positively reinforce those who adhere to current norms with friendship and acceptance. On the other hand, nonconformists experience criticism and even **ostracism,** or rejection by group members. Anyone who has experienced the "silent treatment" from a group of friends knows what a potent social weapon ostracism can be. Norms can be put into proper perspective by understanding how they develop and why they are enforced.

How Norms Are Developed   Experts say norms evolve in an informal manner as the group or organization determines what it takes to be effective. Generally speaking, norms develop in various combinations of the following four ways:

1. *Explicit statements by supervisors or co-workers.* For instance, a group leader might explicitly set norms about not drinking (alcohol) at lunch.

2. *Critical events in the group's history.* At times there is a critical event in the group's history that establishes an important precedent. (For example, a key recruit may have decided to work elsewhere because a group member said too many negative things about the organization. Hence, a norm against such "sour grapes" behavior might evolve.)

3. *Primacy.* The first behavior pattern that emerges in a group often sets group expectations. If the first group meeting is marked by very formal interaction between supervisors and employees, then the group often expects future meetings to be conducted in the same way.

4. *Carryover behaviors from past situations.* Such carryover of individual behaviors from past situations can increase the predictability of group members' behaviors in new settings and facilitate task accomplishment. For instance, students and professors carry fairly constant sets of expectations from class to class.[46]

We would like you to take a few moments and think about the norms that are currently in effect in your classroom. List the norms on a sheet of paper. Do these norms help or hinder your ability to learn? Norms can affect performance either positively or negatively.[47]

Why Norms Are Enforced   Norms tend to be enforced by group members when they

- Help the group or organization survive.
- Clarify or simplify behavioral expectations.

Table 12–2   *Four Reasons Norms Are Enforced*

Norm	Reason for Enforcement	Example
"Make our department look good in top management's eyes."	Group/organization survival	After vigorously defending the vital role played by the Human Resources Management Department at a divisional meeting, a staff specialist is complimented by her boss.
"Success comes to those who work hard and don't make waves."	Clarification of behavioral expectations	A senior manager takes a young associate aside and cautions him to be a bit more patient with co-workers who see things differently.
"Be a team player, not a star."	Avoidance of embarrassment	A project team member is ridiculed by her peers for dominating the discussion during a progress report to top management.
"Customer service is our top priority."	Clarification of central values/unique identity	Two sales representatives are given a surprise Friday afternoon party for having received prestigious best-in-the-industry customer service awards from an industry association.

- Help individuals avoid embarrassing situations.
- Clarify the group's or organization's central values and/or unique identity.[48]

Working examples of each of these four situations are presented in Table 12–2.

Relevant Research Insights and Managerial Implications

Although instruments used to measure role conflict and role ambiguity have questionable validity,[49] two separate meta-analyses indicated that role conflict and role ambiguity negatively affected employees. Specifically, role conflict and role ambiguity were associated with job dissatisfaction, tension and anxiety, lack of organizational commitment, intentions to quit, and, to a lesser extent, poor job performance.[50]

The meta-analyses results hold few surprises for managers. Generally, because of the negative association reported, it makes sense for management to reduce both role conflict and role ambiguity. In this endeavor, managers can use feedback, formal rules and procedures, directive leadership, setting of specific (difficult) goals, and participation. Managers also can use the mentoring process discussed in Chapter 3 to reduce role conflict and ambiguity.

Group Structure and Composition

Work groups of varying size are made up of individuals with varying ability and motivation. Moreover, those individuals perform different roles, on either an assigned or voluntary basis. No wonder some work groups are more productive than others. No wonder some committees are tightly knit while others wallow in conflict. In this section, we examine four important dimensions of group structure and composition: (1) functional roles of group members, (2) group size, (3) gender composition, and (4) group member ability. Each of these dimensions alternatively can enhance or hinder group effectiveness, depending on how it is managed.[51]

Table 12–3   *Functional Roles Performed by Group Members*

Task Roles	Description
Initiator	Suggests new goals or ideas.
Information seeker/giver	Clarifies key issues.
Opinion seeker/giver	Clarifies pertinent values.
Elaborator	Promotes greater understanding through examples or exploration of implications.
Coordinator	Pulls together ideas and suggestions.
Orienter	Keeps group headed toward its stated goal(s).
Evaluator	Tests group's accomplishments with various criteria such as logic and practicality.
Energizer	Prods group to move along or to accomplish more.
Procedural technician	Performs routine duties (e.g., handing out materials or rearranging seats).
Recorder	Performs a "group memory" function by documenting discussion and outcomes.

Maintenance Roles	Description
Encourager	Fosters group solidarity by accepting and praising various points of view.
Harmonizer	Mediates conflict through reconciliation or humor.
Compromiser	Helps resolve conflict by meeting others "half way."
Gatekeeper	Encourages all group members to participate.
Standard setter	Evaluates the quality of group processes.
Commentator	Records and comments on group processes/dynamics.
Follower	Serves as a passive audience.

SOURCE: Adapted from discussion in K D Benne and P Sheats, "Functional Roles of Group Members," *Journal of Social Issues*, Spring 1948; pp 41–49.

Functional Roles Performed by Group Members

As described in Table 12–3, both task and maintenance roles need to be performed if a work group is to accomplish anything.[52]

Task roles

Task-oriented group behavior.

Maintenance roles

Relationship-building group behavior.

Task versus Maintenance Roles   **Task roles** enable the work group to define, clarify, and pursue a common purpose. Meanwhile, **maintenance roles** foster supportive and constructive interpersonal relationships. In short, task roles keep the group *on track* while maintenance roles keep the group *together.* A project team member is performing a task function when he or she stands at an update meeting and says, "What is the real issue here? We don't seem to be getting anywhere." Another individual who says, "Let's hear from those who oppose this plan," is performing a maintenance function. Importantly, each of the various task and maintenance roles may be played in varying combinations and sequences by either the group's leader or any of its members.

Checklist for Managers   The task and maintenance roles listed in Table 12–3 can serve as a handy checklist for managers and group leaders who wish to ensure proper group development. Roles that are not always performed when needed, such as those of coordinator, evaluator, and gatekeeper, can be performed in a timely manner by the formal leader or assigned to other members. The task roles of initiator, orienter, and energizer are especially important because they are *goal-directed* roles. Research studies on group goal setting confirm the motivational power of challenging goals. As with individual goal setting (in Chapter 8), difficult but achievable goals are associated with better group results.[53] Also in line with individual goal-setting theory and research, group goals are more effective if group members clearly understand them and are both individually and collectively committed to achieving them. Initiators, orienters, and energizers can be very helpful in this regard.

International managers need to be sensitive to cultural differences regarding the relative importance of task and maintenance roles. In Japan, for example, cultural tradition calls for more emphasis on maintenance roles, especially the roles of harmonizer and compromiser:

> Courtesy requires that members not be conspicuous or disputatious in a meeting or classroom. If two or more members discover that their views differ—a fact that is tactfully taken to be unfortunate—they adjourn to find more information and to work toward a stance that all can accept. They do not press their personal opinions through strong arguments, neat logic, or rewards and threats. And they do not hesitate to shift their beliefs if doing so will preserve smooth interpersonal relations. (To lose is to win.)[54]

Group Size

How many group members is too many? The answer to this deceptively simple question has intrigued managers and academics for years. Folk wisdom says "two heads are better than one" but that "too many cooks spoil the broth." So where should a manager draw the line when staffing a committee? At 3? At 5 or 6? At 10 or more? Researchers have taken two different approaches to pinpointing optimum group size: mathematical modeling and laboratory simulations. Let us briefly review research evidence from these two approaches.

The Mathematical Modeling Approach   This approach involves building a mathematical model around certain desired outcomes of group action such as decision quality. Due to differing assumptions and statistical techniques, the results of this research are inconclusive. Statistical estimates of optimum group size have ranged from 3 to 13.[55]

The Laboratory Simulation Approach   This stream of research is based on the assumption that group behavior needs to be observed firsthand in controlled laboratory settings. A laboratory study by respected Australian researcher Philip Yetton and his colleague, Preston Bottger, provides useful insights about group size and performance.[56]

A total of 555 subjects (330 managers and 225 graduate management students, of whom 20% were female) were assigned to task teams ranging in size from 2 to 6. The teams worked on the National Aeronautics and Space Administration moon survival exercise. (This exercise involves the rank ordering of 15 pieces of equipment that would enable a spaceship crew on the moon to survive a 200-mile trip between a crash-landing site and home base.)[57] After analyzing the relationships between group size and group performance, Yetton and Bottger concluded the following:

> It would be difficult, at least with respect to decision quality, to justify groups larger than five members. . . . Of course, to meet needs other than high decision quality, organizations may employ groups significantly larger than four or five.[58]

More recent laboratory studies exploring the brainstorming productivity of various size groups (2 to 12 people), in face-to-face versus computer-mediated situations, proved fruitful. In the usual face-to-face brainstorming sessions, productivity of ideas did not increase as the size of the group increased. But brainstorming productivity increased as the size of the group increased when ideas were typed into networked computers.[59] These results suggest that computer networks are helping to deliver on the promise of productivity improvement through modern information technology.[60]

Managerial Implications   Within a contingency management framework, there is no hard-and-fast rule about group size. It depends on the manager's objective for the group. If a high-quality decision is the main objective, then a three- to five-member group would be appropriate. However, if the objective is to generate creative ideas, encourage participation, socialize new members, engage in training, or communicate policies, then groups much larger than five could be justified. But even in this developmental domain, researchers have found upward limits on group size. According to a new meta-analysis, the positive effects of team building activities diminished as group size increased.[61] Managers also need to be aware of *qualitative* changes that occur when group size increases. A meta-analysis of eight studies found the following relationships: as group size increased, group leaders tended to become more directive, and group member satisfaction tended to decline slightly.[62]

Odd-numbered groups (e.g., three, five, seven members) are recommended if the issue is to be settled by a majority vote. Voting deadlocks (e.g., 2-2, 3-3) too often hamper effectiveness of even-numbered groups. A majority decision rule is not necessarily a good idea. One study found that better group outcomes were obtained by negotiation groups that used a unanimous as opposed to majority decision rule. Individuals' self-interests were more effectively integrated when groups used a unanimous decision criterion.[63]

Effects of Men and Women Working Together in Groups

As pointed out in Chapter 2, the female portion of the US labor force has grown significantly in the past 20 years. This demographic shift brought an increase in the number of organizational committees and teams composed of both men and women. Some profound effects on group dynamics might be expected.[64] Let us see what researchers have found in the way of group gender composition effects and what managers can do about them.[65]

Women Face an Uphill Battle in Mixed-Gender Task Groups   Recent laboratory and field studies paint a picture of inequality for women working in mixed-gender groups. Both women and men need to be aware of these often subtle but powerful group dynamics so that corrective steps can be taken.

In a laboratory study of six-person task groups, a clear pattern of gender inequality was found in the way group members interrupted each other. Men interrupted women

One study suggests that females entering male-dominated fields, such as law enforcement, face greater challenges than do males entering female-dominated fields.

(A. Ramey/Stock Boston)

significantly more often than they did other men. Women, who tended to interrupt less frequently and less successfully than men, interrupted men and women equally.[66]

A field study of mixed-gender police and nursing teams in the Netherlands found another group dynamics disadvantage for women. These two particular professions—police work and nursing—were fruitful research areas because men dominate the former while women dominate the latter. As women move into male-dominated police forces and men gain employment opportunities in the female-dominated world of nursing, who faces the greatest resistance? The answer from this study was the women police officers. As the representation of the minority gender (either female police officers or male nurses) increased in the work groups, the following changes in attitude were observed:

> The attitude of the male majority changes from neutral to resistant, whereas the attitude of the female majority changes from favorable to neutral. In other words, men increasingly want to keep their domain for themselves, while women remain willing to share their domain with men.[67]

Again, managers are faced with the challenge of countering discriminatory tendencies in group dynamics.

Social-sexual behavior was the focus of a random survey of 1,232 working men (n = 405) and women (n = 827) in the Los Angeles area.[68] Both harassing and non-harassing sexual conduct were investigated. One-third of the female employees and one-fourth of the male employees reported being sexually harassed in their current job. Nonharassing sexual behavior was much more common, with 80% of the total sample reporting experience with such behavior. Indeed, according to the researchers, increased social contact between men and women in work groups and organizations had led to increased sexualization of the workplace. (To assess the extent of sexualization in your present or former workplace, take a moment to complete the OB Exercise on p 396. What are the ethical implications of your score?)

Constructive Managerial Action   Male and female employees can and often do work well together in groups.[69] A survey of 387 male US government employees sought to determine how they were affected by the growing number of female co-workers. The researchers concluded, "Under many circumstances, including inter-gender interaction in work groups, frequent contact leads to cooperative and supportive social relations."[70] Still, managers need to take affirmative steps to ensure that the documented sexualization of work environments does not erode into sexual harassment. Whether perpetrated against women or men, sexual harassment is demeaning, unethical, and appropriately called "work environment pollution." Moreover, the US Equal Employment Opportunity

What Is the Degree of Sexualization in Your Work Environment?

Instructions

Describe the work environment at your current (or last) job by selecting one number along the following scale for each question.

	Little or Few	Much or Many
1. How much joking or talking about sexual matters do you hear?	1 — 2 — 3 — 4 — 5	
2. How much social pressure are women under to flirt with men?	1 — 2 — 3 — 4 — 5	
3. How much social pressure are men under to flirt with women?	1 — 2 — 3 — 4 — 5	
4. How much of a problem is sexual harassment in your workplace?	1 — 2 — 3 — 4 — 5	
5. How many women dress in a sexually attractive way to men?	1 — 2 — 3 — 4 — 5	

6. How many men dress in a sexually attractive way to women?   1 — 2 — 3 — 4 — 5

7. How many women act in sexually seductive ways toward men?   1 — 2 — 3 — 4 — 5

8. How many men act in sexually seductive ways toward women?   1 — 2 — 3 — 4 — 5

Total score = _____

Norms

8–16	Low degree of sexualization
17–31	Moderate degree of sexualization
32–40	High degree of sexualization

SOURCE: Adapted from B A Gutek, A Gross Cohen, and A M Konrad, "Predicting Social-Sexual Behavior at Work: A Contact Hypothesis," *Academy of Management Journal*, September 1990, p 577.

Commission holds employers legally accountable for behavior it considers sexually harassing. An expert on the subject explains:

> What exactly is sexual harassment? The Equal Employment Opportunity Commission (EEOC) says that unwelcome sexual advances, requests for sexual favors, and other verbal or physical conduct of a sexual nature constitute sexual harassment when submission to such conduct is made a condition of employment; when submission to or rejection of sexual advances is used as a basis for employment decisions; or when such conduct creates an intimidating, hostile, or offensive work environment. These EEOC guidelines interpreting Title VII of the Civil Rights Act of 1964 further state that employers are responsible for the actions of their supervisors and agents and that employers are responsible for the actions of other employees if the employer knows or should have known about the sexual harassment.[71]

Nationwide surveys by *Training* magazine in 1996 and 1997 revealed that 80% of US companies have a formal sexual harassment policy and 74% have training programs targeting sexual harassment.[72]

Beyond avoiding lawsuits by establishing and enforcing anti-discrimination and sexual harassment policies, managers need to take additional steps.[73] Workforce diversity training is a popular approach today. Gender-issue workshops are another option. "Du Pont Co., for example, holds monthly workshops to make managers aware of gender-related attitudes."[74] Phyllis B Davis, a senior vice president at Avon Corporation, has framed the goal of such efforts by saying: "It's a question of consciously creating an environment where everyone has an equal shot at contributing, participating, and most of all advancing."[75]

Importantly, this embracing of organizational and work group diversity goes beyond gender, race, ethnicity, and culture. A recent laboratory study of US college students found a stronger positive relationship between group effectiveness and *value* diversity (as opposed to demographic diversity).[76] Once again we see the importance of managers recognizing and accommodating individual differences rather than relying on stereotypes.

Individual Ability and Group Effectiveness

Imagine that you are a department manager charged with making an important staffing decision amid the following circumstances. You need to form 8 three-person task teams from a pool of 24 employees. Based on each of the employee's prior work records and their scores on ability tests, you know that 12 have high ability and 12 have low ability. The crux of your problem is how to assign the 12 high-ability employees. Should you spread your best talent around by making sure there are both high- and low-ability employees on each team? Then again, you may want to concentrate your best talent by forming four high-ability teams and four low-ability teams. Or should you attempt to find a compromise between these two extremes? What is your decision? Why? One field experiment provided an instructive and interesting answer.

The Israeli Tank-Crew Study Aharon Tziner and Dov Eden, researchers from Tel Aviv University, systematically manipulated the composition of 208 three-man tank crews. All possible combinations of high- and low-ability personnel were studied (high-high-high; high-high-low; high-low-low; and low-low-low). Ability was a composite measure of (1) overall intelligence, (2) amount of formal education, (3) proficiency in Hebrew, and (4) interview ratings. Successful operation of the tanks required the three-man crews to perform with a high degree of synchronized interdependence.[77] Tank-crew effectiveness was determined by commanding officers during military maneuvers for the Israel Defense Forces.

As expected, the high-high-high ability tank crews performed the best and the low-low-low the worst. But the researchers discovered an important *interaction effect:*

> Each member's ability influenced crew performance effectiveness differently depending on the ability levels of the other two members. A high-ability member appears to achieve more in combination with other uniformly high-ability members than in combination with low-ability members.[78]

The tank crews composed of three high-ability personnel far outperformed all other ability combinations. The interaction effect also worked in a negative direction because the low-low-low ability crews performed far below expected levels. Moreover, as illustrated in Figure 12–4, significantly greater performance gains were achieved by creating high-high-high ability crews than by upgrading low-low-low ability crews with one or two high-ability members.

This returns us to the staffing problem at the beginning of this section. Tziner and Eden recommended the following solution:

> Our experimental results suggest that the most productive solution would be to allocate six highs and all 12 lows to six teams of high-low-low ability and to assign the six remaining highs to two teams of high-high-high ability. This avoids the disproportionately low productivity of the low-low-low ability combination, while

Figure 12–4   *Ability of Israeli Tank-Crew Members and Improvements in Effectiveness*

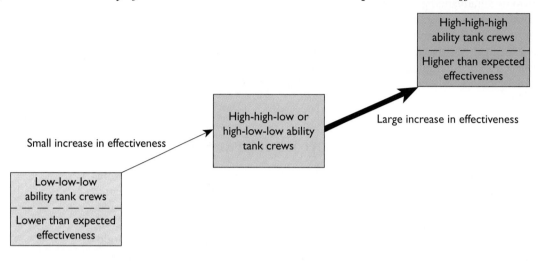

SOURCE: Based on discussion in A Tziner and D Eden, "Effects of Crew Composition on Crew Performance: Does the Whole Equal the Sum of Its Parts?" *Journal of Applied Psychology,* February 1985, pp 85–93.

Figure 12–5   *A Contingency Model for Staffing Work Groups: Effective Use of Available Talent*

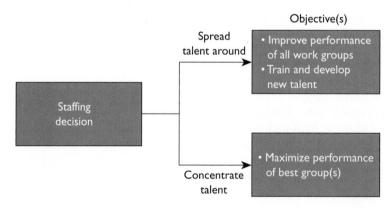

leaving some of the highs for high-high-high ability teams where they are most productive.... Our results show that talent is used more effectively when concentrated than when spread around.[79]

A Managerial Interpretation   While the real-life aspect of the tank-crew study makes its results fairly generalizable, a qualification is in order. Specifically, modern complex organizations demand a more flexible contingency approach. Figure 12–5 shows two basic contingencies. If management seeks to *improve* the performance of *all* groups or train novices, high-ability personnel can be spread around. This option would be appropriate in a high-volume production operation. But if the desired outcome is to *maximize* performance of the *best* group(s), then high-ability personnel should be concentrated. This second option would be advisable in research and development departments, for example, where technological breakthroughs need to be achieved. Extraordinary achievements require clusters of extraordinary talent.[80]

Threats to Group Effectiveness

Even when managers carefully staff and organize task groups, group dynamics can still go haywire. Forehand knowledge of three major threats to group effectiveness—the Asch effect, groupthink, and social loafing—can help managers take necessary preventive steps. Because the first two problems relate to blind conformity, some brief background work is in order.

Very little would be accomplished in task groups and organizations without conformity to norms, role expectations, policies, and rules and regulations. After all, deadlines, commitments, and product/service quality standards have to be established and adhered to if the organization is to survive. But, as pointed out by management consultants Robert Blake and Jane Srygley Mouton, conformity is a two-edged sword:

> Social forces powerful enough to influence members to conform may influence them to perform at a very high level of quality and productivity. All too often, however, the pressure to conform stifles creativity, influencing members to cling to attitudes that may be out of touch with organizational needs and even out of kilter with the times.[81]

Moreover, excessive or blind conformity can stifle critical thinking, the last line of defense against unethical conduct. Almost daily accounts in the popular media of insider trading scandals, price fixing, illegal dumping of hazardous wastes, and other unethical practices make it imperative that future managers understand the mechanics of blind conformity.

The Asch Effect

Nearly 50 years ago, social psychologist Solomon Asch conducted a series of laboratory experiments that revealed a negative side of group dynamics.[82] Under the guise of a "perception test," Asch had groups of seven to nine volunteer college students look at 12 pairs of cards such as the ones in Figure 12–6. The object was to identify the line that was the same length as the standard line. Each individual was told to announce his or her choice to the group. Since the differences among the comparison lines were obvious, there should have been unanimous agreement during each of the 12 rounds. But that was not the case.

Figure 12–6   *The Asch Experiment*

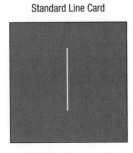
Standard Line Card

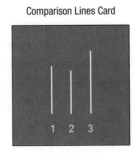
Comparison Lines Card

1   2   3

A Minority of One   All but one member of each group were Asch's confederates who agreed to systematically select the wrong line during seven of the rounds (the other five rounds were control rounds for comparison purposes). The remaining individual was the naive subject who was being tricked. Group pressure was created by having the naive subject in each group be among the last to announce his or her choice. Thirty-one subjects were tested. Asch's research question was: "How often would the naive subjects conform to a majority opinion that was obviously wrong?"

Only 20% of Asch's subjects remained entirely independent; 80% yielded to the pressures of group opinion at least once! Fifty-eight percent knuckled under to the "immoral majority" at least twice. Hence, the **Asch effect,** the distortion of individual judgment by a unanimous but incorrect opposition, was documented. (Do you ever turn your back on your better judgment by giving in to group pressure?)

Asch effect
Giving in to a unanimous but wrong opposition.

A Managerial Perspective   Asch's experiment has been widely replicated with mixed results. Both high and low degrees of blind conformity have been observed with various situations and subjects. Replications in Japan and Kuwait have demonstrated that the Asch effect is not unique to the United States.[83] A 1996 meta-analysis of 133 Asch-line experiments from 17 countries found a *decline* in conformity among US subjects since the 1950s. Internationally, collectivist countries, where the group prevails over the individual, produced higher levels of conformity than individualistic countries.[84] The point is not precisely how great the Asch effect is in a given situation or culture, but rather, managers committed to ethical conduct need to be concerned that the Asch effect exists. Even isolated instances of blind, unthinking conformity seriously threaten the effectiveness and integrity of work groups and organizations. Functional conflict and assertiveness, discussed in Chapters 14 and 15, can help employees respond appropriately when they find themselves facing an immoral majority. Ethical codes mentioning specific practices also can provide support and guidance.

Groupthink

Why did President Lyndon B Johnson and his group of intelligent White House advisers make some very *unintelligent* decisions that escalated the Vietnam War? Those fateful decisions were made despite obvious warning signals, including stronger than expected resistance from the North Vietnamese and withering support at home and abroad. Systematic analysis of the decision-making processes underlying the war in Vietnam and other US foreign policy fiascoes prompted Yale University's Irving Janis to coin the term *groupthink*.[85] Modern managers can all too easily become victims of groupthink, just like President Johnson's staff, if they passively ignore the danger.

Groupthink
Janis's term for a cohesive in-group's unwillingness to realistically view alternatives.

Definition and Symptoms of Groupthink   Janis defines **groupthink** as "a mode of thinking that people engage in when they are deeply involved in a cohesive in-group, when members' strivings for unanimity override their motivation to realistically appraise alternative courses of action."[86] He adds, "Groupthink refers to a deterioration of mental efficiency, reality testing, and moral judgment that results from in-group pressures."[87] Unlike Asch's subjects, who were strangers to each other, members of groups victimized by groupthink are friendly, tightly knit, and cohesive.

The symptoms of groupthink listed in Figure 12–7 thrive in the sort of climate outlined in the following critique of corporate directors in the United States:

Many directors simply don't rock the boat. "No one likes to be the skunk at the garden party," says [management consultant] Victor H. Palmieri. . . . "One does not make

Figure 12–7   *Symptoms of Groupthink Lead to Defective Decision Making*

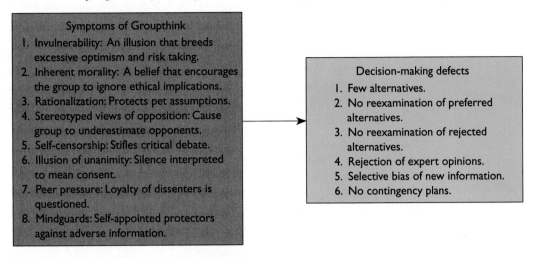

SOURCES: Symptoms adapted from I L Janis, *Groupthink,* 2nd ed (Boston: Houghton Mifflin, 1982), pp 174–75. Defects excerpted from G Moorhead, "Groupthink: Hypothesis in Need of Testing," *Group & Organization Studies,* December 1982, p 434. Copyright © 1982 by Sage Publications. Reprinted by permission of Sage Publications, Inc.

friends and influence people in the boardroom or elsewhere by raising hard questions that create embarrassment or discomfort for management."[88]

In short, policy- and decision-making groups can become so cohesive that strong-willed executives are able to gain unanimous support for poor decisions.[89]

Groupthink Research and Prevention   Laboratory studies using college students as subjects validate portions of Janis's groupthink concept. Specifically, it has been found that

- Groups with a moderate amount of cohesiveness produce better decisions than low- or high-cohesive groups.
- Highly cohesive groups victimized by groupthink make the poorest decisions, despite high confidence in those decisions.[90]

Janis believes prevention is better than cure when dealing with groupthink. He recommends the following preventive measures:

1. Each member of the group should be assigned the role of critical evaluator. This role involves actively voicing objections and doubts.

2. Top-level executives should not use policy committees to rubber-stamp decisions that have already been made.

3. Different groups with different leaders should explore the same policy questions.

4. Subgroup debates and outside experts should be used to introduce fresh perspectives.

5. Someone should be given the role of devil's advocate when discussing major alternatives. This person tries to uncover every conceivable negative factor.

6. Once a consensus has been reached, everyone should be encouraged to rethink their position to check for flaws.[91]

These anti-groupthink measures can help cohesive groups produce sound recommendations and decisions.[92] For example, Kenneth A Macke, the chairman and CEO of Dayton Hudson Corporation, has created a corporate board of directors for the department store giant that is unlikely to be victimized by groupthink:

> Twelve out of 14 directors are outsiders. A vice-chairman chosen from among the outside directors serves as a special liaison between the board and the CEO. The result is a powerful, independent group of directors—a rare species in boardrooms today. How independent? [In 1991], for instance, the board withheld Macke's bonus, which had totaled almost $600,000 in 1990.[93]

The OB in Action Case Study at the end of this chapter explores the possible role of groupthink in the 1986 Challenger Space Shuttle disaster.

Social Loafing

Is group performance less than, equal to, or greater than the sum of its parts? Can three people, for example, working together accomplish less than, the same as, or more than they would working separately? An interesting study conducted more than a half century ago by a French agricultural engineer named Ringelmann found the answer to be "less than."[94] In a rope-pulling exercise, Ringlemann reportedly found that three people pulling together could achieve only two and a half times the average individual rate. Eight pullers achieved less than four times the individual rate. This tendency for individual effort to decline as group size increases has come to be called **social loafing.**[95] Let us briefly analyze this threat to group effectiveness and synergy with an eye toward avoiding it.

Social loafing

Decrease in individual effort as group size increases.

Social Loafing Theory and Research   Among the theoretical explanations for the social loafing effect are (1) equity of effort ("Everyone else is goofing off, so why shouldn't I?"), (2) loss of personal accountability ("I'm lost in the crowd, so who cares?"), (3) motivational loss due to the sharing of rewards ("Why should I work harder than the others when everyone gets the same reward?"), and (4) coordination loss as more people perform the task ("We're getting in each other's way.").

Laboratory studies refined these theories by identifying situational factors that moderated the social loafing effect. Social loafing occurred when

- The task was perceived to be unimportant, simple or not interesting.[96]
- Group members thought their individual output was not identifiable.[97]
- Group members expected their co-workers to loaf.[98]

But social loafing did *not* occur when group members in two laboratory studies expected to be evaluated.[99] Also, recent research suggests that self-reliant "individualists" are more prone to social loafing than are group-oriented "collectivists." But individualists can be made more cooperative by keeping the group small and holding each member personally accountable for results.[100]

Practical Implications   These findings demonstrate that social loafing is not an inevitable part of group effort. Management can curb this threat to group effectiveness by making sure the task is challenging and perceived as important. Additionally, it is a good idea to hold group members personally accountable for identifiable portions of the group's task. One way to do this is with the *stepladder technique,* a group decision-making process proven effective in recent research (see Table 12–4). Compared with

Table 12–4   *How to Avoid Social Loafing in Groups and Teams:*
The Stepladder Technique

The stepladder technique is intended to enhance group decision making by structuring the entry of group members into a core group. Increasing or decreasing the number of group members alters the number of steps. In a four-person group, the stepladder technique has three steps. Initially, two group members (the initial core group) work together on the problem at hand. Next, a third member joins the core group and presents his or her preliminary solutions for the same problem. The entering member's presentation is followed by a three-person discussion. Finally, the fourth group member joins the core group and presents his or her preliminary solutions. This is followed by a four-person discussion, which has as its goal the rendering of a final group decision.

   The stepladder technique has four requirements. First, each group member must be given the group's task and sufficient time to think about the problem before entering the core group. Second, the entering member must present his or her preliminary solutions before hearing the core group's preliminary solutions. Third, with the entry of each additional member to the core group, sufficient time to discuss the problem is necessary. Fourth, a final decision must be purposely delayed until the group has been formed in its entirety.

SOURCE: Excerpted from S G Rogelberg, J L Barnes-Farrell, and C A Lowe, "The Stepladder Technique: An Alternative Group Structure Facilitating Effective Group Decision Making," *Journal of Applied Psychology*, October 1992, vol 77, p 731. Copyright © 1992 by the American Psychological Association. Reprinted with permission.

conventional groups, stepladder groups produced significantly better decisions in the same amount of time. "Furthermore, stepladder groups' decisions surpassed the quality of their best individual members' decisions 56% of the time. In contrast, conventional groups' decisions surpassed the quality of their best members' decisions only 13% of the time."[101] The stepladder technique could be a useful tool for organizations relying on self-managed or total quality management (TQM) teams.

Summary of Key Concepts

1. *Identify the four criteria of a group from a sociological perspective.* Sociologically, a *group* is defined as two or more freely interacting individuals who share collective norms and goals and have a common identity.

2. *Describe the five stages in Tuckman's theory of group development, and discuss the threat of group decay.* The five stages in Tuckman's theory are *forming* (the group comes together), *storming* (members test the limits and each other), *norming* (questions about authority and power are resolved as the group becomes more cohesive), *performing* (effective communication and cooperation help the group get things done), and *adjourning* (group members go their own way). According to recent research, group decay occurs when a work group achieves the "performing" stage and then shifts into reverse. Group decay occurs through *de-norming* (ero-

sion of standards), *de-storming* (growing discontent and loss of cohesiveness), and *de-forming* (fragmentation and breakup of the group).

3. *Distinguish between role conflict and role ambiguity.* Organizational *roles* are sets of behaviors persons expect of occupants of a position. One may experience role overload (too much to do in too little time), role conflict (conflicting role expectations), or role ambiguity (unclear role expectations).

4. *Contrast roles and norms, and specify four reasons norms are enforced in organizations.* While roles are specific to the person's position, norms are shared attitudes that differentiate appropriate from inappropriate behavior in a variety of situations. Norms evolve informally and are

enforced because they help the group or organization survive, clarify behavioral expectations, help people avoid embarrassing situations, and clarify the group's or organization's central values.

5. *Distinguish between task and maintenance functions in groups.* Members of formal groups need to perform both task (goal-oriented) and maintenance (relationship-oriented) roles if anything is to be accomplished.

6. *Summarize the practical contingency management implications for group size and group member ability.* Laboratory simulation studies suggest decision-making groups should be limited to five or fewer members. Larger groups are appropriate when creativity, participation, or socialization are the main objectives. If majority votes are to be taken, odd-numbered groups are recommended to avoid deadlocks. Results of the Israeli tank-crew study prompted researchers to conclude that it is better to concentrate high-ability personnel in separate groups. Within a contingency management perspective, however, there are situations in which it is advisable to spread high-ability people around.

7. *Discuss why managers need to carefully handle mixed-gender task groups.* Women face special group dynamics challenges in mixed-gender task groups. Steps need to be taken to make sure increased sexualization of work environments does not erode into illegal sexual harassment.

8. *Describe groupthink, and identify at least four of its symptoms.* Groupthink plagues cohesive in-groups that shortchange moral judgment while putting too much emphasis on unanimity. Symptoms of groupthink include invulnerability, inherent morality, rationalization, stereotyped views of opposition, self-censorship, illusion of unanimity, peer pressure, and mindguards. Critical evaluators, outside expertise, and devil's advocates are among the preventive measures recommended by Irving Janis, who coined the term *groupthink*.

9. *Define social loafing, and explain how managers can prevent it.* Social loafing involves the tendency for individual effort to decrease as group size increases. This problem can be contained if the task is challenging and important, individuals are held accountable for results and group members expect everyone to work hard. The stepladder technique, a structured approach to group decision making, can reduce social loafing by increasing personal effort and accountability.

Discussion Questions

1. Which of the following would qualify as a sociological group? A crowd watching a baseball game? One of the baseball teams? Explain.

2. What is your opinion about employees being friends with their co-workers (overlapping formal and informal groups)?

3. What is your personal experience with groups that failed to achieve stage 4 of group development? At which stage did they stall? Why? Have you observed group decay? Explain.

4. Considering your current lifestyle, how many different roles are you playing? What sorts of role conflict and role ambiguity are you experiencing?

5. What norms do college students usually enforce in class? How are they enforced?

6. Which roles do you prefer to play in work groups: task or maintenance? How could you do a better job in this regard?

7. How would you respond to a manager who made the following statement? "When it comes to the size of work groups, the bigger the better."

8. Are women typically at a disadvantage in mixed-gender work groups? Give your rationale.

9. Have you ever been a victim of either the Asch effect or groupthink? Explain the circumstances.

10. Have you observed any social loafing recently? What were the circumstances and what could be done to correct the problem?

Internet Exercise

Social skills are a central theme in this chapter, as well as in Chapters 13 through 17. Sexual harassment, in mixed-gender work groups, is a related topic of great importance today. The purpose of this exercise is to assess your basic social and communication skills and build your understanding of sexual harassment.

www.queendom.com
www.de.psu.edu/harass/intro.htm

A Free Self-Assessment Questionnaire for Social Skills

Managers, who are responsible for getting things accomplished with and through others, simply cannot be effective if they are unable to interact skillfully in social settings. As with any skill development program, you need to know *where you are* before constructing a learning agenda for *where you want to be.* Go to the Internet home page for Body-Mind Queen-Dom (www.queendom.com), and select the subheading "Tests, Tests, Tests. . ." under the main menu heading "Tests, Quizzes, Puzzles & Polls." (Note: Our use of this questionnaire is for instructional purposes only and does not constitute an endorsement of any products that may or may not suit your needs. There is no obligation to buy anything.) At the "Tests, Tests, Tests . . . " page, read the brief welcome statement about Queendom's psychological tests, and then scroll down to the category "Relationships." Select the "Communication Skills Test," read the brief instructions, complete all 34 items, and click on the "score" button for automatic scoring. It is possible, if you choose, to print a personal copy of your completed questionnaire and results.

Free Tutorial about Sexual Harassment

As discussed in this chapter, sexual harassment can be a problem when women and men work together in groups. Professor Nancy Wyatt, from The Pennsylvania State University's Delaware County Campus, has compiled a comprehensive and instructive Internet site on the topic of sexual harassment (www.de.psu.edu/harass/intro.htm). Explore this resource for insights.

Questions:

1. Possible scores on the self-assessment questionnaire range from 0 to 100. How did you score? Are you pleasantly (or unpleasantly) surprised by your score?

2. What is your strongest social/communication skill?

3. Reviewing the questionnaire item by item, can you find obvious weak spots in your social/communication skills? For instance, are you a poor listener? Do you interrupt too often? Do you need to be more aware of others, both verbally and nonverbally? Do you have a hard time tuning into others' feelings or expressing your own feelings? How do you handle disagreement?

4. Based on the results of this questionnaire, what is your learning agenda for improving your social and communication skills. (Note: You will find lots of good ideas and practical tips in Chapters 13 through 17.)

5. What insights did you pick up from the sexual harassment Web site? What is your personal experience with sexual harassment in the workplace? Is the problem getting better or worse, in your estimation? What constructive steps need to be taken by today's managers and employees?

OB in Action Case Study   **www.hq.nasa.gov**

A Ten-Year Retrospective of the Challenger Space Shuttle Disaster: Was It Groupthink?

A Fateful Decision . . .

The debate over whether to launch on January 28, 1986, unfolded as follows, according to the report of the Presidential Commission on the Space Shuttle Challenger Accident:

Shortly after 1 PM ET on January 27, NASA's [the National Aeronautic and Space Administration's] booster rocket manager in Cape Canaveral, Larry Wear, asks officials of rocket maker Morton Thiokol in Utah whether cold weather on the 28th would present a problem for launch.

By 2 PM, NASA's top managers are discussing how temperatures in the 30s at the launch pad might affect the shuttle's performance. In Utah, an hour later, Thiokol engineer Roger Boisjoly learns of the forecast for the first time.

By late afternoon, midlevel NASA managers at the Cape are on the phone with Thiokol managers, who point out that the booster's rubbery O-rings, which seal in hot gases, might be affected by cold.

That concern brings in officials from NASA's Marshall Space Flight Center in Huntsville, Alabama, which buys the rockets from Thiokol and readies them for launch.

Marshall managers decide that a three-way telephone conference call is needed, linking NASA and Thiokol engineers and managers in Alabama, Florida, and Utah.

The first conference call begins about 5:45 PM, and Thiokol tells NASA it believes launch should be delayed until noon or afternoon, when the weather turns warmer. It is decided a second conference call would be needed later that evening.

Marshall deputy project manager Judson Lovingood tells shuttle projects manager Stan Reinartz at the Cape that if Thiokol persists, NASA should not launch. Top NASA managers at Marshall are told of Thiokol's concern.

At 8:45 PM, the second conference call begins, involving 34 engineers and managers from NASA and Thiokol at the three sites.

Thiokol engineers Boisjoly and Arnie Thompson present charts showing a history of leaking O-ring joints from tests and previous flights.

The data show that the O-rings perform worse at lower temperatures and that the worst leak of hot gases came in January 1985, when a shuttle launched with the temperature at 53 degrees. Thiokol managers recommend not flying Challenger at temperatures colder than that.

NASA's George Hardy says he's "appalled" at Thiokol's recommendation. Larry Mulloy, Marshall's booster rocket manager, complains that Thiokol is setting down new launch criteria and exclaims, "My God, Thiokol, when do you want me to launch, next April?"

Thiokol Vice President Joe Kilminster asks for five minutes to talk in private. The debate continues for 30 minutes. Boisjoly, Thompson, engineer Bob Ebeling, and others are overruled by Thiokol management, who decide to approve the launch.

At 11 PM, Kilminster tells NASA that Thiokol has changed its mind: Temperature is still a concern but the data are inconclusive. He recommends launch.

Thiokol's concerns that cold weather could hurt the booster joints are not passed up NASA's chain of command beyond officials at the Marshall Space Flight Center.

Challenger is launched at 11:38 AM January 28 in a temperature of 36 degrees.[102]

Shortly after launch on January 28, 1986, Challenger was engulfed in a fiery explosion that led to the deaths of six astronauts and teacher-in-space Christa McAuliffe. As a shocked world watched great billows of smoke trail over the Atlantic, it was clear to those involved that launching Challenger in 36-degree weather was a catastrophic decision.[103]

. . . Ten Years Later

Two who argued the longest and loudest against launch were Thiokol engineers Roger Boisjoly and Arnie Thompson. But their lives took widely differing paths after the accident.

Boisjoly remembers the prelaunch debate this way: "When NASA created the pressure, they all buckled."

He became nationally known as the primary whistle-blower. Thiokol removed Boisjoly from the investigation team and sent him home after he testified before a presidential commission that the company ignored evidence that the booster rocket seals would fail in cold weather.

Boisjoly, 57, says he was blackballed by the industry and run out of town by Thiokol.

For a time, he sought psychiatric help. "It just became unbearable to function," says Boisjoly, who now lives with his wife and daughter in a small mountain town in Utah. He spoke on condition that the town not be named because he fears for his family's safety.

Boisjoly is convinced he is a marked man because some former co-workers believe his testimony contributed to resulting layoffs at Thiokol.

After the accident, he says, drivers would try to run him off the road when he was out on a walk. He got threatening phone calls. Someone tried to break into his house.

"It became so uncomfortable for me that I went out and bought a .38 revolver," he says.

Now retired, Boisjoly earns $1,500 for speeches to universities and business groups. He also runs his own engineering company and teaches Sunday school in the Mormon church, something he says he never would have dreamed of doing before the accident.

Says Thompson, the other voice against launch: "There were the two of us that didn't want to fly and we were defeated. A lot of my top managers were not happy with me."

Yet, with longer ties to Thiokol than Boisjoly, Thompson was promoted to manager and stayed on through the shuttle's redesign.

He retired three years ago at the end of a 25-year-career. Now 66, he spends his time building a small office building in Brigham City, Utah.

"My attitude was, I wanted to stay on and redesign the bird and get back into the air," says Thompson. "I had a personal goal to get flying again." . . .

Thiokol's Bob Ebeling was so sure that Challenger was doomed, he asked his daughter, Leslie, then 33, to his office to watch "a super colossal disaster" unfold on live TV.

When it exploded, "I was in the middle of a prayer for the Lord to do his will and let all these things come to a happy ending and not let this happen," says Ebeling, who managed the rocket ignition system for Thiokol. "We did our level best but it wasn't good enough."

The fact that he foresaw disaster and could not stop it has tortured him since.

Ebeling, 69, says that within a week of the accident he became impotent and suffered high stress and constant headaches, problems he still has today. After 40 years of engineering experience, Thiokol "put me out to pasture on a medical" retirement, he says.

Ebeling still feels "the decision to recommend a launch was pre-ordained by others, by NASA leaning on our upper management. The deck was stacked."

One of those who overruled Ebeling and the others was Jerry Mason, the senior Thiokol manager on the conference call. He took an early retirement from Thiokol five months after the disaster, ending a 25-year career in aerospace.

"I was basically responsible for the operation the day it happened," says Mason, 69. "It was important to the company to put that behind them and get going on the recovery and it would be hard to do that with me sitting there. So I left."

In Mason's case, that meant going abruptly from corporate chieftain to unpaid volunteer. He helped set up a local economic development board and now chairs the Utah Wildlife Federation.

"I had a pretty successful career, and would liked to have gone out with the feeling that I really had done very well all the time instead of having to go out feeling I'd made a mistake at the end."

For Judson Lovingood, the loss was more personal.

Formerly one of NASA's deputy managers for the shuttle project, he wonders still if Challenger contributed to the breakup of his marriage.

"I think (Challenger) had an effect on my personal life," says Lovingood, "a long-term effect."

After the accident, he went to work for Thiokol in Huntsville and retired as director of engineering in 1993. Now remarried, he spends his time puttering in the yard of his Gurley, Alabama, home.

"Sometimes when I think about the seven people (aboard the shuttle), it's pretty painful," says Lovingood.

Besides McAuliffe, on board Challenger were commander Dick Scobee, pilot Mike Smith, and astronauts Ron McNair, Ellison Onizuka, Judy Resnik, and Greg Jarvis.

Their families settled with the government and Thiokol for more than $1.5 billion. Still, "I think people should hold us collectively responsible as a group," Lovingood says. "Every person in that meeting the night before the launch shared in the blame." . . .

Investigations of the Challenger explosion placed much of the blame on NASA's George Hardy, a senior engineering manager.

By saying he was "appalled" by Thiokol's fears of flying in cold weather, critics charged, Hardy pressured Thiokol into approving the launch.

But Hardy refuses to shoulder the blame. "If Thiokol had stuck to their position, there wasn't any way we were going to launch," he says.

Hardy left NASA four months after the accident. Now 65, he runs a small aerospace consulting company in Athens, Alabama.

Whatever else the last decade brought, many of the recollections return to that pressure-packed conference call on the eve of launch.

Questions for Discussion

1. Which task and maintenance roles in Table 12–3 should have been performed or performed better? By whom?

2. Using Figure 12–7 as a guide, which *symptoms* of groupthink are evident in this case?

3. Using Figure 12–7 as a guide, which *decision-making defects* can you identify in this case?

4. Do you think groupthink was a major contributor to the Challenger disaster? Explain.

5. All things considered, who was most to blame for the catastrophic decision to launch? Why?

Personal Awareness and Growth Exercise

Is This a Mature Work Group or Team?

Objectives

1. To increase your knowledge of group processes and dynamics.
2. To give you a tool for assessing the maturity of a work group or task team as well as a diagnostic tool for pinpointing group problems.
3. To help you become a more effective group leader or contributor.

Introduction

Group action is so common today that many of us take it for granted. But are the groups and teams to which we contribute much of our valuable time mature and hence more likely to be effective? Or do they waste our time? How can they be improved? We can and should become tough critical evaluators of group processes.

Instructions

Think of a work group or task team with which you are very familiar (preferably one you worked with in the past or are currently working with). Rate the group's maturity on each of the 20 dimensions.[104] Then add your circled responses to get your total group maturity score. The higher the score, the greater the group's maturity.

	Very False (or Never)				Very True (or Always)
1. Members are clear about group goals.	1 —	2 —	3 —	4 —	5
2. Members agree with the group's goals.	1 —	2 —	3 —	4 —	5
3. Members are clear about their roles.	1 —	2 —	3 —	4 —	5
4. Members accept their roles and status.	1 —	2 —	3 —	4 —	5
5. Role assignments match member abilities.	1 —	2 —	3 —	4 —	5
6. The leadership style matches the group's developmental level.	1 —	2 —	3 —	4 —	5
7. The group has an open communication structure in which all members participate.	1 —	2 —	3 —	4 —	5
8. The group gets, gives, and uses feedback about its effectiveness and productivity.	1 —	2 —	3 —	4 —	5

9. The group spends time planning how it will solve problems and make decisions.   1 — 2 — 3 — 4 — 5

10. Voluntary conformity is high.   1 — 2 — 3 — 4 — 5

11. The group norms encourage high performance and quality.   1 — 2 — 3 — 4 — 5

12. The group expects to be successful.   1 — 2 — 3 — 4 — 5

13. The group pays attention to the details of its work.   1 — 2 — 3 — 4 — 5

14. The group accepts coalition and subgroup formation.   1 — 2 — 3 — 4 — 5

15. Subgroups are integrated into the group as a whole.   1 — 2 — 3 — 4 — 5

16. The group is highly cohesive.   1 — 2 — 3 — 4 — 5

17. Interpersonal attraction among members is high.   1 — 2 — 3 — 4 — 5

18. Members are cooperative.   1 — 2 — 3 — 4 — 5

19. Periods of conflict are frequent but brief.   1 — 2 — 3 — 4 — 5

20. The group has effective conflict-management strategies.   1 — 2 — 3 — 4 — 5

Total score = _____

Arbitrary Norms

20–39   "When in doubt, run in circles, scream and shout!"
40–59   A long way to go
60–79   On the right track
80–100   Ready for group dynamics graduate school

Questions for Discussion

1. Does your evaluation help explain why the group or team was successful or not? Explain.

2. Was (or is) there anything *you* could have done (or can do) to increase the maturity of this group? Explain.

3. How will this evaluation instrument help you be a more effective group member or leader in the future?

Group Exercise

A Committee Decision

Objectives

1. To give you firsthand experience with work group dynamics through a role-playing exercise.[105]
2. To develop your ability to evaluate group effectiveness.

Introduction

Please read the following case before going on.

THE JOHNNY ROCCO CASE

Johnny has a grim personal background. He is the third child in a family of seven. He has not seen his father for several years, and his recollection is that his father used to come home drunk and beat up every member of the family; everyone ran when his father came staggering home.

His mother, according to Johnny, wasn't much better. She was irritable and unhappy, and she always predicted that Johnny would come to no good end. Yet she worked when her health allowed her to do so in order to keep the family in food and clothing. She always decried the fact that she was not able to be the kind of mother she would like to be.

Johnny quit school in the seventh grade. He had great difficulty conforming to the school routine—he misbehaved often, was truant frequently, and fought with schoolmates. On several occasions he was picked up by the police and, along with members of his group, questioned during several investigations into cases of both petty and grand larceny. The police regarded him as "probably a bad one."

The juvenile officer of the court saw in Johnny some good qualities that no one else seemed to sense. Mr O'Brien took it on himself to act as a "big brother" to Johnny. He had several long conversations with Johnny, during which he managed to penetrate to some degree Johnny's defensive shell. He represented to Johnny the first semblance of personal interest in his life. Through Mr O'Brien's efforts, Johnny returned to school and obtained a high school diploma. Afterwards, Mr O'Brien helped him obtain a job.

Now 20, Johnny is a stockroom clerk in one of the laboratories where you are employed. On the whole Johnny's performance has been acceptable, but there have been glaring exceptions. One involved a clear act of insubordination on a fairly unimportant matter. In another, Johnny was accused, on circumstantial grounds, of destroying some expensive equipment. Though the investigation is still open, it now appears the destruction was accidental.

Johnny's supervisor wants to keep him on for at least a trial period, but he wants "outside" advice as to the best way of helping Johnny grow into greater responsibility. Of course, much depends on how Johnny behaves in the next few months. Naturally, his supervisor must follow personnel policies that are accepted in the company as a whole. It is important to note that Johnny is not an attractive young man. He is rather weak and sickly, and he shows unmistakable signs of long years of social deprivation.

A committee is formed to decide the fate of Johnny Rocco. The chairperson of the meeting is Johnny's supervisor and should begin by assigning roles to the group members. These roles [shop steward (representing the union), head of production, Johnny's co-worker, director of personnel, and social worker who helped Johnny in the past] represent points of view the chairperson believes should be included in this meeting. (Johnny is not to be included.) Two observers should also be assigned. Thus, each group will have eight members.

Instructions

After roles have been assigned, each role player should complete the personal preference part of the work sheet, ranking from 1 to 11 the alternatives according to their appropriateness from the vantage point of his or her role.

Once the individual preferences have been determined, the chairperson should call the meeting to order. The following rules govern the meeting: (1) The group must reach a consensus ranking of the alternatives; (2) the group cannot use a statistical aggregation, or majority vote, decision-making process; (3) members should stay "in character" throughout the discussion. Treat this as a committee meeting consisting of members with different backgrounds, orientation, and interests who share a problem.

After the group has completed the assignment, the observers should conduct a discussion of the group process, using the Group Effectiveness Questions here as a guide. Group members should not look at these questions until after the group task has been completed.

Group Effectiveness Questions

A. Referring to Table 12–3, what task roles were performed? By whom?

B. What maintenance roles were performed? By whom?

C. Were any important task or maintenance roles ignored? Which?

D. Was there any evidence of the Asch effect, groupthink, or social loafing? Explain.

Questions for Discussion

1. Did your committee do a good job? Explain.

2. What, if anything, should have been done differently?

3. How much similarity in rankings is there among the different groups in your class? What group dynamics apparently were responsible for any variations in rankings?

Worksheet

Personal Preference	Group Discussion	
___	___	Warn Johnny that at the next sign of trouble he will be fired.
___	___	Do nothing, as it is unclear if Johnny did anything wrong.
___	___	Create strict controls (do's and don'ts) for Johnny with immediate strong punishment for any misbehavior.
___	___	Give Johnny a great deal of warmth and personal attention and affection (overlooking his present behavior) so he can learn to depend on others.
___	___	Fire him. It's not worth the time and effort spent for such a low-level position.
___	___	Talk over the problem with Johnny in an understanding way so he can learn to ask others for help in solving his problems.
___	___	Give Johnny a well-structured schedule of daily activities with immediate and unpleasant consequences for not adhering to the schedule.
___	___	Do nothing now, but watch him carefully and provide immediate punishment for any future behavior.
___	___	Treat Johnny the same as everyone else, but provide an orderly routine so he can learn to stand on his own two feet.
___	___	Call Johnny in and logically discuss the problem with him and ask what you can do to help him.
___	___	Do nothing now, but watch him so you can reward him the next time he does something good.

Chapter Thirteen

Teams and Teamwork for the 21st Century

Learning Objectives

When you finish studying the material in this chapter, you should be able to:

1 Explain how a work group becomes a team.

2 Identify and describe the four types of work teams.

3 Explain the ecological model of work team effectiveness.

4 Discuss why teams fail.

5 List at least three things managers can do to build trust.

6 Distinguish two types of group cohesiveness, and summarize cohesiveness research findings.

7 Define quality circles, virtual teams, and self-managed teams.

8 Discuss what must be done to set the stage for self-managed teams.

9 Describe high-performance teams.

St. Louis—At Monsanto Co. headquarters here, Frederick Perlak and Kevin Holloway are "box buddies." They work in adjoining cubicles, share a secretary and spend hours keeping each other posted about what's happening with the company's global cotton team, which they oversee as co-directors.

"Often I'll lean over from my cubicle and say, 'Kevin, did you get this mail message? Have you discussed this? What did you guys decide on this?' " Dr Perlak says. Adds Mr Holloway, "It's not unusual we'll call each other at home or spend time together after hours."

Monsanto's three-year-old buddy system, known internally as "two in the box," pairs a scientist with a marketing or financial specialist in dozens of critical management positions. In the company's giant agricultural sector, for instance, 30 pairs of box buddies lead most of the crop and geographic teams. In the cotton division, the 45-year-old Dr Perlak is a noted geneticist who has spent years researching bug-

resistant crops, while Mr Holloway, also 45, has a background in marketing, business and human resources.

Monsanto is betting this unusual structure will help it transform itself from a chemical conglomerate into a life-sciences powerhouse. By joining its commercial and research-and-development sides at the head, the company is seeking a jump-start in developing break-through genetic technologies and bringing them to market before competitors.

Robert B. Shapiro,
Monsanto Co., chairman
and CEO.

Chairman and CEO Robert B Shapiro, the champion of two in the box, believes that any competitive edge Monsanto gains over its biotech rivals derives from just how effectively the R&D and commercial staffs work together. "We want to be creative, and we want to be fast," he says.

The fortunes of the paired individuals rise and fall together: Box buddies earn the same pay and benefits, including bonuses.

As co-equals, Messrs Perlak and Holloway together make the key marketing and business decisions on global cotton matters. Twenty-seven associates report to them. "I'm never going to be a financial analyst or an MBA, and Kevin's most likely not ever going to be a molecular biologist. But our diversity of experience really makes us more effective because we can look at problems from very different perspectives," says Dr Perlak, sitting next to his box buddy. The men are wearing identical dark-green sweaters with "Global Cotton Team" emblazoned on them.

"We're two people doing one job, not doing the same job, so we try not to step over each other," he adds. For instance, they try not to attend the same meetings, so Mr Holloway may attend a marketing presentation while Dr Perlak takes in a discussion about teaming up with a seed company. They then compare notes and decide which key decisions they must make jointly. . . .

In between meetings, they huddle for updates and align on positions to take in meetings that affect the cotton business. At day's end, they huddle again to share ideas, counsel each other and respond to electronic mail.

If either man is unavailable when a critical issue arises, the other makes the decision. "We don't want to hamper ourselves in the marketplace by not being able to make quick decisions," says Mr Holloway. "It's not paralysis through analysis here." That was especially important last year, when Dr Perlak spent about three months out of town testifying in three court cases for Monsanto. While they communicated by phone or e-mail, Mr Holloway still had to take the lead on several important matters.

When they disagree, the weight falls on whoever has the expertise. . . .

Mr Shapiro expresses some surprise at how well two in the box is working, noting that most box buddies "are strong personalities with powerful track records and, in many cases, with pretty large and not unreasonable ambitions." One concern, he says: "To what extent will the system be really collaborative, and to what extent will rivalry develop?"[1]

> **FOR DISCUSSION**
> What is the likelihood of other big companies adopting this two-in-the-box approach to teamwork? Explain.

Teams and *teamwork* are popular terms in management circles these days. Cynics might dismiss teamwork as just another management fad or quick-fix gimmick. But a closer look reveals a more profound and durable trend. For instance, former English professor Martin Jack Rosenblum finds fulfillment in Harley-Davidson's motorcycle operations where teamwork is a central feature:

What Rosenblum found at Harley was camaraderie, teamwork, and the sense of accomplishment that made him feel like a contributor to his microcosm. Says Rosenblum, a bearded long-hair who likes to wear snakeskin boots and cowboy shirts to his job as the archivist at Harley's Milwaukee headquarters: "For the first time in my life I feel like I'm part of a community. Harley is the university I've always been looking for."

When Rosenblum was a professor at the University of Wisconsin, he hated all the politics and backstabbing and despaired at all the ineffectual intellectual banter. It was, he says, diametrically opposed to effective teamwork. During those years in the 1980s, he developed an ulcer that nearly killed him. But once he found a more open, goal-oriented environment at Harley, his life improved.[2]

The team approach to managing organizations is having diverse and substantial impacts on organizations and individuals. Teams promise to be a cornerstone of progressive management for the foreseeable future. According to management expert Peter Drucker, tomorrow's organizations will be flatter, information based, and organized around teams.[3] This means virtually all employees will need to polish their team skills. Southwest Airlines, a company that credits a strong team spirit for its success, puts team skills above all else. Case in point:

> Southwest rejected a top pilot from another airline who did stunt work for movie studios because he was rude to a receptionist. Southwest believes that technical skills are easier to acquire than a teamwork and service attitude.[4]

Fortunately, the trend toward teams has a receptive audience today. Both women and younger employees, according to recent studies, thrive in team-oriented organizations.[5]

Examples of the trend toward teams and teamwork abound. Consider this global sampling from the business press:

- *Siemens, the $63-billion-a-year German manufacturing company:* ". . . a new generation of managers is fostering cooperation across the company: They are setting up teams to develop products and attack new markets. They are trying hiking expeditions and weekend workshops to spur ideas and new work methods."[6]

- *Motorola's walkie-talkie plants in Penang, Malaysia, and Plantation, Florida:* "The goal, pursued by Motorola worldwide, is to get employees at all levels to forget narrow job titles and work together in teams to identify and act on problems that hinder quality and productivity. . . . New applicants are screened on the basis of their attitude toward 'teamwork.' "[7]

- *Fiat's new auto plant in Melfi, Italy:* "Fiat slashed the layers between plant managers and workers and spent $64 million training its 7,000 workers and engineers to work in small teams. Now, the 31 independent teams—with 15 to 100 workers apiece—oversee car-assembly tasks from start to finish."[8]

When you buy a new Saturn automobile, you're getting more than a form of transportation. You're getting the product of an incredible amount of *teamwork* in the design, assembly, and marketing of your new vehicle.

(Kevin Horan/Tony Stone Images)

Table 13–1   *The Evolution of a Team*

A work group becomes a team when

1. *Leadership* becomes a shared activity.
2. *Accountability* shifts from strictly individual to both individual and collective.
3. The group develops its own *purpose* or mission.
4. *Problem solving* becomes a way of life, not a part-time activity.
5. *Effectiveness* is measured by the group's collective outcomes and products.

SOURCE: Condensed and adapted from J R Katzenbach and D K Smith, *The Wisdom of Teams: Creating the High-Performance Organization* (New York: HarperBusiness, 1999), p 214.

- *Ford Motor Company's product-development Web site:* "The Web brings 4,500 Ford engineers from labs in the United States, Germany, and England together in cyberspace to collaborate on projects. The idea is to break down the barriers between regional operations so basic auto components are designed once and used everywhere."[9]

All of these huge global companies have staked their future competitiveness on teams and teamwork.

Emphasis in this chapter is on tapping the full and promising potential of work groups. We will (1) identify different types of work teams, (2) introduce a model of team effectiveness, (3) discuss keys to effective teamwork—such as trust, (4) explore applications of the team concept, and (5) review team-building techniques.

Work Teams: Types, Effectiveness, and Stumbling Blocks

Team

Small group with complementary skills who hold themselves mutually accountable for common purpose, goals, and approach.

Jon R Katzenbach and Douglas K Smith, management consultants at McKinsey & Company, say it is a mistake to use the terms *group* and *team* interchangeably. After studying many different kinds of teams—from athletic to corporate to military—they concluded that successful teams tend to take on a life of their own. Katzenbach and Smith define a **team** as "a small number of people with complementary skills who are committed to a common purpose, performance goals, and approach for which they hold themselves mutually accountable."[10] Relative to Tuckman's theory of group development in Chapter 12—forming, storming, norming, performing, and adjourning—teams are task groups that have matured to the *performing* stage (but not slipped into decay). Because of conflicts over power and authority and unstable interpersonal relations, many work groups never qualify as a real team.[11] Katzenbach and Smith clarified the distinction this way: "The essence of a team is common commitment. Without it, groups perform as individuals; with it, they become a powerful unit of collective performance."[12] (See Table 13–1.)

When Katzenbach and Smith refer to "a small number of people" in their definition, they mean between 2 and 25 team members. They found effective teams to typically have fewer than 10 members. This conclusion was echoed in a survey of 400 workplace team members in the United States and Canada: "The average North American team consists of 10 members. Eight is the most common size."[13]

Table 13–2   *Four General Types of Work Teams and Their Outputs*

Types and Examples	Degree of Technical Specialization	Degree of Coordination with Other Work Units	Work Cycles	Typical Outputs
Advice Committees Review panels, boards Quality circles Employee involvement groups Advisory councils	Low	Low	Work cycles can be brief or long; one cycle can be team life span.	Decisions Selections Suggestions Proposals Recommendations
Production Assembly teams Manufacturing crews Mining teams Flight attendant crews Data processing groups Maintenance crews	Low	High	Work cycles typically repeated or continuous process; cycles often briefer than team life span.	Food, chemicals Components Assemblies Retail sales Customer service Equipment repairs
Project Research groups Planning teams Architect teams Engineering teams Development teams Task forces	High	Low (for traditional units) or High (for cross-functional units)	Work cycles typically differ for each new project; one cycle can be team life span.	Plans, designs Investigations Presentations Prototypes Reports, findings
Action Sports team Entertainment groups Expeditions Negotiating teams Surgery teams Cockpit crews Military platoons and squads	High	High	Brief performance events, often repeated under new conditions, requiring extended training and/or preparation.	Combat missions Expeditions Contracts, lawsuits Concerts Surgical operations Competitive events

SOURCE: Excerpted and adapted from E Sundstrom, K P De Meuse, and D Futrell, "Work Teams," *American Psychologist*, February 1990, p 125.

A General Typology of Work Teams

Work teams are created for various purposes and thus face different challenges. Managers can deal more effectively with those challenges when they understand how teams differ. A helpful way of sorting things out is to consider a typology of work teams developed by Eric Sundstrom and his colleagues.[14] Four general types of work teams listed in Table 13–2 are (1) advice, (2) production, (3) project, and (4) action. Each of these labels identifies a basic *purpose*. For instance, advice teams generally make recommendations for managerial decisions. Less commonly do they actually make final decisions. In contrast, production and action teams carry out management's decisions.

Four key variables in Table 13–2 deal with technical specialization, coordination, work cycles, and outputs. Technical specialization is low when the team draws upon members' general experience and problem-solving ability. It is high when team members are required to apply technical skills acquired through higher education and/or extensive training. The degree of coordination with other work units is determined by the team's relative independence (low coordination) or interdependence (high coordination). Work cycles are the amount of time teams need to discharge their missions. The various outputs listed in Table 13–2 are intended to illustrate real-life impacts. A closer look at each type of work team is in order.[15]

Advice Teams   As their name implies, advice teams are created to broaden the information base for managerial decisions. Quality circles, discussed later, are a prime example because they facilitate suggestions for quality improvement from volunteer production or service workers. Advice teams tend to have a low degree of technical specialization. Coordination also is low because advice teams work pretty much on their own. Ad hoc committees (e.g., the annual picnic committee) have shorter life cycles than standing committees (e.g., the grievance committee).

Production Teams   This second type of team is responsible for performing day-to-day operations. Minimal training for routine tasks accounts for the low degree of technical specialization. But coordination typically is high because work flows from one team to another. For example, railroad maintenance crews require fresh information about needed repairs from train crews.

Project Teams   Projects require creative problem solving, often involving the application of specialized knowledge. For example, Boeing's new 777 jumbo jet was designed by project teams consisting of engineering, manufacturing, marketing, finance, and customer service specialists. State-of-the-art computer modeling programs allowed the teams to assemble three-dimensional computer models of the new aircraft. Design and assembly problems were ironed out in project team meetings before production workers started cutting any metal for the first 777. Boeing's 777 design teams required a high degree of coordination among organizational subunits because they were cross functional.[16] A pharmaceutical research team of biochemists, on the other hand, would interact less with other work units because it is relatively self-contained.

Action Teams   This last type of team is best exemplified by a baseball team. High specialization is combined with high coordination. Nine highly trained athletes play specialized defensive positions. But good defensive play is not

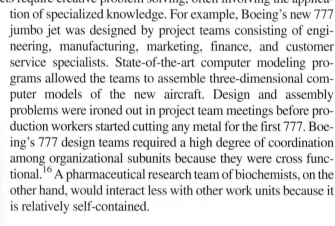

Thanks to the strong team spirit emphasized by Major League Baseball veterans Jay Bell and Matt Williams, the Arizona Diamondbacks won a division pennant in only their second year of existence.

(Reuters/Jeff Topping/Archive Photos)

enough because effective hitting is necessary. Moreover, coordination between the manager, base runners, base coaches, and the bull pen needs to be precise. So it is with airline cockpit crews, hospital surgery teams, mountain-climbing expeditions, rock music groups, labor contract negotiating teams, and police SWAT teams, among others. A unique challenge for action teams is to exhibit peak performance on demand.[17]

This four-way typology of work teams is dynamic and changing, not static. Some teams evolve from one type to another. Other teams represent a combination of types. For example, consider the work of a team at General Foods: "The company launched a line of ready-to-eat desserts by setting up a team of nine people with the freedom to operate like entrepreneurs starting their own business. The team even had to oversee construction of a factory with the technology required to manufacture their product."[18] This particular team was a combination advice-project-action team. In short, the General Foods team did everything but manufacture the end product themselves (that was done by production teams).

Work Team Effectiveness: An Ecological Model

The effectiveness of athletic teams is a straightforward matter of wins and losses. Things become more complicated, however, when the focus shifts to work teams in today's organizations.[19] Figure 13–1 lists two effectiveness criteria for work teams: performance and viability. According to Sundstrom and his colleagues: "*Performance* means acceptability of output to customers within or outside the organization who receive team products, services, information, decisions, or performance events (such as presentations or competitions)."[20] While the foregoing relates to satisfying the needs and expectations of outsiders such as clients, customers, and fans, another team-effectiveness criterion arises. Namely, **team viability,** defined as team member satisfaction and continued willingness to contribute. Are the team members better or worse off for having contributed

Team viability
Team members satisfied and willing to contribute.

Figure 13–1   *An Ecological Model of Work Team Effectiveness*

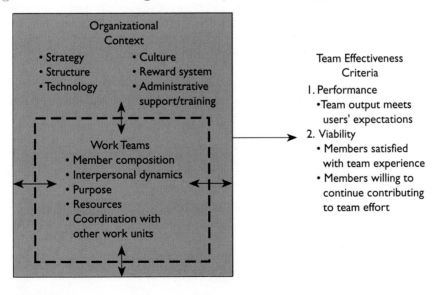

SOURCE: Adapted in part from E Sundstrom, K P De Meuse, and D Futrell, "Work Teams," *American Psychologist,* February 1990, pp 120–33.

to the team effort? A work team is not truly effective if it gets the job done but self-destructs in the process or burns everyone out.

Figure 13–1 is an *ecological* model because it portrays work teams within their organizational environment. In keeping with the true meaning of the word *ecology*—the study of interactions between organisms and their environments—this model emphasizes that work teams need an organizational life-support system. Six critical organizational context variables are listed in Figure 13–1. Work teams have a much greater chance of being effective if they are nurtured and facilitated by the organization. The team's purpose needs to be in concert with the organization's strategy. Similarly, team participation and autonomy require an organizational culture that values those processes. Team members also need appropriate technological tools and training. Teamwork needs to be reinforced by the organizational reward system. Such is not the case when pay and bonuses are tied solely to individual output.

Table 13–3   *Characteristics of an Effective Team*

1. Clear purpose	The vision, mission, goal, or task of the team has been defined and is now accepted by everyone. There is an action plan.
2. Informality	The climate tends to be informal, comfortable, and relaxed. There are no obvious tensions or signs of boredom.
3. Participation	There is much discussion, and everyone is encouraged to participate.
4. Listening	The members use effective listening techniques such as questioning, paraphrasing, and summarizing to get out ideas.
5. Civilized disagreement	There is disagreement, but the team is comfortable with this and shows no signs of avoiding, smoothing over, or suppressing conflict.
6. Consensus decisions	For important decisions, the goal is substantial but not necessarily unanimous agreement through open discussion of everyone's ideas, avoidance of formal voting, or easy compromises.
7. Open communication	Team members feel free to express their feelings on the tasks as well as on the group's operation. There are few hidden agendas. Communication takes place outside of meetings.
8. Clear roles and work assignments	There are clear expectations about the roles played by each team member. When action is taken, clear assignments are made, accepted, and carried out. Work is fairly distributed among team members.
9. Shared leadership	While the team has a formal leader, leadership functions shift from time to time depending on the circumstances, the needs of the group, and the skills of the members. The formal leader models the appropriate behavior and helps establish positive norms.
10. External relations	The team spends time developing key outside relationships, mobilizing resources, and building credibility with important players in other parts of the organization.
11. Style diversity	The team has a broad spectrum of team-player types including members who emphasize attention to task, goal setting, focus on process, and questions about how the team is functioning.
12. Self-assessment	Periodically, the team stops to examine how well it is functioning and what may be interfering with its effectiveness.

SOURCE: G M Parker, *Team Players and Teamwork: The New Competitive Business Strategy* (San Francisco: Jossey-Bass, 1990), Table 2, p 33. Copyright © 1990 by Jossey-Bass Inc., Publishers. Reprinted by permission of John Wiley & Sons, Inc.

Regarding the internal processes of work teams, five important factors are listed in Figure 13–1. Table 13–3 contains an expanded list of characteristics of effective teams that can be useful for evaluating task teams both in school and on the job.[21]

Why Do Work Teams Fail?

Advocates of the team approach to management paint a very optimistic and bright picture. Yet there is a dark side to teams.[22] While exact statistics are not available, they can and often do fail. Anyone contemplating the use of team structures in the workplace needs a balanced perspective of advantages and limitations. One dissenting opinion comes from Gerald A Kraines, head of a major management consulting company, who "denounces trends toward employee empowerment and work teams."[23] In a recent exchange with *The Wall Street Journal,* Kraines offered this unconventional view:

> Q: Isn't hierarchy a dirty word these days?
>
> A: This is the greatest disservice that business schools and the business media have perpetrated on the public. They say hierarchies stifle initiative, creativity, and job fulfillment. They say work groups should form and dissolve flexibly, and without regard to accountability.
>
> The assumption is that employees would be so relieved to be freed from their chains of enslavement that they will act very responsibly and creatively. But they have been so discouraged, beaten, and demoralized that they essentially give up. Then the CEO says, "Poof, you're empowered." What people say, under their breath, is, "I haven't been empowered, I've been poofed."[24]

Team advocates may find these words harsh, but they challenge us to reject the myth that teams can magically replace traditional authority and accountability links. If teams are to be effective, both management and team members must make a concerted effort to think and do things differently.

Common Management Mistakes with Teams   The main threats to team effectiveness, according to the center of Figure 13–2 on p 420, are *unrealistic expectations* leading to *frustration.* Frustration, in turn, encourages people to abandon teams. Both managers and team members can be victimized by unrealistic expectations.[25]

On the left side of Figure 13–2 is a list of common management mistakes. These mistakes generally involve doing a poor job of creating a supportive environment for teams and teamwork. Recalling our discussion of team-based rewards in Chapter 9, reward plans that encourage individuals to compete with one another erode teamwork. As mentioned earlier, teams need a good organizational life-support system.

Problems for Team Members   The lower-right portion of Figure 13–2 lists common problems for team members. Contrary to critics' Theory X contention about employees lacking the motivation and creativity for real teamwork, it is common for teams to take on too much too quickly and to drive themselves too hard for fast results. Important group dynamics and team skills get lost in the rush for results. Consequently, team members' expectations need to be given a reality check by management and team members themselves. Also, teams need to be counseled against quitting when they run into an unanticipated obstacle. Failure is part of the learning process with teams, as it is elsewhere in life. Comprehensive training in interpersonal skills can prevent many common teamwork problems.

Additional insights lie ahead as we turn our attention to cooperation, trust, and cohesiveness.

Figure 13–2   *Why Work Teams Fail*

Mistakes typically made by management

- Teams cannot overcome weak strategies and poor business practices.
- Hostile environment for teams (command-and-control culture; competitive/individual reward plans; management resistance).
- Teams adopted as a fad, a quick-fix; no long-term commitment.
- Lessons from one team not transferred to others (limited experimentation with teams).
- Vague or conflicting team assignments.
- Inadequate team skills training.
- Poor staffing of teams.
- Lack of trust.

Unrealistic expectations resulting in frustration

Problems typically experienced by team members

- Team tries to do too much too soon.
- Conflict over differences in personal work styles (and/or personality conflicts).
- Too much emphasis on results, not enough on team processes and group dynamics.
- Unanticipated obstacle causes team to give up.
- Resistance to doing things differently.
- Poor interpersonal skills (aggressive rather than assertive communication, destructive conflict, win-lose negotiation).
- Poor interpersonal chemistry (loners, dominators, self-appointed experts do not fit in).
- Lack of trust.

SOURCES: Adapted from discussion in S R Rayner, "Team Traps: What They Are, How to Avoid Them," *National Productivity Review,* Summer 1996, pp 101–15; L Holpp and R Phillips, "When Is a Team Its Own Worst Enemy?" *Training,* September 1995, pp 71–82; and B Richardson, "Why Work Teams Flop—and What Can Be Done About It," *National Productivity Review,* Winter 1994/95, pp 9–13.

Effective Teamwork through Cooperation, Trust, and Cohesiveness

As competitive pressures intensify, experts say organizational success increasingly will depend on teamwork rather than individual stars. If this emphasis on teamwork has a familiar ring, it is because sports champions generally say they owe their success to it. For example, teamwork is paramount to Mike Krzyzewski, coach of the two-time National Champion Duke University men's basketball team. Here's a brief exchange during a recent recruiting talk by "Coach K:"

What makes your heart beat, a young man asks.

"I love interacting with people," Krzyzewski replies. "I love molding a team, getting them to be as one."[26]

Whether in the athletic arena or the world of business, three components of teamwork receiving the greatest attention are cooperation, trust, and cohesiveness. Let us explore the contributions each can make to effective teamwork.

Cooperation

Individuals are said to be cooperating when their efforts are systematically *integrated* to achieve a collective objective. The greater the integration, the greater the degree of cooperation.

Cooperation versus Competition   A widely held assumption among American managers is that "competition brings out the best in people." From an economic standpoint, business survival depends on staying ahead of the competition. But from an interpersonal standpoint, critics contend competition has been overemphasized, primarily at the expense of cooperation.[27] According to Alfie Kohn, a strong advocate of greater emphasis on cooperation in our classrooms, offices, and factories,

> My review of the evidence has convinced me that there are two … important reasons for competition's failure. First, success often depends on sharing resources efficiently, and this is nearly impossible when people have to work against one another. Cooperation takes advantage of all the skills represented in a group as well as the mysterious process by which that group becomes more than the sum of its parts. By contrast, competition makes people suspicious and hostile toward one another and actively discourages this process. . . .
>
> Second, competition generally does not promote excellence because trying to do well and trying to beat others simply are two different things. Consider a child in class, waving his arm wildly to attract the teacher's attention, crying, "Oooh! Oooh! Pick me!" When he is finally recognized, he seems befuddled. "Um, what was the question again?" he finally asks. His mind is focused on beating his classmates, not on the subject matter.[28]

Research Support for Cooperation   After conducting a meta-analysis of 122 studies encompassing a wide variety of subjects and settings, one team of researchers concluded that

1. Cooperation is superior to competition in promoting achievement and productivity.
2. Cooperation is superior to individualistic efforts in promoting achievement and productivity.
3. Cooperation without intergroup competition promotes higher achievement and productivity than cooperation with intergroup competition.[29]

Given the size and diversity of the research base, these findings strongly endorse cooperation in modern organizations. Cooperation can be encouraged by reward systems that reinforce teamwork, along with individual achievement.

Another study involving 84 male US Air Force trainees uncovered an encouraging link between cooperation and favorable race relations. After observing the subjects interact in three-man teams during a management game, the researchers concluded: "[Helpful] teammates, both black and white, attract greater respect and liking than do teammates who have not helped. This is particularly true when the helping occurs voluntarily."[30] These findings suggest that managers can enhance equal employment opportunity and diversity programs by encouraging *voluntary* helping behavior in interracial work teams. Accordingly, it is reasonable to conclude that voluntary helping behavior could build cooperation in mixed-gender teams and groups as well.

A more recent study involving 72 health care professionals in a US Veterans Affairs Medical Center found a negative correlation between cooperation and team size. In other words, cooperation diminished as the health care team became larger.[31] Managers thus need to restrict the size of work teams if they desire to facilitate cooperation.

Trust

These have not been good times for trust in the corporate world. Years of mergers, downsizings, layoffs, bloated executive bonuses, and broken promises have left many employees justly cynical about trusting management. After conducting a series of annual workplace surveys, one management consultant recently concluded: "Trust in corporate America is at a low point."[32] Clearly, managers need to take constructive action to close what *Fortune* magazine has called "the trust gap."[33] General Electric's Jack Welch framed the challenge this way:

> Trust is enormously powerful in a corporation. People won't do their best unless they believe they'll be treated fairly—that there's no cronyism and everybody has a real shot. The only way I know to create that kind of trust is by laying out your values and then walking the talk. You've got to do what you say you'll do, consistently, over time.[34]

One encouraging sign: Interest in the topic of trust has blossomed recently in the management literature.[35]

In this section, we examine the concept of trust and introduce six practical guidelines for building trust.

Trust
Reciprocal faith in others' intentions and behavior.

A Cognitive Leap   **Trust** is defined as reciprocal faith in others' intentions and behavior.[36] Experts on the subject explain the reciprocal (give-and-take) aspect of trust as follows:

> When we see others acting in ways that imply that they trust us, we become more disposed to reciprocate by trusting in them more. Conversely, we come to distrust those whose actions appear to violate our trust or to distrust us.[37]

In short, we tend to give what we get: trust begets trust; distrust begets distrust.

Propensity to trust
A personality trait involving one's general willingness to trust others.

A newer model of organizational trust includes a personality trait called **propensity to trust.** The developers of the model explain:

> Propensity might be thought of as the *general willingness to trust others*. Propensity will influence how much trust one has for a trustee prior to data on that particular party being available. People with different developmental experiences, personality types, and cultural backgrounds vary in their propensity to trust. . . . An example of an extreme case of this is what is commonly called blind trust. Some individuals can be observed to repeatedly trust in situations that most people would agree do not warrant trust. Conversely, others are unwilling to trust in most situations, regardless of circumstances that would support doing so.[38]

What is your propensity to trust? How did you develop that personality trait? (See the trust questionnaire in the Personal Awareness and Growth Exercise at the end of this chapter.)

Trust involves "a cognitive 'leap' beyond the expectations that reason and experience alone would warrant"[39] (see Figure 13–3). For example, suppose a member of a newly formed class project team works hard, based on the assumption that her teammates also are working hard. That assumption, on which her trust is based, is a cognitive leap that goes beyond her actual experience with her teammates. When you trust someone, you have *faith* in their good intentions. The act of trusting someone, however, carries with it the inherent risk of betrayal.[40] Progressive managers believe that the benefits of interpersonal trust far outweigh any risks of betrayed trust. For example, Michael Powell, who founded the chain of bookstores bearing his name more than 25 years ago, built his business around the principles of open-book management, empowerment, and trust. Powell's propensity to trust was sorely tested when one of his employees stole more than $60,000 in a used book purchasing scheme. After putting in some accounting safeguards, Powell's propensity to trust remains intact. He observed:

Figure 13–3   *Interpersonal Trust Involves a Cognitive Leap*

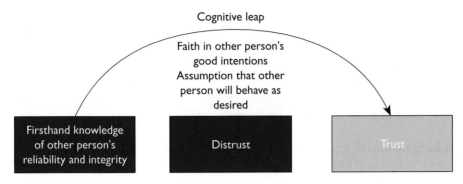

The incident was a watershed for me and my staff, dispelling any naïveté we may have had about crime. We realized that not only *can* theft happen; it *will* happen. At the same time, dealing with the matter forced us to revisit our basic values and managerial philosophies. We believe that the modern demands of business call for an empowered and fully flexible staff, and we know that such a staff will often have to handle valuable commodities and money. We also believe that most people are not going to abuse our trust if they are put in a position with a reasonable amount of review and responsibility.[41]

How to Build Trust   Management professor/consultant Fernando Bartolomé offers the following six guidelines for building and maintaining trust:

1. *Communication.* Keep team members and employees informed by explaining policies and decisions and providing accurate feedback. Be candid about one's own problems and limitations. Tell the truth.[42]

2. *Support.* Be available and approachable. Provide help, advice, coaching, and support for team members' ideas.

3. *Respect.* Delegation, in the form of real decision-making authority, is the most important expression of managerial respect. Actively listening to the ideas of others is a close second. (Empowerment is not possible without trust.)[43]

4. *Fairness.* Be quick to give credit and recognition to those who deserve it. Make sure all performance appraisals and evaluations are objective and impartial.[44]

5. *Predictability.* As mentioned previously, be consistent and predictable in your daily affairs. Keep both expressed and implied promises.

6. *Competence.* Enhance your credibility by demonstrating good business sense, technical ability, and professionalism.[45]

Trust needs to be earned; it cannot be demanded.

Ethics at Work

Karen Stephenson, Anthropologist and UCLA management professor:

How do we create networks of trust that allow for diversity? As an anthropologist, I've learned that, primordially, trust is formed around the campfire. Trust is all about homogeneity: You look like me, you dress like me, you talk like me—I can trust you. But today, if I'm going to learn something new, I've got to trust people who are different from me—and that means diversity. Not diversity for reasons of political correctness, but for reasons of innovation. The challenge today is to build networks of diversity that fuel innovation, even when our primordial instincts tell us otherwise.

Source: "Fast Pack 1999," *Fast Company,* February–March 1999, p 148.

You Decide . . .

How can you, as a manager, build trust among work teams of women and men from diverse cultural, racial, ethnic, and religious backgrounds?

For an interpretation of this situation, visit our Web site **www.mhhe.com/kreitner.**

Cohesiveness

Cohesiveness
A sense of "we-ness"
helps group stick
together.

Cohesiveness is a process whereby "a sense of 'we-ness' emerges to transcend individual differences and motives."[46] Members of a cohesive group stick together. They are reluctant to leave the group. Cohesive group members stick together for one or both of the following reasons: (1) because they enjoy each others' company or (2) because they need each other to accomplish a common goal. Accordingly, two types of group cohesiveness, identified by sociologists, are socio-emotional cohesiveness and instrumental cohesiveness.[47]

**Socio-emotional
cohesiveness**
Sense of togetherness
based on emotional
satisfaction.

**Instrumental
cohesiveness**
Sense of togetherness
based on mutual
dependency needed to
get the job done.

Socio-Emotional and Instrumental Cohesiveness **Socio-emotional cohesiveness** is a sense of togetherness that develops when individuals derive emotional satisfaction from group participation. Most general discussions of group cohesiveness are limited to this type. However, from the standpoint of getting things accomplished in task groups and teams, we cannot afford to ignore instrumental cohesiveness. **Instrumental cohesiveness** is a sense of togetherness that develops when group members are mutually dependent on one another because they believe they could not achieve the group's goal by acting separately. A feeling of "we-ness" is *instrumental* in achieving the common goal. Team advocates generally assume both types of cohesiveness are essential to productive teamwork. But is this really true?

Lessons from Group Cohesiveness Research What is the connection between group cohesiveness and performance? A landmark meta-analysis of 49 studies involving 8,702 subjects provided these insights:

- There is a small but statistically significant cohesiveness→performance effect.
- The cohesiveness→performance effect was stronger for smaller and real groups (as opposed to contrived groups in laboratory studies).
- The cohesiveness→performance effect becomes stronger as one moves from non-military real groups to military groups to sports teams.
- Commitment to the task at hand (meaning the individual sees the performance standards as legitimate) has the most powerful impact on the cohesiveness→performance linkage.
- The *performance→cohesiveness* linkage is stronger than the cohesiveness→performance linkage. Thus, success tends to bind group or team members together rather than closely knit groups being more successful.
- Contrary to the popular view, cohesiveness is not "a 'lubricant' that minimizes friction due to the human 'grit' in the system."[48]
- All this evidence led the researchers to this practical conclusion: "Efforts to enhance group performance by fostering interpersonal attraction or 'pumping up' group pride are not likely to be effective."[49]

A second meta-analysis found no significant relationship between cohesiveness and the quality of group decisions. However, support was found for Janis's contention that *groupthink* tends to afflict cohesive in-groups with strong leadership. Groups whose members liked each other a great deal tended to make poorer quality decisions.[50]

Getting Some Positive Impact from Group Cohesiveness Research tells us that group cohesiveness is no "secret weapon" in the quest for improved group or team performance. The trick is to keep task groups small, make sure performance stan-

Table 13–4   *Steps Managers Can Take to Enhance the Two Types of Group Cohesiveness*

Socio-Emotional Cohesiveness

Keep the group relatively small.

Strive for a favorable public image to increase the status and prestige of belonging.

Encourage interaction and cooperation.

Emphasize members' common characteristics and interests.

Point out environmental threats (e.g., competitors' achievements) to rally the group.

Instrumental Cohesiveness

Regularly update and clarify the group's goal(s).

Give every group member a vital "piece of the action."

Channel each group member's special talents toward the common goal(s).

Recognize and equitably reinforce every member's contributions.

Frequently remind group members they need each other to get the job done.

dards and goals are clear and accepted, achieve some early successes, and follow the tips in Table 13–4. A good example is Westinghouse's highly automated military radar electronics plant in College Station, Texas. Compared with their counterparts at a traditional factory in Baltimore, each of the Texas plant's 500 employees produces eight times more, at half the per-unit cost:

> The key, says Westinghouse, is not the robots but the people. Employees work in teams of 8 to 12. Members devise their own solutions to problems. Teams measure daily how each person's performance compares with that of other members and how the team's performance compares with the plant's. Joseph L Johnson, 28, a robotics technician, says that is a big change from a previous hourly factory job where he cared only about "picking up my paycheck." Here, peer pressure "makes sure you get the job done."[51]

Self-selected work teams (in which people pick their own teammates) and off-the-job social events can stimulate socio-emotional cohesiveness.[52] The fostering of socio-emotional cohesiveness needs to be balanced with instrumental cohesiveness. The latter can be encouraged by making sure everyone in the group recognizes and appreciates each member's vital contribution to the group goal. While balancing the two types of cohesiveness, managers need to remember that groupthink theory and research cautions against too much cohesiveness.

Teams in Action: Quality Circles, Virtual Teams, and Self-Managed Teams

All sorts of interesting approaches to teams and teamwork can be found in the workplace today. A great deal of experimentation is taking place as organizations struggle to be more flexible and responsive. New information technologies also have spurred experimentation with team formats. This section profiles three different approaches to teams: quality circles, virtual teams, and self-managed teams. We have selected these particular types of teams for three reasons: (1) They have recognizable labels. (2) They have at least some research evidence. (3) They range from low to mixed to high degrees of empowerment (refer to Figure 16–2 in Chapter 16).

Table 13–5 *Basic Distinctions among Quality Circles, Virtual Teams, and Self-Managed Teams*

	Quality Circles	Virtual Teams	Self-Managed Teams
Type of team (see Table 13–2)	Advice	Advice or project (usually project)	Production, project, or action
Type of empowerment (see Figure 16–2)	Consultation	Consultation, participation, or delegation	Delegation
Members	Production/service personnel	Managers and technical specialists	Production/service, technical specialists
Basis of membership	Voluntary	Assigned (some voluntary)	Assigned
Relationship to organization structure	Parallel	Parallel or integrated	Integrated
Amount of face-to-face communication	Strictly face to face	Periodic to none	Varies, depending on use of information technology

As indicated in Table 13–5, the three types of teams are distinct, but not totally unique. Overlaps exist. For instance, computer-networked virtual teams may or may not have volunteer members and may or may not be self-managed. Another point of overlap involves the fifth variable in Table 13–5: relationship to organization structure. Quality circles are called *parallel* structures because they exist outside normal channels of authority and communication.[53] Self-managed teams, on the other hand, are *integrated* into the basic organizational structure. Virtual teams vary in this regard, although they tend to be parallel because they are made up of functional specialists (engineers, accountants, marketers, etc.) who team up on temporary projects. Keeping these basic distinctions in mind, let us explore quality circles, virtual teams, and self-managed teams.

Quality Circles

Quality circles

Small groups of volunteers who strive to solve quality-related problems.

Quality circles are small groups of people from the same work area who voluntarily get together to identify, analyze, and recommend solutions for problems related to quality, productivity, and cost reduction. Some prefer the term *quality control circles*. With an ideal size of 10 to 12 members, they typically meet for about 60 to 90 minutes on a regular basis. Some companies allow meetings during work hours, others encourage quality circles to meet after work on employees' time. Once a week or twice a month are common schedules. Management facilitates the quality circle program through skills training and listening to periodic presentations of recommendations. Monetary rewards for suggestions tend to be the exception rather than the rule. Intrinsic motivation, derived from learning new skills and meaningful participation, is the primary payoff for quality circle volunteers.

The Quality Circle Movement   American quality control experts helped introduce the basic idea of quality circles to Japanese industry soon after World War II. The idea eventually returned to the United States and reached fad proportions during the 1970s and 1980s. Proponents made zealous claims about how quality circles were the key to higher productivity, lower costs, employee development, and improved job attitudes. At its zenith during the mid-1980s, the quality circle movement claimed millions of employee participants around the world.[54] Hundreds of US companies and government agencies adopted the idea under a variety of labels.[55] Dramatic growth of quality circles in the United States was attributed to (1) a desire to replicate Japan's industrial success, (2) America's penchant for business fads, and (3) the relative ease of installing quality circles without restructuring the organization.[56] All too often, however, early enthusiasm gave way to disappointment, apathy, and abandonment.[57]

But quality circles, if properly administered and supported by management, can be much more than a management fad seemingly past its prime. According to USC researchers Edward E Lawler and Susan A Mohrman, "quality circles can be an important first step toward organizational effectiveness through employee involvement."[58]

Insights from Field Research on Quality Circles   There is a body of objective field research on quality circles. Still, much of what we know comes from testimonials and case histories from managers and consultants who have a vested interest in demonstrating the technique's success. Although documented failures are scarce, one expert concluded that quality circles have failure rates of more than 60%.[59] Poor implementation is probably more at fault than the quality circle concept itself.[60]

To date, field research on quality circles has been inconclusive. Lack of standardized variables is the main problem, as it typically is when comparing the results of field studies.[61] Team participation programs of all sizes and shapes have been called quality circles. Here's what we have learned to date. A case study of military and civilian personnel at a US Air Force base found a positive relationship between quality circle participation and desire to continue working for the organization. The observed effect on job performance was slight. A longitudinal study spanning 24 months revealed that quality circles had only a marginal impact on employee attitudes but had a positive impact on productivity. In a more recent study, utility company employees who participated in quality circles received significantly better job performance ratings and were promoted more frequently than nonparticipants. This suggests that quality circles live up to their billing as a good employee development technique.[62]

Overall, quality circles are a promising participative management tool, *if they are carefully implemented and supported by all levels of management.*

Virtual Teams

Virtual teams are a product of modern times. They take their name from *virtual reality* computer simulations, where "it's almost like the real thing." Thanks to evolving information technologies such as the Internet, E-mail, videoconferencing, groupware, and fax machines, you can be a member of a work team without really being there.[63] Traditional team meetings are location specific. Team members are either physically present or absent. Virtual teams, in contrast, convene electronically with members reporting in from different locations, different organizations, and even different time zones (see the International OB, p 428).

Because virtual teams are so new, there is no consensual definition. Our working definition of a **virtual team** is a physically dispersed task group that conducts its business through modern information technology.[64] Advocates say virtual teams are very flexible and efficient because they are driven by information and skills, not by time and location. People with needed information and/or skills can be team members, regardless of where or when they actually do their work. On the negative side, lack of face-to-face interaction can weaken trust, communication, and accountability.

Virtual team
Information technology allows group members in different locations to conduct business.

International OB   A Virtual Shell Game for the Seven-Time-Zone Team

About the time the sun starts to go down in the Netherlands, Russ Conser's workday kicks into high gear. As a member of a team responsible for evaluating business opportunities for Shell Technology Ventures, a subsidiary of the oil giant Royal Dutch/Shell, Conser has been helping set up an office near The Hague. Thus far, much of his work has focused on hiring staff and figuring out the logistics of how to get the work done.

What often complicates Conser's day isn't so much the challenges that go along with opening a new office, it's keeping up with his team members—about half of whom are seven time zones away in Houston.

Conser and his colleagues rely heavily on E-mail and videoconferences to communicate with one another. But getting the right message to the right people on both sides of the Atlantic hasn't been easy. "We routinely find out we're miscommunicating, that we forgot to inform a person in the loop, that some people had different expectations as to what's going to happen," he says.

The time difference adds another wrinkle. "We have about a three-hour window each day when we can interact in real time," he explains. Consequently, phone conversations often extend into the night, when the Houston staff is at the office. Other times, the team members in the Netherlands have to wait until the sun comes up in Houston to get information they need. "When they get back to us, we've lost another day on the calendar," says Conser, who has been in the Netherlands since August.

Conser isn't alone in his struggle to communicate with colleagues an ocean away. Rather, he is part of a growing community of people who work as members of "virtual" teams, separated by time, distance, culture and organizational boundaries.

SOURCE: K Kiser, "Working on World Time," *Training*, March 1999, pp 29–30. Reprinted with permission from the March 1999 issue of Training magazine. Copyright © 1999, Lakewood Publications, Minneapolis, MN. All rights reserved. Not for resale.

Research Insights   As one might expect with a new and ill-defined area, research evidence to date is a bit spotty. Here is what we have learned so far from recent studies of computer-mediated groups:

- Virtual groups formed over the Internet follow a group development process similar to that for face-to-face groups.[65] (Recall or discussion of Tuckman's model in Chapter 12.)

- Internet chat rooms create more work and yield poorer decisions than face-to-face meetings and telephone conferences.[66]

- Successful use of groupware (software that facilitates interaction among virtual group members) requires training and hands-on experience.[67]

- Inspirational leadership has a positive impact on creativity in electronic brainstorming groups.[68]

Practical Considerations   Virtual teams may be in fashion, but they are not a cure-all. In fact, they may be a giant step backward for those not well versed in modern information technology. Managers who rely on virtual teams agree on one point: *Meaningful face-to-face contact, especially during early phases of the group development process, is absolutely essential.* Virtual group members need "faces" in their minds to go with names and electronic messages (see the OB in Action Case Study at the end of this chapter). Additionally, virtual teams cannot succeed without some old-fashioned factors such as top-management support, hands-on training, a clear mission and specific objectives, effective leadership, and schedules and deadlines.[69]

Self-Managed Teams

Have you ever thought you could do a better job than your boss? Well, if the trend toward self-managed work teams continues to grow as predicted, you just may get your chance. Entrepreneurs and artisans often boast of not having a supervisor. The same generally cannot be said for employees working in organizational offices and factories. But things are changing. In fact, an estimated half of the employees at *Fortune* 500 companies are working on teams.[70] A growing share of those teams are self-managing, as exemplified by the following situations:

> At a General Mills cereal plant in Lodi, California, teams … schedule, operate, and maintain machinery so effectively that the factory runs with no managers present during the night shift.[71]
>
> [Teams of United Steel Worker's Union members] run Inland Steel Industries Inc. and Nippon Steel Corp.'s $1.1 billion joint venture in New Carlisle, Indiana—with no foremen. Workers share profits and production bonuses, and all make the same pay—about $50,000.[72]

At Texas Instruments' electronics factory near Kuala Lumpur, Malaysia, quality circles have evolved into a system made up almost entirely of self-managing teams:

> Daily administration, explains A Subramaniam, [the factory's] … training manager, involves teams taking on routine activities formerly performed by supervisors. "Now," he says, "they are expected to take care of the daily operations like marking attendance, setup, control of material usage, quality control, monitoring cycle time, safety, and line audits." …
>
> Low Say Sun, training and development administrator, adds, "They [team members] are expected in daily management to detect abnormality and take corrective action as well as make improvements in their work area using problem-solving techniques and quality control tools. It will be just like running a business company. Of course," he adds, "there will be facilitators or managers whom they can turn to for help. In other words, there will be somebody to take care of the team. Training will be provided to enable them to manage their operation and process well."[73]

General Mills has found that, when it comes to management, less can mean more. At the Lodi plant, some of the self-managed teams have set higher production goals for themselves than those formerly set by management. Self-managed teamwork does have its price tag, however. "Training alone costs $70,000 per worker"[74] at the New Carlisle steel plant. Each team member at Texas Instruments' Malaysian facility undergoes 50 hours of intensive training in everything from quality control tools to problem solving to team building and communication.

This section explores self-managed teams by looking at their past, present, and future.

What Are Self-Managed Teams?   Something much more complex is involved than this apparently simple label suggests. The term *self-managed* does not mean simply turning workers loose to do their own thing. Indeed, as we will see, an organization embracing self-managed teams should be prepared to undergo revolutionary changes in management philosophy, structure, staffing and training practices, and reward systems. Moreover, the traditional notions of managerial authority and control are turned on their heads. Not surprisingly, many managers strongly resist giving up the reins of power to people they view as subordinates. They see self-managed teams as a threat to their job security.[75] Texas Instruments has constructively dealt with this problem at its Malaysian factory by making former production supervisors part of the all-important training function.

Self-managed teams
Groups of employees granted administrative oversight for their work.

Cross-functionalism
Team made up of technical specialists from different areas.

Self-managed teams are defined as groups of workers who are given administrative oversight for their task domains. Administrative oversight involves delegated activities such as planning, scheduling, monitoring, and staffing. These are chores normally performed by managers. In short, employees in these unique work groups act as their own supervisor.[76] Self-managed teams are variously referred to as semiautonomous work groups, autonomous work groups, and superteams. A common feature of self-managed teams, particularly among those above the shop-floor or clerical level, is **cross-functionalism.**[77] In other words, specialists from different areas are put on the same team. Amgen, a rapidly growing biotechnology company in Thousand Oaks, California, is literally run by cross-functional, self-managed teams:

> There are two types: product development teams, known as PDTs, which are concerned with everything that relates to bringing a new product to market, and task forces, which do everything else. The members of both come from all areas of the company, including marketing and finance as well as the lab bench. The groups range from five or six employees up to 80 and usually report directly to senior management. In a reversal of the normal process, department heads called facilitators don't run teams; they work for them, making sure they have the equipment and money they need. Teams may meet weekly, monthly, or whenever the members see fit.[78]

Among companies with self-managed teams, the most commonly delegated tasks are work scheduling and dealing directly with outside customers (see Table 13–6). The least common team chores are hiring and firing. Most of today's self-managed teams remain bunched at the shop-floor level in factory settings. Experts predict growth of the practice in the managerial ranks and in service operations.[79]

Historical and Conceptual Roots of Self-Managed Teams   Self-managed teams are an outgrowth of a blend of behavioral science and management practice.[80] Group dynamics research of variables such as cohesiveness initially paved the way. A later stimulus was the socio-technical systems approach in which first British, and then American researchers, tried to harmonize social and technical factors. Their goal

Table 13–6   *Survey Evidence: What Self-Managing Teams Manage*

Percentage of Companies Saying Their Self-Managing Teams Perform These Traditional Management Functions by Themselves.	
Schedule work assignments	67%
Work with outside customers	67
Conduct training	59
Set production goals/quotas	56
Work with suppliers/vendors	44
Purchase equipment/services	43
Develop budgets	39
Do performance appraisals	36
Hire co-workers	33
Fire co-workers	14

SOURCE: Adapted from "1996 Industry Report: What Self-Managing Teams Manage," *Training*, October 1996, p 69.

OB Exercise   Measuring Work Group Autonomy

Instructions

Think of your current (or past) job and work groups. Characterize the group's situation by circling one number on the following scale for each statement. Add your responses for a total score:

Strongly Disagree						Strongly Agree
1 ——	2 ——	3 ——	4 ——	5 ——	6 ——	7

Work Method Autonomy

1. My work group decides how to get the job done. _____

2. My work group determines what procedures to use. _____

3. My work group is free to choose its own methods when carrying out its work. _____

Work Scheduling Autonomy

4. My work group controls the scheduling of its work. _____

5. My work group determines how its work is sequenced. _____

6. My work group decides when to do certain activities. _____

Work Criteria Autonomy

7. My work group is allowed to modify the normal way it is evaluated so some of our activities are emphasized and some deemphasized. _____

8. My work group is able to modify its objectives (what it is supposed to accomplish). _____

9. My work group has some control over what it is supposed to accomplish. _____

Total score = _____

Norms

9–26 = Low autonomy
27–45 = Moderate autonomy
46–63 = High autonomy

SOURCE: Adapted from an individual autonomy scale in J A Breaugh, "The Work Autonomy Scales: Additional Validity Evidence," *Human Relations*, November 1989, pp 1033–56.

---

was to simultaneously increase productivity and employees' quality of work life. More recently, the idea of self-managed teams has gotten a strong boost from job design and participative management advocates. Recall our discussion of Hackman and Oldham's job characteristics model in Chapter 7. According to their model, internal motivation, satisfaction, and performance can be enhanced through five core job characteristics. Of those five core factors, increased *autonomy* is a major benefit for members of self-managed teams. Three types of autonomy are method, scheduling, and criteria autonomy (see the OB Exercise). Members of self-managed teams score high on group autonomy. Autonomy empowers those who are ready and able to handle added responsibility. How did you score? Finally, the social learning theory of self-management, as discussed in Chapter 10, has helped strengthen the case for self-managed teams.

The net result of this confluence is the continuum in Figure 13–4. The traditional clear-cut distinction between manager and managed is being blurred as nonmanagerial employees are delegated greater authority and granted increased autonomy. Importantly, self-managed teams do not eliminate the need for all managerial control (see the upper right-hand corner of Figure 13–4). Semiautonomous work teams represent a balance between managerial and group control.[81]

Are Self-Managed Teams Effective? Research Evidence

As with quality circles and virtual teams, much of what we know about self-managed teams comes from testimonials and case studies. Fortunately, a body of higher quality field research

Figure 13–4   *The Evolution of Self-Managed Work Teams*

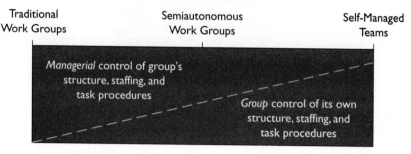

is slowly developing. A review of three meta-analyses covering 70 individual studies concluded that self-managed teams had

- A positive impact on productivity.
- A positive impact on specific attitudes relating to self-management (e.g., responsibility and control).
- No significant impact on general attitudes (e.g., job satisfaction and organizational commitment).
- No significant impact on absenteeism or turnover.[82]

Although encouraging, these results do not qualify as a sweeping endorsement of self-managed teams. Nonetheless, experts say the trend toward self-managed work teams will continue upward in North America because of a strong cultural bias in favor of direct participation. Managers need to be prepared for the resulting shift in organizational administration.

Setting the Stage for Self-Managed Teams   Experience shows that it is better to build a new production or service facility around self-managed teams than to attempt to convert an existing one. The former approach involves so-called "green field sites." General Foods, for example, pioneered the use of autonomous work teams in the United States in 1971 by literally building its Topeka, Kansas, Gravy Train pet food plant around them.[83] Green field sites give management the advantage of selecting appropriate technology and carefully screening job applicants likely to be good team players.

But the fact is, most organizations are not afforded green field opportunities. They must settle for introducing self-managed teams into an existing organization structure.[84]

Making the Transition to Self-Managed Teams   Extensive *management training and socialization* are required to deeply embed Theory Y and participative management values into the organization's culture. This new logic necessarily has to start with top management and filter down. Otherwise, resistance among middle- and lower-level managers will block the transition to teams.[85] Some turnover can be expected among managers who refuse to adjust to broader empowerment. Both *technical and organizational redesign* are necessary. Self-managed teams may require special technology. Volvo's team-based auto assembly plant, for example, relies on portable assembly platforms rather than traditional assembly lines. Structural redesign of the organization must take place because self-managed teams are an integral part of the organization, not patched onto it as in the case of quality circles. For example, in one of Texas Instruments' computer chip factories a hierarchy of teams operates within the traditional structure. Four levels of teams are responsible for different domains. Reporting to the steering team that deals with strategic issues are quality-improvement, corrective-action, and effectiveness teams. TI's quality-improvement and corrective-action teams are cross-functional teams made up of middle managers and functional specialists such as accountants and engineers. Production workers make up the effectiveness teams. The corrective-action teams are unique because they are formed to deal with short-term problems and are disbanded when a solution is found. All the other teams are long-term assignments.[86]

In turn, *personnel, goal setting, and reward systems* need to be adapted to encourage teamwork. Staffing decisions may shift from management to team members who hire their own co-workers. A recent study of 60 self-managing teams involving 540 employees suggests how goal setting should be reoriented. Teams with highly *cooperative* goals functioned more smoothly and had better results than teams with competitive goals.[87] Accordingly, individual bonuses must give way to team bonuses. *Supervisory development workshops* are needed to teach managers to be facilitators rather than order givers.[88] Finally, extensive *team training* is required to help team members learn more about technical details, the business as a whole, and how to be team players. This is where team building enters the picture.

Team Building

Team building is a catch-all term for a whole host of techniques aimed at improving the internal functioning of work groups. Whether conducted by company trainers or outside consultants, team-building workshops strive for greater cooperation, better communication, and less dysfunctional conflict. Experiential learning techniques such as interpersonal trust exercises, conflict-handling role play sessions, and interactive games are common. For example, Germany's Opel uses Lego blocks to teach its auto workers the tight teamwork necessary for just-in-time production.[89] In the mountains of British Columbia, Canada, DowElanco employees try to overcome fear and build trust as they help each other negotiate a difficult tree-top rope course.[90] Meanwhile, in the United States, the Target department store chain has its salesclerks learn cooperation and teamwork with this exercise: "employees linked in a human chain must each wriggle through two Hula-Hoops moving in opposite directions, without breaking the chain or letting the hoops touch the ground."[91] And in Prescott, Arizona, trainees at Motorola's Advanced Leadership Academy polish their teamwork skills by trying to make music with an odd assortment of percussion instruments.[92]

Team building
Experiential learning aimed at better internal functioning of groups.

The University of Chicago Business School promotes "hands-on" learning through team-building exercises. These blindfolded students can accomplish their task only with the help of their teammates. The message is clear: today's business leaders cannot do the job alone.

(Marc Pokempner/Tony Stone Images)

Rote memorization and lecture/discussion are discouraged by teambuilding experts who prefer this sort of *active* versus passive learning. Greater emphasis is placed on *how* work groups get the job done than on the job itself.

Complete coverage of the many team-building techniques would require a separate book. Consequently, the scope of our current discussion is limited to the goal of team building and the day-to-day development of self-management skills. This foundation is intended to give you a basis for selecting appropriate team-building techniques from the many you are likely to encounter in the years ahead.[93]

The Goal of Team Building: High-Performance Teams

Team building allows team members to wrestle with simulated or real-life problems. Outcomes are then analyzed by the group to determine what group processes need improvement. Learning stems from recognizing and addressing faulty group dynamics. Perhaps one subgroup withheld key information from another, thereby hampering group progress. With cross-cultural teams becoming commonplace in today's global economy, team building is more important than ever[94] (see the International OB, p 435).

A nationwide survey of team members from many organizations, by Wilson Learning Corporation, provides a useful model or benchmark of what we should expect of teams. The researchers' question was simply: "What is a high-performance team?"[95] The respondents were asked to describe their peak experiences in work teams. Analysis of the survey results yielded the following eight attributes of high-performance teams:

1. *Participative leadership.* Creating an interdependency by empowering, freeing up, and serving others.

2. *Shared responsibility.* Establishing an environment in which all team members feel as responsible as the manager for the performance of the work unit.

3. *Aligned on purpose.* Having a sense of common purpose about why the team exists and the function it serves.

4. *High communication.* Creating a climate of trust and open, honest communication.

5. *Future focused.* Seeing change as an opportunity for growth.

6. *Focused on task.* Keeping meetings focused on results.

7. *Creative talents.* Applying individual talents and creativity.

8. *Rapid response.* Identifying and acting on opportunities.[96]

These eight attributes effectively combine many of today's most progressive ideas on management,[97] among them being participation, empowerment, service ethic, individual responsibility and development, self-management, trust, active listening, and envisioning. But patience and diligence are required. According to a manager familiar with work teams, "high-performance teams may take three to five years to build."[98] Let us keep this inspiring model of high-performance teams in mind as we conclude our discussion of team building.

Self-management leadership

Process of leading others to lead themselves.

Developing Team Members' Self-Management Skills

A promising dimension of team building has emerged in recent years. It is an extension of the behavioral self-management approach discussed in Chapter 10. Proponents call it **self-management leadership,** defined as the process of leading others to lead them-

International OB   The Wild World of Cross-Cultural Team Building

Brussels—Anyone can talk about cultural differences. Fons Trompenaars tries to make his students feel them.

To do that, the Dutch leader of workshops on "multicultural" management teaches his students (mostly executives) to play a game invented by one of his colleagues, L J P Brug. The object: building towers made of paper.

Mr Trompenaars, a 39-year-old former Royal Dutch/Shell executive, divides a group of several dozen Swedish managers into two groups. Four are designated as "international experts" in building paper towers. Everyone else becomes a native of a make-believe village called Derdia.

"Your culture loves towers but doesn't know how to build them," Mr Trompenaars tells the Derdians. "It's a bit like the British car industry."

The experts are sent out of the room to learn to make paper towers and prepare to pass that skill on to Derdia. Meanwhile, Mr Trompenaars initiates the Swedes into the strange customs of Derdia.

Derdians' greetings involve kissing one another on the shoulder. Holding out a hand to someone means "Please go away." If they disagree, Derdians say "Yes!" and nod their heads vigorously.

What's more, Derdian women have a taboo against using paper or scissors in the presence of men, while men would never use a pencil or a ruler in front of women.

The Swedes, reserved a moment ago, throw themselves into the task of acting like Derdians. They merrily tap one another, kiss shoulders and bray "Yessss!"

Soon, two "experts" are allowed back into the room for a brief study of Derdian culture. The Derdians flock to the experts and gleefully kiss their shoulders. The experts turn red. They seem lost already.

"Would you please sit?" asks Hans Olav Friberg, a young "expert" who, back home in Sweden, works for a company that makes flooring.

"Yessss!" the Derdians say in a chorus. But they don't sit down.

"Who is in charge here?" Mr Friberg inquires. "Yessss!" the Derdians reply.

Mr Friberg leaves the room to confer with his fellow experts. "They didn't understand us," he tells them. But fellow expert Hakan Kalmermo isn't about to be deterred by strange habits. He is taking charge. As he briskly practices making a paper tower, Mr Kalmermo says firmly to the other experts: "The target is to have them produce one tower."

The four experts carry paper and other supplies to the adjoining room, now known as Derdia. They begin to explain the process to the Derdians very slowly, as if speaking to small children. When one of the Derdians shows he understands the workings of a scissors, Mr Kalmermo exclaims: "Good boy!"

Although Mr Kalmermo works hard at making himself clear, the Derdians' customs and taboos obstruct progress. The men won't use rulers as long as women are around but don't explain this behavior to the experts. The answer to every question seems to be "yes." At the end of 30 minutes, no tower has been completed.

The game is over; now comes the self-criticism. "They treated us like idiots," protests one of the Derdians.

The lessons are clear, but Mr Trompenaars drives them home: If you don't figure out basics of a foreign culture, you won't get much accomplished. And if your biases lead you to think of foreign ways as childish, the foreigners may well respond by acting childish.

Still, Mr Kalmermo, the take-charge expert, thinks his team was on the right track. "If we'd had another hour," he says, "I think we would have had 15 towers built."

SOURCE: B Hagerty, "Learning to Turn the Other Shoulder," *The Wall Street Journal*, June 14, 1993, pp B1, B3. Reprinted by permission of *The Wall Street Journal*, © 1993 Dow Jones & Company, Inc. All Rights Reserved Worldwide.

selves. An underlying assumption is that self-managed teams likely will fail if team members are not expressly taught to engage in self-management behaviors. This makes sense because it is unreasonable to expect employees who are accustomed to being managed and led to suddenly manage and lead themselves. Transition training is required, as discussed in the prior section. A key transition to self-management involves *current managers* engaging in self-management leadership behaviors. This is team building in the fullest meaning of the term.

Six self-management leadership behaviors were isolated in a field study of a manufacturing company organized around self-managed teams. The observed behaviors were

1. *Encourages self-reinforcement* (e.g., getting team members to praise each other for good work and results).

2. *Encourages self-observation/evaluation* (e.g., teaching team members to judge how well they are doing).

3. *Encourages self-expectation* (e.g., encouraging team members to expect high performance from themselves and the team).

4. *Encourages self-goal-setting* (e.g., having the team set its own performance goals).

5. *Encourages rehearsal* (e.g., getting team members to think about and practice new tasks).

6. *Encourages self-criticism* (e.g., encouraging team members to be critical of their own poor performance).[99]

According to the researchers, Charles Manz and Henry Sims, this type of leadership is a dramatic departure from traditional practices such as giving orders and/or making sure everyone gets along. Empowerment, not domination, is the overriding goal.

Summary of Key Concepts

1. *Explain how a work group becomes a team.* A team is a mature group where leadership is shared, accountability is both individual and collective, the members have developed their own purpose, problem solving is a way of life, and effectiveness is measured by collective outcomes.

2. *Identify and describe the four types of work teams.* Four general types of work teams are advice, production, project, and action teams. Each type has its characteristic degrees of specialization and coordination, work cycle, and outputs.

3. *Explain the ecological model of work team effectiveness.* According to the ecological model, two effectiveness criteria for work teams are performance and viability. The performance criterion is met if the group satisfies its clients/customers. A work group is viable if its members are satisfied and continue contributing. An ecological perspective is appropriate because work groups require an organizational life-support system. For instance, group participation is enhanced by an organizational culture that values employee empowerment.

4. *Discuss why teams fail.* Teams fail because unrealistic expectations cause frustration and failure. Common management mistakes include weak strategies, creating a hostile environment for teams, faddish use of teams, not learning from team experience, vague team assignments, poor team staffing, inadequate training, and lack of trust. Team members typically try too much too soon, experience conflict over differing work styles and personalities, ignore important group dynamics, resist change, exhibit poor interpersonal skills and chemistry, and display a lack of trust.

5. *List at least three things managers can do to build trust.* Six recommended ways to build trust are through communication, support, respect (especially delegation), fairness, predictability, and competence.

6. *Distinguish two types of group cohesiveness, and summarize cohesiveness research findings.* Cohesive groups have a shared sense of togetherness or a "we" feeling. Socioemotional cohesiveness involves emotional satisfaction. Instrumental cohesiveness involves goal-directed togetherness. There is a small but significant relationship between cohesiveness and performance. The effect is stronger for smaller groups. Commitment to task among group members strengthens the cohesiveness→performance linkage. Success can build group cohesiveness. Cohesiveness is not a cure-all for group problems. Too much cohesiveness can lead to groupthink.

7. *Define quality circles, virtual teams, and self-managed teams.* Quality circles are small groups of volunteers who meet regularly to solve quality-related problems in their work area. Virtual teams are physically dispersed work groups that conduct their business via modern information technologies such as the Internet, E-mail, and videoconferences. Self-managed teams are work groups that perform

their own administrative chores such as planning, scheduling, and staffing.

8. *Discuss what must be done to set the stage for self-managed teams.* Management must embed a new Theory Y logic in the organization's culture. Technology and the organization need to be redesigned to accommodate self-managed teams. Personnel changes, goals, and reward systems that reinforce cooperation and teamwork are necessary. Supervisory training helps managers learn to be facilitators rather than traditional order givers. Team members need lots of training and team building to make them cooperative team players.

9. *Describe high-performance teams.* Eight attributes of high-performance teams are (*a*) participative leadership, (*b*) shared responsibility, (*c*) aligned on purpose, (*d*) high communication, (*e*) future focused for growth, (*f*) focused on task, (*g*) creative talents applied, and (*h*) rapid response.

Discussion Questions

1. Do you agree or disagree with Drucker's vision of more team-oriented organizations? Explain your assumptions and reasoning.

2. Which of the factors listed in Table 13–1 is most crucial to a successful team? Explain.

3. Why bother taking an ecological perspective of work team effectiveness?

4. In your personal friendships, how do you come to trust someone? How fragile is that trust? Explain.

5. Why is delegation so important to building organizational trust?

6. Why should a group leader strive for both socio-emotional and instrumental cohesiveness?

7. Are virtual teams likely to be just a passing fad? Why or why not?

8. Would you like to work on a self-managed team? Explain.

9. How would you respond to a manager who said, "Why should I teach my people to manage themselves and work myself out of a job?"

10. Have you ever been a member of a high-performing team? If so, explain the circumstances and success factors.

Internet Exercise

www.briefings.com
www.akgroup.com

As covered in this chapter, teams are the organizational unit of choice today. Auto companies have design and production teams. Hospitals have patient care teams. Team policing is practiced by many law enforcement agencies. Airlines have ground crew teams. Current and future managers (indeed, all employees) need to know as much as possible about teams and teamwork. The purpose of this exercise is to continue building your knowledge of workplace teams and to assess your readiness for Internet-age teamwork.

Instructive Updates on Teams and Teamwork

Start with the home page of Briefings Publishing Group (www.briefings.com), and select the navigation tab "Team management." At the "Team Management Briefings" page, click on topics from the latest issue that seem relevant and interesting. Next, select relevant categories in the TMB archives menu for helpful advice and tips. This is quick reading intended for busy managers.

A Free Virtual Team Readiness Questionnaire

Virtual teams, where members attempt to complete projects despite being geographically dispersed, will grow more common as advanced computer networks and communication technologies becomes even more sophisticated. Are you (and your organization) ready to work in this sort of electronically connected team environment? You can find out, thanks to the Web site of The Applied Knowledge Group, a consulting company. Call up their home page (www.akgroup.com), and select "Assessment Tool" from the main menu. (Note: Our use of this questionnaire is for instructional purposes only and does not constitute an endorsement of any products that may or may not suit your needs. There is no obligation to buy anything.) Complete the single organizational question (for your current or past employer), complete the next 25 individual questions, and then click on the "Score Test" button. You will be given a virtual team readiness score and a brief interpretation. A personal copy of the questionnaire and results can be printed, if you desire.

Questions

1. If you consulted the Team Management Briefings, what useful ideas, advice, or tips did you pick up?

2. What are your main concerns about today's rush to adopt team-based organizations?

3. How did you score on the Virtual Team Readiness questionnaire? Did you score higher or lower than you might have expected? What are the practical implications of your score?

4. Regarding the first response category on the questionnaire, is your target organization an appropriate place for virtual teams? Explain.

OB in Action Case Study

With the Stakes High, A Lucent Duo Conquers Distance and Culture[100]

Imagine designing the most complex product in your company's history. You need 500 engineers for the job. They will assemble the world's most delicate hardware and write more than a million lines of code. In communicating, the margin for error is minuscule.

Now, scatter those 500 engineers over 13 time zones. Over three continents. Over five states in the United States alone. The Germans schedule to perfection. The Americans work on the fly. In Massachusetts, they go to work early. In New Jersey, they stay late.

Now you have some idea of what Bill Klinger and Frank Polito have been through in the past 18 months. As top software-development managers in Lucent Technologies' Bell Labs division, they played critical roles in creating a new fiber-optic phone switch called the Bandwidth Manager, which sells for about $1 million, the kind of global product behind the company's surging earnings. The high-stakes development was Lucent's most complex undertaking by far since its spin-off from AT&T in 1996.

Managing such a far-flung staff ("distributed development," it's called) is possible only because of technology. But as the two Lucent leaders painfully learned, distance still magnifies differences, even in a high-tech age. "You lose informal interaction—going to lunch, the water cooler," Mr Klinger says. "You can never discount how many issues get solved that way."

The product grew as a hybrid of exotic, widely dispersed technologies: "light-wave" science from Lucent's Merrimack Valley plant, north of Boston, where Mr Polito works; "cross-connect" products here in New Jersey, where Mr Klinger works; timing devices from the Netherlands; and optics from Germany.

Development also demanded multiple locations because Lucent wanted a core model as a platform for special versions for foreign and other niche markets. Involving overseas engineers in the flagship product would speed the later development of spinoffs and impress foreign customers.

And rushing to market meant tapping software talent wherever it was available—ultimately at Lucent facilities in Colorado, Illinois, North Carolina, and India. "The scary thing, scary but exciting, was that no one had really pulled this off on this scale before," says Mr Polito.

Communication technology was the easy part. Lashing together big computers in different cities assured everyone was working on the same up-to-date software version. New project data from one city were instantly available on Web pages everywhere else. Test engineers in India could tweak prototypes in New Jersey. The project never went to sleep.

Technology, however, couldn't conquer cultural problems, especially acute between Messrs Klinger's and Polito's respective staffs in New Jersey and Massachusetts. Each had its own programming traditions and product histories. Such basic words as "test" could mean different things. A programming chore requiring days in one context might take weeks in another. Differing work schedules and physical distance made each location suspect the other of slacking off. "We had such clashes," says Mr Klinger.

Personality tests revealed deep geographic differences. Supervisors from the sleek, glass-covered New Jersey office, principally a research facility abounding in academics, scored as "thinking" people who used cause-and-effect analysis. Those from the old, brick facility in Massachusetts, mainly a manufacturing plant, scored as "feeling" types who based decisions on subjective, human values. Sheer awareness of the differences ("Now I know why you get on my nerves!") began to create common ground.

Amid much cynicism, the two directors hauled their technical managers into team exercises—working in small groups to scale a 14-foot wall and solve puzzles. It's corny, but such methods can accelerate trust-building when time is short and the stakes are high. At one point Mr Klinger asked managers to show up with the product manuals from their previous projects—then, in a ritualistic break from technical parochialism, instructed everyone to tear the covers to pieces.

More than anything else, it was sheer physical presence—face time—that began solidifying the group. Dozens of managers began meeting fortnightly in rotating cities, socializing as much time as their technical discussions permitted. (How better to grow familiar than over hot dogs, beer, and nine innings with the minor league Durham Bulls?) Foreign locations found the direct interaction especially valuable. "Going into the other culture is the only way to understand it," says Sigrid Hauenstein, a Lucent executive in Nuremberg, Germany. "If you don't have a common understanding, it's much more expensive to correct it later."

Eventually the project found its pace. People began wearing beepers to eliminate time wasted on voice-mail tag. Conference calls at varying levels kept everyone in the loop. Staffers posted their photos in the project's Web directory. Many created personal pages. "It's the ultimate democracy of the Web," Mr Klinger says.

The product is now shipping—on schedule, within budget, and with more technical versatility than Lucent expected. Distributed development "paid off in spades," says Gerry Butters, Lucent optical-networking chief.

Even as it helps build the infrastructure of a digitally connected planet, Lucent is rediscovering the importance of face-to-face interaction. All the bandwidth in the world can convey only a fraction of what we are.

Questions for Discussion

1. Could the 500 Lucent engineers who worked on the Bandwidth Manager project be called a *team?* Why or why not? Could Bill Klinger and Frank Polito be called a team? Explain.

2. What role, if any, did trust play in this case?

3. What lessons about managing virtual teams does this case teach us?

4. Which of the eight attributes of high-performance teams are evident in this case?

5. Based on what you have read, what was the overriding key to success in this case?

Personal Awareness and Growth Exercise

How Trusting Are You?

Objectives

1. To introduce you to different dimensions of interpersonal trust.
2. To measure your trust in another person.
3. To discuss the managerial implications of your propensity to trust.

Introduction

The trend toward more open and empowered organizations where teamwork and self-management are vital requires heightened interpersonal trust. Customers need to be able to trust organizations producing the goods and services they buy, managers need to trust nonmanagers to carry out the organization's mission, and team members need to trust each other in order to get the job done. As with any other interpersonal skill, we need to be able to measure and improve our ability to trust others. This exercise is a step in that direction.

Instructions[101]

Think of a specific individual who currently plays an important role in your life (e.g., current or future spouse, friend, supervisor, co-worker, team member, etc.), and rate his or her trustworthiness for each statement according to the following scale. Total your responses, and compare your score with the arbitrary norms provided.

Strongly Disagree									Strongly Agree
1 — 2 — 3 — 4 — 5 — 6 — 7 — 8 — 9 — 10									

Overall Trust   Score

1. I can expect this person to play fair.   _____
2. I can confide in this person and know she/he desires to listen.   _____
3. I can expect this person to tell me the truth.   _____
4. This person takes time to listen to my problems and worries.   _____

Emotional Trust

5. This person would never intentionally misrepresent my point of view to other people.   _____
6. I can confide in this person and know that he/she will not discuss it with others.   _____
7. This person responds constructively and caringly to my problems.   _____

Reliableness

8. If this person promised to do me a favor, she/he would carry out that promise.   _____

9. If I had an appointment with this person, I could count on him/her showing up.   _____

10. I could lend this person money and count on getting it back as soon as possible.   _____

11. I do not need a backup plan because I know this person will come through for me.   _____

Total score = _____

Trustworthiness Scale

77–110 = High (Trust is a precious thing.)

45–76 = Moderate (Be careful; get a rearview mirror.)

11–44 = Low (Lock up your valuables!)

Questions for Discussion

1. Which particular items in this trust questionnaire are most central to your idea of trust? Why?

2. Does your score accurately depict the degree to which you trust (or distrust) the target person?

3. Why do you trust (or distrust) this individual?

4. If you trust this person to a high degree, how hard was it to build that trust? Explain. What would destroy that trust?

5. Based on your responses to this questionnaire, how would you rate your "propensity to trust"? Low? Moderate? High?

6. What are the managerial implications of your propensity to trust?

Group Exercise

Student Team Development Project

Objectives

1. To help you better understand the components of teamwork.

2. To give you a practical diagnostic tool to assess the need for team building.

3. To give you a chance to evaluate and develop an actual group/team.

Introduction

Student teams are very common in today's college classrooms. They are an important part of the move toward cooperative and experiential learning. In other words, learning by doing. Group dynamics and teamwork are best learned by doing. Unfortunately, many classroom teams wallow in ambiguity, conflict, and ineffectiveness. This team development questionnaire can play an important role in the life cycle of your classroom team or group. All members of your team can complete this evaluation at one or more of the following critical points in your team's life cycle: (1) when the team reaches a crisis point and threatens to break up, (2) about halfway through the life of the team, and (3) at the end of the team's life cycle. Discussion of the results by all team members can enhance the group's learning experience.

Instructions

Either at the prompting of your instructor or by group consensus, decide at what point in your team's life cycle this exercise should be completed. *Tip:* Have each team member write their responses to the 10 items on a sheet of paper with no names attached. This will permit the calculation of a group mean score for each item and for all 10 items. Attention should then turn to the discussion questions provided to help any team development problems surface and to point the way toward solutions.

(An alternative to these instructions is to evaluate a team or work group you are associated with in your current job. You may also draw from a group experience in a past job.)

Questionnaire[102]

1. To what extent do I feel a real part of the team?

5	4	3	2	1
Completely a part all the time.	A part most of the time.	On the edge— sometimes in, sometimes out.	Generally outside except for one or two short periods.	On the outside, not really a part of the team.

2. How safe is it in this team to be at ease, relaxed, and myself?

5	4	3	2	1
I feel perfectly safe to be myself; they won't hold mistakes against me.	I feel most people would accept me if I were completely myself, but there are some I am not sure about.	Generally one has to be careful what one says or does in this team.	I am quite fearful about being completely myself in this team.	I am not a fool; I would never be myself in this team.

3. To what extent do I feel "under wraps," that is, have private thoughts, unspoken reservations, or unexpressed feelings and opinions that I have not felt comfortable bringing out into the open?

1	2	3	4	5
Almost completely under wraps.	Under wraps many times.	Slightly more free and expressive than under wraps.	Quite free and expressive much of the time.	Almost completely free and expressive.

4. How effective are we, in our team, in getting out and using the ideas, opinions, and information of all team members in making decisions?

1	2	3	4	5
We don't really encourage everyone to share their ideas, opinions, and information with the team in making decisions.	Only the ideas, opinions, and information of a few members are really known and used in making decisions.	Sometimes we hear the views of most members before making decisions, and sometimes we disregard most members.	A few are sometimes hesitant about sharing their opinions, but we generally have good participation in making decisions.	Everyone feels his or her ideas, opinions, and information are given a fair hearing before decisions are made.

5. To what extent are the goals the team is working toward understood, and to what extent do they have meaning for you?

5	4	3	2	1
I feel extremely good about the goals of our team.	I feel fairly good, but some things are not too clear or meaningful.	A few things we are doing are clear and meaningful.	Much of the activity is not clear or meaningful to me.	I really do not understand or feel involved in the goals of the team.

6. How well does the team work at its tasks?

1	2	3	4	5
Coasts, loafs, makes no progress.	Makes a little progress, but most members loaf.	Progress is slow; spurts of effective work.	Above average in progress and pace of work.	Works well; achieves definite progress.

7. Our planning and the way we operate as a team are largely influenced by:

1	2	3	4	5
One or two team members.	A clique.	Shifts from one person or clique to another.	Shared by most of the members, but some are left out.	Shared by all members of the team.

8. What is the level of responsibility for work in our team?

5	4	3	2	1
Each person assumes personal responsibility for getting work done.	A majority of the members assume responsibility for getting work done.	About half assume responsibility; about half do not.	Only a few assume responsibility for getting work done.	Nobody (except perhaps one) really assumes responsibility for getting work done.

9. How are differences or conflicts handled in our team?

1	2	3	4	5
Differences or conflicts are denied, suppressed, or avoided at all costs.	Differences or conflicts are recognized but remain mostly unresolved.	Differences or conflicts are recognized, and some attempts are made to work them through by some members, often outside the team meetings.	Differences and conflicts are recognized, and some attempts are made to deal with them in our team.	Differences and conflicts are recognized, and the team usually is working them through satisfactorily.

10. How do people relate to the team leader, chairperson, or "boss"?

1	2	3	4	5
The leader dominates the team, and people are often fearful or passive.	The leader tends to control the team, although people generally agree with the leader's direction.	There is some give and take between the leader and the team members.	Team members relate easily to the leader and usually are able to influence leader decisions.	Team members respect the leader, but they work together as a unified team, with everyone participating and no one dominant.

Total score = _____

Questions for Discussion

1. Have any of the items on the questionnaire helped you better understand why your team has had problems? What problems?

2. Based on Table 13–1, are you part of a group or team? Explain.

3. How do your responses to the items compare with the average responses from your group? What insights does this information provide?

4. Refer back to Tuckman's five-stage model of group development in Figure 12–2. Which stage is your team at? How can you tell? Did group decay set in?

5. If you are part way through your team's life cycle, what steps does your team need to take to become more effective?

6. If this is the end of your team's life cycle, what should your team have done differently?

7. What lasting lessons about teamwork have you learned from this exercise?

Chapter Fourteen

Managing Conflict and Negotiation

Learning Objectives

When you finish studying the material in this chapter, you should be able to:

1 Define the term *conflict,* distinguish between functional and dysfunctional conflict, and identify three desired conflict outcomes.

2 Define *personality conflicts,* and explain how managers should handle them.

3 Distinguish between instrumental and terminal values, identify three types of value conflict, and explain how value conflicts can be handled.

4 Discuss the role of in-group thinking in intergroup conflict, and explain what management can do about intergroup conflict.

5 Discuss what can be done about cross-cultural conflict.

6 Explain how managers can stimulate functional conflict, and identify the five conflict-handling styles.

7 Explain the nature and practical significance of conflict triangles and alternative dispute resolution for third-party conflict intervention.

8 Explain the difference between distributive and integrative negotiation, and discuss the concept of added-value negotiation.

. . . when Barry Sternlicht seized control of ITT last year and coaxed his best friend, Richard Nanula, away from Disney to help him run it, nobody predicted a mess like this. Investors in their company, Starwood Hotels & Resorts Worldwide, have lost billions. The friendship is unraveling—and so is the business relationship. "Why did I do this?" wails Sternlicht, strung out by life at the top. "Am I stupid, or am I a jerk? Half the time, I think I'm stupid. The other half, I think I'm a jerk."

So it goes when two smart guys have the money and the résumés to be masters of the universe—and think they have the talent and the temperament too. Sternlicht and Nanula, both 38, had been best friends since their days at Harvard Business School. They were in each other's weddings. They went on family vacations and trips to the Super Bowl together. Even when they lived on opposite coasts, they talked almost daily. "We were each other's biggest fans," says Nanula, who was Michael Eisner's protégé at Disney and, at 31,

the youngest CFO [Chief Financial Officer] ever of a *Fortune* 500 company.

It's not that Sternlicht and Nanula now despise each other. Nor are they warring over the vision for Starwood, which Sternlicht built from a near-bankrupt shell into the world's largest hotel and gaming company, with name brands like Sheraton and Westin and trophy assets from Caesars Palace in Las Vegas to the Gritti Palace in Venice.

Both men want to make Starwood the No. 1 broad-based leisure company and a champion of shareholder value. One of their models is Disney.

The core problem, these longtime pals have discovered, is that their "complementary" styles—Nanula is as calm and cautious as Sternlicht is intense and impetuous—aren't complementary after all. And—who could have guessed it?—they are clashing over power. Sternlicht got upset last summer when the *New York Times* ran a glowing profile of Nanula, identified as Starwood's boss, and photographed him perched regally at the company's posh St Regis Hotel. According to insiders, Sternlicht griped that Nanula "looked like King Tut." Tut, tut. Sounds like plain old envy on the part of a kid who should learn to share credit. But Sternlicht is not a sharer. In January he demoted Nanula from CEO to president. "We're not equals," says Sternlicht, now chairman and CEO. "I think of myself as captain of the ship. Richard is my first mate."

The Wonderful World of Starwood this is not. The relationship between the captain and his first mate got so stormy last fall that Sternlicht, to his credit, brought in an organizational consultant named Michael Feiner. A former senior vice president of personnel at Pepsi-Cola, Feiner (whom some Starwood employees nicknamed "the marriage counselor") has been working with Sternlicht and Nanula much the way a therapist would with warring couples. But can this partnership be saved? Probably not. Sternlicht seems too egocentric to lead a *Fortune* 500 company. Nanula, so far, hasn't made the grade. [1]

FOR DISCUSSION

Putting yourself in Michael Feiner's place, what would you have done to help turn Sternlicht and Nanula into an effective leadership team? *Note:* Soon after this case was written, Nanula quit to become CEO of Broadband Sports.

How would you handle this situation?

Your name is Annie and you are a product development manager for Amazon.com. As you were eating lunch today in your cubicle, Laura, a software project manager with an office nearby, asked if she could talk to you for a few minutes. You barely know Laura and you have heard both good and bad things about her work habits. Although your mind was more on how to meet Friday's deadline than on lunch, you waved her in.

She proceeded to pour out her woes about how she is having an impossible time partnering with Hans on a new special project. He is regarded as a top-notch software project manager, but Laura has found him to be ill-tempered and uncooperative. Laura thought you and Hans were friends because she has seen the two of you talking in the cafeteria and parking lot. You told Laura you have a good working relationship with Hans, but he's not really a friend. Still, Laura pressed on. "Would you straighten Hans out for me?" she asked. "We've got to get moving on this special project."

"Why this?" "Why now?" "Why me?!!" you thought as your eyes left Laura and drifted back to your desk.

Write down some ideas about how to handle this all-too-common conflict situation. Set it aside. We'll revisit your recommendation later in the chapter. In the meantime, we need to explore the world of conflict. After discussing a modern view of conflict and four major types of conflict, we learn how to manage conflict both as a participant and as a third party. The related topic of negotiation is examined next. We conclude with a contingency approach to conflict management and negotiation.

Make no mistake about it. Conflict is an unavoidable aspect of modern life. These major trends conspire to make *organizational* conflict inevitable:

Conflict: A Modern Perspective

- Constant change.
- Greater employee diversity.
- More teams (virtual and self-managed).
- Less face-to-face communication (more electronic interaction).
- A global economy with increased cross-cultural dealings.

Dean Tjosvold, from Canada's Simon Fraser University, notes that "Change begets conflict, conflict begets change"[2] and challenges us to do better with this sobering global perspective:

> Learning to manage conflict is a critical investment in improving how we, our families, and our organizations adapt and take advantage of change. Managing conflicts well does not insulate us from change, nor does it mean that we will always come out on top or get all that we want. However, effective conflict management helps us keep in touch with new developments and create solutions appropriate for new threats and opportunities.
>
> Much evidence shows we have often failed to manage our conflicts and respond to change effectively. High divorce rates, disheartening examples of sexual and physical abuse of children, the expensive failures of international joint ventures, and bloody ethnic violence have convinced many people that we do not have the abilities to cope with our complex interpersonal, organizational, and global conflicts.[3]

But respond we must. As outlined in this chapter, tools and solutions are available, if only we develop the ability and will to use them persistently. The choice is ours: Be active managers of conflict, or be managed by conflict.

A comprehensive review of the conflict literature yielded this consensus definition: "**conflict** is a process in which one party perceives that its interests are being opposed or negatively affected by another party."[4] The word *perceives* reminds us that sources of conflict and issues can be real or imagined. The resulting conflict is the same. Conflict can escalate (strengthen) or deescalate (weaken) over time. "The conflict process unfolds in a context, and whenever conflict, escalated or not, occurs the disputants or third parties can attempt to manage it in some manner."[5] Consequently, current and future managers need to understand the dynamics of conflict and know how to handle it effectively (both as disputants and as third parties).

Conflict
One party perceives its interests are being opposed or set back by another party.

A Conflict Continuum

Ideas about managing conflict underwent an interesting evolution during the 20th century. Initially, scientific management experts such as Frederick W Taylor believed all conflict ultimately threatened management's authority and thus had to be avoided or quickly resolved. Later, human relationists recognized the inevitability of conflict and advised managers to learn to live with it. Emphasis remained on resolving conflict whenever possible, however. Beginning in the 1970s, OB specialists realized conflict had both positive and negative outcomes, depending on its nature and intensity. This perspective introduced the revolutionary idea that organizations could suffer from *too little* conflict. Figure 14–1 illustrates the relationship between conflict intensity and outcomes.

Work groups, departments, or organizations that experience too little conflict tend to be plagued by apathy, lack of creativity, indecision, and missed deadlines. Excessive

Figure 14–1   *The Relationship between Conflict Intensity and Outcomes*

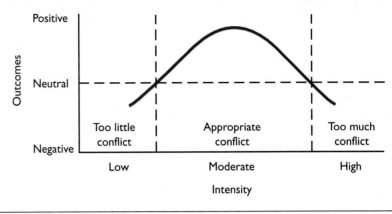

SOURCE: L D Brown, *Managing Conflict of Organizational Interfaces,* © 1986, Addison-Wesley Publishing Co., Inc., Reading, Massachusetts. Figure 1.1 on page 8. Reprinted with permission.

conflict, on the other hand, can erode organizational performance because of political infighting, dissatisfaction, lack of teamwork, and turnover. Workplace aggression and violence can be manifestations of excessive conflict.[6] Appropriate types and levels of conflict energize people in constructive directions.[7]

Functional versus Dysfunctional Conflict

Functional conflict
Serves organization's interests.

Dysfunctional conflict
Threatens organization's interests.

The distinction between **functional conflict** and **dysfunctional conflict** pivots on whether the organization's interests are served. According to one conflict expert,

> Some [types of conflict] support the goals of the organization and improve performance; these are functional, constructive forms of conflict. They benefit or support the main purposes of the organization. Additionally, there are those types of conflict that hinder organizational performance; these are dysfunctional or destructive forms. They are undesirable and the manager should seek their eradication.[8]

Functional conflict is commonly referred to in management circles as constructive or cooperative conflict.[9]

An interesting test of functional conflict will unfold during the next few years at Ford Motor Company. When Alex Trotman retired as CEO at the end of 1998, he was replaced by a two-man team. Australian-born Jacques Nasser became president and CEO. Henry Ford's great-grandson, William Clay Ford, Jr, became chairman of the board. According to *Fortune* magazine:

> Bill acknowledges the possibility of tensions. "I think Jac wanted to make sure I wasn't going to be a shadow CEO, and I wanted to make sure that he wasn't trying to do absolutely everything," he says. "We're both opinionated and not bashful about it. But that's fine—we'll close the door and yell at each other and work it out in private."[10]

In contrast, managers such as Fred Ackman, former chairman of Superior Oil Corporation, foster dysfunctional conflict by dealing with personalities rather than with issues:

> Employees say Ackman proved thoroughly autocratic, refusing even to discuss staff suggestions. He tended to treat disagreement as disloyalty. Many were put off by Ackman's

(DILBERT reprinted by permission of United Feature Syndicate, Inc.)

abusive temper, which together with his stature (5 feet 8 ½ inches) and red hair earned him the nickname "Little Red Fred." Says a former subordinate, "He couldn't stand it when somebody disagreed with him, even in private. He'd eat you up alive, calling you a dumb S.O.B. or asking if you had your head up your ass. It happened all the time."[11]

Not surprisingly, of 13 top executives at Superior Oil, 9 left within one year after Ackman joined the company.

Antecedents of Conflict

Certain situations produce more conflict than others. By knowing the antecedents of conflict, managers are better able to anticipate conflict and take steps to resolve it if it becomes dysfunctional. Among the situations that tend to produce either functional or dysfunctional conflict are

- Incompatible personalities or value systems.
- Overlapping or unclear job boundaries.
- Competition for limited resources.
- Interdepartment/intergroup competition.
- Inadequate communication.
- Interdependent tasks (e.g., one person cannot complete his or her assignment until others have completed their work).
- Organizational complexity (conflict tends to increase as the number of hierarchical layers and specialized tasks increase).
- Unreasonable or unclear policies, standards, or rules.
- Unreasonable deadlines or extreme time pressure.
- Collective decision making (the greater the number of people participating in a decision, the greater the potential for conflict).
- Decision making by consensus.
- Unmet expectations (employees who have unrealistic expectations about job assignments, pay, or promotions are more prone to conflict).
- Unresolved or suppressed conflicts.[12]

Proactive managers carefully read these early warnings and take appropriate action. For example, in North America, group conflict can be reduced by making decisions on the basis of a majority vote rather than seeking a consensus.

Desired Conflict Outcomes

Within organizations, conflict management is more than simply a quest for agreement. If progress is to be made and dysfunctional conflict minimized, a broader agenda is in order. Tjosvold's cooperative conflict model calls for three desired outcomes:

1. *Agreement.* But at what cost? Equitable and fair agreements are best. An agreement that leaves one party feeling exploited or defeated will tend to breed resentment and subsequent conflict.

2. *Stronger relationships.* Good agreements enable conflicting parties to build bridges of goodwill and trust for future use. Moreover, conflicting parties who trust each other are more likely to keep their end of the bargain.

3. *Learning.* Functional conflict can promote greater self-awareness and creative problem solving. Like the practice of management itself, successful conflict handling is learned primarily by doing. Knowledge of the concepts and techniques in this chapter is a necessary first step, but there is no substitute for hands-on practice. In a contentious world, there are plenty of opportunities to practice conflict management.[13]

Types of Conflict

Certain antecedents of conflict, highlighted earlier, deserve a closer look. This section probes the nature and organizational implications of four basic types of conflict: personality conflict, value conflict, intergroup conflict, and cross-cultural conflict. Our discussion of each type of conflict includes some practical tips and techniques.

Personality Conflict

We visited the topic of personalities in our Chapter 2 discussion of diversity. Also, recall the Big Five personality dimensions introduced in Chapter 5. Once again, your *personality* is the package of stable traits and characteristics creating your unique identity. According to experts on the subject:

> Each of us has a unique way of interacting with others. Whether we are seen as charming, irritating, fascinating, nondescript, approachable, or intimidating depends in part on our personality, or what others might describe as our style.[14]

Please take a moment to refer back to the OB Exercise on p 39 in Chapter 2 titled "Drawing Your Personality Profile." If you have not completed the exercise yet, it would be instructive to do so now. How helpful is this contrast of profiles (for yourself and another person) for pinpointing specific sources of personality conflict? Given the many possible combinations of personality traits, it is clear why personality conflicts are inevitable. We define a **personality conflict** as interpersonal opposition based on personal dislike and/or disagreement.

Personality conflict
Interpersonal opposition driven by personal dislike or disagreement.

Workplace Incivility: The Seeds of Personality Conflict   Somewhat akin to physical pain, chronic personality conflicts often begin with seemingly insignificant irritations. For instance, a manager can grow to deeply dislike someone in the next cubicle who persistently whistles off-key while drumming their foot on the side of a filing cabinet. Sadly, grim little scenarios such as this are all too common today, given the steady erosion of civility in the workplace. Researchers recently noted how increased

Workplace incivility can wreak havoc in a crowded and pressure-packed workplace. Conflict can be avoided by embedding civility and respect for others in the organization's culture. A simple "please" or "thank you" can build a needed bridge of goodwill between coworkers.

(Terry Vine/Tony Stone Images)

informality, pressure for results, and employee diversity have fostered an "anything goes" atmosphere in today's workplaces. They view incivility as a self-perpetuating vicious cycle that can end in violence.[15]

Vicious cycles of incivility need to be avoided (or broken early) with an organizational culture that places a high value on respect for co-workers. This requires managers and leaders to act as caring and courteous role models. A positive spirit of cooperation, as opposed to one based on negativism and aggression, also helps. Some organizations have resorted to workplace etiquette training. More specifically, constructive feedback and/or skillful behavior modification can keep a single irritating behavior from precipitating a full-blown personality conflict (or worse).

Dealing with Personality Conflicts   Personality conflicts are a potential minefield for managers. Let us frame the situation. Personality traits, by definition, are stable and resistant to change. Moreover, according to the American Psychiatric Association's *Diagnostic and Statistical Manual of Mental Disorders,* there are 410 psychological disorders that can and do show up in the workplace.[16] This brings up legal issues. Employees in the United States suffering from psychological disorders such as depression and mood-altering diseases such as alcoholism are protected from discrimination by the Americans with Disabilities Act.[17] (Other nations have similar laws.) Also, sexual harassment and other forms of discrimination can grow out of apparent personality conflicts.[18] Finally, personality conflicts can spawn workplace aggression and violence.[19]

Traditionally, managers dealt with personality conflicts by either ignoring them or transferring one party. In view of the legal implications, just discussed, both of these options may be open invitations to discrimination lawsuits. Table 14–1 presents practical tips for both

Ethics at Work

Examples of incivility in the workplace abound: answering the phone with a "yeah," neglecting to say thank you or please, using voice mail to screen calls, leaving a half cup of coffee behind to avoid having to brew the next pot, standing uninvited but impatiently over the desk of someone engaged in a telephone conversation, dropping trash on the floor and leaving it for the maintenance crew to clean up, and talking loudly on the phone about personal matters.

SOURCE: Excerpted from L M Andersson and C M Pearson, "Tit for Tat? The Spiraling Effect of Incivility in the Workplace," *Academy of Management Review,* July 1999, p 453.

You Decide . . .

If personally confronted with them, how would you handle each of these workplace incivilities? What other incivilities have you encountered on the job recently? What did you do?

For an interpretation of this situation, visit our Web site **www.mhhe.com/kreitner.**

Table 14–1   *How to Deal with Personality Conflicts*

Tips for Employees Having a Personality Conflict	Tips for Third-Party Observers of a Personality Conflict	Tips for Managers Whose Employees Are Having a Personality Conflict
• Follow company policies for diversity, anti-discrimination, and sexual harassment.	• Follow company policies for diversity, anti-discrimination, and sexual harassment.	• Follow company policies for diversity, anti-discrimination, and sexual harassment.
• Communicate directly with the other person to resolve the perceived conflict (emphasize problem solving and common objectives, not personalities).	• Do not take sides in someone else's personality conflict.	• Investigate and document conflict.
• Avoid dragging co-workers into the conflict.	• Suggest the parties work things out themselves in a constructive and positive way.	• If appropriate, take corrective action (e.g., feedback or B Mod).
• If dysfunctional conflict persists, seek help from direct supervisors or human resource specialists.	• If dysfunctional conflict persists, refer the problem to parties' direct supervisors.	• If necessary, attempt informal dispute resolution.
		• Refer difficult conflicts to human resource specialists or hired counselors for formal resolution attempts and other interventions.

nonmanagers and managers who are involved in or affected by personality conflicts. Our later discussions of handling dysfunctional conflict and alternative dispute resolution techniques also apply.

Value Conflict

In Chapter 3, we discussed organizational values, both espoused and enacted. We also looked at organizational value systems. Here, we look at *personal* values and how they can trigger various forms of conflict.

Value
(personal) Durable belief in a way of behaving or an end-state.

According to Milton Rokeach, a pioneering values researcher, a **value** is "an enduring belief that a specific mode of conduct or end-state of existence is personally or socially preferable to an opposite or converse mode of conduct or end-state of existence."[20] An individual's **value system** is defined by Rokeach as an "enduring organization of beliefs concerning preferable modes of conduct or end-states of existence along a continuum of relative importance."[21] Lifelong behavior patterns are dictated by values that are fairly well set by the time people are in their early teens. However, significant life-altering events—such as having a child, business failure, death of a loved one, going to war, or surviving a serious accident or disease—can reshape one's value system during adulthood.

Value system
The organization of one's beliefs about preferred ways of behaving and end-states of belief.

Extensive research supports Rokeach's contention that differing value systems go a long way toward explaining individual differences in behavior. Value → behavior connections have been documented for a wide variety of behaviors, ranging from weight loss to shopping selections to political party affiliation to religious involvement to choice of college major.[22] *Value conflict* can erupt when opposition is based on interpersonal differences in instrumental and terminal values.

Instrumental and Terminal Values   In line with his distinction between modes of conduct and end-states, Rokeach distinguishes between instrumental values and terminal values. **Instrumental values** are alternative behaviors or means by which we achieve desired ends. Sample instrumental values from Rokeach's original list of 18 are ambitious, honest, independent, loving, and obedient.[23] Someone who ranks the instrumental value "honest" highly, relative to the other instrumental values, is likely to be more honest than someone who gives it a low ranking.

> **Instrumental values**
> Personally preferred ways of behaving.

Highly ranked **terminal values**—such as a sense of accomplishment, happiness, pleasure, salvation, and wisdom—are desired end-states or life goals. Some would say terminal values are what life is all about. History is full of examples of people who were persecuted or put to death for their passionately held terminal values. Longitudinal evidence from value surveys during the 1960s, 1970s, and 1980s showed relative stability of terminal values among Americans, despite turbulent social and economic times. Six terminal values consistently ranked in the top one-third were family security, a world at peace, freedom, self-respect, happiness, and wisdom.[24]

> **Terminal values**
> Personally preferred end-states.

Now let us turn our attention to three kinds of value conflict: intrapersonal value conflict, interpersonal value conflict, and individual-organization value conflict. The sources of conflict are, respectively, from inside the person, between people, and between the person and the organization.

Intrapersonal Value Conflict   Inner conflict and resultant stress typically are experienced when highly ranked instrumental and terminal values pull the individual in different directions. This is somewhat akin to role conflict, as discussed in Chapter 12. The main difference is locus of influence: Role conflict involves *outside* social expectations; intrapersonal value conflict involves *internal* priorities. For employees who want balance in their lives, a stressful conflict arises when one values, for example, "being ambitious" (instrumental value) and "ending up happy" (terminal value). As the experience of Intel's director of new business development, Kirby Dyess, attests, it takes discipline to achieve balance in the face of intrapersonal value conflict.

> I can tell that I've hit the wall at work, and that I need to recalibrate my life, when I can no longer empathize with others, when I'm focused only on results, when I ignore other people's goals, and when I become frustrated with life's interruptions. Or when my daughter has to tell me, "It'll be all right, Kirby."
>
> To reorient my life, I take several important steps: Every day, I do something that's totally for myself. I constantly look for ways to simplify my life. And when I start to run out of creative juices, I avoid the temptation to work harder. Instead, I do something recreational, like gardening.[25]

Interpersonal Value Conflict   This type of value conflict parallels personality conflict. Just as people have different styles that may or may not mesh, they also embrace unique combinations of instrumental and terminal values that inevitably spark disagreement. Consider, for example, the situation of Chad Myers, a Peace Corps volunteer who spent his two-year tour of duty building latrines in Bolivia:

> "A lot of my friends were going into high-paying, good jobs," said Chad, a recent graduate of North Carolina State. "They look at me in shock and disgust and ask, 'Why are you working for free when you could be making $50,000 a year?' "
>
> Chad's rationale for joining the Peace Corps was apparent a few minutes later when he explained: "I've set a goal, and this is pretty high. If I can get 20 kids to wash their hands after going to the bathroom, I will have accomplished something that will have changed their lives and someday those of their children."[26]

Chad's goal would seem laughable to classmates acting out more selfish and material-istic values. But his unconventional value-driven behavior certainly means a lot to the health of his Bolivian friends.

Individual-Organization Value Conflict   As we saw in Chapter 3, companies actively seek to embed certain values into their corporate cultures. Conflict can occur when values espoused and enacted by the organization collide with employees' personal values.[27] This is a very common and persistent problem. For example, a culture shift at Time Warner, the huge entertainment company, hit some bumps. Time Warner began a program in 1999 to shed its reputation for internal warfare and get everyone to embrace "what the company calls its 'core values and guiding principles'—among them 'diversity,' 'respect,' and 'integrity.' "[28] One thousand executives were slated to attend two-day seminars to acquaint them with the "new" corporate values. As *The Wall Street Journal* reported at the time, it was not love at first sight:

> Not surprisingly for a company filled with cynical journalists and media executives, the program has met with some initial derision. For all the expensive management talent involved in the process, the values strike some employees as a bit obvious. In addition to diversity, respect, and integrity, other central values are "creativity," "community," and "teamwork."
>
> One senior executive who has attended innumerable meetings involved in the process describes the company's values statement as "The Boy Scout's oath. No nuclear bombs." (Even though the values statement says that Time Warner welcomes "divergent voices even if we risk controversy or loss," none of the internal critics of the program would allow their names to be used.)[29]

Like personalities, personal values are resistant to change.

Handling Value Conflicts through Values Clarification   For intrapersonal conflict, a Toronto management writer and consultant recommends getting out of what she calls "the busyness trap" by asking these questions:

- Is your work really meeting your most important needs?
- Are you defining yourself purely in terms of your accomplishments?
- Why are you working so hard? To what personal ends?
- Are you making significant sacrifices in favor of your work?
- Is your work schedule affecting other people who are important in your life?[30]

Meanwhile, a New Jersey management consultant tells us to fight interpersonal and individual-organization conflict by being value-centered leaders who consistently role model positive personal values.[31]

Yet another approach for dealing with all forms of value conflict is a career-counseling and team-building technique called *values clarification*. To gain useful hands-on experience, take a break from your reading and complete the OB Exercise on p 455. (Note: Rokeach's original value survey with 18 instrumental and 18 terminal values is ideal for this exercise, but the copyright holder does not permit mass reproduction.) The values listed in the OB Exercise, although not broken neatly into instrumental and terminal values, are a good substitute. Our key learning point is to get people to identify and talk about their personal values to establish common ground as a basis for teamwork and conflict avoidance and resolution.

OB Exercise Personal Values Clarification

Instructions for Individuals Working Alone

Review the following list of 30 values and then rank your top 6 values (1 = most important; 6 = least important). What *intra*personal value conflicts can you detect? How can you resolve them? Which, if any, of your cherished values likely conflict with those deemed important by your family, friends, co-workers, and employer? What could be done to reduce this interpersonal and individual-organizational value conflict?

Instructions for Teams

Each team member should begin by ranking their top six personal values, as specified above. Have someone record each team member's top-ranked value on a flip chart or chalkboard (no names attached). Then spend a few minutes discussing both differences and commonalities. Try to find common ground among seemingly different values. If your group is a task team, an additional step could be to derive four or more consensus values to guide the team's work. (Do not short-cut consensus seeking by voting.) How do your personal values align with your teammates' values and the team's consensus values? What needs to be done to reduce actual or threatened value conflict?

_____	Responsibility (joint and/or individual)	_____	Accomplishment
_____	Involvement in decision making	_____	Satisfying relationships
_____	Competence	_____	Creativity
_____	Meaning	_____	Self-worth
_____	Autonomy	_____	Self-expression
_____	Recognition	_____	Leadership opportunities
_____	Personal and professional growth	_____	Financial security
_____	New and different experiences	_____	Diversity
_____	Collaboration on common tasks	_____	Career mobility
_____	Harmony or an absence of conflict	_____	A sense of belonging
_____	Competition	_____	Shared fun and experiences
_____	Meeting deadlines in a timely manner	_____	Peace and serenity
_____	A high standard of excellence	_____	Good health
_____	Status, position	_____	Loyalty
_____	Stimulation from challenge and change	_____	Duty to family
		_____	Other _____

SOURCE: List of values quoted from L Gardenswartz and A Rowe, *Diverse Teams at Work: Capitalizing on the Power of Diversity* (New York: McGraw-Hill, 1994), p 85. © 1994. Reproduced with permission of the McGraw-Hill Companies.

Intergroup Conflict

Conflict among work groups, teams, and departments is a common threat to organizational competitiveness. For example, when Michael Volkema became CEO of Herman Miller in the mid-1990s, he found an inward-focused company with divisions fighting over budgets. He has since curbed intergroup conflict at the Michigan-based furniture maker by emphasizing collaboration and redirecting everyone's attention outward, to the customer.[32] Managers who understand the mechanics of intergroup conflict are better equipped to face this sort of challenge.

In-Group Thinking: The Seeds of Intergroup Conflict   As we discussed in previous chapters, *cohesiveness*—a "we feeling" binding group members together—can be a good or bad thing. A certain amount of cohesiveness can turn a group of individuals into a smooth-running team. Too much cohesiveness, however, can breed groupthink because a desire to get along pushes aside critical thinking. The study of in-groups by small group researchers has revealed a whole package of changes associated with increased group cohesiveness. Specifically,

- Members of in-groups view themselves as a collection of unique individuals, while they stereotype members of other groups as being "all alike."
- In-group members see themselves positively and as morally correct, while they view members of other groups negatively and as immoral.
- In-groups view outsiders as a threat.
- In-group members exaggerate the differences between their group and other groups. This typically involves a distorted perception of reality.[33]

Avid sports fans who simply can't imagine how someone would support the opposing team exemplify one form of in-group thinking. Also, this pattern of behavior is a form of ethnocentrism, discussed as a cross-cultural barrier in Chapter 4. Reflect for a moment on evidence of in-group behavior in your life. Does your circle of friends make fun of others because of their race, gender, nationality, sexual preference, or major in college?

In-group thinking is one more fact of organizational life that virtually guarantees conflict. Managers cannot eliminate in-group thinking, but they certainly should not ignore it when handling intergroup conflicts.

 Research Lessons for Handling Intergroup Conflict   Sociologists have long recommended the contact hypothesis for reducing intergroup conflict. According to the *contact hypothesis,* the more the members of different groups interact, the less intergroup conflict they will experience. Those interested in improving race, international, and union-management relations typically encourage cross-group interaction. The hope is that *any* type of interaction, short of actual conflict, will reduce stereotyping and combat in-group thinking. But recent research has shown this approach to be naive and limited. For example, one recent study of 83 health center employees (83% female) at a midwest US university probed the specific nature of intergroup relations and concluded:

> The number of *negative* relationships was significantly related to higher perceptions of intergroup conflict. Thus, it seems that negative relationships have a salience that overwhelms any possible positive effects from friendship links across groups.[34]

Intergroup friendships are still desirable, as documented in many studies,[35] but they are readily overpowered by negative intergroup interactions. Thus, *priority number 1 for managers faced with intergroup conflict is to identify and root out specific negative linkages among groups.* A single personality conflict, for instance, may contaminate the entire intergroup experience. The same goes for an employee who voices negative opinions or spreads negative rumors about another group. Our updated contact model in Figure 14–2 is based on this and other recent research insights, such as the need to foster positive attitudes toward other groups.[36] Also, notice how conflict within the group and negative gossip from third parties are threats that need to be neutralized if intergroup conflict is to be minimized.

As demonstrated by British Airways in the International OB on p 458, the quest for good intergroup relations needs to be creative, systematic, and relentless.

Figure 14–2   *An Updated Contact Model for Minimizing Intergroup Conflict*

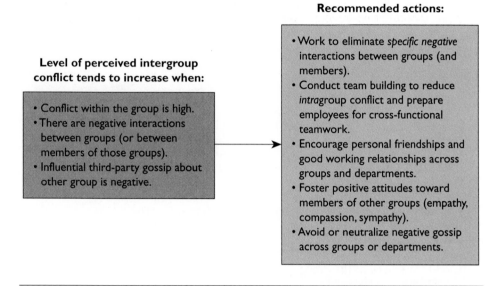

Recommended actions:

Level of perceived intergroup conflict tends to increase when:

- Conflict within the group is high.
- There are negative interactions between groups (or between members of those groups).
- Influential third-party gossip about other group is negative.

- Work to eliminate *specific negative* interactions between groups (and members).
- Conduct team building to reduce *intragroup* conflict and prepare employees for cross-functional teamwork.
- Encourage personal friendships and good working relationships across groups and departments.
- Foster positive attitudes toward members of other groups (empathy, compassion, sympathy).
- Avoid or neutralize negative gossip across groups or departments.

SOURCE: Based on research evidence in G Labianca, D J Brass, and B Gray, "Social Networks and Perceptions of Intergroup Conflict: The Role of Negative Relationships and Third Parties," *Academy of Management Journal,* February 1998, pp 55–67; C D Batson et al., "Empathy and Attitudes: Can Feeling for a Member of a Stigmatized Group Improve Feelings toward the Group?" *Journal of Personality and Social Psychology,* January 1997, pp 105–18; and S C Wright et al., "The Extended Contact Effect: Knowledge of Cross-Group Friendships and Prejudice," *Journal of Personality and Social Psychology,* July 1997, pp 73–90.

Cross-Cultural Conflict

Doing business with people from different cultures is commonplace in our global economy where cross-border mergers, joint ventures, and alliances are the order of the day.[37] Because of differing assumptions about how to think and act, the potential for cross-cultural conflict is both immediate and huge.[38] Success or failure, when conducting business across cultures, often hinges on avoiding and minimizing actual or perceived conflict. For example, consider this cultural mismatch:

> Mexicans place great importance on saving face, so they tend to expect any conflicts that occur during negotiations to be downplayed or kept private. The prevailing attitude in the [United States], however, is that conflict should be dealt with directly and publicly to prevent hard feelings from developing on a personal level.[39]

This is not a matter of who is right and who is wrong; rather it is a matter of accommodating cultural differences for a successful business transaction. Awareness of the cross-cultural differences we discussed in Chapters 4 and 6—individualism/collectivism, perceptions of time, interpersonal space, language, religion, and universalist(rules)/particularist(relationships)—is an important first step. Beyond that, cross-cultural conflict can be moderated by using international consultants and building cross-cultural relationships.

International Consultants   In response to broad demand, there is a growing army of management consultants specializing in cross-cultural relations. Competency

International OB — Breaking Barriers at British Airways

Who Marcia Bradley, 45, marketing manager, culture-change projects, British Airways.

What's Your Problem? "We're quality fanatics. There's a 'BA way,' and there's a wrong way. But sometimes we go outside the company for ideas. How do I turn outsiders into insiders without compromising their ideas? How do I convince insiders to give outsiders a chance?"

Tell Me About It "I'm part of a major initiative to rethink the experience of being at an airport. I work with lots of vendors and consultants. But we have such a strong way of doing things at BA that there's a tendency to keep outsiders at arm's length. We risk creating great proposals that collect dust—or rolling out initiatives that don't meet expectations. I need to show my BA colleagues and my outside colleagues what they can learn from each other."

What's Your Solution? "Total immersion. Before we even think about a proposal, we might spend three months introducing our partners to BA, and vice versa. We make sure that the consultants experience our product. We arrange for them to fly BA to meetings—both in Club Class (first class) and in World Traveller (economy class). We ask for their impressions: How comfortable were the seats? How long did you wait at the counter? We open a dialogue about the company.

Courtesy of British Airways

"Partners also meet key BA players—in structured get-to-know-you gatherings as well as for brainstorming. We even ask these partners to spend time with people whom they won't be working with. They visit departments; they drop in on meetings.

"Finally, they get a formal education in BA's values and in our brand integrity. It's part history lesson, part rules-of-the-road orientation. We cover everything from our principles of customer service to the choice of colors on our aircraft.

"The payoff is huge. When it's time to sign off on budgets or to approve designs, we do it faster and more confidently."

SOURCE: C Olofson, "Let Outsiders In, Turn Your Insiders Out," *Fast Company*, March 1999, p 46.

---

and fees vary widely, of course. But a carefully selected cross-cultural consultant can be helpful, as this illustration shows:

> Last year, when electronics-maker Canon planned to set up a subsidiary in Dubai through its Netherlands division, it asked consultant Sahid Mirza of Glocom, based in Dubai, to find out how the two cultures would work together.
>
> Mirza sent out the test questionnaires and got a sizeable response. "The findings were somewhat surprising," he recalls. "We found that, at the bedrock level, there were relatively few differences. Many of the Arab businessmen came from former British colonies and viewed business in much the same way as the Dutch."
>
> But at the level of behavior, there was a real conflict. "The Dutch are blunt and honest in expression, and such expression is very offensive to Arab sensibilities." Mirza offers the example of a Dutch executive who says something like, "We can't meet the deadline." Such a negative expression—true or not—would be gravely offensive to an Arab. As a result of Mirza's research, Canon did start the subsidiary in Dubai, but it trained both the Dutch and the Arab executives first.[40]

Consultants also can help untangle possible personality, value, and intergroup conflicts from conflicts rooted in differing national cultures. Note: Although we have discussed

Table 14–2   *Ways to Build Cross-Cultural Relationships*

Behavior	Rank
Be a good listener	1
Be sensitive to needs of others	2
Be cooperative, rather than overly competitive	2
Advocate inclusive (participative) leadership	3
Compromise rather than dominate	4
Build rapport through conversations	5
Be compassionate and understanding	6
Avoid conflict by emphasizing harmony	7
Nurture others (develop and mentor)	8

(Rank 2 and 2 are marked with a brace labeled "Tie")

SOURCE: Adapted from R L Tung, "American Expatriates Abroad: From Neophytes to Cosmopolitans," *Journal of World Business*, Summer 1998, Table 6, p 136.

these four basic types of conflict separately, they typically are encountered in complex, messy bundles.

Building Cross-Cultural Relationships to Avoid Dysfunctional Conflict

Rosalie L Tung's recent study of 409 expatriates from US and Canadian multinational firms, mentioned in Chapter 4, is very instructive.[41] Her survey sought to pinpoint success factors for the expatriates (14% female) who were working in 51 different countries worldwide. Nine specific ways to facilitate interaction with host-country nationals, as ranked from most useful to least useful by the respondents, are listed in Table 14–2. Good listening skills topped the list, followed by sensitivity to others and cooperativeness rather than competitiveness. Interestingly, US managers are culturally characterized as just the opposite: poor listeners, blunt to the point of insensitivity, and excessively competitive. Some managers need to add self-management to the list of ways to minimize cross-cultural conflict.

As we have seen, conflict has many faces and is a constant challenge for managers who are responsible for reaching organizational goals. Our attention now turns to the active management of both functional and dysfunctional conflict. We discuss how to stimulate functional conflict, how to handle dysfunctional conflict, and how third parties can deal effectively with conflict. Relevant research lessons also are examined.

Managing Conflict

Stimulating Functional Conflict

Sometimes committees and decision-making groups become so bogged down in details and procedures that nothing substantive is accomplished. Carefully monitored functional conflict can help get the creative juices flowing once again. Managers basically have two options. They can fan the fires of naturally occurring conflict—but this approach can be unreliable and slow. Alternatively, managers can resort to programmed

Programmed conflict

Encourages different opinions without protecting management's personal feelings.

conflict. Experts in the field define **programmed conflict** as "conflict that raises different opinions *regardless of the personal feelings of the managers.*"[42] The trick is to get contributors to either defend or criticize ideas based on relevant facts rather than on the basis of personal preference or political interests. This requires disciplined role playing. Two programmed conflict techniques with proven track records are devil's advocacy and the dialectic method. Let us explore these two ways of stimulating functional conflict.

Devil's Advocacy   This technique gets its name from a traditional practice within the Roman Catholic Church. When someone's name came before the College of Cardinals for elevation to sainthood, it was absolutely essential to ensure that he or she had a spotless record. Consequently, one individual was assigned the role of *devil's advocate* to uncover and air all possible objections to the person's canonization. In accordance with this practice, **devil's advocacy** in today's organizations involves assigning someone the role of critic.[43] Recall from Chapter 12, Irving Janis recommended the devil's advocate role for preventing groupthink.

Devil's advocacy

Assigning someone the role of critic.

In the left half of Figure 14–3, note how devil's advocacy alters the usual decision-making process in steps 2 and 3. This approach to programmed conflict is intended to generate critical thinking and reality testing.[44] It is a good idea to rotate the job of devil's advocate so no one person or group develops a strictly negative reputation. Moreover, periodic devil's advocacy role-playing is good training for developing analytical and communication skills.

The Dialectic Method   Like devil's advocacy, the dialectic method is a time-honored practice. This particular approach to programmed conflict traces back to the dialectic school of philosophy in ancient Greece. Plato and his followers attempted to synthesize truths by exploring opposite positions (called thesis and antithesis). Court systems in the United States and elsewhere rely on directly opposing points of view for determining guilt or innocence. Accordingly, today's **dialectic method** calls for managers to foster a structured debate of opposing viewpoints prior to making a decision.[45] Steps 3 and 4 in the right half of Figure 14–3 set the dialectic approach apart from the normal decision-making process. Here is how Anheuser-Busch's corporate policy committee uses the dialectic method:

Dialectic method

Fostering a debate of opposing viewpoints to better understand an issue.

> When the policy committee … considers a major move—getting into or out of a business, or making a big capital expenditure—it sometimes assigns teams to make the case for each side of the question. There may be two teams or even three. Each is knowledgeable about the subject; each has access to the same information. Occasionally someone in favor of the project is chosen to lead the dissent, and an opponent to argue for it. Pat Stokes, who heads the company's beer empire, describes the result: "We end up with decisions and alternatives we hadn't thought of previously," sometimes representing a synthesis of the opposing views. "You become a lot more anticipatory, better able to see what might happen, because you have thought through the process."[46]

A major drawback of the dialectic method is that "winning the debate" may overshadow the issue at hand. Also, the dialectic method requires more skill training than does devil's advocacy. Regarding the comparative effectiveness of these two approaches to stimulating functional conflict, however, a laboratory study ended in a tie. Compared with groups that strived to reach a consensus, decision-making groups using either devil's advocacy or the dialectic method yielded equally higher

Figure 14–3   *Techniques for Stimulating Functional Conflict: Devil's Advocacy and the Dialectic Method*

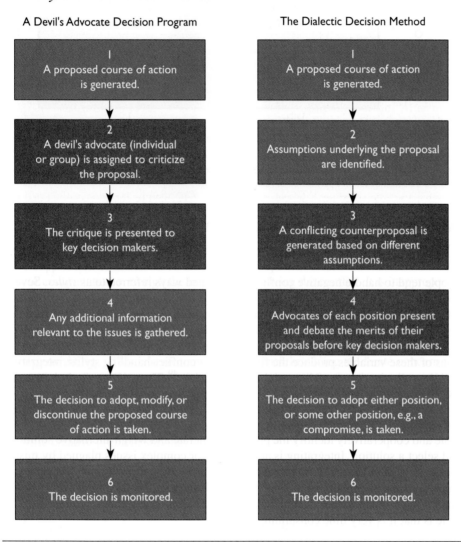

SOURCE: R A Cosier and C R Schwenk, "Agreement and Thinking Alike: Ingredients for Poor Decisions," *Academy of Management Executive,* February 1990, pp 72–73. Used with permission.

quality decisions.[47] But, in a more recent laboratory study, groups using devil's advocacy produced more potential solutions and made better recommendations for a case problem than did groups using the dialectic method.[48] In light of this mixed evidence, managers have some latitude in using either devil's advocacy or the dialectic method for pumping creative life back into stalled deliberations. Personal preference and the role players' experience may well be the deciding factors in choosing one approach over the other. The important thing is to actively stimulate functional conflict when necessary (such as when the risk of blind conformity or groupthink is high).

5. *Discuss what can be done about cross-cultural conflict.* International consultants can prepare people from different cultures to work effectively together. Cross-cultural conflict can be minimized by having expatriates build strong cross-cultural relationships with their hosts (primarily by being good listeners, being sensitive to others, and being more cooperative than competitive).

6. *Explain how managers can stimulate functional conflict, and identify the five conflict-handling styles.* There are many antecedents of conflict—including incompatible personalities, competition for limited resources, and unrealized expectations—that need to be monitored. Functional conflict can be stimulated by permitting antecedents of conflict to persist and/or programming conflict during decision making with devil's advocates or the dialectic method. The five conflict-handling styles are integrating (problem solving), obliging (smoothing), dominating (forcing), avoiding, and compromising. There is no single best style.

7. *Explain the nature and practical significance of conflict triangles and alternative dispute resolution for third-party conflict inter-*vention. A conflict triangle occurs when one member of a conflict seeks the help of a third party rather than facing the opponent directly. Detriangling is advised, whereby the third-party redirects the disputants' energy toward each other in a positive and constructive manner. Alternative dispute resolution (ADR) involves avoiding costly court battles with more informal and user-friendly techniques such as facilitation, conciliation, peer review, ombudsman, mediation, and arbitration.

8. *Explain the difference between distributive and integrative negotiation, and discuss the concept of added-value negotiation.* Distributive negotiation involves fixed-pie and win-lose thinking. Integrative negotiation is a win-win approach to better results for both parties. The five steps in added value negotiation are as follows: Step 1, clarify interests; Step 2, identify options; Step 3, design alternative deal packages; Step 4, select a deal; and Step 5, perfect the deal. Elements of value, multiple deals, and creative agreement are central to this approach.

Discussion Questions

1. What examples of functional and dysfunctional conflict have you observed lately?

2. Which of the antecedents of conflict do you think are most common (or most troublesome) in today's workplaces?

3. Have you ever been directly involved in a personality conflict? Explain. Was it handled well? Explain. What could have been done differently?

4. Does your personal value profile in the OB Exercise help explain any intrapersonal, interpersonal, or individual-organization value conflict you may have experienced? Explain.

5. How could in-group thinking affect the performance of a manager living and working in a foreign country?

6. Which of the five conflict-handling styles is your strongest (your weakest)? How can you improve your ability to handle conflict?

7. What is your personal experience with conflict triangles? Based on what you have learned in this chapter, do you think you could do a better job of handling conflict triangles in the future? Explain.

8. Which of the six ADR techniques appeals the most to you? Why?

9. Has your concept of negotiation, prior to reading this chapter, been restricted to "fixed-pie" thinking? Explain.

10. How could added-value negotiation make your life a bit easier? Explain in terms of a specific problem, conflict, or deadlock.

Internet Exercise

www.books.mcgraw-hill.com
www.adrr.com
www.cybersettle.com/
www.pon.harvard.edu

A great deal of interesting and useful material about conflict and negotiation can be found on the Internet. This is a good thing because the more than six billion inhabitants of this planet have a lot to learn about getting along. The purpose of this exercise is to help develop your conflict-handling skills and broaden your understanding of alternative dispute resolution (ADR) and negotiation.

An Exercise on Dealing with a Poor Working Relationship

McGraw-Hill, the publisher of this textbook, has an extensive online collection of free training games and exercises gleaned from McGraw-Hill publications. Start with the Internet home page www.books.mcgraw-hill.com, and select the main menu item "Education & Training." (Note: Although this is a commercial Web site, you need not buy anything to complete this exercise.) On successive pages, select the following chain of items from the main menus: "Training McGraw-Hill," "Trainer's Toolchest," and "Free Training Games." At the "Free Training Games" page, scroll down to the heading "Conflict Resolution" and select "Dialogue with an Imaginary Guru." (Note: Although this exercise is intended to be administered to a group, you can work through it yourself.) Be sure to read the "D.A.R.R.N.-It!" handout for step 1. In step 2, complete the "Dialogue" handout. You probably will want to print personal copies of these handouts. Be creative and have fun when writing the dialogue with your imaginary guru.

Background Information on ADR

Stephen R Marsh, a lawyer and mediator from Dallas, Texas, has compiled an extensive and user-friendly Internet site on alternative dispute resolution (www.adrr.com). In volume one of the Mediation Essays, be sure to select and read the material under the headings "What Is Mediation?" and "Negotiation in Mediation." In volume three of the Mediation Essays, the heading "Defining Conflict" presents an instructive perspective. There are many other good readings, depending on your interests and circumstances. Also, pay a quick visit to www.cybersettle.com/ to get an idea of how the power and scope of the Internet is being used to avoid costly lawsuits through ADR.

Research Updates on Negotiation

Harvard Law School, in cooperation with other leading universities, hosts the Internet site "Program on Negotiation" (www.pon.harvard.edu). Select the heading "Publications" from the main menu. Next, click on "Negotiation Journal" and survey the brief article summaries from recent issues of that quarterly journal. Focus on topics and findings related to managing organizational behavior.

Questions

1. If you completed the Imaginary Guru exercise, was it helpful to take a different perspective of your poor working relationship? Explain. How important is it to "walk in the other person's shoes" when trying to avoid or resolve a conflict? Explain.

2. Why is there so much interest in ADR these days? Are you presently involved in a dispute or conflict that could be mediated? Explain. What do you think of Cybersettle.com? Does it seem practical?

3. What new insights did you pick up from the *Negotiation Journal?* Explain.

OB in Action Case Study

www.rowefurniture.com

Charlene Pedrolie Rearranged Furniture and Lifted a Business[81]

When business picked up, the knives came out. Charlene Pedrolie had just introduced the latest management methods at the big, old flagship factory of Rowe Furniture Corp. [in Salem, Virginia]. Workers had been organized into "cells." Cross-training had been instituted. Four layers of supervision had been wiped out.

But when orders surged for the 1995 fall season, the cells couldn't keep up. Workers were pressured by stress under the new rules and frazzled by change; one had a nervous breakdown. Skeptics questioned not only the new processes but the new boss—a 34-year-old Yankee female, a complete outsider in an old-line Dixie company.

Yet today, attitudes have changed 180 degrees. Output and earnings are surging, making Rowe a hot stock in the furniture group. How Ms Pedrolie pulled it off teaches a valuable lesson not only in the management of change but also in the attainment of corporate power.

Rowe Furniture was stuck midway through a major transformation when it recruited her in April 1995 from a plant manager's job at General Electric. Rowe's research showed that people hate buying upholstered furniture. They want a much wider selection than any showroom can display, yet they refuse to wait months for a special order. So Rowe created a computer network on which customers could match fabrics and styles, promising speedy delivery and a midrange price.

The marketing solution, however, created problems upstream. Rowe's factory had to produce a much wider variety of products in much less time, all with no increase in cost. Making that happen was Ms Pedrolie's assignment.

In her mind, there was little mystery about the method. She would annihilate the inefficient old assembly line. Sewers, gluers, staplers, and stuffers would be brought together in cells of roughly 35. Through cross training, everyone in the cell could do every job related to making a sofa, instead of doing one job on every piece. When anyone had time to spare they could help someone getting backed up.

Supervisors, used to pushing for the maximum performance in a single task (more cushions! faster sewing!), would be eliminated. Perhaps most important, workers could act on their own ideas for improving productivity.

When Ms Pedrolie outlined the plan to her fellow officers during a meeting at the local Holiday Inn, "We sat there and thought, 'She's crazy,' " recalls Steve Sherlor, a company vice president.

So Ms Pedrolie resolved to pull off the plan with blinding speed, leaving no time for second-guessing. Though given to spontaneous cheers ("all right!" "way to go!"), she was stern. Some managers who resisted her changes got the ax.

The production workers, for their part, returned after the brief plant makeover agog to see their power tools dangling from the ceiling in clusters instead of in a long, straight line. Suddenly they were working alongside—and forced to communicate with—three dozen cell members. Accustomed to having the parts come to them, they were dragging raw materials to their cells and bumping into one another along the way. Productivity fell as staplers learned to glue and gluers to staple.

The success of Rowe's retailing initiative only worsened the problems at the plant. Schedules swelled to 58 hours a week; tempers grew short. "It was really touch and go," recalls General Manager John Sisson. The naysayers began their I-told-you-sos, and Ms Pedrolie began losing sleep, worrying management would call everything off.

Thankfully, the passage of a few weeks—and the regular Christmas shutdown—proved therapeutic. As workers returned from vacation to a less frenzied schedule, cells began to function as teams. Workers realized they could snuff out problems instantly when they occurred within the cell, whereas solutions were slow to come on the old assembly lines. As productivity recovered and then surpassed previous levels, incentive payments inched higher.

People also noticed that the factory was bathed in sunlight; the company had scraped the paint from the windows, the legacy of a past energy crisis. "It's important to make the environment part of the change," Ms Pedrolie says. "It prevents people from wanting to go back to the old."

Most important of all, shop-floor workers were stunned to see their ideas triggering action, which in turn triggered more ideas. One task force found a better way to stuff pillows. A loading crew made the case for larger truck trailers. Another group created a new revenue source by selling spare kiln capacity to lumber-drying operations. (Workers can leave their jobs to join task forces because of cross-training.)

Today, the plant operates at record productivity. "Everybody's a lot happier," says shop worker Sally Huffman. Ms Pedrolie is now turning her attention to the office, cross-training the credit, order, and customer-service people so that any one employee can handle all of a dealer's needs.

What is the lesson? Partly that Ms Pedrolie played the change game shrewdly. But more fundamentally, that she followed an enduring precept in the exercise of power: The more widely that true authority is dispersed, the firmer the foundations of management.

Questions for Discussion

1. What antecedents of conflict can you detect in this case? Which one(s) presented the greatest obstacle to Pedrolie's new way of doing things? Explain.

2. How big a problem was in-group thinking in this case? Explain.

3. Which of the cross-cultural relationship building behaviors in Table 14–2 would have served Pedrolie well during the change? Explain.

4. What evidence of functional and dysfunctional conflict can you detect in this case?

5. Which conflict-handling styles did Pedrolie use effectively (or ineffectively)?

Personal Awareness and Growth Exercise

What Is Your Primary Conflict-Handling Style?

Objectives

1. To continue building your self-awareness.
2. To assess your approach to conflict.
3. To provide a springboard for handling conflicts more effectively.

Introduction

Professor Afzalur Rahim, developer of the five-style conflict model in Figure 14–4, created an assessment instrument upon which the one in this exercise is based. The original instrument was validated through a factor analysis of responses from 1,219 managers from across the United States.[82]

Instructions

For each of the 15 items, indicate how often you rely on that tactic by circling the appropriate number.

Conflict-Handling Tactics	Rarely			Always

1. I argue my case with my co-workers to show the merits of my position.   1 — 2 —③— 4 — 5

2. I negotiate with my co-workers so that a compromise can be reached.   1 — 2 — 3 —④— 5

3. I try to satisfy the expectations of my co-workers.   1 — 2 — 3 —④— 5

4. I try to investigate an issue with my co-workers to find a solution acceptable to us.   1 — 2 — 3 — 4 —⑤

5. I am firm in pursuing my side of the issue.   1 — 2 — 3 —④— 5

6. I attempt to avoid being "put on the spot" and try to keep my conflict with my co-workers to myself.   1 —②— 3 — 4 — 5

7. I hold on to my solution to a problem.   1 — 2 —③— 4 — 5

8. I use "give and take" so that a compromise can be made.   1 — 2 — 3 —④— 5

9. I exchange accurate information with my co-workers to solve a problem together.   1 — 2 — 3 —④— 5

10. I avoid open discussion of my differences with my co-workers.   1 —②— 3 — 4 — 5

11. I accommodate the wishes of my co-workers.   1 — 2 —③— 4 — 5

12. I try to bring all our concerns out in the open so that the issues can be resolved in the best possible way.   1 — 2 — 3 —④— 5

13. I propose a middle ground for breaking deadlocks.   1 — 2 — 3 —④— 5

14. I go along with the suggestions of my co-workers.   1 — 2 —③— 4 — 5

15. I try to keep my disagreements with my co-workers to myself in order to avoid hard feelings.   1 —②— 3 — 4 — 5

Scoring and Interpretation

Enter your responses, item by item, in the five categories below, and then add the three scores for each of the styles. Note: There are no right or wrong answers, because individual differences are involved.

Integrating		Obliging		Dominating	
Item	Score	Item	Score	Item	Score
4.	5	3.	4	1	3
9.	4	11.	3	5.	4
12.	4	14.	3	7.	3
Total =	13	Total =	10	Total =	10

Avoiding		Compromising	
Item	Score	Item	Score
6.	2	2.	4
10.	2	8.	4
15.	2	13.	4
Total =	6	Total =	12

Your primary conflict-handling style is : ___Integrating___
(The category with the highest total.)

Your backup conflict-handling style is: ___Avoiding___
(The category with the second highest total.)

Questions for Discussion

1. Are the results what you expected? Explain.

2. Is there a clear gap between your primary and backup styles, or did they score about the same? If they are about the same, does this suggest indecision about handling conflict on your part? Explain.

3. Will your primary conflict-handling style carry over well to many different situations? Explain.

4. What is your personal learning agenda for becoming a more effective conflict handler?

Group Exercise

Bangkok Blowup (A Role-Playing Exercise)

Objectives

1. To further your knowledge of interpersonal conflict and conflict-handling styles.

2. To give you a firsthand opportunity to try the various styles of handling conflict.

Introduction

This is a role-playing exercise intended to develop your ability to handle conflict. There is no single best way to resolve the conflict in this exercise. One style might work for one person, while another gets the job done for someone else.

Instructions

Read the following short case, "Can Larry Fit In?" Pair up with someone else and decide which of you will play the role of Larry and which will play the role of Melissa, the office manager. Pick up the action from where the case leaves off. Try to be realistic and true to the characters in the case. The manager is primarily responsible for resolving this conflict situation. Whoever plays Larry should resist any unreasonable requests or demands and cooperate with any personally workable solution. Note: To conserve time, try to resolve this situation in less than 15 minutes.

CASE: "CAN LARRY FIT IN?"[83]

Melissa, Office Manager

You are the manager of an auditing team sent to Bangkok, Thailand, to represent a major international accounting firm headquartered in New York. You and Larry, one of your auditors, were sent to Bangkok to set up an auditing operation. Larry is about seven years older than you and has five more years seniority in the firm. Your relationship has become very strained since you were recently designated as the office manager. You feel you were given the promotion because you have established an excellent working relationship with the Thai staff as well as a broad range of international clients. In contrast, Larry has told other members of the staff that your promotion simply reflects the firm's heavy emphasis on affirmative action. He has tried to isolate you from the all-male accounting staff by focusing discussions on sports, local night spots, and so forth.

You are sitting in your office reading some complicated new reporting procedures that have just arrived from the home office. Your concentration is suddenly interrupted by a loud knock on your door. Without waiting for an invitation to enter, Larry bursts into your office. He is obviously very upset, and it is not difficult for you to surmise why he is in such a nasty mood.

You recently posted the audit assignments for the coming month, and you scheduled Larry for a job you knew he wouldn't like. Larry is one of your senior auditors, and the company norm is that they get the choice assignments. This particular job will require him to spend two weeks away from Bangkok in a remote town, working with a company whose records are notoriously messy.

Unfortunately, you have had to assign several of these less-desirable audits to Larry recently because you are short of personnel. But that's not the only reason. You have received several complaints from the junior staff (all Thais) recently that Larry treats them in a condescending manner. They feel he is always looking for an opportunity to boss them around, as if he were their supervisor instead of an experienced, supportive mentor. As a result, your whole operation works more smoothly when you can send Larry out of town on a solo project for several days. It keeps him from coming into your office and telling you how to do your job, and the morale of the rest of the auditing staff is significantly higher.

Larry slams the door and proceeds to express his anger over this assignment.

Larry, Senior Auditor

You are really ticked off! Melissa is deliberately trying to undermine your status in the office. She knows that the company norm is that senior auditors get the better jobs. You've paid your dues, and now you expect to be treated with respect. And this isn't the first time this has happened. Since she was made the office manager, she has tried to keep you out of the office as much as possible. It's as if she doesn't want her rival for leadership of the office around. When you were asked to go to Bangkok, you assumed that you would be made the office manager because of your seniority in the firm. You are certain that the decision to pick Melissa is yet another indication of reverse discrimination against white males.

In staff meetings, Melissa has talked about the need to be sensitive to the feelings of the office staff as well as the clients in this multicultural setting. "Where does she come off preaching about sensitivity! What about my feelings, for heaven's sake?" you wonder. This is nothing more than a straightforward power play. She is probably feeling insecure about being the only female accountant in the office and being promoted over someone with more experience. "Sending me out of town," you decide, "is a clear case of 'out of sight, out of mind.'"

Well, it's not going to happen that easily. You are not going to roll over and let her treat you unfairly. It's time for a showdown. If she doesn't agree to change this assignment and apologize for the way she's been treating you, you're going to register a formal complaint with her boss in the New York office. You are prepared to submit your resignation if the situation doesn't improve.

Questions for Discussion

1. What antecedents of conflict appear to be present in this situation? What can be done about them?

2. Having heard how others handled this conflict, did one particular style seem to work better than the others?

Part Four

Organizational Processes

Chapter Fifteen

Organizational Communication in the Internet Age

Learning Objectives

When you finish studying the material in this chapter, you should be able to:

1 Describe the perceptual process model of communication.

2 Explain the contingency approach to media selection.

3 Contrast the communication styles of assertiveness, aggressiveness, and nonassertiveness.

4 Discuss the primary sources of both nonverbal communication and listener comprehension.

5 Identify and give examples of the three different listening styles, and review the 10 keys to effective listening.

6 Describe the communication differences between men and women, and explain the source of these differences.

7 Discuss patterns of hierarchical communication and the grapevine.

8 Demonstrate your familiarity with four antecedents of communication distortion between managers and employees.

9 Explain the information technology of Internet/Intranet/Extranet, E-mail, videoconferencing, and collaborative computing, and explain the related use of telecommuting.

10 Describe the process, personal, physical, and semantic barriers to effective communication.

BusinessWeek Dennis M Kubit, chief executive of Trans-General Group, a Pittsburgh insurance outfit, used to be like most executives in his stodgy industry. He rarely surfed the Internet, and his company's Web site was little more than a shingle emblazoned with the corporate name and a list of services. But last year, customers and brokers began asking about the insurer's Internet strategy. Banks, for instance, wanted to sell Trans-General's products over the Web. So, six months ago, Kubit decided he had to get wired— and fast. Now he spends one to two hours a day online, checking out rivals' Web sites and surfing for industry news. "We felt we were behind and we needed to catch up," he says.

Kubit isn't the only one. Even as electronic commerce is poised to bring sweeping changes to virtually every industry, fewer than one-third of CEOs in the United States consider themselves Web-literate, according to a PricewaterhouseCoopers survey of more than 800 CEOs that was released in January. Only one in four surf the Web regularly, and 69% describe their Internet sophistication as fair or poor. . . .

At Trans-General, Kubit might be considered the house "dot com" these days. Since the fall, he has hired a chief information officer, Charles Klein, and gotten himself some one-on-one training to learn how the Web might be

Going online means dramatic changes both externally and internally for organizations like Levi Strauss & Company.
(Scott Goodwin Photography)

Figure 15–4   *Communication Competence Affects Upward Mobility*

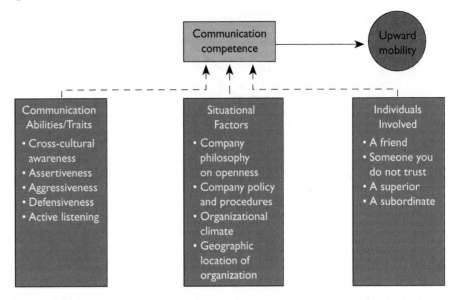

your control: assertiveness, aggressiveness, nonassertiveness, nonverbal communication, and active listening. We conclude this section by discussing gender differences in communication.

Assertiveness, Aggressiveness, and Nonassertiveness

The saying, "You can attract more flies with honey than with vinegar," captures the difference between using an assertive communication style and an aggressive style. Research studies indicate that assertiveness is more effective than aggressiveness in both work-related and consumer contexts.[20] An **assertive style** is expressive and self-enhancing and is based on the "ethical notion that it is not right or good to violate our own or others' basic human rights, such as the right to self-expression or the right to be treated with dignity and respect."[21] In contrast, an **aggressive style** is expressive and self-enhancing and strives to take unfair advantage of others. A **nonassertive style** is characterized by timid and self-denying behavior. Nonassertiveness is ineffective because it gives the other person an unfair advantage.

Managers may improve their communication competence by trying to be more assertive and less aggressive or nonassertive. This can be achieved by using the appropriate nonverbal and verbal behaviors listed in Table 15–2. For instance, managers should attempt to use the nonverbal behaviors of good eye contact, a strong, steady, and audible voice, and selective interruptions. They should avoid nonverbal behaviors such as glaring or little eye contact, threatening gestures, slumped posture, and a weak or whiny voice. Appropriate verbal behaviors include direct and unambiguous language and the use of "I" messages instead of "you" statements. For example, when you say, "Mike, I was disappointed with your report because it contained typographical errors," rather than "Mike, your report was poorly done," you reduce defensiveness. "I" statements describe your feelings about someone's performance or behavior instead of laying blame on the person.

Assertive style
Expressive and self-enhancing, but does not take advantage of others.

Aggressive style
Expressive and self-enhancing, but takes unfair advantage of others.

Nonassertive style
Timid and self-denying behavior.

International OB — Cross-Cultural Awareness Affects Interpersonal Communication

John Gillespie—vice president of Clarke Consulting Group, based in Redwood City, California—recalls a meeting in Tokyo in which the Japanese participants had carefully arranged the room. When the American and European participants arrived, they rearranged the chairs to form a "U." The Japanese watched and said nothing. In the meeting, they also said nothing. Unwittingly, the Western participants had silenced their Japanese colleagues by assuming that the Western way was the only way.

Pacing is another factor influenced by culture. Westerners' typical "do it now" approach can work against them in Asia.... In fact, Gillespie says that Asians say in confidential interviews that Americans interrupt and never listen.

"In Buddhist societies, silence is admired. In a Japanese context, when you finish saying something, you expect silence. In Asian cultures, too many words are considered suspicious."

SOURCE: C C Hebard, "Managing Effectively in Asia," *Training & Development*, April 1996, p 36.

Table 15–2 *Communication Styles*

Communication Style	Description	Nonverbal Behavior Pattern	Verbal Behavior Pattern
Assertive	Pushing hard without attacking; permits others to influence outcome; expressive and self-enhancing without intruding on others	Good eye contact Comfortable but firm posture Strong, steady, and audible voice Facial expressions matched to message Appropriately serious tone Selective interruptions to ensure understanding	Direct and unambiguous language No attributions or evaluations of other's behavior Use of "I" statements and cooperative "we" statements
Aggressive	Taking advantage of others; expressive and self-enhancing at other's expense	Glaring eye contact Moving or leaning too close Threatening gestures (pointed finger; clenched fist) Loud voice Frequent interruptions	Swear words and abusive language Attributions and evaluations of other's behavior Sexist or racist terms Explicit threats or put-downs
Nonassertive	Encouraging others to take advantage of us; inhibited; self-denying	Little eye contact Downward glances Slumped posture Constantly shifting weight Wringing hands Weak or whiny voice	Qualifiers ("maybe"; "kind of") Fillers ("uh," "you know," "well") Negaters ("It's not really that important"; "I'm not sure")

SOURCE: Adapted in part from J A Waters, "Managerial Assertiveness," *Business Horizons*, September–October 1982, pp 24–29.

Remember that nonverbal and verbal behaviors should complement and reinforce each other. James Waters, a communication expert, further recommends that assertiveness can be enhanced by using various combinations of the following assertiveness elements:

1. *Describe* the situation or the behavior of people to which you are reacting.

2. *Express* your feelings, and/or *explain* what impact the other's behavior has on you.

t is questionnaire is for instructional purposes only and does not constitute an endorsement of any products that may or may not suit your needs. There is no obligation to buy anything.) At the "Tests, Tests, Tests . . ." page, read the brief welcome statement about Queendom's psychological tests, and then scroll down to the category "Career/Job." Select the "Assertiveness Test," read the instructions, complete all 32 items, and click on the "score" button for automatic scoring. Read the interpretation of your results.

Questions

1. Possible scores on the self-assessment questionnaire range from 0 to 100. How did you score? Are you surprised by the results? Do you agree with the interpretation of your score?

2. Reviewing the questionnaire item by item, can you find aspects of communication in which you are either nonassertive or possibly too assertive? Do you think that your communication style can be improved by making adjustments within these areas of communication?

3. Based on the results of this questionnaire, develop an action plan for improving your communication style. Table 15–2 is a helpful source.

OB in Action Case Study   www.viacom.com

Collaborative Computing Dramatically Affects Organizational Communication[90]

Employees of Chemical Banking Corp. had been shaken by workforce cuts, reorganizations, and a pending merger. Rumors often raced through the ranks, sapping productivity and morale.

But Bruce Hasenyager found a way to squelch the gossip in the bank's corporate-systems division: The senior vice president let employees post anonymous questions on an electronic bulletin board, accessible to anyone who was on the office computer network. Then he responded to the questions on-line.

"It became a powerful tool for building trust," Mr Hasenyager says. "We could kill off the crazy rumors. When it was whispered around the water cooler that part of our group's work might be contracted out to IBM, I had a way to tell everyone at once that it was baloney."

But Chemical's electronic water cooler soon spun out of control. When Mr Hasenyager resigned last year, following the completion of Chemical's merger with Manufacturers Hanover Trust, his successor became uncomfortable with this unruly forum. After barbed criticism of management began appearing on the system, the new executive pulled the plug.

Computer networks—and the sticky management issues they present—are spreading across the workplace. In the first wave of desktop computerization, workers generally used their machines to perform tasks in isolation, such as writing, creating a financial spreadsheet, or designing graphics or products. But as more and more office computers are tied together in networks—using cables or phone lines, "servers" that store data and direct traffic, and a new class of software called groupware—the nature of personal computing is changing. And office life is changing along with it.

Electronic mail is probably the simplest and most familiar form of groupware, in which notes are zapped across a network between two desktop PCs. More sophisticated groupware programs connect many people together at the same time, often functioning like a suite of electronic conference rooms where many conversations can take place at the same time. The programs can also collect these silent conversations and create an electronic transcript. And they are not limited to words: Some groupware programs can sift, sort, and transmit scanned images, sound, and even video.

Because they enable hundreds of workers to share information simultaneously, groupware networks can give lowly office workers intelligence previously available only to their bosses. Networks also can give the rank-and-file new access: the ability to join in on-line discussions with senior executives. In these interactions, people are judged more by what they say than by their rank on the corporate ladder.

"The cultural effect is enormous," says Bill Wilson, a manager at Johnson & Higgins, a New York insurance brokerage firm that links its professional staff with new network software. "It's helping to dissolve the old corporate hierarchy." . . .

But the proliferation of networks can also bring unintended tensions. In a corporate culture where information is already jealously guarded, some companies are finding employees unwilling to share their best work in network discussions. Managers like the ones at Chemical often feel the need to control what goes out across the network. . . .

This new electronic landscape can foster an egalitarian sense of empowerment among employees. Or it can be a tool of authoritarian managers, leading to loss of workplace privacy. For better or worse, "it's a powerful means of amplifying the style and character of a company and its managers," Mr Hasenyager says.

At MTV Networks, groupware became a new weapon for the affiliate salesforce. When the Viacom Inc. unit was battling last summer against rival Turner Broadcasting System Inc.'s Cartoon Channel, trying to get cable operators to carry MTV's new Comedy Central network instead, salesmen in some areas were meeting unexpected resistance. Then a saleswoman in Chicago discovered that a cable system in her territory had been offered a special two-year, rock-bottom price by Cartoon Channel.

She typed this intelligence into a groupware network that tracks most day-to-day activity of the sales force. Others noticed that another salesman in Florida had also heard something about a new, more aggressive deal from the competition. "Suddenly it clicked; we'd figured out their game," says Kris Bagwell, the young MTV salesman who helped design the new network. Top MTV executives were told of the tactic and were able to counterattack by changing their own pricing and terms, saving several pending deals, according to Mr Bagwell.

He says groupware gives management a better tool to follow what's going on in the field. "Let's say we need to know about every sales call last month on a Cox system where Nickelodeon was discussed," he says. "Or we need to know what people were hearing about Comedy Central's local ad sales in the Southeast last quarter. With a couple of mouse clicks, you can drill in and find what you need."

At Coopers & Lybrand's Atlanta office, William Jennings, director of fraud investigation services, used groupware to win a contract that he says he wouldn't have known about otherwise. Using a system that electronically clips and categorizes news wires, he came across a report of a food-service company in Hawaii that had an inventory-theft problem, apparently covered up by fraud. He quickly turned to an in-house Notes database and discovered that people in Coopers & Lybrand's Los Angeles office knew people at the victimized company.

After on-line consultations, he decided to offer Coopers & Lybrand's services to ferret out the fraud. Clicking into another groupware database, which cross-indexed the background and skills of 900 auditors, he searched for someone with prior law-enforcement experience, a CPA, and familiarity with food-service inventories. "We found him in Dallas, and put him on a plane the next day. Coopers got the contract, and the client got the right man for the job."

In some organizations, networks and groupware breach the lines of command. At Wright-Patterson Air Force Base in Ohio, which uses network software made by Quality Decision Management, of Taunton, Massachusetts, "rank doesn't really matter when you're on-line," says Lt Col Donald Potter. "An enlisted man could send a message to a colonel."Five years ago, he says, "there wouldn't have been an easy way for a sergeant to share an idea with a colonel short of making a formal appointment to go see him in his office." . . .

But at some organizations, knowledge is power, and sharing doesn't come easily. This became clear at Price Waterhouse, which uses Notes to connect 18,000 professionals. In an MIT study of an unnamed company—which others confirm was the big accounting firm—Prof Wanda Orlikowsky found evidence that some junior employees wouldn't share information on the network because of the firm's intensely competitive culture.

As one explained to Ms Orlikowsky: "The corporate psychology makes the use of Notes difficult, particularly in the consultant career path, which creates a back-stabbing, aggressive environment." Another said: "I'm trying to develop an area of expertise that makes me stand out. If I shared that with you, you'd get the credit and not me. . . . Power in this firm is client base and technical ability. Now if you put this information in a Notes database, you lose power." Price Waterhouse says it is happy with Notes.

Questions for Discussion

1. How does collaborative computing influence the amount of noise in the communication process? Explain.

2. Is using networked computers to communicate consistent with the contingency model for selecting media? Discuss your rationale.

3. How does collaborative computing affect the grapevine and communication distortion? Explain.

4. What are the major benefits and limitations of collaborative computing? Discuss your conclusions.

5. Do you think people say things on a computer network that they would not say face-to-face? Discuss the implications for organizational behavior.

Personal Awareness and Growth Exercise

Assessing Your Listening Skills

Objectives

1. To assess your listening skills.
2. To develop a personal development plan aimed at increasing your listening skills.

Introduction

Listening is a critical component of effective communication. Unfortunately, research and case studies suggest that many of us are not very good at actively listening. This is particularly bad in light of the fact that managers spend more time listening than they do speaking or writing. This exercise provides you the opportunity to assess your listening skills and develop a plan for improvement.

Instructions

The following statements reflect various habits we use when listening to others. For each statement, indicate the extent to which you agree or disagree with it by selecting one number from the scale provided. Circle your response for each statement. Remember, there are no right or wrong answers. After completing the survey, add up your total score for the 17 items, and record it in the space provided.

Listening Skills Survey

1 = Strongly disagree

2 = Disagree

3 = Neither agree nor disagree

4 = Agree

5 = Strongly agree

1. I daydream or think about other things when listening to others.   1 — 2 — 3 — 4 — 5

2. I do not mentally summarize the ideas being communicated by a speaker.   1 — 2 — 3 — 4 — 5

3. I do not use a speaker's body language or tone of voice to help interpret what he or she is saying.   1 — 2 — 3 — 4 — 5

4. I listen more for facts than overall ideas during classroom lectures.   1 — 2 — 3 — 4 — 5

5. I tune out dry speakers.   1 — 2 — 3 — 4 — 5

6. I have a hard time paying attention to boring people.   1 — 2 — 3 — 4 — 5

7. I can tell whether someone has anything useful to say before he or she finishes communicating a message.   1 — 2 — 3 — 4 — 5

8. I quit listening to a speaker when I think he or she has nothing interesting to say.   1 — 2 — 3 — 4 — 5

9. I get emotional or upset when speakers make jokes about issues or things that are important to me.   1 — 2 — 3 — 4 — 5

10. I get angry or distracted when speakers use offensive words.   1 — 2 — 3 — 4 — 5

11. I do not expend a lot of energy when listening to others.   1 — 2 — 3 — 4 — 5

12. I pretend to pay attention to others even when I'm not really listening.   1 — 2 — 3 — 4 — 5

13. I get distracted when listening to others.   1 — 2 — 3 — 4 — 5

14. I deny or ignore information and comments that go against my thoughts and feelings.   1 — 2 — 3 — 4 — 5

15. I do not seek opportunities to challenge my listening skills.   1 — 2 — 3 — 4 — 5

16. I do not pay attention to the visual aids used during lectures.   1 — 2 — 3 — 4 — 5

17. I do not take notes on handouts when they are provided.   1 — 2 — 3 — 4 — 5

Total Score = _____

Preparing a Personal Development Plan

1. Use the following norms to evaluate your listening skills:
   17–34 = Good listening skills
   35–53 = Moderately good listening skills
   54–85 = Poor listening skills.
   How would you evaluate your listening skills?

2. Do you agree with the assessment of your listening skills? Why or why not?

3. The 17-item listening skills survey was developed to assess the extent to which you use the keys to effective listening presented in Table 15–3. Use Table 15–3 and the development plan format shown on the following page to prepare your development plan. First, identify the five statements from the listening skills survey that received your highest ratings—high ratings represent low skills. Record the survey numbers in the space provided in the development plan. Next, compare the content of these survey items to the descriptions of bad and good listeners shown in Table 15–3. This comparison will help you identify the keys to effective listening being measured by each survey item. Write down the keys to effective listening that correspond to each of the five items you want to improve. Finally, write down specific actions or behaviors that you can undertake to improve the listening skill being considered.

Development Plan

Survey Items	Key to Effective Listening I Want to Improve	Action Steps Required (What Do You Need to Do to Build Listening Skills for This Listening Characteristic?)
#		
#		
#		
#		
#		

Group Exercise

Practicing Different Styles of Communication

Objectives

1. To demonstrate the relative effectiveness of communicating assertively, aggressively, and nonassertively.
2. To give you hands-on experience with different styles of communication.

Introduction

Research shows that assertive communication is more effective than either an aggressive or nonassertive style. This *role-playing exercise* is designed to increase your ability to communicate assertively. Your task is to use different communication styles while attempting to resolve the work-related problems of a poor performer.

Instructions

Divide into groups of three, and read the "Poor Performer" and "Store Manager" roles provided here. Then decide who will play the poor performer role, who will play the managerial role, and who will be the observer. The observer will be asked to provide feedback to the manager after each role play. When playing the managerial role, you should first attempt to resolve the problem by using an aggressive communication style. Attempt to achieve your objective by using the nonverbal and verbal behavior patterns associated with the aggressive style shown in Table 15–2. Take about four to six minutes to act out the instructions. The observer should give feedback to the manager after completing the role play. The observer should comment on how the employee responded to the aggressive behaviors displayed by the manager.

After feedback is provided on the first role play, the person playing the manager should then try to resolve the problem with a nonassertive style. Observers once again should provide feedback. Finally, the manager should confront the problem with an assertive style. Once again, rely on the relevant nonverbal and verbal behavior patterns presented in Table 15–2, and take four to six minutes to act out each scenario. Observers should try to provide detailed feedback on how effectively the manager exhibited nonverbal and verbal assertive behaviors. Be sure to provide positive and constructive feedback.

After completing these three role plays, switch roles: manager becomes observer, observer becomes poor performer, and poor performer becomes the manager. When these role plays are completed, switch roles once again.

ROLE: POOR PERFORMER

You sell shoes full-time for a national chain of shoe stores. During the last month you have been absent three times without giving your manager a reason. The quality of your work has been slipping. You have a lot of creative excuses when your boss tries to talk to you about your performance.

When playing this role, feel free to invent a personal problem that you may eventually want to share with your manager. However, make the manager dig for information about this problem. Otherwise, respond to your manager's comments as you normally would.

ROLE: STORE MANAGER

You manage a store for a national chain of shoe stores. In the privacy of your office, you are talking to one of your salespeople who has had three unexcused absences from work during the last month. (This is excessive, according to company guidelines, and must be corrected.) The quality of his or her work has been slipping. Customers have complained that this person is rude, and co-workers have told you this individual isn't carrying his or her fair share of the work. You are fairly sure this person has some sort of personal problem. You want to identify that problem and get him or her back on the right track.

Questions for Discussion

1. What drawbacks of the aggressive and nonassertive styles did you observe?
2. What were major advantages of the assertive style?
3. What were the most difficult aspects of trying to use an assertive style?
4. How important was nonverbal communication during the various role plays? Explain with examples.

Chapter Sixteen

Influence Tactics, Empowerment, and Politics

Learning Objectives

When you finish studying the material in this chapter, you should be able to:

1 Explain the concept of mutuality of interest.

2 Name at least three "soft" and two "hard" influence tactics, and summarize the practical lessons from influence research.

3 Identify and briefly describe French and Raven's five bases of power, and discuss the responsible use of power.

4 Define the term *empowerment,* and discuss the realities of open-book management.

5 Explain why delegation is the highest form of empowerment, and discuss the connections among delegation, trust, and personal initiative.

6 Define *organizational politics,* and explain what triggers it.

7 Distinguish between favorable and unfavorable impression management tactics.

8 Explain how to manage organizational politics.

"Imagine a world without the Supremes, Smokey Robinson, Marvin Gaye, Stevie Wonder, Diana Ross, Michael Jackson, Lionel Richie, the Temptations, and the Four Tops," someone once said, "and you've just imagined a world without Berry Gordy."

Gordy, who worked on the Ford assembly line and sold cookware door to door, submitted in the end to his passion for songwriting and transforming no-names into stars.

As a songwriter, Gordy found early success with hits like "Lonely Teardrops," sung by Jackie Wilson. But Gordy soon realized he wanted more control. "To protect my songs, which are my loves, I had to find singers who could sing and record them like I heard them in my head."

At 29, with an $800 loan from his family, Gordy founded Motown. He leased a two-story house at 2648 West Grand Boulevard in Detroit. "Everything was makeshift," he says. "We used the bathroom as an echo chamber."

Gordy borrowed from his assembly-line experience in refining Motown acts. The kids learned harmony from the vocal coach, steps from the choreography coach, and manners from the etiquette coach. Meanwhile, Motown's songwriters pounded out new tunes. When it was time to perform, the kids—Diana, Marvin, Stevie, Smokey,

Motown legend Berry Gordy gets his star on Hollywood's Walk of Fame. Surrounding Mr. Gordy are some of his star "students": Stevie Wonder, Otis Williams of the Temptations, Smokey Robinson, and Diana Ross.
(AP/Wide World Photos)

SCENARIOS[95]

1. A high school ballplayer buoys the spirits of a teammate who struck out at a key moment by emphasizing the latter's game-winning hit last week and noting that even the greatest big-league hitters fail about 7 times out of 10. He may privately suspect his teammate has only mediocre baseball talent, but by putting the best side to his comments and not sharing his doubts, he makes the teammate feel better, builds his confidence so he can face tomorrow's game in a more optimistic frame of mind, and boosts the teammate's image in front of the other players who can hear his reassuring words.

2. At a party, a college student describes her roommate to a potential date she knows her friend finds extremely attractive. She stresses her friend's intelligence, attractiveness, and common interests but fails to mention that her friend can also be quite arrogant.

Stage 2 (10 to 15 minutes): Join two or three others in a discussion group and compare scores for both scenarios.

Are there big differences of opinion, or is there a general consensus? Next, briefly discuss these questions: "How do *you* create a good first impression in *specific* situations?" "What goes through your mind when you see someone trying to make a good impression for themselves or for someone else?" Note: Your instructor may ask you to pick a spokesperson to briefly report the results of your discussion to the class. If so, be sure to keep notes during the discussion.

Questions for Discussion

1. Is the whole practice of impression management a dishonest waste of time, or does it have a proper place in society? Why?

2. In what situations can impression management attempts backfire?

3. How do you know when someone has taken impression management too far?

4. How would you respond to a person who made this statement? "I never engage in impression management."

Chapter Seventeen

Leadership

Learning Objectives

When you finish studying the material in this chapter, you should be able to:

1 Define the term leadership, and explain the difference between leading versus managing.

2 Review trait theory research, and discuss the idea of one best style of leadership, using the Ohio State studies and the Leadership Grid® as points of reference.

3 Explain, according to Fiedler's contingency model, how leadership style interacts with situational control.

4 Discuss House's path–goal theory, and Hersey and Blanchard's situational leadership theory.

5 Define and differentiate transactional and charismatic leadership.

6 Explain how charismatic leadership transforms followers and work groups.

7 Summarize the managerial implications of charismatic leadership.

8 Explain the leader–member exchange model of leadership.

9 Describe the substitutes for leadership, and explain how they substitute for, neutralize, or enhance the effects of leadership.

10 Describe servant-leadership and superleadership.

Catherine Hapka is executive vice president, markets US West Communications, and oversees a $6.8 billion telecommunications business. Her leadership style is represented by her favorite saying and secret to success. Her favorite saying is "winning begets winning," and her secret is "make your own luck through hard work and perseverance."

Amid washed-out white shirts and nonconfrontational neckties, Catherine Hapka is wearing a searingly red jacket, one that puts the blaze back in blazer. She's at US West's Minneapolis office conducting a meeting—an "event" in her lexicon—to discuss how the company can win back market share in the local long-distance telephone business. Hapka is known around the company as a master motivator, a trait she credits for her success. Today her stated goal is to "raise the temperature in the room."

Hapka kicks off by exhorting her charges: "We need to retake Pork Chop Hill." A half-dozen executives proceed to lay out their battle plans. Hapka listens intently, tapping her pen, rocking back and forth, literally vibrating with energy. She makes frequent interjections. "What's the headline," she demands when confronted with insufficiently digested data. At another point, she simply urges: "Speed, speed, speed, speed!" She wraps up the meeting with a rousing, "I smell victory already."

Equal parts intensity and acumen, Hapka is charged with supercharging US West Communications, which provides phone service to 25 million customers in 14 states. Marketing, sales,

Catherine Hapka.
(Brian Smale)

customer service, and new-venture development are all her bailiwick. "My job is to get us ready for brutal competition," she explains. "No one believes a Baby Bell can be a lean, mean machine." But Hapka seems to relish the challenge and states with a grin: "I love to do things that people say can't be done."

Hapka learned this aggressive style early in her career. Her first job after graduating from the University of Minnesota was as a financial management trainee with GE in Syracuse, New York. Driving to work each day, Hapka passed a brand new Schlitz brewery in nearby Baldwinsville. "It looked like more fun," she says. So she signed on as a supervisor, overseeing 40 union workers through two shifts a day. In this gritty environment, Hapka began to evolve her management philosophy, what she terms "existential leadership." In essence: Try to involve workers in big ideas that matter to the survival of the company rather than small processes. Within the brewery, the big idea was ever-increasing productivity. End-of-shift beer blasts proved a potent incentive. Says Hapka: "I learned to be more of a coach and less of a supervisor." . . . Her existential approach means finding the big ideas that will motivate unionized phone workers in one breath, entrepreneurs in the next. The process, she says, leaves her feeling like "Jekyll and Hyde."

As for her future, "My goal is to be the CEO of a major corporation. Period." After a pause to let that sink in, she continues: "Ambition is good for the people who hire me, good for the people who follow me. I don't know why people are so worried about talking about ambition. It's what drives this country."[1]

Someone once observed that a leader is a person who finds out which way the parade is going, jumps in front of it, and yells "Follow me!" The plain fact is that this approach to leadership has little chance of working in today's rapidly changing world. Admired leaders, such as civil rights activist Martin Luther King, John Kennedy, and Microsoft's Bill Gates, led people in bold new directions. They envisioned how things could be improved, rallied followers, and refused to accept failure. In short, successful leaders are those individuals who can step into a difficult situation and make a noticeable difference. But how much of a difference can leaders make in modern organizations?

OB researchers have discovered that leaders can make a difference. One study, for example, tracked the relationship between net profit and leadership in 167 companies from 13 industries. It also covered a time span of 20 years. Higher net profits were earned by companies with effective leaders.[2] A more recent study examined the relationship between leadership and performance within major-league baseball teams. The sample consisted of all managers who directed a major-league baseball team during any season from 1945 to 1965. The researchers then tracked the performance of their teams up to the year the manager retired. Using a sophisticated measure of managerial effectiveness, results demonstrated that effective managers won more games with player performance held constant than did less effective managers.[3] Leadership makes a difference!

After formally defining the term *leadership,* this chapter focuses on the following areas: (1) trait and behavioral approaches to leadership, (2) alternative situational theories of leadership, (3) charismatic leadership, and (4) additional perspectives on leadership. Because there are many different leadership theories within each of these areas, it is impossible to discuss them all. This chapter is based on reviewing those theories with the most research support.

Because the topic of leadership has fascinated people for centuries, definitions abound. This section presents a definition of leadership and highlights the similarities and differences between leading versus managing.

What Does Leadership Involve?

What Is Leadership?

Disagreement about the definition of leadership stems from the fact that it involves a complex interaction among the leader, the followers, and the situation. For example, some researchers define leadership in terms of personality and physical traits, while others believe leadership is represented by a set of prescribed behaviors. In contrast, other researchers believe that leadership is a temporary role that can be filled by anyone. There is a common thread, however, among the different definitions of leadership. The common thread is social influence.

As the term is used in this chapter, **leadership** is defined as "a social influence process in which the leader seeks the voluntary participation of subordinates in an effort to reach organizational goals."[4] Tom Peters and Nancy Austin, authors of the best-seller, *A Passion for Excellence,* describe leadership in broader terms:

> Leadership means vision, cheerleading, enthusiasm, love, trust, verve, passion, obsession, consistency, the use of symbols, paying attention as illustrated by the content of one's calendar, out-and-out drama (and the management thereof), creating heroes at all levels, coaching, effectively wandering around, and numerous other things. Leadership must be present at all levels of the organization. It depends on a million little things done with obsession, consistency, and care, but all of those million little things add up to nothing if the trust, vision, and basic belief are not there.[5]

Leadership
Influencing employees to voluntarily pursue organizational goals.

As you can see from this definition, leadership clearly entails more than wielding power and exercising authority and is exhibited on different levels. At the individual level, for example, leadership involves mentoring, coaching, inspiring, and motivating. Leaders build teams, create cohesion, and resolve conflicts at the group level. Finally, leaders build culture and create change at the organizational level.[6]

Figure 17–1 provides a conceptual framework for understanding leadership. It was created by integrating components of the different theories and models discussed in this chapter. Figure 17–1 indicates that certain leader characteristics/traits are the foundation of effective leadership. In turn, these characteristics affect an individual's ability to carry out various managerial behaviors/roles. Effective leadership also depends on various situational variables. These variables are important components of the contingency leadership theories discussed later in this chapter. Finally, leadership is results oriented.

Leading versus Managing

It is important to appreciate the difference between leadership and management to fully understand what leadership is all about. Bernard Bass, a leadership expert, concluded that "leaders manage and managers lead, but the two activities are not synonymous."[7] Bass tells us that although leadership and management overlap, each entails a unique set of activities or functions. Broadly speaking, managers typically perform functions associated with planning, investigating, organizing, and control, and leaders deal with the interpersonal aspects of a manager's job. Leaders inspire others, provide emotional support, and try to get employees to rally around a common goal. Leaders also play a

Figure 17–1   *A Conceptual Framework for Understanding Leadership*

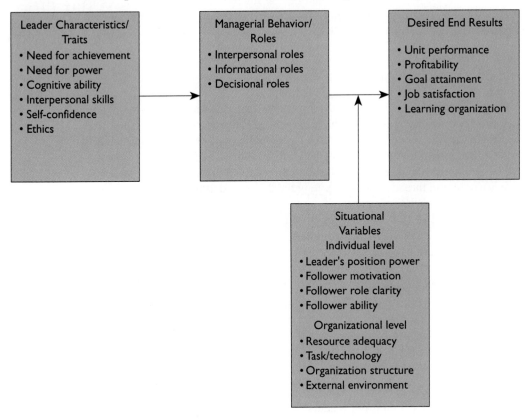

SOURCE: Adapted in part from G Yukl, "Managerial Leadership: A Review of Theory and Research," *Journal of Management,* June 1989, p 274.

key role in creating a vision and strategic plan for an organization. Managers, in turn, are charged with implementing the vision and strategic plan. Table 17–1 summarizes the key differences found between leaders and managers.[8]

The distinction between leaders and managers is more than a semantic issue for four reasons:

1. It is important from a hiring standpoint. Because leaders and managers perform a subset of unique functions, it is important to recruit and select people who have the required intellectual abilities, experience, and job-relevant knowledge to perform their jobs.[9]

2. Differences may affect group effectiveness. Work group performance can be increased by staffing a productive mix of leaders and managers.

3. Successful organizational change is highly dependent upon effective leadership throughout an organization. Senior executives cannot create change on their own. According to organizational change expert John Kotter, successful organizational transformation is 70% to 90% leadership and 10% to 30% management.[10]

4. Distinctions between leading and managing highlight the point that leadership is not restricted to people in particular positions or roles. Anyone from the bottom to the top of an organization can be a leader. Many an informal leader have con-

Table 17–1   *Differences between Leaders and Managers*

Leaders	Managers
Innovate	Administer
Develop	Maintain
Inspire	Control
Long-term view	Short-term view
Ask what and why	Ask how and when
Originate	Initiate
Challenge the status quo	Accept the status quo
Do the right things	Do things right

SOURCE: Distinctions were taken from W G Bennis, *On Becoming a Leader* (Reading, MA: Addison-Wesley, 1989).

tributed to organizational effectiveness. Consider the behavior exhibited by Skip Tobey, an employee at America West Airlines.

"I'm not just an aircraft cleaner," the 36-year-old Phoenix native said. "That's my title, but that's not the end of my job."

Tobey said he looks for ways to help passengers, lending a hand to young families maneuvering strollers through narrow aircraft aisles and assisting elderly travelers.

"My satisfaction is tied into quality, helping the passengers," he said. "No matter what it takes, if it means going to the furthest extreme, I'll do it."[11]

Skip's behavior is not only inspirational, but it supports leadership expert Warren Bennis's conclusion about leaders and managers. Bennis characterized managers as people who do things right and leaders as individuals who do the "right" things. Skip Tobey is clearly doing the "right" things to help America West provide excellent customer service.

Trait and Behavioral Theories of Leadership

This section examines the two earliest approaches used to explain leadership. Trait theories focused on identifying the personal traits that differentiated leaders from followers. Behavioral theorists examined leadership from a different perspective. They tried to uncover the different kinds of leader behaviors that resulted in higher work group performance. Both approaches to leadership can teach current and future managers valuable lessons about leading.

Trait Theory

At the turn of the 20th century, the prevailing belief was that leaders were born, not made. Selected people were thought to possess inborn traits that made them successful leaders. A **leader trait** is a physical or personality characteristic that can be used to differentiate leaders from followers.

Before World War II, hundreds of studies were conducted to pinpoint the traits of successful leaders. Dozens of leadership traits were identified. During the postwar period,

Leader trait
Personal characteristics that differentiate leaders from followers.

Jack Welch (in the center), chairman and CEO of General Electric Co., laughs during a visit to the floor of the New York Stock Exchange. He is an extraordinary leader who was selected by *Fortune* as one of the best leaders during the 20th century.

(AP/Wide World Photos)

however, enthusiasm was replaced by widespread criticism. Studies conducted by Ralph Stogdill in 1948 and by Richard Mann in 1959, which sought to summarize the impact of traits on leadership, caused the trait approach to fall into disfavor.

Stogdill's and Mann's Findings   Based on his review, Stogdill concluded that five traits tended to differentiate leaders from average followers: (1) intelligence, (2) dominance, (3) self-confidence, (4) level of energy and activity, and (5) task-relevant knowledge.[12] Consider the leadership traits that Jack Welch, chief executive officer of General Electric, indicated that he is looking for in his replacement during an interview with *Fortune*.

> "Vision. Courage. The four E's: energy, ability to energize others, the edge to make tough decisions, and execution, which is key because you can't just decide but have got to follow up in 19 ways. Judgment. The self-confidence to hire always someone who's better than you. Are they growing things? Do they add new insights to the businesses they run? Do they like to nurture small businesses?"
>
> And one more: an insatiable appetite for accomplishment. Too many CEOs, Welch once said, believe that the high point comes the day they land the job. Not Welch, who says, "I'm 63 and finally getting smart."[13]

Although Welch is looking for some of the same traits identified by Ralph Stogdill, research revealed that these five traits did not accurately predict which individuals became leaders in organizations. People with these traits often remained followers.

Mann's review was similarly disappointing for the trait theorists. Among the seven categories of personality traits he examined, Mann found intelligence was the best predictor of leadership. However, Mann warned that all observed positive relationships between traits and leadership were weak (correlations averaged about 0.15).[14]

Together, Stogdill's and Mann's findings dealt a near deathblow to the trait approach. But now, decades later, leadership traits are once again receiving serious research attention.

Contemporary Trait Research   Two OB researchers concluded in 1983 that past trait data may have been incorrectly analyzed. By applying modern statistical techniques to an old database, they demonstrated that the majority of a leader's behavior could be attributed to stable underlying traits.[15] Unfortunately, their methodology did not single out specific traits.

A 1986 meta-analysis by Robert Lord and his associates remedied this shortcoming. Based on a reanalysis of Mann's data and subsequent studies, Lord concluded that people have leadership *prototypes* that affect our perceptions of who is and who is not an effective leader. Your **leadership prototype** is a mental representation of the traits and behaviors that you believe are possessed by leaders. We thus tend to perceive that someone is a leader when he or she exhibits traits or behaviors that are consistent with our prototypes.[16] Lord's research demonstrated that people are perceived as being leaders when they exhibit the traits associated with intelligence, masculinity, and dominance. A more recent study of 200 undergraduate and graduate students also confirmed the idea that leadership prototypes influence leadership perceptions. Results revealed that perceptions of an individual as a leader were affected by that person's sex—males were perceived to be leaders more than females—and behavioral flexibility. People who were more behaviorally flexible were perceived as more leaderlike.[17]

Another pair of leadership researchers attempted to identify key leadership traits by asking the following open-ended question to more than 20,000 people around the world: "What values (personal traits or characteristics) do you look for and admire in your superiors?" The top four traits included honesty, forward-looking, inspiring, and competent.[18] The researchers concluded that these four traits constitute a leader's credibility. This research suggests that people want their leaders to be credible and to have a sense of direction.

Gender and Leadership   The increase of women in the workforce has generated much interest in understanding the similarities and differences in female and male leaders. Important issues concern whether women and men (1) assume varying leadership roles within work groups, (2) use different leadership styles, (3) are relatively more or less effective in leadership roles, and (4) whether there are situational differences that produce gender differences in leadership effectiveness. Three meta-analyses were conducted to summarize research pertaining to these issues.

The first meta-analysis demonstrated that men and women differed in the type of leadership roles they assumed within work groups. Men were seen as displaying more overall leadership and task leadership. In contrast, women were perceived as displaying more social leadership.[19] Results from the second meta-analysis revealed that leadership styles varied by gender. Women used a more democratic or participative style than men. Men employed a more autocratic and directive style than women.[20] Finally, a recent meta-analysis of more than 75 studies uncovered three key findings: (1) Female and male leaders were rated as equally effective. This is a very positive outcome because it suggests that despite barriers and possible negative stereotypes toward female leaders, female and male leaders were equally effective. (2) Men were rated as more effective leaders than women when their roles were defined in more masculine terms, and women were more effective than men in roles defined in less masculine terms. (3) Gender differences in leadership effectiveness were associated with the percentage of male leaders and male subordinates. Specifically, male leaders were seen as more effective than females when there was a greater percentage of male leaders and male subordinates. Interestingly, a similar positive bias in leadership effectiveness was not found for women.[21]

Trait Theory in Perspective   We can no longer afford to ignore the implications of leadership traits. Traits play a central role in how we perceive leaders. Recalling the Chapter 6 discussion of social perception, it is important to determine the traits embodied in people's schemata (or mental pictures) for leaders. If those traits are inappropriate (i.e., foster discriminatory selection and invalid performance appraisals), they need

Leadership prototype
Mental representation of the traits and behaviors possessed by leaders.

Many managers believe that women do not want overseas assignments. It thus is not surprising that men receive more international transfers and promotions than women. This is unfortunate because women actually prefer foreign assignments just as much as men and are equally effective once there.

(Julie Houck/Stock Boston)

to be corrected through training and development. Consider the stereotypes associated with who gets selected for corporate assignments overseas.

While women represent about half of the global workforce, surveys indicate they count for less than 12% of the expatriate population. Why? Because many male managers still believe women aren't interested in overseas jobs or won't be effective at them. The managers cite dual-career complications, gender prejudice in many countries, and the risk of sexual harassment. That's hogwash, according to researchers at Loyola University (Chicago). Their recent survey of 261 female expats and their supervisors concluded that women are just as interested as men in foreign assignments and just as effective once there. In fact, contends Linda Stroh, one of the researchers, the traits considered crucial for success overseas—knowing when to be passive, being a team player, soliciting a variety of perspectives—are more often associated with women's management styles than men's.[22]

It appears that managers should be careful to avoid using gender-based stereotypes when making overseas assignments. Moreover, organizations may find it beneficial to consider selected leadership traits when choosing among candidates for leadership positions. Gender should not be used as one of these traits. Consider, for example, the qualities that Colin Powell, former chairman of the Joint Chiefs of Staff and White House national security advisor, believes that effective leaders need to have in the 21st century:

Leadership will always require people who have a vision of where they wish to take "the led." Leadership will always require people who are able to organize the effort of [others] to accomplish the objectives that flow from the vision. And leadership will always put a demand on leaders to pick the right people. . . .

Leadership also requires motivating people. And that means pushing the vision down to every level of the organization.

What will make things different in the 21st century, however, is that the world is going through a transformation . . . At the same time, the world is being fundamentally reshaped by the information and technology revolution, which is supplanting the industrial revolution. . . . The leaders of this new industrial-information era have to be able to use these tools and understand the power of information and technology—and how that gives them new opportunities.[23]

In contrast to these traits, the International OB on p 557, outlines the relevant leadership traits of Russian leaders from the 1400s to the present time. As you can see, Russian organizations need to nurture and develop a similar but different set of leadership traits.

International OB   Russian Leadership Traits in Three Eras

Leadership Trait	Traditional Russian Society (1400s to 1917)	The Red Executive (1917 to 1991)	The Market-Oriented Manager (1991 to Present)
Leadership Motivation			
Power	Powerful autocrats	Centralized leadership stifled grass-roots democracy	Shared power and ownership
Responsibility	Centralization of responsibility	Micromanagers and macropuppets	Delegation and strategic decision making
Drive			
Achievement motivation	Don't rock the boat	Frustrated pawns	The sky's the limit
Ambition	Equal poverty for all	Service to party and collective good	Overcoming the sin of being a winner
Initiative	Look both ways	Meticulous rule following and behind-the-scenes finessing	Let's do business
Energy	Concentrated spasms of labor	"8-hour day," 8 to 8, firefighting	8-day week, chasing opportunities
Tenacity	Life is a struggle	Struggling to accomplish the routine	Struggling to accomplish the new
Honesty and Integrity			
Dual ethical standard	Deception in dealings, fealty in friendship	Two sets of books, personal integrity	Wild capitalism, personal trust
Using connections (*blat*)	Currying favor with landowners	Greasing the wheels of the state	Greasing palms, but learning to do business straight
Self-Confidence			
	From helplessness to bravado	From inferior quality to "big is beautiful"	From cynicism to overpromising

SOURCE: S M Puffer, "Understanding the Bear: A Portrait of Russian Business Leaders," *Academy of Management Executive*, February 1994, p 42. Used with permission.

Behavioral Styles Theory

This phase of leadership research began during World War II as part of an effort to develop better military leaders. It was an outgrowth of two events: the seeming inability of trait theory to explain leadership effectiveness and the human relations movement, an outgrowth of the Hawthorne Studies. The thrust of early behavioral leadership theory was to focus on leader behavior, instead of on personality traits. It was believed that leader behavior directly affected work group effectiveness. This led researchers to identify patterns of behavior (called leadership styles) that enabled leaders to effectively influence others.

Consideration
Creating mutual respect and trust with followers.

Initiating structure
Organizing and defining what group members should be doing.

The Ohio State Studies   Researchers at Ohio State University began by generating a list of behaviors exhibited by leaders. At one point, the list contained 1,800 statements that described nine categories of leader behavior. Ultimately, the Ohio State researchers concluded there were only two independent dimensions of leader behavior: consideration and initiating structure. **Consideration** involves leader behavior associated with creating mutual respect or trust and focuses on a concern for group members' needs and desires. **Initiating structure** is leader behavior that organizes and defines what group members should be doing to maximize output. These two dimensions of leader behavior were oriented at right angles to yield four behavioral styles of leadership (see Figure 17–2).

It initially was hypothesized that a high-structure, high-consideration style would be the one best style of leadership. Through the years, the effectiveness of the high-high style has been tested many times. Overall, results have been mixed. Researchers thus concluded that there is not one best style of leadership.[24] Rather, it is argued that effectiveness of a given leadership style depends on situational factors.

University of Michigan Studies   As in the Ohio State studies, this research sought to identify behavioral differences between effective and ineffective leaders. Researchers identified two different styles of leadership: one was employee centered, the other was job centered. These behavioral styles parallel the consideration and initiating-structure styles identified by the Ohio State group. In summarizing the results from these studies, one management expert concluded that effective leaders (1) tend to have supportive or employee-centered relationships with employees, (2) use group rather than individual methods of supervision, and (3) set high performance goals.[25]

Blake and Mouton's Managerial/Leadership Grid®   Perhaps the most widely known behavioral styles model of leadership is the Managerial Grid.® Behavioral scientists Robert Blake and Jane Srygley Mouton developed and trademarked the grid. They use it to demonstrate that there *is* one best style of leadership. Blake and Mouton's Managerial Grid® (renamed the **Leadership Grid®** in 1991) is a matrix formed by the intersection of two dimensions of leader behavior (see Figure 17–3). On the horizontal axis is "concern for production." "Concern for people" is on the vertical axis.

Blake and Mouton point out that "the variables of the Managerial Grid® are *attitudinal and conceptual,* with *behavior* descriptions derived from and connected with the thinking that lies behind action."[26] In other words, concern for production and concern for people involve attitudes and patterns of thinking, as well as specific behaviors. By scaling each axis of the grid from 1 to 9, Blake and Mouton were able to plot five leadership styles. Because it emphasizes teamwork and interdependence, the 9,9 style is considered by Blake and Mouton to be the best, regardless of the situation.

Ethics at Work

The following situation involved Paul Orfalea, founder and chairman of Kinko's, and one of his employees:

About 20 years ago, I had a manager working for me who lied and was quick to fire people. Nobody liked this guy. He was real bad. Then the bookkeeper caught him stealing. I was too weak to deal with the situation, and I just let it go on. When I finally confronted him, he gave me some excuse about his father having a heart attack. The stress had driven him to steal, he said. I really should have fired him and sent him to jail. But I was gutless, and I felt sorry for him. In those days we had three or four workers at every store, and my job was to get all those people to like one another. I tried to get people out of their stores to talk with one another.

SOURCE: Excerpted from P Orfalea, "My Biggest Mistake," *Inc.,* March 1999 p 88.

You Decide . . .

Was Mr Orfalea being too considerate by not firing the employee? What is the effect of letting the behavior of stealing go unpunished?

For an interpretation of this issue, visit our Web site **www.mhhe.com/kreitner**

Leadership Grid®
Represents four leadership styles found by crossing concern for production and concern for people.

Figure 17–2   *Four Leadership Styles Derived from the Ohio State Studies*

	Low structure, high consideration Less emphasis is placed on structuring employee tasks while the leader concentrates on satisfying employee needs and wants.	High structure, high consideration The leader provides a lot of guidance about how tasks can be completed while being highly considerate of employee needs and wants.
High		
Low	Low structure, low consideration The leader fails to provide necessary structure and demonstrates little consideration for employee needs and wants.	High structure, low consideration Primary emphasis is placed on structuring employee tasks while the leader demonstrates little consideration for employee needs and wants.

Consideration (vertical axis)

Low   High

Initiating Structure

Figure 17–3   *The Leadership Grid®*

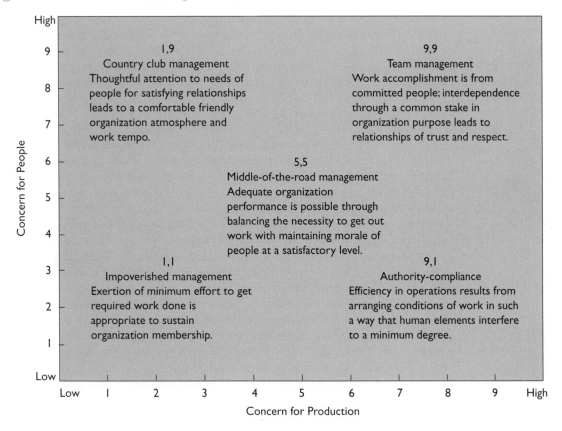

In support of the 9,9 style, Blake and Mouton cite the results of a study in which 100 experienced managers were asked to select the best way of handling 12 managerial situations. Between 72% and 90% of the managers selected the 9,9 style for each of the 12 situations.[27] Moreover, Blake and Mouton report, "The 9,9, orientation . . . leads to productivity, satisfaction, creativity, and health."[28] Critics point out that Blake and Mouton's research may be self-serving. At issue is the grid's extensive use as a training and consulting tool for diagnosing and correcting organizational problems.

Behavioral Styles Theory in Perspective   By emphasizing leader *behavior,* something that is learned, the behavioral style approach makes it clear that leaders are made, not born. This is the opposite of the trait theorists' traditional assumption. Given what we know about behavior shaping and model-based training, leader *behaviors* can be systematically improved and developed. Consider, for example, how Steve Sitek, director of performance development and training at Ernst and Young's Finance, Technology, and Administration Division, is striving to grow and develop leadership talent within the organization:

> Sitek oversees a senior development program that helps executives gain feedback on how they measure up against 11 critical leadership characteristics. Internal studies have shown a direct correlation between executive performance and the 11 characteristics, which include being innovative, excited, persuasive, and strategic. In one-on-one encounters with superiors, managers discuss their assessments to identify characteristics that need strengthening and are charged with structuring their own development plans. . . . Managers are encouraged to work on the characteristics they need to grow incrementally over a multi-year period. Sitek produces specific training geared to each characteristic. "I have a training program for each one," he says. "For example, the No. 1 development gap that we discovered was the characteristic of persuasiveness. I offer a one-day program on this characteristic.[29]

Behavioral styles research also revealed that there is no one best style of leadership. The effectiveness of a particular leadership style depends on the situation at hand. For instance, employees prefer structure over consideration when faced with role ambiguity.[30] Finally, research also reveals that it is important to consider the difference between how frequently and how effectively managers exhibit various leader behaviors. For example, a manager might ineffectively display a lot of considerate leader behaviors. Such a style is likely to frustrate employees and possibly result in lowered job satisfaction and performance. Because the frequency of exhibiting leadership behaviors is secondary in importance to effectiveness, managers are encouraged to concentrate on improving the effective execution of their leader behaviors.[31] At this time we would like you to complete the OB Exercise on p 561. The exercise gives you the opportunity to test the behavioral styles theory by assessing your teacher's leadership style and your associated class satisfaction and role clarity. Are you satisfied with this class? If yes, the behavioral styles approach is supported if your teacher displayed both high consideration and initiating structure. In contrast, the behavioral style approach is not supported if you are satisfied with this class and your teacher exhibits something other than the standard high-high style. Do your results support the proposition that there is one best style of leadership? Are your results consistent with past research that showed leadership behavior depends on the situation at hand? The answer is yes if you prefer initiating structure over consideration when faced with high

OB Exercise Assessing Teacher Leadership Style, Class Satisfaction, and Student Role Clarity

Instructions

A team of researchers converted a set of leadership measures for application in the classroom. For each of the items shown here, use the following rating scale to circle the answer that best represents your feelings. Next, use the scoring key to compute scores for your teacher's leadership style and your class satisfaction and role clarity.

1 = Strongly disagree
2 = Disagree
3 = Neither agree nor disagree
4 = Agree
5 = Strongly agree

1. My instructor behaves in a manner which is thoughtful of my personal needs.   1 — 2 — 3 — 4 — 5

2. My instructor maintains a friendly working relationship with me.   1 — 2 — 3 — 4 — 5

3. My instructor looks out for my personal welfare.   1 — 2 — 3 — 4 — 5

4. My instructor gives clear explanations of what is expected of me.   1 — 2 — 3 — 4 — 5

5. My instructor tells me the performance goals for the class.   1 — 2 — 3 — 4 — 5

6. My instructor explains the level of performance that is expected of me.   1 — 2 — 3 — 4 — 5

7. I am satisfied with the variety of class assignments.   1 — 2 — 3 — 4 — 5

8. I am satisfied with the way my instructor handles the students.   1 — 2 — 3 — 4 — 5

9. I am satisfied with the spirit of cooperation among my fellow students.   1 — 2 — 3 — 4 — 5

10. I know exactly what my responsibilities are.   1 — 2 — 3 — 4 — 5

11. I am given clear explanations of what has to be done.   1 — 2 — 3 — 4 — 5

Scoring Key

Teacher consideration (1, 2, 3)   _____
Teacher initiating structure (4, 5, 6)   _____
Class satisfaction (7, 8, 9)   _____
Role clarity (10, 11)   _____

Arbitrary Norms

Low consideration = 3–8
High consideration = 9–15
Low structure = 3–8
High structure = 9–15
Low satisfaction = 3–8
High satisfaction = 9–15
Low role clarity = 2–5
High role clarity = 6–10

SOURCE: The survey was adapted from A J Kinicki and C A Schriesheim, "Teachers as Leaders: A Moderator Variable Approach," *Journal of Educational Psychology,* 1978, pp 928–35.

role ambiguity. The answer also is yes if you prefer consideration over structure when role ambiguity is low. We now turn our attention to discussing alternative situational theories of leadership.

Situational theories
Propose that leader styles should match the situation at hand.

Situational Theories

Situational leadership theories grew out of an attempt to explain the inconsistent findings about traits and styles. **Situational theories** propose that the effectiveness of a particular style of leader behavior depends on the situation. As situations change, different styles become appropriate. This directly challenges the idea of one best style of leadership. Let us closely examine three alternative situational theories of leadership that reject the notion of one best leadership style.

Fiedler's Contingency Model

Fred Fiedler, an OB scholar, developed a situational model of leadership. It is the oldest and one of the most widely known models of leadership. Fiedler's model is based on the following assumption:

> The performance of a leader depends on two interrelated factors: (1) the degree to which the situation gives the leader control and influence—that is, the likelihood that [the leader] can successfully accomplish the job; and (2) the leader's basic motivation—that is, whether [the leader's] self-esteem depends primarily on accomplishing the task or on having close supportive relations with others.[32]

With respect to a leader's basic motivation, Fiedler believes that leaders are either task motivated or relationship motivated. These basic motivations are similar to initiating structure/concern for production and consideration/concern for people. Consider the basic leadership motivation possessed by Cynthia Danaher, general manager of Hewlett-Packard's Medical Products Group:

> Once a manager is in charge of thousands of employees, the ability to set direction and delegate is more vital than team-building and coaching, she believes....When Ms Danaher changed her top management team and restructured the Medical Products Group, moving out of slow-growth businesses to focus on more-profitable clinical equipment, she had to relinquish her need for approval. "Change is painful, and someone has to be the bad guy," she says. Suddenly employees she considered friends avoided her and told her she was ruining the group. "I didn't use to be able to tolerate that, and I'd try to explain over and over why change had to occur," she says. Over time, she has learned to simply "charge ahead," accepting that not everyone will follow and that some won't survive.[33]

Danaher clearly has used a task motivation to create organizational change within Hewlett-Packard.

Fiedler's theory also is based on the premise that leaders have one dominant leadership style that is resistant to change. He suggests that leaders must learn to manipulate or influence the leadership situation in order to create a "match" between their leadership style and the amount of control within the situation at hand. After discussing the components of situational control and the leadership matching process, we review relevant research and managerial implications.[34]

Situational Control   Situational control refers to the amount of control and influence the leader has in her or his immediate work environment. Situational control ranges from high to low. High control implies that the leader's decisions will produce predictable results because the leader has the ability to influence work outcomes. Low control implies that the leader's decisions may not influence work outcomes because the leader has very little influence. There are three dimensions of situational control: leader–member relations, task structure, and position power. These dimensions vary independently, forming eight combinations of situational control (see Figure 17–4).

The three dimensions of situational control are defined as follows:

Leader–member relations

Extent that leader has the support, loyalty, and trust of work group.

- **Leader–member relations** reflect the extent to which the leader has the support, loyalty, and trust of the work group. This dimension is the most important component of situational control. Good leader–member relations suggest that the leader can depend on the group, thus ensuring that the work group will try to meet the leader's goals and objectives.

Figure 17–4   *Representation of Fiedler's Contingency Model*

Situational Control	High Control Situations			Moderate Control Situations			Low Control Situations	
Leader-member relations	Good	Good	Good	Good	Poor	Poor	Poor	Poor
Task structure	High	High	Low	Low	High	High	Low	Low
Position power	Strong	Weak	Strong	Weak	Strong	Weak	Strong	Weak
Situation	I	II	III	IV	V	VI	VII	VIII
Optimal Leadership Style		Task-Motivated Leadership			Relationship-Motivated Leadership			Task-Motivated Leadership

SOURCE: Adapted from F E Fiedler, "Situational Control and a Dynamic Theory of Leadership," in *Managerial Control and Organizational Democracy,* eds B King, S Streufert, and F E Fiedler (New York: John Wiley & Sons, 1978), p 114.

- **Task structure** is concerned with the amount of structure contained within tasks performed by the work group. For example, a managerial job contains less structure than that of a bank teller. Because structured tasks have guidelines for how the job should be completed, the leader has more control and influence over employees performing such tasks. This dimension is the second most important component of situational control.

- **Position power** refers to the degree to which the leader has formal power to reward, punish, or otherwise obtain compliance from employees.[35]

Task structure
Amount of structure contained within work tasks.

Position power
Degree to which leader has formal power.

Linking Leadership Motivation and Situational Control   Fiedler's complete contingency model is presented in Figure 17–4. The last row under the Situational Control column shows that there are eight different leadership situations. Each situation represents a unique combination of leader–member relations, task structure, and position power. Situations I, II, and III represent high control situations. Figure 17–4 shows that task-motivated leaders are hypothesized to be most effective in situations of high control. Under conditions of moderate control (situations IV, V, and VI), relationship-motivated leaders are expected to be more effective. Finally, the results orientation of task-motivated leaders is predicted to be more effective under conditions of low control (situations VII and VIII).

Research and Managerial Implications   The overall accuracy of Fiedler's contingency model was tested through a meta-analysis of 35 studies containing 137 leader style–performance relations. According to the researchers' findings, (1) the contingency theory was correctly induced from studies on which it was based; (2) for laboratory studies testing the model, the theory was supported for all leadership situations except situation II; and (3) for field studies testing the model, three of the eight situations (IV, V, and VII) produced completely supportive results, while partial support was obtained for situations I, II, III, VI, and VIII. A more recent meta-analysis of data obtained from 1,282 groups also provided mixed support for the contingency model.[36] These findings suggest that Fiedler's model needs theoretical refinement.[37]

The major contribution of Fiedler's model is that it prompted others to examine the contingency nature of leadership. This research, in turn, reinforced the notion that there is no one best style of leadership. Leaders are advised to alter their task and relationship orientation to fit the demands of the situation at hand.

Path–Goal Theory

Path–goal theory is based on the expectancy theory of motivation discussed in Chapter 8. Expectancy theory proposes that motivation to exert effort increases as one's effort→performance→outcome expectations improve. Path–goal theory focuses on how leaders influence followers' expectations.

Robert House originated the path–goal theory of leadership. He proposed a model that describes how expectancy perceptions are influenced by the contingent relationships among four leadership styles and various employee attitudes and behaviors (see Figure 17–5).[38] According to the path–goal model, leader behavior is acceptable when employees view it as a source of satisfaction or as paving the way to future satisfaction. In addition, leader behavior is motivational to the extent it (1) reduces roadblocks that interfere with goal accomplishment, (2) provides the guidance and support needed by employees, and (3) ties meaningful rewards to goal accomplishment. Because the model deals with pathways to goals and rewards, it is called the path–goal theory of leadership. House sees the leader's main job as helping employees stay on the right paths to challenging goals and valued rewards.

Leadership Styles   House believes leaders can exhibit more than one leadership style. This contrasts with Fiedler, who proposes that leaders have one dominant style. The four leadership styles identified by House are as follows:

- *Directive leadership.* Providing guidance to employees about what should be done and how to do it, scheduling work, and maintaining standards of performance.
- *Supportive leadership.* Showing concern for the well-being and needs of employees, being friendly and approachable, and treating workers as equals.
- *Participative leadership.* Consulting with employees and seriously considering their ideas when making decisions.
- *Achievement-oriented leadership.* Encouraging employees to perform at their highest level by setting challenging goals, emphasizing excellence, and demonstrating confidence in employee abilities.[39]

Research evidence supports the idea that leaders exhibit more than one leadership style.[40] Descriptions of business leaders reinforce these findings. For example, PepsiCo's CEO, Roger Enrico, uses multiple leadership styles to influence others:

"Roger is at once one of the warmest and most personable people, and so cold," says a former PepsiCo executive. "His strength is his ability to charm you and get you on his side, and also dispassionately evaluate a business and fix it. He never gets sucked

Figure 17–5   *A General Representation of House's Path–Goal Theory*

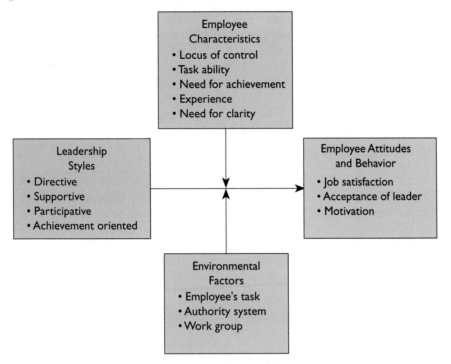

into the culture, the history of a business. So he's not afraid to cut the fat, storm ahead, reorganize, shut the factory, kill the product line. He's agile and he's cunning."

He challenges everything and assumes nothing. For example, when Enrico took charge at PepsiCo's Frito-Lay division five years ago, the numbers looked fine. But Enrico smelled something rotten at the food company. Profits were rising, it turned out, because management was pumping up prices on Doritos and other snacks. Frito was scrimping on product quality. Enrico slashed costs, firing 1,700 workers and sweeping out management.[41]

Contingency Factors   **Contingency factors** are situational variables that cause one style of leadership to be more effective than another. In this context, these variables affect expectancy or path–goal perceptions. This model has two groups of contingency variables (see Figure 17–5). They are employee characteristics and environmental factors. Five important employee characteristics are locus of control, task ability, need for achievement, experience, and need for clarity. Three relevant environmental factors are (1) the employee's task, (2) the authority system, and (3) the work group. All these factors have the potential for hindering or motivating employees.

Research has focused on determining whether the various contingency factors influence the effectiveness of different leadership styles. A recent summary of this research revealed that only 138 of 562 (25%) contingency relationships tested confirmed the theory. Although these results were greater than chance, they provided limited support for the moderating relationships predicted within path–goal theory. On the positive side, however, the *task characteristics* of autonomy, variety, and significance and the *employee characteristics* of ability, experience, training and knowledge, professional orientation, indifference to organizational rewards, and need for independence obtained results that were semiconsistent with the theory.[42]

Contingency factors
Variables that influence the appropriateness of a leadership style.

Managerial Implications   There are two important managerial implications. First, leaders possess and use more than one style of leadership. Managers thus should not be hesitant to try new behaviors when the situation calls for them. Second, a small set of task and employee characteristics are relevant contingency factors. Managers are encouraged to modify their leadership style to fit these various task and employee characteristics. For example, supportive and achievement leadership are more likely to be satisfying when employees have a lot of ability and experience.

Hersey and Blanchard's Situational Leadership Theory

Readiness

Follower's ability and willingness to complete a task.

Situational leadership theory (SLT) was developed by management writers Paul Hersey and Kenneth Blanchard.[43] According to the theory, effective leader behavior depends on the readiness level of a leader's followers. **Readiness** is defined as the extent to which a follower possesses the ability and willingness to complete a task. Willingness is a combination of confidence, commitment, and motivation.

The SLT model is summarized in Figure 17–6. The appropriate leadership style is found by cross referencing follower readiness, which varies from low to high, with one

Figure 17–6   *Situational Leadership Model*

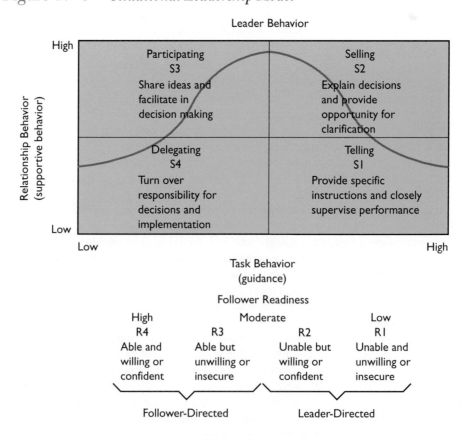

of four leadership styles. The four leadership styles represent combinations of task and relationship-oriented leader behaviors (S_1 to S_4). Leaders are encouraged to use a "telling style" for followers with low readiness. This style combines high task-oriented leader behaviors, such as providing instructions, with low relationship-oriented behaviors, such as close supervision (see Figure 17–6). As follower readiness increases, leaders are advised to gradually move from a telling, to a selling, to a participating, and, ultimately, to a delegating style. In the most recent description of this model, the four leadership styles depicted in Figure 17–6 are referred to as telling or directing (S_1), persuading or coaching (S_2), participating or supporting (S_3), and delegating (S_4).[44]

Although SLT is widely used as a training tool, it is not strongly supported by scientific research. For instance, leadership effectiveness was not attributable to the predicted interaction between follower readiness and leadership style in a study of 459 salespeople.[45] Moreover, a study of 303 teachers indicated that SLT was accurate only for employees with low readiness. This finding is consistent with a survey of 57 chief nurse executives in California. These executives did not delegate in accordance with SLT.[46] Finally, researchers have concluded that the self-assessment instrument used to measure leadership style and follower readiness is inaccurate and should be used with caution.[47] In summary, managers should exercise discretion when using prescriptions from SLT.

From Transactional to Charismatic Leadership

New perspectives of leadership theory have emerged in the past 15 years, variously referred to as "charismatic," "heroic," "transformational," or "visionary" leadership.[48] These competing but related perspectives have created confusion among researchers and practicing managers. Fortunately, Robert House and Boas Shamir have given us a practical, integrated theory. It is referred to as *charismatic leadership*.

This section begins by highlighting the differences between transactional and charismatic leadership. We then discuss a model of the charismatic leadership process and its research and management implications.

What Is the Difference between Transactional and Charismatic Leadership?

Most of the models and theories previously discussed in this chapter represent transactional leadership. **Transactional leadership** focuses on the interpersonal transactions between managers and employees. Leaders are seen as engaging in behaviors that maintain a quality interaction between themselves and followers. The two underlying characteristics of transactional leadership are that (1) leaders use contingent rewards to motivate employees and (2) leaders exert corrective action only when subordinates fail to obtain performance goals.

In contrast, **charismatic leadership** emphasizes "symbolic leader behavior, visionary and inspirational messages, nonverbal communication, appeal to ideological values, intellectual stimulation of followers by the leader, display of confidence in self and followers, and leader expectations for follower self-sacrifice and for performance beyond the call of duty."[49] Charismatic leadership can produce significant organizational change and results because it "transforms" employees to pursue organizational goals in lieu of self-interests. Ken Chenault, chief operating officer of American Express Company, is a good example of a charismatic leader. Consider what others have to say about his leadership style:

Transactional leadership
Focuses on interpersonal interactions between managers and employees.

Charismatic leadership
Transforms employees to pursue organizational goals over self-interests.

An elegant, quietly charismatic man of even temper and unrelenting drive, Chenault tends to inspire his admirers to extravagant praise. "Ken radiates such a depth of belief that people would do anything for him," says Rochelle Lazarus, chairman and CEO of Ogilvy & Mather Worldwide Inc., AmEx's lead advertising agency. "He is a true leader," adds Amy DiGeso, a former AmEx executive who is chief executive of Mary Kay Inc.: "I can say unequivocally that I admire Ken more than anyone else I've ever worked with. I think he will be our generation's Jack Welch." . . . A former management consultant himself, Chenault is said to be as hard-driving and pragmatic as his boss [Harvey Golub]. Unlike Golub, though, he has always been able to engage the emotions of his colleagues as well as their intellects. "Harvey is a brilliant man, but Ken has the hearts and minds of the people at the TRS [Travel Related Services] company," says Thomas O Ryder, a longtime AmEx exec who recently became CEO of Reader's Digest Assn.[50]

Let us now examine how charismatic leadership transforms followers.

How Does Charismatic Leadership Transform Followers?

Charismatic leaders transform followers by creating changes in their goals, values, needs, beliefs, and aspirations. They accomplish this transformation by appealing to followers' self-concepts—namely, their values and personal identity. Figure 17–7 presents a model of how charismatic leadership accomplishes this transformation process.

Figure 17–7 shows that organizational culture is a key precursor of charismatic leadership. You may recall from our discussion of organizational culture in Chapter 3 that long-term financial performance was highest for organizations with an adaptive culture. Organizations with adaptive cultures anticipate and adapt to environmental changes and focus on leadership that emphasizes the importance of service to customers, stockholders, and employees. This type of management orientation involves the use of charismatic leadership.

Charismatic leaders first engage in three key sets of leader behavior. If done effectively, these behaviors positively affect individual followers and their work groups. These positive effects, in turn, influence a variety of outcomes. Before discussing the model of charismatic leadership in more detail, it is important to note two general conclusions about charismatic leadership.[51] First, the two-headed arrow between organizational culture and leader behavior in Figure 17–7 reveals that individuals with charismatic behavioral tendencies are able to influence culture. This implies that charismatic leadership reinforces the core values of an adaptive culture and helps to change dysfunctional aspects of an organization's culture that develop over time. Second, charismatic leadership has effects on multiple levels within an organization. For example, Figure 17–7 shows that charismatic leadership can positively influence individual outcomes (e.g., motivation), group outcomes (e.g., group cohesion), and organizational outcomes (e.g., financial performance). You can see that the potential for positive benefits from charismatic leadership is quite widespread.

Charismatic Leader Behavior   The first set of charismatic leader behaviors involves establishing a common vision of the future. A vision is "a realistic, credible, attractive future for your organization."[52] According to Burt Nanus, a leadership expert, the "right" vision unleashes human potential because it serves as a beacon of hope and common purpose. It does this by attracting commitment, energizing workers, creating

Figure 17–7   *A Charismatic Model of Leadership*

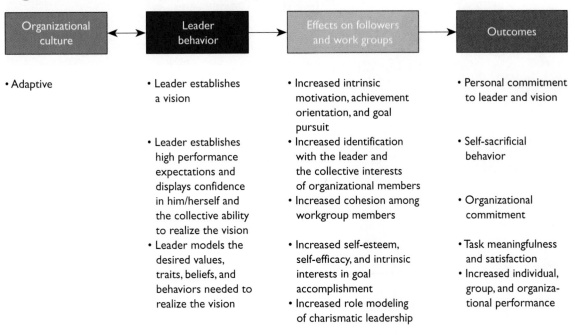

Organizational culture	Leader behavior	Effects on followers and work groups	Outcomes

- Adaptive

- Leader establishes a vision

- Leader establishes high performance expectations and displays confidence in him/herself and the collective ability to realize the vision
- Leader models the desired values, traits, beliefs, and behaviors needed to realize the vision

- Increased intrinsic motivation, achievement orientation, and goal pursuit
- Increased identification with the leader and the collective interests of organizational members
- Increased cohesion among workgroup members

- Increased self-esteem, self-efficacy, and intrinsic interests in goal accomplishment
- Increased role modeling of charismatic leadership

- Personal commitment to leader and vision

- Self-sacrificial behavior

- Organizational commitment

- Task meaningfulness and satisfaction
- Increased individual, group, and organizational performance

SOURCE: Based in part on D A Waldman and F J Yammarino, "CEO Charismatic Leadership: Levels-of-Management and Levels-of-Analysis Effects," *Academy of Management Review,* April 1999, pp 266–85; and B Shamir, R J House, and M B Arthur, "The Motivational Effects of Charismatic Leadership: A Self-Concept Based Theory," *Organization Science,* November 1993, pp 577–94.

meaning in employees' lives, establishing a standard of excellence, promoting high ideals, and bridging the gap between an organization's present problems and its future goals and aspirations.[53] In contrast, the "wrong" vision can be very damaging to an organization.

Consider what happened to Coastal Physician Group Inc. as it pursued the vision of its founder Dr Steven Scott. Dr Scott's vision was to create networks of physician practices and then sell the network services to health care providers:

> Today, his dream of a physician-led revolution has turned into a nightmare. Major clients and top executives have fled. Coastal is abandoning many of its businesses, selling clinics and trying to resuscitate its original activity, staffing hospitals. . . .
>
> Dr Scott himself, a 48-year-old workaholic obstetrician turned entrepreneur, sits in his fenced-in two-story brick home here, cooling his heels and sipping iced tea. In May, his hand-picked board ousted him as chief executive officer and put him on "sabbatical." The CEO who made a practice of calling subordinates at home at night is now barred, by motion of the board, from speaking to Coastal's employees. He also can't enter its offices, even though he owns the building. . . .
>
> Current management describes him as an arrogant boss who ruined Coastal through a series of missteps and can't bear to let go.[54]

As you can see, Coastal Physician Group's vision produced disastrous results. This highlights the fact that charismatic leaders do more than simply establish a vision. They also must gain input from others in developing an effective implementation plan. For example, Johnson & Johnson obtained input about its vision and implementation plan by surveying all of its 80,000 employees.[55]

Lloyd Ward, CEO of Maytag, is a charismatic leader who is transforming the organization. Maytag's revenue and profits have grown under Ward's leadership.

Courtesy of Maytag Corporation

The second set of leader behaviors involves two key components:

1. Charismatic leaders set high performance expectations and standards because they know challenging, attainable goals lead to greater productivity.

2. Charismatic leaders need to publicly express confidence in the followers' ability to meet high performance expectations. This is essential because employees are more likely to pursue difficult goals when they believe they can accomplish what is being asked of them.

The third and final set of leader behaviors involves being a role model. Through their actions, charismatic leaders model the desired values, traits, beliefs, and behaviors needed to realize the vision.

Motivational Mechanisms Underlying the Positive Effects of Charismatic Leadership
Charismatic leadership positively affects employee motivation (see Figure 17–7). One way in which this occurs is by increasing the intrinsic value of an employee's effort and goals. Leaders do this by emphasizing the symbolic value of effort; that is, charismatic leaders convey the message that effort reflects important organizational values and collective interests. Followers come to learn that their level of effort represents a moral statement. For example, high effort represents commitment to the organization's vision and values, whereas low effort reflects a lack of commitment.

Charismatic leadership also increases employees' effort → performance expectancies by positively contributing to followers' self-esteem and self-efficacy. Leaders also increase the intrinsic value of goal accomplishment by explaining the organization's vision and goals in terms of the personal values they represent. This helps employees to personally connect with the organization's vision. Charismatic leaders further increase the meaningfulness of actions aimed toward goal accomplishment by showing how goals move the organization toward its positive vision, which then gives followers a sense of "growth and development," both of which are important contributors to a positive self-concept.

Research and Managerial Implications

The charismatic model of leadership presented in Figure 17–7 was partially supported by previous research. A study of 50 field companies in the Israel Defense Forces revealed that charismatic leader behavior was positively related to followers' identification with and trust in the leader, motivation, self-sacrifice, identification with the work group, and attachment to the work group.[56] A meta-analysis of 54 studies further indicated that charismatic leaders were viewed as more effective leaders by both supervisors and followers and had followers who exerted more effort and reported higher levels of job satisfaction than noncharismatic leaders.[57] Other studies showed that charismatic leadership was positively associated with followers' individual performance, job satisfaction, and satisfaction with the leader.[58] At the organizational level, a second meta-analysis demonstrated that charismatic leadership was positively correlated with organizational measures of effectiveness.[59] Two additional studies demonstrated that both charismatic and transactional leadership were positively associated with a variety of important employee outcomes.[60] Finally, a study of 31 presidents of the United States indicated that charisma significantly predicted presidential performance.[61]

These results underscore four important managerial implications. First, the best leaders are not just charismatic, they are both transactional and charismatic. Leaders should attempt these two types of leadership while avoiding a "laissez-faire" or "wait-and-see" style. Laissez-faire leadership is the most ineffective leadership style.[62]

Second, charismatic leadership is not applicable in all organizational situations. According to a team of experts, charismatic leadership is most likely to be effective when

1. The situation offers opportunities for "moral" involvement.
2. Performance goals cannot be easily established and measured.
3. Extrinsic rewards cannot be clearly linked to individual performance.
4. There are few situational cues or constraints to guide behavior.
5. Exceptional effort, behavior, sacrifices, and performance are required of both leaders and followers.[63]

Third, employees at any level in an organization can be trained to be more transactional and charismatic.[64] This reinforces the organizational value of developing and rolling out a combination of transactional and charismatic leadership training for all employees. Fourth, charismatic leaders can be ethical or unethical. Whereas ethical charismatic leaders enable employees to enhance their self-concepts, unethical ones select or produce obedient, dependent, and compliant followers.[65] Top management can create and maintain ethical charismatic leadership by

1. Creating and enforcing a clearly stated code of ethics.
2. Recruiting, selecting, and promoting people with high morals and standards.
3. Developing performance expectations around the treatment of employees—these expectations can then be assessed in the performance appraisal process.
4. Training employees to value diversity.
5. Identifying, rewarding, and publicly praising employees who exemplify high moral conduct.[66]

Additional Perspectives on Leadership

This section examines four additional approaches to leadership: leader–member exchange theory, substitutes for leadership, servant leadership, and superleadership. We spend more time discussing leader–member exchange theory and substitutes for leadership because they have been more thoroughly investigated.

The Leader–Member Exchange (LMX) Model of Leadership

The leader–member exchange model of leadership revolves around the development of dyadic relationships between managers and their direct reports. This model is quite different from those previously discussed in that it focuses on the quality of relationships between managers and subordinates as opposed to the behaviors or traits of

Figure 17–8   *A Role-Making Model of Leadership*

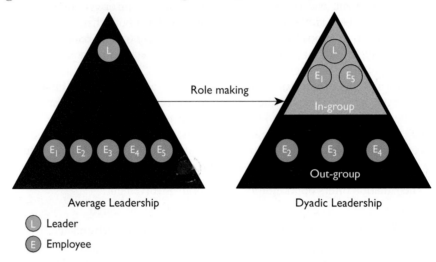

SOURCE: Adapted from F Dansereau, Jr., G Graen, and W J Haga, "A Vertical Dyad Linkage Approach to Leadership within Formal Organizations," *Organizational Behavior and Human Performance*, February 1975, p 72.

either leaders or followers. It also is different in that it does not assume that leader behavior is characterized by a stable or average leadership style as does the Leadership Grid® and Fiedler's contingency theory. In other words, these models assume a leader treats all subordinates in about the same way. This traditional approach to leadership is shown in the left side of Figure 17–8. In this case, the leader (designated by the circled L) is thought to exhibit a similar pattern of behavior toward all employees (E_1 to E_5). In contrast, the LMX model is based on the assumption that leaders develop unique one-to-one relationships with each of the people reporting to them. Behavioral scientists call this sort of relationship a *vertical dyad.* The forming of vertical dyads is said to be a naturally occurring process, resulting from the leader's attempt to delegate and assign work roles. As a result of this process, two distinct types of leader–member exchange relationships are expected to evolve.[67]

In-group exchange
A partnership characterized by mutual trust, respect, and liking.

One type of leader–member exchange is called the **in-group exchange.** In this relationship, leaders and followers develop a partnership characterized by reciprocal influence, mutual trust, respect and liking, and a sense of common fates. Figure 17–8 shows that E_1 and E_5 are members of the leader's in-group. In the second type of exchange, referred to as an **out-group exchange,** leaders are characterized as overseers who fail to create a sense of mutual trust, respect, or common fate.[68] E_2, E_3, and E_4 are members of the out-group on the right side of Figure 17–8.

Out-group exchange
A partnership characterized by a lack of mutual trust, respect, and liking.

Research Findings   If the leader–member exchange model is correct, there should be a significant relationship between the type of leader–member exchange and job-related outcomes. Research supports this prediction. For example, a positive leader–member exchange was positively associated with job satisfaction, job performance, goal commitment, organizational citizenship behaviors (organizational citizenship behavior was discussed in Chapter 7), and satisfaction with leadership.[69] Positive leader–member exchange also was correlated with greater safety communication, safety commitment, and a reduction in the number of accidents at work.[70] The type of leader–member exchange was found to predict not only turnover among nurses and computer analysts, but also career outcomes, such as promotability, salary level, and receipt of bonuses over a seven-year period.[71] Finally, studies also have identified a variety of variables that influence the quality of an LMX. For example, LMX was related to personality similarity and demographic similarity.[72] Further, the quality of an LMX was positively related with the extent to which leaders and followers like each other, the leaders' positive expectations of their subordinates, and employees' impression management techniques (recall the discussion of impression management in Chapter 16).[73] The quality of an LMX also was negatively associated with the number of employees reporting to a manager and the work load.[74]

Managerial Implications   There are three important implications associated with the LMX model of leadership. First, leaders are encouraged to establish high-performance expectations for all of their direct reports because setting high-performance standards fosters high-quality LMXs. Second, because personality and demographic similarity between leaders and followers is associated with higher LMXs, managers need to be careful that they don't create a homogeneous work environment in the spirit of having positive relationships with their direct reports. Our discussion of diversity in Chapter 2 clearly documented that there are many positive benefits of having a diverse workforce. The third implication pertains to those of us who find ourselves in a poor LMX. Before providing advice about what to do in this situation, we would like you to assess the quality of your current leader–member exchange. The OB Exercise on p 574, contains a measure of leader–member exchange that segments an LMX into four subdimensions: mutual affection, loyalty, contribution to work activities, and professional respect.[75]

What is the overall quality of your LMX? Do you agree with this assessment? Which subdimensions are high and low? If your overall LMX and associated subdimensions are all high, you should be in a very good situation with respect to the relationship between you and your manager. Having a low LMX overall score or a low dimensional score, however, reveals that part of the relationship with your manager may need improvement. OB researcher Robert Vecchio offers the following tips to both followers and leaders for improving the quality of leader–member exchanges:

1. New employees should offer their loyalty, support, and cooperativeness to their manager.
2. If you are an out-group member, either accept the situation, try to become an in-group member by being cooperative and loyal, or quit.
3. Managers should consciously try to expand their in-groups.
4. Managers need to give employees ample opportunity to prove themselves.[76]

Finally, you may want to try using some of the impression management techniques discussed in Chapter 16 in order to improve your LMX.

Substitutes for Leadership

Virtually all leadership theories assume that some sort of formal leadership is necessary, whatever the circumstances. But this basic assumption is questioned by this model of leadership. Specifically, some OB scholars propose that there are a variety of situational variables that can substitute for, neutralize, or enhance the effects of leadership. These situational variables are referred to as **substitutes for leadership.**[77] Substitutes for leadership can thus increase or diminish a leader's ability to influence the work group. For example, leader behavior that initiates structure would tend to be resisted by independent-minded employees with high ability and vast experience. Consequently, such employees would be guided more by their own initiative than by managerial directives.

Substitutes for leadership
Situational variables that can substitute for, neutralize, or enhance the effects of leadership.

OB Exercise   Assessing Your Leader–Member Exchange

Instructions

For each of the items shown below, use the following scale to circle the answer that best represents how you feel about the relationship between you and your current manager/supervisor. If you are not currently working, complete the survey by thinking about a previous manager. Remember, there are no right or wrong answers. After circling a response for each of the 12 items, use the scoring key to compute scores for the subdimensions within your leader–member exchange.

1 = Strongly disagree
2 = Disagree
3 = Neither agree nor disagree
4 = Agree
5 = Strongly agree

1. I like my supervisor very much
   as a person.   1 — 2 — 3 — 4 — 5

2. My supervisor is the kind of
   person one would like to have
   as a friend.   1 — 2 — 3 — 4 — 5

3. My supervisor is a lot of fun to
   work with.   1 — 2 — 3 — 4 — 5

4. My supervisor defends my work
   actions to a superior, even
   without complete knowledge
   of the issue in question.   1 — 2 — 3 — 4 — 5

5. My supervisor would come to
   my defense if I were "attacked"
   by others.   1 — 2 — 3 — 4 — 5

6. My supervisor would defend me
   to others in the organization if
   I made an honest mistake.   1 — 2 — 3 — 4 — 5

7. I do work for my supervisor
   that goes beyond what is
   specified in my job description.   1 — 2 — 3 — 4 — 5

8. I am willing to apply extra
   efforts, beyond those normally
   required, to meet my
   supervisor's work goals.   1 — 2 — 3 — 4 — 5

9. I do not mind working my
   hardest for my supervisor.   1 — 2 — 3 — 4 — 5

10. I am impressed with my
    supervisor's knowledge of
    his/her job.   1 — 2 — 3 — 4 — 5

11. I respect my supervisor's
    knowledge of and competence
    on the job.   1 — 2 — 3 — 4 — 5

12. I admire my supervisor's
    professional skills.   1 — 2 — 3 — 4 — 5

Scoring Key

Mutual affection (add items 1–3)   _____
Loyalty (add items 4–6)   _____
Contribution to work activities (add items 7–9)   _____
Professional respect (add items 10–12) _____
Overall score (add all 12 items)   _____

Arbitrary Norms

Low mutual affection = 3–9
High mutual affection = 10–15
Low loyalty = 3–9
High loyalty = 10–15
Low contribution to work activities = 3–9
High contribution to work activities = 10–15
Low professional respect = 3–9
High professional respect = 10–15
Low overall leader–member exchange = 12–38
High overall leader–member exchange = 39–60

SOURCE: Survey items were taken from R C Liden and J M Maslyn, "Multidimensionality of Leader–Member Exchange: An Empirical Assessment through Scale Development," *Journal of Management*, 1998, p 56.

Table 17–2   *Substitutes for Leadership*

Characteristic	Relationship-Oriented or Considerate Leader Behavior Is Unnecessary	Task-Oriented or Initiating Structure Leader Behavior Is Unnecessary
Of the Subordinate		
1. Ability, experience, training, knowledge		X
2. Need for independence	X	X
3. "Professional" orientation	X	X
4. Indifference toward organizational rewards	X	X
Of the Task		
5. Unambiguous and routine		X
6. Methodologically invariant		X
7. Provides its own feedback concerning accomplishment		X
8. Intrinsically satisfying	X	
Of the Organization		
9. Formalization (explicit plans, goals, and areas of responsibility)		X
10. Inflexibility (rigid, unbending rules and procedures)		X
11. Highly specified and active advisory and staff functions		X
12. Closely knit, cohesive work groups	X	X
13. Organizational rewards not within the leader's control	X	X
14. Spatial distance between superior and subordinates	X	X

SOURCE: Adapted from S Kerr and J M Jermier, "Substitutes for Leadership: Their Meaning and Measurement," *Organizational Behavior and Human Performance,* December 1978, pp 375–403.

Kerr and Jermier's Substitutes for Leadership Model   According to Steven Kerr and John Jermier, the OB researchers who developed this model, the key to improving leadership effectiveness is to identify the situational characteristics that can either substitute for, neutralize, or improve the impact of a leader's behavior. Table 17–2 lists the various substitutes for leadership. Characteristics of the subordinate, the task, and the organization can act as substitutes for traditional hierarchical leadership. Further, different characteristics are predicted to negate different types of leader behavior. For example, tasks that provide feedback concerning accomplishment, such as taking a test, tend to negate task-oriented but not relationship-oriented leader behavior (see Table 17–2). Although the list in Table 17–2 is not all-inclusive, it shows that there are more substitutes for task-oriented leadership than for relationship-oriented leadership.

Research and Managerial Implications   Two different approaches have been used to test this model. The first is based on the idea that substitutes for leadership are contingency variables that moderate the relationship between leader behavior and employee attitudes and behavior.[78] A recent summary of this research revealed that only 318 of 3,741 (9%) contingency relationships tested supported the model.[79] This demonstrates that substitutes for leadership do not moderate the effect of a leader's behavior as suggested by Steve Kerr and John Jermier. The second approach to test the substitutes model examined whether substitutes for leadership have a direct effect on employee attitudes and behaviors. A recent meta-analysis of 36 different samples revealed that the combination of substitute variables and leader behaviors significantly explained a variety of employee attitudes and behaviors. Interestingly, the substitutes for leadership were more important than leader behaviors in accounting for employee attitudes and behaviors.[80]

The key implication is that managers should be attentive to the substitutes listed in Table 17–2 because they directly influence employee attitudes and performance. Managers can positively influence the substitutes through employee selection, job design, work group assignments, and the design of organizational processes and systems.[81]

Servant-Leadership

Servant-leadership
Focuses on increased service to others rather than to oneself.

Servant-leadership is more a philosophy of managing than a testable theory. The term *servant-leadership* was coined by Robert Greenleaf in 1970. Greenleaf believes that great leaders act as servants, putting the needs of others, including employees, customers, and community, as their first priority. **Servant-leadership** focuses on increased service to others rather than to oneself.[82] According to Jim Stuart, cofounder of the leadership circle in Tampa, Florida, "Leadership derives naturally from a commitment to service. You know that you're practicing servant-leadership if your followers become wiser, healthier, more autonomous—and more likely to become servant-leaders themselves."[83] Servant-leadership is not a quick-fix approach to leadership. Rather, it is a long-term, transformational approach to life and work. Table 17–3 presents 10 characteristics possessed by servant-leaders. One can hardly go wrong by trying to adopt these characteristics.

Superleadership

Superleader
Someone who leads others to lead themselves.

A **superleader** is someone who leads others to lead themselves. You may recall that we already discussed this approach to leadership in Chapter 13 with respect to developing team members' self-management skills. We briefly highlight it again because superleadership is equally relevant within teams as well as any general leadership situation. Superleaders empower followers by acting as a teacher and coach rather than as a dictator and autocrat. The need for this form of leadership is underscored by a survey of 1,046 Americans. Results demonstrated that only 38% of the respondents ever had an effective coach or mentor.[84]

Productive thinking is the cornerstone of superleadership. Specifically, managers are encouraged to teach followers how to engage in productive thinking.[85] This is expected to increase employees feelings of personal control and intrinsic motivation. Superleadership has the potential to free up a manager's time because employees are encouraged to manage themselves. Future research is needed to test the validity of recommendations derived from this new approach to leadership.

Table 17–3   *Characteristics of the Servant-Leader*

Servant-Leadership Characteristics	Description
1. Listening	Servant-leaders focus on listening to identify and clarify the needs and desires of a group.
2. Empathy	Servant-leaders try to empathize with others' feelings and emotions. An individual's good intentions are assumed even when he or she performs poorly.
3. Healing	Servant-leaders strive to make themselves and others whole in the face of failure or suffering.
4. Awareness	Servant-leaders are very self-aware of their strengths and limitations.
5. Persuasion	Servant-leaders rely more on persuasion than positional authority when making decisions and trying to influence others.
6. Conceptualization	Servant leaders take the time and effort to develop broader based conceptual thinking. Servant-leaders seek an appropriate balance between a short-term, day-to-day focus and a long-term, conceptual orientation.
7. Foresight	Servant-leaders have the ability to foresee future outcomes associated with a current course of action or situation.
8. Stewardship	Servant-leaders assume that they are stewards of the people and resources they manage.
9. Commitment to the growth of people	Servant-leaders are committed to people beyond their immediate work role. They commit to fostering an environment that encourages personal, professional, and spiritual growth.
10. Building community	Servant-leaders strive to create a sense of community both within and outside the work organization.

SOURCE: These characteristics and descriptions were derived from L C Spears, "Introduction: Servant-Leadership and the Greenleaf Legacy," in *Reflections on Leadership: How Robert K Greenleaf's Theory of Servant-Leadership Influenced Today's Top Management Thinkers,* ed L C Spears (New York: John Wiley & Sons, 1995), pp 1–14.

Summary of Key Concepts

1. *Define the term* leadership, *and explain the difference between leading versus managing.* Leadership is defined as a social influence process in which the leader tries to obtain the voluntary participation of employees in an effort to reach organizational objectives. Leadership entails more than having authority and power. Although leadership and management overlap, each entails a unique set of activities or functions. Managers typically perform functions associated with planning, investigating, organizing, and control, and leaders deal with the interpersonal aspects of a manager's job. Table 17–1 summarizes the differences between leading and managing.

2. *Review trait theory research, and discuss the idea of one best style of leadership, using the Ohio State studies and the Leader-*

ship Grid® *as points of reference.* Historical leadership research did not support the notion that effective leaders possessed unique traits from followers. However, teams of researchers reanalyzed this historical data with modern-day statistical procedures. Results revealed that individuals tend to be perceived as leaders when they possess one or more of the following traits: intelligence, dominance, and masculinity. A recent study further demonstrated that employees value credible leaders. Credible leaders are honest, forward-looking, inspiring, and competent. Research also examined the relationship between gender and leadership. Results demonstrated that (a) men and women differed in the type of leadership roles they assume, (b) leadership styles varied by gender, and (c) gender differences in ratings of leadership effectiveness were associated with the percentage of male leaders and male subordinates. The Ohio State studies revealed that there were two key independent dimensions of leadership behavior: consideration and initiating structure. Authors of the Leadership Grid® proposed that leaders should adopt a style that demonstrates high concern for production and people. Research did not support the premise that there is one best style of leadership.

3. *Explain, according to Fiedler's contingency model, how leadership style interacts with situational control.* Fiedler believes leader effectiveness depends on an appropriate match between leadership style and situational control. Leaders are either task motivated or relationship motivated. Situation control is composed of leader–member relations, task structure, and position power. Task-motivated leaders are effective under situations of both high and low control. Relationship-motivated leaders are more effective when they have moderate situational control.

4. *Discuss House's path–goal theory and Hersey and Blanchard's situational leadership theory.* According to path–goal theory, leaders alternately can exhibit directive, supportive, participative, or achievement-oriented styles of leadership. The effectiveness of these styles depends on various employee characteristics and environmental factors. Path–goal theory has received limited support from research. There are two important managerial implications: (a) leaders possess and use more than one style of leadership, and (b) managers are advised to modify their leadership style to fit a small subset of task and employee characteristics. According to situational leadership theory (SLT), effective leader behavior depends on the readiness level of a leader's followers. As follower readiness increases, leaders are advised to gradually move from a telling to a selling to a participating and, finally, to a delegating style. Research does not support SLT.

5. *Define and differentiate transactional and charismatic leadership.* There is an important difference between transactional and charismatic leadership. Transactional leaders focus on the interpersonal transactions between managers and employees. Charismatic leaders motivate employees to pursue organizational goals above their own self-interests. Both forms of leadership are important for organizational success.

6. *Explain how charismatic leadership transforms followers and work groups.* Organizational culture is a key precursor of charismatic leadership, which is composed of three sets of leader behavior. These leader behaviors, in turn, positively affect followers' and work groups' goals, values, beliefs, aspirations, and motivation. These positive effects are then associated with a host of preferred outcomes.

7. *Summarize the managerial implications of charismatic leadership.* There are four managerial implications: (a) The best leaders are both transactional and charismatic. (b) Charismatic leadership is not applicable in all organizational situations. (c) Employees at any level in an organization can be trained to be more transactional and charismatic. (d) Top management needs to promote and reinforce ethical charismatic leadership because charismatic leaders can be ethical or unethical.

8. *Explain the leader–member exchange model of leadership.* This model revolves around the development of dyadic relationships between managers and their direct reports. These leader–member exchanges qualify as either in-group or out-group relationships. Research supports this model of leadership.

9. *Describe the substitutes for leadership, and explain how they substitute for, neutralize, or enhance the effects of leadership.* There are 14 substitutes for leadership (see Table 17–2) that can substitute for, neutralize, or enhance the effects of leadership. These substitutes contain characteristics of the subordinates, the task, and the organization. Research shows that substitutes directly influence employee attitudes and performance.

10. *Describe servant-leadership and superleadership.* Servant-leadership is more a philosophy than a testable theory. It is based on the premise that great leaders act as servants, putting the needs of others, including employees, customers, and community, as their first priority. A superleader is someone who leads others to lead themselves. Superleaders empower followers by acting as a teacher and coach rather than as a dictator and autocrat.

Discussion Questions

1. Is everyone cut out to be a leader? Explain.

2. Has your college education helped you develop any of the traits that characterize leaders?

3. Should organizations change anything in response to research pertaining to gender and leadership? If yes, describe your recommendations.

4. What leadership traits and behavioral styles are possessed by the president of the United States?

5. Does it make more sense to change a person's leadership style or the situation? How would Fred Fiedler and Robert House answer this question?

6. Describe how a college professor might use House's path–goal theory to clarify student's path–goal perceptions.

7. Identify three charismatic leaders, and describe their leadership traits and behavioral styles.

8. Have you ever worked for a charismatic leader? Describe how he or she transformed followers.

9. Have you ever been a member of an in-group or out-group? For either situation, describe the pattern of interaction between you and your manager.

10. In your view, which leadership theory has the greatest practical application? Why?

Internet Exercise

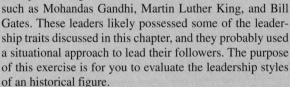

www.leader-values.com

The topic of leadership has been important since the dawn of time. History is filled with examples of great leaders such as Mohandas Gandhi, Martin Luther King, and Bill Gates. These leaders likely possessed some of the leadership traits discussed in this chapter, and they probably used a situational approach to lead their followers. The purpose of this exercise is for you to evaluate the leadership styles of an historical figure.

Go to the Internet home page for Leadership Values (**www.leader-values.com**), and select the subheading "4 E's" on the left side of the screen. This section provides an overview of leadership and suggests four essential traits/behaviors that are exhibited by leaders: to envision, enable, empower, and energize. After reading this material, go back to the home page, and select the subheading

"Historical Leaders" from the list on the left-hand side of the page. Next, choose one of the leaders from the list of historical figures, and read the description about his or her leadership style. You may want to print all of the material you read thus far from this web page to help you answer the following questions.

Questions

1. Describe the 4 E's of leadership.

2. To what extent do the 4 E's overlap with the theories and models of leadership discussed in this chapter?

3. Using any of the theories or models discussed in this chapter, how would you describe the leadership style of the historical figure you investigated?

4. Was this leader successful in using the 4 E's of leadership? Describe how he/she used the 4 E's.

OB in Action Case Study[86]

www.maytag.com

Lloyd Ward Becomes CEO of Maytag

BusinessWeek The journey began on a narrow country road in southern Michigan. There, in a 20-foot-by-20-foot house with no running water, lived the Ward family: mother, father, three sons, and two daughters. In the rare moments during the 1950s and 1960s that Rubert Ward wasn't working—at his day job as postman, his night job as movie house janitor, or his Sunday job as Baptist preacher—he liked to gather his boys and talk about "Ward & Sons." It was the imaginary auto-repair shop that he dreamed about one day running with them.

In reality, he had no training as a mechanic, but he had made himself an expert by checking out manuals from the library, in the same way he later figured out how to remedy the house's sagging roof and install plumbing. "He would take on things he had no clue about, and he would get a book, and he would learn," says the middle Ward child, Lloyd.

Rubert Ward never got to start Ward & Sons. He died of a heart attack in 1967, at 47. But from his tiny house, with its tight quarters and big dreams, would emerge one of the most driven men in America today: a star college basketball

player who studied to become an engineer, an engineer who transformed himself into an inspirational speaker and one of the country's most respected marketers, and a marketer who next month will become only the second African American ever to lead a large US company.

He is Lloyd David Ward, a singular study in ambition, smarts, and resilience. When he assumes the top job at Maytag Corp. on Aug. 12, Ward, 50, will have made a longer journey than any other executive in Corporate America. Some chieftains, such as Lee A Iacocca, have escaped poverty to find their way to the corner office. A few African American executives, such as American Express Co. CEO-in-waiting Kenneth Chenault, have overcome the racism that still plagues the workplace. The country's first black CEO of a major corporation, Fannie Mae's Franklin D Raines, is one of them, but his impressive rise from poverty in Seattle to head of the government-sponsored company has taken place more in the political arena of Washington, DC than in the corporate world.

No one, in fact, has defeated the pincer of poverty and prejudice as Lloyd Ward has. And he has done it at some of the world's best-known companies, from Procter & Gamble to Ford to PepsiCo. Working with Maytag CEO Leonard A Hadley, Ward over the last three years has reinvented the staid appliance company, helping to triple its stock price. A master motivator who listens as well as he speaks, Ward has convinced Maytag veterans that change was both necessary and possible. Colleagues laud his ability to challenge people's beliefs without criticizing them personally, to seize on nuggets of common ground, and then to exploit them. "He is a good thinker," says PepsiCo Inc. CEO Roger A Enrico, "but he is an exceptional leader."

His energy, however, is also the cause of one of Ward's few weaknesses as a manager: impatience. It led to his rash decision to quit P&G in the 1970s when he did not get a transfer he wanted. And it has at times created friction between him and Hadley.

Sincere. Ward's engaging ways seem always on display. He greets people with a firm handshake, pulling himself closer to them, putting a palm on the back of their elbow, and quickly asking questions about their own life, even when he has never before met them. "Were you born here?" "What's your husband's name?" "How long have you worked here?" . . .

But Corporate America's newest star is hardly a stranger to challenges. "My whole life I've been faced with 'No,' " he says. Indeed, his success against all odds demonstrates to what extent bigotry continues to be a part of the American experience. Every step of the way, from a college roommate who wanted nothing to do with Ward to a resident of Maytag's hometown who told Ward his "kind" wasn't wanted there, he has encountered indignities and obstacles that every African American knows and few whites can fathom. . . .

It would have been difficult for anyone to see his way to the corner office from the street where Ward grew up. It was in Romulus, [Michigan], then a rural town about 20 miles west of Detroit and now the site of the sprawling Detroit Metro Airport. His neighborhood was little more than a stretch of gravel, pockmarked by tiny square houses. The Wards and their five children squeezed their lives into three small rooms. The three boys lived in one, with a bunk bed that nearly scraped the ceiling. The girls slept in another, and the parents bedded down on a fold-out couch in a living room full of secondhand furniture covered with dropcloths.

Despite the hardships, the Ward household was a happy place. "It's hard to imagine," Lloyd says now, "but when I think back, it was a wonderful childhood because we were so close." . . .

Finishing high school in 1969, Ward won a college basketball scholarship to Michigan State University. Ward knew how to use it: He wanted to become a doctor. . . .

Other barriers awaited him at Michigan State as well. When the basketball team's academic adviser saw Ward's courses in organic chemistry and calculus, the adviser told him to switch to easier classes such as health and "intro-

ductory basketball." Jordan [his teammate] remembers a coach telling Ward: "We're paying you to be a basketball player." Ward balked. So the adviser called the registrar's office and switched his courses himself. But Ward walked over to the office and changed them right back.

Good grades and a strong record on the court proved the coaches wrong, and they eventually left him alone. . . .

From Michigan State, it was straight to P&G, where Ward confronted an old problem in a new guise. Instead of overt racism, Ward this time encountered the patronizing attitudes of P&G's efforts to hire minorities in those days, say people who were at the company at the time. Despite his B average in engineering and his having been the captain of a Big Ten basketball team, P&G was willing to hire him and a handful of other blacks only for its "qualifiable" program, an early version of affirmative action. "They brought us in under the stigma of being 'qualifiable,' " Ward says. "The idea was that there weren't qualified African Americans."

Ward nonetheless holds no grudge against P&G. In fact, he now praises the company as an early supporter of diversity. "If it were not for the so-called affirmative action of the '60s and '70s," he says, "people like me may not have ever gotten the opportunity to provide the leadership that we have now been able to give." . . .

Back at headquarters, Ward let people know he wanted much more than an engineering career. Floyd Dickens Jr, one of Ward's early supervisors, remembers a meeting in the '70s. Ward was wearing his usual gray suit, white shirt, and red tie. Dickens asked Ward about his goals, and Ward didn't mince words: By the age of 45, he wanted to be chief executive of a major US corporation.

It was an astonishingly bold ambition. When Ward came to P&G in 1970, he was one of just eight African American engineers in a department of around 1,200. In large companies, a black CEO seemed as likely as a black President of the [U.S.]. But that wasn't all. Dickens knew that engineers stood no chance of reaching the top of P&G. That was reserved for marketers and product developers, who knew how to bring money to the bottom line. "You're in the wrong organization if you want that," he told Ward.

So Ward pushed for a transfer that never came. Frustrated, he left P&G to take a job with Ford Motor Co. in 1977 and took his family back to Detroit. The move was a disaster. Ward became lost and struggled inside the massive auto company. A year later, he jumped at the chance to get back to P&G. All he wanted, he said, was, someday, an opportunity to transfer out of engineering.

He got it—and made the most of it. Over the next decade, Ward skipped from one field to the next, often stepping down a rung in the corporate hierarchy in order to earn his spurs. In 1984, for instance, he remade P&G's 100-year-old Ivorydale soap plant, which had been expanded in haphazard fashion over the years. Working with the unionized workforce, Ward redesigned the plant from top to bottom. "Lloyd is a high-energy, very focused, very competitive individual," says John E Pepper, chairman of P&G and Ward's former boss. By 1986, he had made the move to general management, heading up P&G's dishwashing unit.

But Ward was tiring of the P&G bureaucracy. In 1987, he was off again, this time for P&G's corporate opposite: the rough-and-ready culture of PepsiCo Inc., where Ward thrived. As head of Frito-Lay's western and central divisions, Ward led the charge against archrival Anheuser-Busch Cos.' Eagle Snacks. At the time, Eagle was trying to speed the launch of its new corn-chip brand by offering a free bag of potato chips with every purchase. When Ward heard about the strategy, he upped the ante. With a "supersize" bag of Frito-Lay chips, the company threw in a large bag of Doritos, a far more popular and established product than Eagle's entry. Unable to sell its brand, Eagle soon pulled back, and later Anheuser-Busch got out of the snack business altogether. "It was a major victory, and it was a lot of fun," says Ward.

Pep Talks. Pepsi was also the place where Ward began to polish his leadership skills. He was constantly out in the field trying to rev up the troops, even showing up at the loading docks to give an informal pep talk to workers there. Through it all, Ward's go-for-the-throat competitiveness and gung ho motivational tactics helped increase his division's overall market share in the region from 50% to 56%. "People in that division had decided that you couldn't grow market share because it was already so high," says Steven S Reinemund, chairman of Frito-Lay. "Lloyd didn't accept that. He went on a personal crusade."

Winning at business was hardly his only crusade. While at Pepsi, Ward got deeply involved in the Dallas community with his push to get more high school kids into college. Employees became mentors to students. They dropped in at school after work and on weekends to help with homework. Ward tutored kids in his office and brought members of the Dallas Mavericks basketball team to the school to give them a lift. And he whisked kids who passed a state test to a Six Flags amusement park on the Frito-Lay corporate jet. By 1996, 61% of the students passed the state's math test, up from 32% in 1994. "Dare to dream," Ward would tell them. "Learn to love adversity. Perform—good intentions are not enough." To this day, Ward urges self-reliance. "There are many who are systematically excluded. [But] the oppressed have to overcome the prejudices of society," Ward says. "Knock on the door, pull on the handle, and, if you have to, dismantle the hinge."

Meanwhile, Ward was intent on advancing his own career. So when a small Chicago search firm came calling in 1995, with an opportunity to interview for a job that could lead to the CEO's office, Ward convinced Lita [his wife] it was a good idea—even though it was in Newton, Iowa, 40 miles from Des Moines and a world away from big-city life in Dallas. It was a huge leap of faith: Ward was willing to leave a hot career at marketing heavyweight Pepsi to head the appliance division of a sleepy company personified by the hang-dog look of the Maytag repairman in TV ads. But the fast-track shot at the CEO's job made it worthwhile for Ward.

It was also a big risk for Maytag leaders, who typically promoted carefully groomed insiders. CEO Hadley, for example, has been at the company for 40 years. This time, however, he instructed the board that his successor should be an outsider. The company needed "an extroverted marketing man," he says. . . .

In Newton, though, Ward's focus is all on the present. Once Hadley dumped unprofitable units and revamped products, Ward set about reinvigorating the company's unsophisticated marketing culture. He sped up the pace of product introductions: Maytag will launch 20 new products this year, up from only a few in the mid '90s. He lured more than a dozen executives, mostly from Pepsi and P&G, to Newton. He developed new consumer-research methods, sending observers into people's houses to watch them cook and clean, rather than simply asking them to fill out surveys. One result: a new $400 washer to help Maytag compete for the lower end of the business it had long shunned. "Ward has been able to almost reinvent Maytag," says Mike London, a senior vice-president at Best Buy Co., a major client. . . .

Still, Ward's hard-charging ways have led to occasional mis-steps. "There were a few rough spots in front of a dealer group here and there," Beer says. And while Hadley and Ward speak highly of each other, their relationship has been tense at times, say other Maytag executives. Hadley is the veteran, bowing out on a high note and reluctant to relinquish control. Ward is the outsider, fond of shaking things up. "His style is very different from mine," says Hadley. "He holds meetings I wouldn't hold. He invites more people than I would invite. He says to me: 'You have to go out and sell your program.'" Says Ward: "Succession is hard at this level."

Differences aside, the results have made both men look smart. And Maytag's remarkable run has at last paid off for Ward. In May, Maytag's board gathered to announce that Lloyd Ward would become the company's ninth chief executive. Afterward, Lloyd and Lita celebrated at a posh Des Moines restaurant.

When Lloyd and Lita got home that night, exhausted, they climbed the stairs to their bedroom and collapsed in two facing chairs. Neither said anything. "We just looked at each other," Lloyd says. The silence lasted for more than five minutes. Their journey was complete. They had made it to the top, together. Rubert Ward would have been proud. It may not have been "Ward & Sons," but a member of the family finally had a business of his own.

Questions for Discussion

1. What role did Ward's upbringing play in his rise to CEO of Maytag? Discuss.

2. Citing examples, which different leadership traits and styles were exhibited by Lloyd Ward?

3. What did you learn about leadership from this case? Use examples to reinforce your conclusions.

4. Does Ward appear to display more transactional or charismatic leadership? Explain.

5. What career advice can you take from the manner in which Lloyd Ward rose to the top position at Maytag?

Personal Awareness and Growth Exercise

How Ready Are You to Assume the Leadership Role?

Objectives

1. To assess your readiness for the leadership role.
2. To consider the implications of the gap between your career goals and your readiness to lead.

Introduction

Leaders assume multiple roles. Roles represent the expectations that others have of occupants of a position. It is important for potential leaders to consider whether they are ready for the leadership role because mismatches in expectations or skills can derail a leader's effectiveness. This exercise assesses your readiness to assume the leadership role.[87]

Instructions

For each statement, indicate the extent to which you agree or disagree with it by selecting one number from the scale provided. Circle your response for each statement. Remember, there are no right or wrong answers. After completing the survey, add your total score for the 20 items, and record it in the space provided.

1 = Strongly disagree
2 = Disagree
3 = Neither agree nor disagree
4 = Agree
5 = Strongly agree

1. It is enjoyable having people count on me for ideas and suggestions. 1 — 2 — 3 — 4 — 5

2. It would be accurate to say that I have inspired other people. 1 — 2 — 3 — 4 — 5

3. It's a good practice to ask people provocative questions about their work. 1 — 2 — 3 — 4 — 5

4. It's easy for me to compliment others. 1 — 2 — 3 — 4 — 5

5. I like to cheer people up even when my own spirits are down. 1 — 2 — 3 — 4 — 5

6. What my team accomplishes is more important than my personal glory. 1 — 2 — 3 — 4 — 5

7. Many people imitate my ideas. 1 — 2 — 3 — 4 — 5

8. Building team spirit is important to me. 1 — 2 — 3 — 4 — 5

9. I would enjoy coaching other members of the team. 1 — 2 — 3 — 4 — 5

10. It is important to me to recognize others for their accomplishments. 1 — 2 — 3 — 4 — 5

11. I would enjoy entertaining visitors to my firm even if it interfered with my completing a report. 1 — 2 — 3 — 4 — 5

12. It would be fun for me to represent my team at gatherings outside our department. 1 — 2 — 3 — 4 — 5

13. The problems of my teammates are my problems too. 1 — 2 — 3 — 4 — 5

14. Resolving conflict is an activity I enjoy. 1 — 2 — 3 — 4 — 5

15. I would cooperate with another unit in the organization even if I disagreed with the position taken by its members. 1 — 2 — 3 — 4 — 5

16. I am an idea generator on the job. 1 — 2 — 3 — 4 — 5

17. It's fun for me to bargain whenever I have the opportunity. 1 — 2 — 3 — 4 — 5

18. Team members listen to me when I speak. 1 — 2 — 3 — 4 — 5

19. People have asked me to assume the leadership of an activity several times in my life. 1 — 2 — 3 — 4 — 5

20. I've always been a convincing person. 1 — 2 — 3 — 4 — 5

Total score: _____

Norms for Interpreting the Total Score[88]

90–100	=	High readiness for the leadership role
60–89	=	Moderate readiness for the leadership role
40–59	=	Some uneasiness with the leadership role
39 or less	=	Low readiness for the leadership role

Questions for Discussion

1. Do you agree with the interpretation of your readiness to assume the leadership role? Explain why or why not.

2. If you scored below 60 and desire to become a leader, what might you do to increase your readiness to lead? To answer this question, we suggest that you study the statements carefully—particularly those with low responses—to determine how you might change either an attitude or a behavior so that you can realistically answer more questions with a response of "agree" or "strongly agree."

3. How might this evaluation instrument help you to become a more effective leader?

Group Exercise

Exhibiting Leadership within the Context of Running a Meeting[89]

Objectives

1. To consider the types of problems that can occur when running a meeting.

2. To identify the leadership behaviors that can be used to handle problems that occur in meetings.

Introduction

Managers often find themselves playing the role of formal or informal leader when participating in a planned meeting (e.g., committees, work groups, task forces, etc.). As a leader, individuals often must handle a number of interpersonal situations that have the potential of reducing the group's productivity. For example, if an individual has important information that is not shared with the group, the meeting will be less productive. Similarly, two or more individuals who engage in conversational asides could disrupt the normal functioning of the group. Finally, the group's productivity will also be threatened by two or more individuals who argue or engage in personal attacks on one another during a meeting. This exercise is designed to help you practice some of the behaviors necessary to overcome these problems and at the same time share in the responsibility of leading a productive group.[90]

Instructions

Your instructor will divide the class into groups of four to six. Once the group is assembled, briefly summarize the types of problems that can occur when running a meeting—start with the material presented in the preceding introduction. Write your final list on a piece of paper. Next, for each problem on the group's list, the group should brainstorm a list of appropriate leader behaviors that can be used to handle the problem. Use the guidelines for brainstorming discussed in Chapter 11. Try to arrive at a consensus list of leadership behaviors that can be used to handle the various problems encountered in meetings.

Questions for Discussion

1. What type of problems that occur during meetings are most difficult to handle? Explain.

2. Are there any particular leader behaviors that can be used to solve multiple problems during meetings? Discuss your rationale.

3. Was there a lot of agreement about which leader behaviors were useful for dealing with specific problems encountered in meetings? Explain.

Chapter Eighteen

Managing Occupational Stress

Learning Objectives

When you finish studying the material in this chapter, you should be able to:

1 Define the term *stress*.

2 Describe the model of occupational stress.

3 Discuss four reasons why it is important for managers to understand the causes and consequences of stress.

4 Explain how stressful life events create stress.

5 Review the model of burnout, and highlight the managerial solutions to reduce it.

6 Explain the mechanisms of social support.

7 Describe the coping process.

8 Discuss the personality characteristic of hardiness.

9 Discuss the Type A behavior pattern and its management implications.

10 Contrast the four dominant stress-reduction techniques.

David Lundsford, director of advanced technology at Dell Personal Systems Group, discussed how he manages his workload and personal life during an interview with *Fast Company* magazine.

I often hear people proudly claim that they work 100-hour weeks. The first thing I think is, How can a person really be effective for 100 hours? How effective you are is more important than how long you work. Your goal should be to hone your work habits to achieve maximum performance. But a lot of us are hooked on a tangible metric that suggests that more hours must equal better work.

In the 13 years I've worked at Dell, I can remember two times when my work style led to major burnout. I lost the inspiration to perform. I reached a point where nothing mattered. I didn't care: Fire me. Shoot me. Whatever. The work I was doing began to feel futile, a feeling that is hard to translate into productivity. When you realize, as I did, that a lack of balance downgrades your effectiveness, it's easy to make balance a priority. I finally understood that achieving balance would actually help my career.

David Lundsford, Director of Advanced Technology, Dell Personal Systems Group
Courtesy of David Lundsford

More and more, the boundaries between work and life are being blurred by technology—pagers, cellphones, E-mail. It's easy to let your work life migrate into your personal life, so you need to create a reverse migration. I do this by scheduling routine breaks in my workday to have private moments. That can mean sitting and reflecting for 20 minutes, or talking to someone who is important to me. I'm beginning to manage my personal

restructuring are predominant stress-reduction techniques. Slow and deep breathing and a conscious effort to relieve muscle tension are common denominators of muscle relaxation. Biofeedback relies on a machine to train people to detect bodily signs of stress. This awareness facilitates proactive coping with stressors. Meditation activates the relaxation response by redirecting one's thoughts away from oneself. Cognitive restructuring entails identifying irrational or maladaptive thoughts and replacing them with rational or logical thoughts.

Discussion Questions

1. What are the key stressors encountered by students? Which ones are under their control?

2. Describe the behavioral and physiological symptoms you have observed in others when they are under stress.

3. Why do uncontrollable events lead to more stress than controllable events?

4. Why would people in the helping professions become burned out more readily than people in other occupations?

5. Do you think your professors are likely to become burned out? Explain your rationale.

6. Which of the five sources of social support is most likely to provide individuals with social support? Explain.

7. Why would people have difficulty using a control coping strategy to cope with the aftermath of a natural disaster like an earthquake or flood?

8. How can someone increase their hardiness and reduce their Type A behavior?

9. Have you used any of the stress-reduction techniques? Evaluate their effectiveness.

10. What is the most valuable lesson you learned from this chapter? Explain.

Internet Exercise   **www.queendom.com**

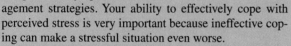

We highlighted in this chapter how people cope with stress by using a variety of control, escape, and symptom management strategies. Your ability to effectively cope with perceived stress is very important because ineffective coping can make a stressful situation even worse.

A Free Self-Assessment Questionnaire to Measure Your Coping Skills

The purpose of this exercise is to provide you with feedback on how well you cope with perceived stress. Go to the Internet home page for Body-Mind QueenDom (**www.queendom.com**), and find the main menu heading "Tests, Quizzes, Puzzles, & Polls." Now select the subheading for "Tests, Tests, Tests." At the "Tests, Tests, Tests. . ." page, read the brief welcome statement about Queendom's psychological tests and then scroll down to the category for "Intelligence." Now select the "Coping Skills" test, read the instructions, complete all items, and click on the "score" button for automatic scoring. (Note: Our use of this questionnaire is for instructional purposes only and does not constitute an endorsement of any product

ucts that may or may not suit your needs. There is no obligation to buy anything.) You will receive an overall coping skills score as well as scores for seven coping subdimension scores: reactivity to stress, ability to assess situations, self-reliance, resourcefulness, adaptability and flexibility, proactive attitudes, and ability to relax. You can print a personal copy of the interpretation of your results for use when answering the following questions.

Questions

Possible scores for overall coping skills range from 0 (extremely poor coping skills) to 100 (extremely good coping skills).

1. How did you score? Are you surprised by the results?

2. How did you score on the coping skills subdimensions of reactivity to stress, ability to assess situations, self-reliance, resourcefulness, adaptability and flexibility, proactive attitudes, and ability to relax? Do you agree with the interpretation of your scores?

3. Based on the interpretation of your results, what can you do to improve your coping skills? How might you also reduce your level of perceived stress?

OB in Action Case Study   **www.inc.com**

Store Managers at Au Bon Pain Have a Stressful Job[88]

As a teenager growing up in a blue-collar family and working in the cabinet factories and shoe mills of New England, Richard Thibeault thought of managers as people "up there on the ladder." They sat behind desks, worked 9 to 5, were pillars of the community.

What he never imagined them doing is his work these predawn hours: wheeling a rack of croissants across a nearly deserted street, past the delivery trucks and the occasional derelict. His tie flaps against his white shirt. He has been at work since 3 AM, baking muffins, preparing soups, worrying about falling sales at the Au Bon Pain bakery cafe he manages.

Inside his store, the 46-year-old Mr Thibeault sags against his desk—a converted counter in a tiny room crammed with croissant warmers and drink dispensers. Rock music from a boombox brought in by his workers pours in from the adjacent kitchen. Mr Thibeault's black briefcase sits on the lone chair. He used to bring paperwork like performance reviews home. But after seven months of 70-hour weeks he began crumpling over his desk at home and falling asleep.

Mr Thibeault earned $34,000 last year. "When I tell people what I do, they don't believe I'm a manager," he says. "Some days I think maybe I should go back to factory work. It was easier."

During the past decade, the percentage of workers classified as "managers" has increased to 14.5% from 11%; the growth has been even greater in the service sector.

But most of these jobs are far from the white-collar status positions normally associated with the term "manager." They are high-pressure, dead-end jobs with little status and low pay: the harried store manager at a fast-food restaurant; the assistant manager at a discount drug store; the manager at a travel agency; the bank-branch head.

These people carry the title manager, but they lead a blue-collar life—working long hours, often doing the same tasks as those they employ, and carrying out orders from above. Their autonomy is tightly circumscribed by corporate headquarters. They are given productivity quotas, told which products to push and which to shed, who and how many to hire. With the shrinking of middle management they have more responsibilities—dealing with personnel, meeting cost and labor targets—but less chance to move up. . . .

Dissatisfaction is mushrooming even as the number of first-line management jobs grows. In a series of surveys of department-store chains, Purdue University found that dissatisfaction among low-level managers increased to 50% in 1995 from 36% in 1986. Turnover is surging, with managers often citing little opportunity for creativity and poor prospects for promotion. A different survey of 1,300 fast-food restaurants this year found that 47% of entry-level managers "often think about quitting." . . .

Recently, Mr Thibeault calculated that he makes $7.83 cents an hour—83 cents more than he pays the part-time college students he employs.

Mr Thibeault's first stop this day, as always, is the computer that hangs over his makeshift desk. It is his constant companion, spitting out hour-by-hour projections, sent down from corporate headquarters, of how much food he should sell and how many workers he should use. This morning it tells a sad story. Last week, he was projected to make $2,100 in sales. He made $1,900. His business this year is down 28%—a drop he blames on the recent opening of a Starbucks Corp. coffee bar and a Dunkin Donuts in the neighborhood and the departure of several hundred construction workers from the area.

Because he missed corporate targets for labor and food costs, Mr Thibeault is known as an "outlyer." He was told a few weeks ago that he wouldn't get a $1,200 quarterly bonus. He appealed the decision and was given the money. But he doubts the company will let him miss targets a second time.

Mr Thibeault would like to run some discount specials to boost business. Au Bon Pain won't let him. Restaurant managers "don't have degrees in marketing," says David Peterman, the company's senior vice president of operations. All specials are determined by corporate headquarters. Mr Thibeault, who only has seven workers, would like to hire more to speed service. The computer printout says no.

Desperate to bring costs down, Mr Thibeault has trimmed staff to a handful of people and has taken on more work himself. "It's not the pressure out there from customers that gets to me," he says as he tapes a printout of the day's sales targets on the wall and runs a yellow highlighter through the key breakfast and lunch hours. "It's the pressure from higher up."

At 3:15 AM, Mr Thibeault lights the first cigarette of the pack he smokes daily, pulls on rubber gloves, and shoves 12 trays of blueberry muffins into the oven. Two years ago he was operated on successfully for stomach cancer. "My doctor

Group Exercise

Reducing the Stressors in Your Environment

Objectives

1. To identify the stressors in your environment.
2. To evaluate the extent to which each stressor is a source of stress.
3. To develop a plan for reducing the impact of stressors in your environment.

Introduction

Stressors are environmental factors that produce stress. They are prerequisites to experiencing the symptoms of stress. As previously discussed in this chapter, people do not appraise stressors in the same way. For instance, having to complete a challenging assignment may be motivational for one person and threatening to another. This exercise was designed to give you the opportunity to identify the stressors in your environment, to evaluate the extent to which these stressors create stress in your life, and to develop a plan for reducing the negative effects of these stressors.

Instructions

Your instructor will divide the class into groups of four to six. Once the group is assembled, the group should brainstorm and record a list of stressors that they believe exist in their environments. Use the guidelines for brainstorming discussed in Chapter 11. After recording all the brainstormed ideas on a piece of paper, remove redundancies and combine like items so that the group has a final list of unique stressors. Next, each group member should individually determine the extent to which each stressor is a source of stress in his or her life. For the purpose of this exercise,

stress is defined as existing whenever you experience feelings of pressure, strain, or emotional upset. The stress evaluation is done by first indicating the frequency with which each stressor is a source of stress to you. Use the six-point rating scale provided. Once everyone has completed their individual ratings, combine the numerical judgments to compute an average stress score for each stressor. Next, identify the five stressors with the highest average stress ratings. Finally, the group should develop a plan for coping with each of these five stressors. Try to make your recommendations as specific as possible.

Rating Scale

Answer the following question for each stressor: To what extent is the stressor a source of stress?

1 = Never
2 = Rarely
3 = Occasionally
4 = Often
5 = Usually
6 = Always

Questions for Discussion

1. Are you surprised by the type of stressors that were rated as creating the most stress in your lives? Explain.

2. Did group members tend to agree or disagree when evaluating the extent to which the various stressors created stress in their lives? What is the source of the different appraisals?

3. Did your coping plans include more forms of control or escape-oriented coping strategies? Explain.

Part Five

The Evolving Organization

Chapter Nineteen

Organizational Effectiveness and Design

Learning Objectives

When you finish studying the material in this chapter, you should be able to:

1 Describe the four characteristics common to all organizations, and explain the difference between closed and open systems.

2 Contrast the following organizational metaphors: military/mechanical, biological, and cognitive systems.

3 Describe the ecosystem model of organizations, and define the term *postmodern organization*.

4 Describe the four generic organizational effectiveness criteria, and discuss how managers can prevent organizational decline.

5 Explain what the contingency approach to organization design involves.

6 Describe the relationship between differentiation and integration in effective organizations.

7 Discuss Burns and Stalker's findings regarding mechanistic and organic organizations.

8 Define and briefly explain the practical significance of centralization and decentralization.

9 Discuss the effective management of organizational size.

10 Describe horizontal, hourglass, and virtual organizations.

On a foggy January morning at Dell Computer Corporation's headquarters in Round Rock, Texas, a receptionist boots up 10 computers that line two sides of the lobby in building RR3. The computers operate a number of programs but default to Dell's home page, which is also available through the Internet.

Among other functions, the page allows applicants who come by in person to view job listings, and directly create and submit resumes into a database that any Dell hiring manager can access. It's a small innovation, perhaps, but one that helps Dell hire the 100 employees per week it needs to sustain its growth.

And that growth has been robust. The company's workforce grew 56% in 1998 from a year earlier, and company earnings increased by 59% over the same period. Small wonder, then, that Dell is now the world's fastest growing major computer sales company, according to industry analyst Dataquest.

The company's growth, however, forces its human resources staff to constantly raise the bar by which it measures success. The challenges HR faces include selecting and developing a workforce that can meet constantly changing requirements without losing Dell's market and customer focus, or its culture.

Here's how they do it.

Dell Computer is a master of E-commerce.

Courtesy of Dell Computer Company

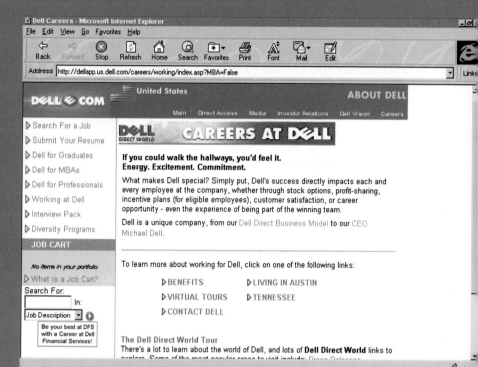

calls soon yields a group of six to eight unofficial "trustees" who steer the company to safety. Trustees are often direct competitors of the ailing business, willing to contribute money and ease competition to rescue their rival. They know implicitly that others would do the same for them. Thanks to this practice, locals aver, there has never been a bankruptcy in Lumezzane.

The town's tight industrial weave is evident after working hours, too. Workmen and bosses play cards together in the same cafés and address each other with the informal "*tu*." Somali, Pakistani, and other foreign workers receive extensive help with housing and job placement. As Putnam's theory of social capital predicts, involvement in city government is also high, with voter turnout in local elections at about 90%. But turnout for regional and national elections is lower.

One-Upmanship

Religion, more than politics, is a strong unifying force—as well as the pretext for business and social activities. Says Don Turla, one local parish priest: "At weddings, feast days, or funerals, after 10 minutes, every conversation turns to business." The town has no fewer than seven parishes, each of which launches projects that frequently become elaborate games of one-upmanship. When one parish funded a nursery school some years ago, others quickly followed suit. (Some of the schools have since been converted into vocational training centers.)

All is not sweetness and light. Every industrialist complains of unfair business practices by competitors, and many are locked in bitter lawsuits (though disputes are set aside when bankruptcy threatens).

Nevertheless, people are fiercely loyal to Lumezzane. They don't sell their businesses to outsiders, and they endure skyrocketing housing costs, even though they could do better in nearby Brescia. Above all, the people of Lumezzane appear to live to work, not the other way around.

Questions for Discussion

1. Which of the organizational metaphors in Table 19–1 is exemplified in this case? Why?

2. What can Americans, who culturally tend to be more competitive than cooperative, learn from the business climate in Lumezzane, Italy?

3. Do you think this particular situation is unique to Italian culture, or could it be replicated in other countries? Explain. Which countries? Why?

Personal Awareness and Growth Exercise

Organization Design Field Study

Objectives

1. To get out into the field and talk to a practicing manager about organizational structure.

2. To increase your understanding of the important distinction between mechanistic and organic organizations.

3. To broaden your knowledge of contingency design, in terms of organization-environment fit.

Introduction

A good way to test the validity of what you have just read about organizational design is to interview a practicing manager. (Note: If you are a manager, simply complete the questionnaire yourself.)

Instructions

Your objective is to interview a manager about aspects of organizational structure, environmental uncertainty, and organizational effectiveness. A *manager* is defined as anyone who supervises other people in an organizational setting. The organization may be small or large and for-profit or not-for-profit. Higher-level managers are preferred, but middle managers and first-line supervisors are acceptable. If you interview a lower-level manager, be sure to remind him or her that you want a description of the overall organization, not just an isolated subunit. Your interview will center on the adaptation of Table 19–2, as discussed below.

When conducting your interview, be sure to explain to the manager what you are trying to accomplish. But assure the manager that his or her name will not be mentioned in class discussion or any written projects. Try to keep side notes during the interview for later reference.

Questionnaire

The following questionnaire, adapted from Table 19–2, will help you determine if the manager's organization is relatively mechanistic or relatively organic in structure. Note: For items 1 and 2 on the following questionnaire, have the manager respond in terms of the average nonmanagerial employee. (Circle one number for each item.)

Characteristics

1. Task definition and knowledge required	Narrow; technical	1—2—3—4—5—6—7	Broad; general
2. Linkage between individual's contribution and organization's purpose	Vague or indirect	1—2—3—4—5—6—7	Clear or direct
3. Task flexibility	Rigid; routine	1—2—3—4—5—6—7	Flexible; varied
4. Specification of techniques, obligations, and rights	Specific	1—2—3—4—5—6—7	General
5. Degree of hierarchical control	High	1—2—3—4—5—6—7	Low (self-control emphasized)
6. Primary communication pattern	Top-down	1—2—3—4—5—6—7	Lateral (between peers)
7. Primary decision-making style	Authoritarian	1—2—3—4—5—6—7	Democratic; participative
8. Emphasis on obedience and loyalty	High	1—2—3—4—5—6—7	Low

Total score =

Additional Question about the Organization's Environment

This organization faces an environment that is (circle one number):

Stable and certain   1—2—3—4—5—6—7—8—9—10   Unstable and uncertain

Additional Questions about the Organization's Effectiveness

1. Profitability (if a profit-seeking business):
   Low   1—2—3—4—5—6—7—8—9—10   High

2. Degree of organizational goal accomplishment:
   Low   1—2—3—4—5—6—7—8—9—10   High

3. Customer or client satisfaction:
   Low   1—2—3—4—5—6—7—8—9—10   High

4. Employee satisfaction:
   Low   1—2—3—4—5—6—7—8—9—10   High

Total effectiveness score = _____

(Add responses from above)

Questions for Discussion

1. Using the following norms, was the manager's organization relatively mechanistic or organic?

   8–24   =   Relatively mechanistic

   25–39   =   Mixed

   40–56   =   Relatively organic

2. In terms of Burns and Stalker's contingency theory, does the manager's organization seem to fit its environment? Explain.

3. Does the organization's degree of effectiveness reflect how well it fits its environment? Explain.

Group Exercise

Stakeholder Audit Team

Objectives

1. To continue developing your group interaction and teamwork skills.

2. To engage in open-system thinking.

3. To conduct a stakeholder audit and thus more fully appreciate the competing demands placed on today's managers.

4. To establish priorities and consider trade-offs for modern managers.

Introduction

According to open-system models of organizations, environmental factors—social, political, legal, technological, and economic—greatly affect what managers can and cannot do. This exercise gives you an opportunity to engage in open-system thinking within a team setting. It requires a team meeting of about 20 to 25 minutes followed by a 10- to 15-minute general class discussion. Total time required for this exercise is about 30 to 40 minutes.

Instructions

Your instructor will randomly assign you to teams with five to eight members each. Choose one team member to act as recorder/spokesperson. Either at your instructor's prompting or as a team, choose one of these two options:

1. Identify an organization that is familiar to everyone on your team (it can be a local business, your college or university, or a well-known organization such as McDonald's, Wal-Mart, or American Airlines).

2. Select an organization from any of the OB in Action Case Studies following each chapter in this book.

Next, using Figure 19–5 as a model, do a *stakeholder audit* for the organization in question. This will require a team brainstorming session followed by brief discussion. Your team will need to make reasonable assumptions about the circumstances surrounding your target organization.

Finally, your team should select the three (or more) *high-priority* stakeholders on your team's list. Rank them number one, number two, and so on. (Tip: A top-priority stakeholder is one with the greatest short-term impact on the success or failure of your target organization.) Be pre-pared to explain to the entire class your rationale for selecting each high-priority stakeholder.

Questions for Discussion

1. How does this exercise foster open-system thinking? Give examples.

2. Did this exercise broaden your awareness of the complexity of modern organizational environments? Explain.

3. Why do managers need clear priorities when it comes to dealing with organizational stakeholders?

4. How many *trade-offs* (meaning one party gains at another's expense) can you detect in your team's list of stakeholders? Specify them.

5. Does your experience with doing a stakeholder audit strengthen or weaken the validity of the ecosystem model of organizations? Explain.

6. How difficult was it for your team to complete this assignment? Explain.

Chapter Twenty

Managing Change in Learning Organizations

Learning Objectives

When you finish studying the material in this chapter, you should be able to:

1 Discuss the external and internal forces that create the need for organizational change.

2 Describe Lewin's change model and the systems model of change.

3 Discuss Kotter's eight steps for leading organizational change.

4 Demonstrate your familiarity with the four identifying characteristics of organization development (OD).

5 Discuss the 10 reasons employees resist change.

6 Identify alternative strategies for overcoming resistance to change.

7 Define a learning organization.

8 Discuss the process organizations use to build their learning capabilities.

9 Review the reasons organizations naturally resist learning.

10 Discuss the role of leadership in creating a learning organization.

BusinessWeek Dawn G Lepore, Charles Schwab Corp.'s chief information officer, likes to tell the story of a recent panel she sat on that featured executives from several Internet upstarts. At first, her fellow panelists seemed surprised to see her. "But when I mentioned that our site gets 76 million hits per day, the eBay guy sitting next to me gasped," she laughs. "I got a lot more respect after that."

The wired world may not have noticed, but Schwab has been far more successful than most brick-and-mortar companies at moving the core of its business online. In doing so, it has already worked through many of the tough challenges that are bedeviling managers who are just arriving at the online party. If everyone now knows that the Net is revolutionizing business, Lepore warns, "actually living that on a daily basis is pretty difficult."

Account Explosion. Of course, the rewards of success are pretty high, too. Having captured 42% of the assets invested in online-trading accounts today, the San Francisco–based dis-count broker has made itself the player to beat in online financial services....

So how did Schwab make the switch so quickly? For starters, its managers recognized the Web's potential long before Internet frenzy spread beyond Silicon Valley. Their wake-up call came in 1995, the first year more personal computers were sold in the United States than televisions. Although no techie, founder Charles R Schwab quickly got on board. That gave the initiative a big

Dawn Lepore, Charles Schwab Corporation's chief information officer.
©1999 John Swanda/Donald Jones
Photography/Courtesy of The Charles Schwab & Co.

boost and helped win it adequate funding, even though any payoff was highly uncertain.

The decision to launch the online business as a separate unit was another key move. "Those people were completely focused, so it's not, 'I have now 20 things to do, and by the way, the Internet is my 21st thing,'" recalls Lepore.

Early on, she and her colleagues also worked hard to end resistance from Schwab's branch staff, who felt threatened by the online unit. The company sent frequent E-mails to employees highlighting the rapid growth in online trading. And the branch staff was trained first, so they, not the tech staff, trained customers to use online services. Lepore says that ensured that "they felt like part of the change."

Risky Shift. The staffers' backing proved vital when customers began to rebel against the two-tiered pricing system that schwab.com initially set up. Full-service customers were charged an average of $65 to trade on the Net, while Schwab.com users were paying just $29.95. Faced with complaints, the branch staff warned that the price differential needed to go. So in January, 1998, David Pottruck, Schwab's co-CEO, brushed aside fears that a shift would cannibalize Schwab's traditional business and priced all Net trades at $29.95. The move cut $150 million from expected revenue and sent Schwab's shares tumbling from 41 to 28.

But soon, the risk paid off, as volume soared. That made Schwab a Net rarity: Unlike a lot of other online ventures, it makes money. "E-commerce has been very profitable for us," Lepore says. And that's how she plans to keep it.[1]

FOR DISCUSSION

What were the forces for change at Schwab Corporation, and how did the company handle resistance to change?

Dawn Lepore's experiences at Schwab Corporation are not the exception. Increased competition and startling breakthroughs in information technology are forcing companies to change the way they do business. Customers are demanding greater value and lower prices. The rate of organizational and societal change is clearly accelerating. For example, a survey of 750 corporations revealed that all of them were involved in at least one organizational change program. Another survey of 259 executives indicated that 84% had one change initiative under way, while nearly 50% had three or more change programs being implemented.[2]

Companies no longer have a choice—they must change to survive. Unfortunately, it is not easy to successfully implement organizational change. As Lepore experienced at Schwab, people frequently resist organizational change even when change is occurring for good reason. Peter Senge, a well-known expert on the topic of organizational change, made the following comment about organizational change during an interview with *Fast Company* magazine:

> When I look at efforts to create change in big companies over the past 10 years, I have to say that there's enough evidence of success to say that change is possible—and enough evidence of failure to say that it isn't likely.[3]

If Senge is correct, then it is all the more important for current and future managers to learn how they can successfully implement organizational change. This final chapter was written to help managers navigate the journey of change.

Specifically, we discuss the forces that create the need for organization change, models of planned change, resistance to change, and creating a learning organization.

Forces of Change

How do organizations know when they should change? What cues should an organization look for? Although there are no clear-cut answers to these questions, the "cues" that signal the need for change are found by monitoring the forces for change.

Organizations encounter many different forces for change. These forces come from external sources outside the organization and from internal sources. This section examines the forces that create the need for change. Awareness of these forces can help managers determine when they should consider implementing an organizational change. The external and internal forces for change are presented in Figure 20–1.

External Forces

External forces for change originate outside the organization. Because these forces have global effects, they may cause an organization to question the essence of what business it is in and the process by which products and services are produced. There are four key external forces for change: demographic characteristics, technological advancements, market changes, and social and political pressures. Each is now discussed.

External forces for change
Originate outside the organization.

Figure 20–1   *The External and Internal Forces for Change*

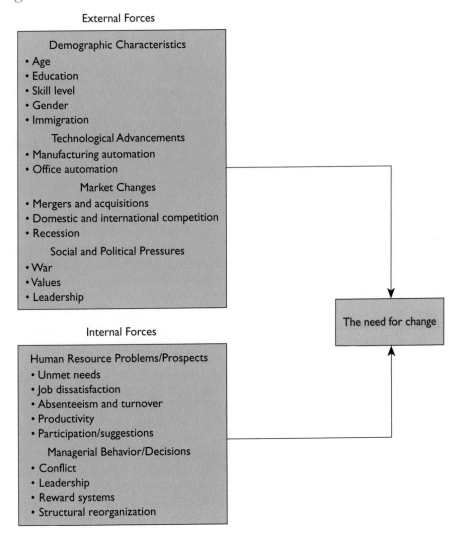

External Forces

Demographic Characteristics
• Age
• Education
• Skill level
• Gender
• Immigration

Technological Advancements
• Manufacturing automation
• Office automation

Market Changes
• Mergers and acquisitions
• Domestic and international competition
• Recession

Social and Political Pressures
• War
• Values
• Leadership

Internal Forces

Human Resource Problems/Prospects
• Unmet needs
• Job dissatisfaction
• Absenteeism and turnover
• Productivity
• Participation/suggestions

Managerial Behavior/Decisions
• Conflict
• Leadership
• Reward systems
• Structural reorganization

The need for change

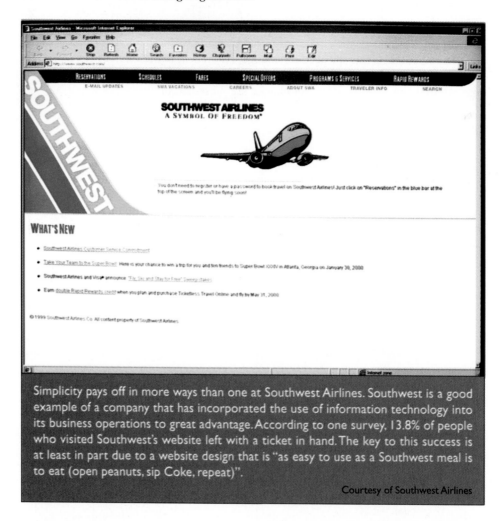

Simplicity pays off in more ways than one at Southwest Airlines. Southwest is a good example of a company that has incorporated the use of information technology into its business operations to great advantage. According to one survey, 13.8% of people who visited Southwest's website left with a ticket in hand. The key to this success is at least in part due to a website design that is "as easy to use as a Southwest meal is to eat (open peanuts, sip Coke, repeat)".

Courtesy of Southwest Airlines

Demographic Characteristics   Chapter 2 provided a detailed discussion of the demographic changes occurring in the US workforce. Two key trends identified in this discussion were that (1) the workforce is more diverse and (2) there is a business imperative to effectively manage diversity. Organizations need to effectively manage diversity if they are to receive maximum contribution and commitment from employees.

Technological Advancements   Both manufacturing and service organizations are increasingly using technology as a means to improve productivity and market competitiveness. Manufacturing companies, for instance, have automated their operations with robotics, computerized numerical control (CNC), which is used for metal cutting operations, and computer-aided design (CAD). CAD is a computerized process of drafting and designing engineering drawings of products. Companies also are using computer-integrated manufacturing (CIM). This highly technical process attempts to integrate product design with product planning, control, and operations. In contrast to these manufacturing technologies, the service sector of the US economy is using office automation. Office automation consists of a host of computerized technologies that are used to obtain, store, analyze, retrieve, and communicate information.

Development and use of information technologies is probably one of the biggest forces for change. Organizations, large and small, private and public, for profit and not-

International OB Japanese Firms Discontinue the Jobs-for-Life Philosophy

Sony President Nobuyuki Idei must think he's in Silicon Valley. How does he rev up his staff and goose flagging profits? By tossing the whole organization chart in the air, pulling vagrant subsidiaries back into the parent company, and committing to scrapping 20% of his factories by 2003 while escorting some 17,000 workers to the door.

Idei's mid-March restructuring proposal dashes most hopes in Japan that the country's jobs-for-life policy would survive the recession. Facing hefty losses this month at the close of Japan's fiscal year, companies have been falling over each other to announce restructurings. NEC Corp. plans to slash 15,000 jobs worldwide over three years. Parts maker Omron Corp.'s payroll will shrink by 2,000. And it's not just high tech: In a bid for public funds, Japan's top 15 banks have agreed to ax almost 20,000 jobs by 2004.

SOURCE: Excerpted from I M Kunii, E Thornton, and J Rae-Dupree, "Sony's Shake Up," *Business Week*, March 22, 1999, p 52.

---

for-profit, all must adapt to using a host of information technologies. Consider how Southwest Airlines is using the Internet to obtain customers:

> According to Nielsen/Net Ratings' August survey, 13.8% of people who visited Southwest's site left with a ticket in hand. The company's "look-to-book" ratio is twice that of Travelocity and higher than that of any traditional retailer on the Web. Southwest, it seems, has found a way to turn eyeballs into buyers. . . . The key is a design that's as simple to use as a Southwest meal is to eat (open peanuts, sip Coke, repeat). Instead of the infinity of choices that dot.coms assume customers want, Southwest delivers a page where a transaction takes just 10 quick clicks to complete. Up pops a fare, plus options to help you get a better flight or better prices. Arranging a ticket is so simple that it seems like real customer service.[4]

Experts believe that E-business will continue to create evolutionary changes in organizations throughout the world. Organizations are encouraged to join the E-volution!

Market Changes   The emergence of a global economy is forcing companies to change the way they do business. For example, many Japanese companies are having to discontinue their jobs-for-life philosophy because of increased international competition (see the

Starbucks has become a favorite place for people to enjoy coffee, tea, and pastries. Their outlets are particularly popular around college campuses. Starbucks is an example of a growing number of companies that create alliances with other organizations in order to provide quality products.

(Sonda Dawes/The Image Works)

International OB on p 661). US companies are also forging new partnerships and alliances with their suppliers and potential competitors.

For example, AOL has created alliances with drkoop.com, GTE, US West, Sun, and Nintendo, while Oracle has between 15,000 and 16,000 business alliances.[5] Consider the type of alliances that affect a day in the life of David Ernst, a consulting partner at McKinsey & Company in Washington, DC:

The gas pumped into his car is the product of an alliance between Shell and Texaco Inc. Payment for the gas is thrown on a credit card co-branded by Royal/Dutch Shell Group and Mastercard. A cup of Starbucks Corp. coffee that Ernst grabs as he careens through an airport that whisks Ernst to his destination is part of a grouping of several international carriers. Says Ernst, an alliance expert: "For most companies, the basis of competition has shifted to groups of companies competing against groups of companies."[6]

This example highlights that organizations must learn how to create collaborative win-win relationships with other organizations if they are to survive in the world-wide restructuring of alliances and partnerships.

Social and Political Pressures   These forces are created by social and political events. For example, tobacco companies are experiencing a lot of pressure to alter the way they market their products within the United States. This pressure is being exerted through legislative bodies that represent the American populace. Political events can create substantial change. For instance, the collapse of the Berlin Wall and communism in Russia created many new business opportunities. Although it is difficult for organizations to predict changes in political forces, many organizations hire lobbyists and consultants to help them detect and respond to social and political changes.

Internal Forces

Internal forces for change come from inside the organization. These forces may be subtle, such as low job satisfaction, or can manifest in outward signs, such as low productivity and conflict. Internal forces for change come from both human resource problems and managerial behavior/decisions.

Human Resource Problems/Prospects   These problems stem from employee perceptions about how they are treated at work and the match between individual and organization needs and desires. Chapter 7 highlighted the relationship between an employee's unmet needs and job dissatisfaction. Dissatisfaction is a symptom of an underlying employee problem that should be addressed. Unusual or high levels of absenteeism and turnover also represent forces for change. Organizations might respond to

---

Internal forces for change
Originate inside the organization.

these problems by using the various approaches to job design discussed in Chapter 7, by reducing employees' role conflict, overload, and ambiguity (recall our discussion in Chapter 12), and by removing the different stressors discussed in Chapter 18. Prospects for positive change stem from employee participation and suggestions.

Managerial Behavior/Decisions   Excessive interpersonal conflict between managers and their subordinates is a sign that change is needed. Both the manager and the employee may need interpersonal skills training, or the two individuals may simply need to be separated. For example, one of the parties might be transferred to a new department. Inappropriate leader behaviors such as inadequate direction or support may result in human resource problems requiring change. As discussed in Chapter 17, leadership training is one potential solution for this problem. Inequitable reward systems—recall our discussion in Chapters 8 and 9—and the type of structural reorganizations discussed in Chapter 19 are additional forces for change.

Models and Dynamics of Planned Change

American managers are criticized for emphasizing short-term, quick-fix solutions to organizational problems. When applied to organizational change, this approach is doomed from the start. Quick-fix solutions do not really solve underlying problems, and they have little staying power. Researchers and managers alike have thus tried to identify effective ways to manage the change process. This section sheds light on their insights. After discussing different types of organizational changes, we review Lewin's change model, a systems model of change, Kotter's eight-stages for leading organizational change, and organizational development.

Types of Change

A useful three-way typology of change is displayed in Figure 20–2.[7] This typology is generic because it relates to all sorts of change, including both administrative and technological changes. Adaptive change is lowest in complexity, cost, and uncertainty. It involves reimplementation of a change in the same organizational unit at a later time or imitation of a similar change by a different unit. For example, an adaptive change for a

Figure 20–2   *A Generic Typology of Organizational Change*

Adaptive change — Reintroducing a familiar practice

Innovative change — Introducing a practice new to the organization

Radically innovative change — Introducing a practice new to the industry

Low ⊢————————————————————⊣ High

- Degree of complexity, cost, and uncertainty
- Potential for resistance to change

department store would be to rely on 12-hour days during the annual inventory week. The store's accounting department could imitate the same change in work hours during tax preparation time. Adaptive changes are not particularly threatening to employees because they are familiar.

Innovative changes fall midway on the continuum of complexity, cost, and uncertainty. An experiment with flexible work schedules by a farm supply warehouse company qualifies as an innovative change if it entails modifying the way other firms in the industry already use it. Unfamiliarity, and hence greater uncertainty, make fear of change a problem with innovative changes.

At the high end of the continuum of complexity, cost, and uncertainty are radically innovative changes. Changes of this sort are the most difficult to implement and tend to be the most threatening to managerial confidence and employee job security.[8] They can tear the fabric of an organization's culture. Resistance to change tends to increase as changes go from adaptive to innovative to radically innovative.

Lewin's Change Model

Most theories of organizational change originated from the landmark work of social psychologist Kurt Lewin. Lewin developed a three-stage model of planned change which explained how to initiate, manage, and stabilize the change process.[9] The three stages are unfreezing, changing, and refreezing. Before reviewing each stage, it is important to highlight the assumptions that underlie this model:[10]

1. The change process involves learning something new, as well as discontinuing current attitudes, behaviors, or organizational practices.

2. Change will not occur unless there is motivation to change. This is often the most difficult part of the change process.

3. People are the hub of all organizational changes. Any change, whether in terms of structure, group process, reward systems, or job design, requires individuals to change.

4. Resistance to change is found even when the goals of change are highly desirable.

5. Effective change requires reinforcing new behaviors, attitudes, and organizational practices.

Let us now consider the three stages of change.

Benchmarking
Process by which a company compares its performance with that of high-performing organizations.

Unfreezing   The focus of this stage is to create the motivation to change. In so doing, individuals are encouraged to replace old behaviors and attitudes with those desired by management. Managers can begin the unfreezing process by disconfirming the usefulness or appropriateness of employees' present behaviors or attitudes. In other words, employees need to become dissatisfied with the old way of doing things. Benchmarking is a technique that can be used to help unfreeze an organization. **Benchmarking** "describes the overall process by which a company compares its performance with that of other companies, then learns how the strongest-performing companies achieve their results."[11] For example, one company for which we consulted discovered through benchmarking that their costs to develop a computer system were twice as high as the best companies in the industry, and the time it took to get a new product to market was four times longer than the benchmarked organizations. These data were ultimately used to unfreeze employees' attitudes and motivate people to change the organization's internal processes in order to remain competitive.[12] Managers also need to devise ways to reduce the barriers to change during this stage.

Changing   Because change involves learning, this stage entails providing employees with new information, new behavioral models, or new ways of looking at things. The purpose is to help employees learn new concepts or points of view. Role models, mentors, experts, benchmarking results, and training are useful mechanisms to facilitate change. Experts recommend that it is best to convey the idea that change is a continuous learning process rather than a one-time event.

Refreezing   Change is stabilized during refreezing by helping employees integrate the changed behavior or attitude into their normal way of doing things. This is accomplished by first giving employees the chance to exhibit the new behaviors or attitudes. Once exhibited, positive reinforcement is used to reinforce the desired change (recall our discussion in Chapter 10). Additional coaching and modeling also are used at this point to reinforce the stability of the change.[13]

A Systems Model of Change

A systems approach takes a "big picture" perspective of organizational change. It is based on the notion that any change, no matter how large or small, has a cascading impact throughout an organization. For example, promoting an individual to a new work group affects the group dynamics in both the old and new groups. Similarly, creating project or work teams may necessitate the need to revamp compensation practices. These examples illustrate that change creates additional change. Today's solutions are tomorrow's problems. A systems model of change offers managers a framework to understand the broad complexities of organizational change.[14] The three main components of a systems model are inputs, target elements of change, and outputs (see Figure 20–3).

Inputs   All organizational changes should be consistent with an organization's mission, vision, and resulting strategic plan. A **mission statement** represents the "reason" an organization exists. In Chapter 3 we defined an organization's *vision* as a long-term goal that describes "what" an organization wants to become. Consider how the difference between mission and vision affects organizational change. Your university probably has a mission to educate people. This mission does not necessarily imply anything about change. It simply defines the university's overall purpose. In contrast, the university may have a vision to be recognized as the "best" university in the country. This vision requires the organization to benchmark itself against other world-class universities and to create plans for achieving the vision. Ameritech, for example, is trying to transform itself in order to accomplish the following vision:

> Ameritech will be the world's premier provider of full-service communications—for people at work, at home, or on the move. Our goal will be to improve the quality of life for individuals and to increase the competitive effectiveness of the businesses we serve.
>
> As we move and manage information for our customers, we will set the standards for value and quality.
>
> Ameritech's competence will reach worldwide, building on our strength in America's vibrant upper Midwest. Customers can be assured that we will assume no task we cannot do exceedingly well.[15]

While vision statements point the way, strategic plans contain the detail needed to create organizational change.

A **strategic plan** outlines an organization's long-term direction and actions necessary to achieve planned results. Strategic plans are based on considering an organization's

Mission statement
Summarizes "why" an organization exists.

Strategic plan
A long-term plan outlining actions needed to achieve planned results.

Figure 20–3   *A Systems Model of Change*

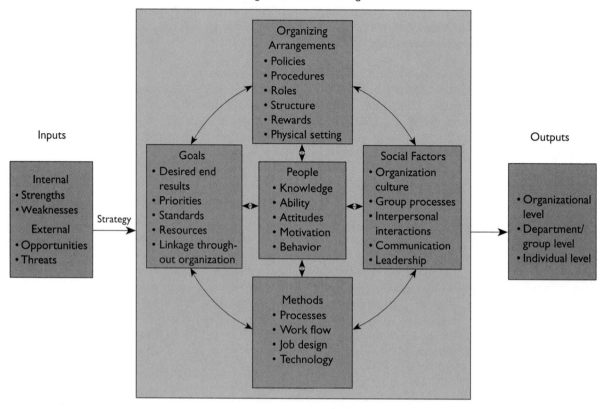

Target Elements of Change

Organizing Arrangements
• Policies
• Procedures
• Roles
• Structure
• Rewards
• Physical setting

Inputs

Internal
• Strengths
• Weaknesses
External
• Opportunities
• Threats

Strategy

Goals
• Desired end results
• Priorities
• Standards
• Resources
• Linkage throughout organization

People
• Knowledge
• Ability
• Attitudes
• Motivation
• Behavior

Social Factors
• Organization culture
• Group processes
• Interpersonal interactions
• Communication
• Leadership

Outputs

• Organizational level
• Department/group level
• Individual level

Methods
• Processes
• Work flow
• Job design
• Technology

SOURCES: Adapted from D R Fuqua and D J Kurpius, "Conceptual Models in Organizational Consultation," *Journal of Counseling & Development,* July/August 1993, pp 602–18; and D A Nadler and M L Tushman, "Organizational Frame Bending: Principles for Managing Reorientation," *Academy of Management Executive,* August 1989, pp 194–203.

strengths and weaknesses relative to its environmental opportunities and threats. This comparison results in developing an organizational strategy to attain desired outputs such as profits, customer satisfaction, quality, adequate return on investment, and acceptable levels of turnover and employee commitment (see Figure 20–3). In summary, organizations tend to commit resources to counterproductive or conflicting activities when organizational changes are not consistent with its strategic plan.

Target elements of change

Components of an organization that may be changed.

Target Elements of Change   **Target elements of change** represent the components of an organization that may be changed. As shown in Figure 20–3, change can be directed at realigning organizing arrangements, social factors, methods, goals, and people.[16] The choice is based on the strategy being pursued or the organizational problem at hand. For example, Hershey Foods Corporation targeted a technological change in order to improve the distribution and sales of its products. Unfortunately, the organization struggled with the technological intervention, and competitors benefited from Hershey's problems:

> For the nation's largest candy maker, with revenue of $4.44 billion last year, this could turn out to be a very scary Halloween. New technology that came on line in July has

gummed up its ordering-and-distribution system, leaving many stores nationwide reporting spot shortages of Kisses, Kit Kats, Twizzlers, and other stalwarts of the trick-or-treating season. In mid-July, Hershey flipped the switch on a $112 million computer system that was supposed to automate and modernize everything from taking candy orders to putting pallets on trucks. Two months later, the company announced that something was wrong. Now, an additional six weeks later—and with Halloween looming—it's still working out the kinks and says it hopes to have everything running smoothly by early December. . . . Already, rivals are benefiting without making much effort.[17]

This example also highlights that change begets change. Specifically, a change in methods—a new computer system—led to additional changes in organizing arrangements and goals.

Moreover, there are two additional points to note about the systems model shown in Figure 20–3. First, the double-headed arrows among the target elements of change indicate that a change in one organizational component affects the others. Second, people are the hub of all change. Change will not succeed unless individuals embrace it in one way or another.

Outputs   Outputs represent the desired end results of a change. Once again, these end results should be consistent with an organization's strategic plan. Figure 20–3 indicates that change may be directed at the organizational level, department/group level, or individual level. Change efforts are more complicated and difficult to manage when they are targeted at the organizational level. This occurs because organizational-level changes are more likely to affect multiple target elements of change shown in the model.

Kotter's Eight Steps for Leading Organizational Change

John Kotter, an expert in leadership and change management, believes that organizational change typically fails because senior management commits one or more of the following errors:[18]

1. Failure to establish a sense of urgency about the need for change.
2. Failure to create a powerful-enough guiding coalition that is responsible for leading and managing the change process.
3. Failure to establish a vision that guides the change process.
4. Failure to effectively communicate the new vision.
5. Failure to remove obstacles that impede the accomplishment of the new vision.
6. Failure to systematically plan for and create short-term wins. Short-term wins represent the achievement of important results or goals.
7. Declaration of victory too soon. This derails the long-term changes in infrastructure that are frequently needed to achieve a vision.
8. Failure to anchor the changes into the organization's culture. It takes years for long-term changes to be embedded within an organization's culture.

Kotter recommends that organizations should follow eight sequential steps to overcome these problems (see Table 20–1).

Each of the steps shown in Table 20–1 is associated with the eight fundamental errors just discussed. These steps also subsume Lewin's model of change. The first four

Table 20–1   *Steps to Leading Organizational Change*

Step	Description
1. Establish a sense of urgency	Unfreeze the organization by creating a compelling reason for why change is needed.
2. Create the guiding coalition	Create a cross-functional, cross-level group of people with enough power to lead the change.
3. Develop a vision and strategy	Create a vision and strategic plan to guide the change process.
4. Communicate the change vision	Create and implement a communication strategy that consistently communicates the new vision and strategic plan.
5. Empower broad-based action	Eliminate barriers to change, and use target elements of change to transform the organization. Encourage risk taking and creative problem solving.
6. Generate short-term wins	Plan for and create short-term "wins" or improvements. Recognize and reward people who contribute to the wins.
7. Consolidate gains and produce more change	The guiding coalition uses credibility from short-term wins to create more change. Additional people are brought into the change process as change cascades throughout the organization. Attempts are made to reinvigorate the change process.
8. Anchor new approaches in the culture	Reinforce the changes by highlighting connections between new behaviors and processes and organizational success. Develop methods to ensure leadership development and succession.

SOURCE: The steps were developed by J P Kotter, *Leading Change* (Boston: Harvard Business School Press, 1996).

steps represent Lewin's "unfreezing" stage. Steps 5, 6, and 7 represent "changing," and step 8 corresponds to "refreezing." The value of Kotter's steps is that it provides specific recommendations about behaviors that managers need to exhibit to successfully lead organizational change. It is important to remember that Kotter's research reveals that it is ineffective to skip steps and that successful organizational change is 70% to 90% leadership and only 10% to 30% management. Senior managers are thus advised to focus on leading rather than managing change.[19]

Organization Development

Organization development (OD) is an applied field of study and practice. A pair of OD experts defined **organization development** as follows:

Organization development
A set of techniques or tools that are used to implement organizational change.

> Organization development is concerned with helping managers plan change in organizing and managing people that will develop requisite commitment, coordination, and competence. Its purpose is to enhance both the effectiveness of organizations and the well-being of their members through planned interventions in the organization's human processes, structures, and systems, using knowledge of behavioral science and its intervention methods.[20]

As you can see from this definition, OD constitutes a set of techniques or interventions that are used to implement organizational change. These techniques or interventions apply to each of the change models discussed in this section. For example, OD is used during Lewin's "changing" stage. It also is used to identify and implement targeted elements of change within the systems model of change. Finally, OD might be used during Kotter's steps 1, 3, 5, 6, and 7. In this section, we briefly review the four identifying characteristics of OD and its research and practical implications.[21]

OD Involves Profound Change   Change agents using OD generally desire deep and long-lasting improvement. OD consultant Warner Burke, for example, who strives for fundamental *cultural* change, wrote: "By fundamental change, as opposed to fixing a problem or improving a procedure, I mean that some significant aspect of an organization's culture will never be the same."[22]

OD Is Value-Loaded   Owing to the fact that OD is rooted partially in humanistic psychology, many OD consultants carry certain values or biases into the client organization. They prefer cooperation over conflict, self-control over institutional control, and democratic and participative management over autocratic management. In addition to OD being driven by a consultant's values, some OD practitioners now believe that there is a broader "value perspective" that should underlie any organizational change. Specifically, OD should always be customer focused. This approach implies that organizational interventions should be aimed at helping to satisfy customers' needs and thereby provide enhanced value of an organization's products and services. Consider the OD intervention used by Andersen Windows of Bayport, Minnesota—a $1 billion manufacturer of windows—to enhance customer value:

> Until about 15 years ago, Andersen was a mass producer of a variety of standard windows in large batches. In an effort to meet customer needs, Andersen kept adding to its product line, which led to fatter catalogues and a bewildering set of choices for both home owners and contractors. In a six-year period, the number of products almost tripled. The order systems became so complex that calculating a price quote for windows in a new home could take several hours and run over a dozen pages. Furthermore, this complexity almost doubled the error rate, which began to damage the company's reputation for superior quality.
>
> In order to bring order out of chaos, Andersen developed an interactive computer version of the paper catalogues it sold to distributors and retailers. With this system, the outlet salesperson can help customers customize each window to meet their needs, check the design for structural soundness, and generate a price quote. The system reduces the time involved by more than 75% and is virtually error free. And of course, customers get precisely what they want, promptly, and without hassle—true customer value.[23]

OD Is a Diagnosis/Prescription Cycle   OD theorists and practitioners have long adhered to a medical model of organization. Like medical doctors, internal and external OD consultants approach the "sick" organization, "diagnose" its ills, "prescribe" and implement an intervention, and "monitor" progress.[24]

OD Is Process-Oriented   Ideally, OD consultants focus on the form and not the content of behavioral and administrative dealings. For example, product design engineers and market researchers might be coached on how to communicate more effectively with one another without the consultant knowing the technical details of their conversations. In addition to communication, OD specialists focus on other processes, including problem solving, decision making, conflict handling, trust, power sharing, and career development.

OD Research and Practical Implications   Before discussing OD research, it is important to note that many of the topics contained in this book are used during OD interventions. For example, role analysis, which was discussed in Chapter 12, is used to enhance cooperation among work group members by getting them to discuss their mutual expectations. Team building also is commonly used as an OD technique. It is used to improve the functioning of work groups and was reviewed in Chapter 13. The point is that OD research has practical implications for a variety of OB applications previously discussed. OD-related interventions produced the following insights:

- A meta-analysis of 18 studies indicated that employee satisfaction with change was higher when top management was highly committed to the change effort.[25]

- A meta-analysis of 52 studies provided support for the systems model of organizational change. Specifically, varying one target element of change created changes in other target elements. Also, there was a positive relationship between individual behavior change and organizational-level change.[26]

- A meta-analysis of 126 studies demonstrated that multifaceted interventions using more than one OD technique were more effective in changing job attitudes and work attitudes than interventions that relied on only one human-process or technostructural approach.[27]

There are three practical implications derived from this research. First, planned organization change works. However, management and change agents are advised to rely on multifaceted interventions. As indicated elsewhere in this book, goal setting, feedback, recognition and rewards, training, participation, and challenging job design have good track records relative to improving performance and satisfaction. Second, change programs are more successful when they are geared toward meeting both short-term and long-term results. Managers should not engage in organizational change for the sake of change. Change efforts should produce positive results.[28] Finally, organizational change is more likely to succeed when top management is truly committed to the change process and the desired goals of the change program. This is particularly true when organizations pursue large-scale transformation.[29]

Understanding and Managing Resistance to Change

We are all creatures of habit. It generally is difficult for people to try new ways of doing things. It is precisely because of this basic human characteristic that most employees do not have enthusiasm for change in the workplace. Rare is the manager who does not have several stories about carefully cultivated changes that died on the vine because of resistance to change. It is important for managers to learn to manage resistance because failed change efforts are costly. Costs include decreased employee loyalty, lowered probability of achieving corporate goals, a waste of money and resources, and difficulty in fixing the failed change effort. This section examines employee resistance to change, relevant research, and practical ways of dealing with the problem.

Why People Resist Change in the Workplace

No matter how technically or administratively perfect a proposed change may be, people make or break it. Individual and group behavior following an organizational change can take many forms (see Figure 20–4). The extremes range from acceptance to active resistance. **Resistance to change** is an emotional/behavioral response to real or imagined threats to an established work routine.

Figure 20–4 shows that resistance can be as subtle as passive resignation and as overt as deliberate sabotage. Managers need to learn to recognize the manifestations of resistance both in themselves and in others if they want to be more effective in creat-

Resistance to change
Emotional/behavioral response to real or imagined work changes.

Figure 20–4   *The Continuum of Resistance to Change*

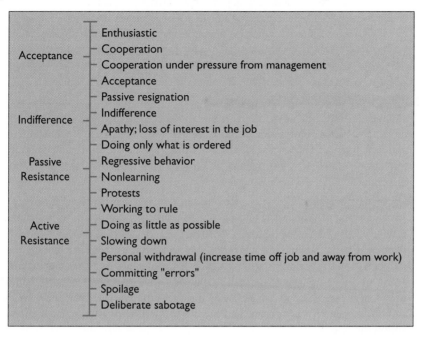

SOURCE: A S Judson, *Changing Behavior in Organizations: Minimizing Resistance to Change* (Cambridge, MA: Basil Blackwell, Inc., 1991), p 48. Used with permission.

ing and supporting change. For example, managers can use the list in Figure 20–4 to prepare answers and tactics to combat the various forms of resistance.

Now that we have examined the manifestations of resistance to change, let us consider the reasons employees resist change in the first place. Ten of the leading reasons are listed here:[30]

1. *An individual's predisposition toward change.* This predisposition is highly personal and deeply ingrained. It is an outgrowth of how one learns to handle change and ambiguity as a child. Consider the hypothetical examples of Mary and Jim. Mary's parents were patient, flexible, and understanding. From the time Mary was weaned from a bottle, she was taught that there were positive compensations for the loss of immediate gratification. She learned that love and approval were associated with making changes. In contrast, Jim's parents were unreasonable, unyielding, and forced him to comply with their wishes. They forced him to take piano lessons even though he hated them. Changes were demands for compliance. This taught Jim to be distrustful and suspicious of change. These learned predispositions ultimately affect how Mary and Jim handle change as adults.[31] Dell Computer Corporation recognizes how important an individual's predisposition toward change can be and tries to hire people with positive predispositions:

   . . . Dell actively seeks and cultivates a certain type of employee mind-set. For example, potential employees are told early on that their former titles may not correlate exactly with positions at Dell because the company structure is relatively flat. "We have to strip the paradigm that titles and levels mean anything," says Price [Steve Price is vice president of human resources for Dell's Public and Americas International Group]. "People have to park their egos at the door. Furthermore, Dell's employees have to move away from the paradigm that more means better. "It's just the reverse," says Price. "When we take half of what you have away from you and tell you to go rebuild it, that's a sign of success." …"We typically attract people for whom change is not a problem," says Koster [Jim Koster is director of human resources for customer service].[32]

2. *Surprise and fear of the unknown.* When innovative or radically different changes are introduced without warning, affected employees become fearful of the implications. Grapevine rumors fill the void created by a lack of official announcements. Harvard's Rosabeth Moss Kanter recommends appointing a transition manager charged with keeping all relevant parties adequately informed.[33]

3. *Climate of mistrust.* Trust, as discussed in Chapter 13, involves reciprocal faith in others' intentions and behavior. Mutual mistrust can doom to failure an otherwise well-conceived change. Mistrust encourages secrecy, which begets deeper mistrust. Managers who trust their employees make the change process an open, honest, and participative affair. Employees who, in turn, trust management are more willing to expend extra effort and take chances with something different. Robert Shapiro, CEO of Monsanto, believes that trust plays a key role in building employee morale and leading organizational change. He made the following comments during an interview for *USA Today* about this issue:

> You can't get to good morale by lying. You can get to illusion that way. If I was faced with a decision that might hurt morale at a crucial time, I might delay the decision. In companies there is reciprocity. If you manipulate workers, they're going to manipulate you. The old Marxist class model was the people on top tried to manipulate the people on the bottom and the people on the bottom tried to manipulate the people on the top. You can't get innovation that way. You find an enormous amount of time and effort is dealing with the lack of trust of others. Look at all the inefficiencies of lack of trust. It tells you that an honest organization is going to be much more efficient. It just makes good business sense.[34]

4. *Fear of failure.* Intimidating changes on the job can cause employees to doubt their capabilities. Self-doubt erodes self-confidence and cripples personal growth and development.

5. *Loss of status and/or job security.* Administrative and technological changes that threaten to alter power bases or eliminate jobs generally trigger strong resistance. For example, most corporate restructuring involves the elimination of managerial jobs. One should not be surprised when middle managers resist restructuring and participative management programs that reduce their authority and status.

6. *Peer pressure.* Someone who is not directly affected by a change may actively resist it to protect the interest of his or her friends and co-workers.

7. *Disruption of cultural traditions and/or group relationships.* Whenever individuals are transferred, promoted, or reassigned, cultural and group dynamics are thrown into disequilibrium.

8. *Personality conflicts.* Just as a friend can get away with telling us something we would resent hearing from an adversary, the personalities of change agents can breed resistance.

9. *Lack of tact and/or poor timing.* Undue resistance can occur because changes are introduced in an insensitive manner or at an awkward time.

10. *Nonreinforcing reward systems.* Individuals resist when they do not foresee positive rewards for changing. For example, an employee is unlikely to support a change effort that is perceived as requiring him or her to work longer with more pressure.

Research on Resistance to Change

The classic study of resistance to change was reported in 1948 by Lester Coch and John R P French. They observed the introduction of a new work procedure in a garment factory. The change was introduced in three different ways to separate groups of workers. In the "no participation" group, the garment makers were simply told about the new procedure. Members of a second group, called the "representative" group, were introduced to the change by a trained co-worker. Employees in the "total participation" group learned of the new work procedure through a graphic presentation of its cost-saving potential. Mixed results were recorded for the representative group. The no participation and total participation groups, meanwhile, went in opposite directions. Output dropped sharply for the no participation group, while grievances and turnover climbed. After a small dip in performance, the total participation group achieved record-high output levels while experiencing no turnover.[35] Since the Coch and French study, participation has been the recommended approach for overcoming resistance to change.[36]

Empirical research uncovered five additional personal characteristics related to resistance to change. A recent study of 514 employees from six organizations headquartered in four different continents (North America, Europe, Asia, and Australia) revealed that personal dispositions pertaining to having a "positive self-concept" and "tolerance for risk" were positively related to coping with change. That is, people with a positive self-concept and a tolerance for risk handled organizational change better than those without these dispositions.[37] A second study also found that high self-efficacy and an internal locus of control were negatively associated with resistance to change.[38] Finally, a study of 305 college students and 15 university staff members revealed that attitudes toward a specific change were positively related to respondents' general attitudes toward change and content within their change schema. You may recall from Chapter 6 that a change schema relates to various perceptions, thoughts, and feelings that people have when they encounter organizational change.[39]

The preceding research is based on the assumption that individuals directly or consciously resist change. Some experts contend that this is not the case. Rather, there is a growing belief that resistance to change really represents employees' responses to obstacles in the organization that prevent them from changing.[40] For example, John Kotter, the researcher who developed the eight steps for leading organizational change that were discussed earlier in this chapter, studied more than 100 companies and concluded that employees generally wanted to change but were unable to do so because of obstacles that prevented execution. He noted that obstacles in the organization's structure or in a "performance appraisal system [that] makes people choose between the new vision and their own self-interests" impeded change more than an individual's direct resistance.[41] This new perspective implies that a systems model such as that shown in Figure 20–3 should be used to determine the causes of failed change. Such an approach would likely reveal that ineffective organizational change is due to faulty organizational processes and systems as opposed to employees' direct

Instructions

Circle the number that best represents your opinions about the company being evaluated.

3 = Yes
2 = Somewhat
1 = No

1. Is the change effort being sponsored by a senior-level executive (CEO, COO)? 3—2—1
2. Are all levels of management committed to the change? 3—2—1
3. Does the organization culture encourage risk taking? 3—2—1
4. Does the organization culture encourage and reward continuous improvement? 3—2—1
5. Has senior management clearly articulated the need for change? 3—2—1
6. Has senior management presented a clear vision of a positive future? 3—2—1
7. Does the organization use specific measures to assess business performance? 3—2—1
8. Does the change effort support other major activities going on in the organization? 3—2—1
9. Has the organization benchmarked itself against world-class companies? 3—2—1
10. Do all employees understand the customers' needs? 3—2—1
11. Does the organization reward individuals and/or teams for being innovative and for looking for root causes of organizational problems? 3—2—1
12. Is the organization flexible and cooperative? 3—2—1
13. Does management effectively communicate with all levels of the organization? 3—2—1
14. Has the organization successfully implemented other change programs? 3—2—1
15. Do employees take personal responsibility for their behavior? 3—2—1
16. Does the organization make decisions quickly? 3—2—1

Total score: _____

Arbitrary Norms

40–48 = High readiness for change
24–39 = Moderate readiness for change
16–23 = Low readiness for change

SOURCE Based on the discussion contained in T A Stewart, "Rate Your Readiness to Change," *Fortune*, February 7, 1994, pp 106–10.

resistance.[42] In conclusion, a systems perspective suggests that people do not resist change, per se, but rather that individual's "anti-change" attitudes and behaviors are caused by obstacles within the work environment.

Alternative Strategies for Overcoming Resistance to Change

Before recommending specific approaches to overcome resistance, there are four key conclusions that should be kept in mind. First, an organization must be ready for change. Just as a table must be set before you can eat, so must an organization be ready for change before it can be effective.[43] The OB Exercise contains a survey that assesses an organization's readiness for change. Use the survey to evaluate a company that you worked for or are familiar with that undertook a change effort. What was the company's readiness for change, and how did this evaluation relate to the success of the change effort?

Second, organizational change is less successful when top management fails to keep employees informed about the process of change. Third, do not assume that people are consciously resisting change. Managers are encouraged to use a systems model of change to identify the obstacles that are affecting the implementation process. Fourth, employees' perceptions or interpretations of a change significantly affect resistance. Employees are less likely to resist when they perceive that the benefits of a change overshadow the personal costs. At a minimum then, managers are advised to (1) provide as much information as possible to employees about the change, (2) inform employees about the reasons/rationale for the change, (3) conduct meetings to address employees' questions regarding the change, and (4) provide employees the opportunity to discuss how the proposed change might affect them.[44] These recommendations underscore the importance of communicating with employees throughout the process of change.

In addition to communication, employee participation in the change process is another generic approach for reducing resistance. Consider how George Bauer, president of the US affiliate of Mercedes-Benz Credit Corp., used participation and employee involvement to reengineer operations and downsize the workforce:

> The first step is delegating reengineering efforts to those who know best where to cut: the people actually doing the work. The second step is comforting them with a guarantee: Anyone bold enough to eliminate his own job will receive a new job—and probably a better one—helping to create new growth.
>
> So to the shock (and skepticism) of his superiors in Stuttgard, Mr Bauer delegated the problem of streamlining to groups of employees and managers, partly in the cold calculation that a grassroots effort would help workers "buy in" and partly in the sincere belief that the best ideas would come from outside the executive suite.
>
> The outcome shook the operation to its core. Managers proposed reducing or even wiping out their own departments through automation or restructuring. Four entire layers of management vanished. Employees were assigned to functional teams with almost complete authority to execute decisions.[45]

Bauer's radical approach to change management resulted in a 31% increase in assets between 1992 and 1995 and a 19% increase in staff. JD Power & Associates also rated Mercedes-Benz Credit number one in customer satisfaction among all import captive-finance companies in 1995.[46] In spite of positive results like those found by Bauer, organizational change experts have nonetheless criticized the tendency to treat participation as a cure-all for resistance to change. They prefer a contingency approach because resistance can take many forms and, furthermore, because situational factors vary (see Table 20–2). As seen in Table 20–2, Participation + Involvement does have its place, but it takes time that is not always available. Also as indicated in Table 20–2, each of the other five methods has its situational niche, advantages, and drawbacks. In short, there is no universal strategy for overcoming resistance to change. Managers need a complete repertoire of change strategies.[47]

Creating a Learning Organization

Organizations are finding that yesterday's competitive advantage is becoming the minimum entrance requirement for staying in business. This puts tremendous pressure on organizations to learn how best to improve and stay ahead of competitors. In fact, both researchers and practicing managers agree that an organization's capability to learn is a key strategic weapon.[48] It thus is important for organizations to enhance and nurture their capability to learn.

So how do organizations create a learning organization? It is not easy! To help clarify what this process entails, this section begins by defining a learning organization. We then present a model of how to build an organization's learning capability and discuss

Table 20-2 *Six Strategies for Overcoming Resistance to Change*

Approach	Commonly Used in Situations	Advantages	Drawbacks
Education + Communication	Where there is a lack of information or inaccurate information and analysis.	Once persuaded, people will often help with the implementation of the change.	Can be very time consuming if lots of people are involved.
Participation + Involvement	Where the initiators do not have all the information they need to design the change and where others have considerable power to resist.	People who participate will be committed to implementing change, and any relevant information they have will be integrated into the change plan.	Can be very time consuming if participators design an inappropriate change.
Facilitation + Support	Where people are resisting because of adjustment problems.	No other approach works as well with adjustment problems.	Can be time consuming, expensive, and still fail.
Negotiation + Agreement	Where someone or some group will clearly lose out in a change and where that group has considerable power to resist.	Sometimes it is a relatively easy way to avoid major resistance.	Can be too expensive in many cases if it alerts others to negotiate for compliance.
Manipulation + Co-optation	Where other tactics will not work or are too expensive.	It can be a relatively quick and inexpensive solution to resistance problems.	Can lead to future problems if people feel manipulated.
Explicit+ Implicit coercion	Where speed is essential and where the change initiators possess considerable power.	It is speedy and can overcome any kind of resistance.	Can be risky if it leaves people mad at the initiators.

SOURCE: Reprinted by permission of the *Harvard Business Review*. An exhibit from "Choosing Strategies for Change" by J P Kotter and L A Schlesinger (March/April 1979). Copyright © 1979 by the President and Fellows of Harvard College; all rights reserved.

some reasons organizations naturally resist learning. The chapter concludes by reviewing new roles and skills required of leaders to create a learning organization and several management practices that must be unlearned.

Defining a Learning Organization

Peter Senge, a professor at the Massachusetts Institute of Technology, popularized the term *learning organization* in his best-selling book entitled *The Fifth Discipline*. He described a learning organization as "a group of people working together to collectively enhance their capacities to create results that they truly care about."[49] A practical interpretation of these ideas results in the following definition. A **learning organization** is one that proactively creates, acquires, and transfers knowledge and that changes its behavior on the basis of new knowledge and insights.[50]

By breaking this definition into its three component parts, we can clearly see the characteristics of a learning organization. First, new ideas are a prerequisite for learn-

Learning organization
Proactively creates, acquires, and transfers knowledge throughout the organization.

The Motorola employees shown here share their knowledge and experiences with each other as they engage in a classroom discussion during a Motorola University training session.

Courtesy of Motorola, Inc.

ing. Learning organizations actively try to infuse their organizations with new ideas and information. They do this by constantly scanning their external environments, hiring new talent and expertise when needed, and by devoting significant resources to train and develop their employees. For example, Motorola and Saturn Corporation, two companies noted for cultivating learning environments, send employees to 40 and 100 hours of training per year, respectively.[51] Second, new knowledge must be transferred throughout the organization. Learning organizations strive to reduce structural, process, and interpersonal barriers to the sharing of information, ideas, and knowledge among organizational members. Finally, behavior must change as a result of new knowledge. Learning organizations are results oriented. They foster an environment in which employees are encouraged to use new behaviors and operational processes to achieve corporate goals.[52]

Building an Organization's Learning Capability

Figure 20–5 presents a model of how organizations build and enhance their learning capability. **Learning capabilities** represent the set of core competencies, which are defined as the special knowledge, skills, and technological know-how that differentiate an organization from its competitors, and processes that enable an organization to adapt to its environment.[53] The general idea underlying Figure 20–5 is that learning capabilities are the fuel for organizational success. Just like gasoline enables a car's engine to perform, learning capabilities equip an organization to foresee and respond to internal and external changes. This capability, in turn, increases the chances of satisfying customers and boosting sales and profitability.[54] Let us now consider the two major contributors to an organization's learning capability: facilitating factors and learning mode.

Learning capabilities
The set of core competencies and internal processes that enable an organization to adapt to its environment.

Facilitating Factors *Facilitating factors* represent "the internal structure and processes that affect how easy or hard it is for learning to occur and the amount of effective learning that takes place."[55] Table 20–3 contains a list of 10 key facilitating factors. Keep in mind as you read them that these factors can either enable or impede an organization's ability to respond to its environment. Consider, for example, the "concern for measurement" factor. A recent national survey of 203 executives compared companies that did and did not focus on measurement-management. Results revealed that those companies who focused on measurement-management were identified as industry leaders, had financial performance that put them in the top third of their industry, and were more successful at implementing and managing major change initiatives.[56] This

Figure 20–5   *Building an Organization's Learning Capability*

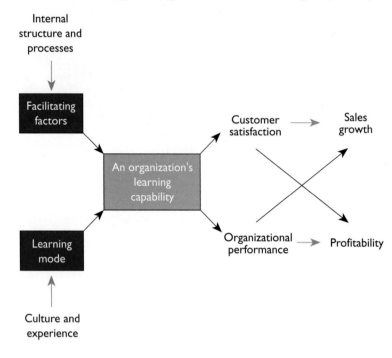

study suggests that concern for measurement enhanced these organizations' learning capabilities. Ernst & Young is a good example of a company that used several of the listed facilitating factors to increase its learning capability:

> Ernst & Young figures that its knowledge falls into three categories of "content." The first is benchmark data—studies, surveys, industry facts, and figures. "Each year we buy about $30 million of this stuff in the United States alone, so that's valuable right there," says Peetz [John Peetz is the chief knowledge officer]. "The second content is point-to-point knowledge, which is people sharing what they know. And finally, we've got expert knowledge, or the best people in a given area who know how to solve specific problems." To tie this together, Ernest & Young created "power packs," or databases on specific business areas that employees load into laptops. Those packs also contain contact information for the firm's network of subject matter experts. If a consultant runs into a glitch in a supply-chain management proposal, for example, he or she can instantly find and get help from Ernst & Young's most experienced supply-chain master.[57]

Learning modes
The various ways in which organizations attempt to create and maximize their learning.

Learning Mode   **Learning modes** represent the various ways in which organizations attempt to create and maximize their learning. Figure 20–5 shows that learning modes are directly influenced by an organization's culture and experience or past history. Consider how the culture at Siemens Power Transmission and Distribution in Raleigh, North Carolina, affected its learning modes:

> Concerned that the company cafeteria was becoming a place for inappropriate socializing, management had walled off part of the room, believing that decreasing the cafeteria's size would make it less convenient for workers to linger there. "It was the exact wrong thing to do," says training director Barry Blystone. As it turned out,

Table 20–3   *Factors That Facilitate Organizational Learning Capabilities*

1. Scanning imperative	Interest in external happenings and in the nature of one's environment. Valuing the processes of awareness and data generation. Curious about what is "out there" as opposed to "in here."
2. Performance gap	Shared perception of a gap between actual and desired state of performance. Disconfirming feedback interrupts a string of successes. Performance shortfalls are seen as opportunities for learning.
3. Concern for measurement	Spend considerable effort in defining and measuring key factors when venturing into new areas; strive for specific, quantifiable measures; discourse over metrics is seen as a learning activity.
4. Experimental mindset	Support for trying new things; curiosity about how things work; ability to "play" with things. Small failures are encouraged, not punished. See changes in work processes, policies, and structures as a continuous series of graded tryouts.
5. Climate of openness	Accessibility of information; relatively open boundaries. Opportunities to observe others; problems/errors are shared, not hidden; debate and conflict are acceptable.
6. Continuous education	Ongoing commitment to education at all levels; support for growth and development of members.
7. Operational variety	Variety exists in response modes, procedures, systems; significant diversity in personnel. Pluralistic rather than monolithic definition of valued internal capabilities.
8. Multiple advocates	Top-down and bottom-up initiatives are possible; multiple advocates and gatekeepers exist.
9. Involved leadership	Leadership at significant levels articulates vision and is very actively engaged in its actualization; takes ongoing steps to implement vision; "hands-on" involvement in educational and other implementation steps.
10. Systems perspective	Strong focus on how parts of the organization are interdependent; seek optimization of organizational goals at the highest levels; see problems and solutions in terms of systemic relationships.

SOURCE: Reprinted by permission of Sage Publications Ltd. from B Moingeon and A Edmondson, in *Organizational Learning and Competitive Advantage*, (Thousand Oaks, CA: Sage,© 1996), p 43.

workers were using the cafeteria as a de facto meeting place where they could gather in a corner to discuss work issues (along with all the other things managers assumed they were talking about—cars, families, the Duke University Blue Devils, etc.).…"By shrinking the size of the cafeteria, we're taking important space and time away from an informal learning opportunity," Blystone says. Ironically, the company used the walled-off space for a conference room—one where meetings had to be scheduled in advance.[58]

"The Mad Hatter's Tea-Party"
From the Peter Newell "Alice in Wonderland"

Just as Alice had to learn to navigate in a world full of the unknown, so must organizations adopt a "learning mode" to cope with the ever-changing landscape of the business environment.
(North Wind Pictures)
North Wind Picture Archives

This example illustrates how Siemen's suspicious and low trusting culture detracted from the spontaneous learning that is critical within learning organizations.

OB researcher Danny Miller reviewed the literature on organizational learning and identified six dominant modes of learning.[59]

1. *Analytic learning.* Learning occurs through systematic gathering of internal and external information. Information tends to be quantitative and analyzed via formal systems. The emphasis is on using deductive logic to numerically analyze objective data.

2. *Synthetic learning.* Synthetic learning is more intuitive and generic than the analytic mode. It emphasizes the synthesis of large amounts of complex information by using systems thinking. That is, employees try to identify interrelationships between issues, problems, and opportunities.

3. *Experimental learning.* This mode is a rational methodological approach that is based on conducting small experiments and monitoring the results.

4. *Interactive learning.* This mode involves learning-by-doing. Rather than using systematic methodological procedures, learning occurs primarily through the exchange of information. Learning is more intuitive and inductive.

5. *Structural learning.* This mode is a methodological approach that is based on the use of organizational routines. Organizational routines represent standardized processes and procedures that specify how to carry out tasks and roles. People learn from routines because they direct attention, institutionalize standards, and create consistent vocabularies.

6. *Institutional learning.* This mode represents an inductive process by which organizations share and model values, beliefs, and practices either from their external environments or from senior executives. Employees learn by observing environmental examples or senior executives. Socialization and mentoring play a significant role in institutional learning.

How Facilitating Factors and Learning Modes Produce Learning Capability   Researchers suspect there is some type of optimal matching between the facilitating factors and learning modes that affects learning capability.[60] For example, the "experimental mindset" facilitating factor should enhance the learning capability of a company that predominately uses an "experimental learning" mode. In contrast, the inconsistency between an "experimental mindset" and a "structural learning" mode would most likely impede organizational learning. Because the concept of a learning organization is very new to the field of OB, we really do not know how the facilitating factors combine with learning modes to influence an organization's learning capability. Future empirical research is needed to examine this issue. Nonetheless, we do know that an organization's learning capability is an important contributor to organizational effectiveness.[61] Managers are thus advised to develop, nurture, and reinforce their organizations' learning capabilities. Let us now consider the reasons organizations unfortunately have a natural tendency to resist learning.

Organizations Naturally Resist Learning

You may be wondering why any rational person or organization would resist learning. It just does not make sense. Well, organizations do not consciously resist learning. They do it because of three fundamental problems that plague society at large: focusing on fragmentation rather than systems, emphasizing competition over collaboration, and a tendency to be reactive rather than proactive.[62] Overcoming these problems requires a fundamental shift in how we view the world.

Focusing on Fragmentation Rather than Systems   Fragmentation involves the tendency to break down a problem, project, or process into smaller pieces. For example, as students you are taught to memorize isolated facts, study abstract theories, and learn ideas and concepts that bear no resemblance to your personal life experiences. This reinforces the use of an analytic strategy that entails solving complex problems by studying subcomponents rather than wholes. Unfortunately, modern-day problems such as the United States' runaway health care costs or national debt cannot be solved with piecemeal linear approaches.

In organizations, fragmentation creates functional "walls" or "silos" that separate people into independent groups. In turn, this results in creating specialists who work within specific functional areas. It also generates internal fiefdoms that battle over power, resources, and control. Learning, sharing, cooperation, and collaboration are ultimately lost on the battlefield.

Emphasizing Competition over Collaboration   Competition is a dominant societal and management paradigm: A **paradigm** represents a generally accepted way of viewing the world. Although nothing is intrinsically wrong with competition, this paradigm results in employees competing with the very people with whom they need to collaborate for success. Moreover, it creates an overemphasis on looking good rather than being good, which prohibits learning because people become reluctant to admit when they do not know something. This is especially true of leaders. In turn, employees hesitate to accept tasks or assignments that they are not good at. Finally, competition produces a fixation on short-term measurable results rather than on long-term solutions to root causes of problems.

> **Paradigm**
> A generally accepted way of viewing the world.

Being Reactive Rather than Creative and Proactive   People are accustomed to changing only when they need to because life is less stressful and frustrating when we stay within our comfort zones. This contrasts with the fundamental catalyst of real learning. The drive to learn is fueled by personal interest, curiosity, aspiration, imagination, experimentation, and risk taking. The problem is that all of us have been conditioned to respond and react to others' directions and approval. This undermines the intrinsic drive to learn. When this tendency is coupled with management by fear, intimidation, and crisis, people not only resist learning, they become paralyzed by the fear of taking risks.

Table 20–4   *Leadership Roles and Activities for Building a Learning Organization*

Leadership Activities	Role 1: Build a Commitment to Learning	Role 2: Work to Generate Ideas with Impact	Role 3: Work to Generalize Ideas with Impact
Make learning a component of the vision and strategic objectives	X		
Invest in learning	X		
Publicly promote the value of learning	X		
Measure, benchmark, and track learning	X		
Create rewards and symbols of learning	X		
Implement continuous improvement programs		X	
Increase employee competence through training, or buy talent from outside the organization		X	
Experiment with new ideas, processes, and structural arrangements		X	
Go outside the organization to identify world-class ideas and processes		X	
Identify mental models of organizational processes		X	
Instill systems thinking throughout the organization		X	
Create an infrastructure that moves ideas across organizational boundaries			X
Rotate employees across functional and divisional boundaries			X

SOURCE: Based in part on D Ulrich, T Jick, and M Von Glinow, "High-Impact Learning: Building and Diffusing Learning Capability," *Organizational Dynamics,* Autumn 1993, pp 52–66.

Effective Leadership Is the Solution

There is hope! Effective leadership chisels away at these natural tendencies and paves the way for organizational learning. Leaders can create an organizational culture that promotes systems thinking over fragmentation, collaboration and cooperation over competition, and innovation and proaction over reactivity. Leaders must, however, adopt new roles and associated activities to create a learning organization.

Specifically, leaders perform three key functions in building a learning organization: (1) building a commitment to learning, (2) working to generate ideas with impact, and (3) working to generalize ideas with impact.[63] Table 20–4 contains a list of leadership activities needed to support each role.

Building a Commitment to Learning   Leaders need to instill an intellectual and emotional commitment to learning by using the ideas shown in Table 20–4. For example, Harley Davidson has identified "intellectual curiosity" as one of its core corporate values. Leaders can promote the value of learning by modeling the desired attitudes and behaviors. They can attend seminars as presenters or participants, share effective managerial practices with peers, and disseminate readings, videos, and other educational materials. Leaders also need to invest the financial resources needed to create a learning infrastructure. Consider the experience of BP Amoco and the World Bank:

> BP Amoco's management spent $12.5 million up front to install the right technologies for knowledge management and to coach employees. Over the years, it has spent more than $20 million on coaching. But that investment has paid off quickly as the company saved huge sums through the sharing of best practices worldwide. The World Bank devotes approximately 4% of its administrative budget to knowledge management. According to Stephen Denning, program director of knowledge management, this percentage is at the lower end of corporate spending, but represents a significant amount for his nonprofit organization. Senior leaders lend support to the initiative and provide the resources each of the bank's 20 sectors need to form local partnerships, provide ad hoc advice, and disseminate knowledge.[64]

Working to Generate Ideas with Impact   Ideas with impact are those that add value to one or more of an organization's three key stakeholders: employees, customers, and shareholders. The leadership activities shown in Table 20–4 reveal six ways to generate ideas with impact.

Working to Generalize Ideas with Impact   Leaders must make a concerted effort to reduce interpersonal, group, and organizational barriers to learning. This can be done by creating a learning infrastructure. This is a large-scale effort that includes the following activities:

- Measuring and rewarding learning.
- Increasing open and honest dialogue among organizational members.
- Reducing conflict.
- Increasing horizontal and vertical communication.
- Promoting teamwork.
- Rewarding risk taking and innovation.
- Reducing the fear of failure.
- Increasing the sharing of successes, failures, and best practices across organizational members.
- Reducing stressors and frustration.
- Reducing internal competition.
- Increasing cooperation and collaboration.
- Creating a psychologically safe and comforting environment.[65]

Unlearning the Organization

In addition to implementing the ideas listed in Table 20–4, organizations must concurrently unlearn organizational practices and paradigms that made them successful. Quite simply, traditional organizations and the associated organizational behaviors they created have outlived their usefulness. Management must seriously question and challenge the ways of thinking that worked in the past if they want to create a learning organization.[66] For example, the old management paradigm of planning, organizing, and control might be replaced with one of vision, values, and empowerment. The time has come for management and employees to think as owners, not as "us" and "them" adversaries.

Let us close our study of organizational behavior by considering a mission statement that promotes this new managerial paradigm:

> This is a company of owners, of partners, of businesspeople. We are in business together. Our economic figures—which is to say, our jobs and our financial security—depend not on management's generosity ("them") or on the strength of a union ("us") but on our collective success in the marketplace. We will share in the rewards just as—by definition—we share in the risks.
>
> No one in this company is just an employee. People have different jobs, make different salaries, have different levels of authority. But all workers will see the same basic information and will have a voice in matters affecting them. And it will be everyone's responsibility to understand how the business operates, to keep track of its results, and to make decisions that contribute to its success in the marketplace.[67]

Summary of Key Concepts

1. *Discuss the external and internal forces that create the need for organizational change.* Organizations encounter both external and internal forces for change. There are four key external forces for change: demographic characteristics, technological advancements, market changes, and social and political pressures. Internal forces for change come from both human resource problems and managerial behavior/decisions.

2. *Describe Lewin's change model and the systems model of change.* Lewin developed a three-stage model of planned change that explained how to initiate, manage, and stabilize the change process. The three states were *unfreezing,* which entails creating the motivation to change, *changing,* and stabilizing change through *refreezing.* A systems model of change takes a big picture perspective of change. It focuses on the interaction among the key components of change. The three main components of change are inputs, target elements of change, and outputs. The target elements of change represent the components of an organization that may be changed. They include organizing arrangements, social factors, methods, goals, and people.

3. *Discuss Kotter's eight steps for leading organizational change.* John Kotter believes that organizational change fails for one or more of eight common errors. He proposed eight steps that organizations should follow to overcome these errors. The eight steps are as follows: (*a*) establish a sense of urgency, (*b*) create the guiding coalition, (*c*) develop a vision and strategy, (*d*) communicate the change vision, (*e*) empower broad-based action, (*f*) generate short-term wins, (*g*) consolidate gains and produce more change, and (*h*) anchor new approaches in the culture.

4. *Demonstrate your familiarity with the four identifying characteristics of organization development (OD).* The identifying characteristics of OD are that it (*a*) involves profound change, (*b*) is value loaded, (*c*) is a diagnosis/prescription cycle, and (*d*) is process oriented.

5. *Discuss the 10 reasons employees resist change.* Resistance to change is an emotional/behavioral response to real or imagined threats to an established work routine. Ten reasons employees resist change are (*a*) an individual's predisposition toward change, (*b*) surprise and fear of the unknown, (*c*) climate of mistrust, (*d*) fear of failure, (*e*) loss of status and/or job security, (*f*) peer pressure, (*g*) disruption of cultural traditions and/or group relationships, (*h*) personality conflicts, (*i*) lack of tact and/or poor timing, and (*j*) nonreinforcing reward systems.

6. *Identify alternative strategies for overcoming resistance to change.* Organizations must be ready for change. Assuming an organization is ready for change, the alternative strategies for overcoming resistance to change are education + communication, participation + involvement, facilitation + support, negotiation + agreement, manipulation + co-optation, and explicit + implicit coercion. Each has its situational appropriateness and advantages and drawbacks.

7. *Define a learning organization.* A learning organization is one that proactively creates, acquires, and transfers knowledge and changes its behavior on the basis of new knowledge and insights.

8. *Discuss the process organizations use to build their learning capabilities.* Learning capabilities represent the set of core competencies and processes that enable an organization to adapt to its environment. Learning capabilities are directly affected by organizational facilitating factors and learning modes. Facilitating factors constitute the internal structure and processes that either encourage or impede learning within an organization. Learning modes repre-

sent the various ways by which organizations attempt to create and maximize their learning. Researchers believe that there is some type of optimal matching between the facilitating factors and learning modes that affects learning capability.

9. *Review the reasons organizations naturally resist learning.* There are three underlying reasons. The first involves the tendency to focus on fragmentation rather than systems. Fragmentation involves the tendency to break down a problem, project, or process into smaller pieces. It reinforces a linear analytic strategy that examines subcomponents rather than wholes. A dominant management paradigm that emphasizes competition over collabora-

tion is the second reason. The third reason organizations naturally resist learning is that people have a tendency to be reactive rather than creative and proactive. This tendency stems from the fact that all of us have been conditioned to respond and react to others' directions and approval.

10. *Discuss the role of leadership in creating a learning organization.* Leaders perform three key functions in building a learning organization: (*a*) building a commitment to learning, (*b*) working to generate ideas with impact, and (*c*) working to generalize ideas with impact. There are 13 different leadership activities needed to support each role (see Table 20–4).

Discussion Questions

1. Which of the external forces for change do you believe will prompt the greatest change between now and the year 2010?

2. Have you worked in an organization where internal forces created change? Describe the situation and the resulting change.

3. How would you respond to a manager who made the following statement? "Unfreezing is not important, employees will follow my directives."

4. What are some useful methods that can be used to refreeze an organizational change?

5. Have you ever observed the systems model of change in action? Explain what occurred.

6. Have you ever resisted a change at work? Explain the circumstances and your thinking at the time.

7. Which source of resistance to change do you think is the most common? Which is the most difficult for management to deal with?

8. Does the company you work for act like a learning organization? Explain your rationale.

9. Which of the three reasons for organizations' natural resistance to learning is the most powerful? Explain.

Internet Exercise   **www.sei.com**

In this chapter we reviewed several models of organizational change. Because these models are based on different sets of assumptions, each one offers managers a unique set of recommendations for how organizational change should be implemented. We also discussed a variety of recommendations for how managers might better implement organizational change. The purpose of this exercise is for you to expand your knowledge about how organizations should implement organizational change by considering recommendations provided by The Software Engineering Institute (SEI). The SEI is a federally funded research and development center sponsored by the US Department of Defense. This organization focuses on assisting organizations to improve the process of software engineering. In so doing, the SEI has learned much about how to implement organizational change. Go to the Internet home

page for the SEI (**www.sei.com**), and select the "search" option. This will enable you to search the SEI's database on selected topics. Search on the keyword "organizational change." Use the sources identified through this search to answer the following questions.

Questions

1. What are the key elements of organizational change? How do these compare to the components contained in the systems model of organizational change presented in Figure 20–3?

2. What specific recommendations does the SEI offer about managing organizational change?

3. What roles do change agents, sponsors, champions, and participants play in the process of implementing organizational change?

OB in Action Case Study

Levi Strauss Struggles with Creating Organizational Change[68]

When Robert Haas led the most recent LBO of Levi Strauss & Co. in 1996, he took one of the world's most successful brands and placed its entire future in the hands of four people: himself, an uncle, and two cousins. Other family shareholders had two choices: Cede all power to this group for 15 years, or cash out. Most stayed in.

It seemed a good bet at the time. Haas was the guy who had saved the troubled family company back in 1984. . . .

If the family shareholders had been paying careful attention to what was really going on at Levi's well before the '96 LBO, they might have bet differently. Sometime around 1990, a great brand began coming apart at the seams. Levi's market share among males ages 14 to 19 has since dropped in half, it hasn't had a successful new product in years, its advertising campaigns have been failures, its in-store presentations are embarrassing, and its manufacturing costs are bloated. The reengineering—with an $850 million budget—was a disaster. J.C. Penney, Levi's biggest customer, reports that last fall Levi's delivered its all-important back-to-school line—get ready—45 days late. Says Levi's Thomas Kasten, who led the reengineering: "I don't think we fully accomplished anything, to be honest."

Since 1997 the company has announced plans to shut 29 factories in North America and Europe and to eliminate 16,310 jobs. A month ago it said 1998 sales had dropped 13%, to just under $6 billion. *Fortune* estimates that since the '96 LBO—since Bob Haas became unaccountable to anyone but his three relatives—Levi Strauss' market value has shrunk from $14 billion to about $8 billion. By comparison, crosstown San Francisco rival Gap has grown from $7 billion to over $40 billion during the same period. . . .

Haas envisions Levi Strauss as a company where a factory worker's voice is as likely to be heard as the CEO's. "He's not the sort of manager who says, 'Here's what you did wrong,' " explains Levi's former CFO George James. "Instead, he sits down, looks you in the eye, and asks, 'What do you think you did wrong?' " Because of his obvious sincerity, Levi's employees are fiercely loyal to him, although they don't always approve of his management style. "I love Bob to death, but he has a tendency to want to involve everybody in decision-making. He's compassionate to a fault," says Peter Thigpen, former president of Levi Strauss USA.

No matter how well-intentioned, group decision-making usually degenerates into endless meetings, task forces, memos, and E-mails. That's what happened at Levi Strauss. "Everything had to go into a corporate process, so nothing ever got resolved," says Robert Siegel, who left the company after 29 years to become CEO of Stride Rite in 1993. "Almost half my time was spent in meetings that were absolutely senseless." Clearly frustrated even now, Siegel adds, "If you asked [Levi's executives] for the time, they would build you a clock, and still not be able to tell you the time." . . .

Levi Strauss has always believed in corporate philanthropy and social responsibility. When the firm went public in 1971, its offering prospectus made corporate history by warning that profits might be affected by a commitment to social programs. But Bob Haas wanted to go further—much further. In 1987 he developed the Levi Strauss Mission and Aspirations Statement, which promoted teamwork, trust, diversity, empowerment, etc., etc. Printed on recycled blue denim, the aspirations statement was hung on office walls, posted in factories, enclosed in Lucite paperweights, and laminated on wooden plaques. For most CEOs, that would have done it: State your mission, act accordingly, and expect your employees to do the same. Haas, however, had something to prove: that a company driven by social values could outperform one driven by profits.

He changed Levi's compensation plans so that one-third of executives' bonuses reflected their ability to manage "aspirationally." He assigned 80 task forces to make the company more "aspirational." The work-and-family task force sent a 25-page questionnaire to 17,000 employees. The global-sourcing task force spent nine months creating guidelines that would hold Levi's overseas contractors to the highest possible standards of labor practices. A diversity focus group organized off-site sessions that paired white, male managers with women and minorities to discuss racial and gender stereotypes.

By the early 1990s, Levi's employees were attending the company's "core curriculum," a three-part, ten-day course that covered leadership, diversity, and ethical decision-making. Joined by at least one senior manager, groups of 20 employees discussed their vulnerabilities, shared their deepest fears, even composed their obituaries. . . .

In hindsight, the wusses did get in the way. For even as Bob Haas pioneered utopian management, the business began to look threadbare. Despite its enlightened benevolence, Levi's clung to old ways of doing things. It stopped innovating. It ignored, or was oblivious to, the marketplace. The "principled reasoning approach" to decision-making taught in the core curriculum didn't help. "Unless you could convince everyone to agree with your idea, you didn't have the authority to make a decision," says former CFO George James. "That made it very difficult to be responsive."

Case in point: Dockers, launched by Levi's in 1986. Dockers khakis were an immediate success, hitting the market just as American men began replacing suits with more casual attire. But in 1993, Dockers missed one of the biggest trends in the khaki market: wrinkle-resistant pants. As other manufacturers began selling them, Dockers stayed put. Sales collapsed. That same year, Levi's reported its first decline in profits since 1988.

The denim market was changing too. Levi's 501s used to be the hot jeans. "But in '93, kids started telling us the legs were too narrow," says Gross of Millers Outpost. In response, Millers Outpost created its own line of jeans with legs as wide as 23 inches. Then J.C. Penney and Sears got into the act, making jeans with flared legs and boot cuts. Tommy Jeans splashed the Hilfiger logo all over its baggy pants. JNCO introduced jeans with 40-inch-wide legs and 17-inch-deep pockets. Through it all, Levi Strauss kept on pushing its basic jeans, with 16-inch-wide legs and 6-inch pockets. . . .

In 1993, Levi Strauss embarked on something called the Customer Service Supply Chain initiative. Once again, what began as a well-intentioned project morphed into a monster. The stated goal of the initiative was to make Levi's more responsive to retailers. The company wanted to get new products to market in three months, down from 15 months, and to reduce the time needed to restock a pair of jeans from three weeks to 72 hours. Amazingly, no one seriously considered the possibility that getting a pair of jeans to stores in 72 hours might double or triple Levi's costs. "There was no cost boundary," says Tom Kasten, who headed the effort. "I mean, we talked a little about how it shouldn't cost more, but it really was an afterthought."

In June 1993, 200 of Levi's best people began designing a new supply chain. Many were vice presidents of important divisions, divisions that would now be without leaders. Others left work behind, forcing colleagues to do double duty. Joined by at least 100 Andersen consultants, the group took over the third floor of headquarters, soon covering the walls with vast organizational charts and maps. The place resembled a war room. The members of the Third Floor Brigade weren't just on a mission, they were, in their words, "creating a revolution." To convince skeptics at Levi's that this was serious stuff, they collected magazine cover stories on companies like IBM, GM, and Digital that were in turmoil because they had ignored their changing markets. Proselytizing, the Brigade blew up the covers, pasted them to poster boards, and carried them around the organization. "It created huge battle lines," says Jacobi, Levi's president. "There were Moonies and there were nonbelievers, and they avoided each other and said bad things about each other. But there was no way to get out of it. It was like quicksand."

The Customer Service Supply Chain initiative was no longer just about improving service to retail customers. It was about improving everything. Whole new categories of jobs were created. The Third Floor Brigade rewrote more than 600 job descriptions; all over the company people had to reapply for their positions. To help employees evaluate their aptitudes and handle the imminent changes, the Brigade put together a 145-page handbook called *Individual Readiness for a Changing Environment*. "Let yourself feel the loss, then let go and move on," it advised. "New ways should be viewed as neither right nor wrong, neither better nor worse, than the previous ones."

Levi's employees freaked out. Some who didn't get the jobs they had applied for, or reapplied for, broke down. Others simply quit. "It pushed me over the edge," says a former employee. The retailers—the people actually meant to benefit from all this—shook their heads in disbelief. "The reengineering changes had us confused as hell," says a buyer at one major Levi's account. "One minute there was no customer service, the next minute they'd overdo it." By the time Levi's board of directors put an end to the nonsense in late 1995, the reengineering team's budget had swollen by 70%, to $850 million. As for restocking basic product, J.C. Penney's standard is 20 days; Levi's average last year was 27 days.

How did this go on for so long? Simple. Haas has the power, and most family members seem content with the arrangement—despite the sagging value of their shares (which have declined by about 40% in three years), despite the fact that they get no dividends. "I've always looked on it as a long-term investment," says Robert Friedman, cousin to Bob Haas and a member of the Levi's board. Rumor has it some family members want out, or at the very least would like a new CEO. They won't get one. Other than the four men who control the votes, no one has any say in the company until 2011, when the shareholder agreement expires. . . .

Last year, Levi's redefined its utopian mission. The old one, which appeared in the preamble to the mission and aspirations statement, was: "To sustain responsible commercial success." The new one is simply, and ambiguously: "To be the casual apparel authority." So, once again, the company is in the midst of major organizational changes. It recently shifted to a brand-management structure long popular with consumer companies like Procter & Gamble and Sara Lee. So, once again, people are moving into new jobs, being given new titles. Because management now recognizes that one of Levi's problems was inbreeding, an urgent mandate is to fill one-third of all openings with outsiders.

On Wednesday, June 12, 1996, a crowd of Levi Strauss employees gathered in San Francisco to hear a major announcement. Standing proudly before them, Bob Haas revealed a new incentive plan. With the company now fully in family hands, Haas could not offer employees stock options. Instead, he promised that if Levi's reached $7.6 billion in cumulative cash flow by 2001 (after three years, it's just $2.8 billion), every employee in the world, all 37,000 of them—from sewing machine operators in El Paso to salesmen in Barcelona—would receive a bonus worth one year's salary. Giddy employees cheered. Here was the latest confirmation that they were working for the world's most enlightened employer. Sincere notes of gratitude poured in to headquarters: "Bob, thanks for this great opportunity. Only 1,895 days to go! Many thanks, Estelle." And: "Bob, many thanks for your generous & exciting idea. What a great challenge to rise to, Paul T." And: "Bob, see you in 2001 for the big party! Kel."

One more thing: The party will be in utopia.

Questions for Discussion

1. What were the internal and external forces for change at Levi Straus?

2. How effectively did Levi Straus apply Lewin's model of change when implementing the "Customer Service Supply Chain" initiative? Explain.

3. Use the systems model of change shown in Figure 20–3 to discuss how Levi Straus has attempted to create organizational change. Based on this assessment, what would you have done differently if you were Bob Haas? Discuss.

4. To what extent is Levi Straus a learning organization?

5. Based on everything that you have learned about organizational behavior, what is your opinion about the new incentive plan that Bob Haas revealed at the end of the case?

Personal Awareness and Growth Exercise

Applying the Systems Model of Change

Objectives

1. To help you understand the diagnosis step of planned organizational change.

2. To give you a practical diagnostic tool to assess which target elements of change in Figure 20–3 should be changed during a change process.

Introduction

Diagnosis is the first step in planned organizational change. It is used to identify past or current organizational problems that inhibit organizational effectiveness. As indicated in Figure 20–3, there are five organizational areas in which to look for problems: organizing arrangements, social factors, methods, goals, and people. In this exercise, you will be asked to complete a brief survey assessing these five areas of an organization.

Instructions

If you currently have a full- or part-time job, think of your organization and describe it by circling an appropriate response for each of the following 18 statements. Calculate a total score for each diagnostic area. Then connect the set of points for your organization in a vertical profile. If you are not currently employed, describe the last organization you worked for. If you have never worked, use your current university or school as your frame of reference.

After completing the survey, think of an "ideal" organization: an organization that you believe would be most effective. How do you believe this organization would stand in terms of the five diagnostic areas? We would like you to assess this organization with the same diagnostic survey. Circle your responses with a different color or marking. Then vertically connect the set of points for your "ideal" organization. Calculate a total score for each diagnostic area.

Organizational Diagnostic Survey

1 = Strongly disagree
2 = Disagree
3 = Neutral
4 = Agree
5 = Strongly agree

Organizing Arrangements

1. The company has the right recognition and rewards in place to support its vision and strategies.   1—2—3—4—5

2. The organizational structure facilitates goal accomplishment.   1—2—3—4—5

3. Organizational policies and procedures are administered fairly.   1—2—3—4—5

Total Organizing Arrangements score = _____   _____

Social Factors

4. The culture promotes adaptability and flexibility.   1—2—3—4—5

5. Interpersonal and group conflict are handled in a positive manner.   1—2—3—4—5

6. Horizontal and vertical communication is effective.   1—2—3—4—5

7. Leaders are good role models and decision makers.   1—2—3—4—5

Total Social Factors score = _____   _____

Methods

8. The work flow promotes higher quality and quantity of performance.   1—2—3—4—5

9. Technology is effectively utilized.   1—2—3—4—5

10. People focus on solving root cause problems rather than symptoms.   1—2—3—4—5

Total Methods score = _____   _____

Goals

11. I am aware of the organization's
vision and strategic goals.   1—2—3—4—5

12. I have all the tools and resources I
need to do my job.   1—2—3—4—5

13. Corporate goals are cascaded down
the organization.   1—2—3—4—5

14. I am evaluated against specific
standards of performance.   1—2—3—4—5

Total Goals score = _____ _____

People

15. This organization inspires the very
best in me in the way of job
performance.   1—2—3—4—5

16. I understand my job duties and
responsibilities.   1—2—3—4—5

17. I like working in this company.   1—2—3—4—5

18. People are motivated to do the best
job they can.   1—2—3—4—5

Total People score = _____ _____

Questions for Discussion

1. Based on your evaluation of your current organization, which diagnostic area(s) is most in need of change?

2. Based on a comparison of your current and ideal organizations, which diagnostic area(s) is most in need of change? If your answer is different from the first question, explain the difference.

3. What sort of intervention would be appropriate for your work group or organization? Give details.

Group Exercise

Creating Personal Change through Force-Field Analysis[69]

Objectives

1. To apply force-field analysis to a behavior or situation you would like to change.

2. To receive feedback on your strategies for bringing about change.

Introduction

The theory of force-field analysis is based on the premise that people resist change because of counteracting positive and negative forces. Positive forces for change are called *thrusters*. They propel people to accept change and modify their behavior. In contrast, *counterthrusters* or *resistors* are negative forces that motivate an individual to maintain the status quo. People frequently fail to change because they experience equal amounts of positive and negative forces to change.

Force-field analysis is a technique used to facilitate change by first identifying the thrusters and resistors that exist in a specific situation. To minimize resistance to change, it is generally recommended to first reduce or remove the negative forces to change. Removing counterthrusters should create increased pressure for an individual to change in the desired direction. Managers can also further increase motivation to change by following up the reduction of resistors with an increase in the number of positive thrusters of change.

Instructions

Your instructor will pair you up with another student. The two of you will serve as a team that evaluates the completeness of each other's force-field analysis and recommendations. Once the team is assembled, each individual should independently complete the Force-Field Analysis Form presented after these instructions. Once both of you complete this activity, one team member should present results from steps 2 through 5 from the five-step Force-Field Analysis Form. The partner should then evaluate the results by considering the following questions with his or her team member:

1. Are there any additional thrusters and counterthrusters that should be listed? Add them to the list.

2. Do you agree with the "strength" evaluations of thrusters and counterthrusters in step 4? Ask your partner to share his or her rationale for the ratings. Modify the ratings as needed.

3. Examine the specific recommendations for change listed in step 5, and evaluate whether you think they will produce the desired changes. Be sure to consider whether the focal person has the ability to eliminate, reduce, or increase each thruster and counterthruster that is the basis for a specific recommendation. Are there any alternative strategies you can think of?

4. What is your overall evaluation of your partner's intervention strategy?

FORCE-FIELD ANALYSIS FORM[70]

Step 1

In the space provided, please identify a number of personal problems you would like to solve or aspects of your life you would like to change. Be as imaginative as possible. You are not limited to school situations. For example, you may want to consider your work environment if you are currently employed, family situation, interpersonal relationships, club situations, and so forth. It is important that you select some aspects of your life that you would like to change but which up to now have made no effort to do.

_____
_____
_____
_____
_____
_____
_____

Step 2

Review in your mind the problems or aspects listed in step 1. Now select one that you would really like to change and which you believe lends itself easily to force-field analysis. Select one that you will feel comfortable talking about to other people.

_____

Step 3

On the form following step 4, indicate existing forces that are pushing you in the direction of change. Thrusters may be forces internal to the self (pride, regret, and fear) or they may be external to the self (friends, the boss, a professor). Also list existing forces that are preventing you from changing. Again, the counterthruster may be internal to the self (uncertainty, fear) or external to the self (poor instruction, limited resources, lack of support mechanisms).

Step 4

In the space to the right of your list of thrusters and counterthrusters indicate the relative strength. For consistency, use a scale of 1 to 10, with 1 indicating a weak force and 10 indicating a high force.

Thrusters	Strength
_____	_____
_____	_____
_____	_____
_____	_____
_____	_____
_____	_____

Counterthrusters	Strength
_____	_____
_____	_____
_____	_____
_____	_____
_____	_____
_____	_____

Step 5

Analyze your thrusters and counterthrusters, and develop a strategy for bringing about the desired change. Remember that it is possible to produce the desired results by strengthening existing thrusters, introducing new thrusters, weakening or removing counterthrusters, or some combination of these. Consider the impact of your change strategy on the system's internal stress (i.e., on yourself and others), the likelihood of success, the availability of resources, and the long-term consequences of planned changes. Be prepared to discuss your recommendations with the partner in your group.

_____
_____
_____
_____
_____
_____
_____

Questions for Discussion

1. What was your reaction to doing a force-field analysis? Was it insightful and helpful?

2. Was it valuable to receive feedback about your force-field analysis from a partner? Explain.

3. How would you assess the probability of effectively implementing your recommendations?

Video Case: Specialized Bicycle Components

Organizational Behavior: Working for "Psychic Income" at Specialized Bicycle

Sequence of Activities for Part 1 of This Video Case Study:

1. Read all or portions of Chapters 1–4, as assigned by your instructor.
2. Read the following introduction to Specialized Bicycle Components.
3. View Part 1 of the video.
4. Answer the questions for Part 1.

The Dream: "Live to Ride, Ride to Live"

Imagine it's early summer in the Canadian Rockies. Scattered puffy clouds signal a beautiful day ahead as the new sun peeks over glacier-scarred mountains. You and three friends are spending the week mountain biking near Banff, Alberta. The overall goal, aside from having lots of fun, is to sharpen your conditioning at higher elevation in preparation for summer races in Utah, West Virginia, and Colorado. Someday you'd like to do nothing but train in neat places like this and race in equally neat places, but for now you have to settle for a patchwork schedule of work and play. Life is here and now and you want to squeeze everything from it you possibly can. Time to ride.

You're in third position on today's ride along a remote forest trail that's still in rough shape from a harsh winter. Pine scent and the musty smell of a damp forest floor give way periodically to open patches of meadow with new grass and explosions of wild flowers. Birds and rabbits are everywhere. Loose rocks, wash outs, and snow-damaged tree branches litter the trail. Still, you push your speed to keep up with what your gut tells you is too fast a pace for these conditions. Of course, the deep red sands and slick rock trails of Moab, Utah, will be no picnic either.[1] Out of the corner of your eye, as you flash by, you catch sight of a porcupine enjoying a breakfast of pine bark.

About 20 meters ahead, a cow elk the size of a horse leaps across the trail. Your imagination ponders the chances of a hungry bear in hot pursuit. Without warning, your front tire glances off a mossy rock and you barely stay upright as your right knee ricochets off a huge rotting tree stump. As you overcorrect to the left, a low hemlock branch lashes your face, knocking your glasses askew. "Whew, that was close," you mutter to yourself, as you adjust your glasses and rivet your attention on the rough trail ahead.

Part 1: How Organizational Behavior Impacts Specialized Bicycle—"All You Need Is Love" of Cycling

Certainly a deep bruise to boast about tomorrow, but no major damage to the knee, thank goodness. You lean into the pedals and take your speed to the edge. Stunning scenery flies past. Still, on a perfect day like this your mind can't help but turn freely in a kaleidoscope of thoughts. People, places, things. One name that likely won't enter your mind is Mike Sinyard, without whose pioneering efforts today's exhilarating mountain bike ride might never have occurred.

The Legend

After graduating with a business degree from San Jose State University in 1974, Mike Sinyard took his life-long fascination with bicycles to Europe.[2] Cycling from one European bicycle manufacturer to another, Sinyard wondered if the awakening US cycling movement could someday rival the scope and sophistication of Europe's. He purchased $1,200 of bike parts and sold everything in just two days back home in San Jose. By negotiating advance payments from local bike shops, Sinyard was able to start a modest business importing bike components from Europe, Japan, and Taiwan. Thus, Specialized Bicycle Components, now based in Morgan Hill, California, was born.

Sales of European-style road bicycles started to decline in the US during the late 1970s. Complaints of uncomfortable saddles, hand-numbing grips, and flat tires prevailed. Sinyard responded in 1981 by designing and commercializing the first fat-tired "mountain bike." It was named the Stumpjumper and carried a $750 price tag. Specialized sold 500 Stumpjumpers that first year. *Success* magazine recently offered this historical perspective:

> When Sinyard first unveiled the Stumpjumper, he offered more than a new bike and sport; he sold an attitude. In the late 1970s the public perceived bicycling as an exclusive European sport. To ride seriously, you had to have special equipment and clothes, and that was intimidating for a lot of people. But mountain biking was a California phenomenon. It was about having fun, and anybody could do it. "That was the primary thing we wanted to get across to people," says Sinyard. "Not the bike but the fun, the freedom. So, our early ads evoked a wild, surfing, hippie kind of attitude. The bike was just the vehicle to get you to the feeling."[3]

Competitors Trek, Cannondale, and Schwinn-Scott jumped on the mountain bike bandwagon and sales rocketed upward during the 1980s. In fact, 90% of all bikes sold in the United States during the 1980s were mountain bikes and fitness bikes. So, today, the name *Mike Sinyard* is to mountain biking as the name Jake Burton is to snowboarding and the name Scott Olson is to in-line skating—each a legend whose innovative ideas created entirely new sports and spawned new industries.

The Company

Specialized Bicycle's first 25 years were much like a mountainous bike ride. Lots of adrenalin-pumping ups and downs. Sinyard's passion for making cutting-edge mountain bikes proved to be a mixed blessing for Specialized. While competitors were selling mountain bikes through mass marketers such as Kmart for an average price of $300, Specialized's high-end bikes were sold only through specialty bicycle shops for upwards to $3,000. Trek took a dominant leadership position in the industry Sinyard pioneered. Sinyard's obsession with innovation led to missed product launch deadlines and delayed shipping dates. A lower-end, popularly-priced bike called the Full Force slotted for mass marketers became a failed experiment.

Having tripped over the classic entrepreneur's dilemma of evolving from a seat-of-the-pants innovator to a professional manager, Sinyard realized Specialized needed to become a well-managed company if it was to survive. Design, finance, human resource, and product quality experts were brought on board. Quality improved along with dealer relations. By 1998, Specialized's revenues from the sale of high-end mountain bikes and biking accessories topped $300 million (a healthy 26 percent annual growth rate).[4]

The Road Ahead

Today, Specialized Bicycle Components is building strong brand recognition and becoming adept at E-commerce on the Internet (**www.specialized.com**). Structuring a strong dealer network is a top priority. Innovation is still a driving passion. The "ride" remains paramount.

Questions for Discussion

1. How many people-centered practices, as discussed in the beginning of Chapter 1, are evident in Part 1 of the video? Explain.

2. What evidence of the 4-P cycle of continuous improvement, in Figure 1–1, is apparent in Part 1 of this video case?

3. Would you call Specialized a Theory X or Theory Y company? Explain.

4. Would W Edwards Deming likely approve of the way business is done at Specialized? Explain.

5. What aspects of TQM can you find in this video case?

6. Part 1 of this video case reveals a limited degree of gender and racial diversity among Specialized Bicycle's leadership team. How would you explain the "business case" for greater diversity to Sinyard and his fellow executives?

7. What are the main espoused and enacted values of Specialized Bicycle's culture? Does the company seem to "walk the talk?" Explain.

8. Which label in Table 3–1 would you use to describe Specialized Bicycle's culture?

9. How strong is the bike company's culture? What are the positive and negative implications of your assessment of the culture's strength?

10. Regarding the distinction between individualistic and collectivist cultures in Chapter 4, how effective has Specialized Bicycle been at getting employees from America's characteristically individualistic culture to think and work collectively? Explain.

Sequence of Activities for Part 2 of This Video Case Study:

1. Read all or portions of Chapters 5–10, as assigned by your instructor.

2. Read the following comments on Specialized Bicycle Components.

3. View Part 2 of the video.

4. Answer questions for Part 2.

Tony M. Herdrich, Director, International Sales: "The Motivation is You're Doing Something That You Love. Something You Enjoy Doing Because You're So Involved in the Sport."

Employees at Specialized Bicycle often use words like "passion" and "love" when referring to their work. Many of today's employees would laugh at the notion of having a passion for the job or loving their work. We are challenged to figure out what sets Specialized Bicycle apart from the typical workplace.

Part 2: Individual Behavior in Organizations and How It Affects Specialized Bicycle—"You Mean I Can Have Fun at Work?"

Questions for Discussion

1. How important are the concepts of self-efficacy, organizational identification, and locus of control—as discussed in Chapter 5—to the success of Specialized Bicycle?

2. Recall Specialized Bicycle's mission statement from Part 1 of the video case:

   Number one—We love the sport.

   Number two—We want to build products that help people like you enjoy the sport as much as we do. period.

   How could this mission statement affect the social perception process, as described in Figure 6–1?

3. Could the mission statement have a Pygmalion effect on the employees? Explain.

4. What motivational lessons can Herzberg's motivator-hygiene theory teach the managers at Specialized?

5. Which of the five core job dimensions, discussed in Chapter 7, are clearly evident in Parts 1 and 2 of the video case?

6. Using Locke's goal-setting model in Chapter 8 as an explanatory device, how do the goals posted on the wall at Specialized Bicycle likely influence job performance?

7. How important are intrinsic rewards, as defined in Chapter 9, at Specialized Bicycle? Explain.

8. What are the chances that team-based pay, as covered in Chapter 9, would work at Specialized Bicycle? Explain.

9. What can the managers at Specialized Bicycle do to ensure that rewards become positive reinforcement?

Part 3: Group and Social Processes at Specialized Bicycle—One Very Large Cycling Team

Sequence of Activities for Part 3 of This Video Case Study:

1. Read all or portions of Chapters 11–14, as assigned by your instructor.

2. Read the following comments on Specialized Bicycle Components.

3. View Part 3 of the video.

4. Answer questions for Part 3.

Company Publication: "We Are All—Staff, Riders, Retailers—the Life Blood."

Except for tandem bikes, cycling begins at the individual level. One person rides one bike. But teamwork inevitably enters the picture as support teams enable individual riders to stay in the race and hopefully win. Race formats involving teams, such as the famed *Tour de France,* also are very common today. In short, competitive bike racers cannot succeed alone, they need to be part of a high-performance team. Likewise, employees at Specialized Bicycle are members of lots of small teams and one big company-retailer-customer team. Management, like bicycling, is a *team sport*.

Questions for Discussion

1. How can Simon's normative model, as described in Chapter 11, help us better understand decision making at Specialized Bicycle?

2. How can the garbage can model of decision making, as discussed in Chapter 11, help Specialized Bicycle's managers better understand how they make important decisions?

3. In view of the company's slogan "innovate or die," why is it important for all employees at Specialized Bicycle to understand that creativity is a *process* with identifiable steps, rather than a sudden brilliant flash of insight?

4. What *norms,* as covered in Chapter 12, are evident in the video segments you have viewed so far?

5. What are the chances of groupthink occurring at Specialized Bicycle? Explain your reasoning.

6. Using Figure 13–2 as a reference point, what must Specialized Bicycle do to make its team-based structure work properly?

7. What should Specialized Bicycle do to build necessary trust in its "pods" of employees and between its dealers and the company?

8. Given Specialized Bicycle's extensive commitment to cross-functional work groups, called *pods,* is there room for virtual teams and self-managed teams? Explain.

9. What do members of the company's "pods" need to know about managing functional and dysfunctional conflict, as discussed in Chapter 14?

Part 4: Evolving Organizational Processes at Specialized Bicycle— "Innovate or Die."

Sequence of Activities for Part 4 of this Video Case Study:

1. Read all or portions of Chapters 15–18, as assigned by your instructor.
2. Read the following comments on Specialized Bicycle Components.
3. View Part 4 of the video.
4. Answer questions for Part 4.

Ariadne Delon Scott, Sales Support Manager, "You Can Dream Big Here."

In a manner of speaking, company founder Mike Sinyard walks a narrow tightrope as a leader. On the one hand, his legendary status as the creator of mountain bikes can inspire his employees to reach for greatness. On the other hand, such an imposing figure can intimidate and dominate. Just like in bike riding, *balance* is the key.

Questions for Discussion

1. Based on what you have seen and heard, are Specialized Bicycle's organizational culture and structure conducive to free and open communication? Explain.

2. How will the restructuring project, whereby the strategically-important product development group will be housed at headquarters, facilitate effective organizational communication?

3. Which of the nine generic influence tactics listed in Chapter 16 does Mike Sinyard apparently rely upon to get things accomplished at Specialized?

4. Which bases of power does Mike Sinyard apparently rely upon the most?

5. Does company founder and chairman Mike Sinyard deserve to be called an "empowering" manager? Explain.

6. Using Table 17–1 as a guide, would you describe Mike Sinyard as a leader or a manager? Explain.

7. Where would you plot Mike Sinyard's leadership style on the Leadership Grid (Figure 17-3)? Explain.

8. Are founder and chairman Mike Sinyard and president and CEO Tom Albers an effective leadership *team?* Explain.

9. Is Mike Sinyard a transactional or charismatic leader? Explain. What are the potential drawbacks of this particular type of leadership?

10. Are stress and burnout, as defined in Chapter 18, likely to be widespread problems at Specialized Bicycle? Explain.

Endnotes

CHAPTER I

[1] P LaBarre, ed, "What's New, What's Not: David Duffield," *Fast Company,* January 1999, p 80.

[2] As quoted in T A Stewart, "Who Will Run GE?" *Fortune,* January 11, 1999, p 27.

[3] Scott Adams, *The Dilbert Principle* (New York: HarperBusiness, 1996), p 51. Also see A Bryant, "Make That Mr. Dilbert," *Newsweek,* March 22, 1999, pp 46–47.

[4] J Pfeffer and J F Veiga, "Putting People First for Organizational Success," *Academy of Management Executive,* May 1999, p 37.

[5] Adapted from Ibid.

[6] See the brief report on layoffs in the United States in G Koretz, "Quick to Fire and Quick to Hire," *Business Week,* May 31, 1999, p 34. For the case against layoffs, see J R Morris, W F Cascio, and C E Young, "Downsizing After All These Years: Questions and Answers About Who Did It, How Many Did It, and Who Benefited from It," *Organizational Dynamics,* Winter 1999, pp 78–87.

[7] Data from Pfeffer and Veiga, "Putting People First for Organizational Success," p 47.

[8] Learn what the US Postal Service is doing in "Growing Leaders: U.S. Postal Service," *HRMagazine,* February 1999, p 38.

[9] H Mintzberg, "The Manager's Job: Folklore and Fact," *Harvard Business Review,* July–August 1975, p 61. For an alternative perspective, see R J Samuelson, "Why I Am Not a Manager," *Newsweek,* March 22, 1999, p 47.

[10] See, for example, H Mintzberg, "Managerial Work: Analysis from Observation," *Management Science,* October 1971, pp B97–B110; and F Luthans, "Successful vs. Effective Real Managers," *Academy of Management Executive,* May 1988, pp 127–32. For an instructive critique of the structured observation method, see M J Martinko and W L Gardner, "Beyond Structured Observation: Methodological Issues and New Directions," *Academy of Management Review,* October 1985, pp 676–95. Also see N Fondas, "A Behavioral Job Description for Managers," *Organizational Dynamics,* Summer 1992, pp 47–58.

[11] See L B Kurke and H E Aldrich, "Mintzberg Was Right!: A Replication and Extension of *The Nature of Managerial Work,*" *Management Science,* August 1983, pp 975–84.

[12] For example, see A I Kraut, P R Pedigo, D D McKenna, and M D Dunnette, "The Role of the Manager: What's Really Important in Different Management Jobs," *Academy of Management Executive,* November 1989, pp 286–93; J C McCune, "Brave New World," *Management Review,* October 1997, pp 11–14; and N H Woodward, "The Coming of the X Managers," *HRMagazine,* March 1999, pp 74–80.

[13] Validation studies can be found in E Van Velsor and J B Leslie, *Feedback to Managers, Volume II: A Review and Comparison of Sixteen Multi-Rater Feedback Instruments* (Greensboro, NC: Center for Creative Leadership, 1991); and F Shipper, "A Study of the Psychometric Properties of the Managerial Skill Scales of the Survey of Management Practices," *Educational and Psychological Measurement,* June 1995, pp 468–79.

[14] For example, see S B Parry, "Just What Is a Competency? (And Why Should You Care?)" *Training,* June 1998, pp 58–64.

[15] See F Shipper, "Mastery and Frequency of Managerial Behaviors Relative to Sub-Unit Effectiveness," *Human Relations,* April 1991, pp 371–88.

[16] Ibid.

[17] Data from F Shipper, "A Study of Managerial Skills of Women and Men and Their Impact on Employees' Attitudes and Career Success in a Nontraditional Organization," paper presented at the Academy of Management Meeting, August 1994, Dallas, Texas. The same outcome for on-the-job studies is reported in A H Eagly and B T Johnson, "Gender and Leadership Style: A Meta-Analysis," *Psychological Bulletin,* September 1990, pp 233–56.

[18] For instance, see J B Rosener, "Ways Women Lead," *Harvard Business Review,* November–December 1990, pp 119–25; and C Lee, "The Feminization of Management," *Training,* November 1994, pp 25–31.

[19] See, for example, N Munk, "The New Organization Man," *Fortune,* March 16, 1998, pp 62–74; D T Hall and J E Moss, "The New Protean Career Contract: Helping Organizations and Employees Adapt," *Organizational Dynamics,* Winter 1998, pp 22–37; N Munk, "Finished at Forty," *Fortune,* February 1, 1999, pp 50–66; and B E Bellesi, "The Changing American Workforce," *Management Review,* March 1999, p 9. For a collection of eight articles on the related topic of psychological contracts, see the special issue of *Journal of Organizational Behavior,* 1998.

[20] Drawn from W J Byron, "Coming to Terms with the New Corporate Contract," *Business Horizons,* January–February 1995, pp 8–15.

[21] C Lee, "Trust," *Training,* January 1997, p 32.

[22] See T J Tetenbaum, "Shifting Paradigms: From Newton to Chaos," *Organizational Dynamics,* Spring 1998, pp 21–32; and R W Oliver, *The Shape of Things to Come* (New York: McGraw-Hill, 1999).

[23] Essential sources on reengineering are M Hammer and J Champy, *Reengineering the Corporation: A Manifesto for Business Revolution* (New York: HarperCollins, 1993); and J Champy, *Reengineering Management: The Mandate for New Leadership* (New York: HarperCollins, 1995). Also see "Anything Worth Doing Is Worth Doing from Scratch," *Inc.,* May 18, 1999 (20th Anniversary Issue), pp 51–52.

[24] For thoughtful discussion, see G G Dess, A M A Rasheed, K J McLaughlin, and R L Priem, "The New Corporate Architecture," *Academy of Management Executive,* August 1995, pp 7–20.

[25] See, for example, "The Dreaded 'E Word,'" *Training,* September 1998, p 19; K Dover, "Avoiding Empowerment Traps," *Management Review,* January 1999, pp 51–55; and G B Weathersby, "Management May Never Be the Same," *Management Review,* February 1999, p 5. A brief case study of empowerment in action can be found in C Dahle, "Big Learning, Fast Futures," *Fast Company,* June 1999, pp 46, 48.

[26] See J B Miner, "The Validity and Usefulness of Theories in an Emerging Organizational Science," *Academy of Management Review,* April 1984, pp 296–306.

[27] B S Lawrence, "Historical Perspective: Using the Past to Study the Present," *Academy of Management Review,* April 1984, p 307.

[28] Evidence indicating that the original conclusions of the famous Hawthorne studies were unjustified may be found in R G Greenwood, A A Bolton, and R A Greenwood, "Hawthorne a Half Century Later: Relay Assembly Participants Remember," *Journal of Management,* Fall–Winter 1983, pp 217–31; and R H Franke and J D Kaul, "The Hawthorne Experiments: First Statistical Interpretation," *American Sociological Review,* October 1978, pp 623–43. For a positive interpretation of the Hawthorne studies, see J A Sonnenfeld, "Shedding Light on the Hawthorne Studies," *Journal of Occupational Behaviour,* April 1985, pp 111–30.

[29] See M Parker Follett, *Freedom and Coordination* (London: Management Publications Trust, 1949).

[30] See D McGregor, *The Human Side of Enterprise* (New York: McGraw-Hill, 1960).

[31] J Hall, "Americans Know How to Be Productive if Managers Will Let Them," *Organizational Dynamics,* Winter 1994, p 38.

[32] See, for example, R Zemke, "TQM: Fatally Flawed or Simply Unfocused?" *Training,* October 1992, p 8.

33 See S Alsop, "The Dawn of E-Service," *Fortune,* November 9, 1998, p 243; L Grant, "Customer Service Key to Web Success," *USA Today,* February 4, 1999, p 12B; A Slywotzky, "How Digital Is Your Company?" *Fast Company,* February–March 1999, pp 94–113; and T Merriden, "Measured for Success," *Management Review,* April 1999, pp 27–32.

34 L Wah, "The Almighty Customer," *Management Review,* February 1999, p 17.

35 Data from "AMA Global Survey on Key Business Issues," *Management Review,* December 1998, p 30. Also see "1999 Annual Survey: Corporate Concerns," *Management Review,* March 1999, pp 55–56.

36 Instructive background articles on TQM are R Zemke, "A Bluffer's Guide to TQM," *Training,* April 1993, pp 48–55; R R Gehani, "Quality Value-Chain: A Meta-Synthesis of Frontiers of Quality Movement," *Academy of Management Executive,* May 1993, pp 29–42; P Mears, "How to Stop Talking About, and Begin Progress Toward, Total Quality Management," *Business Horizons,* May–June 1993, pp 11–14; and the Total Quality Special Issue of *Academy of Management Review,* July 1994.

37 M Sashkin and K J Kiser, *Putting Total Quality Management to Work* (San Francisco: Berrett-Koehler, 1993), p 39.

38 R J Schonberger, "Total Quality Management Cuts a Broad Swath—Through Manufacturing and Beyond," *Organizational Dynamics,* Spring 1992, p 18. Also see K Y Kim, J G Miller, and J Heineke, "Mastering the Quality Staircase, Step by Step," *Business Horizons,* January–February 1997, pp 17–21; R Bell and B Keys, "A Conversation with Curt W Reimann on the Background and Future of the Baldrige Award," *Organizational Dynamics,* Spring 1998, pp 51–61; and B Kasanoff, "Are You Ready for Mass Customization?" *Training,* May 1998, pp 70–78.

39 See R K Reger, L T Gustafson, S M Demarie, and J V Mullane, "Reframing the Organization: Why Implementing Total Quality Is Easier Said than Done," *Academy of Management Review,* July 1994, pp 565–84.

40 Deming's landmark work is W E Deming, *Out of the Crisis* (Cambridge, MA: MIT, 1986).

41 See M Trumbull, "What Is Total Quality Management?" *The Christian Science Monitor,* May 3, 1993, p 12; and J Hillkirk, "World-Famous Quality Expert Dead at 93," *USA Today,* December 21, 1993, pp 1B–2B.

42 Based on discussion in M Walton, *Deming Management at Work* (New York: Putnam/Perigee, 1990).

43 Ibid., p 20.

44 Adapted from D E Bowen and E E Lawler III "Total Quality-Oriented Human Resources Management," *Organizational Dynamics,* Spring 1992, pp 29–41.

45 See T F Rienzo, "Planning Deming Management for Service Organizations," *Business Horizons,* May–June 1993, pp 19–29. Also see M R Yilmaz and S Chatterjee, "Deming and the Quality of Software Development," *Business Horizons,* November–December 1997, pp 51–58.

46 For example, see J Shea and D Gobeli, "TQM: The Experiences of Ten Small Businesses," *Business Horizons,* January–February 1995, pp 71–77; T L Zeller and D M Gillis, "Achieving Market Excellence through Quality: The Case of Ford Motor Company," *Business Horizons,* May–June 1995, pp 23–31; and P McLagan and C Nel, "A New Leadership Style for Genuine Total Quality," *Journal for Quality and Participation,* June 1996, pp 14–16.

47 H L Tosi, Jr., and J W Slocum, Jr., "Contingency Theory: Some Suggested Directions," *Journal of Management,* Spring 1984, p 9.

48 For empirical evidence in a cross-cultural study, see D I Jung and B J Avolio, "Effects of Leadership Style and Followers' Cultural Orientation on Performance in Groups and Individual Task Conditions," *Academy of Management Journal,* April 1999, pp 208–18.

49 M Chase, "You Think Your Pain Is the Boss's Fault? It's Really Bacteria," *The Wall Street Journal,* September 11, 1995, p B1. Reprinted by permission of *The Wall Street Journal,* © 1995 Dow Jones & Company, Inc. All Rights Reserved Worldwide. Also see "Tracing Ulcers to a Bacterial Infection," *USA Today,* February 26, 1998, p 6D.

50 See R L Daft, "Learning the Craft of Organizational Research," *Academy of Management Review,* October 1983, pp 539–46.

51 See K E Weick, "Theory Construction as Disciplined Imagination," *Academy of Management Review,* October 1989, pp 516–31. Also see D A Whetten's article in the same issue, pp 490–95.

52 Theory-focused versus problem-focused research is discussed in K E Weick, "Agenda Setting in Organizational Behavior: A Theory-Focused Approach," *Journal of Management Inquiry,* September 1992, pp 171–82. Also see K J Klein, H Tosi, and A A Cannella, Jr., "Multilevel Theory Building: Benefits, Barriers, and New Developments," *Academy of Management Review,* April 1999, pp 243–48. (Note: The special forum on multilevel theory building in the April 1999 issue of *Academy of Management Review* includes an additional five articles.)

53 For instance, see M R Buckley, G R Ferris, H J Bernardin, and M G Harvey, "The Disconnect between the Science and Practice of Management," *Business Horizons,* March–April 1998, pp 31–38.

54 Complete discussion of this technique can be found in J E Hunter, F L Schmidt, and G B Jackson, *Meta-Analysis. Cumulating Research Findings across Studies* (Beverly Hills, CA: Sage Publications, 1982); and J E Hunter and F L Schmidt, *Methods of Meta-Analysis: Correcting Error and Bias in Research Findings* (Newbury Park, CA: Sage Publications, 1990). Also see R Hutter Epstein, "The Number-Crunchers Drugmakers Fear and Love," *Business Week,* August 22, 1994, pp 70–71.

55 Limitations of meta-analysis technique are discussed in P Bobko and E F Stone-Romero, "Meta-Analysis May Be Another Useful Tool, But It Is Not a Panacea," in *Research in Personnel and Human Resources Management,* vol. 16, ed G R Ferris (Stamford, CT: JAI Press, 1998), pp 359–97.

56 For an interesting debate about the use of students as subjects, see J Greenberg, "The College Sophomore as Guinea Pig: Setting the Record Straight," *Academy of Management Review,* January 1987, pp 157–59; and M E Gordon, L A Slade, and N Schmitt, "Student Guinea Pigs: Porcine Predictors and Particularistic Phenomena," *Academy of Management Review,* January 1987, pp 160–63.

57 Good discussions of case studies can be found in A S Lee, "Case Studies as Natural Experiments," *Human Relations,* February 1989, pp 117–37; and K M Eisenhardt, "Building Theories from Case Study Research," *Academy of Management Review,* October 1989, pp 532–50. The case survey technique is discussed in R Larsson, "Case Survey Methodology: Analysis of Patterns across Case Studies," *Academy of Management Journal,* December 1993, pp 1515–46.

58 Based on discussion found in J M Beyer and H M Trice, "The Utilization Process: A Conceptual Framework and Synthesis of Empirical Findings," *Administrative Science Quarterly,* December 1982, pp 591–622.

59 See J J Martocchio, "Age-Related Differences in Employee Absenteeism: A Meta-Analysis," *Psychology & Aging,* December 1989, pp 409–14.

60 L Wah, "Making Knowledge Stick," *Management Review,* May 1999, p 25. For more on knowledge management, see R Nurmi, "Knowledge-Intensive Firms," *Business Horizons,* May–June 1998, pp 26–32; R A Spinello, "The Knowledge Chain," *Business Horizons,* November–December 1998, pp 4–14; D Stamps, "Is Knowledge Management a Fad?" *Training,* March 1999, pp 36–42; and L Wah, "Behind the Buzz," *Management Review,* April 1999, pp 16–26.

61 Steve Hamm, "I'm Trying to Let Other People Dive in Before I Do," *Business Week,* May 17, 1999, pp 110–11.

62 These research results are discussed in detail in J B Miner and N R Smith, "Decline and Stabilization of Managerial Motivation Over a 20-Year Period," *Journal of Applied Psychology,* June 1982, pp 297–305.

63 See J B Miner, J M Wachtel, and B Ebrahimi, "The Managerial Motivation of Potential Managers in the United States and Other Countries of the World: Implications for National Competitiveness and the Productivity Problem," in *Advances in International Comparative Management,* vol. 4, ed B Prasad (Greenwich, CT: JAI Press, 1989), pp 147–70; and J B Miner, C C Chen, and K C Yu, "Theory Testing under Adverse Conditions: Motivation to Manage in the People's Republic of China," *Journal of Applied Psychology,* June 1991, pp 343–49.

64 See J B Miner, B Ebrahimi, and J M Wachtel, "How Deficiencies in Motivation to Manage Contribute to the United States' Competitiveness

Problem (and What Can Be Done about It)," *Human Resource Management,* Fall 1995, pp 363–87.
[65] Based on K M Bartol and D C Martin, "Managerial Motivation among MBA Students: A Longitudinal Assessment," *Journal of Occupational Psychology,* March 1987, pp 1–12.

LEARNING MODULE A

[1] See "Do Americans Trust Media Polls?" *USA Today,* May 18, 1999, p 1A.
[2] This study is discussed in A Finkbeiner, "Some Science Is Baloney; Learn to Tell the Difference," *USA Today,* September 11, 1997, p 15A.
[3] "Buckle Up in the Rear Seat?" *University of California, Berkeley Wellness Letter,* August 1987, p 1.
[4] F N Kerlinger, *Foundations of Behavioral Research* (New York: Holt, Rinehart & Winston, 1973), p 18. (Emphasis added.)
[5] See A H Winefield and M Tiggemann, "Employment Status and Psychological Well-Being: A Longitudinal Study," *Journal of Applied Psychology,* August 1990, pp 455–59.
[6] See P J Frost and R E Stablein, eds, *Doing Exemplary Research* (Newbury Park, CA: Sage, 1992); and S Begley, "The Meaning of Junk," *Newsweek,* March 22, 1993, pp 62–64.
[7] S S Stevens, "Mathematics, Measurement, and Psychophysics," in *Handbook of Experimental Psychology,* ed S S Stevens (New York: John Wiley & Sons, 1951), p 1.
[8] A thorough discussion of the importance of measurement is provided by D P Schwab, "Construct Validity in Organizational Behavior," in *Research in Organizational Behavior,* eds B M Staw and L L Cummings (Greenwich, CT: JAI Press, 1980), pp 3–43.
[9] See J L Komaki, "Toward Effective Supervision: An Operant Analysis and Comparison of Managers at Work," *Journal of Applied Psychology,* May 1986, pp 270–79. Results from the sailing study can be found in J L Komaki, M L Desselles, and E D Bowman, "Definitely Not a Breeze: Extending an Operant Model of Effective Supervision to Teams," *Journal of Applied Psychology,* June 1989, pp 522–29.
[10] A thorough discussion of the pros and cons of using surveys or questionnaires is provided by J A Krosnick, "Survey Research," in *Annual Review of Psychology,* eds J T Spence, J M Darley, and D J Foss (Palo Alto, CA: 1999), pp 537–67.
[11] See F L Schmidt and M Rader, "Exploring the Boundary Conditions for Interview Validity: Meta-Analytic Validity Findings for a New Interview Type," *Personnel Psychology,* Summer 1999, pp 445–64; and M A McDaniel, D Whetzel, F L Schmidt, and S Maurer, "The Validity of Employment Interviews: A Comprehensive Review and Meta-Analysis," *Journal of Applied Psychology,* August 1994, pp 599–616.
[12] A complete discussion of research methods is provided by T D Cook and D T Campbell, *Quasi-Experimentation: Design & Analysis Issues for Field Settings* (Chicago: Rand McNally, 1979).
[13] Ibid.
[14] For a thorough discussion of the guidelines for conducting good research, see L Wilkinson, "Statistical Methods in Psychology Journals," *American Psychologist,* August 1999, pp 594–604.
[15] This discussion is based on material presented in the *Publication Manual of the American Psychological Association,* 4th ed (Washington, DC: American Psychological Association, 1994).
[16] Ibid., p 5.
[17] "Buckle Up in the Rear Seat?"

CHAPTER 2

[1] Excerpted from E Thornton, "Make Way for Women with Welding Guns: Japanese Women Are Winning More Rights—and Factory Jobs," *Business Week,* April 19, 1999, p 54.
[2] Details of this example were taken from S McCartney, "Tension in the Air: What Some Call Racist at American Eagle, Others Say Was in Jest," *The Wall Street Journal,* April 20, 1999, pp A1, A8.
[3] Ibid.

[4] This discussion is based on material in R R Thomas, Jr, *Redefining Diversity* (New York: AMACOM, 1996), pp 4–9.
[5] The following discussion is based on L Gardenswartz and A Rowe, *Diverse Teams at Work* (New York: McGraw-Hill, 1994), pp 31–57.
[6] This distinction is made by M Loden, *Implementing Diversity* (Chicago: Irwin, 1996).
[7] H Collingwood, "Who Handles a Diverse Work Force Best?" *Working Women,* February 1996, p 25.
[8] See A Karr, "Work Week: A Special News Report about Life on the Job—and Trends Taking Shape There," *The Wall Street Journal,* June 1, 1999, p A1.
[9] See M Minehan, "Islam's Growth Affects Workplace Policies," *HRMagazine,* November 1998, p 216.
[10] See R R Thomas, Jr, "From Affirmative Action to Affirming Diversity," *Harvard Business Review,* March–April 1990, pp 107–17.
[11] Opposition to affirmative action was investigated by J Swim and D Miller, "White Guilt: Its Antecedents and Consequences for Attitudes toward Affirmative Action," *Personality and Social Psychology Bulletin,* April 1999, pp 500–14; and J D Leck, D M Saunders, and M Charbonneau, "Affirmative Action Programs: An Organizational Justice Perspective," *Journal of Organizational Behavior,* January 1996, pp 79–89.
[12] For a thorough review of relevant research, see M E Heilman, "Affirmative Action: Some Unintended Consequences for Working Women," in *Research in Organizational Behavior,* vol 16, eds B M Staw and L L Cummings (Greenwich, CT: JAI Press, 1994), pp 125–69.
[13] Results from this study can be found in M E Heilman, W S Battle, C E Keller, and R A Lee, "Type of Affirmative Action Policy: A Determinant of Reactions to Sex-Based Preferential Selection?" *Journal of Applied Psychology,* April 1998, pp 190–205.
[14] See J Kaufman, "How Workplaces May Look without Affirmative Action," *The Wall Street Journal,* March 20, 1995, pp B1, B7.
[15] Valuing diversity is discussed by R R Thomas, Jr, *Beyond Race and Gender* (New York: American Management Association, 1991).
[16] Different types of diversity training programs are discussed by P L Nemetz and S L Christensen, "The Challenge of Cultural Diversity: Harnessing a Diversity of Views to Understand Multiculturalism," *Academy of Management Review,* April 1996, pp 434–62.
[17] See P Digh, "Coming to Terms with Diversity," *HRMagazine,* November 1998, pp 117–20.
[18] See S Rynes and B Rosen, "A Field Survey of Factors Affecting the Adoption and Perceived Success of Diversity Training," *Personnel Psychology,* Summer 1995, pp 247–70.
[19] J Crockett, "Diversity as a Business Strategy," *Management Review,* May 1999, p 62.
[20] Results can be found in Rynes and Rosen, "A Field Survey of Factors Affecting the Adoption and Perceived Success of Diversity Training."
[21] A M Morrison, *The New Leaders: Guidelines on Leadership Diversity in America* (San Francisco: Jossey-Bass, 1992), p 78.
[22] Results can be found in N London-Vargas, *Faces of Diversity* (New York: Vantage Press, 1999).
[23] Crockett, "Diversity as a Business Strategy."
[24] R W Judy, "America's Worker Dearth: The US Labor Market Is Going to Stay Tight, and the Winners Will Learn to Cope with It," *Outlook,* Summer 1998, pp 24–28.
[25] D Jones, "Lower Birth Rate Drains Labor Pool," *USA Today,* April 12, 1999, p B1.
[26] Data were obtained from H N Fullerton, Jr, "Employment Projections: Entrants to the Labor Force by Sex, Race, and Hispanic Origin," *Bureau of Labor Statistics Online,* Table 6, January 1998 (http://stats.bls.gov/emptab3.htm).
[27] Earning statistics were obtained from "Table 3: Median Usual Weekly Earnings of Full-Time Wage and Salary Workers by Occupation and Sex, Quarterly Averages, not Seasonally Adjusted," *Bureau of Labor Statistics,* April 15, 1999 (http://stats.bls.gov/news.release/wkyeng.t03.htm).
[28] Results can be found in K S Lyness and D E Thompson, "Above the Glass Ceiling: A Comparison of Matched Samples of Female and Male Executives," *Journal of Applied Psychology,* June 1997, pp 359–75.

[29] This study was conducted by K S Lyness and M K Judiesch, "Are Women More Likely to Be Hired or Promoted into Management Positions?" *Journal of Vocational Behavior,* February 1999, pp 158–73.

[30] Statistics were obtained from "Catalyst Census: Equal Pay and Highest Executive Ranks Still Elude Women," *CWBN Resources-Catalyst Reports,* November 9, 1998 (http://www.cdnbizwomen.com/resources/census5.shtm).

[31] See C Daniels, "The Global Glass Ceiling: And Ten Women Who Broke Through It," *Fortune,* October 12, 1998, pp 102–3.

[32] Information on women-owned businesses can be found in P Thomas, "Closing the Gender Gap," *The Wall Street Journal,* May 24, 1999, p R12.

[33] Details of this study can be found in B R Ragins, B Townsend, and M Mattis, "Gender Gap in the Executive Suite: CEOs and Female Executives Report on Breaking the Glass Ceiling," *Academy of Management Executive,* February 1998, pp 28–42.

[34] Here are the ranks for each career strategy: Strategy 1 = 12; Strategy 2 = 6; Strategy 3 = 5; Strategy 4 = 11; Strategy 5 = 9; Strategy 6 = 3; Strategy 7 = 10; Strategy 8 = 1; Strategy 9 = 7; Strategy 10 = 8; Strategy 11 = 4; Strategy 12 = 2; and Strategy 13 = 13.

[35] "Employed White, Black, and Hispanic-Origin Workers by Sex, Occupation, Class of Worker, and Full- or Part-Time Status," *Bureau of Labor Statistics,* February 13, 1997 (http://ferret.bls.census.gov/macro/171996/empearn/aa12.txt).

[36] See D Jones, "African-Americans Take Reins at 'Fortune' Firms," *USA Today,* April 27, 1999, pp 1B, 2B.

[37] Data were reported in G D Paulin, "A Growing Market: Expenditures by Hispanic Consumers," *Monthly Labor Review,* March 1998, pp 3–21.

[38] See S Kravetz, "Work Week: A Special News Report about Life on the Job—And Trends Taking Shape There," *The Wall Street Journal,* April 13, 1999, p. A1; and C Comeau-Kirschner, "Navigating the Roadblocks," *Management Review,* May 1999, p 8.

[39] See Y F Niemann and J F Dovidio, "Relationship of Solo Status, Academic Rank, and Perceived Distinctiveness to Job Satisfaction of Racial/Ethnic Minorities," *Journal of Applied Psychology,* February 1998, pp 55–71; J I Sanchez and P Brock, "Outcomes of Perceived Discrimination among Hispanic Employees: Is Diversity Management a Luxury or a Necessity?" *Academy of Management Journal,* June 1996, pp 704–19; and T H Cox, Jr, and J A Finley, "An Analysis of Work Specialization and Organization Level as Dimensions of Workforce Diversity," in *Diversity in Organizations,* eds M M Chemers, S Oskamp, and M A Costanzo (Thousand Oaks, CA: Sage Publications, 1995), pp 62–88.

[40] See "No 630. Civilian Labor Force and Participation Rates, by Educational Attainment, Sex, Race, and Hispanic Origin: 1992 to 1994," *Statistical Abstract of the United States,* September 1995, p 401.

[41] These statistics were drawn from E S Rubenstein, "The College Payoff Illusion," *American Outlook,* Fall 1998, pp 14–18.

[42] See D Dooley and J Prause, "Underemployment and Alcohol Misuse in the National Longitudinal Survey of Youth," *Journal of Studies on Alcohol,* November 1998, pp 669–80; and D C Feldman, "The Nature, Antecedents and Consequences of Underemployment," *Journal of Management,* 1966, pp 385–407.

[43] The relationship between income and education is discussed by E S Rubenstein, "The College Payoff Illusion"; and R W Judy and C D'Amico, *Workforce 2020* (Indianapolis, IN: Hudson Institute, 1997).

[44] See J C Day and A E Curry, "School Enrollment—Social and Economic Characteristics of Students: October 1996 (Update)," *Current Population Reports,* October 1996 (http://www.census.gov); and "Facts on Literacy," *National Literacy Facts,* August 27, 1998 (http://www.svs.net/wpci/Litfacts.htm).

[45] "Facts on Literacy."

[46] See "Literacy in America and the District," *Washington Literacy Council,* June 4, 1999 (http://www.erols.com/washlc/litfats/htm); and T L Smith, "The Resource Center: Finding Solutions for Illiteracy," *HRFocus,* February 1995, p 7.

[47] See A R Karr, "Work Week: A Special News Report about Life on the Job—And Trends Taking Shape There," *The Wall Street Journal,* May 18, 1999, p A1.

[48] See H London, "The Workforce, Education, and the Nation's Future," Summer 1998 (http://www.hudson.org/american_outlook/articles_sm98/london.htm).

[49] For a discussion of what women want from employers, see N Enbar, "Corporate Culture: What Do Women Want? Ask 'Em," *Business Week,* March 29, 1999, p 8.

[50] Employee training is discussed by C D'Amico, "Got Skills?" *American Outlook,* Fall 1998, pp 36–38.

[51] See R Balu, "Work Week: A Special Report about Life on the Job—And Trends Taking Shape There," *The Wall Street Journal,* April 27, 1999, p A1.

[52] P M Elsass and D A Ralston, "Individual Responses to the Stress of Career Plateauing," *Journal of Management,* Spring 1989, p 35.

[53] Supportive findings can be found in D R Ettington, "Successful Career Plateauing," *Journal of Vocational Behavior,* February 1998, pp 72–88; and N Nicholson, "Purgatory or Place of Safety? The Managerial Plateau and Organizational Agegrading," *Human Relations,* December 1993, pp 1369–89.

[54] Strategies for dealing with an aging workforce are discussed by R W Judy, "The Coming Retirement Torrent," *American Outlook,* Fall 1998, pp 28–31.

[55] Statistics were reported in S Shellenbarger, "Work & Family: Planning Ahead for the Inevitable, An Elder's Illness," *The Wall Street Journal,* March 22, 1995, p B1.

[56] See K Walter, "Elder Care Obligations Challenge the Next Generation," *HRMagazine,* July 1996, pp 98–103.

[57] Discrimination lawsuits are discussed by S Steinhauser, "Is Your Corporate Culture in Need of an Overhaul?" *HRMagazine,* July 1998, pp 87–91.

[58] Lactation programs are discussed by K Tyler, "Got Milk?" *HRMagazine,* March 1999, pp 68–73.

[59] A A Johnson, "The Business Case for Work-Family Programs," *Journal of Accountancy,* August 1995, pp 55–56.

[60] This research is summarized in F J Milliken and L L Martins, "Searching for Common Threads: Understanding the Multiple Effects of Diversity in Organizational Groups," *Academy of Management Review,* April 1996, pp 402–33; and T H Cox, Jr, and J A Finley, "An Analysis of Work Specialization and Organization Level as Dimensions of Workforce Diversity," in *Diversity in Organizations,* eds M M Chemers, S Oskamp, and M A Costanzo (Thousand Oaks, CA: Sage Publications, 1995), pp 62–88.

[61] Research on gay and lesbian employees can be found in C Waldo, "Working in a Majority Context: A Structural Model of Heterosexism as Minority Stress in the Workplace," *Journal of Counseling Psychology,* April 1999, pp 218–32; and J M Croteau, "Research on the Work Experiences of Lesbian, Gay, and Bisexual People: An Integrative Review of Methodology and Findings," *Journal of Vocational Behavior,* April 1996, pp 195–209.

[62] Results can be found in B E Whitley, Jr, and M E Kite, "Sex Differences in Attitudes toward Homosexuality: A Comment on Oliver and Hyde (1993)," *Psychological Bulletin,* January 1995, pp 146–54.

[63] *The Human Rights Campaign Manual,* 1998 (http://www.hrc.org/manual.html).

[64] See P Digh, "People with Disabilities Show What They Can Do," *HRMagazine,* June 1998, pp 141–45; and D Kruse, "Persons with Disabilities: Demographic, Income, and Health Care Characteristics, 1993," *Monthly Labor Review,* September 1998, pp 13–22.

[65] Accommodation statistics are discussed by Digh, "People with Disabilities Show What They Can Do."

[66] J T Ferguson and W R Johnston, "Managing Diversity," *Mortgage Banking,* September 1995, p 36.

[67] C Y Coleman, "Attention, Shoppers: Target Makes a Play for Minority Group Sears Has Cultivated," *The Wall Street Journal,* April 12, 1999, p A1.

[68] See R W Thompson, "Diversity among Managers Translates into Profitability," *HRMagazine,* April 1999, p 10.

[69] For research on TMT demographics, see K Y Williams, "Demography and Diversity in Organizations: A Review of 100 Years of Research," in *Research in Organizational Behavior,* vol 20, eds B M Staw and

L L Cummings (Greenwich, CT: JAI Press, 1998), pp 77–140; C Miller, L Burke, and W Glick, "Cognitive Diversity among Upper-Echelon Executives: Implications for Strategic Decision Processes," *Strategic Management Journal*, 1998, pp 39–58; and S B Lawrence, "The Black Box of Organizational Demography," *Organization Science*, 1997, pp 61–72.

[70] See R Moss-Kanter, *The Change Masters* (New York: Simon and Schuster, 1983); and L K Larkey, "Toward a Theory of Communicative Interactions in Culturally Diverse Workgroups," *Academy of Management Review*, April 1996, pp 463–91.

[71] See Williams, "Demography and Diversity in Organizations: A Review of 100 Years of Research."

[72] Ibid.

[73] See W E Watson, K Kumar, and L K Michaelson, "Cultural Diversity's Impact on Interaction Process and Performance: Comparing Homogeneous and Diverse Task Groups," *Academy of Management Journal*, June 1993, pp 590–602; and V I Sessa and S E Jackson, "Diversity in Decision-Making Teams: All Differences Are Not Created Equal," in *Diversity in Organizations*, eds M M Chemers, S Oskamp, and M A Costanzo (Thousand Oaks, CA: Sage Publications, 1995), pp 133–56.

[74] The relationship between conflict and stages of group development is discussed by D C Lau and J K Murnighan, "Demographic Diversity and Faultlines: The Compositional Dynamics of Organizational Groups," *Academy of Management Review*, April 1998, pp 325–40.

[75] See J A Chatman, J T Polzer, S G Barsade, and M A Neale, "Being Different Yet Feeling Similar: The Influence of Demographic Composition and Organizational Culture on Work Processes and Outcomes," *Administrative Science Quarterly*, December 1998, pp 749–80; and D A Harrison, K H Price, and M P Bell, "Beyond Relational Demography: Time and the Effects of Surface-and Deep-Level Diversity on Work Group Cohesion," *Academy of Management Journal*, February 1998, pp 96–107.

[76] These barriers were taken from discussions in Loden, *Implementing Diversity;* E E Spragins, "Benchmark: The Diverse Work Force," *Inc.*, January 1993, p 33; and Morrison, *The New Leaders: Guidelines on Leadership Diversity in America.*

[77] For a discussion of ethnocentrism, see M Kiselica, "Confronting My Own Ethnocentrism and Racism: A Process of Pain and Growth," *Journal of Counseling & Development*, Winter 1999, pp 14–17; and S Perreault and R Y Bourhis, "Ethnocentrism, Social Identification, and Discrimination," *Personality & Social Psychology Bulletin*, January 1999, pp 92–103.

[78] See the related discussion in G R Ferris, D D Frink, D P S Bhawuk, and D C Gilmore, "Reactions of Diverse Groups to Politics in the Workplace," *Journal of Management*, 1996, pp 23–44.

[79] This discussion is based on Thomas, *Redefining Diversity.*

[80] D J Gaiter, "Eating Crow: How Shoney's, Belted by a Lawsuit, Found the Path to Diversity," *The Wall Street Journal*, April 16, 1996, pp A1, A11.

[81] Excerpted from P Dass and B Parker, "Strategies for Managing Human Resource Diversity: From Resistance to Learning," *Academy of Management Executive*, May 1999, p 69.

[82] Gaiter, "Eating Crow: How Shoney's, Belted by a Lawsuit, Found the Path to Diversity."

[83] Dass and Parker, "Strategies for Managing Human Resource Diversity: From Resistance to Learning," p. 73.

[84] Excerpted from S Branch, "The 100 Best Companies to Work for in America," *Fortune*, January 11, 1999, pp 121, 130, 134.

[85] For complete details and results from this study, see Morrison, *The New Leaders: Guidelines on Leadership Diversity in America.*

[86] A Karr, "Work Week: A Special News Report about Life on the Job—And Trends Taking Shape There," *The Wall Street Journal*, March 9, 1999, p A1.

[87] Results are presented in P Digh, "The Next Challenge: Holding People Accountable," *HRMagazine*, October 1998, pp 63–69.

[88] Ibid, pp 66–67.

[89] Empirical support is provided by H Ibarra, "Race, Opportunity, and Diversity of Social Circles in Managerial Networks," *Academy of Management Journal*, June 1995, pp 673–703; and P J Ohlott, M N Ruderman, and C D McCauley, "Gender Differences in Managers' Developmental Job Experiences," *Academy of Management Journal*, February 1994, pp 46–67.

[90] R Kazel, "Hotel Speaks Employees' Languages," *Business Insurance*, November 24, 1997, p 14.

[91] Excerpted from M Adams, "Building a Rainbow, One Stripe at a Time," *HRMagazine*, August 1998, p 73.

[92] Reprinted by permission of *Harvard Business Review.* An excerpt from "Diversity and Competitive Advantage at Merck" by R V Gilmartin, January–February 1999. Copyright © 1999 by the President and Fellows of Harvard College; all rights reserved.

[93] This exercise was modified from Gardenswartz and Rowe, *Diverse Teams at Work* (New York: McGraw-Hill, 1994), pp 60–61 © 1994. Reproduced with permission of The McGraw-Hill Companies.

CHAPTER 3

[1] Excerpted from C Yang and P Elstrom, "Doc Ebbers' Miracle Diet," *Business Week*, March 1, 1999, pp 58, 60.

[2] For a comprehensive review of recent research, see D R Denison, "What IS the Difference between Organizational Culture and Organizational Climate? A Native's Point of View on a Decade of Paradigm Wars," *Academy of Management Review*, July 1996, pp 619–54.

[3] E H Schein, "Culture: The Missing Concept in Organization Studies," *Administrative Science Quarterly*, June 1996, p 236.

[4] This discussion is based on E H Schein, *Organizational Culture and Leadership*, 2nd ed (San Francisco: Jossey-Bass, 1992), pp 16–48.

[5] Q Hardy, "Strained Relations: A Software Star Sees Its Family Culture Turn Dysfunctional," *The Wall Street Journal*, May 9, 1999, p A1.

[6] S H Schwartz, "Universals in the Content and Structure of Values: Theoretical Advances and Empirical Tests in 20 Countries," in *Advances in Experimental Social Psychology*, ed M P Zanna (New York: Academic Press, 1992), p 4.

[7] The discussion between espoused and enacted values is based on Schein, *Organizational Culture and Leadership.*

[8] See E Shapiro, "Time Warner Defines, Defends System of Values," *The Wall Street Journal*, March 9, 1999, pp B1, B4.

[9] Results can be found in S Clarke, "Perceptions of Organizational Safety: Implications for the Development of Safety Culture," *Journal of Organizational Behavior*, March 1999, pp 185–98.

[10] See Schwartz, "Universals in the Content and Structure of Values: Theoretical Advances and Empirical Tests in 20 Countries."

[11] Excerpted from S L Payne, "Recognizing and Reducing Transcultural Ethical Tension," *The Academy of Management Executive*, August 1998, p 84.

[12] This typology and related discussion was derived from B Kabanoff and J Holt, "Changes in the Espoused Values of Australian Organizations 1986–1990," *Journal of Organizational Behavior*, May 1996, pp 201–19.

[13] For an example of profiling organizational values see T J Kalliath, A C Bluedorn, and D F Gillespie, "A Confirmatory Factor Analyses of the Competing Values Instrument," *Educational and Psychological Measurement*, February 1999, pp 143–58.

[14] See T J Galpin, *The Human Side of Change* (San Francisco: Jossey-Bass, 1996); and J Kotter, *Leading Change* (Boston: Harvard Business School Press, 1996).

[15] Results can be found in Kabanoff and Holt, "Changes in the Espoused Values of Australian Organizations 1986–1990."

[16] Details of this study and the general trend toward cooperation and participation is discussed by J T DeLaney, "Workplace Cooperation: Current Problems, New Approaches," *Journal of Labor Research*, Winter 1996, pp 45–61.

[17] Adapted from L Smircich, "Concepts of Culture and Organizational Analysis," *Administrative Science Quarterly*, September 1983, pp 339–58.

[18] The 3M example was based on material contained in S Branch, "The 100 Best Companies to Work for in America," *Fortune*, January 11, 1999, pp 118–44; and D Anfuso, "3M's Staffing Strategy Promotes Productivity and Pride," *Personnel Journal*, February 1995, pp 28–34.

[19] J M Higgins, "Innovate or Evaporate: Seven Secrets of Innovative Corporations," *The Futurist*, September–October 1995, p 45.

[20] Anfuso, "3M's Staffing Strategy Promotes Productivity and Pride," p 28.

[21] Branch, "The 100 Best Companies to Work for in America," p 144.

[22] See A Xenikou and A Furnham, "A Correlated and Factor Analytic Study of Four Questionnaire Measures of Organizational Culture," *Human Relations,* March 1996, pp 349–71; and Denison, "What IS the Difference between Organizational Culture and Organizational Climate? A Native's Point of View on a Decade of Paradigm Wars."

[23] The validity of these cultural types was investigated and supported by R A Cooke and J L Szumal, "Measuring Normative Beliefs and Shared Behavioral Expectations in Organizations: The Reliability and Validity of the Organizational Culture Inventory," *Psychological Reports,* June 1993, pp 1299–1330.

[24] Excerpted from D Takahashi, "Intel Trial Plan: Argue Legality, Not the Facts," *The Wall Street Journal,* March 5, 1999, pp B1, B2.

[25] See V González-Romá, J M Peiró, S Lloret, and A Zornoza, "The Validity of Collective Climates," *Journal of Organizational Behavior,* March 1999, pp 25–40; and Schein, *Organizational Culture and Leadership.*

[26] Excerpted from D Weimer, "3M: The Heat Is on the Boss," *Business Week,* March 15, 1999, p 82.

[27] An historical overview of research on organizational culture is provided by H M Trice and J M Beyer, *The Cultures of Work Organizations* (Englewood Cliffs, NJ: Prentice-Hall, 1993).

[28] See W G Ouchi, *Theory Z: How American Business Can Meet the Japanese Challenge* (Reading, MA: Addison-Wesley Publishing, 1981).

[29] See T E Deal and A A Kennedy, *Corporate Cultures: The Rites and Rituals of Corporate Life* (Reading, MA: Addison-Wesley Publishing, 1982).

[30] See T J Peters and R H Waterman, Jr, *In Search of Excellence* (New York: Harper & Row, 1982).

[31] Ibid., pp 75–76.

[32] The measurement of organizational culture is discussed by Xenikou and Furnham, "A Correlated and Factor Analytic Study of Four Questionnaire Measures of Organizational Culture"; Denison, "What IS the Difference between Organizational Culture and Organizational Climate? A Native's Point of View on a Decade of Paradigm Wars"; and Cooke and Szumal, "Measuring Normative Beliefs and Shared Behavioral Expectations in Organizations: The Reliability and Validity of the Organizational Culture Inventory."

[33] Results can be found in J P Kotter and J L Heskett, *Corporate Culture and Performance* (New York: The Free Press, 1992); and D R Denison and A K Mishra, "Toward a Theory of Organizational Culture and Effectiveness," *Organization Science,* March–April 1995, pp 204–23.

[34] See S Tully, "Northwest and KLM: The Alliance from Hell," *Fortune,* June 24, 1996, pp 64–72; and J Marren, *Mergers & Acquisitions: A Valuation Handbook* (Homewood, IL: Business One Irwin, 1993).

[35] See S Kravetz, "Work Week: A Special News Report about Life on the Job—And Trends Taking Shape There," *The Wall Street Journal,* February 16, 1999, p A1.

[36] The success rate of mergers is discussed in R J Grossman, "Irreconcilable Differences," *HRMagazine,* April 1999, pp 42–48.

[37] Results can be found in Cooke and Szumal, "Measuring Normative Beliefs and Shared Behavioral Expectations in Organizations: The Reliability and Validity of the Organizational Culture Inventory."

[38] Supportive findings are discussed by C Vandenberghe, "Organizational Culture, Person-Culture Fit, and Turnover: A Replication in the Health Care Industry," *Journal of Organizational Behavior,* March 1999, pp 175–84; S G Harris and K W Mossholder, "The Affective Implications of Perceived Congruence with Culture Dimensions during Organizational Transformation," *Journal of Management,* 1996, pp 527–48; and B Schneider, H W Goldstein, and D B Smith, "The ASA Framework: An Update," *Personnel Psychology,* Winter 1995, pp 747–73.

[39] Results can be found in S Zamanou and S R Glaser, "Moving Toward Participation and Involvement," *Group & Organization Management,* December 1994, pp 475–502.

[40] The relationship between organizational change and culture is discussed by J Silvester, N R Anderson, and F Patterson, "Organizational Culture Change: An Inter-Group Attributional Analysis," *Journal of Occupational and Organizational Psychology,* March 1999, pp 1–23; and T E Vollman, *The Transformation Imperative: Achieving Market Dominance through Radical Change* (Boston, MA: Harvard Business School Press, 1996).

[41] The IBM example was taken from J A Byrne, "Strategic Planning," *Business Week,* August 26, 1996, pp 46–52.

[42] This perspective was promoted by Deal and Kennedy, *Corporate Cultures: The Rites and Rituals of Corporate Life.*

[43] Excerpted from H Lancaster, "Managing Your Career: Traditional Managers Have to Jump Hurdles to Join Internet Firms," *The Wall Street Journal,* March 30, 1999, p B1.

[44] This perspective is discussed in "The Culture Wars," *Inc.,* May 15, 1999, pp 107–8.

[45] R H Kilman, M J Saxton, and R Serpa, *Gaining Control of the Corporate Culture* (San Francisco: Jossey-Bass, 1986), p 356.

[46] Results from this study can be found in Kotter and Heskett, *Corporate Culture and Performance.*

[47] K Bemowski, "Leaders on Leadership," *Quality Progress,* January 1996, p 43.

[48] S McCartney, "Airline Industry's Top-Ranked Woman Keeps Southwest's Small-Fry Spirit Alive," *The Wall Street Journal,* November 30, 1996, pp B1, B11.

[49] The mechanisms were based on material contained in E H Schein, "The Role of the Founder in Creating Organizational Culture," *Organizational Dynamics,* Summer 1983, pp 13–28.

[50] Excerpted from M Apgar IV, "The Alternative Workplace: Changing Where and How People Work," *Harvard Business Review,* May–June 1998, p 123.

[51] Ibid, pp 121–136.

[52] See E J Hawk, "Culture and Rewards," *Personnel Journal,* April 1995, pp 30–37.

[53] See N M Tichy and C DeRose, "The Pepsi Challenge: Building a Leader-Driven Organization," *Training & Development,* May 1996, pp 58–66.

[54] J Van Maanen, "Breaking In: Socialization to Work," in *Handbook of Work, Organization, and Society,* ed R Dubin (Chicago: Rand-McNally, 1976), p 67.

[55] A M Nicotera and D P Cushman, "Organizational Ethics: A Within-Organization View," *Journal of Applied Communication,* November 1992, p 447.

[56] For an instructive capsule summary of the five different organizational socialization models, see J P Wanous, A E Reichers, and S D Malik, "Organizational Socialization and Group Development: Toward an Integrative Perspective," *Academy of Management Review,* October 1984, pp 670–83, Table 1. Also see D C Feldman, *Managing Careers in Organizations* (Glenview, IL: Scott, Foresman, 1988), Ch. 5.

[57] Supportive results can be found in P W Hom, R W Griffeth, L E Palich, and J S Bracker, "Revisiting Met Expectations as a Reason Why Realistic Job Previews Work," *Personnel Psychology,* Spring 1999, pp 97–112.

[58] See J M Phillips, "Effects of Realistic Job Previews on Multiple Organizational Outcomes: A Meta-Analysis," *Academy of Management Journal,* December 1998, pp 673–90.

[59] J Van Maanen, "People Processing: Strategies of Organizational Socialization," *Organizational Dynamics,* Summer 1978, p 21.

[60] Excerpted from R Ganzel, "Putting Out the Welcome Mat," *Training,* March 1998, pp 56, 58.

[61] For a thorough review of socialization research, see T N Bauer, E W Morrison, and R R Callister, "Organizational Socialization: A Review and Directions for Future Research," *Research in Personnel and Human Resources Management,* vol 16 (Stamford, CT: JAI Press, 1998), pp 149–214.

[62] Results can be found in B E Ashforth, A M Saks, and R T Lee, "Socialization and Newcomer Adjustment: The Role of Organizational Context," *Human Relations,* July 1998, pp 897–926; and B E Ashforth and A M Saks, "Socialization Tactics: Longitudinal Effects on Newcomer Adjustment," *Academy of Management Journal,* February 1996, pp 149–78.

[63] Results from two separate studies can be found in E W Morrison, "Longitudinal Study of the Effects of Information Seeking," *Journal of Applied Psychology,* April 1993, pp 173–83; and E W Morrison, "Newcomer Information Seeking: Exploring Types, Modes, Sources, and Outcomes," *Academy of Management Journal,* June 1993, pp 557–89.

[64] See T N Bauer and S G Green, "Testing the Combined Effects of Newcomer Information Seeking and Manager Behavior on Socialization," *Journal of Applied Psychology,* February 1998, pp 72–83.

[65] See Bauer, Morrison, and Callister, "Organizational Socialization: A Review and Directions for Future Research."

[66] See A M Saks and B E Ashforth, "Proactive Socialization and Behavioral Self-Management," *Journal of Vocational Behavior,* June 1996, pp 301–23.

[67] For a thorough review of research on the socialization of diverse employees with disabilities see A Colella, "Organizational Socialization of Newcomers with Disabilities: A Framework for Future Research," in *Research in Personnel and Human Resources Management,* ed G R Ferris (Greenwich, CT: JAI Press, 1996), pp 351–417.

[68] See K E Kram, "Phases of the Mentor Relationship," *Academy of Management Journal,* December 1983, pp 608–25.

[69] H Lancaster, "Managing Your Career: It's Harder, but You Still Can Rise Up from the Mail Room," *The Wall Street Journal,* June 18, 1996, p B1.

[70] See S Seibert, "The Effectiveness of Facilitated Mentoring: A Longitudinal Quasi-Experiment," *Journal of Vocational Behavior,* June 1999, pp 483–502; and T A Scandura, "Dysfunctional Mentoring Relationships and Outcomes," *Journal of Management,* 1998, pp 449–67.

[71] Results can be found in G F Dreher and T H Cox, Jr, "Race, Gender, and Opportunity: A Study of Compensation Attainment and the Establishment of Mentoring Relationships," *Journal of Applied Psychology,* June 1996, pp 297–308.

[72] Results from this study can be found in G F Dreher and J A Chargois, "Gender, Mentoring Experiences, and Salary Attainment among Graduates of an Historically Black University," *Journal of Vocational Behavior,* December 1998, pp 401–16.

[73] See S G Green and T N Bauer, "Supervisory Mentoring by Advisers: Relationships with Doctoral Student Potential, Productivity, and Commitment," *Personnel Psychology,* Autumn 1995, pp 537–61; and T D Allen, S E McManus, and J E Russell, "Newcomer Socialization and Stress: Formal Peer Relationships as a Source of Support," *Journal of Vocational Behavior,* June 1999, pp 453–70.

[74] Excerpted from I Mochari, "Roll Out the Welcome Mat," *Inc.,* May 1999, p 101.

[75] See R M O'Neill, S Horton, and J F Crosby, "Gender Issues in Developmental Relationships," in *Mentoring Dilemmas: Developmental Relationships within Multicultural Organizations. Applied Social Research,* eds A J Murrell et al. (Mahwah, NJ: Lawrence Erlbaum Associates, 1999), pp 63–80; and B R Ragins, "Diversity, Power, and Mentorship in Organizations," in *Diversity in Organizations: New Perspectives for a Changing Workplace,* eds M M Chemers, S Oskamp, and M A Costanzo (Thousand Oaks, CA: Sage, 1995), pp 91–132.

[76] See Dreher and Cox, "Race, Gender, and Opportunity: A Study of Compensation Attainment and the Establishment of Mentoring Relationships."

[77] See B J Tepper, "Upward Maintenance Tactics in Supervisory Mentoring and Nonmentoring Relationships," *Academy of Management Journal,* August 1995, pp 1191–1205; A Vincent and J Seymour, "Profile of Women Mentors: A National Survey," *SAM Advanced Management Journal,* Spring 1995, pp 4–10; and V A Parker and K E Kram, "Women Mentoring Women: Creating Conditions for Connection," *Business Horizons,* March–April 1993, pp 42–51.

[78] For a discussion of the practical guidelines for implementing mentoring programs see K Tyler, "Mentoring Programs Link Employees and Experienced Execs," *HRMagazine,* April 1998, pp 99–103.

[79] Details of these examples can be found in L Wah, "Lip-Service Ethics Programs Prove Ineffective," *Management Review,* June 1999, p 9; and "Workplace Ethics Dilemma," *USA Today,* February 15, 1999, p 1B.

[80] L Wah, "Lies in the Executive Wing," *Management Review,* May 1999, p 9.

[81] Excerpted from L Grensing-Pophal, "Walking the Tightrope, Balancing Risks & Gains," *HRMagazine,* October 1998, p 112.

[82] See C Gilligan, "In a Different Voice: Women's Conceptions of Self and Morality," *Harvard Educational Review,* November 1977, pp 481–517; and C Gilligan, *In a Different Voice: Psychological Theory and Women's Development* (Cambridge, MA: Harvard University Press, 1982).

[83] Branch, "The 100 Best Companies to Work for in America."

[84] The role of incentives and ethical behavior was investigated by A E Tenbrunsel, "Misrepresentation and Expectations of Misrepresentation in an Ethical Dilemma: The Role of Incentives and Temptation," *Academy of Management Journal,* June 1998, pp 330–39.

[85] A new model of ethical behavior that is based on the interaction between person and situation factors is proposed by D J Brass, K D Butterfield, and B C Skaggs, "Relationships and Unethical Behavior: A Social Network Perspective," *The Academy of Management Review,* January 1998, pp 14–31.

[86] See S J Pharr, " 'Moralism' and the Gender Gap: Judgments of Political Ethics in Japan," *Political Psychology,* March 1998, pp 211–36; L M Dawson, "Women and Men, Morality, and Ethics," *Business Horizons,* July–August 1995, pp 61–68; D K Johnston, "Adolescents' Solutions to Dilemmas in Fables: Two Moral Orientations—Two Problem Solving Strategies," in *Moral Development: Caring Voices and Women's Moral Frames,* ed B Puka (New York: Garland Publishing, 1994) pp 99–121; and C Gilligan and J Attanucci, "Two Moral Orientations: Gender Differences and Similarities," *Merril-Palmer Quarterly,* July 1988, pp 223–37.

[87] Gilligan and Attanucci, "Two Moral Orientations: Gender Differences and Similarities," pp 224–25.

[88] These conclusions were derived from J Dobson and J White, "Toward the Feminine Firm: An Extension to Thomas White," *Business Ethics Quarterly,* July 1995, pp 463–78.

[89] See Ch. 6 in K Hodgson, *A Rock and a Hard Place: How to Make Ethical Business Decisions When the Choices Are Tough* (New York: AMACOM, 1992), pp 66–77.

[90] Adapted from W E Stead, D L Worrell, and J Garner Stead, "An Integrative Model for Understanding and Managing Ethical Behavior in Business Organizations," *Journal of Business Ethics,* March 1990, pp 233–42.

[91] For an excellent review of integrity testing, see D S Ones and C Viswesvaran, "Integrity Testing in Organizations," in *Dysfunctional Behavior in Organizations: Violent and Deviant Behavior,* eds R W Griffin et al. (Stamford, CT: JAI Press, 1998), pp 243–76.

[92] C M Solomon, "Prepare to Walk a Moral Tightrope: Put Your Ethics to a Global Test," *Personnel Journal,* January 1996, p 70.

[93] See "Open Business Is Good for Business," *People Management,* January 1996, pp 24–27.

[94] "Doing the Right Thing," *The Economist,* May 20, 1995, p 64. © 1995, The Economist Newspaper Group, Inc. Reprinted with permission. Further reproduction prohibited. www.economist.com

[95] See D Takahashi, "Workers of the World, Unite: Leave This on Your Boss's Desk," *The Wall Street Journal,* May 19, 1999, p B1.

[96] This exercise was adapted from Richard Pascale, "The Paradox of 'Corporate Culture': Reconciling Ourselves to Socialization," pp 26–41. © 1985 by the Regents of the University of California. Reprinted/condensed

from the *California Management Review,* 27, no. 2, by permission of The Regents.

[97] These scenarios were excerpted from Dawson, "Women and Men, Morality and Ethics," pp 62, 65.

[98] Comparative norms were obtained from Dawson, "Women and Men, Morality and Ethics." Scenario 1: would sell (28% males, 57% females); would not sell (66% males, 28% females); unsure (6% males, 15% females). Scenario 2: would consult (84% males, 32% females); would not consult (12% males, 62% females); unsure (4% males, 6% females).

[99] The following trends were taken from Dawson, "Women and Men, Morality and Ethics." Women were likely to primarily respect feelings, ask "who will be hurt?", avoid being judgmental, search for compromise, seek solutions that minimize hurt, rely on communication, believe in contextual relativism, be guided by emotion, and challenge authority. Men were likely to primarily respect rights, ask "who is right?", value decisiveness, make unambiguous decisions, seek solutions that are objectively fair, rely on rules, believe in blind impartiality, be guided by logic, and accept authority.

ANSWERS TO OB EXERCISE

[1] Although there are no clear examples of shared objects such as plaques or logos in the Ritz-Carlton example, the policies, practices, procedures, and routines designed to reward employees for providing excellent customer service partially represent shared objects or things. There are two potential shared sayings for the Ritz. One might be "do whatever it takes," and the second could be "we are ladies and gentlemen serving ladies and gentlemen." The "Gold Standards" constitute shared behavior or doings in that they specify desired employee behavior within the Ritz.

Hamburger University represents a shared object or thing within McDonald's. McDonald's vision and its associated acronym of QSCV might well constitute a shared saying. The detailed policies and procedures manual and Francising 2000 reflect shared behavior or doings because they clearly specify desired forms of employee behavior. Franchisees at McDonald's are likely to share positive emotions about providing customers with quality, service, convenience, and value because their income is directly tied to these customer outcomes.

[2] McDonald's culture appears to be more control oriented than that at the Ritz-Carlton. The Ritz is known for empowering its employees to make decisions, whereas McDonald's directly influences employee behavior through its meticulous policies and procedures. Both organizations are likely to have a competitive component within their cultures because they operate in very competitive markets.

CHAPTER 4

[1] Excerpted from D McGinn and S Theil, "Hands on the Wheel," *Newsweek,* April 12, 1999, pp 49–52. For more, see B Vlasic, "The First Global Car Colossus," *Business Week,* May 18, 1998, pp 40–43; K Lowry, "The Auto Baron," *Business Week,* November 16, 1998, pp 82–90; M Maynard, "Merger of Two Equals Appears To Be Unequal," *USA Today,* March 26, 1999, pp 1B–2B; and M Maynard, "DaimlerChrysler Rides High," *USA Today,* April 28, 1999, p 3B.

[2] Based on J S Lublin, "An Overseas Stint Can Be a Ticket to the Top," *The Wall Street Journal,* January 29, 1996, pp B1, B5.

[3] G Dutton, "Building a Global Brain," *Management Review,* May 1999, p 35.

[4] For helpful practical advice, see Table 1 in N J Adler and S Bartholomew, "Managing Globally Competent People," *Academy of Management Executive,* August 1992, pp 52–65. Also see A J Marsella, "Toward a 'Global-Community Psychology,' " *American*

Psychologist, December 1998, pp 1282–91; and B Kogut, "What Makes a Company Global?" *Harvard Business Review,* January–February 1999, pp 165–70.

[5] M Mabry, "Pin a Label on a Manager—And Watch What Happens," *Newsweek,* May 14, 1990, p 43.

[6] Ibid.

[7] E H Schein, *Organizational Culture and Leadership* (San Francisco: Jossey-Bass, 1985), p 9. Also see H H Baligh, "Components of Culture: Nature, Interconnections, and Relevance to the Decisions on the Organization Structure," *Management Science,* January 1994, pp 14–27.

[8] For instructive discussion, see J S Black, H B Gregersen, and M E Mendenhall, *Global Assignments: Successfully Expatriating and Repatriating International Managers* (San Francisco: Jossey-Bass, 1992), Ch. 2.

[9] F Trompenaars and C Hampden-Turner, *Riding the Waves of Culture: Understanding Cultural Diversity in Global Business,* 2nd ed (New York: McGraw-Hill, 1998), pp 6–7.

[10] "How Cultures Collide," *Psychology Today,* July 1976, p 69.

[11] See M Mendenhall, "A Painless Approach to Integrating 'International' into OB, HRM, and Management Courses," *Organizational Behavior Teaching Review,* no. 3 (1988–89), pp 23–27.

[12] See C L Sharma, "Ethnicity, National Integration, and Education in the Union of Soviet Socialist Republics," *The Journal of East and West Studies,* October 1989, pp 75–93; and R Brady and P Galuszka, "Shattered Dreams," *Business Week,* February 11, 1991, pp 38–42.

[13] J Main, "How to Go Global—And Why," *Fortune,* August 28, 1989, p 73.

[14] An excellent contrast between French and American values can be found in C Gouttefarde, "American Values in the French Workplace," *Business Horizons,* March–April 1996, pp 60–69.

[15] W D Marbach, "Quality: What Motivates American Workers?" *Business Week,* April 12, 1993, p 93.

[16] See G A Sumner, *Folkways* (New York: Ginn, 1906). Also see J G Weber, "The Nature of Ethnocentric Attribution Bias: Ingroup Protection or Enhancement?" *Journal of Experimental Social Psychology,* September 1994, pp 482–504.

[17] "House English-only Bill Aims at Federal Agencies," *USA Today,* July 25, 1996, p 3A. For another example of ethnocentric behavior, see J Cox, "Summers Has Slightly Tense Relationship with Japanese," *USA Today,* May 13, 1999, p 2B.

[18] D A Heenan and H V Perlmutter, *Multinational Organization Development* (Reading, MA: Addison-Wesley, 1979), p 17.

[19] Data from R Kopp, "International Human Resource Policies and Practices in Japanese, European, and United States Multinationals," *Human Resource Management,* Winter 1994, pp 581–99.

[20] See "How Cultures Collide," pp 66–74, 97; and M Munter, "Cross-Cultural Communication for Managers," *Business Horizons,* May–June 1993, pp 69–78.

[21] D C Barnlund, "Public and Private Self in Communicating with Japan," *Business Horizons,* March–April 1989, p 38.

[22] See E W K Tsang, "Can *Guanxi* Be a Source of Sustained Competitive Advantage for Doing Business in China?" *Academy of Management Executive,* May 1998, pp 64–73.

[23] The concept of "face" and good tips on saving face in Far East Asia are presented in J A Reeder, "When West Meets East: Cultural Aspects of Doing Business in Asia," *Business Horizons,* January–February 1987, pp 69–74. Also see B Stout, "Interviewing in Japan," *HRMagazine,* June 1998, pp 71–77; and J A Quelch and C M Dinh-Tan, "Country Managers in Transitional Economies: The Case of Vietnam," *Business Horizons,* July–August 1998, pp 34–40.

[24] The German management style is discussed in R Stewart, "German Management: A Challenge to Anglo-American Managerial Assumptions," *Business Horizons,* May–June 1996, pp 52–54.

[25] See D Stauffer, "No Need for Inter-American Culture Clash," *Management Review,* January 1998, p 8; J Scarborough, "Comparing Chinese and Western Cultural Roots: Why 'East Is East and . . . ,' " *Business Horizons,* November–December 1998, pp 15–24; and C B Meek, "*Ganbatte:* Understanding the Japanese Employee," *Business Horizons,* January–February 1999, pp 27–36.

[26] This list is based on E T Hall, "The Silent Language in Overseas Business," *Harvard Business Review,* May–June 1960, pp 87–96; and R Knotts, "Cross-Cultural Management: Transformations and Adaptations," *Business Horizons,* January–February 1989, pp 29–33; and Trompenaars and Hampden-Turner, *Riding the Waves of Culture: Understanding Cultural Diversity in Global Business.*

[27] A discussion of Japanese stereotypes in America can be found in L Smith, "Fear and Loathing of Japan," *Fortune,* February 26, 1990, pp 50–57. Diversity in so-called Eastern Bloc countries in Central and Eastern Europe is discussed in F Luthans, R R Patrick, and B C Luthans, "Doing Business in Central and Eastern Europe: Political, Economic, and Cultural Diversity," *Business Horizons,* September–October 1995, pp 9–16.

[28] Based on discussion in P R Harris and R T Moran, *Managing Cultural Differences,* 3rd ed (Houston: Gulf Publishing, 1991) p 12. Also see "Workers' Attitudes Similar Worldwide," *HRMagazine,* December 1998, pp 28–30; and C Comeau-Kirschner, "It's a Small World," *Management Review,* March 1999, p 8.

[29] Data from Trompenaars and Hampden-Turner, *Riding the Waves of Culture: Understanding Cultural Diversity in Global Business,* Ch 5. For relevant research evidence, see Y A Fijneman, M E Willemsen, and Y H Poortinga, "Individualism–Collectivism: An Empirical Study of a Conceptual Issue," *Journal of Cross-Cultural Psychology,* July 1996, pp 381–402; D I Jung and B J Avolio, "Effects of Leadership Style and Followers' Cultural Orientation on Performance in Groups and Individual Task Conditions," *Academy of Management Journal,* April 1999, pp 208–18; T M Singelis, M H Bond, W F Sharkey, and C S Y Lai, "Unpacking Culture's Influence on Self-Esteem and Embarrassability: The Role of Self-Construals," *Journal of Cross-Cultural Psychology,* May 1999, pp 315–41; and M J Bresnahan, R Ohashi, W Y Liu, R Nebashi, and C Liao, "A Comparison of Response Styles in Singapore and Taiwan," *Journal of Cross-Cultural Psychology,* May 1999, pp 342–58.

[30] As quoted in E E Schultz, "Scudder Brings Lessons to Navajo, Gets Some of Its Own," *The Wall Street Journal,* April 29, 1999, p C12.

[31] Trompenaars and Hampden-Turner, *Riding the Waves of Culture: Understanding Cultural Diversity in Global Business,* p 56.

[32] See, for example, N R Mack, "Taking Apart the Ticking of Time," *The Christian Science Monitor,* August 29, 1991, p 17.

[33] For a comprehensive treatment of time, see J E McGrath and J R Kelly, *Time and Human Interaction: Toward a Social Psychology of Time* (New York: The Guilford Press, 1986). Also see L A Manrai and A K Manrai, "Effects of Cultural-Context, Gender, and Acculturation on Perceptions of Work versus Social/Leisure Time Usage," *Journal of Business Research,* February 1995, pp 115–28.

[34] A good discussion of doing business in Mexico is G K Stephens and C R Greer, "Doing Business in Mexico: Understanding Cultural Differences," *Organizational Dynamics,* Summer 1995, pp 39–55.

[35] R W Moore, "Time, Culture, and Comparative Management: A Review and Future Direction," in *Advances in International Comparative Management,* vol. 5, ed S B Prasad (Greenwich, CT: JAI Press, 1990), pp 7–8.

[36] See A C Bluedorn, C F Kaufman, and P M Lane, "How Many Things Do You Like to Do at Once? An Introduction to Monochronic and Polychronic Time," *Academy of Management Executive,* November 1992, pp 17–26.

[37] "Multitasking" term drawn from S McCartney, "The Breaking Point: Multitasking Technology Can Raise Stress and Cripple Productivity," *The Arizona Republic,* May 21, 1995, p D10.

[38] O Port, "You May Have To Reset This Watch—In a Million Years," *Business Week,* August 30, 1993, p 65.

[39] See E T Hall, *The Hidden Dimension* (Garden City, NY: Doubleday, 1966).

[40] "How Cultures Collide," p 72.

[41] D Raybeck and D Herrmann, "A Cross-Cultural Examination of Semantic Relations," *Journal of Cross-Cultural Psychology,* December 1990, p 470.

[42] G A Michaelson, "Global Gold," *Success,* March 1996, p 16.

[43] Translation services are discussed in D Pianko, "Smooth Translations," *Management Review,* July 1996, p 10; and R Ganzel, "Universal Translator? Not Quite," *Training,* April 1999, pp 22–24.

[44] For example, see "When in Rio. . . ," *Training,* December 1998, p 25.

[45] From *Managing Cultural Differences,* 4th ed, p 23. Phillip R Harris and Robert T Moran. Copyright 1996 © by Gulf Publishing Company. Used with permission. All rights reserved.

[46] "Going Global? Stifle Yourself!" *Training,* August 1995, p 14. (Italics added.)

[47] Results adapted from and value definitions quoted from S R Safranski and I-W Kwon, "Religious Groups and Management Value Systems," in *Advances in International Comparative Management,* vol. 3, eds R N Farner and E G McGoun (Greenwich, CT: JAI Press, 1988), pp 171–83.

[48] Ibid., p 180.

[49] N J Adler, *International Dimensions of Organizational Behavior,* 2nd ed (Boston: PWS–Kent, 1991), p 10. Also see P C Earley and H Singh, "International and Intercultural Management Research: What's Next?" *Academy of Management Journal,* April 1995, pp 327–40; M B Teagarden et al., "Toward a Theory of Comparative Management Research: An Idiographic Case Study of the Best International Human Resources Management Project," *Academy of Management Journal,* October 1995, pp 1261–87; M H Segall, W J Lonner, and J W Berry, "Cross-Cultural Psychology as a Scholarly Discipline: On the Flowering of Culture in Behavioral Research," *American Psychologist,* October 1998, pp 1101–10; and M Easterby-Smith and D Malina, "Cross-Cultural Collaborative Research: Toward Reflexivity," *Academy of Management Journal,* February 1999, pp 76–86.

[50] For complete details, see G Hofstede, *Culture's Consequences: International Differences in Work-Related Values,* abridged ed (Newbury Park, CA: Sage Publications, 1984); G Hofstede, "The Interaction between National and Organizational Value Systems," *Journal of Management Studies,* July 1985, pp 347–57; and G Hofstede, "Management Scientists Are Human," *Management Science,* January 1994, pp 4–13. Also see V J Shackleton and A H Ali, "Work-Related Values of Managers: A Test of the Hofstede Model," *Journal of Cross-Cultural Psychology,* March 1990, pp 109–18; R Hodgetts, "A Conversation with Geert Hofstede," *Organizational Dynamics,* Spring 1993, pp 53–61; and P B Smith, S Dugan, and F Trompenaars, "National Culture and the Values of Organizational Employees: A Dimensional Analysis Across 43 Nations," *Journal of Cross-Cultural Psychology,* March 1996, pp 231–64.

[51] See G Hofstede and M H Bond, "Hofstede's Culture Dimensions: An Independent Validation Using Rokeach's Value Survey," *Journal of Cross-Cultural Psychology,* December 1984, pp 417–33. A recent study using the Chinese Value Survey (CVS) is reported in D A Ralston, D J Gustafson, P M Elsass, F Cheung, and R H Terpstra, "Eastern Values: A Comparison of Managers in the United States, Hong Kong, and the People's Republic of China," *Journal of Applied Psychology,* October 1992, pp 664–71.

[52] G Hofstede, "Cultural Constraints in Management Theories," *Academy of Management Executive,* February 1993, p 90.

[53] See Y Paik and J H D Sohn, "Confucius in Mexico: Korean MNCs and the Maquiladoras," *Business Horizons,* November–December 1998, pp 25–33.

[54] For complete details, see G Hofstede and M H Bond, "The Confucius Connection: From Cultural Roots to Economic Growth," *Organizational Dynamics,* Spring 1988, pp 4–21.

[55] See P M Rosenzweig, "When Can Management Science Research Be Generalized Internationally?" *Management Science,* January 1994, pp 28–39.

[56] A follow-up study is J P Johnson and T Lenartowicz, "Culture, Freedom and Economic Growth: Do Cultural Values Explain Economic Growth?" *Journal of World Business,* Winter 1998, pp 332–56.

[57] See C A Rodrigues, "The Situation and National Culture as Contingencies for Leadership Behavior: Two Conceptual Models," in *Advances in International Comparative Management,* vol. 5, ed S B Prasad (Greenwich, CT: JAI Press, 1990), pp 51–68. For a study that found consistent perception of six leadership styles across four countries (Norway, United States,

Sweden, and Australia), see C B Gibson and G A Marcoulides, "The Invariance of Leadership Styles across Four Countries," *Journal of Managerial Issues,* Summer 1995, pp 176–93.

[58] For details, see D H B Welsh, F Luthans, and S M Sommer, "Managing Russian Factory Workers: The Impact of US-Based Behavioral and Participative Techniques," *Academy of Management Journal,* February 1993, pp 58–79. Also see F Luthans, S J Peterson, and E Ibrayeva, "The Potential for the 'Dark Side' of Leadership in Post-Communist Countries," *Journal of World Business,* Summer 1998, pp 185–201.

[59] Data from J Kahn, "The World's Most Admired Companies," *Fortune,* October 26, 1998, pp 206–26.

[60] J S Black and H B Gregersen, "The Right Way to Manage Expats," *Harvard Business Review,* March–April 1999, p 53. A more optimistic picture is presented in R L Tung, "American Expatriates Abroad: From Neophytes to Cosmopolitans," *Journal of World Business,* Summer 1998, pp 125–44.

[61] Adapted from R L Tung, "Expatriate Assignments: Enhancing Success and Minimizing Failure," *Academy of Management Executive,* May 1987, pp 117–26.

[62] S Dallas, "Rule No. 1: Don't Diss the Locals," *Business Week,* May 15, 1995, p 8.

[63] These insights come from Tung, "American Expatriates Abroad: From Neophytes to Cosmopolitans"; P M Caligiuri and W F Cascio, "*Can We Send Her There?* Maximizing the Success of Western Women on Global Assignments," *Journal of World Business,* Winter 1998, pp 394–416; and T L Speer, "Gender Barriers Crumbling, Traveling Business Women Report," *USA Today,* March 16, 1999, p 5E.

[64] Data from B Hagerty, "Trainers Help Expatriate Employees Build Bridges to Different Cultures," *The Wall Street Journal,* June 14, 1993, pp B1, B3. Also see A Weiss, "Global Doesn't Mean 'Foreign' Anymore," *Training,* July 1998, pp 50–55; and G Dutton, "Do You Think Globally?" *Management Review,* February 1999, p 6.

[65] C M Farkas and P De Backer, "There Are Only Five Ways to Lead," *Fortune,* January 15, 1996, p 111. The shortage of global managers is discussed in L K Stroh and P M Caligiuri, "Increasing Global Competitiveness through Effective People Management," *Journal of World Business,* Spring 1998, pp 1–16.

[66] An excellent reference book in this area is Black, Gregersen, and Mendenhall, *Global Assignments: Successfully Expatriating and Repatriating International Managers.* Also see K Roberts, E E Kossek, and C Ozeki, "Managing the Global Workforce: Challenges and Strategies," *Academy of Management Executive,* November 1998, pp 93–106.

[67] Ibid., p 97.

[68] J S Lublin, "Younger Managers Learn Global Skills," *The Wall Street Journal,* March 31, 1992, p B1.

[69] See P C Earley, "Intercultural Training for Managers: A Comparison of Documentary and Interpersonal Methods," *Academy of Management Journal,* December 1987, pp 685–98; and J S Black and M Mendenhall, "Cross-Cultural Training Effectiveness: A Review and a Theoretical Framework for Future Research," *Academy of Management Review,* January 1990, pp 113–36. Also see M R Hammer and J N Martin, "The Effects of Cross-Cultural Training on American Managers in a Japanese-American Joint Venture," *Journal of Applied Communication Research,* May 1992, pp 161–81; and J K Harrison, "Individual and Combined Effects of Behavior Modeling and the Cultural Assimilator in Cross-Cultural Management Training," *Journal of Applied Psychology,* December 1992, pp 952–62.

[70] See G P Ferraro, "The Need for Linguistic Proficiency in Global Business," *Business Horizons,* May–June 1996, pp 39–46. For a study demonstrating that employees tend to prefer foreign assignments in culturally similar locations, see S Aryee, Y W Chay, and J Chew, "An Investigation of the Willingness of Managerial Employees to Accept an Expatriate Assignment," *Journal of Organizational Behavior,* May 1996, pp 267–83.

[71] See Harris and Moran, *Managing Cultural Differences,* pp 223–28; M Shilling, "Avoid Expatriate Culture Shock," *HRMagazine,* July 1993, pp 58–63; and D Stamps, "Welcome to America: Watch Out for Culture Shock," *Training,* November 1996, pp 22–30.

[72] S Tully, "The Modular Corporation," *Fortune,* February 8, 1993, pp 108, 112.

[73] Additional instructive resources on the expatriate cycle are C M Solomon, "One Assignment, Two Lives," *Personnel Journal,* May 1996, pp 36–47; L A Collins Allard, "Managing Globe-Trotting Expats," *Management Review,* May 1996, pp 39–43; J S Lublin, "Is Transfer to Native Land a Passport to Trouble?" *The Wall Street Journal,* June 3, 1996, pp B1, B4; and M Richey, "Global Families: Surviving an Overseas Move," *Management Review,* June 1996, pp 57–61.

[74] See H H Nguyen, L A Messe, and G E Stollak, "Toward a More Complex Understanding of Acculturation and Adjustment," *Journal of Cross-Cultural Psychology,* January 1999, pp 5–31.

[75] K L Miller, "How a Team of Buckeyes Helped Honda Save a Bundle," *Business Week,* September 13, 1993, p 68.

[76] B Newman, "For Ira Caplan, Re-Entry Has Been Strange," *The Wall Street Journal,* December 12, 1995, p A12.

[77] See Black, Gregersen, and Mendenhall, *Global Assignments: Successfully Expatriating and Repatriating International Managers,* p 227. Also see H B Gregersen, "Commitments to a Parent Company and a Local Work Unit During Repatriation," *Personnel Psychology,* Spring 1992, pp 29–54; and H B Gregersen and J S Black, "Multiple Commitments upon Repatriation: The Japanese Experience," *Journal of Management,* no. 2, 1996, pp 209–29.

[78] Ibid., pp 226–27.

[79] See J R Engen, "Coming Home," *Training,* March 1995, pp 37–40; and L K Stroh, H B Gregersen, and J S Black, "Closing the Gap: Expectations versus Reality among Repatriates," *Journal of World Business,* Summer 1998, pp 111–24.

[80] Excerpted from J S Lublin, "Companies Use Cross-Cultural Training to Help Their Employees Adjust Abroad," *The Wall Street Journal,* August 4, 1992, pp B1, B6.

[81] This list of work goals is quoted from I Harpaz, "The Importance of Work Goals: An International Perspective," *Journal of International Business Studies,* First Quarter 1990, p 79.

[82] Adapted from a seven-country summary in Ibid., Table 2, p 81.

[83] See A Nimgade, "American Management as Viewed by International Professionals," *Business Horizons,* November–December 1989, pp 98–105; R Calori and B Dufour, "Management European Style," *Academy of Management Executive,* August 1995, pp 61–71; and W A Hubiak and S J O'Donnell, "Do Americans Have Their Minds Set Against TQM?" *National Productivity Review,* Summer 1996, pp 19–32.

CHAPTER 5

[1] Excerpted from C Hymowitz, "Here's a Career Path: M.B.A., Eye Surgeon, and Twins at 53," *The Wall Street Journal,* June 1, 1999, p B1.

[2] D Seligman, "The Trouble with Buyouts," *Fortune,* November 30, 1992, p 125.

[3] S I Cheldelin and L A Foritano, "Psychometrics: Their Use in Organisation Development," *Journal of Managerial Psychology,* no. 4, 1989, p 21.

[4] See "A Market Solution for Diversity?" *Training,* June 1998, p 14; R W Thompson, "Diversity among Managers Translates into Profitability," *HRMagazine,* April 1999, p 10; J Crockett, "DIVERSITY as a Business Strategy," *Management Review,* May 1999, p 62; and P Dass and B Parker, "Strategies for Managing Human Resource Diversity: From Resistance to Learning," *Academy of Management Executive,* May 1999, pp 68–80.

[5] V Gecas, "The Self-Concept," in *Annual Review of Sociology,* eds R H Turner and J F Short, Jr. (Palo Alto, CA: Annual Reviews Inc., 1982), vol. 8, p 3. Also see A P Brief and R J Aldag, "The 'Self' in Work Organizations: A Conceptual Review," *Academy of Management Review,* January 1981, pp 75–88; J J Sullivan, "Self Theories and Employee Motivation," *Journal of Management,* June 1989, pp 345–63; P Cushman, "Why the Self Is Empty," *American Psychologist,* May 1990, pp 599–611; and L Gaertner, C Sedikides, and K Graetz, "In Search of Self-Definition: Motivational Primacy of the Individual Self, Motivational Primacy of the Collective Self, or Contextual Primacy?" *Journal of Personality and Social Psychology,* January 1999, pp 5–18.

[6] L Festinger, *A Theory of Cognitive Dissonance* (Stanford, CA: Stanford University Press, 1957), p 3.

[7] See J Holt and D M Keats, "Work Cognitions in Multicultural Interaction," *Journal of Cross-Cultural Psychology,* December 1992, pp 421–43.

[8] A Canadian versus Japanese comparison of self-concept can be found in J D Campbell, P D Trapnell, S J Heine, I M Katz, L F Lavallee, and D R Lehman, "Self-Concept Clarity: Measurement, Personality Correlates, and Cultural Boundaries," *Journal of Personality and Social Psychology,* January 1996, pp 141–56.

[9] See D C Barnlund, "Public and Private Self in Communicating with Japan," *Business Horizons,* March–April 1989, pp 32–40; and the section on "Doing Business with Japan" in P R Harris and R T Moran, *Managing Cultural Differences,* 4th ed (Houston: Gulf Publishing, 1996), pp 267–76.

[10] Based in part on a definition found in Gecas, "The Self-Concept." Also see N Branden, *Self-Esteem at Work: How Confident People Make Powerful Companies* (San Francisco: Jossey-Bass, 1998).

[11] H W Marsh, "Positive and Negative Global Self-Esteem: A Substantively Meaningful Distinction or Artifacts?" *Journal of Personality and Social Psychology,* April 1996, p 819.

[12] Ibid.

[13] For related research, see R C Liden, L Martin, and C K Parsons, "Interviewer and Applicant Behaviors in Employment Interviews," *Academy of Management Journal,* April 1993, pp 372–86; M B Setterlund and P M Niedenthal, " 'Who Am I? Why Am I Here?': Self-Esteem, Self-Clarity, and Prototype Matching," *Journal of Personality and Social Psychology,* October 1993, pp 769–80; and G J Pool, W Wood, and K Leck, "The Self-Esteem Motive in Social Influence: Agreement with Valued Majorities and Disagreement with Derogated Minorities," *Journal of Personality and Social Psychology,* October 1998, pp 967–75.

[14] See S J Rowley, R M Sellers, T M Chavous, and M A Smith, "The Relationship between Racial Identity and Self-Esteem in African American College and High School Students," *Journal of Personality and Social Psychology,* March 1998, pp 715–24.

[15] N Hellmich, "Emphasizing Achievement, Not Faint Praise," *USA Today,* October 24, 1995, p 1D.

[16] See J A Stein, M D Newcomb, and P M Bentler, "The Relative Influence on Vocational Behavior and Family Involvement on Self-Esteem: Longitudinal Analyses of Young Adult Women and Men," *Journal of Vocational Behavior,* June 1990, pp 320–38.

[17] Based on P G Dodgson and J V Wood, "Self-Esteem and the Cognitive Accessibility of Strengths and Weaknesses after Failure," *Journal of Personality and Social Psychology,* July 1998, pp 178–97.

[18] Details may be found in B R Schlenker, M F Weigold, and J R Hallam, "Self-Serving Attributions in Social Context: Effects of Self-Esteem and Social Pressure," *Journal of Personality and Social Psychology,* May 1990, pp 855–63.

[19] See R F Baumeister, L Smart, and J M Boden, "Relation of Threatened Egotism to Violence and Aggression: The Dark Side of High Self-Esteem," *Psychological Review,* January 1996, pp 5–33; and D Seligman, "Down with Esteem," *Fortune,* April 29, 1996, pp 211–14.

[20] For related reading, see M Kaeter, "False Identities," *Business Ethics,* March–April 1994, p 46.

[21] E Diener and M Diener, "Cross-Cultural Correlates of Life Satisfaction and Self-Esteem," *Journal of Personality and Social Psychology,* April 1995, p 662. For cross-cultural evidence of a similar psychological process for self-esteem, see T M Singelis, M H Bond, W F Sharkey, and C S Y Lai, "Unpackaging Culture's Influence on Self-Esteem and Embarrassability," *Journal of Cross-Cultural Psychology,* May 1999, pp 315–41.

[22] Based on data in F L Smoll, R E Smith, N P Barnett, and J J Everett, "Enhancement of Children's Self-Esteem through Social Support Training for Youth Sports Coaches," *Journal of Applied Psychology,* August 1993, pp 602–10.

[23] W J McGuire and C V McGuire, "Enhancing Self-Esteem by Directed-Thinking Tasks: Cognitive and Affective Positivity Asymmetries," *Journal of Personality and Social Psychology,* June 1996, p 1124.

[24] J L Pierce, D G Gardner, L L Cummings, and R B Dunham, "Organization-Based Self-Esteem: Construct Definition, Measurement, and Validation," *Academy of Management Journal,* September 1989, p 625. Also see J L Pierce, D G Gardner, R B Dunham, and L L Cummings, "Moderation by Organization-Based Self-Esteem of Role Condition-Employee Response Relationships," *Academy of Management Journal,* April 1993, pp 271–88.

[25] Practical steps are discussed in M Kaeter, "Basic Self-Esteem," *Training,* August 1993, pp 31–35. Also see G Koretz, "The Vital Role of Self-Esteem," *Business Week,* February 2, 1998, p 26; and T A Judge, E A Locke, C C Durham, and A N Kluger, "Dispositional Effects on Job and Life Satisfaction: The Role of Core Evaluations," *Journal of Applied Psychology,* February 1998, pp 17–34.

[26] Adapted from discussion in J K Matejka and R J Dunsing, "Great Expectations," *Management World,* January 1987, pp 16–17. Also see P Pascarella, "It All Begins with Self-Esteem," *Management Review,* February 1999, pp 60–61.

[27] M E Gist, "Self-Efficacy: Implications for Organizational Behavior and Human Resource Management," *Academy of Management Review,* July 1987, p 472. Also see A Bandura, "Self-Efficacy: Toward a Unifying Theory of Behavioral Change," *Psychological Review,* March 1977, pp 191–215; and M E Gist and T R Mitchell, "Self-Efficacy: A Theoretical Analysis of Its Determinants and Malleability," *Academy of Management Review,* April 1992, pp 183–211.

[28] D Rader, " 'I Knew What I Wanted to Be,' " *Parade Magazine,* November 1, 1992, p 4.

[29] Based on D H Lindsley, D A Brass, and J B Thomas, "Efficacy-Performance Spirals: A Multilevel Perspective," *Academy of Management Review,* July 1995, pp 645–78.

[30] See, for example, V Gecas, "The Social Psychology of Self-Efficacy," in *Annual Review of Sociology,* eds W R Scott and J Blake (Palo Alto, CA: Annual Reviews, Inc., 1989), vol. 15, pp 291–316; C K Stevens, A G Bavetta, and M E Gist, "Gender Differences in the Acquisition of Salary Negotiation Skills: The Role of Goals, Self-Efficacy, and Perceived Control," *Journal of Applied Psychology,* October 1993, pp 723–35; and D Eden and Y Zuk, "Seasickness as a Self-Fulfilling Prophecy: Raising Self-Efficacy to Boost Performance at Sea," *Journal of Applied Psychology,* October 1995, pp 628–35.

[31] For more on learned helplessness, see Gecas, "The Social Psychology of Self-Efficacy"; M J Martinko and W L Gardner, "Learned Helplessness: An Alternative Explanation for Performance Deficits," *Academy of Management Review,* April 1982, pp 195–204; and C R Campbell and M J Martinko, "An Integrative Attributional Perspective of Empowerment and Learned Helplessness: A Multimethod Field Study," *Journal of Management,* no. 2, 1998, pp 173–200.

[32] Research on this connection is reported in R B Rubin, M M Martin, S S Bruning, and D E Powers, "Test of a Self-Efficacy Model of Interpersonal Communication Competence," *Communication Quarterly,* Spring 1993, pp 210–20.

[33] Excerpted from T Petzinger Jr, "Bob Schmonsees Has a Tool for Better Sales, and It Ignores Excuses," *The Wall Street Journal,* March 26, 1999, p B1.

[34] Data from A D Stajkovic and F Luthans, "Self-Efficacy and Work-Related Performance: A Meta-Analysis," *Psychological Bulletin,* September 1998, pp 240–61.

[35] Based in part on discussion in Gecas, "The Social Psychology of Self-Efficacy."

[36] See S K Parker, "Enhancing Role Breadth Self-Efficacy: The Roles of Job Enrichment and Other Organizational Interventions," *Journal of Applied Psychology,* December 1998, pp 835–52.

[37] The positive relationship between self-efficacy and readiness for retraining is documented in L A Hill and J Elias, "Retraining Midcareer Managers: Career History and Self-Efficacy Beliefs," *Human Resource Management,* Summer 1990, pp 197–217. Also see A M Saks, "Longitudinal Field Investigation of the Moderating and Mediating Effects of Self-Efficacy on the Relationship between Training and Newcomer Adjustment," *Journal of Applied Psychology,* April 1995, pp 211–25.

[38] See A D Stajkovic and Fred Luthans, "Social Cognitive Theory and Self-Efficacy: Going Beyond Traditional Motivational and Behavioral Approaches," *Organizational Dynamics,* Spring 1998, pp 62–74.

[39] See P C Earley and T R Lituchy, "Delineating Goal and Efficacy Effects: A Test of Three Models," *Journal of Applied Psychology,* February 1991, pp 81–98.

[40] See W S Silver, T R Mitchell, and M E Gist, "Response to Successful and Unsuccessful Performance: The Moderating Effect of Self-Efficacy

on the Relationship between Performance and Attributions," *Organizational Behavior and Human Decision Processes,* June 1995, pp 286–99; R Zemke, "The Corporate Coach," *Training,* December 1996, pp 24–28; and J P Masciarelli, "Less Lonely at the Top," *Management Review,* April 1999, pp 58–61.

41 M Snyder and S Gangestad, "On the Nature of Self-Monitoring: Matters of Assessment, Matters of Validity," *Journal of Personality and Social Psychology,* July 1986, p 125.

42 T Morganthau, "Throwing Long," *Newsweek,* August 19, 1996, p 29.

43 Data from M Kilduff and D V Day, "Do Chameleons Get Ahead? The Effects of Self-Monitoring on Managerial Careers," *Academy of Management Journal,* August 1994, pp 1047–60.

44 Data from D B Turban and T W Dougherty, "Role of Protege Personality in Receipt of Mentoring and Career Success," *Academy of Management Journal,* June 1994, pp 688–702.

45 See F Luthans, "Successful vs. Effective Managers," *Academy of Management Executive,* May 1988, pp 127–32.

46 For related research evidence on *self-silencing,* see L V Gratch, M E Bassett, and S L Attra, "The Relationship of Gender and Ethnicity to Self-Silencing and Depression among College Students," *Psychology of Women Quarterly,* December 1995, pp 509–15. Also see W G Graziano and W H M Bryant, "Self-Monitoring and the Self-Attribution of Positive Emotions," *Journal of Personality and Social Psychology,* January 1998, pp 250–61.

47 M G Pratt, "To Be or Not to Be? Central Questions in Organizational Identification," in *Identity in Organizations,* eds D A Whetten and P C Godfrey (Thousand Oaks, CA: Sage Publications, 1998), p 172. Also see S Albert, B E Ashforth, and J E Dutton, "Organizational Identity and Identification: Charting New Waters and Building New Bridges," *Academy of Management Review,* January 2000, pp 13–17.

48 See G Dessler, "How to Earn Your Employees' Commitment," *Academy of Management Executive,* May 1999, pp 58–67.

49 For more, see B Filipczak, "The Soul of the Hog," *Training,* February 1996, pp 38–42.

50 For evidence of the stability of adult personality dimensions, see R R McCrae, "Moderated Analyses of Longitudinal Personality Stability," *Journal of Personality and Social Psychology,* September 1993, pp 577–85. Adult personality changes are documented in L Kaufman Cartwright and P Wink, "Personality Change in Women Physicians from Medical Student to Mid-40s," *Psychology of Women Quarterly,* June 1994, pp 291–308. Also see L Pulkkinen, M Ohranen, and A Tolvanen, "Personality Antecedents of Career Orientation and Stability among Women Compared to Men," *Journal of Vocational Behavior,* February 1999, pp 37–58.

51 The landmark report is J M Digman, "Personality Structure: Emergence of the Five-Factor Model," *Annual Review of Psychology,* vol. 41, 1990, pp 417–40. Also see M R Barrick and M K Mount, "Autonomy as a Moderator of the Relationships between the Big Five Personality Dimensions and Job Performance," *Journal of Applied Psychology,* February 1993, pp 111–18; J A Johnson and F Ostendorf, "Clarification of the Five-Factor Model with the Abridged Big Five Dimensional Circumplex," *Journal of Personality and Social Psychology,* September 1993, pp 563–76; and M Zuckerman, D M Kuhlman, J Joireman, P Teta, and M Kraft, "A Comparison of Three Structural Models for Personality: The Big Three, the Big Five, and the Alternative Five," *Journal of Personality and Social Psychology,* October 1993, pp 757–68.

52 For a review of research on the relationship between introversion–extroversion, motivation, and performance, see M S Humphreys and W Revelle, "Personality, Motivation, and Performance: A Theory of the Relationship between Individual Differences and Information Processing," *Psychological Review,* April 1984, pp 153–84. Also see D F Caldwell and J M Burger, "Personality Characteristics of Job Applicants and Success in Screening Interviews," *Personnel Psychology,* Spring 1998, pp 119–36; J B Asendorpf and S Wilpers, "Personality Effects on Social Relationships," *Journal of Personality and Social Psychology,* June 1998, pp 1531–44; K M DeNeve and H Cooper, "The Happy Personality: A Meta-Analysis of 137 Personality Traits and Subjective Well-Being," *Psychological Bulletin,* September 1998, pp 197–229; and D P Skarlicki,

R Folger, and P Tesluk, "Personality as a Moderator in the Relationship between Fairness and Retaliation," *Academy of Management Journal,* February 1999, pp 100–8.

53 Data from S V Paunonen et al., "The Structure of Personality in Six Cultures," *Journal of Cross-Cultural Psychology,* May 1996, pp 339–53. Also see M S Katigbak, A T Church, and T X Akamine, "Cross-Cultural Generalizability of Personality Dimensions: Relating Indigenous and Imported Dimensions in Two Cultures," *Journal of Personality and Social Psychology,* January 1996, pp 99–114; V Benet-Martinez and O P John, "*Los Cinco Grandes* Across Cultures and Ethnic Groups: Multitrait Multimethod Analyses of the Big Five in Spanish and English," *Journal of Personality and Social Psychology,* September 1998, pp 729–750; and G Saucier and F Ostendorf, "Hierarchical Subcomponents of the Big Five Personality Factors: A Cross-Language Replication," *Journal of Personality and Social Psychology,* April 1999, pp 613–27.

54 See M R Barrick and M K Mount, "The Big Five Personality Dimensions and Job Performance: A Meta-Analysis," *Personnel Psychology,* Spring 1991, pp 1–26. Also see R P Tett, D N Jackson, and M Rothstein, "Personality Measures as Predictors of Job Performance: A Meta-Analytic Review," *Personnel Psychology,* Winter 1991, pp 703–42.

55 Barrick and Mount, "The Big Five Personality Dimensions and Job Performance: A Meta-Analysis," p 18. See O Behling, "Employee Selection: Will Intelligence and Conscientiousness Do the Job?" *Academy of Management Executive,* February 1998, pp 77–86.

56 Barrick and Mount, "The Big Five Personality Dimensions and Job Performance: A Meta-Analysis," p 21. Also see D M Tokar, A R Fischer, and L M Subich, "Personality and Vocational Behavior: A Selective Review of the Literature, 1993–1997," *Journal of Vocational Behavior,* October 1998, pp 115–53; and K C Wooten, T A Timmerman, and R Folger, "The Use of Personality and the Five-Factor Model to Predict New Business Ventures: From Outplacement to Start-up," *Journal of Vocational Behavior,* February 1999, pp 82–101.

57 See S B Gustafson and M D Mumford, "Personal Style and Person-Environment Fit: A Pattern Approach," *Journal of Vocational Behavior,* April 1995, pp 163–88.

58 See discussion in Barrick and Mount, "The Big Five Personality Dimensions and Job Performance: A Meta-Analysis," pp 21–22. Also see J M Cortina, M L Doherty, N Schmitt, G Kaufman, and R G Smith, "The 'Big Five' Personality Factors in the IPI and MMPI: Predictors of Police Performance," *Personnel Psychology,* Spring 1992, pp 119–40; M J Schmit and A M Ryan, "The Big Five in Personnel Selection: Factor Structure in Applicant and Nonapplicant Populations," *Journal of Applied Psychology,* December 1993, pp 966–74; and C Caggiano, "Psychopath," *Inc.,* July 1998, pp 77–85.

59 M K Mount and M R Barrick, "The Big Five Personality Dimensions: Implications for Research and Practice in Human Resources Management," in *Research in Personnel and Human Resources Management,* ed G R Ferris (Greenwich, CT: JAI Press, 1995), vol. 13, p 189. See J M Collins and D H Gleaves, "Race, Job Applicants, and the Five-Factor Model of Personality: Implications for Black Psychology, Industrial/Organizational Psychology, and the Five-Factor Theory," *Journal of Applied Psychology,* August 1998, pp 531–44.

60 W Lambert, "Psychological Tests Designed to Weed Out Rogue Cops Get a 'D,' " *The Wall Street Journal,* September 1995, p A1. Also see A M Ryan, R E Ployhart, and L A Friedel, "Using Personality Testing to Reduce Adverse Impact: A Cautionary Note," *Journal of Applied Psychology,* April 1998, pp 298–307.

61 Other sources relating to Table 5–2 are "Testing . . . Testing," *Training,* September 1998, p 14; and B Leonard, "Reading Employees," *HRMagazine,* April 1999, pp 67–73.

62 R Lieber, "Wired for Hiring: Microsoft's Slick Recruiting Machine," *Fortune,* February 5, 1996, p 124.

63 See C M Solomon, "Testing at Odds with Diversity Efforts?" *Personnel Journal,* April 1996, pp 131–40; and J C McCune, "Testing, Testing 1-2-3," *Management Review,* January 1996, pp 50–52.

64 For example, see J C Connor, "The Paranoid Personality at Work," *HRMagazine,* March 1999, pp 120–26; and "Your Sleep Has a Personality," *Management Review,* May 1999, p 9.

[65] For an instructive update, see J B Rotter, "Internal versus External Control of Reinforcement: A Case History of a Variable," *American Psychologist,* April 1990, pp 489–93. A critical review of locus of control and a call for a meta-analysis can be found in R W Renn and R J Vandenberg, "Differences in Employee Attitudes and Behaviors Based on Rotter's (1966) Internal-External Locus of Control: Are They All Valid?" *Human Relations,* November 1991, p 1161–77.

[66] J Fierman, "What's Luck Got to Do with It?" *Fortune,* October 16, 1995, p 149.

[67] For an overall review of research on locus of control, see P E Spector, "Behavior in Organizations as a Function of Employee's Locus of Control," *Psychological Bulletin,* May 1982, pp 482–97; the relationship between locus of control and performance and satisfaction is examined in D R Norris and R E Niebuhr, "Attributional Influences on the Job Performance–Job Satisfaction Relationship," *Academy of Management Journal,* June 1984, pp 424–31; salary differences between internals and externals were examined by P C Nystrom, "Managers' Salaries and Their Beliefs about Reinforcement Control," *The Journal of Social Psychology,* August 1983, pp 291–92.

[68] See S R Hawk, "Locus of Control and Computer Attitude: The Effect of User Involvement," *Computers in Human Behavior,* no. 3, 1989, pp 199–206. Also see A S Phillips and A G Bedeian, "Leader-Follower Exchange Quality: The Role of Personal and Interpersonal Attributes," *Academy of Management Journal,* August 1994, pp 990–1001.

[69] These recommendations are from Spector, "Behavior in Organizations as a Function of Employee's Locus of Control."

[70] See "What Men Think About," *Training,* March 1995, p 14; and P Cappelli, "Is the 'Skills Gap' Really about Attitudes?" *California Management Review,* Summer 1995, pp 108–24.

[71] M Fishbein and I Ajzen, *Belief, Attitude, Intention and Behavior: An Introduction to Theory and Research* (Reading, MA: Addison-Wesley Publishing, 1975), p 6. For more, see D Andrich and I M Styles, "The Structural Relationship between Attitude and Behavior Statements from the Unfolding Perspective," *Psychological Methods,* December 1998, pp 454–69; A P Brief, *Attitudes In and Around Organizations* (Thousand Oaks, CA: Sage Publications, 1998); and "Tips to Pick the Best Employee," *Business Week,* March 1, 1999, p 24.

[72] For a discussion of the difference between values and attitudes, see B W Becker and P E Connor, "Changing American Values—Debunking the Myth," *Business,* January–March 1985, pp 56–59.

[73] See B M Staw and J Ross, "Stability in the Midst of Change: A Dispositional Approach to Job Attitudes," *Journal of Applied Psychology,* August 1985, pp 469–80. Also see J Schaubroeck, D C Ganster, and B Kemmerer, "Does Trait Affect Promote Job Attitude Stability?" *Journal of Organizational Behavior,* March 1996, pp 191–96.

[74] Data from P S Visser and J A Krosnick, "Development of Attitude Strength Over the Life Cycle: Surge and Decline," *Journal of Personality and Social Psychology,* December 1998, pp 1389–1410.

[75] For a brief overview and update of the model, see M Fishbein and M Stasson, "The Role of Desires, Self-Predictions, and Perceived Control in the Prediction of Training Session Attendance," *Journal of Applied Social Psychology,* February 1990, pp 173–98. Alternative models are discussed in M Sverke and S Kuruvilla, "A New Conceptualization of Union Commitment: Development and Test of an Integrated Theory," *Journal of Organizational Behavior,* Special Issue, 1995, pp 505–32; and R C Thompson and J G Hunt, "Inside the Black Box of Alpha, Beta, and Gamma Change: Using a Cognitive-Processing Model to Assess Attitude Structure," *Academy of Management Review,* July 1996, pp 655–90.

[76] See R P Steel and N K Ovalle II, "A Review and Meta-Analysis of Research on the Relationship between Behavioral Intentions and Employee Turnover," *Journal of Applied Psychology,* November 1984, pp 673–86. Also see J A Ouellette and W Wood, "Habit and Intention in Everyday Life: The Multiple Processes by Which Past Behavior Predicts Future Behavior," *Psychological Bulletin,* July 1998, pp 54–74; and "Worker Retention Presents Challenge to US Employers," *HRMagazine,* September 1998, p 22.

[77] I Ajzen and M Fishbein, *Understanding Attitudes and Predicting Social Behavior* (Englewood Cliffs, NJ: Prentice-Hall, 1980), p 7. Also

see J Barling, K E Dupre, and C G Hepburn, "Effects of Parents' Job Insecurity on Children's Work Beliefs and Attitudes," *Journal of Applied Psychology,* February 1998, pp 112–18; and J W Dean, Jr, P Brandes, and R Dharwadkar, "Organizational Cynicism," *Academy of Management Review,* April 1998, pp 341–52.

[78] Drawn from J M Grant and T S Bateman, "An Experimental Test of the Impact of Drug-Testing Programs on Potential Job Applicants' Attitudes and Intentions," *Journal of Applied Psychology,* April 1990, pp 127–31.

[79] For an overall review of attitude formation research, see Ajzen and Fishbein, *Understanding Attitudes and Predicting Social Behavior.* Also see S Chaiken and C Stangor, "Attitudes and Attitude Change," in *Annual Review of Psychology,* eds M R Rosenzweig and L W Porter (Palo Alto, CA: Annual Reviews, 1987), pp 575–630; and Fishbein and Stasson, "The Role of Desires, Self-Predictions, and Perceived Control in the Prediction of Training Session Attendance."

[80] See P W Hom and C L Hulin, "A Competitive Test of the Prediction of Reenlistment by Several Models," *Journal of Applied Psychology,* February 1981, pp 23–39. Also see P R Warshaw, R Calantone, and M Joyce, "A Field Study Application of the Fishbein and Ajzen Intention Model," *The Journal of Social Psychology,* February 1986, pp 135–365.

[81] Data from D A Kravitz and J Platania, "Attitudes and Beliefs about Affirmative Action: Effects of Target and of Respondent Sex and Ethnicity," *Journal of Applied Psychology,* December 1993, pp 928–38.

[82] Based on evidence in C J Thomsen, A M Basu, and M Tippens Reinitz, "Effects of Women's Studies Courses on Gender-Related Attitudes of Women and Men," *Psychology of Women Quarterly,* September 1995, pp 419–26.

[83] See B Fishel, "A New Perspective: How to Get the Real Story from Attitude Surveys," *Training,* February 1998, pp 91–94.

[84] S B Parry, "The Quest for Competencies," *Training,* July 1996, p 48. Also see S B Parry, "Just What Is a Competency? (And Why Should You Care?)," *Training,* June 1998, pp 58–64.

[85] For interesting reading on intelligence, see E Cose, "Teaching Kids to Be Smart," *Newsweek,* August 21, 1995, pp 58–60; A Farnham, "Are You Smart Enough to Keep Your Job?" *Fortune,* January 15, 1996, pp 34–48; D Stamps, "Are We Smart Enough for Our Jobs?" *Training,* April 1996, pp 44–50; K S Peterson, "Do New Definitions of Smart Dilute Meaning?" *USA Today,* February 18, 1997, pp 1D–2D; and J R Flynn, "Searching for Justice: The Discovery of IQ Gains Over Time," *American Psychologist,* January 1999, pp 5–20.

[86] For an excellent update on intelligence, including definitional distinctions and a historical perspective of the IQ controversy, see R A Weinberg, "Intelligence and IQ," *American Psychologist,* February 1989, pp 98–104.

[87] Ibid.

[88] S L Wilk, L Burris Desmarais, and P R Sackett, "Gravitation to Jobs Commensurate with Ability: Longitudinal and Cross-Sectional Tests," *Journal of Applied Psychology,* February 1995, p 79.

[89] B Azar, "People Are Becoming Smarter—Why?" *APA Monitor,* June 1996, p 20. Also see " 'Average' Intelligence Higher than It Used to Be," *USA Today,* February 18, 1997, p 6D.

[90] For related research, see M J Ree and J A Earles, "Predicting Training Success: Not Much More Than g," *Personnel Psychology,* Summer 1991, pp 321–32.

[91] See F L Schmidt and J E Hunter, "Employment Testing: Old Theories and New Research Findings," *American Psychologist,* October 1981, p 1128. Also see Y Ganzach, "Intelligence and Job Satisfaction," *Academy of Management Journal,* October 1998, pp 526–39.

[92] D Goleman, *Emotional Intelligence* (New York: Bantam Books, 1995), p 34. For more, see Q N Huy, "Emotional Capability, Emotional Intelligence, and Radical Change," *Academy of Management Review,* April 1999, pp 325–45.

[93] M N Martinez, "The Smarts That Count," *HRMagazine,* November 1997, pp 72–78.

[94] "What's Your EQ at Work?" *Fortune,* October 26, 1998, p 298.

[95] Based on M Davies, L Stankov, and R D Roberts, "Emotional Intelligence: In Search of an Elusive Construct," *Journal of Personality and Social Psychology,* October 1998, pp 989–1015.

[96] A Fisher, "Success Secret: A High Emotional IQ," *Fortune,* October 26, 1998, p 294.

[97] See I Briggs Myers (with P B Myers), *Gifts Differing* (Palo Alto, CA: Consulting Psychologists Press, 1980). Mentions of the MBTI can be found in B O'Reilly, "Does Your Fund Manager Play the Piano?" *Fortune,* December 29, 1997, pp 139–44; T A Stewart, "Escape from the Cult of Personality Tests," *Fortune,* March 16, 1998, p 80; J T Adams III, "What's Your Type?" *HRMagazine,* June 1999, p 8; and T Petzinger Jr, "With the Stakes High, a Lucent Duo Conquers Distance and Culture," *The Wall Street Journal,* April 23, 1999, p B1.

[98] For a complete discussion of each cognitive style, see J W Slocum, Jr, and D Hellriegel, "A Look at How Managers' Minds Work," *Business Horizons,* July–August 1983, pp 58–68; and W Taggart and D Robey, "Minds and Managers: On the Dual Nature of Human Information Processing and Management," *Academy of Management Review,* April 1981, pp 187–95. Also see M Wood Daudelin, "Learning from Experience through Reflection," *Organizational Dynamics,* Winter 1996, pp 36–48.

[99] See B K Blaylock and L P Rees, "Cognitive Style and the Usefulness of Information," *Decision Sciences,* Winter 1984, pp 74–91.

[100] Additional material on cognitive styles may be found in F A Gul, "The Joint and Moderating Role of Personality and Cognitive Style on Decision Making," *The Accounting Review,* April 1984, pp 264–77; B H Kleiner, "The Interrelationship of Jungian Modes of Mental Functioning with Organizational Factors: Implications for Management Development," *Human Relations,* November 1983, pp 997–1012; and J L McKenney and P G W Keen, "How Managers' Minds Work," *Harvard Business Review,* May–June 1974, pp 79–90.

[101] See G H Rice, Jr, and D P Lindecamp, "Personality Types and Business Success of Small Retailers," *Journal of Occupational Psychology,* June 1989, pp 177–82.

[102] W L Gardner and M J Martinko, "Using the Myers-Briggs Type Indicator to Study Managers: A Literature Review and Research Agenda," *Journal of Management,* no. 1, 1996, p 77.

[103] For example, see F Ramsoomair, "Relating Theoretical Concepts to Life in the Classroom: Applying the Myers-Briggs Type Indicator," *Journal of Management Education,* February 1994, pp 111–16. For related material, see S Shapiro and M T Spence, "Managerial Intuition: A Conceptual and Operational Framework," *Business Horizons,* January–February 1997, pp 63–68.

[104] S Hamm, "Bill's Co-Pilot," *Business Week,* September 14, 1998, pp 85, 87.

[105] Quoted in B Schlender, "Why Andy Grove Can't Stop," *Fortune,* July 10, 1995, p 91.

[106] D Lieberman, "Fear of Failing Drives Diller," *USA Today,* February 10, 1999, p 3B.

[107] R S Lazarus, *Emotion and Adaptation* (New York: Oxford University Press, 1991), p 6. Also see, Goleman, *Emotional Intelligence,* pp 289–90; and J A Russell and L F Barrett, "Core Affect, Prototypical Emotional Episodes, and Other Things Called *Emotion:* Dissecting the Elephant," *Journal of Personality and Social Psychology,* May 1999, pp 805–19.

[108] Based on discussion in R D Arvey, G L Renz, and T W Watson, "Emotionality and Job Performance: Implications for Personnel Selection," in *Research in Personnel and Human Resources Management,* vol. 16, ed G R Ferris (Stamford, CT: JAI Press, 1998), pp 103–47. Also see L A King, "Ambivalence Over Emotional Expression and Reading Emotions," *Journal of Personality and Social Psychology,* March 1998, pp 753–62.

[109] See G Smith, " 'It's Nice to Have This Stuff in Your Blood,' " *Business Week,* August 12, 1996, p 74.

[110] See S V Brull, "Eight Wings and a Prayer," *Business Week,* October 19, 1998, pp 77–79; C Sittenfeld, "Good Ways to Deliver Bad News," *Fast Company,* April 1999, pp 58–60; and M Hickins, "A Day at the Races," *Management Review,* May 1999, pp 56–61.

[111] Based on J M Kidd, "Emotion: An Absent Presence in Career Theory," *Journal of Vocational Behavior,* June 1998, pp 275–88.

[112] Data from A M Kring and A H Gordon, "Sex Differences in Emotions: Expression, Experience, and Physiology," *Journal of Personality and Social Psychology,* March 1998, pp 686–703.

[113] Drawn from P Totterdell, S Kellett, K Teuchmann, and R B Briner, "Evidence of Mood Linkage in Work Groups," *Journal of Personality and Social Psychology,* June 1998, pp 1504–15.

[114] See A M O'Leary-Kelly, R W Griffin, and D J Glew, "Organization-Motivated Aggression: A Research Framework," *Academy of Management Review,* January 1996, pp 225–53. Also see J H Neuman and R A Baron, "Workplace Violence and Workplace Aggression: Evidence Concerning Specific Forms, Potential Causes, and Preferred Targets," *Journal of Management,* no. 3, 1998, pp 391–419; and D Cohen, "Culture, Social Organization, and Patterns of Violence," *Journal of Personality and Social Psychology,* August 1998, pp 408–19.

[115] J C McCune, "And You Thought TV Was Violent," *Management Review,* June 1999, p 8.

[116] C Joinson, "Controlling Hostility," *HRMagazine,* August 1998, p 65.

[117] Excerpted from K Morris, "The Reincarnation of Mike Milken," *Business Week,* May 10, 1999, pp 92–104.

[118] The questionnaire and scoring key are excerpted from J W Slocum, Jr, and D Hellriegel, "A Look at How Managers' Minds Work," *Business Horizons,* July–August 1983, pp 58–68.

CHAPTER 6

[1] Excerpted from P Black, "Keeping Memory Lane Unclogged," *Business Week,* March 8, 1999, pp 116–17.

[2] For a review of memory research, see D L Schacter, "The Seven Sins of Memory," *American Psychologist,* March 1999, pp 182–203.

[3] Details may be found in R Eisenberger, P Fasolo, and V Davis–LaMastro, "Perceived Organizational Support and Employee Diligence, Commitment, and Innovation," *Journal of Applied Psychology,* February 1990, pp 51–59.

[4] S T Fiske and S E Taylor, *Social Cognition,* 2nd ed (Reading, MA: Addison-Wesley Publishing, 1991), pp 1–2.

[5] Adapted from discussion in Fiske and Taylor, *Social Cognition,* 2nd ed, pp 247–50.

[6] The negativity bias was examined and supported by O Ybarra and W G Stephan, "Misanthropic Person Memory," *Journal of Personality and Social Psychology,* April 1996, pp 691–700; and Y Ganzach, "Negativity (and Positivity) in Performance Evaluation: Three Field Studies," *Journal of Applied Psychology,* August 1995, pp 491–99.

[7] E Rosch, C B Mervis, W D Gray, D M Johnson, and P Boyes-Braem, "Basic Objects in Natural Categories," *Cognitive Psychology,* July 1976, p 383.

[8] Washing clothes.

[9] See B R Ragins, B Townsend, and M Mattis, "Gender Gap in the Executive Suite: CEOs and Female Executives Report on Breaking the Glass Ceiling," *The Academy of Management Executive,* February 1998, pp 28–42; and P A Giuffre and C L Williams, "Boundary Lines: Labeling Sexual Harassment in Restaurants," *Gender and Society,* September 1994, pp 378–401.

[10] See J P Forgas, "On Being Happy and Mistaken: Mood Effects on the Fundamental Attribution Error," *Journal of Personality and Social Psychology,* August 1998, 318–31; and A Varma, A S DeNisi, and L H Peters, "Interpersonal Affect and Performance Appraisal: A Field Study," *Personnel Psychology,* Summer 1996, pp 341–60.

[11] See I Ajzen and J Sexton, "Depth of Processing, Belief Congruence, and Attitude-Behavior Correspondence," in *Dual-Process Theories in Social Psychology,* eds S Chaiken, and Y Trope (New York: The Guilford Press, 1999), pp 117–38; and A J Kinicki, P W Hom, M R Trost, and K J Wade, "Effects of Category Prototypes on Performance-Rating Accuracy," *Journal of Applied Psychology,* June 1995, pp 354–70.

[12] The relationship between depression and information processing is discussed by A Zelli and K A Dodge, "Personality Development from the Bottom Up," in *The Coherence of Personality,* eds D Cervone and Y Shoda (New York: The Guilford Press, 1999), pp 94–126.

[13] For a thorough discussion about the structure and organization of memory, see L R Squire, B Knowlton, and G Musen, "The Structure and Organization of Memory," in *Annual Review of Psychology,* eds L W Porter and

M R Rosenzweig (Palo Alto, CA: Annual Reviews Inc., 1993), vol. 44, pp 453–95.

[14] A thorough discussion of the reasoning process used to make judgments and decisions is provided by S A Sloman, "The Empirical Case for Two Systems of Reasoning," *Psychological Bulletin,* January 1996, pp 3–22.

[15] Results can be found in C M Marlowe, S L Schneider, and C E Nelson, "Gender and Attractiveness Biases in Hiring Decisions: Are More Experienced Managers Less Biased?" *Journal of Applied Psychology,* February 1996, pp 11–21.

[16] Details of this study can be found in C K Stevens, "Antecedents of Interview Interactions, Interviewers' Ratings, and Applicants' Reactions," *Personnel Psychology,* Spring 1998, pp 55–85.

[17] See R C Mayer and J H Davis, "The Effect of the Performance Appraisal System on Trust for Management: A Field Quasi-Experiment," *Journal of Applied Psychology,* February 1999, pp 123–36.

[18] Results can be found in W H Bommer, J L Johnson, G A Rich, P M Podsakoff, and S B Mackenzie, "On the Interchangeability of Objective and Subjective Measures of Employee Performance: A Meta-Analysis," *Personnel Psychology,* Autumn 1995, pp 587–605.

[19] See J I Sanchez and P D L Torre, "A Second Look at the Relationship between Rating and Behavioral Accuracy in Performance Appraisal," *Journal of Applied Psychology,* February 1996, pp 3–10; and Kinicki, Hom, Trost, and Wade, "Effects of Category Prototypes on Performance-Rating Accuracy."

[20] The effectiveness of rater training was supported by D V Day and L M Sulsky, "Effects of Frame-of-Reference Training and Information Configuration on Memory Organization and Rating Accuracy," *Journal of Applied Psychology,* February 1995, pp 158–67.

[21] Results can be found in J S Phillips and R G Lord, "Schematic Information Processing and Perceptions of Leadership in Problem-Solving Groups," *Journal of Applied Psychology,* August 1982, pp 486–92.

[22] C Leerhsen, "How Disney Does It," *Newsweek,* April 3, 1989, p 52.

[23] C M Judd and B Park, "Definition and Assessment of Accuracy in Social Stereotypes," *Psychological Review,* January 1993, p 110.

[24] For a thorough discussion of stereotype accuracy, see M C Ashton and V M Esses, "Stereotype Accuracy: Estimating the Academic Performance of Ethnic Groups," *Personality and Social Psychology Bulletin,* February 1999, pp 225–36.

[25] See C Comeau-Kirschner, "Navigating the Roadblocks," *Management Review,* May 1999, p 8; and S Shellenbarger, "Work-Force Study Finds Loyalty Is Weak, Division of Race and Gender Are Deep, *The Wall Street Journal,* September 3, 1993, pp B1, B9.

[26] The process of stereotype formation and maintenance is discussed by S T Fiske, M Lin, and S L Neuberg, "The Continuum Model: Ten Years Later," in *Dual-Process Theories in Social Psychology,* eds S Chaiken and Y Trope (New York: The Guilford Press, 1999) pp 231–54.

[27] This discussion is based on material presented in G V Bodenhausen, C N Macrae, and J W Sherman, "On the Dialectics of Discrimination," in *Dual-Process Theories in Social Psychology,* eds S Chaiken and Y Trope (New York: The Guilford Press, 1999) pp 271–90.

[28] See A H Eagly, S J Karu, and B T Johnson, "Gender and Leadership Style among School Principals: A Meta-Analysis," *Educational Administration Quarterly,* February 1992, pp 76–102; and I K Broverman, S Raymond Vogel, D M Broverman, F E Clarkson, and P S Rosenkrantz, "Sex-Role Stereotypes: A Current Appraisal," *Journal of Social Issues,* 1972, p 75.

[29] See B P Allen, "Gender Stereotypes Are Not Accurate: A Replication of Martin (1987) Using Diagnostic vs. Self-Report and Behavioral Criteria," *Sex Roles,* May 1995, pp 583–600.

[30] Results can be found in V E Schein, R Mueller, T Lituchy, and J Liu, "Think Manager—Think Male: A Global Phenomenon?" *Journal of Organizational Behavior,* January 1996, pp 33–41.

[31] See J D Olian, D P Schwab, and Y Haberfeld, "The Impact of Applicant Gender Compared to Qualifications on Hiring Recommendations: A Meta-Analysis of Experimental Studies," *Organizational Behavior and Human Decision Processes,* April 1988, pp 180–95.

[32] Results from the meta-analyses are discussed in K P Carson, C L Sutton, and P D Corner, "Gender Bias in Performance Appraisals:

A Meta-Analysis," paper presented at the 49th Annual Academy of Management Meeting, Washington, DC: 1989. Results from the field study can be found in T J Maurer and M A Taylor, "Is Sex by Itself Enough? An Exploration of Gender Bias Issues in Performance Appraisal," *Organizational Behavior and Human Decision Processes,* November 1994, pp 231–51.

[33] See J Landau, "The Relationship of Race and Gender to Managers' Ratings of Promotion Potential," *Journal of Organizational Behavior,* July 1995, pp 391–400.

[34] Results from this study can be found in M Biernat, C S Crandall, L V Young, D Kobrynowicz, and S M Halpin, "All That You Can Be: Stereotyping of Self and Others in a Military Context," *Journal of Personality and Social Psychology,* August 1998, pp 301–317.

[35] For a complete review, see S R Rhodes, "Age-Related Differences in Work Attitudes and Behavior: A Review and Conceptual Analysis," *Psychological Bulletin,* March 1983, pp 328–67. Supporting evidence was also provided by G Burkins, "Work Week: A Special News Report about Life on the Job—and Trends Taking Shape There," *The Wall Street Journal,* May 5, 1996, p A1.

[36] See G M McEvoy, "Cumulative Evidence of the Relationship between Employee Age and Job Performance," *Journal of Applied Psychology,* February 1989, pp 11–17.

[37] A thorough discussion of the relationship between age and performance is contained in D A Waldman and B J Avolio, "Aging and Work Performance in Perspective: Contextual and Developmental Considerations," in *Research in Personnel and Human Resources Management,* ed G R Ferris (Greenwich, CT: JAI Press, 1993), vol. 11, pp 133–62.

[38] For details, see B J Avolio, D A Waldman, and M A McDaniel, "Age and Work Performance in Nonmanagerial Jobs: The Effects of Experience and Occupational Type," *Academy of Management Journal,* June 1990, pp 407–22.

[39] D H Powell, "Aging Baby Boomers: Stretching Your Workforce Options," *HRMagazine,* July 1998, p 83.

[40] See P W Hom and R W Griffeth, *Employee Turnover* (Cincinnati, OH: SouthWestern, 1995), pp 35–50; and J J Martocchio, "Age-Related Differences in Employee Absenteeism: A Meta-Analysis," *Psychology and Aging,* December 1989, pp 409–14.

[41] Various racial stereotypes are discussed by N London-Vargas, *Faces of Diversity* (New York: Vantage Press, 1999); and M Shih, T L Pittinsky, and N Ambady, "Stereotypes Susceptibility: Identity Salience and Shifts in Quantitative Performance," *Psychological Science,* January 1999, pp 80–83.

[42] See "Employed White, Black, and Hispanic-Origin Workers by Sex, Occupation, Class of Worker, and Full- or Part-Time Status," *Bureau of Labor Statistics,* February 13, 1997 (http://ferret.bls.census.gov/macro/171996/empearn//aa12.txt); and D Jones, "African-Americans Take Reins at 'Fortune' Firms," *USA Today,* April 27, 1999, pp 1B, 2B.

[43] Details of the study on race and attitudes may be found in J H Greenhaus, S Parasuraman, W M Wormley, "Effects of Race on Organizational Experiences, Job Performance Evaluations, and Career Outcomes," *Academy of Management Journal,* March 1990, pp 64–86.

[44] Results from these studies can be found in A I Huffcutt and P L Roth, "Racial Group Differences in Employment Interview Evaluations," *Journal of Applied Psychology,* April 1998, pp 179–89; and T-R Lin, G H Dobbins, and J-L Farh, "A Field Study of Race and Age Similarity Effects on Interview Ratings in Conventional and Situational Interviews," *Journal of Applied Psychology,* June 1992, pp 363–71.

[45] See D A Waldman and B J Avolio, "Race Effects in Performance Evaluations: Controlling for Ability, Education, and Experience," *Journal of Applied Psychology,* December 1991, pp 897–901; and E D Pulakos, L A White, S H Oppler, and W C Borman, "Examination of Race and Sex Effects on Performance Ratings," *Journal of Applied Psychology,* October 1989, pp 770–80.

[46] Results can be found in Landau, "The Relationship of Race and Gender to Managers' Ratings of Promotion Potential."

[47] C M Schall, "The Americans with Disabilities Act—Are We Keeping Our Promise? An Analysis of the Effect of the ADA on the Employment of Persons with Disabilities," *Journal of Vocational Rehabilitation,* June 1998, p 191.

[48] P Digh, "People with Disabilities Show What They Can Do," *HRMagazine,* June 1998, pp 141–45.

[49] Statistics pertaining to the employment of persons with disabilities are presented in T W Hale, H V Hayghe, and J M McNeil, "Persons with Disabilities: Labor Market Activity in 1994, " *Monthly Labor Review,* September 1998, pp 3–12.

[50] The discussion about the performance of disabled employees and the costs of their employment was based on P Digh, "People with Disabilities Show What They Can Do."

[51] Supporting studies were conducted by A J Kinicki, C A Lockwood, P W Hom, and R W Griffeth, "Interviewer Predictions of Applicant Qualifications and Interviewer Validity," *Journal of Applied Psychology,* October 1990, pp 477–86; and Day and Sulsky, "Effects of Frame-of-Reference Training and Information Configuration on Memory Organization and Rating Accuracy."

[52] Skill based pay is discussed by T P Flannery, D A Hofrichter, P E Platten, *People, Performance, and Pay: Dynamic Compensation for Changing Organizations* (New York: The Free Press, 1996).

[53] Research is reviewed by R Rodgers, J E Hunter, and D L Rogers, "Influence of Top Management Commitment on Management Program Success," *Journal of Applied Psychology,* February 1993, pp 151–55.

[54] The background and results for this study are presented in R Rosenthal and L Jacobson, *Pygmalion in the Classroom: Teacher Expectation and Pupils' Intellectual Development* (New York: Holt, Rinehart & Winston, 1968).

[55] See D Eden and Y Zuk, "Seasickness as a Self-Fulfilling Prophecy: Raising Self-Efficacy to Boost Performance at Sea," *Journal of Applied Psychology,* October 1995, pp 628–35. For a thorough review of research on the Pygmalion effect, see D Eden, *Pygmalion in Management: Productivity as a Self-Fulfilling Prophecy* (Lexington, MA: Lexington Books, 1990), ch 2.

[56] This study was conducted by T Dvir, D Eden, M L Banjo, "Self-Fulfilling Prophecy and Gender: Can Women Be Pygmalion and Galatea?" *Journal of Applied Psychology,* April 1995, pp 253–70.

[57] See J-F Manzoni and J-L Barsoux, "The Set-up-to-Fail Syndrome," *Harvard Business Review,* March–April 1998, pp 101–13.

[58] This example was based on Ibid; and "Living Down to Expectations," *Training,* July 1998, p 15.

[59] The role of positive expectations at Microsoft is discussed by S Hamm and O Port, "The Mother of All Software Projects," *Business Week,* February 22, 1999, pp 69, 72.

[60] These recommendations were adapted from J Keller, "Have Faith—In You," *Selling Power,* June 1996, pp 84, 86; and R W Goddard, "The Pygmalion Effect," *Personnel Journal,* June 1985, p 10.

[61] Kelley's model is discussed in detail in H H Kelley, "The Processes of Causal Attribution," *American Psychologist,* February 1973, pp 107–28.

[62] For examples, see J Susskind, K Maurer, V Thakkar, D L Hamilton, and J W Sherman, "Perceiving Individuals and Groups: Expectancies, Dispositional Inferences, and Causal Attributions," *Journal of Personality and Social Psychology,* February 1999, pp 181–91; and J McClure, "Discounting Causes of Behavior: Are Two Reasons Better than One?" *Journal of Personality and Social Psychology,* January 1998, pp 7–20.

[63] See P D Sweeney, K Anderson, and S Bailey, "Attributional Style in Depression: A Meta-Analytic Review," *Journal of Personality and Social Psychology,* May 1986, pp 974–91.

[64] Results can be found in P J Corr and J A Gray, "Attributional Style as a Personality Factor in Insurance Sales Performance in the UK," *Journal of Occupational Psychology,* March 1996, pp 83–87.

[65] Supportive results can be found in J Silvester, N R Anderson, F Patterson, "Organizational Culture Change: An Inter-Group Attributional Analysis," *Journal of Occupational and Organizational Psychology,* March 1999, pp 1–23; J Greenberg, "Forgive Me, I'm New: Three Experimental Demonstrations of the Effects of Attempts to Excuse Poor Performance," *Organizational Behavior and Human Decision Processes,* May 1996, pp 165–78; and G E Prussia, A J Kinicki, and J S Bracker, "Psychological and Behavioral Consequences of Job Loss: A Covariance Structure Analysis Using Weiner's (1985) Attribution Model," *Journal of Applied Psychology,* June 1993, pp 382–94.

[66] Results from these studies can be found in D A Hofmann and A Stetzer, "The Role of Safety Climate and Communication in Accident Interpretation: Implications for Learning from Negative Events," *Academy of Management Journal,* December 1998, pp 644–57; and I Choi, R E Nisbett, and A Norenzayan, "Causal Attribution Across Cultures: Variation and Universality," *Psychological Bulletin,* January 1999, pp 47–63.

[67] The effect of the self-serving bias was tested and supported by P E De Michele, B Gansneder, G B Solomon, "Success and Failure Attributions of Wrestlers: Further Evidence of the Self-Serving Bias," *Journal of Sport Behavior,* August 1998, pp 242–55; and C Sedikides, W K Campbell, G D Reeder, and A J Elliot, "The Self-Serving Bias in Relational Context," *Journal of Personality and Social Psychology,* February 1998, pp 378–86.

[68] Details may be found in S E Moss and M J Martinko, "The Effects of Performance Attributions and Outcome Dependence on Leader Feedback Behavior Following Poor Subordinate Performance," *Journal of Organizational Behavior,* May 1998, pp 259–74; and E C Pence, W C Pendelton, G H Dobbins, and J A Sgro, "Effects of Causal Explanations and Sex Variables on Recommendations for Corrective Actions Following Employee Failure," *Organizational Behavior and Human Performance,* April 1982, pp 227–40.

[69] See D Konst, R Vonk, and R V D Vlist, "Inferences about Causes and Consequences of Behavior of Leaders and Subordinates," *Journal of Organizational Behavior,* March 1999, pp 261–71.

[70] See M Miserandino, "Attributional Retraining as a Method of Improving Athletic Performance," *Journal of Sport Behavior,* August 1998, pp 286–97; and F Forsterling, "Attributional Retraining: A Review," *Psychological Bulletin,* November 1985, pp 496–512.

[71] Excerpted from A Fisher, "Finished at Forty," *Fortune,* February 1, 1999, pp 50–54, 60.

[72] This exercise was modified from one contained in L Gardenwartz and A Rowe, *Diverse Teams at Work* (New York: McGraw-Hill, 1994), p 169. © 1994. Reproduced with permission of The McGraw-Hill Companies.

[73] The worksheet was adapted from Ibid, p 169.

CHAPTER 7

[1] Excerpted from M Conlin, "9 to 5 Isn't Working Anymore," *Business Week,* September 20, 1999, pp 94, 98.

[2] T R Mitchell, "Motivation: New Direction for Theory, Research, and Practice," *Academy of Management Review,* January 1982, p 81.

[3] This discussion is based on T R Mitchell, "Matching Motivational Strategies with Organizational Contexts," in *Research in Organizational Behavior* (vol 19), eds L L Cummings and B M Staw (Greenwich, CT: JAI Press, 1997), pp 57–149.

[4] A Karr, "Work Week: A Special News Report about Life on the Job—And Trends Taking Shape There," *The Wall Street Journal,* February 9, 1999, p A1.

[5] Mitchell, "Motivation: New Direction for Theory, Research, and Practice," p 83.

[6] The effects of feelings and emotions on work motivation are discussed by J M George and A P Brief, "Motivational Agendas in the Workplace: The Effects of Feelings on Focus of Attention and Work Motivation," in *Research in Organizational Behavior,* eds B M Staw and L L Cummings (Greenwich, CT: JAI Press, 1996), vol. 18, pp 75–109.

[7] For a complete discussion of the organizational criterion of interest to managers and researchers, see J T Austin and P Villanova, "The Criterion Problem: 1917–1992," *Journal of Applied Psychology,* December 1992, pp 836–74.

[8] For a complete description of Maslow's theory, see A H Maslow, "A Theory of Human Motivation," *Psychological Review,* July 1943, pp 370–96.

[9] C C Pinder, *Work Motivation: Theory, Issues, and Applications* (Glenview, IL: Scott, Foresman, 1984), p 52.

[10] Excerpted from D Fenn, "Workplace: Managing Generation X," *Inc.,* August 1996, p 91.

[11] Excerpted from W Band, "Targeting Quality Efforts to Build Customer Loyalty," *The Quality Observer,* December 1995, p 34.

[12] Layoff statistics were obtained from "Table 1. Mass Layoff Events and Initial Claimants for Unemployment Insurance, January 1997, to

March 1999," *Bureau of Labor Statistics,* May 20, 1999 (http://www.bls.gov/news.release/mmls.t01.htm).

[13] The impact of job loss on displaced workers well-being was investigated by A J Kinicki, G E Prussia, and F M Mckee-Ryan, "A Panel Study of Coping with Involuntary Job Loss," *Academy of Management Journal,* in press.

[14] See R A Starkweather and C L Steinbacher, "Job Satisfaction Affects the Bottom Line," *HRMagazine,* September 1998, pp 110–12.

[15] Results can be found in W D Spangler, "Validity of Questionnaire and TAT Measures of Need for Achievement: Two Meta-Analyses," *Psychological Bulletin,* July 1992, pp 140–54.

[16] Results can be found in S D Bluen, J Barling, and W Burns, "Predicting Sales Performance, Job Satisfaction, and Depression by Using the Achievement Strivings and Impatience–Irritability Dimensions of Type A Behavior," *Journal of Applied Psychology,* April 1990, pp 212–16; and D C McClelland, *The Achieving Society* (New York: Free Press, 1961).

[17] H A Murray, *Explorations in Personality* (New York: John Wiley & Sons, 1938), p 164.

[18] Recent studies of achievement motivation can be found in H Grant and C S Dweck, "A Goal Analysis of Personality and Personality Coherence," in *The Coherence of Personality,* eds D Cervone and Y Shoda (New York: The Guilford Press, 1999), pp 345–71; and D Y Dai, S M Moon, and J F Feldhusen, "Achievement Motivation and Gifted Students: A Social Cognitive Perspective," *Educational Psychologist,* Spring/Summer 1998, pp 45–63.

[19] See K G Shaver, "The Entrepreneurial Personality Myth," *Business and Economic Review,* April/June 1995, pp 20–23.

[20] Research on the affiliative motive can be found in S C O'Connor and L K Rosenblood, "Affiliation Motivation in Everyday Experience: A Theoretical Comparison," *Journal of Personality and Social Psychology,* March 1996, pp 513–22; and R F Baumeister and M R Leary, "The Need to Belong: Desire for Interpersonal Attachments as a Fundamental Human Motivation," *Psychological Bulletin,* May 1995, pp 497–529.

[21] See the following series of research reports: D K McNeese-Smith, "The Relationship between Managerial Motivation, Leadership, Nurse Outcomes and Patient Satisfaction," *Journal of Organizational Behavior,* March 1999, pp 243–59; A M Harrell and M J Stahl, "A Behavioral Decision Theory Approach for Measuring McClelland's Trichotomy of Needs," *Journal of Applied Psychology,* April 1981, pp 242–47; and M J Stahl, "Achievement, Power and Managerial Motivation: Selecting Managerial Talent with the Job Choice Exercise," *Personnel Psychology,* Winter 1983, pp 775–89.

[22] For a review of the foundation of achievement motivation training, see D C McClelland, "Toward a Theory of Motive Acquisition," *American Psychologist,* May 1965, pp 321–33. Evidence for the validity of motivation training can be found in H Heckhausen and S Krug, "Motive Modification," in *Motivation and Society,* ed A J Stewart (San Francisco: Jossey-Bass, 1982).

[23] Results can be found in D B Turban and T L Keon, "Organizational Attractiveness: An Interactionist Perspective," *Journal of Applied Psychology,* April 1993, pp 184–93.

[24] See D Steele Johnson and R Perlow, "The Impact of Need for Achievement Components on Goal Commitment and Performance," *Journal of Applied Social Psychology,* November 1992, pp 1711–20.

[25] J L Bowditch and A F Buono, *A Primer on Organizational Behavior* (New York: John Wiley & Sons, 1985), p 210.

[26] Supporting results can be found in B Melin, U Lundberg, J Söderlund, and M Granqvist, "Psychological and Physiological Stress Reactions of Male and Female Assembly Workers: A Comparison between Two Different Forms of Work Organization," *Journal of Organizational Behavior,* January 1999, pp 47–61; and S Melamed, I Ben-Avi, J Luz, and M S Green, "Objective and Subjective Work Monotony: Effects on Job Satisfaction, Psychological Distress, and Absenteeism in Blue-Collar Workers," *Journal of Applied Psychology,* February 1995, pp 29–42.

[27] Excerpted from T Aeppel, "More, More, More: Rust-Belt Factor Lifts Productivity, and Staff Finds It's No Picnic," *The Wall Street Journal,* May 18, 1999, p A1.

[28] See Ibid, pp A1, A10.

[29] This type of program was developed and tested by M A Campion and C L McClelland, "Follow-Up and Extension of the Interdisciplinary Costs and Benefits of Enlarged Jobs," *Journal of Applied Psychology,* June 1993, pp 339–51.

[30] K Walter, "The MTA Travels Far with Its Future Managers Program," *Personnel Journal,* March 1995, pp 70–71. Used with permission of ACC Communications, Inc., Costa Mesa, CA. All rights reserved.

[31] An empirical test of the relationship between job rotation and career-related outcomes was conducted by M A Campion, L Cheraskin, and M J Stevens, "Career-Related Antecedents and Outcomes of Job Rotation," *Academy of Management Journal,* December 1994, pp 1518–42.

[32] See F Herzberg, B Mausner, and B B Snyderman, *The Motivation to Work* (New York: John Wiley & Sons, 1959).

[33] Two tests of Herzberg's theory can be found in I O Adigun and G M Stephenson, "Sources of Job Motivation and Satisfaction among British and Nigerian Employees," *The Journal of Social Psychology,* June 1992, pp 369–76; and E A Maidani, "Comparative Study of Herzberg's Two-Factor Theory of Job Satisfaction Among Public and Private Sectors," *Public Personnel Management,* Winter 1991, pp 441–48.

[34] F Herzberg, "One More Time: How Do You Motivate Employees?" *Harvard Business Review,* January/February 1968, p 56.

[35] Results are presented in "Are Your Staffers Happy? They're in the Minority," *Supervisory Management,* March 1996, p 11.

[36] Both sides of the Herzberg controversy are discussed by N King, "Clarification and Evaluation of the Two-Factor Theory of Job Satisfaction," *Psychological Bulletin,* July 1970, pp 18–31; and B Grigaliunas and Y Weiner, "Has the Research Challenge to Motivation–Hygiene Theory Been Conclusive? An Analysis of Critical Studies," *Human Relations,* December 1974, pp 839–71.

[37] Pinder, *Work Motivation: Theory, Issues, and Applications,* p 28.

[38] J R Hackman, G R Oldham, R Janson, and K Purdy, "A New Strategy for Job Enrichment," *California Management Review,* Summer 1975, p 58.

[39] Ibid., p 58. (Emphasis added.)

[40] C V Clarke, "Be All You Can Be!" *Black Enterprise,* February 1996, pp 72–73.

[41] Definitions of the job characteristics were adapted from J R Hackman and G R Oldham, "Motivation through the Design of Work: Test of a Theory," *Organizational Behavior and Human Performance,* August 1976, pp 250–79.

[42] A review of this research can be found in M L Ambrose and C T Kulik, "Old Friends, New Faces: Motivation Research in the 1990s," *Journal of Management,* 1999, pp 231–92.

[43] The complete JDS and norms for the MPS are presented in J R Hackman and G R Oldham, *Work Redesign* (Reading, MA: Addison-Wesley Publishing, 1980). Studies that revised the JDS were conducted by J L Cordery and P P Sevastos, "Responses to the Original and Revised Job Diagnostic Survey: Is Education a Factor in Responses to Negatively Worded Items?" *Journal of Applied Psychology,* February 1993, pp 141–43; and J R Idaszak and F Drasgow, "A Revision of the Job Diagnostic Survey: Elimination of a Measurement Artifact," *Journal of Applied Psychology,* February 1987, pp 69–74.

[44] Excerpted from A Taylor III, "Rally of the Dolls: It Worked for Toyota. Can It Work for Toys?" *Fortune,* January 11, 1999, p 36.

[45] See M L Ambrose and C T Kulik, "Old Friends, New Faces: Motivation Research in the 1990s;" C Wong, C Hui, and K S Law, "A Longitudinal Study of the Job Perception-Job Satisfaction Relationship: A Test of the Three Alternative Specifications," *Journal of Occupational and Organizational Psychology,* June 1998, pp 127–46; and T Loher, R A Noe, N L Moeller, and M P Fitzgerald, "A Meta-Analysis of the Relation of Job Characteristics to Job Satisfaction," *Journal of Applied Psychology,* May 1985, pp 280–89.

[46] Results can be found in S K Parker, "Enhancing Role Breadth Self-Efficacy: The Roles of Job Enrichment and Other Organizational Interventions," *Journal of Applied Psychology,* December 1998, pp 835–52.

[47] Results can be found in M R Kelley, "New Process Technology, Job Design, and Work Organization: A Contingency Model," *American Sociological Review,* April 1990, pp 191–208.

[48] Productivity studies are reviewed in R E Kopelman, *Managing Productivity in Organizations* (New York: McGraw-Hill, 1986).

[49] Absenteeism results are discussed in Y Fried and G R Ferris, "The Validity of the Job Characteristics Model: A Review and Meta-Analysis," *Personnel Psychology,* Summer 1987, pp 287–322. The turnover meta-analysis was conducted by G M McEvoy and W F Cascio, "Strategies for Reducing Turnover: A Meta-Analysis," *Journal of Applied Psychology,* May 1985, pp 342–53.

[50] See J R Rentsch and R P Steel, "Testing the Durability of Job Characteristics as Predictors of Absenteeism Over a Six-Year Period," *Personnel Psychology,* Spring 1998, pp 165–90.

[51] A thorough discussion of reengineering and associated outcomes can be found in J Champy, *Reengineering Management: The Mandate for New Leadership* (New York: Harper Business, 1995); and M Hammer and J Champy, *Reengineering the Corporation: A Manifesto for Business Revolution* (New York: Harper Business, 1993).

[52] See J D Jonge and W B Schaufeli, "Job Characteristics and Employee Well-Being: A Test of Warr's Vitamin Model in Health Care Workers Using Structural Equation Modelling," *Journal of Organizational Behavior,* July 1998, pp 387–407; and D C Ganster and D J Dwyer, "The Effects of Understaffing on Individual and Group Performance in Professional and Trade Occupations," *Journal of Management,* 1995, pp 175–90.

[53] G R Oldham and J R Hackman, "Work Design in the Organizational Context," in *Research in Organizational Behavior,* eds B M Staw and L L Cummings (Greenwich, CT: JAI Press, 1980), pp 248–49.

[54] Excerpted from S Nearman, "The Simple Billionaire," *Selling Power,* June 1999, p 48.

[55] For a review of the development of the JDI, see P C Smith, L M Kendall, and C L Hulin, *The Measurement of Satisfaction in Work and Retirement* (Skokie, IL: Rand McNally, 1969).

[56] For norms on the MSQ, see D J Weiss, R V Dawis, G W England, and L H Lofquist, *Manual for the Minnesota Satisfaction Questionnaire* (Minneapolis: Industrial Relations Center, University of Minnesota, 1967).

[57] For a review of these models, see A P Brief, *Attitudes In and Around Organizations* (Thousand Oaks, CA: Sage Publications, 1998).

[58] See A R Karr, "Work Week: A Special News Report about Life on the Job—And Trends Taking Shape There," *The Wall Street Journal,* June 29, 1999, p A1.

[59] For a review of need satisfaction models, see E F Stone, "A Critical Analysis of Social Information Processing Models of Job Perceptions and Job Attitudes," in *Job Satisfaction: How People Feel about Their Jobs and How It Affects Their Performance,* eds C J Cranny, P Cain Smith, and E F Stone (New York: Lexington Books, 1992), pp 21–52.

[60] See J P Wanous, T D Poland, S L Premack, and K S Davis, "The Effects of Met Expectations on Newcomer Attitudes and Behaviors: A Review and Meta-Analysis," *Journal of Applied Psychology,* June 1992, pp 288–97; and P W Hom, R W Griffeth, L E Palich, and J S Bracker, "Revisiting Met Expectations as a Reason Why Realistic Job Previews Work," *Personnel Psychology,* Spring 1999, pp 97–112.

[61] A complete description of this model is provided by E A Locke, "Job Satisfaction," in *Social Psychology and Organizational Behavior,* eds M Gruneberg and T Wall (New York: John Wiley & Sons, 1984).

[62] For a test of the value fulfillment value, see W A Hochwarter, P L Perrewe, G R Ferris, and R A Brymer, "Job Satisfaction and Performance: The Moderating Effects of Value Attainment and Affective Disposition," *Journal of Vocational Behavior,* April 1999, pp 296–313.

[63] Results from the meta-analysis can be found in L A Witt and L G Nye, "Gender and the Relationship between Perceived Fairness of Pay or Promotion and Job Satisfaction," *Journal of Applied Psychology,* December 1992, pp 910–17.

[64] A thorough discussion of this model is provided by T A Judge, E A Locke, and C C Durham, "The Dispositional Causes of Job Satisfaction: A Core Evaluations Approach," in *Research in Organizational Behavior* (vol 19), eds L L Cummings and B M Staw (Greenwich, CT: JAI Press, 1997), pp 151–88.

[65] Supportive results can be found in H M Weiss, J P Nicholas, and C S Daus, "An Examination of the Joint Effects of Affective Experiences and Job Beliefs on Job Satisfaction and Variances in Affective Experiences Over Time," *Organizational Behavior and Human Decision Processes,* April 1999, pp 1–24; J D Shaw, M K Duffy, G D Jenkins, Jr, and N Gupta, "Positive and Negative Affect, Signal Sensitivity, and Pay Satisfaction," *Journal of Management,* 1999, pp 189–206; R P Steel and J R Rentsch, "The Dispositional Model of Job Attitudes Revisited: Findings of a 10-Year Study," *Journal of Applied Psychology,* December 1997, pp 873–79; and B M Staw and J Ross, "Stability in the Midst of Change: A Dispositional Approach to Job Attitudes," *Journal of Applied Psychology,* August 1985, pp 469–80.

[66] See E Diener and C Diener, "Most People Are Happy," *Psychological Science,* May 1996, pp 181–85; D Lykken and A Tellegen, "Happiness Is a Stochastic Phenomenon," *Psychological Science,* May 1996, pp 186–89; and R D Arvey, T J Bouchard, Jr, N L Segal, and L M Abraham, "Job Satisfaction: Environmental and Genetic Components," *Journal of Applied Psychology,* April 1989, pp 187–92.

[67] Results can be found in A J Kinicki, F M McKee-Ryan, C A Schriesheim, and K P Carson, "Assessing the Construct Validity of the Job Descriptive Index (JDI): A Review and Analysis," 2000, manuscript submitted for publication.

[68] See S P Brown, "A Meta-Analysis and Review of Organizational Research on Job Involvement," *Psychological Bulletin,* September 1996, pp 235–55.

[69] D W Organ, "The Motivational Basis of Organizational Citizenship Behavior," in *Research in Organizational Behavior,* eds B M Staw and L L Cummings (Greenwich, CT: JAI Press, 1990), p 46.

[70] See D W Organ and K Ryan, "A Meta-Analytic Review of Attitudinal and Dispositional Predictors of Organizational Citizenship Behavior," *Personnel Psychology,* Winter 1995, pp 775–802.

[71] Supportive results can be found in M A Konovsky and D W Organ, "Dispositional and Contextual Determinants of Organizational Citizenship Behavior," *Journal of Organizational Behavior,* May 1996, pp 253–66; and P M Podsakoff, S B MacKenzie, and W H Bommer, "Transformational Leader Behaviors and Substitutes for Leadership as Determinants of Employee Satisfaction, Commitment, Trust, and Organizational Citizenship Behaviors," *Journal of Management,* pp 259–98.

[72] See T D Allen and M C Rush, "The Effects of Organizational Citizenship Behavior on Performance Judgments: A Field Study and a Laboratory Experiment," *Journal of Applied Psychology,* April 1998, pp 247–60.

[73] See R P Tett and J P Meyer, "Job Satisfaction, Organizational Commitment, Turnover Intention, and Turnover: Path Analysis Based on Meta-Analytic Findings," *Personnel Psychology,* Summer 1993, pp 259–93.

[74] See J E Mathieu and D Zajac, "A Review and Meta-Analysis of the Antecedents, Correlates, and Consequences of Organizational Commitment," *Psychological Bulletin,* September 1990, pp 171–94.

[75] See R D Hackett, "Work Attitudes and Employee Absenteeism: A Synthesis of the Literature," *Journal of Occupational Psychology,* 1989, pp 235–48.

[76] The results can be found in P W Hom and R W Griffeth, *Employee Turnover* (Cincinnati, OH: SouthWestern, 1995), pp 35–50.

[77] See Ibid; and C Kalb and A Rogers, "Stress," *Newsweek,* June 14, 1999, pp 56–63.

[78] See P A McGuire, "Worker Stress, Health Reaching Critical Point," *APA Monitor,* May 1999, pp 1, 27.

[79] Results can be found in M A Blegen, "Nurses' Job Satisfaction: A Meta-Analysis of Related Variables," *Nursing Research,* January/February 1993, pp 36–41.

[80] The relationship between performance and satisfaction was reviewed by M T Iaffaldano and P M Muchinsky, "Job Satisfaction and Job Performance: A Meta-Analysis," *Psychological Bulletin,* March 1985, pp 251–73.

[81] The relationship between satisfaction and performance is discussed by P C Smith and C Cranny, "Psychology of Men at Work," *Annual Review of Psychology,* 1968, pp 467–96; and R A Katzell, D E Thompson, and R A Guzzo, "How Job Satisfaction and Job Performance Are and Are Not Linked," in *Job Satisfaction: How People Feel about Their Jobs and How It Affects Their Performance,* eds C J Cranny, P Cain Smith, and E F Stone (New York: Lexington Books, 1992), pp 195–217.

Responsivity to Challenge," *Journal of Applied Psychology,* February 1993, pp 73–85.

[14] See J M Plas, *Person-Centered Leadership: An American Approach to Participatory Management* (Thousand Oaks, CA: Sage, 1996).

[15] Excerpted from R Ganzel, "Feeling Squeezed by Technology?" *Training,* April 1998, p 62.

[16] Ibid, pp 62–70.

[17] See G Stern, "Take a Bite, Do Some Work, Take a Bite," *The Wall Street Journal,* January 17, 1994, pp B1, B2; R F Bettendorf, "Curing the New Ills of Technology: Proper Ergonomics Can Reduce Cumulative Trauma Disorders among Employees," *HRMagazine,* March 1990, pp 35–36, 80; and S Overman, "Prescriptions for a Healthier Office," *HRMagazine,* February 1990, pp 30–34.

[18] Amparano, "On-Job Stress Is Making Workers Sick," p A12.

[19] See R Lazarus, *Stress and Emotion: A New Synthesis* (New York: Springer Publishing, 1999).

[20] Research on job loss is summarized by K A Hanisch, "Job Loss and Unemployment Research from 1994 to 1998: A Review and Recommendations for Research and Intervention," *Journal of Vocational Behavior,* October 1999, pp 188–220.

[21] Supportive results can be found in A A Grandey and R Cropanzano, "The Conservation of Resources Model Applied to Work-Family Conflict and Strain," *Journal of Vocational Behavior,* April 1999, pp 350–70; J R Edwards and N P Rothbard, "Work and Family Stress and Well-Being; An Examination of Person-Environment Fit in the Work and Family Domains," *Organizational Behavior and Human Decision Processes,* February 1999, pp 85–129; and A J Kinicki, F M McKee, and K J Wade, "Annual Review, 1991–1995; Occupational Health," *Journal of Vocational Behavior,* October 1996, pp 190–220.

[22] Results from this study were reported in "Poll: 1 in 6 Workers Want to Hit Someone," *The Arizona Republic,* September 6, 1999, p A11.

[23] Reviews of this research can be found in R S DeFrank and J M Ivancevich, "Stress on the Job: An Executive Update," *Academy of Management Executive,* August 1998, pp 55–66; and M Koslowsky, *Modeling the Stress-Strain Relationship in Work Settings* (New York: Routledge, 1998).

[24] Results can be found in L Narayanan, S Menon, and P E Spector, "Stress in the Workplace: A Comparison of Gender and Occupations," *Journal of Organizational Behavior,* 1999, pp 63–73.

[25] See M E Lachman and S L Weaver, "The Sense of Control as a Moderator of Social Class Differences in Health and Well-Being," *Journal of Personality and Social Psychology,* March 1998, pp 763–73.

[26] These findings are reported in B Melin, U Lundberg, J Soderlund, and M Granqvist, "Psychological and Physiological Stress Reactions of Male and Female Assembly Workers: A Comparison between Two Different Forms of Work Organization," *Journal of Organizational Behavior,* January 1999, pp 47–61.

[27] Research on chronic hostility is discussed by "Healthy Lives: A New View of Stress," *University of California, Berkeley Wellness Letter,* June 1990, pp 4–5. Also see R S Jorgensen, B T Johnson, M E Kolodziej, and G E Schreer, "Elevated Blood Pressure and Personality: A Meta-Analytic Review," *Psychological Bulletin,* September 1996, pp 293–320.

[28] These statistics were reported in U L McFarling, "Depression Costs Business Billions," *The Arizona Republic,* September 11, 1999, p A15.

[29] The economic cost of stress is discussed by V M Gibson, "Stress in the Workplace: A Hidden Cost Factor," *HR Focus,* January 1993, p 15.

[30] M Bordwin, "Overwork: The Cause of Your Next Workers' Comp Claim?" *American Management Association,* March 1996, p 50.

[31] F A McMorris, "Can Post-Traumatic Stress Arise from Office Battles?" *The Wall Street Journal,* February 5, 1996, p B1.

[32] P A McGuire, "Worker Stress, Health Reaching Critical Point," *American Psychological Association Monitor,* May 1999, p 1.

[33] This landmark study was conducted by T H Holmes and R H Rahe, "The Social Readjustment Rating Scale," *Journal of Psychosomatic Research,* August 1967, pp 213–18.

[34] The rating scale was recently revised by C J Hobson, J Kamen, J Szostek, C M Nethercut, J W Tiedmann, and S Wojnarowicz, "Stressful Life Events: A Revision and Update of the Social Readjustment Rat-

ing Scale," *International Journal of Stress Management,* January 1998, pp 1–23.

[35] Normative predictions are discussed in O Behling and A L Darrow, "Managing Work-Related Stress," in *Modules in Management,* eds J E Rosenzweig and F E Kast (Chicago: Science Research Associates, 1984).

[36] This research is discussed by K S Kendler, L M Karkowski, and C A Prescott, "Causal Relationship between Stressful Life Events and the Onset of Major Depression," *American Journal of Psychiatry,* June 1999, pp 837–48; C Segrin, "Social Skills, Stressful Life Events, and the Development of Psychosocial Problems," *Journal of Social and Clinical Psychology,* Spring 1999, pp 14–34; and R S Bhagat, "Effects of Stressful Life Events on Individual Performance Effectiveness and Work Adjustment Processes within Organizational Settings: A Research Model," *Academy of Management Review,* October 1983, pp 660–71.

[37] See D R Pillow, A J Zautra, and I Sandler, "Major Life Events and Minor Stressors: Identifying Mediational Links in the Stress Process," *Journal of Personality and Social Psychology,* February 1996, pp 381–94; R C Barnett, S W Raudenbush, R T Brennan, J H Pleck, and N L Marshall, "Change in Job and Marital Experiences and Change in Psychological Distress: A Longitudinal Study of Dual-Earner Couples," *Journal of Personality and Social Psychology,* November 1995, pp 839–50; and S Cohen, D A J Tyrell, and A P Smith, "Negative Life Events, Perceived Stress, Negative Affect, and Susceptibility to the Common Cold," *Journal of Personality and Social Psychology,* January 1993, pp 131–40.

[38] See Hobson, Kamen, Szostek, Nethercut, Tiedmann, and Wojnarowicz, "Stressful Life Events: A Revision and Update of the Social Readjustment Rating Scale," pp 1–23; and R H Rahe, "Life Changes Scaling: Other Results; Gender Differences," *International Journal of Stress Management,* October 1998, pp 249–50.

[39] J Kaufman and E J Pollack, "Making the Best of It," *The Wall Street Journal* (Eastern Edition), February 26, 1996, p R6.

[40] Excerpted from L Kaufman, "Companies Start to Address Burnout," *The Arizona Republic,* May 16, 1999, p AZ12.

[41] Results are presented in T D Schellhardt, "Off the Track: Is Your Job Going Nowhere? That May Be Natural, but It Doesn't Have to Be Permanent," *The Wall Street Journal* (Eastern Edition), February 26, 1996, p R4.

[42] Excerpted from R Johnson, "Owners Pressured to Work through Vacation Season," *The Wall Street Journal,* July 27, 1999, p B3.

[43] The phases are thoroughly discussed by C Maslach, *Burnout: The Cost of Caring* (Englewood Cliffs, NJ: Prentice-Hall, 1982).

[44] The discussion of the model is based on C L Cordes and T W Dougherty, "A Review and Integration of Research on Job Burnout," *Academy of Management Review,* October 1993, pp 621–56.

[45] H Levinson, "When Executives Burn Out," *Harvard Business Review,* July–August 1996, p 153.

[46] Results and conclusions can be found in R T Lee and B E Ashforth, "A Meta-Analytic Examination of the Correlates of the Three Dimensions of Burnout," *Journal of Applied Psychology,* April 1996, pp 123–33.

[47] See Ibid; E Babakus, D W Cravens, M Johnston, and W C Moncrief, "The Role of Emotional Exhaustion in Sales Force Attitude and Behavior Relationships," *Journal of the Academy of Marketing Science,* 1999, pp 58–70; and R D Iverson, M Olekalns, and P J Erwin, "Affectivity, Organizational Stressors, and Absenteeism: A Causal Model of Burnout and Its Consequences," *Journal of Vocational Behavior,* February 1998, pp 1–23.

[48] Recommendations for reducing burnout are discussed by J E Moore, "Are You Burning Out Valuable Resources," *HRMagazine,* January 1999, pp 93–97; and L Grensing-Pophal, "Recognizing and Conquering On-the-Job Burnout: HR, Heal Thyself," *HRMagazine,* March 1999, pp 82–88.

[49] Excerpted from S Shellenbarger, "Work & Family: Three Myths That Make Managers Push Staff to the Edge of Burnout," *The Wall Street Journal,* March 17, 1999, p B1.

[50] S Armour, "Employers Urge Workers to Chill Out Before Burning Out," *USA Today,* June 22, 1999, p 5B.

[51] Types of support are discussed by S Cohen and T A Wills, "Stress, Social Support, and the Buffering Hypothesis," *Psychological Bulletin,* September 1985, pp 310–57.

[52] S Shellenbarger, "Work & Family: Five Friends Get the Lift They Need from a Girl's Night Out," *The Wall Street Journal,* May 29, 1996, p B1. Reprinted by permission of *The Wall Street* Journal © 1996 Dow Jones & Company, Inc. All Rights Reserved Worldwide.

[53] The perceived availability and helpfulness of social support was discussed by B P Buunk, J D Jonge, J F Ybema, and C J D Wolff, "Psychosocial Aspects of Occupational Stress," in *Handbook of Work and Organizational Psychology,* 2nd ed, P J D Drenth, H Thierry, and C J D Wolff (New York: Psychology Press, 1998), pp 145–82.

[54] See B N Uchino, J T Cacioppo, and J K Kiecolt-Glaser, "The Relationship between Social Support and Physiological Processes: A Review with Emphasis on Underlying Mechanisms and Implications for Health," *Psychological Bulletin,* May 1996, pp 488–531; and H Benson and M Stark, *Timeless Healing: The Power and Biology of Belief* (New York: Scribner, 1996).

[55] Supporting results can be found in C J Holahan, R H Moos, C K Holahan, and R C Cronkite, "Resource Loss, Resource Gain, and Depressive Symptoms: A 10-Year Model," *Journal of Personality and Social Psychology,* September 1999, pp 620–29; D S Carlson and P L Perrewe, "The Role of Social Support in the Stressor-Strain Relationship: An Examination of Work-Family Conflict," *Journal of Management,* 1999, pp 513–40; and M H Davis, M M Morris, and L A Kraus, "Relationship-Specific and Global Perceptions of Social Support: Associations with Well-Being and Attachment," *Journal of Personality and Social Psychology,* February 1998, pp 468–81.

[56] See S Aryee, V Luk, A Leung, and S Lo, "Role Stressors, Interrole Conflict, and Well-Being: The Moderating Influence of Spousal Support and Coping Behaviors among Employed Parents in Hong Kong," *Journal of Vocational Behavior,* April 1999, pp 259–78; and C Viswesvaran, J I Sanchez, and J Fisher, "The Role of Social Support in the Process of Work Stress: A Meta-Analysis," *Journal of Vocational Behavior,* April 1999, pp 314–34.

[57] For details, see B P Buunk, B J Doosje, L G J M Jans, and L E M Hopstaken, "Perceived Reciprocity, Social Support, and Stress at Work: The Role of Exchange and Communal Orientation," *Journal of Personality and Social Psychology,* October 1993, pp 801–11; and C E Cutrona, "Objective Determinants of Perceived Social Support," *Journal of Personality and Social Psychology,* February 1986, pp 349–55.

[58] R S Lazarus and S Folkman, "Coping and Adaptation," in *Handbook of Behavioral Medicine,* ed W D Gentry (New York: The Guilford Press, 1984), p 283.

[59] The antecedents of appraisal were investigated by G J Fogarty, M A Machin, M J Albion, L F Sutherland, G I Lalor, and S Revitt, "Predicting Occupational Strain and Job Satisfaction: The Role of Stress, Coping, Personality, and Affectivity Variables," *Journal of Vocational Behavior,* June 1999, pp 429–52; E C Chang, "Dispositional Optimism and Primary and Secondary Appraisal of a Stressor: Controlling Influences and Relations to Coping and Psychological and Physical Adjustment," *Journal of Personality and Social Psychology,* April 1998, pp 1109–20; and J C Holder and A Vaux, "African American Professionals: Coping with Occupational Stress in Predominantly White Work Environments," *Journal of Vocational Behavior,* December 1988, pp 315–33.

[60] Lazarus and Folkman, "Coping and Adaptation," p 289.

[61] This example was taken from S N Mehta, "Hear Them Roar: More Women Quit Lucrative Jobs to Start Their Own Businesses," *The Wall Street Journal,* November 11, 1996, pp A1, A4.

[62] See C R Leana, D C Feldman, and G Y Tan, "Predictors of Coping Behavior after a Layoff," *Journal of Organizational Behavior,* 1998, pp 85–97; and B Major, C Richards, M L Cooper, C Cozzarelli, and J Zubek, "Personal Resilience, Cognitive Appraisals, and Coping: An Integrative Model of Adjustment to Abortion," *Journal of Personality and Social Psychology,* March 1998, pp 735–52.

[63] See results presented in M A Gowan, C M Riordan, and R D Gatewood, "Test of a Model of Coping with Involuntary Job Loss Following a Company Closing," *Journal of Applied Psychology,* February 1999, pp 75–86; and T M Begley, "Coping Strategies as Predictors of Employee Distress and Turnover after an Organizational Consolidation: A Longitudinal Analysis," *Journal of Occupational and Organizational Psychology,* December 1998, pp 305–29.

[64] This pioneering research is presented in S C Kobasa, "Stressful Life Events, Personality, and Health: An Inquiry into Hardiness," *Journal of Personality and Social Psychology,* January 1979, pp 1–11.

[65] See S C Kobasa, S R Maddi, and S Kahn, "Hardiness and Health: A Prospective Study," *Journal of Personality and Social Psychology,* January 1982, pp 168–77.

[66] Results can be found in V Florian, M Mikulincer, and O Taubman, "Does Hardiness Contribute to Mental Health during a Stressful Real-Life Situation? The Roles of Appraisal and Coping," *Journal of Personality and Social Psychology,* April 1995, pp 687–95; and K L Horner, "Individuality in Vulnerability: Influences on Physical Health," *Journal of Health Psychology,* January 1998, pp 71–85.

[67] See C Robitschek and S Kashubeck, "A Structural Model of Parental Alcoholism, Family Functioning, and Psychological Health: The Mediating Effects of Hardiness and Personal Growth Orientation," *Journal of Counseling Psychology,* April 1999, pp 159–72; and "Basic Behavioral Science Research for Mental Health," *American Psychologist,* January 1996, pp 22–28.

[68] B Priel, N Gonik, and B Rabinowitz, "Appraisals of Childbirth Experience and Newborn Characteristics: The Role of Hardiness and Affect," *Journal of Personality,* September 1993, pp 299–315.

[69] M Friedman and R H Rosenman, *Type A Behavior and Your Heart* (Greenwich, CT: Fawcett Publications, 1974), p 84. (Boldface added.)

[70] H Olen, "The Pitfalls of Perfectionism," *Working Woman,* March 1996, p 55.

[71] See C Lee, L F Jamieson, and P C Earley, "Beliefs and Fears and Type A Behavior: Implications for Academic Performance and Psychiatric Health Disorder Symptoms," *Journal of Organizational Behavior,* March 1996, pp 151–77; S D Bluen, J Barling, and W Burns, "Predicting Sales Performance, Job Satisfaction, and Depression by Using the Achievement Strivings and Impatience-Irritability Dimensions of Type A Behavior," *Journal of Applied Psychology,* April 1990, pp 212–16; and M S Taylor, E A Locke, C Lee and M E Gist, "Type A Behavior and Faculty Research Productivity: What Are the Mechanisms?" *Organizational Behavior and Human Performance,* December 1984, pp 402–18.

[72] Results from the meta-analysis are contained in S A Lyness, "Predictors of Differences between Type A and B Individuals in Heart Rate and Blood Pressure Reactivity," *Psychological Bulletin,* September 1993, pp 266–95.

[73] See S Booth-Kewley and H S Friedman, "Psychological Predictors of Heart Disease: A Quantitative Review" *Psychological Bulletin,* May 1987, pp 343–62. More recent results can be found in T Q Miller, T W Smith, C W Turner, M L Guijarro, A J Hallet, "A Meta-Analytic Review of Research on Hostility and Physical Health," *Psychological Bulletin,* March 1996, pp 322–48.

[74] B Boshnack, "Quick Hints: Just Forget It," *Selling Power,* January/February 1996, p 78.

[75] See J Rothman, "Wellness and Fitness Programs," in *Source-book of Occupational Rehabilitation,* ed P M King (New York: Plenum Press, 1998), pp 127–44; and S Shellenbarger, "Work & Family: Rising Before Dawn, Are You Getting Ahead or Just Getting Tired?" *The Wall Street Journal,* February 17, 1999, p B1.

[76] Results are presented in "Employers Promote Healthy Habits," *HRMagazine,* February 1999, pp 32, 34.

[77] Supportive results can be found in W E Holden, M M Deichmann, and J D Levy, "Empirically Supported Treatments in Pediatric Psychology: Recurrent Pediatric Headache," *Journal of Pediatric Psychology,* April 1999, pp 91–109; and V Barcia, P Maria, J Sanz, and F J Labrador, "Psychological Changes Accompanying and Mediating Stress-Management Training for Essential Hypertension." *Applied Psychophysiology and Biofeedback,* September 1998, pp 159–78.

[78] See H Benson, *The Relaxation Response* (New York: William Morrow and Co., 1975).

[79] Research pertaining to meditation is discussed by A G Marlatt and J L Kristeller, "Mindfulness and Mediation," in *Integrating Spirituality Into Treatment: Resources for Practitioners,* ed W R Miller (Washington, DC: American Psychological Association, 1999), pp 67–84; and H Benson and M Stark, *Timeless Healing* (New York: Scribner, 1996).

[80] Results are presented in "Your Blood Pressure: Think It Down," *Cooking Light,* October 1996, p 24.

[81] See M W Otto, "Cognitive Behavioral Therapy for Social Anxiety Disorder: Model, Methods, and Outcome," *Journal of Clinical Psychiatry,* 1999, pp 14–19.

[82] See S Reynolds, E Taylor, and D A Shapiro, "Session Impact in Stress Management Training," *Journal of Occupational Psychology,* June 1993, pp 99–113; and J M Ivancevich, M T Matteson, S M Freedman, and J S Phillips, "Worksite Stress Management Interventions," *American Psychologist,* February 1990, pp 252–61.

[83] An evaluation of stress-reduction programs is conducted by P A Landsbergis and E Vivona-Vaughan, "Evaluation of an Occupational Stress Intervention in a Public Agency," *Journal of Organizational Behavior,* January 1996, pp 29–48; and D C Ganster, B T Mayes, W E Sime, and G D Tharp, "Managing Organizational Stress: A Field Experiment," *Journal of Applied Psychology,* October 1982, pp 533–42.

[84] R Kreitner, "Personal Wellness: It's Just Good Business," *Business Horizons,* May–June 1982, p 28.

[85] Results are presented in "The 18-Year Gap," *University of California, Berkeley Wellness Letter,* January 1991, p 2.

[86] A thorough review of this research is provided by D L Gebhardt and C E Crump, "Employee Fitness and Wellness Programs in the Workplace," *American Psychologist,* February 1990, pp 262–72. Also see A J Daley and G Parfitt, "Good Health—Is It Worth It? Mood States, Physical Well-Being, Job Satisfaction and Absenteeism in Members and Non-Members of a British Corporate Health and Fitness Club," *Journal of Occupational and Organizational Psychology,* June 1996, pp 121–34.

[87] Excerpted from Rothman, "Wellness and Fitness Programs," in P M King (ed.) *Sourcebook of Occupational Rehabilitation* (New York: Plenum Press, 1998), pp 140, 141, 143. Use with permission of Plenum Publishing.

[88] Excerpted from J Kaufman, "In Name Only: For Richard Thibeault, Being a 'Manager' Is a Blue-Collar Life," *The Wall Street Journal,* October 1, 1996, pp A1, A4. Reprinted by permission of *The Wall Street Journal* © 1996 Dow Jones & Company, Inc. All Rights Reserved Worldwide.

[89] Adapted from C Maslach and S E Jackson, "The Measurement of Experienced Burnout," *Journal of Occupational Behavior,* April 1981, pp 99–113.

CHAPTER 19

[1] Excerpted from C Joinson, "Moving at the Speed of Dell," *HRMagazine,* April 1999, pp 51–52. Also see J W Gurley, "A Dell for Every Industry," *Fortune,* October 12, 1998, pp 167–72.

[2] See P F Drucker, "The New Society of Organizations," *Harvard Business Review,* September–October 1992, pp 95–104; J R Galbraith, E E Lawler III, and Associates, eds, *Organizing for the Future: The New Logic for Managing Complex Organizations,* (San Francisco: Jossey-Bass, 1993); and R W Oliver, *The Shape of Things to Come: Seven Imperatives for Winning in the New World of Business* (New York: McGraw-Hill, 1999).

[3] C I Barnard, *The Functions of the Executive* (Cambridge, MA: Harvard University Press, 1938), p 73. Also see M C Suchman, "Managing Legitimacy: Strategic and Institutional Approaches," *Academy of Management Review,* July 1995, pp 571–610.

[4] Drawn from E H Schein, *Organizational Psychology,* 3rd ed (Englewood Cliffs, NJ: Prentice-Hall, 1980), pp 12–15.

[5] For interesting and instructive insights about organization structure, see G Morgan, *Images of Organization* (Newbury Park, CA: Sage, 1986); G Morgan, *Creative Organization Theory: A Resource Book* (Newbury Park, CA: Sage, 1989); G Hofstede, "An American in Paris: The Influence of Nationality on Organization Theories," *Organization Studies,* no. 3, 1996,

pp 525–37; and J G March, "Continuity and Change in Theories of Organizational Action," *Administrative Science Quarterly,* June 1996, pp 278–87.

[6] For related research, see S Finkelstein and R A D'Aveni, "CEO Duality as a Double-Edged Sword: How Boards of Directors Balance Entrenchment Avoidance and Unity of Command," *Academy of Management Journal,* October 1994, pp 1079–1108.

[7] For an interesting historical perspective of hierarchy, see P Miller and T O'Leary, "Hierarchies and American Ideals, 1900–1940," *Academy of Management Review,* April 1989, pp 250–65.

[8] For an excellent overview of the span of control concept, see D D Van Fleet and A G Bedeian, "A History of the Span of Management," *Academy of Management Review,* July 1977, pp 356–72. Also see E E Lawler III and J R Galbraith, "New Roles for the Staff: Strategic Support and Service," in *Organizing for the Future: The New Logic for Managing Complex Organizations,* eds J R Galbraith, E E Lawler III, and Associates (San Francisco: Jossey-Bass, 1993), pp 65–83.

[9] M Koslowsky, "Staff/Line Distinctions in Job and Organizational Commitment," *Journal of Occupational Psychology,* June 1990, pp 167–73.

[10] See, for example, R J Marshak, "Managing the Metaphors of Change," *Organizational Dynamics,* Summer 1993, pp 44–56; R Garud and S Kotha, "Using the Brain as a Metaphor to Model Flexible Production Systems," *Academy of Management Review,* October 1994, pp 671–98; and R W Keidel, "Rethinking Organizational Design," *Academy of Management Executive,* November 1994, pp 12–30.

[11] D S Brown, "Managers' New Job Is Concert Building," *HRMagazine,* September 1990, p 42.

[12] K S Cameron, "Effectiveness as Paradox: Consensus and Conflict in Conceptions of Organizational Effectiveness," *Management Science,* May 1986, pp 540–41. Also see S Sackmann, "The Role of Metaphors in Organization Transformation," *Human Relations,* June 1989, pp 463–84; and H Tsoukas, "The Missing Link: A Transformational View of Metaphors in Organizational Science," *Academy of Management Review,* July 1991, pp 566–85.

[13] See W R Scott, "The Mandate Is Still Being Honored: In Defense of Weber's Disciples," *Administrative Science Quarterly,* March 1996, pp 163–71.

[14] Based on M Weber, *The Theory of Social and Economic Organization,* translated by A M Henderson and T Parsons (New York: Oxford University Press, 1947). An instructive analysis of the mistranslation of Weber's work may be found in R M Weiss, "Weber on Bureaucracy: Management Consultant or Political Theorist?" *Academy of Management Review,* April 1983, pp 242–48.

[15] For a critical appraisal of bureaucracy, see R P Hummel, *The Bureaucratic Experience,* 3rd ed (New York: St. Martin's Press, 1987). The positive side of bureaucracy is presented in C T Goodsell, *The Case for Bureaucracy: A Public Administration Polemic* (Chatham, NJ: Chatham House Publishers, 1983).

[16] See G Pinchot and E Pinchot, "Beyond Bureaucracy," *Business Ethics,* March–April 1994, pp 26–29; and O Harari, "Let the Computers Be the Bureaucrats," *Management Review,* September 1996, pp 57–60.

[17] J Huey and G Colvin, "The Jack and Herb Show," *Fortune,* January 11, 1999, p 164.

[18] A management-oriented discussion of general systems theory—an interdisciplinary attempt to integrate the various fragmented sciences—may be found in K E Boulding, "General Systems Theory—The Skeleton of Science," *Management Science,* April 1956, pp 197–208.

[19] J D Thompson, *Organizations in Action* (New York: McGraw-Hill, 1967), pp 6–7. Also see A C Bluedorn, "The Thompson Interdependence Demonstration," *Journal of Management Education,* November 1993, pp 505–09.

[20] For more on this subject, see V-W Mitchell, "Organizational Homoeostasis: A Role for Internal Marketing," *Management Decision,* no. 2, 1992, pp 3–7. Biological metaphors are explored in T Petzinger Jr, "A New Model for the Nature of Business: It's Alive!" *The Wall Street Journal,* February 26, 1999, pp B1, B4; and T Petzinger Jr, "Two Doctors Give New Meaning to Taking Your Business to Heart," *The Wall Street Journal,* April 30, 1999, p B1.

[21] R L Daft and K E Weick, "Toward a Model of Organizations as Inter-pretation Systems," *Academy of Management Review,* April 1984, p 293.

[22] For good background reading, see the entire Autumn 1998 issue of *Organizational Dynamics;* D Lei, J W Slocum, and R A Pitts, "Design-ing Organizations for Competitive Advantage: The Power of Unlearning and Learning," *Organizational Dynamics,* Winter 1999, pp 24–38; L Baird, P Holland, and S Deacon, "Learning from Action: Imbedding More Learning into the Performance Fast Enough to Make a Differ-ence," *Organizational Dynamics,* Spring 1999, pp 19–32; "Leading-Edge Learning: Two Views," *Training & Development,* March 1999, pp 40–42; and A M Webber, "Learning for a Change," *Fast Company,* May 1999, pp 178–88.

[23] K Kelly, "Motorola: Training for the Millennium," *Business Week,* March 28, 1994, p 158. For updates, see R O Crockett, "How Motorola Lost Its Way," *Business Week,* May 4, 1998, pp 140–48; and R O Crockett, "Motorola: Slow and Steady Isn't Winning Any Races," *Business Week,* August 10, 1998, pp 62, 64.

[24] See J F Moore, *The Death of Competition: Leadership and Strategy in the Age of Business Ecosystems* (New York: HarperBusiness, 1996), pp 153–54; and "Falcon May Be Taken Off Endangered List," *USA Today,* August 25, 1998, p 3A.

[25] J A C Baum, "Organizational Ecology," in *Handbook of Organization Studies,* eds S R Clegg, C Hardy, and W R Nord (Thousand Oaks, CA: Sage Publications, 1996), p 77. (Emphasis added.) Also see C S Hunt and H E Aldrich, "The Second Ecology: Creation and Evolution of Organizational Communities," in *Research in Organizational Behavior,* vol. 20, eds B M Staw and L L Cummings (Greenwich, CT: JAI Press, 1998), pp 267–301; and W Tsai and S Ghoshal, "Social Capital and Value Creation: The Role of Intrafirm Networks," *Academy of Manage-ment Journal,* August 1998, pp 464–76.

[26] Moore, *The Death of Competition,* pp 11–12.

[27] Ibid., pp 15–16. (Emphasis added.) For updates, see D Kirkpatrick, "Is the PC Dead? Not Even Close," *Fortune,* December 21, 1998, pp 211–14; D B Yoffie and M A Cusumano, "Judo Strategy: The Com-petitive Dynamics of Internet Time," *Harvard Business Review,* Janu-ary–February 1999, pp 71–81; B Gates, "Why the PC Will Not Die," *Newsweek,* May 31, 1999, p 64; and J Dreyfuss, "Death to the Personal Computer," *Fortune,* July 19, 1999, p 138[N].

[28] For example, see O Harari, "The Marrying Kind," *Management Review,* June 1998, pp 23–26; and P Burrows and R Grover, "Steve Jobs, Movie Mogul," *Business Week,* November 23, 1998, pp 140–54.

[29] M Maynard, "It's Not Easy Being Green, So Carmakers Unite," *USA Today,* April 20, 1999, p 1B.

[30] Based on discussion in S R Clegg and C Hardy, "Introduction: Orga-nizations, Organization and Organizing," in *Handbook of Organization Studies,* eds S R Clegg, C Hardy, and W R Nord (Thousand Oaks, CA: Sage Publications, 1996), pp 1–28. Also see B Ettorre, "A Conversation with Charles Handy: On the Future of Work and an End to the 'Century of the Organization,'" *Organizational Dynamics,* Summer 1996, pp 15–26.

[31] As quoted in L McCauley, "Measure What Matters," *Fast Company,* May 1999, pp 97–98.

[32] K Cameron, "Critical Questions in Assessing Organizational Effec-tiveness," *Organizational Dynamics,* Autumn 1980, p 70. Also see J Pfeffer, "When It Comes to 'Best Practices'—Why Do Smart Organi-zations Occasionally Do Dumb Things?" *Organizational Dynamics,* Summer 1996, pp 33–44; G N Powell, "Reinforcing and Extending Today's Organizations: The Simultaneous Pursuit of Person-Organization Fit and Diversity," *Organizational Dynamics,* Winter 1998, pp 50–61; R C Vergin and M W Qoronfleh, "Corporate Reputation and the Stock Market," *Business Horizons,* January–February 1998, pp 19–26; K Gawande and T Wheeler, "Measures of Effectiveness for Governmental Organizations," *Management Science,* January 1999, pp 42–58; and E V McIntyre, "Accounting Choices and EVA," *Busi-ness Horizons,* January–February 1999, pp 66–72.

[33] See B Wysocki Jr, "Rethinking a Quaint Idea: Profits," *The Wall Street Journal,* May 19, 1999, pp B1, B6; and J Collins, "Turning Goals into

Results: The Power of Catalytic Mechanisms," *Harvard Business Review,* July–August 1999, pp 71–82.

[34] See, for example, R O Brinkerhoff and D E Dressler, *Productivity Measurement: A Guide for Managers and Evaluators* (Newbury Park, CA: Sage Publications, 1990); J McCune, "The Productivity Paradox," *Management Review,* March 1998, pp 38–40; and R J Samuelson, "Cheerleaders vs. The Grumps," *Newsweek,* July 26, 1999, p 78.

[35] See A Reinhardt, "Log On, Link Up, Save Big," *Business Week,* June 22, 1998, pp 132–38; and R W Oliver, "Happy 150th Birthday, Elec-tronic Commerce!" *Management Review,* July–August 1999, pp 12–13.

[36] Data from M Maynard, "Toyota Promises Custom Order in 5 Days," *USA Today,* August 6, 1999, p 1B.

[37] "Interview: M Scott Peck," *Business Ethics,* March–April 1994, p 17.

[38] Cameron, "Critical Questions in Assessing Organizational Effective-ness," p 67. Also see W Buxton, "Growth from Top to Bottom," *Man-agement Review,* July–August 1999, p 11.

[39] See R K Mitchell, B R Agle, and D J Wood, "Toward a Theory of Stakeholder Identification and Salience: Defining the Principle of Who and What Really Counts," *Academy of Management Review,* October 1997, pp 853–96; W Beaver, "Is the Stakeholder Model Dead?" *Busi-ness Horizons,* March–April 1999, pp 8–12; J Frooman, "Stakeholder Influence Strategies," *Academy of Management Review,* April 1999, pp 191–205; and T M Jones and A C Wicks, "Convergent Stakeholder Theory," *Academy of Management Review,* April 1999, pp 206–21.

[40] See N C Roberts and P J King, "The Stakeholder Audit Goes Public," *Organizational Dynamics,* Winter 1989, pp 63–79; and I Henriques and P Sadorsky, "The Relationship between Environmental Commitment and Managerial Perceptions of Stakeholder Importance," *Academy of Management Journal,* February 1999, pp 87–99.

[41] E M Reingold, "America's Hamburger Helper," *Time,* June 29, 1992, p 66.

[42] See C Ostroff and N Schmitt, "Configurations of Organizational Effectiveness and Efficiency," *Academy of Management Journal,* December 1993, pp 1345–61.

[43] K S Cameron, "Effectiveness as Paradox: Consensus and Conflict in Conceptions of Organizational Effectiveness," *Management Science,* May 1986, p 542.

[44] Alternative effectiveness criteria are discussed in Ibid.; A G Bedeian, "Organization Theory: Current Controversies, Issues, and Directions," in *International Review of Industrial and Organizational Psychology,* eds C L Cooper and I T Robertson (New York: John Wiley & Sons, 1987), pp 1–33; and M Keeley, "Impartiality and Participant-Interest Theories of Organizational Effectiveness," *Administrative Science Quarterly,* March 1984, pp 1–25.

[45] D N Sull, "Why Good Companies Go Bad," *Harvard Business Review,* July–August 1999, pp 42–52. Also see H B Cohen, "The Perfor-mance Paradox," *Academy of Management Executive,* August 1998, pp 30–40.

[46] M A Mone, W McKinley, and V L Barker III, "Organizational Decline and Innovation: A Contingency Framework," *Academy of Management Review,* January 1998, p 117.

[47] P Lorange and R T Nelson, "How to Recognize—and Avoid—Orga-nizational Decline," *Sloan Management Review,* Spring 1987, p 47.

[48] Excerpted from Ibid., pp 43–45. Also see E E Lawler III and J R Galbraith, "Avoiding the Corporate Dinosaur Syndrome," *Organiza-tional Dynamics,* Autumn 1994, pp 5–17; and K Labich, "Why Compa-nies Fail," *Fortune,* November 14, 1994, pp 52–68.

[49] For details, see K S Cameron, M U Kim, and D A Whetten, "Organi-zational Effects of Decline and Turbulence," *Administrative Science Quarterly,* June 1987, pp 222–40. Also see A G Bedeian and A A Armenakis, "The Cesspool Syndrome: How Dreck Floats to the Top of Declining Organizations," *Academy of Management Executive,* February 1998, pp 58–63.

[50] Twelve dysfunctional consequences of decline are discussed and empirically tested in K S Cameron, D A Whetten, and M U Kim, "Orga-nizational Dysfunctions of Decline," *Academy of Management Journal,* March 1987, pp 126–38. Also see D K Hurst, *Crisis and Renewal:*

Meeting the Challenge of Organizational Change (Boston: Harvard Business School Press, 1995).

[51] Data from V L Barker III and P W Patterson, Jr, "Top Management Team Tenure and Top Manager Causal Attributions at Declining Firms Attempting Turnarounds," *Group & Organization Management,* September 1996, pp 304–36. Stories of organizational decline can be found in G Colvin, "How Rubbermaid Managed to Fail," *Fortune,* November 23, 1998, pp 32–33; W C Symonds, "Paddling Harder at L L Bean," *Business Week,* December 7, 1998, pp 72, 75; J Weiner, "How Nordictrack Lost Its Footing," *Business Week,* December 14, 1998, p 138; "The Apple Story," p 38 in J Pfeffer and J F Veiga, "Putting People First for Organizational Success," *Academy of Management Executive,* May 1999, pp 37–48; and R A Melcher, "I'm Working My Tail Off to Fix It," *Business Week,* August 16, 1999, pp 72, 74.

[52] For related reading, see C R Eitel, "The Ten Disciplines of Business Turnaround," *Management Review,* December 1998, p 13; J R Morris, W F Cascio, and C E Young, "Downsizing After All These Years: Questions and Answers about Who Did It, How Many Did It, and Who Benefited from It," *Organizational Dynamics,* Winter 1999, pp 78–87; and S Kuczynski, "Help! I Shrunk the Company!" *HRMagazine,* June 1999, pp 40–45.

[53] A culture of "entitlement" also hastens organizational decline. See J M Bardwick, *Danger in the Comfort Zone: From Boardroom to Mailroom—How to Break the Entitlement Habit That's Killing American Business* (New York: AMACOM, 1991). Also see D W Organ, "Argue with Success," *Business Horizons,* November–December 1995, pp 1–2; and J P Kotter, "Kill Complacency," *Fortune,* August 5, 1996, pp 168–70.

[54] J Greenwald, "Are America's Corporate Giants a Dying Breed?" *Time,* December 28, 1992, p 28. Procter & Gamble's fight against decline is discussed in B Saporito, "Behind the Tumult at P&G," *Fortune,* March 7, 1994, pp 74–82. Also see B Saporito, "The Eclipse of Mars," *Fortune,* November 28, 1994, pp 82–92.

[55] Excerpted from A Taylor III, "Why Toyota Keeps Getting Better and Better and Better," *Fortune,* November 19, 1990, pp 66–67.

[56] For updates, see J M Pennings, "Structural Contingency Theory: A Reappraisal," *Research in Organizational Behavior* (Greenwich, CT: JAI Press, 1992), vol. 14, pp 267–309; A D Meyer, A S Tsui, and C R Hinings, "Configurational Approaches to Organizational Analysis," *Academy of Management Journal,* December 1993, pp 1175–95; and D H Doty, W H Glick, and G P Huber, "Fit, Equifinality, and Organizational Effectiveness: A Test of Two Configurational Theories," *Academy of Management Journal,* December 1993, pp 1196–1250.

[57] An interesting distinction between three types of environmental uncertainty can be found in F J Milliken, "Three Types of Perceived Uncertainty about the Environment: State, Effect, and Response Uncertainty," *Academy of Management Review,* January 1987, pp 133–43.

[58] R Duncan, "What Is the Right Organization Structure?" *Organizational Dynamics,* Winter 1979, p 63.

[59] Ibid.

[60] See P Sellers, "Crunch Time for Coke," *Fortune,* July 19, 1999, pp 72–78.

[61] See T J Tetenbaum, "Shifting Paradigms: From Newton to Chaos," *Organizational Dynamics,* Spring 1998, pp 21–32; W Miller, "Building the Ultimate Resource," *Management Review,* January 1999, pp 42–45; D P Ellerman, "Global Institutions: Transforming International Development Agencies into Learning Organizations," *Academy of Management Executive,* February 1999, pp 25–35; and K Maani and C Benton, "Rapid Team Learning: Lessons from Team New Zealand America's Cup Campaign," *Organizational Dynamics,* Spring 1999, pp 48–62.

[62] P R Lawrence and J W Lorsch, *Organization and Environment* (Homewood, IL: Richard D Irwin, 1967), p 157.

[63] Pooled, sequential, and reciprocal integration are discussed in J W Lorsch, "Organization Design: A Situational Perspective," *Organizational Dynamics,* Autumn 1977, pp 2–14. Also see J E Ettlie and E M Reza, "Organizational Integration and Process Innovation," *Academy of Management Journal,* October 1992, pp 795–827; and A L Patti and J P Gilbert, "Collocating New Product Development Teams: Why,

When, Where, and How?" *Business Horizons,* November–December 1997, pp 59–64.

[64] See B Dumaine, "Ability to Innovate," *Fortune,* January 29, 1990, pp 43, 46. For good reading on innovation and technology, see O Port, "Getting to 'Eureka!' " *Business Week,* November 10, 1997, pp 72–75; J W Gurley, "Got a Good Idea? Better Think Twice," *Fortune,* December 7, 1998, pp 215–16; J C McCune, "The Technology Treadmill," *Management Review,* December 1998, pp 10–12; and L Yates and P Skarzynski, "How Do Companies Get to the Future First?" *Management Review,* January 1999, pp 16–22.

[65] K Deveny, "Bag Those Fries, Squirt That Ketchup, Fry That Fish," *Business Week,* October 13, 1986, p 86.

[66] See D A Morand, "The Role of Behavioral Formality and Informality in the Enactment of Bureaucratic versus Organic Organizations," *Academy of Management Review,* October 1995, pp 831–72.

[67] See J Huey, "The New Post-Heroic Leadership," *Fortune,* February 21, 1994, pp 42–50; and F Shipper and C C Manz, "Employee Self-Management without Formally Designated Teams: An Alternative Road to Empowerment," *Organizational Dynamics,* Winter 1992, pp 48–61.

[68] See G P Huber, C C Miller, and W H Glick, "Developing More Encompassing Theories about Organizations: The Centralization-Effectiveness Relationship as an Example," *Organization Science,* no. 1, 1990, pp 11–40; and C Handy, "Balancing Corporate Power: A New Federalist Paper," *Harvard Business Review,* November–December 1992, pp 59–72. Also see W R Pape, "Divide and Conquer," *Inc. Technology,* no. 2, 1996, pp 25–27; and J Schmidt, "Breaking Down Fiefdoms," *Management Review,* January 1997, pp 45–49.

[69] P Kaestle, "A New Rationale for Organizational Structure," *Planning Review,* July–August 1990, p 22.

[70] Details of this study can be found in T Burns and G M Stalker, *The Management of Innovation* (London: Tavistock, 1961).

[71] D J Gillen and S J Carroll, "Relationship of Managerial Ability to Unit Effectiveness in More Organic versus More Mechanistic Departments," *Journal of Management Studies,* November 1985, pp 674–75.

[72] J D Sherman and H L Smith, "The Influence of Organizational Structure on Intrinsic versus Extrinsic Motivation," *Academy of Management Journal,* December 1984, p 883.

[73] See J A Courtright, G T Fairhurst, and L E Rogers, "Interaction Patterns in Organic and Mechanistic Systems," *Academy of Management Journal,* December 1989, pp 773–802.

[74] See J Woodward, *Industrial Organization: Theory and Practice* (London: Oxford University Press, 1965); and P D Collins and F Hull, "Technology and Span of Control: Woodward Revisited," *Journal of Management Studies,* March 1986, pp 143–64.

[75] See L W Fry, "Technology-Structure Research: Three Critical Issues," *Academy of Management Journal,* September 1982, pp 532–52.

[76] Ibid., p 548. Also see R Reese, "Redesigning for Dial Tone: A Socio-Technical Systems Case Study," *Organizational Dynamics,* Autumn 1995, pp 80–90.

[77] For example, see C C Miller, W H Glick, Y-D Wang, and G P Huber, "Understanding Technology-Structure Relationships: Theory Development and Meta-Analytic Theory Testing," *Academy of Management Journal,* June 1991, pp 370–99; and K H Roberts and M Grabowski, "Organizations, Technology and Structuring," in *Handbook of Organization Studies,* eds S R Clegg, C Hardy, and W R Nord (Thousand Oaks, CA: Sage Publications, 1996), pp 409–23.

[78] The phrase "small is beautiful" was coined by the late British economist E F Schumacher. See E F Schumacher, *Small Is Beautiful: Economics as If People Mattered* (New York: Harper & Row, 1973).

[79] T J Peters and R H Waterman, Jr, *In Search of Excellence* (New York: Harper & Row, 1982), p 321. Also see T Peters, "Rethinking Scale," *California Management Review,* Fall 1992, pp 7–29.

[80] See, for example, W McKinley, "Decreasing Organizational Size: To Untangle or Not to Untangle?" *Academy of Management Review,* January 1992, pp 112–23; W Zellner, "Go-Go Goliaths," *Business Week,* February 13, 1995, pp 64–70; T Brown, "Manage 'BIG!' " *Management Review,* May 1996, pp 12–17; and E Shapiro, "Power, Not Size, Counts," *Management Review,* September 1996, p 61.

[81] C Handy, *The Hungry Spirit* (New York: Broadway Books, 1998), pp 107–8. Also see C Handy, "The Doctrine of Enough," *Management Review,* June 1998, pp 52–54.

[82] P L Zweig, "The Case against Mergers," *Business Week,* October 30, 1995, p 122. Also see O Harari, "Too Big for Your Own Good?" *Management Review,* November 1998, pp 30–32; G Colvin, "The Year of the Mega Merger," *Fortune,* January 11, 1999, pp 62–64; A Taylor III, "More Mergers. Dumb Idea." *Fortune,* February 15, 1999, pp 26–27; P Troiano, "Mergers: Good or Bad?" *Management Review,* April 1999, p 9; and R J Grossman, "Irreconcilable Differences," *HRMagazine,* April 1999, pp 42–48.

[83] S Crock, "A Lean, Mean Fighting Machine It Ain't," *Business Week,* January 11, 1999, p 41.

[84] R Z Gooding and J A Wagner III, "A Meta-Analytic Review of the Relationship between Size and Performance: The Productivity and Efficiency of Organizations and Their Subunits," *Administrative Science Quarterly,* December 1985, pp 462–81.

[85] Ibid., p 477.

[86] Results are presented in P G Benson, T L Dickinson, and C O Neidt, "The Relationship between Organizational Size and Turnover: A Longitudinal Investigation," *Human Relations,* January 1987, pp 15–30. Also see M Yasai-Ardekani, "Effects of Environmental Scarcity and Munificence on the Relationship of Context to Organizational Structure," *Academy of Management Journal,* March 1989, pp 131–56.

[87] See E E Lawler III, "Rethinking Organization Size," *Organizational Dynamics,* Autumn 1997, pp 24–35; O Harari, "Honey, I Shrunk the Company!" *Management Review,* December 1998, pp 39–41; and J C McCune, "Stuck in the Middle?" *Management Review,* February 1999, pp 44–49.

[88] See V Sathe, "Fostering Entrepreneurship in the Large, Diversified Firm," *Organizational Dynamics,* Summer 1989, pp 20–32; J R Galbraith and E E Lawler III, "Effective Organizations: Using the New Logic of Organizing," in *Organizing for the Future: The New Logic for Managing Complex Organizations,* eds J R Galbraith, E E Lawler III, and Associates (San Francisco: Jossey-Bass, 1993), pp 290–92; and J Kim, "Welch Thinks Small, Acts Big," *USA Today,* February 26, 1993, p 2B.

[89] C Palmeri, "A Process That Never Ends," *Forbes,* December 21, 1992, p 55.

[90] See J Child, "Organizational Structure, Environment and Performance: The Role of Strategic Choice," *Sociology,* January 1972, pp 1–22.

[91] See J Galbraith, *Organization Design* (Reading, MA: Addison-Wesley Publishing, 1977); J R Montanari, "Managerial Discretion: An Expanded Model of Organization Choice," *Academy of Management Review,* April 1978, pp 231–41; and H R Bobbitt, Jr, and J D Ford, "Decision-Maker Choice as a Determinant of Organizational Structure," *Academy of Management Review,* January 1980, pp 13–23.

[92] For an alternative model of strategy making, see S L Hart, "An Integrative Framework for Strategy-Making Processes," *Academy of Management Review,* April 1992, pp 327–51. Also see F E Harrison and M A Pelletier, "A Typology of Strategic Choice," *Technological Forecasting and Social Change,* November 1993, pp 245–63; H Mintzberg, "The Rise and Fall of Strategic Planning," *Harvard Business Review,* January–February 1994, pp 107–14; M Valle, "Buy High, Sell Low: Why CEOs Kiss Toads, and How Shareholders Get Warts," *Academy of Management Executive,* May 1998, pp 97–98; G R Weaver, L K Trevino, and P L Cochran, "Corporate Ethics Programs as Control Systems: Influences of Executive Commitment and Environmental Factors," *Academy of Management Journal,* February 1999, pp 41–57; and C McDermott and K K Boyer, "Strategic Consensus: Marching to the Beat of a Different Drummer?" *Business Horizons,* July–August 1999, pp 21–28.

[93] See A Bhide, "How Entrepreneurs Craft Strategies That Work," *Harvard Business Review,* March–April 1994, pp 150–61; and J W Dean, Jr, and M P Sharfman, "Does Decision Process Matter? A Study of Strategic Decision-Making Effectiveness," *Academy of Management Journal,* April 1996, pp 368–96; R L Osborne, "Strategic Values: The Corporate Performance Engine," *Business Horizons,* September–October 1996,

pp 41–47; and B Ettorre, "When Patience Is a Corporate Virtue," *Management Review,* November 1996, pp 28–32.

[94] S Perlstein, "Less Is More," *Business Ethics,* September–October 1993, p 15. Reprinted with permission from *Business Ethics,* P.O. Box 8439, Minneapolis, MN 55408. 612/879-0695.

[95] Details may be found in D Miller, "Strategy Making and Structure: Analysis and Implications for Performance," *Academy of Management Journal,* March 1987, pp 7–32. For more, see T L Amburgey and T Dacin, "As the Left Foot Follows the Right? The Dynamics of Strategic and Structural Change," *Academy of Management Journal,* December 1994, pp 1427–52; and M W Peng and P S Heath, "The Growth of the Firm in Planned Economies in Transition: Institutions, Organizations, and Strategic Choice," *Academy of Management Review,* April 1996, pp 492–528.

[96] T A Stewart, "Welcome to the Revolution," *Fortune,* December 13, 1993, p 66. Also see R B Reich, "The Company of the Future," *Fast Company,* November 1998, pp 124–50.

[97] See Galbraith and Lawler, "Effective Organizations: Using the New Logic of Organizing," pp 285–99.

[98] R Jacob, "The Struggle to Create an Organization for the 21st Century," *Fortune,* April 3, 1995, pp 91–92. © 1995 Time Inc. Reprinted by permission.

[99] See S Sonnesyn Brooks, "Managing a Horizontal Revolution," *HRMagazine,* June 1995, pp 52–58; and M Hequet, "Flat and Happy," *Training,* April 1995, pp 29–34.

[100] For related discussion, see B Filipczak, "The Ripple Effect of Computer Networking," *Training,* March 1994, pp 40–47.

[101] See O Harari, "Transform Your Organization into a Web of Relationships," *Management Review,* January 1998, pp 21–24; R J Alford, "Going Virtual, Getting Real," *Training & Development,* January 1999, pp 34–44; S Greco, "Go Right to the Outsource," *Inc.,* February 1999, p 39; M Minehan, "Forecasting Future Trends for the Workplace," *HRMagazine,* February 1999, p 176; and W B Werther, Jr, "Structure-Driven Strategy and Virtual Organization Design," *Business Horizons,* March–April 1999, pp 13–18.

[102] G McWilliams, "Got a Grand? Get a Pentium PC," *Business Week,* November 4, 1996, p 52.

[103] Handy, *The Hungry Spirit,* p 186. (Emphasis added.)

[104] Excerpted from T Mueller, "A Town Where Cooperation Is King," *Business Week,* December 15, 1997, p 155.

CHAPTER 20

[1] Excerpted from N Byrnes, "How Schwab Grabbed the Lion's Share," *Business Week,* June 28, 1999, p 88.

[2] These statistics were taken from J A Lopez, "Corporate Change: You Can Count on It," *The Arizona Republic,* March 3, 1996, pp D1, D3; and J J Laabs, "Expert Advice on How to Move Forward with Change," *Personnel Journal,* July 1996, pp 54–63.

[3] A M Webber, "Learning for a Change," *Fast Company,* May 1999, p 180.

[4] Excerpted from D Roth, "10 Companies That Get It: Southwest Airlines," *Fortune,* November 8, 1999, p 115.

[5] A discussion of strategic alliances and partnerships is contained in D Sparks, "Special Report: Partners," *Business Week,* October 25, 1999, pp 106–12.

[6] Ibid, p 106.

[7] This three-way typology of change was adapted from discussion in P C Nutt, "Tactics of Implementation," *Academy of Management Journal,* June 1986, pp 230–61.

[8] Types of organizational change are discussed by K E Weick and R E Quinn, "Organizational Change and Development," in *Annual Review of Psychology,* eds J T Spence, J M Darley, and D J Foss (Palo Alto, CA: Annual Reviews, 1999), vol. 50, pp 361–86.

[9] For a thorough discussion of the model, see K Lewin, *Field Theory in Social Science* (New York: Harper & Row, 1951).

[10] These assumptions are discussed in E H Schein, *Organizational Psychology,* 3rd ed (Englewood Cliffs, NJ: Prentice-Hall, 1980).

[11] C Goldwasser, "Benchmarking: People Make the Process," *Management Review,* June 1995, p 40.

[12] Benchmark data for "America's Best Plants" can be found in
J H Sheridan, "Lessons from the Best," *Industry Week,* February 1996,
pp 13–20.

[13] Top management's role in implementing change according to Lewin's
model is discussed by E H Schein, "The Role of the CEO in the Management of Change: The Case of Information Technology," in *Transforming
Organizations,* eds T A Kochan and M Useem (New York: Oxford University Press, 1992), pp 80–95.

[14] Systems models of change are discussed by D W Haines, "Letting
'The System' Do the Work," *Journal of Applied Behavioral Science,*
September 1999, pp 306–24; and D A Nadler and M L Tushman,
"Strategic Imperatives and Core Competencies for the 21st Century,"
Organizational Dynamics, Summer 1999, pp 45–59.

[15] N Tichy, "Simultaneous Transformation and CEO Succession: Key to
Global Competitiveness," *Organizational Dynamics,* Summer 1996, p 55.

[16] A thorough discussion of the target elements of change can be found
in M Beer and B Spector, "Organizational Diagnosis: Its Role in Organizational Learning," *Journal of Counseling & Development,* July/August
1993, pp 642–50; and P Dainty, "Organizational Change: A Strategy for
Successful Implementation," *Journal of Business and Psychology,* Summer 1990, pp 463–81.

[17] Excerpted from E Nelson and E Ramstad, "Trick or Treat: Hershey's
Biggest Dud Has Turned Out to Be New Computer System," *The Wall
Street Journal,* October 29, 1999, p A1.

[18] These errors are discussed by J P Kotter, "Leading Change: The Eight
Steps to Transformation," in *The Leader's Change Handbook,* eds
J A Conger, G M Spreitzer, and E E Lawler III (San Francisco, CA:
1999) pp 87–99.

[19] The type of leadership needed during organizational change is dis-
cussed by J P Kotter, *Leading Change* (Boston: Harvard Business
School Press, 1996); and B Ettorre, "Making Change," *Management
Review,* January 1996, pp 13–18.

[20] M Beer and E Walton, "Developing the Competitive Organization:
Interventions and Strategies," *American Psychologist,* February 1990,
p 154.

[21] An historical overview of the field of OD can be found in N A M
Worren, K Ruddle, and K Moore, "From Organizational Development to
Change Management," *Journal of Applied Behavioral Science,* Septem-
ber 1999, pp 273–86; and A H Church, J Waaclawski, and W Siegal,
"Will the Real OD Practitioner Please Stand Up? A Call for Change in
the Field," *Organization Development Journal,* Summer 1999, pp 49–59.

[22] W W Burke, *Organization Development: A Normative View* (Reading,
MA: Addison-Wesley Publishing, 1987), p 9.

[23] Excerpted from L D Goodstein and H E Butz, "Customer Value: The
Linchpin of Organizational Change," *Organizational Dynamics,* Summer
1998, p 26. © 1998 American Management Association International.
Reprinted by permission of American Management Association International, New York, NY. All rights reserved. http://www.amanet.org.

[24] An example of using employee surveys to conduct OD is provided by
B Schneider, S D Ashworth, A C Higgs, and L Carr, "Design, Validity,
and Use of Strategically Focused Employee Attitude Surveys," *Personnel Psychology,* Autumn 1996, pp 695–705.

[25] See R Rodgers, J E Hunter, and D L Rogers, "Influence of Top Management Commitment on Management Program Success," *Journal of
Applied Psychology,* February 1993, pp 151–55.

[26] Results can be found in P J Robertson, D R Roberts, and J I Porras,
"Dynamics of Planned Organizational Change: Assessing Empirical
Support for a Theoretical Model," *Academy of Management Journal,*
June 1993, pp 619–34.

[27] Results from the meta-analysis can be found in G A Neuman,
J E Edwards, and N S Raju, "Organizational Development Interventions:
A Meta-Analysis of Their Effects on Satisfaction and Other Attitudes,"
Personnel Psychology, Autumn 1989, pp 461–90.

[28] The importance of results-oriented change efforts is discussed by
R J Schaffer and H A Thomson, "Successful Change Programs Begin
with Results," *Harvard Business Review,* January–February 1992,
pp 80–89.

[29] See the related discussion in D M Schneider and C Goldwasser, "Be a
Model Leader of Change: Here's How to Get the Results You Want from
the Change You're Leading," *Management Review,* March 1998,
pp 41–45.

[30] Adapted in part from B W Armentrout, "Have Your Plans for
Change Had a Change of Plan?" *HRFOCUS,* January 1996, p 19; and
A S Judson, *Changing Behavior in Organizations: Minimizing Resis-
tance to Change* (Cambridge, MA: Blackwell, Inc., 1991).

[31] See "Vulnerability and Resilience," *American Psychologist,* January
1996, pp 22–28.

[32] Excerpted from C Joinson, "Moving at the Speed of Dell,"
HRMagazine, April 1999, p 52.

[33] See R Moss Kanter, "Managing Traumatic Change: Avoiding the
'Unlucky 13,' " *Management Review,* May 1987, pp 23–24.

[34] Excerpted from D Jones, "Driving Change—Too Fast? *USA Today,*
August 11, 1999, p 6B.

[35] See L Coch and J R P French, Jr, "Overcoming Resistance to
Change," *Human Relations,* 1948, pp 512–32.

[36] For a thorough review of the role of participation in organizational
change, see W A Pasmore and M R Fagans, "Participation, Individual
Development, and Organizational Change: A Review and Synthesis,"
Journal of Management, June 1992, pp 375–97.

[37] Results from this study can be found in T A Judge, C J Thoresen,
V Pucik, and T W Welbourne, "Managerial Coping with Organizational
Change: A Dispositional Perspective," *Journal of Applied Psychology,*
February 1999, pp 107–22.

[38] L Morris, "Research Capsules," *Training & Development,* April 1992,
pp 74–76; and T Hill, N D Smith, and M F Mann, "Role of Efficacy
Expectations in Predicting the Decision to Use Advanced Technologies:
The Case of Computers," *Journal of Applied Psychology,* May 1987,
pp 307–14.

[39] Results can be found in C-M Lau and R W Woodman, "Understanding Organizational Change: A Schematic Perspective," *Academy of Management Journal,* April 1995, pp 537–54.

[40] See the related discussion in E B Dent and S G Goldberg, "Challenging 'Resistance to Change,' " *Journal of Applied Behavioral Science,*
March 1999, pp 25–41.

[41] J P Kotter, "Leading Change: Why Transformation Efforts Fail," *Harvard Business Review,* 1995, p 64.

[42] See Dent and Goldberg, "Challenging 'Resistance to Change;' "
J Krantz, "Comment on 'Challenging Resistance to Change,' " *Journal
of Applied Behavioral Science,* March 1999, pp 42–44; and E B Dent
and S G Goldberg, " 'Resistance to Change:' A Limiting Perspective,"
Journal of Applied Behavioral Science, March 1999, pp 45–47.

[43] Readiness for change is discussed by B Trahant and W W Burke,
"Traveling through Transitions," *Training & Development,* February
1996, pp 37–41.

[44] For a discussion of how managers can reduce resistance to change by
providing different explanations for an organizational change, see
D M Rousseau and S A Tijoriwala, "What's a Good Reason to Change?
Motivated Reasoning and Social Accounts in Promoting Organizational
Change," *Journal of Applied Psychology,* August 1999, pp 514–28.

[45] T Petzinger, Jr, "The Front Lines: Georg Bauer Put Burden of Downsizing into Employees' Hands," *The Wall Street Journal,* May 10, 1996,
p B1.

[46] Ibid.

[47] Additional strategies for managing resistance are discussed by
T J Galpin, *The Human Side of Change: A Practical Guide to Organiza-
tional Redesign* (San Francisco: Jossey-Bass, 1996); and D May and
M Kettelhut, "Managing Human Issues in Reengineering Projects,"
Journal of Systems Management, January/February 1996, pp 4–11.

[48] See L Baird, P Holland, and S Deacon, "Learning from Action:
Imbedding More Learning into the Performance Fast Enough to Make a
Difference," *Organizational Dynamics,* Spring 1999, pp 19–32; and
K Kuwada, "Strategic Learning: The Continuous Side of Discontinuous
Strategic Change," *Organization Science,* November–December 1998,
pp 719–36.

[49] R M Fulmer and J B Keys, "A Conversation with Peter Senge: New Development in Organizational Learning," *Organizational Dynamics,* Autumn 1998, p 35.

[50] This definition was based on D A Garvin, "Building a Learning Organization," *Harvard Business Review,* July/August 1993, pp 78–91.

[51] See D Stamps, "Learning Ecologies," *Training,* January 1998, pp 32–38.

[52] Organizational learning is discussed by K Maani and C Benton, "Rapid Team Learning: Lessons from Team New Zealand America's Cup Campaign," *Organizational Dynamics,* Spring 1999, pp 48–62; and A Edmondson and B Moingeon, "From Organizational Learning to the Learning Organization," *Management Learning,* 1998, pp 5–20.

[53] A discussion of learning capabilities and core competencies is provided by W Miller, "Building the Ultimate Resource," *Management Review,* January 1999, pp 42–45; and C Long and M Vickers-Koch, "Using Core Capabilities to Create Competitive Advantage," *Organizational Dynamics,* Summer 1995, pp 7–22.

[54] The relationship between organizational learning and various effectiveness criteria is discussed by S F Slater and J C Narver, "Market Orientation and the Learning Organization," *Journal of Marketing,* July 1995, pp 63–74.

[55] A J DiBella, E C Nevis, and J M Gould, "Organizational Learning Style as a Core Capability," in *Organizational Learning and Competitive Advantage,* eds B Moingeon and A Edmondson (Thousand Oaks, CA: Sage, 1996), pp 41–42.

[56] Details of this study can be found in J H Lingle and W A Schiemann, "From Balanced Scorecard to Strategic Gauges: Is Measurement Worth It?" *American Management Association,* March 1996, pp 56–61.

[57] Excerpted from J Stuller, "Chief of Corporate Smarts," *Training,* April 1998, p 32.

[58] Excerpted from Stamps, "Learning Ecologies," p 35.

[59] This discussion and definitions are based on D Miller, "A Preliminary Typology of Organizational Learning: Synthesizing the Literature," *Journal of Management,* 1996, pp 485–505.

[60] See the related discussion in DiBella, Nevis, and Gould, "Organizational Learning Style as a Core Capability."

[61] See D Collis, "Organizational Capability as a Source of Profit," in *Organizational Learning and Competitive Advantage,* eds B Moingeon and A Edmondson (Thousand Oaks, CA: Sage, 1996), pp 139–63.

[62] This discussion is based on material presented in P Senge, *The Dance of Change: The Challenges to Sustaining Momentum in Learning Organizations* (New York: Doubleday, 1999); and J B Keys, R M Fulmer, and S A Stumpf, "Microworlds and Simuworlds: Practice Fields for the Learning Organization," *Organizational Dynamics,* Spring 1996, pp 36–49.

[63] The role of leadership in building a learning organization is discussed by M Beer, "Leading Learning and Learning to Lead," in *The Leader's Change Handbook,* eds J A Conger, G M Spreitzer, and E E Lawler III (San Francisco, CA: Jossey-Bass, 1999), pp 127–61; and Senge, *The Dance of Change: The Challenges to Sustaining Momentum in Learning Organizations.*

[64] Excerpted from L Wah, "Making Knowledge Stick," *Management Review,* May 1999, p 27.

[65] See N A Wishart, J J Elam, D Robey, "Redrawing the Portrait of a Learning Organization: Inside Knight-Ridder, Inc.," *Academy of Management Executive,* February 1996, pp 7–20; C Argyris, "Good Communication That Blocks Learning," *Harvard Business Review,* July–August 1994, pp 77–85; and D A Garvin, "Building a Learning Organization," *Harvard Business Review,* July–August 1993, pp 78–91.

[66] See the related discussion in D Lei, J W Slocum, and R A Pitts, "Designing Organizations for Competitive Advantage: The Power of Unlearning and Learning," *Organizational Dynamics,* Winter 1999, pp 24–38.

[67] J Case, "A Company of Businesspeople," *Inc.,* April 1993, p 86.

[68] Excerpted from N Munk, "How Levi's Trashed a Great American Brand," *Fortune,* April 12, 1999, pp 83–86, 88, 90.

[69] Based on a group exercise in L W Mealiea, *Skills for Managers in Organizations* (Burr Ridge, IL: Irwin, 1994), pp 198–201. © 1994. Reproduced with permission of the McGraw-Hill Companies.

[70] The force-field analysis form was quoted directly from Ibid, pp 199, 201.

VIDEO CASE

[1] For a good first-hand account of mountain bike racing in Moab, Utah, see Todd Balf, "Midnight Riders," *Fast Company,* January–February 2000, pp 280–288.

[2] Based on Steve Kaufman, "California High-End Bicycle Firm Steers Back onto Profitable Course," *San Jose Mercury News,* December 20, 1996.

[3] David Carnoy, "Sporting Chance," *Success,* January 1998, pp 52–53.

[4] Data from Lenny Liebmann, "E-Service at Hub of Online Push," *Information Week,* September 27, 1999.

Glossary

ability Stable characteristic responsible for a person's maximum physical or mental performance.

accountability practices Focus on treating diverse employees fairly.

adaptive perspective Assumes that adaptive cultures enhance a firm's financial performance.

affirmative action Focuses on achieving equality of opportunity in an organization.

aggressive style Expressive and self-enhancing, but takes unfair advantage of others.

aided-analytic Using tools to make decisions.

alternative dispute resolution Avoiding costly lawsuits by resolving conflicts informally or through mediation or arbitration.

Americans with Disabilities Act Prohibits discrimination against the disabled.

asch effect Giving in to a unanimous but wrong opposition.

assertive style Expressive and self-enhancing, but does not take advantage of others.

attention Being consciously aware of something or someone.

attitude Learned predisposition toward a given object.

availability heuristic Tendency to base decisions on information readily available in memory.

baseline data Preintervention data collected by someone other than the target person.

behavior chart Program evaluation graph with baseline and intervention data.

behavior modification Making specific behavior occur more or less often by managing its cues and consequences.

behavioral contingencies Antecedent →behavior→consequence (A→B→C) relationships.

behavioral self-management Modifying one's own behavior by managing cues, cognitive processes, and consequences.

benchmarking Process by which a company compares its performance with that of high-performing organizations.

bounded rationality Constraints that restrict decision making.

brainstorming Process to generate a quantity of ideas.

buffers Resources or administrative changes that reduce burnout.

bureaucracy Max Weber's idea of the most rationally efficient form of organization.

burnout A condition of emotional exhaustion and negative attitudes.

care perspective Involves compassion and an ideal of attention and response to need.

career plateauing The end result when the probability of being promoted is very small.

case study In-depth study of a single person, group, or organization.

causal attributions Suspected or inferred causes of behavior.

centralized decision making Top managers make all key decisions.

charismatic leadership Transforms employees to pursue organizational goals over self-interests.

closed system A relatively self-sufficient entity.

coalition Temporary groupings of people who actively pursue a single issue.

coercive power Obtaining compliance through threatened or actual punishment.

cognitions A person's knowledge, opinions, or beliefs.

cognitive categories Mental depositories for storing information.

cognitive style A perceptual and judgmental tendency, according to Jung's typology.

cohesiveness A sense of "we-ness" helps group stick together.

collaborative computing Using computer software and hardware to help people work better together.

collectivist culture Personal goals less important than community goals and interests.

communication Interpersonal exchange of information and understanding.

communication competence Ability to effectively use communication behaviors in a given context.

communication distortion Purposely modifying the content of a message.

conflict One party perceives its interests are being opposed or set back by another party.

conflict triangle Conflicting parties involve a third person rather than dealing directly with each other.

consensus Presenting opinions and gaining agreement to support a decision.

consideration Creating mutual respect and trust with followers.

contingency approach Using management tools and techniques in a situationally appropriate manner; avoiding the one-best-way mentality.

contingency approach to organization design Creating an effective organization–environment fit.

contingency factors Variables that influence the appropriateness of a leadership style.

continuous reinforcement Reinforcing every instance of a behavior.

control strategy Coping strategy that directly confronts or solves problems.

coping Process of managing stress.

core job dimensions Job characteristics found to various degrees in all jobs.

creativity Process of developing something new or unique.

cross-cultural management Understanding and teaching behavioral patterns in different cultures.

cross-cultural training Structured experiences to help people adjust to a new culture/country.

cross-functionalism Team made up of technical specialists from different areas.

culture Socially derived, taken-for-granted assumptions about how to think and act.

culture shock Anxiety and doubt caused by an overload of new expectations and cues.

decentralized decision making Lower-level managers are empowered to make important decisions.

decision making Identifying and choosing solutions that lead to a desired end result.

decision-making style A combination of how individuals perceive and respond to information.

delegation Granting decision-making authority to people at lower levels.

delphi technique Process to generate ideas from physically dispersed experts.

development practices Focus on preparing diverse employees for greater responsibility and advancement.

devil's advocacy Assigning someone the role of critic.

dialectic method Fostering a debate of opposing viewpoints to better understand an issue.

differentiation Division of labor and specialization that causes people to think and act differently.

distributive justice The perceived fairness of how resources and rewards are distributed.

diversity The host of individual differences that make people different from and similar to each other.

dysfunctional conflict Threatens organization's interests.

electronic mail Uses the Internet/Intranet to send computer-generated text and documents.

emotions Complex human reactions to personal achievements and setbacks that may be felt and displayed.

employment contract Mutual written and implied expectations between employer and employee.

empowerment   Sharing varying degrees of power with lower-level employees to better serve the customer.

enacted values   The values and norms that are exhibited by employees.

equity theory   Holds that motivation is a function of fairness in social exchanges.

escalation of commitment   Sticking to an ineffective course of action too long.

escape strategy   Coping strategy that avoids or ignores stressors and problems.

espoused values   The stated values and norms that are preferred by an organization.

ethics   Study of moral issues and choices.

ethnocentrism   Belief that one's native country, culture, language, and behavior are superior.

eustress   Stress that is good or produces a positive outcome.

expectancy   Belief that effort leads to a specific level of performance.

expectancy theory   Holds that people are motivated to behave in ways that produce valued outcomes.

experienced meaningfulness   Feeling that one's job is important and worthwhile.

experienced responsibility   Believing that one is accountable for work outcomes.

expert power   Obtaining compliance through one's knowledge or information.

external factors   Environmental characteristics that cause behavior.

external forces for change   Originate outside the organization.

external locus of control   Attributing outcomes to circumstances beyond one's control.

extinction   Making behavior occur less often by ignoring or not reinforcing it.

extranet   Connects internal employees with selected customers, suppliers, and strategic partners.

extrinsic rewards   Financial, material, or social rewards from the environment.

feedback   Objective information about performance.

field study   Examination of variables in real-life settings.

fight-or-flight response   To either confront stressors or try to avoid them.

fit perspective   Assumes that culture must align with its business or strategic context.

formal group   Formed by the organization.

functional analysis   Reducing person–environment interaction to A→B→C terms.

functional conflict   Serves organization's interests.

functional social support   Support sources that buffer stress in specific situations.

fundamental attribution bias   Ignoring environmental factors that affect behavior.

gainsharing   Bonuses tied to measurable productivity increases.

garbage can model   Holds that decision making is sloppy and haphazard.

genderflex   Temporarily using communication behaviors typical of the other gender.

glass ceiling   Invisible barrier blocking women and minorities from top management positions.

global social support   The total amount of social support available.

goal   What an individual is trying to accomplish.

goal commitment   Amount of commitment to achieving a goal.

goal difficulty   The amount of effort required to meet a goal.

goal specificity   Quantifiability of a goal.

grapevine   Unofficial communication system of the informal organization.

group   Two or more freely interacting people with shared norms and goals and a common identity.

group cohesiveness   A "we feeling" binding group members together.

groupthink   Janis's term for a cohesive in-group's unwillingness to realistically view alternatives.

hardiness   Personality characteristic that neutralizes stress.

hierarchical communication   Exchange of information between managers and employees.

high-context cultures   Primary meaning derived from nonverbal situational cues.

holistic wellness approach   Advocates personal responsibility in reducing stressors and stress.

hygiene factors   Job characteristics associated with job dissatisfaction.

impression management   Getting others to see us in a certain manner.

individualistic culture   Primary emphasis on personal freedom and choice.

informal group   Formed by friends.

information richness   Information-carrying capacity of data.

in-group exchange   A partnership characterized by mutual trust, respect, and liking.

initiating structure   Organizing and defining what group members should be doing.

instrumental cohesiveness   Sense of togetherness based on mutual dependency needed to get the job done.

instrumental values   Personally preferred ways of behaving.

instrumentality   A performance→outcome perception.

integration   Cooperation among specialists to achieve common goal.

intelligence   Capacity for constructive thinking, reasoning, problem solving.

interactional justice   The perceived fairness of the decision maker's behavior in the process of decision making.

intermittent reinforcement   Reinforcing some but not all instances of behavior.

internal factors   Personal characteristics that cause behavior.

internal forces for change   Originate inside the organization.

internal locus of control   Attributing outcomes to one's own actions.

internal motivation   Motivation caused by positive internal feelings.

internet   A global network of computer networks.

intranet   An organization's private Internet.

intrinsic rewards   Self-granted, psychic rewards.

job design   Changing the content and/or process of a specific job to increase job satisfaction and performance.

job enlargement   Putting more variety into a job.

job enrichment   Building achievement, recognition, stimulating work, responsibility, and advancement into a job.

job rotation   Moving employees from one specialized job to another.

job satisfaction   An affective or emotional response to one's job.

judgmental heuristics   Rules of thumb or shortcuts that people use to reduce information-processing demands.

justice perspective   Based on the ideal of reciprocal rights and driven by rules and regulations.

knowledge of results   Feedback about work outcomes.

laboratory study   Manipulation and measurement of variables in contrived situations.

law of effect   Behavior with favorable consequences is repeated; behavior with unfavorable consequences disappears.

leader–member relations   Extent that leader has the support, loyalty, and trust of work group.

leader trait   Personal characteristics that differentiate leaders from followers.

leadership   Influencing employees to voluntarily pursue organizational goals.

leadership Grid®   Represents four leadership styles found by crossing concern for production and concern for people.

leadership prototype   Mental representation of the traits and behaviors possessed by leaders.

learned helplessness   Debilitating lack of faith in one's ability to control the situation.

learning capabilities   The set of core competencies and internal processes that enable an organization to adapt to its environment.

learning modes   The various ways in which organizations attempt to create and maximize their learning.

learning organization   Proactively creates, acquires, and transfers knowledge throughout the organization.

legitimate power   Obtaining compliance through formal authority.

liaison individuals   Consistently pass along grapevine information to others.

line managers   Have authority to make organizational decisions.

linguistic style   A person's typical speaking pattern.

listening   Actively decoding and interpreting verbal messages.

low-context cultures   Primary meaning derived from written and spoken words.

maintenance roles   Relationship-building group behavior.

management   Process of working with and through others to achieve organizational objectives efficiently and ethically.

management by objectives   Management system incorporating participation in decision making, goal setting, and feedback.

managing diversity   Creating organizational changes that enable all people to perform up to their maximum potential.

mechanistic organizations   Rigid, command-and-control bureaucracies.

mentoring   Process of forming and maintaining developmental relationships between a mentor and a junior person.

met expectations   The extent to which one receives what he or she expects from a job.

meta-analysis   Pools the results of many studies through statistical procedure.

mission statement   Summarizes "why" an organization exists.

monochronic time   Preference for doing one thing at a time because time is limited, precisely segmented, and schedule driven.

motivating potential score   The amount of internal work motivation associated with a specific job.

motivation   Psychological processes that arouse and direct goal-directed behavior.

motivators   Job characteristics associated with job satisfaction.

mutuality of interest   Balancing individual and organizational interests through win-win cooperation.

natural rewards   Normal social interactions such as praise or recognition.

need for achievement   Desire to accomplish something difficult.

need for affiliation   Desire to spend time in social relationships and activities.

need for power   Desire to influence, coach, teach, or encourage others to achieve.

needs   Physiological or psychological deficiencies that arouse behavior.

negative inequity   Comparison in which another person receives greater outcomes for similar inputs.

negative reinforcement   Making behavior occur more often by contingently withdrawing something negative.

negotiation   Give-and-take process between conflicting interdependent parties.

noise   Interference with the transmission and understanding of a message.

nominal group technique   Process to generate ideas and evaluate solutions.

nonanalytic   Using preformulated rules to make decisions.

nonassertive style   Timid and self-denying behavior.

nonverbal communication   Messages sent outside of the written or spoken word.

norm   Shared attitudes, opinions, feelings, or actions that guide social behavior.

open system   Organism that must constantly interact with its environment to survive.

operant behavior   Skinner's term for learned, consequence-shaped behavior.

optimizing   Choosing the best possible solution.

organic organizations   Fluid and flexible network of multitalented people.

organization   System of consciously coordinated activities of two or more people.

organization-based self-esteem   An organization member's self-perceived value.

organization chart   Boxes-and-lines illustration showing chain of formal authority and division of labor.

organization development   A set of techniques or tools that are used to implement organizational change.

organizational behavior   Inter-disciplinary field dedicated to better understanding and managing people at work.

organizational culture   Shared values and beliefs that underlie a company's identity.

organizational decline   Decrease in organization's resource base (money, customers, talent, innovations).

organizational ecologists   Those who study the effect of environmental factors on organizational success/failure and interrelationships among populations and communities of organizations.

organizational identification   Organizational values or beliefs become part of one's self-identity.

organizational moles   Use the grapevine to enhance their power and status.

organizational politics   Intentional enhancement of self-interest.

organizational socialization   Process by which employees learn an organization's values, norms, and required behaviors.

ostracism   Rejection by other group members.

out-group exchange   A partnership characterized by a lack of mutual trust, respect, and liking.

paradigm   A generally accepted way of viewing the world.

participative management   Involving employees in various forms of decision making.

pay for performance   Monetary incentives tied to one's results or accomplishments.

perception   Process of interpreting one's environment.

perceptual model of communication   Consecutively linked elements within the communication process.

performance appraisal   Judgmental evaluation of one's traits, behavior, or accomplishments as basis for personnel decisions and development plans.

persistence   Extent to which effort is expended on a task over time.

personal initiative   Going beyond formal job requirements and being an active self-starter.

personality   Stable physical and mental characteristics responsible for a person's identity.

personality conflict   Interpersonal opposition driven by personal dislike or disagreement.

personalized power   Directed at helping oneself.

polychronic time   Preference for doing more than one thing at a time because time is flexible and multidimensional.

position power   Degree to which leader has formal power.

positive inequity   Comparison in which another person receives lesser outcomes for similar inputs.

positive reinforcement   Making behavior occur more often by contingently presenting something positive.

postmodern organizations   Flexible organizations that are decentralized, computer linked, and less hierarchical than bureaucracies.

problem   Gap between an actual and desired situation.

procedural justice   The perceived fairness of the process and procedures used to make allocation decisions.

process style   Likes to discuss issues in detail.

profit sharing   Portion of bottom-line economic profits given to employees.

programmed conflict   Encourages different opinions without protecting management's personal feelings.

propensity to trust   A personality trait involving one's general willingness to trust others.

proxemics   Hall's term for the study of cultural expectations about interpersonal space.

punishment   Making behavior occur less often by contingently presenting something negative or withdrawing something positive.

quality circles   Small groups of volunteers who strive to solve quality-related problems.

rational model   Logical four-step approach to decision making.

readiness   Follower's ability and willingness to complete a task.

realistic job preview   Presents both positive and negative aspects of a job.

reality shock   A newcomer's feeling of surprise after experiencing unexpected situations or events.

reasons style   Interested in hearing the rationale behind a message.

reciprocity   Widespread belief that people should be paid back for their positive and negative acts.

recruitment practices   Attempts to attract qualified, diverse employees at all levels.

referent power   Obtaining compliance through charisma or personal attraction.

relaxation response   State of peacefulness.

representativeness heuristic   Tendency to assess the likelihood of an event occurring based on impressions about similar occurrences.

resistance to change   Emotional/behavioral response to real or imagined work changes.

respondent behavior   Skinner's term for unlearned stimulus–response reflexes.

results style   Interested in hearing the bottom line or result of a message.

reward equality norm   Everyone should get the same rewards.

reward equity norm   Rewards should be tied to contributions.

reward power   Obtaining compliance with promised or actual rewards.

role ambiguity   Others' expectations are unknown.

role conflict   Others have conflicting or inconsistent expectations.

role overload   Others' expectations exceed one's ability.

roles   Expected behaviors for a given position.

sample survey   Questionnaire responses from a sample of people.

satisficing   Choosing a solution that meets a minimum standard of acceptance.

scenario technique   Speculative forecasting method.

schema   Mental picture of an event or object.

self-concept   Person's self-perception as a physical, social, spiritual being.

self-efficacy   Belief in one's ability to do a task.

self-esteem   One's overall self-evaluation.

self-fulfilling prophecy   People's expectations determine behavior and performance.

self-managed teams   Groups of employees granted administrative oversight for their work.

self-management leadership   Process of leading others to lead themselves.

self-monitoring   Observing one's own behavior and adapting it to the situation.

self-serving bias   Taking more personal responsibility for success than failure.

self-talk   Evaluating thoughts about oneself.

servant-leadership   Focuses on increased service to others rather than to oneself.

sex-role stereotype   Beliefs about appropriate roles for men and women.

shaping   Reinforcing closer and closer approximations to a target behavior.

situational theories   Propose that leader styles should match the situation at hand.

skill   Specific capacity to manipulate objects.

social loafing   Decrease in individual effort as group size increases.

social power   Ability to get things done with human, informational, and material resources.

social support   Amount of helpfulness derived from social relationships.

socialized power   Directed at helping others.

socio-emotional cohesiveness   Sense of togetherness based on emotional satisfaction.

span of control   The number of people reporting directly to a given manager.

spillover model   Describes the reciprocal relationship between job and life satisfaction.

staff personnel   Provide research, advice, and recommendations to line managers.

stakeholder audit   Systematic identification of all parties likely to be affected by the organization.

stereotype   Beliefs about the characteristics of a group.

strategic constituency   Any group of people with a stake in the organization's operation or success.

strategic plan   A long-term plan outlining actions needed to achieve planned results.

strength perspective   Assumes that the strength of corporate culture is related to a firm's financial performance.

stress   Behavioral, physical, or psychological response to stressors.

stressful life events   Life events that disrupt daily routines and social relationships.

stressors   Environmental factors that produce stress.

superleader   Someone who leads others to lead themselves.

symptom management strategy   Coping strategy that focuses on reducing the symptoms of stress.

target elements of change   Components of an organization that may be changed.

task roles   Task-oriented group behavior.

task structure   Amount of structure contained within work tasks.

team   Small group with complementary skills who hold themselves mutually accountable for common purpose, goals, and approach.

team-based pay   Linking pay to teamwork behavior and/or team results.

team building   Experiential learning aimed at better internal functioning of groups.

team viability   Team members satisfied and willing to contribute.

telecommuting   Doing work that is generally performed in the office away from the office using different information technologies.

terminal values   Personally preferred end-states of belief.

theory   A story defining key terms, providing a conceptual framework, and explaining why something occurs.

theory Y   McGregor's modern and positive assumptions about employees being responsible and creative.

360-degree feedback   Comparison of anonymous feedback from one's superior, subordinates, and peers with self-perceptions.

total quality management   An organizational culture dedicated to training, continuous improvement, and customer satisfaction.

transactional leadership   Focuses on interpersonal interactions between managers and employees.

trust   Reciprocal faith in others' intentions and behavior.

type A behavior pattern   Aggressively involved in a chronic, determined struggle to accomplish more in less time.

unaided-analytic   Analysis is limited to processing information in one's mind.

underemployment   The result of taking a job that requires less education, training, or skills than possessed by a worker.

unity of command principle   Each employee should report to a single manager.

upward feedback   Subordinates evaluate their boss.

valence   The value of a reward or outcome.

value   (personal) Durable belief in a way of behaving or an end-state.

value attainment   The extent to which a job allows fulfillment of one's work values.

values   Enduring belief in a mode of conduct or end-state.

value system   Pattern of values within an organization.

valuing diversity   Emphasizes the awareness, recognition, understanding, and appreciation of human differences.

virtual team   Information technology allows group members in different locations to conduct business.

vision   Long-term goal describing "what" an organization wants to become.

workforce demographics   Statistical profiles of adult workers.

Indexes

NAME

COMPANY

Visit the Kreitner and Kinicki website and download a free wolf screen saver developed exclusively for the book.